C0-BPZ-080

Actors' Television Credits

Supplement III: 1982-1985

JAMES ROBERT PARISH
and
VINCENT TERRACE

The Scarecrow Press, Inc.
Metuchen, N.J., & London
1986

Also published by Scarecrow Press, Inc.:

Actors' Television Credits: 1950-1972 (1973)
Actors' Television Credits: Supplement I (1978)
Actors' Television Credits: Supplement II (1982)

Library of Congress Cataloging-in-Publication Data

Parish, James Robert.
Actors' television credits. Supplement III, 1982-1985.

Bibliography: p.
1. Television actors and actresses--Credits.
2. Television programs--United States. I. Terrace, Vincent, 1948- . II. Title.
PN1992.4.A2P3 Suppl. 3 791.45'028'0922 86-17691
ISBN 0-8108-1928-7

Manufactured in the United States of America

DEDICATION

Each year many new performers hope for success in the entertainment field. Thirteen-year-old Samantha Smith was a fresh, new talent with a seemingly bright future in show business. After filming only four episodes of the TV series "Lime Street," she died, tragically, in a plane crash.

To Samantha Smith, and her dream of peace throughout the world, we dedicate this book.

CONTENTS

FOREWORD

Actors' Television Credits, 1982-1985 is the fourth volume in a highly regarded series of books that document the individual performances of actors on television. (The prior volumes cover the years 1950-1972; 1973-1976; and 1977-1981.)

As with past editions, the New York Market edition of TV Guide has been a major source of information. However, with TV Guide's decreasing cast information, we have found it necessary to supplement our research with additional sources. This edition strongly reflects the use of network press releases, which have provided us with a wealth of information, including one very difficult aspect of chronicling individual episodes--titles. Actual viewings and network information not available to the public have also been a major source of information. We have tried our best to make this edition as complete as possible.

This edition also reflects the first inclusion of cable credits. Although cable is comprised primarily of theatrical feature films, we have chronicled only the made-for-cable dramatic and comedy specials and series. Theatrical credits are not included in any performer's listing.

We have also tried to make this edition reflect as many new and up-and-coming performers as possible (names that should be easily recognizable) as well as to continue to compile the performances of older actors whose credits date back to the 1950s.

We are grateful also to several readers, in particular Steve Eberly, Mark Speck, and Dennis Tucker for their time and efforts in compiling most of the A&C's that appear in this edition.

When utilizing this supplement, or the previous three volumes, it is suggested that the reader take advantage of the following source materials:

For television movies: Movies Made for Television: The Telefeature and the Miniseries, 1964-1984 (New York Zoetrope, 1984)

For TV series: The Encyclopedia of Television: Series, Pilots and Specials, Vol. 1: 1937-1973; Vol. 2: 1974-1984; Vol. 3: Index (New York Zoetrope, 1985)

For episode-by-episode listings: Television Drama Series Programming: A Comprehensive Chronicle, 5 vols.: 1947-1959, 1959-1975, 1975-1980, 1980-1982, 1982-1984 [forthcoming] (Scarecrow Press)

For individual storyline information: Any market edition of TV Guide; but the New York edition for NN entries.

Please keep in mind when using this volume that our aim has been three-fold: 1) to update performers' entries for the years 1982 through 1985; 2) to amplify (e.g., with full episode titles wherever possible), correct (e.g., erroneous telecast dates, improper titles) and delete (e.g., repeat episodes) data from the prior volumes; and 3) to add new performers' entries, giving listings for their TV work from January 1, 1982, through December 31, 1985 (or earlier, depending on the performer).

For future supplements to this work, the authors would be grateful for data concerning corrections, additions, and amplifications of published entries.

James Robert Parish
2255 Ben Lomond Drive
Los Angeles, California 90027

Vincent Terrace
1830 Delancey Place
Bronx, New York 10462

ACKNOWLEDGMENTS

We are grateful to the following people, who have helped to make possible this third supplement of *Actors' Television Credits*:

Steve Eberly

Barry Gillam

Alvin H. Marill

Robert Reed

Ted Serrell

Mark Speck

Dennis Tucker

KEY

A&C[1]	Additions and Corrections to materials found in the base volume and Supplements 1 and 2. Each A&C has been designed to refer the reader to the volume to which the information belongs. B.V. refers to the Base Volume (1950-1972), Supp. 1 to Supplement 1 (1973-1976), and Supp. 2 to Supplement 2 (1977-1981)
A&E	Arts and Entertainment (cable)
ABC	The American Broadcasting Company (broadcast)
CBS	The Columbia Broadcasting System (broadcast)
DIS	The Disney Channel (cable)
ep	episode
ep hos	episode host or hostess
ESPN	The Entertainment & Sports Network (cable)
HBO	Home Box Office (cable)
MM	Metromedia Television (broadcast)
ms	miniseries
nar	narrator
NBC	The National Broadcasting Company (broadcast)
NN	non-network program (a.k.a. syndicated)
OPT	Operation Prime Time (syndicated network)
PBS	The Public Broadcasting Service (broadcast)
pt	pilot (test program for a potential series)
ret to sr	indicates a performer who returns to a series after a leave of absence
SHO	Showtime (cable)
sp	special
sr	series
sr ret	series return
SUPP.	Supplement: covering the years 1982-1985
TEC	The Entertainment Channel (cable; defunct)
tf	telefeature
tf/pt	combination telefeature and pilot film
TMC	The Movie Channel (cable)
*	new subject entry in this volume
vo	voice only

1. Information listed as A&C indicates additional episode information not found in any of the previous volumes and corrected information to the previous volumes (indicated with an underscore).

AREAS NOT COVERED IN THIS VOLUME

- Documentaries
- Game Shows
- News Broadcasts
- Reality Programs
- Sports Programs
- Talk Shows
- Theatrical Motion Pictures
- Variety Programs

-A-

AAKER, LEE
A&C, B.V.:
Tales of the 77th Bengal Lancers ep The Glass Necklace 3.24.57 NBC
The Danny Thomas Show ep Rusty Meets Little Lord Fauntleroy 5.16.60 CBS

AAMES, ANGELA*
The Comeback Kid tf 4.11.80 ABC
Moviola: This Year's Blonde tf 5.18.80 NBC
Cheers ep Sam's Women 10.7.82 NBC
Automan sr 12.15.83 ABC
The Cracker Brothers pt 9.14.84 NBC
Alice ep 10.14.85 CBS

AAMES, WILLIE*
Adam-12 ep Credit Risk 12.17.74 NBC
We'll Get By sr 3.6.75 CBS
Little House on the Prairie ep Injun Kid 1.31.77 NBC
Eight Is Enough sr 8.10.77 (through 8.29.81 ABC)
The Love Boat ep Doc's Nephew 11.6.82 ABC
The Tom Swift and Linda Craig Mystery Hour pt 7.3.83 ABC
Dungeons and Dragons sr vo 9.17.83 CBS
Charles in Charge sr 10.3.84 CBS
The New Love, American Style ep Love and New Year's Eve 12.27.85 ABC

ABBOTT, PHILIP*
Studio One ep Music and Mrs. Pratt 10.12.53 CBS
Philco Television Playhouse ep The Girl with the Stop Watch 10.25.53 NBC
The Big Story ep 12.11.53 NBC
The Big Story ep 5.15.54 NBC
Danger ep The Big Man 6.15.54 CBS
Philco Television Playhouse ep Friday the 13th 6.27.54 NBC
Goodyear Theater ep Recoil 8.15.54 NBC
Studio One ep U.F.O. 9.6.54 CBS
The Man Behind the Badge ep The Case of Strategic Air Command 9.12.54 NN
Armstrong Circle Theater ep The Runaway 10.5.54 NBC
Armstrong Circle Theater ep Flare-up 11.16.54 NBC
Goodyear Theater ep The Rabbit Trap 2.13.55 NBC

Armstrong Circle Theater ep Trapped 3.15.55 NBC
Philco Television Playhouse ep The Ghost Writer 5.29.55 NBC
Armstrong Circle Theater ep Five Who Shook the World 3.20.56 NBC
Alfred Hitchcock Presents ep Portrait of Jocelyn 4.8.56 CBS
U.S. Steel Hour ep Noon on Doomsday 4.25.56 CBS
Studio One ep Snap Your Fingers 6.18.56 CBS
U.S. Steel Hour ep A Matter of Pride 4.29.57 CBS
Gunsmoke ep How to Kill a Friend 11.22.58 CBS
Armstrong Circle Theater ep And Bring Home a Baby 1.7.59 NBC
Alcoa Presents (a.k.a. One Step Beyond) ep The Dead Part of the House 3.17.59 ABC
Black Saddle ep Client: Jessup 4.18.59 NBC
Naked City ep Memory of Crying 4.12.60 ABC
Hotel de Paree ep Sundance and the Man in the Shadows 4.15.60 CBS
Diagnosis: Unknown ep Final Performance 8.18.60 CBS
Perry Mason ep The Case of the Envious Editor 1.7.61 CBS
Naked City ep The Well Dressed Termites 2.8.61 ABC
The Twilight Zone ep Long Distance Call 3.3.61 CBS
Cain's Hundred ep The Left Side of Canada 5.1.62 NBC
The Detectives ep The Airtight Case 5.5.61 ABC
The Defenders ep A Quality of Mercy 9.16.61 CBS
Bus Stop ep A Lion Walks Among Us 12.3.61 ABC
Stoney Burke ep The Contender 10.1.62 ABC
Alcoa Premiere ep Guest in the House 10.11.62 CBS
Saints and Sinners ep A Night of Horns and Bells 12.24.62 NBC
Route 66 ep Suppose I Said I Was the Queen of Spain 2.8.63 CBS
Empire ep The Tiger Inside 2.12.63 ABC
The Twilight Zone ep The Parallel 3.14.63 CBS
Ben Casey ep Lullaby for Billy Digman 5.6.63 ABC
Dr. Kildare ep A Hand Held Out in Darkness 5.30.63 NBC
77 Sunset Strip ep Never to Have Loved 6.14.63 ABC
Gunsmoke ep Tobe 10.19.63 CBS
Bonanza ep The Toy Soldier 10.20.63 NBC
Great Adventure ep The Great Diamond Mountain 11.8.63 CBS
Kraft Suspense Theater ep The Long Lost Life of Edward Smalley 1.12.63 NBC
The Outer Limits ep The Borderland 12.16.63 ABC
The Outer Limits ep Zzzz 1.27.64 ABC
The Eleventh Hour ep Does My Mother Have to Know? 3.25 and 4.1.64 NBC
Kraft Suspense Theater ep Once Upon a Savage Night 4.2.64 NBC
Slattery's People ep What is Honor? What is Death? 11.23.64 CBS
Mr. Broadway ep Sticks and Stones May Break My Bones 12.12.64 CBS
Rawhide ep No Dogs or Drovers 12.18.64 CBS
The Fugitive ep Devil's Carnival 12.22.64 ABC

Kentucky Jones ep 1.30.65 NBC
The Wonderful World of Color ep Kilroy 3.14, 3.21, 4.4.65 NBC
Perry Mason ep The Case of the Wrongful Writ 5.6.65 CBS
The FBI sr 9.19.65 ABC
The FBI sr ret 9.18.66 ABC
The FBI sr ret 9.17.67 ABC
The FBI sr ret 9.22.68 ABC
The FBI sr ret 9.14.69 ABC
The FBI sr ret 9.20.70 ABC
The FBI sr ret 9.12.71 ABC
The FBI sr ret 9.17.72 ABC
The FBI sr ret 9.16.73 ABC
Medical Center ep Torment 9.22.75 CBS
The Bionic Woman ep The Jailing of Jaime 5.12.76 ABC
Delvecchio ep Hot Spell 11.14.76 CBS
Tail Gunner Joe tf 2.6.77 ABC
Kingston: Confidential ep 7.6.77 NBC
Escape from Bogan County tf 10.7.77 CBS
The Bionic Woman ep Escape to Love 11.26.77 NBC
The Cops and Robin tf 3.28.78 ABC
Quincy, M.E. ep 10.19.78 NBC
The Paper Chase ep 10.31.78 CBS
Quincy, M.E. ep Last Rites 9.16.80 NBC
Lou Grant ep Business 3.23.81 CBS
Palmerstown, U.S.A. ep 5.19.81 CBS
The Fantastic World of D.C. Collins tf 2.10.84 NBC
Santa Barbara ep 7.30.84 NBC
Dynasty ep The Mortgage 10.10.84 ABC
Airwolf ep Flight #903 is Missing 11.17.84 CBS
Highway to Heaven ep Birds of a Feather 11.6.85 NBC

ABDUL-JABBAR, KAREEM (a.k.a. Lew Alcindor)*
Mannix ep A Day Filled with Shadows 2.13.71 CBS
The Man from Atlantis ep Giant 10.25.77 NBC
Diff'rent Strokes ep Substitute Teacher 11.6.82 NBC
Tales from the Darkside ep Djinn, No Chaser 11.10.84 NN
Pryor's Place ep 12.15.84 CBS
The ABC Afterschool Special ep The Hero Who Couldn't Read 1.9.85 ABC
Diff'rent Strokes ep A Tale of Two Teachers 11.8.85 ABC

ACKER, SHARON
A&C, Supp. 1:
Harry O ep The Admiral's Lady 9.19.74 ABC
Cannon ep The Deadly Conspiracy 9.19.75 CBS
A&C, Supp. 2:
The Rockford Files ep Rosenthal and Gilda Stern Are Dead 9.29.78 NBC
The Rockford Files ep The Man Who Saw Alligators 2.10.79 NBC
Stone ep Deep Sleeper 1.14.80 ABC
SUPP.:

The Murder That Wouldn't Die tf 3.9.80 NBC
The Powers of Matthew Star ep Brain Drain 3.4.83 NBC
Matt Houston ep The Centerfold Murders 9.30.83 ABC
Trapper John, M.D. ep 10.16.83
The Whiz Kids ep 4.7.84
Crazy Like a Fox ep Sunday in the Park with Harry 10.13.85 CBS
Knight Rider ep Knight Song 11.15.85 NBC

ACKERMAN, LESLIE
SUPP.:
Trapper John, M.D. ep Is There a Doctor in the House? 11.29.81 CBS
Simon and Simon ep Psyched Out 1.13.83 CBS
Washingtoon pt 10.15.84 SHO
Malice in Wonderland tf 5.12.85 CBS
Royal Match pt 8.2.85 CBS

ACKROYD, DAVID*
Exo-Man tf/pt 6.18.77 NBC
The Defection of Simas Kudirka tf 1.23.78 CBS
The Paper Chase ep 100 Voices of Silence 10.10.78 CBS
The Word ms 11.12-15.78 CBS
And I Alone Survived tf 11.27.78 NBC
Women in White ms 2.8, 2.15, 2.22.79 NBC
Mind Over Murder tf 10.23.79 CBS
The Yeagers sr 6.1.80 ABC
A Gun in the House tf 2.11.81 CBS
Trapper John, M.D. ep Victims 1.10.82
McClain's Law ep The Last Hero 3.20.82
The Academy pt 3.31.82 NBC
The Academy II pt 12.8.82 NBC
Cocaine: One Man's Seduction tf 2.27.83 NBC
Deadly Lessons tf 3.7.83 ABC
Teacher's Only ep Leather and Lace 4.23.83 NBC
Two Marriages ep The Prize 9.14.83 ABC
Whiz Kids ep Fatal Error 10.12.83 CBS
Dynasty ep The Bungalow 10.5.83 ABC
Dynasty ep The Note 10.19.83 ABC
When Your Lover Leaves tf 10.31.83 NBC
The Sky's No Limit tf 2.7.84 CBS
AfterMASH sr 1.16.84 CBS
AfterMASH sr ret 9.25.84 CBS
Cover Up ep Murder in Malibu 12.1.84 CBS
Hardcastle and McCormick ep Undercover McCormick 3.11.85 ABC
Picking Up the Pieces tf 10.22.85 CBS
MacGyver ep Trumbo's World 11.10.85 ABC
St. Elsewhere ep Lost and Found in Space 11.13.85 NBC
St. Elsewhere ep Close Encounters 11.20.85 NBC
St. Elsewhere ep Watch the Skies 11.27.85 NBC
Cagney and Lacey ep Bold Ghosts 12.9.85 CBS

ADAIR, DEBORAH*
The Young and the Restless sr 1981 CBS
Dynasty sr (with ep "Tracy") 11.16.83 ABC
Matt Houston ep The Beach Club Murders 2.1.85 ABC
The Love Boat ep The Love Boat Fall Preview Party Special 9.15.84 ABC
Finder of Lost Loves sr 9.22.84 ABC
Hotel ep Fantasies 10.17.84 ABC
The Love Boat ep Starting Over 11.10.84 ABC
Hotel ep 12.4.85 ABC

ADAMS, BROOKE*
F. Scott Fitzgerald and "The Last of the Belles" tf 1.7.74 ABC
The Daughters of Joshua Cabe Return tf 1.28.75 ABC
Who Is the Black Dahlia? tf 3.1.75 NBC
Black Bart pt 4.4.75 CBS
Murder on Flight 502 tf 11.21.75 ABC
Police Woman ep Angela 1.27.76 NBC
James Dean tf 2.19.76 NBC
Flatbush/Avenue J pt 8.24.76 CBS
Kojak ep Dead Again 12.19.76 CBS
Family ep Acts of Love 9.13, 9.20.77 ABC
Nero Wolfe tf/pt 12.19.79 ABC
Lace tf 2.26, 2.27.84 ABC
Special People: Based on a True Story tf 9.11.84 CBS
Lace II tf 5.5, 5.6.85 ABC

ADAMS, DON
A&C, Supp. 1:
Wait Til Your Father Gets Home ep (vo) Don for the Defense Spring 1974 NN
SUPP.:
The Love Boat ep Safety Last 1.2.82 ABC
The Love Boat ep A Very Temporary Secretary 2.12.83 ABC
Inspector Gadget sr (vo) 9.83 NN
The Love Boat ep Novelties 3.17.84 ABC
The Fall Guy ep Losers Weepers 9.19.84 ABC
Check It Out sr 9.85 USA

ADAMS, EDIE
A&C, Supp. 2:
Harry O ep Past Imperfect 1.22.76 ABC
The Eddie Capra Mysteries ep How Do I Kill Thee? 11.3.78 NBC

ADAMS, JULIE
A&C, B.V.:
The Rifleman ep Nora 5.24.60 ABC
Markham ep Crash in the Desert 8.18.60 CBS
The Andy Griffith Show ep The County Nurse 3.19.62 CBS
The Big Valley ep Target 10.31.66 ABC
SUPP.:
Cagney and Lacey ep Better Than Equal 8.9.82 CBS

Quincy, M.E. ep Science for Sale 11.24.82 NBC
Capitol sr 1983 CBS

ADAMS, MAUD
SUPP.:
Chicago Story sr 3.6.82 NBC
Emerald Point, N.A.S. sr 9.26.83 CBS

ADAMS, NICK
A&C, B.V.:
Wanted: Dead or Alive ep The Martin Poster 9.6.58 CBS
Trackdown ep The Gang 2.25.59 CBS
Trackdown ep The Trick 4.15.59 CBS
Burke's Law ep Who Killed Billy Joe? 11.8.63 ABC
The Monroes ep Gun Bound 1.25.67 ABC

AGUTTER, JENNY*
The Snow Goose sp 11.15.71 NBC
A War of Children tf 12.5.72 CBS
Classic Theater ep The Wild Duck 11.14.75 PBS
The Man in the Iron Mask tf 1.17.77 NBC
The Six Million Dollar Man ep Deadly Countdown 9.25, 10.2.77 ABC
Mayflower: The Pilgrim's Adventure tf 11.21.79 CBS
Beulah Land ms 10.7, 10.8, 10.9.80 NBC
Magnum, P.I. ep Little Games 1.3.85 CBS

AHN, PHILIP
A&C, B.V.:
Wanted: Dead Or Alive ep Rope Law 1.3.59 CBS
Wanted: Dead Or Alive ep Pay Off At Pinto 5.21.60 CBS
The Big Valley ep The Emperor of Rice 2.12.68 ABC
My Three Sons ep Honorable Guest 3.68 CBS
Switch ep Death Tong 1.9.78 CBS

AIDMAN, CHARLES
A&C, Supp. 2:
Wanted: Dead Or Alive ep Competition 1.31.59 CBS
Trackdown ep The Samaritan 2.18.59 CBS
Black Saddle ep Client: Neal Adams 5.9.59 NBC
Wanted: Dead Or Alive ep Estralita 10.3.59 CBS
Zane Grey Theater ep Confession 10.15.59 CBS
Wagon Train ep The Amos Gibbon Story 4.20.60 NBC
Johnny Ringo ep The Stranger 5.19.60 CBS
Wagon Train ep The River Crossing 12.14.60 NBC
The Dick Van Dyke Show ep My Husband Is Not a Drunk 10.31.62 CBS
The Dick Van Dyke Show ep Laura's Little Lie 10.9.63 CBS
The Andy Griffith Show ep Andy's Rival 9.20.65 CBS
Gomer Pyle, USMC ep A Visit from Cousin Goober Fall 1965 CBS

Hawaii Five-O ep Nightmare Road 2.18.70 CBS
The Rockford Files ep The Mayor's Committee from Deer Lick Falls 11.25.77 NBC
SUPP.:
Bosom Buddies ep Waterballoongate 12.11.81 ABC
Walt Disney ... One Man's Dream sp 12.12.81 CBS
Magnum, P.I. ep Computer Date 1.14.82 CBS
Marian Rose White tf 1.19.82 CBS
Prime Suspect tf 1.20.82 CBS
Today's FBI ep Blue Collar 2.21.82
Quincy, M.E. ep Sleeping Dogs 11.17.82 NBC
Seven Brides for Seven Brothers ep 3.9.83 CBS
It Takes Two ep Only When I Laugh 3.10.83 ABC
Dallas ep 11.11.83, 11.18.83 CBS
Crazy Like a Fox ep Turn of the Century Fox 1.6.85 CBS
The Twilight Zone sr (nar) 9.27.85 CBS
Cagney and Lacey ep Mothers and Sons 11.25.85 CBS

AKERS, ANDRA*
Police Woman ep Glitter with a Bullet 11.18.75 NBC
Rafferty ep Rafferty (pt/first ep) 9.5.77 CBS
Baretta ep Who Can Make the Sun Shine? 11.30.77 ABC
Dallas ep Love and Marriage 12.20.79 CBS
Hart to Hart ep Death in the Slow Lane 6.3.80 ABC
Flamingo Road ep The Intruder 11.24.81 NBC
Hardcase pt 12.6.81 NBC
Pen 'n' Inc pt 8.15.81 NBC
Hart to Hart ep Harts and Palms 2.9.82 ABC
The Dukes of Hazzard ep Birds Gotta Fly 2.26.82 CBS
Voyagers ep Old Hickory and the Pirate 11.28.82 NBC
Copacabana tf 12.3.85 CBS

AKINS, CLAUDE
A&C, Supp. 2:
I Love Lucy ep Desert Island 11.25.56 CBS
Zane Grey Theater ep Courage Is a Gun 12.14.56 CBS
Zane Grey Theater ep Man Unforgiving 1.3.58 CBS
The Rifleman ep The Safe Guard 11.18.58 ABC
Law of the Plainsman ep A Question of Courage 2.25.60 NBC
Wanted: Dead or Alive ep Prison Trail 5.14.60 CBS
The Rifleman ep Meeting At Midnight 5.17.60 ABC
The Rifleman ep Strange Town 10.25.60 ABC
Zane Grey Theater ep Ransom 11.17.60 CBS
Wagon Train ep The Roger Bigelow Story 12.21.60 NBC
The Monroes ep Ride With Terror 9.21.66 ABC
Toma ep The Accused 5.10.74 ABC
SUPP.:
Desperate Intruder tf 7.31.83 NN
The Love Boat ep Looking for Mr. Wilson 12.17.83 ABC
The Master ep Max 1.20.84 NBC
Celebrity ms 2.12, 2.13, 2.14.84 NBC

Masquerade ep Winnings 4.6.84 ABC
The Legmen ep Woman's Work 8.6.84 NBC
Murder, She Wrote ep Deadly Lady 10.7.84 CBS
Murder, She Wrote ep Hooray for Homicide 10.28.84 CBS
The Baron and the Kid tf 11.21.84 CBS
Murder, She Wrote ep Hit, Run and Homicide 11.25.84 CBS
The Love Boat ep Country Blues 12.8.84 ABC
Murder, She Wrote ep Death Takes a Curtain Call 12.16.84 CBS
Hotel ep Love and Honor 1.16.85 ABC
Hotel ep 12.6.85 ABC

ALBERT, EDDIE
A&C, B.V.:
Tales of Wells Fargo ep A Field of Pride 11.18.61 NBC
Wagon Train ep The Kurt Davis Story 11.28.62 ABC
Mr. Novak ep Visions of Sugar Plums 10.6.64 NBC
The Beverly Hillbillies ep Thanksgiving Story 11.68 CBS
SUPP.:
Beyond Witch Mountain pt 2.20.82 CBS
Rooster tf/pt 8.19.82 ABC
Simon and Simon ep Pirate's Key 1.20.83 CBS
The Love Boat ep The Dean and the Flunkie 2.5.83 ABC
The Demon Murder Case tf 3.6.83 NBC
Burning Rage tf 9.21.84 CBS
In Like Flynn tf/pt 9.14/85 ABC
Hotel ep Pathways 10.30.85 ABC

ALBERT, EDWARD
SUPP.:
Blood Feud tf 4.25 and 5.2.83 OPT
The Yellow Rose sr 10.2.83 NBC
Murder, She Wrote ep Hit, Run and Homicide 11.25.84 CBS
The Hitchhiker ep Man at the Window 3.3.85 HBO

ALBERTSON, JACK
A&C, Supp. 2:
I Love Lucy ep Bon Voyage 1.16.56 CBS
Our Miss Brooks ep Travel Crazy Fall 1956 CBS
Bachelor Father ep Woman of the House Spring 1957 CBS
Bachelor Father ep The Finishing School Spring 1958 CBS
Richard Diamond ep 3.15.59 CBS
The Danny Thomas Show ep The Double Dinner 4.59 CBS
The Many Loves of Dobie Gillis ep Deck the Halls 12.22.59 CBS
The Donna Reed Show ep The Fatal Leap 3.60 ABC
The Many Loves of Dobie Gillis ep Competition Is the Life of Trade 5.24.60 CBS
Dobie Gillis ep You Ain't Nothing But a Houn' Dog 10.4.60 CBS
Pete and Gladys ep Movie Bug 10.17.60 CBS
The Donna Reed Show ep Alex's Twin Fall 1960 ABC
Dobie Gillis ep Maynard G. Krebs--Boy Millionaire 11.22.60 CBS
The Tab Hunter Show ep My Darling Teacher 11.27.60 NBC

Michael Shayne, Private Eye ep Dolls Are Deadly 9.30.60 NBC
Riverboat ep Listen To the Nightingale 1.2.61 NBC
The Tab Hunter Show ep Weekend on Ice 1.15.61 NBC
Dobie Gillis ep Have You Stopped Beating Your Wife? 1.31.61 CBS
The Tab Hunter Show ep Me and My Shadow 2.19.61 NBC
The Tab Hunter Show ep Crazy Over Horses 2.26.61 NBC
Peter Loves Mary ep The Bridey Lindsey Story 5.17.61 NBC
87th Precinct ep Killer's Payoff 11.6.61 NBC
Klondike ep Sure Thing, Man 11.28.61 NBC
The Joey Bishop Show ep Ham in the Family 12.61 NBC
Room For One More sr 1.27.62
The Dick Van Dyke Show ep The Twizzle 2.28.62 CBS
Saints and Sinners ep All the Fine Young Men 9.24.62 NBC
The Lieutenant ep Cool of the Evening 9.21.63 NBC
The Lucy Show ep Lucy and Viv Open a Restaurant Spring 1964 CBS
The Trials of O'Brien ep Charlie Has All the Luck 11.24.65 CBS
Run, Buddy, Run ep Death of Buddy Overstreet 10.3.66 CBS
Hey, Landlord! ep The Long, Hot Bus 10.30.66 NBC
Run For Your Life ep The Treasure Seekers 11.14.66 NBC
It's About Time ep Cave Family Swingers 2.5.67 CBS
Run For Your Life ep Cry Hard, Cry Fast 11.22.67, 11.29.67 NBC
The Andy Griffith Show ep Aunt Bee's Cousin 12.4.67 CBS
Here Come the Brides ep A Man and His Magic 12.4.68 ABC
Gunsmoke ep Danny 10.13.69 CBS
Land of the Giants ep Panic 1.25.70 ABC
Marcus Welby, M.D. ep Go Get 'em Tiger 2.10.70 ABC
Bracken's World ep Papa Never Spanked Me 2.27.70 NBC
Nanny and the Professor ep The Haunted House 10.70 ABC
The Men From Shiloh ep With Love, Bullets and Valentines 10.7.70 NBC
The Immortal ep Reflections on a Lost Tomorrow 10.8.70 ABC
Love, American Style ep Love and the Second Time Around 2.12.71 ABC
Sarge ep A Terminal Case of Vengeance 9.21.71 NBC
SUPP.:
My Body, My Child tf 4.12.82 ABC
Terror at Alcatraz tf/pt 7.4.82 NBC
Grandpa, Will You Run with Me? sp 4.3.83 NBC

ALBRIGHT, LOLA
A&C, B.V.:
Love That Bob ep Bob Falls in Love 10.20.55 CBS
Love That Bob ep Hawaii Calls 10.27.55 CBS
Love That Bob ep Hawaii Stays 11.3.55 CBS
Love That Bob ep Wedding, Wedding, Who's Got the Wedding 11.10.55 CBS
Love That Bob ep Bob Calls Kay's Bluff Spring 1957 CBS
Love That Bob ep Bob Goes Fishing ... Gets Caught Spring

1957 CBS
The Dick Van Dyke Show ep How to Spank a Star 3.11.64 CBS
Burke's Law ep Who Killed Who IV? 4.3.64 ABC
Cimarron Strip ep The Beast That Walks Like a Man 11.3.67 CBS
A&C, Supp. 2:
Switch ep Who Killed Lila Craig? 1.16.78 CBS
The Eddie Capra Mysteries ep Where There's Smoke 9.22.78 NBC
SUPP.:
Quincy, M.E. ep Murder on Ice 3.9.83 NBC
Airwolf ep Sins of the Past 10.27.84 CBS

ALDA, ALAN
SUPP.:
M*A*S*H sr ret 10.25.82 CBS
The Four Seasons ep 1.29.84 CBS

ALDA, ROBERT
A&C, Supp. 1:
Get Christie Love ep For the Family Honor 10.23.74 ABC
A&C, Supp. 2:
The Rockford Files ep A Three Day Affair With a Thirty Day Escrow 11.10.78 NBC
SUPP.:
The Days of Our Lives sr 1981 NBC
Trapper John, M.D. ep 10.24.82 CBS
Private Benjamin ep The Real Thing 4.26.82 CBS
Matt Houston ep The Visitors 2.27.83 ABC
Amanda's ep Aunt Sonia 3.24.83 ABC

ALDEN, NORMAN
A&C, Supp. 2:
Love That Bob ep Bob Meets Miss Sweden Spring 1957 CBS
Leave It To Beaver ep Water Anyone? Fall 1957 CBS
The Adventures of Rin Tin Tin ep Foot Soldier 10.16.58 ABC
The Adventures of Rin Tin Tin ep The Luck of O'Hara 4.3.59 ABC
Lawless Years ep The Lion and the Mouse 5.21.59 NBC
Lawless Years ep Frames 7.16.59 NBC
Hennessy ep Hennessy Meets Honeyboy 10.5.59 CBS
Philip Marlowe ep Lilli, Sweet Lilli 1.19.60 ABC
The Life and Legend of Wyatt Earp ep Requiem For Old Man Clanton 5.30.61 ABC
The Life and Legend of Wyatt Earp ep Just Before the Battle 6.13.61 ABC
The Life and Legend of Wyatt Earp ep The Outlaws Cry Murder 6.27.61 ABC
Lawless Years ep Ginny 7.14.61 NBC
The Rifleman ep The Anvil Chorus 12.17.62 ABC
Saints and Sinners ep The Homecoming Bit 1.7.63 NBC

Temple Houston ep The Law and Big Annie 1.16.64 NBC
Combat ep The Silver Service 10.13.64 ABC
Mr. Broadway ep Between the Rats and the Finks 10.17.64 CBS
Ben Casey ep Three Lil Lambs 3.29.65 ABC
My Favorite Martian ep Hate Me a Little 11.7.65 CBS
Amos Burke, Secret Agent ep The Weapon 11.10.65 ABC
The Andy Griffith Show ep The Battle of Mayberry 4.4.66 CBS
The Andy Griffith Show ep Howard the Bowler 9.18.67 CBS
The Big Valley ep Guilty 10.30.67 ABC
Gunsmoke ep Death Train 11.27.67 CBS
Gunsmoke ep Wonder 12.18.67 CBS
Mod Squad ep Bad Man on Campus 10.1.68 ABC
The Queen and I ep Who's Holding the Bag? 2.13.69 CBS
My Three Sons sr 9.26.70 CBS
Hawaii Five-O ep Rest in Peace, Somebody 11.16.71 CBS
The FBI ep The Wizard 11.12.72 ABC
Owen Marshall, Counselor at Law ep They've Got to Blame Somebody 2.14.73 ABC
Gunsmoke ep Lynch Town 11.19.73 CBS
Apple's Way ep The Outsider 12.15.74 CBS
Baretta ep Under the City 11.3.76 ABC
McMillan ep Bets Off 12.5.76 NBC
The Rockford Files ep Heartaches of a Fool 9.22.78 NBC
SUPP.:
The Facts of Life ep The Marriage Brokers 1.27.82 NBC
The Fall Guy ep Goin' For It 1.27.82 ABC
Desperate Lives tf 3.3.82 CBS
The Greatest American Hero ep The Newlywed Game 1.6.83 ABC
Falcon Crest ep 1.21.83 CBS
The A-Team ep A Small and Deadly War 2.15.83 NBC
Matt Houston ep A Novel Way to Die 4.17.83 ABC
Webster ep Consulting Adults 9.30.83 ABC
Hardcastle and McCormick ep Pennies from Dead Man's Eyes 12.9.84 ABC
Matt Houston ep Break Point 1.11.85 ABC
The Heart of a Champion: The Ray Mancini Story tf 5.1.85 CBS

ALETTER, FRANK
A&C, Supp. 2:
Mrs. G Goes to College ep The Bird 4.62 CBS
Perry Mason ep The Case of the Skeleton's Closet 5.5.62 CBS
Hazel ep Ain't Walter Nice Fall 1962 NBC
The Lloyd Bridges Show ep The Testing Ground 10.23.62 CBS
The Lucy Show ep Lucy, the Music Lover 11.62 CBS
My Favorite Martian ep Russians "R" in Season 10.20.63 CBS
Ben Casey ep There Should Be an Outfit Called Families Anonymous! 12.11.63 ABC
Perry Mason ep The Case of the Arrogant Arsonist 3.5.64 CBS
Great Adventure ep The Henry Bergh Story 3.20.64 CBS

Twelve O'Clock High ep Grant Me No Favor 11.15.65 ABC
Twelve O'Clock High ep Angel Babe 2.28.66 ABC
Petticoat Junction ep The Invisible Mr. Dobble Spring 1966 CBS
Nanny and the Professor ep Nanny and Her Witch's Brew 11.71 ABC
Cannon ep Blood Lines 2.25.76 CBS
Switch ep Thirty Thousand Witnesses 12.26.77 CBS
SUPP.:
The ABC Weekend Special ep Mayday! Mayday! 1.24, 1.31.81 ABC
CHiPs ep Trained for Trouble 4.4.82 NBC
The Fall Guy ep A Piece of Cake 12.1.82 ABC
Alice ep 3.7.83 CBS
Love, Sidney ep One Is Enough 3.28.83 NBC
Automan ep Ships in the Night 1.5.84 ABC
Simon and Simon ep 10.11.84 CBS
Hotel ep New Beginnings 1.23.85 ABC
Three's A Crowd ep One Ego to Go 2.5.85 ABC
Detective in the House ep 4.5.85 CBS
The Golden Girls ep (pt/first ep) 9.14.85 NBC

ALEXANDER, JANE
SUPP.:
In the Custody of Strangers tf 5.26.82 ABC
When She Says No tf 1.30.84 ABC
Calamity Jane tf 3.6.84 CBS
An American Portrait ep Rosina "Rosie the Riveter" Bonavita 4.11.85 CBS
Malice in Wonderland tf 5.12.85 CBS

ALICIA, ANA (a.k.a. Ana-Alicia)*
Battlestar Galactica ep Take the Celestra 4.1.79 ABC
The Sacketts tf 5.15, 5.16.79 NBC
Buck Rogers in the 25th Century ep Vegas in Space 10.4.79 NBC
Quincy, M.E. ep No Way to Treat a Patient 4.3.80 NBC
Roughnecks tf 7.15, 7.16.80 NN
Condominium tf 11.20, 11.24.80 OPT
B.J. and the Bear ep Seven Lady Captives 3.24.81 NBC
Coward of the Country tf 10.7.81 CBS
The Ordeal of Bill Carney tf 12.23.81 CBS
McClain's Law ep A Matter of Honor 1.15.82 NBC
Falcon Crest sr (with ep "House of Cards") 3.12.82 CBS
Happy Endings tf 3.1.83 CBS
Falcon Crest sr ret 9.30.83 CBS
Falcon Crest sr ret 9.28.84 CBS
The Love Boat ep My Mother, My Chaperone 11.24.84 ABC
Falcon Crest sr ret 10.4.85 CBS

ALLEN, DEBBIE*
The Greatest Thing That Almost Happened tf 10.26.77 CBS

Roots: The Next Generation ms 2.18.79 to 2.25.79 ABC
The Love Boat ep The Decision 2.24.79 ABC
Ebony, Ivory and Jade tf/pt 8.3.79 CBS
Fame sr 1.7.82 NBC
Fame sr ret 9.30.82 NBC
The Love Boat ep Isaac's Aegean Affair 2.5.83 ABC
Fame sr ret 10/83 NN
Women of San Quentin tf 10.23.83 NBC
Celebrity ms 2.12, 2.13, 2.14.84 NBC
Fame sr ret 10/84 NN
Fame sr ret 10/85 NN

ALLEN, KAREN*
Lovey: A Circle of Children, Part 2 tf 12.13.78 CBS
Knots Landing ep (pt/first episode) 12.27.79 CBS
East of Eden ms 2.8, 2.9, 2.11.81 ABC

ALLEN, SIAN BARBARA
A&C, Supp. 1:
Alias Smith and Jones ep Six Strangers at Apache Springs 10.28.71 ABC
The Rockford Files ep Tall Woman in Red Wagon 10.11.74 NBC

ALLEN, STEVE
SUPP.:
Hart to Hart ep Deep in the Hart of Dixieland 3.9.82 ABC
Nurse ep The Clown Prince Is Indisposed 4.30.82 CBS
Fantasy Island ep What's the Matter with Kids? 4.16.83 ABC
Hotel ep Detours 11.7.84 ABC
Alice in Wonderland tf 12.9, 12.10.85 CBS

ALLEY, KIRSTIE*
The Highway Honeys pt 1.13.83 NBC
The Love Boat ep Don't Take My Wife, Please 11.26.83 ABC
Masquerade sr 12.22.83 ABC
Sins of the Past tf 4.2.84 ABC
A Bunny's Tale tf 2.25.85 ABC
The Hitchhiker ep Out of the Night 10.29.85 HBO
North and South ms ep 11.3.85 ABC

ALLYSON, JUNE
SUPP.:
The Kid with the Broken Halo tf/pt 4.5.82 NBC
Simon and Simon ep The Last Time I Saw Michael 12.9.82 CBS
Hart to Hart ep Always, Elizabeth 5.15.84 ABC
Murder, She Wrote ep Hit, Run and Homicide 11.25.84 CBS
The Misfits of Science ep Steer Crazy (a.k.a. Old Folk) 11.29.85 NBC

ALVARADO, TRINI
SUPP.:
American Playhouse ep Private Contentment 4.27.82 PBS

Dreams Don't Die tf 5.21.82 ABC
Jacob Timerman: Prisoner Without a Name, Cell Without a Number tf 5.22.83 NBC

AMECHE, DON
SUPP.:
Mr. Smith ep Mr. Smith Goes Public 12.16.83 NBC
The Love Boat ep The Lady and the Maid 3.3.84 ABC
Not in Front of the Kids pt 6.16.84 ABC
Detective in the House ep Father and Other Strangers 3.22.85 CBS

AMES, LEON
A&C, B.V.:
Please Don't Eat the Daisies ep Monster in the Basement 2.66 NBC
The Andy Griffith Show ep The Senior Play 11.14.66 CBS
My Three Sons ep Big Ol' Katie 12.21.68 CBS
My Three Sons ep Expendable Katie 12.28.68 CBS

AMOS, JOHN
SUPP.:
The Love Boat ep Final Score 2.12.83 ABC
The A-Team ep Pure-Dee Poison 1.31.84 NBC
Trapper John, M.D. ep 3.11.84
Hunter sr 9.18.84 NBC
Hunter sr ret 3.23.85 NBC

AMSTERDAM, MOREY
A&C, B.V.:
December Bride ep Mountain Climbing 9.57 CBS
How to Marry a Millionaire ep The Three Pretenders 10.57 NN
The Phil Silvers Show ep Bilko's Giveaway 12.58 CBS

ANDERMAN, MAUREEN*
Kojak ep Where Do You Go When You Have No Place To Go? 12.12.76 CBS
The Andros Targets ep In the Event of My Death 2.14.77 CBS
Once Upon a Family tf 1.22.80 CBS
King Crab tf 6.15.80 ABC
Every Stray Dog and Kid pt 9.21.81 NBC
St. Elsewhere ep Down's Syndrome 11.16.82 NBC
Cocaine and Blue Eyes tf/pt 1.2.83 NBC
The Equalizer ep The Lockbox 10.9.85 CBS
Macbeth sp 11.26.85 A&E
Spenser: For Hire ep Blood Money 11.26.85 ABC

ANDERSON, BARBARA
A&C, Supp. 1:
Harry O ep Material Witness 11.14.74 ABC
A&C, Supp. 2:
Switch ep Net Loss 9.23.77

SUPP.:
Simon and Simon ep Design for Killing 2.10.83 CBS
Star of the Family ep Save My Life, Please 10.21.82 ABC
Simon and Simon ep 2.10.84 CBS

ANDERSON, BRIDGETTE*
Washington Mistress tf 1.13.82 CBS
King's Crossing ep Triangle 2.6.82 ABC
Mae West tf 5.2.82 ABC
Gun Shy sr 3.15.83 CBS
The Return of Marcus Welby, M.D. tf/pt 5.16.84 ABC
Hotel ep Lost and Found 2.13.85 ABC
A Summer to Remember tf 3.27.85 CBS

ANDERSON, HARRY*
Cheers ep Sam at Eleven 12.30.82 NBC
Cheers ep Pick a Con, Any Con 2.24.83 NBC
Night Court sr 1.4.84 NBC
Night Court sr ret 9.27.84 NBC
Tales from the Darkside ep All a Clone By the Telephone 1.19.85 NN
Night Court sr ret 9.26.85 NBC
Hello Sucker! sp 10.11.85 SHO

ANDERSON, JOHN
A&C, Supp. 1:
Trackdown ep End of an Outlaw 11.29.57 CBS
Have Gun--Will Travel ep No Visitors 11.30.57 CBS
Zane Grey Theater ep Hang the Heart High 1.15.59 CBS
The Rifleman ep The Retired Gun 1.20.59 ABC
The Rifleman ep The Shivaree 2.3.59 ABC
The Rifleman ep The Hawk 4.14.59 ABC
Perry Mason ep The Case of the Calendar Girl 4.18.59 CBS
Trackdown ep Toss-Up 5.20.59 CBS
Have Gun--Will Travel ep First Catch a Tiger 9.21.59 CBS
The Rifleman ep The Patsy 9.29.59 ABC
Law of the Plainsman ep Appointment in Santa Fe 11.19.59 NBC
Perry Mason ep The Case of the Battered Bikini 12.5.59 CBS
The Rifleman ep Day of the Hunter 1.5.60 ABC
Detectives ep Karate 1.8.60 ABC
The Rifleman ep Mail Order Groom 1.12.60 ABC
Law of the Plainsman ep Endurance 1.14.60 NBC
Black Saddle ep The Indian Tree 2.19.60 ABC
Lawman ep Left Hand of the Law 3.27.60 ABC
The Rifleman ep Shotgun Man 4.12.60 ABC
Law of the Plainsman ep Jeb's Daughter 4.14.60 NBC
Detectives ep The Prowler 4.22.60 ABC
The Rebel ep Paint a Horse with Scarlet 5.15.60 ABC
Johnny Ringo ep The Derelict 5.26.60 CBS
The Westerner ep School Days 10.7.60 NBC
Bat Masterson ep The Court-Martial of Mayor Mays 1.12.61 NBC

The Rifleman ep Face of Yesterday 1.31.61 ABC
The Twilight Zone ep Odyssey of Flight 33 2.4.61 CBS
Peter Loves Mary ep Last Train from Oakdale 2.8.61 NBC
Lawman ep Hassayampa 2.12.61 ABC
Adventures in Paradise ep Captain Butcher 2.20.61 ABC
87th Precinct ep The Modus Man 10.16.61 NBC
The Rifleman ep The Journey Back 10.31.61 ABC
Cheyenne ep Retaliation 11.13.61 ABC
Bonanza ep The Countess 11.19.61 NBC
Laramie ep The Perfect Gift 1.2.62 NBC
Tall Man ep Night of the Hawk 3.3.62 NBC
Thriller ep Innocent Bystanders 4.9.62 NBC
Sam Benedict ep Nor Practice Makes Perfect 9.29.62 NBC
The Virginian ep Throw a Long Rope 10.3.62 NBC
Eleventh Hour ep 10.24.62 NBC
Stoney Burke ep Spin a Golden Web 11.26.62 ABC
Laramie ep Bad Blood 12.4.62 NBC
The Rifleman ep Incident at Line Shack Six 1.7.63 ABC
Alcoa Premiere ep Blow Hard, Blow Clear 2.14.63 CBS
Laramie ep The Violent Ones 3.5.63 NBC
The Twilight Zone ep Of Late I Think of Cliffordville 4.11.63 CBS
Perry Mason ep The Case of the Greek Goddess 4.18.63 CBS
Kraft Mystery Theater ep Shadow of a Man 6.19.63 NBC
Dr. Kildare ep The Good Samaritan 10.3.63 NBC
Bonanza ep Rain from Heaven 10.6.63 NBC
The Twilight Zone ep The Old Man in the Cave 11.8.63 CBS
The Outer Limits ep Nightmare 12.2.63 ABC
The Fugitive ep Come Watch Me Die 1.21.64 ABC
Rawhide ep Incident at Hourglass 3.12.64 CBS
Ben Casey ep But Who Shall Beat the Drum? 9.24.64 ABC
Ben Casey ep You Fish Or You Can Bait 10.12.64 ABC
Voyage to the Bottom of the Sea ep Cradle of the Deep 3.1.65 ABC
Rawhide ep Retreat 3.26.65 CBS
The Alfred Hitchcock Hour ep The Second Wind 4.26.65 NBC
A Man Called Shenandoah ep Survival 9.20.65 ABC
The Virginian ep Day of the Scorpion 9.22.65 NBC
The Big Valley ep Boots with My Father's Name 9.29.65 ABC
The Big Valley ep The Guilt of Matt Bertell 12.8.65 ABC
The Big Valley ep Invaders 12.29.65 ABC
The FBI ep The Forests of the Night 1.2.66 ABC
The Wackiest Ship in the Army ep 1.2.66 and 1.9.66 NBC
Gunsmoke ep 1.22.66 and 1.29.66 CBS
Branded ep Nice Day for a Hanging 2.6.66 NBC
The Virginian ep Harvest of Strangers 2.16.66 NBC
The Legend of Jesse James ep The Hunted and the Hunters 4.11.66 ABC
The Virginian ep Echo of Thunder 10.5.66 NBC
The Felony Squad ep The Deadly Panther 1.9.67 ABC
Cimarron Strip ep Whitey 10.19.67 CBS

The Virginian ep Bitter Autumn 11.1.67 NBC
Dundee and the Culhane ep 11.15.67 CBS
Mannix ep 12.30.67 CBS
The Rat Patrol ep The Pipeline to Disaster Raid 1.1.68 ABC
Here Come the Brides ep A Man's Errand 3.19.69 ABC
Here Come the Brides ep The Road to the Cradle 11.7.69 ABC
Bonanza ep The Fence 12.28.69 NBC
Hollywood Television Theater ep The Andersonville Trial 5.17.70 PBS
Cade's County ep 10.24.71 CBS
The Sixth Sense ep Through the Flame, Darkly 11.4.72 ABC
Cannon ep Deadly Heritage 3.21.73 CBS
Kung Fu ep The Third Man 4.26.73 ABC
Kung Fu ep Cross-Ties 3.21.74 ABC
Petrocelli ep A Life for a Life 10.9.74 NBC
Born Free ep The White Rhino 11.25.74 NBC
Little House on the Prairie ep Haunted House 9.24.75 NBC
Bronk ep Deception 12.7.75 CBS
SUPP.:
Hart to Hart ep Hart of Darkness 12.8.81 ABC
Bret Maverick ep The Vulture Also Rises 3.16.82 NBC
Silver Spoons ep The Great Computer Caper 11.6.82 NBC
The First Time tf 11.8.82 ABC
Quincy, M.E. ep Sleeping Dogs 11.17.82 NBC
Voyagers ep The Day the Rebs Took Lincoln 11.21.82 NBC
Missing Children: A Mother's Story tf 12.1.82 CBS
The Fall Guy ep Happy Trails 1.12.83 ABC
M*A*S*H ep 1.24.83 CBS
Matt Houston ep The Monster 1.6.84 ABC
Scarecrow and Mrs. King ep 2.13.84 CBS
Sins of the Past tf 4.2.84 ABC
Matt Houston ep New Orleans Nightmare 2.8.85 ABC
Riptide ep Diamonds Are for Never 2.21.85 NBC
North and South ms ep 11.3.85 ABC
MacGyver ep Target: MacGyver 12.22.85 ABC

ANDERSON, LONI
A&C, Supp. 2:
Barnaby Jones ep Deadly Reunion 2.12.76 CBS
Three's Company ep Coffee, Tea Or Jack? 3.78 ABC
SUPP.:
Country Gold tf 11.23.82 CBS
My Mother's Secret Life tf 2.5.84 ABC
Partners in Crime sr 9.22.84 NBC
Amazing Stories ep Guilt Trip 12.1.85 NBC
A Letter to Three Wives tf 12.16.85 NBC

ANDERSON, MELISSA SUE
SUPP.:
An Innocent Love tf 3.2.82 CBS
First Affair tf 10.25.83 CBS

Hotel ep Lifelines 5.9.84 ABC
Finder of Lost Loves ep (pt/first ep) 9.22.84 ABC
Murder, She Wrote ep Hooray for Homicide 10.28.84 CBS
Glitter ep A Minor Miracle 12.18.84 ABC
Hotel ep Imperfect Union 10.9.85 ABC

ANDERSON, MELODY*
Pleasure Cove tf/pt 1.3.79 NBC
Elvis tf 2.11.79 ABC
Archie Bunker's Place ep 10.3.82 CBS
Dallas ep 10.22.82 CBS
T.J. Hooker ep 11.6.82 ABC
The Fall Guy ep Colt's Outlaws (a.k.a. The Backlot Gang) 11.10.82 ABC
CHiPs ep Day of the Robot 1.2.83 NBC
The A-Team ep (pt/first ep) 1.23.83 NBC
St. Elsewhere ep Remission 2.15.83 NBC
St. Elsewhere ep Brothers 3.15.83 NBC
St. Elsewhere ep Working 4.5.83 NBC
St. Elsewhere ep Addiction 5.3.83 NBC
Manimal sr 9.30.83 NBC
Police Woman Centerfold tf 10.17.83 NBC
Ernie Kovacs: Between the Laughter tf 5.14.84 ABC

ANDERSON, RICHARD
A&C, Supp. 2:
Playhouse 90 ep The 80 Yard Run 1.16.58 CBS
The Rifleman ep One Went to Denver 3.17.59 ABC
Wagon Train ep The Matthew Lowry Story 4.1.59 NBC
The Rifleman ep The Lariat 3.29.60 ABC
Law of the Plainsman ep Cavern of the Wind 4.21.60 NBC
Thriller ep The Purple Room 10.25.60 NBC
Checkmate ep Murder Game 12.17.60 CBS
Wanted: Dead or Alive ep Three for One 12.21.60 CBS
The Rifleman ep Miss Birdie 12.27.60 ABC
The Rifleman ep Flowers By the Door 1.10.61 ABC
Wanted: Dead or Alive ep Epitaph 2.8.61 CBS
Hong Kong ep Murder By Proxy 3.1.61 ABC
Kraft Mystery Theater ep The House on Rue Riviera 8.30.61 NBC
The Rifleman ep Milly's Brother 4.23.62 ABC
The Rifleman ep The Bullet 2.25.63 ABC
Dr. Kildare ep Who Ever Heard of a Two-Headed Doll? 9.26.63 NBC
The Lieutenant ep The Two-Star Giant 10.5.63 NBC
Redigo ep The Crooked Circle 10.22.63 ABC
Combat ep A Silent Cry 2.18.64 ABC
Gunsmoke ep Big Man, Little Target 11.21.64 CBS
Kraft Suspense Theater ep Jungle of Fear 4.22.65 NBC
Big Valley ep Last Train to the Fair 4.27.66 ABC
The Man from UNCLE ep The Candidate's Wife Affair 11.4.66 NBC

The Felony Squad ep Prologue to Murder 11.7.66 ABC
The FBI ep Collision Course 11.13.66 ABC
Twelve O'Clock High ep To Seek and Destroy 11.18.66 ABC
Twelve O'Clock High ep Burden of Guilt 12.2.66 ABC
I Spy ep Little Boy Lost 12.14.66 NBC
Twelve O'Clock High ep Six Feet Under 12.16.66 ABC
The Fugitive ep The Judgement 8.22, 8.29.67 ABC
Cimarron Strip ep The Legend of Jud Starr 9.14.67 CBS
The FBI ep Traitor 10.15.67 ABC
The Felony Squad ep The Love Victim 2.5.68 ABC
The FBI ep The Enemies 11.3.68 ABC
The Felony Squad ep Conspiracy of Power 1.10, 1.17.69 ABC
Mod Squad ep Ride the Man Down 10.14.69 ABC
Bracken's World ep Stop Date 12.19.69 NBC
The High Chaparral ep The Long Shadow 1.2.70 NBC
Gunsmoke ep The War Priest 1.5.70 CBS
Alias Smith and Jones ep Never Trust an Honest Man 4.15.71 ABC
The Delphi Bureau ep The Face That Never Was Project 4.7.73 ABC
SUPP.:
Fantasy Island ep Wuthering Heights 1.9.82 ABC
Simon and Simon ep The List 2.17.83 CBS
The Whiz Kids ep Deadly Access 10.26.83 CBS
The Fall Guy ep Inside, Outside 11.16.83 ABC
Automan ep Renegade Run 3.5.84 ABC
Fantasy Island ep The Obsolete Man 3.24.84 ABC
Cover Up sr 9.22.84 CBS
Kane and Abel ms 11.17 to 11.19.85 CBS
Perry Mason Returns tf 12.1.85 NBC
The A-Team ep The Doctor Is Out 12.10.85 NBC

ANDES, KEITH
A&C, B.V.:
The Rifleman ep The Debt 3.5.62 ABC
Branded ep Piece of a Name 5.23.65 NBC
The Lucy Show ep Lucy and the Golden Greek 10.11.65 CBS
The Andy Griffith Show ep Helen, the Authoress 2.27.67 CBS

ANDREWS, DANA
SUPP.:
The Love Boat ep Hyde and Seek 10.30.82 ABC
The Love Boat ep The Groupies 11.6.82 ABC

ANDREWS, TIGE*
Steve Canyon ep Operation Jettison 10.11.58 NBC
The Lawless Years ep 7.30.59 NBC
The Detectives sr 10.16.59 ABC
Playhouse 90 ep Seven Against the Wall 12.11.59 CBS
The Detectives sr ret 9.16.60 ABC
Adventures in Paradise ep Wild Mangoes 5.8.61 ABC

The Detectives sr ret 9.29.61 ABC
Alcoa Premiere ep Flashing Spikes 10.4.62 CBS
Sam Benedict ep Green Room, Green Day 1.19.63 NBC
Mr. Novak ep A Single Isolated Incident 10.22.63 NBC
Slattery's People ep Who You Taking to the Main Event, Eddie? 3.12.65 CBS
12 O'Clock High ep Rx for a Sick Bird 9.20.65 ABC
Jericho ep Wall to Wall Kaput 10.27.66 CBS
Run for Your Life ep A Game of Violence 11.28.66 NBC
The Big Valley ep Wagonload of Dreams 1.2.67 ABC
The Fugitive ep Walls of Night 4.4.67 ABC
The FBI ep Force of Nature 4.9.67 ABC
The Bob Hope Chrysler Theater ep Deadlock 5.17.67 NBC
Dundee and the Culhane ep 10.18.67 CBS
Star Trek ep Friday's Child 12.1.67 NBC
Gunsmoke ep The Jackals 2.12.68 CBS
The Mod Squad sr 9.24.68 ABC
The Mod Squad sr ret 9.23.69 ABC
The Mod Squad sr ret 9.22.70 ABC
The Mod Squad sr ret 9.14.71 ABC
The Mod Squad sr ret 9.14.72 ABC
Marcus Welby, M.D. ep For Services Rendered 9.25.73 ABC
Police Story ep Countdown 1.15, 1.22.74 NBC
Skyway to Death tf 1.19.74 ABC
Kojak ep The Chinatown Murders 9.15.74 CBS
Amy Prentiss ep Portrait of Evil 2.2.75 NBC
The Barbary Coast ep 10.31.75 ABC
Police Woman ep The Purge 11.25.75 NBC
Kojak ep Justice Deferred 2.15.76 CBS
Raid on Entebbe tf 1.9.77 NBC
Kojak ep Photo Must Credit Joe Paxton 3.4.78 CBS
Return of the Mod Squad tf 5.18.79 ABC
Vegas ep 1.9.80 ABC
Quincy, M.E. ep Experiment in Murder 3.31.82 NBC
Tucker's Witch ep Big Mouth 10.13.82 CBS
Seven Brides for Seven Brothers ep 12.22.82 CBS
Hawaiian Heat ep Old Dues 11.16.84 ABC
Street Hawk ep Fire on the Wing 2.8.85 ABC
Hell Town ep The Wedding at St. Dominics 12.4.85 NBC
The Misfits of Science ep Fumble on the One 12.6.85 NBC

ANN-MARGRET*
Who Will Love My Children? tf 2.14.83 ABC
A Streetcar Named Desire tf 3.4.84 ABC

ANSARA, MICHAEL
A&C, B.V.:
The Adventures of Rin Tin Tin ep Yo-o Rinty 10.12.56 ABC
Tales of the 77th Bengal Lancers ep The Enemy 2.24.57 ABC
Hawkeye and the Last of the Mohicans ep Hawkeye's Homecoming 4.57 NN

The Westerner ep Hand on the Gun 12.23.60 NBC
The Farmer's Daughter ep Comes the Revolution 11.63 ABC
Daniel Boone ep The Search 3.3.66 NBC
I Dream of Jeannie ep The Battle of Waikiki 1.68 NBC
Here Come the Brides ep Wives for Wakando 1.22.69 ABC
The High Chaparral ep For the Love of Carlos 4.4.69 NBC
A&C, Supp. 1:
Hawaii Five-O ep Death Is a Company Policy 9.12.72 CBS
The Rockford Files ep Joey Blue Eyes 1.30.76 NBC
SUPP.:
Simon and Simon ep A Recipe for Disaster 12.22.81 CBS
Gavilan ep Designated Hero 12.14.82 NBC
The Fantastic World of D.C. Collins tf 2.10.84 NBC
George Burns Comedy Week ep The Assignment 10.30.85 CBS
Hunter ep Rape and Revenge: The Revenge 11.9.85 NBC
Hardcastle and McCormick ep Mirage à Trois 12.2.85 ABC

ANTON, SUSAN*
The Great American Beauty Contest tf 2.13.73 ABC
The Love Boat ep East Meets West 10.1.83 ABC
Mickey Spillane's Mike Hammer ep Deadly Prey 11.10.84 CBS

ARCHER, ANNE*
The Storefront Lawyers ep Shadows of Doubt 11.11.70 CBS
Hawaii Five-O ep Beautiful Screamer 12.2.70 CBS
Love, American Style ep 12.17.70 ABC
The FBI ep Downfall 2.21.71 ABC
The Mod Squad ep Color of Laughter, Color of Tears 10.12.71 ABC
Ironside ep Murder Impromptu 11.2.71 NBC
Alias Smith and Jones ep Shootout at Diablo Station 12.2.71 ABC
The Sixth Sense ep Can a Dead Man Strike from the Grave? 2.26.72 ABC
Mannix ep A Problem of Innocence 3.4.73 ABC
Bob & Carol & Ted & Alice sr 9.25.73 ABC
The Blue Knight ms 11.13, 11.14, 11.15, 11.16.73 NBC
Harry O ep Guardian at the Gates 9.26.74 ABC
The Mark of Zorro tf 10.29.74 ABC
The Log of the Black Pearl tf 1.4.75 NBC
Little House on the Prairie ep Doctor's Lady 1.22.75 NBC
Petrocelli ep One Killer Too Many 10.1.75 NBC
Switch ep Big Deal in Paradise 2.24.76 CBS
Harry O ep The Mysterious Case of Lester and Dr. Fong 3.18.76 ABC
A Matter of Wife ... And Death tf 4.10.76 NBC
The Dark Side of Innocence tf 5.20.76 NBC
Seventh Avenue ms 2.10, 2.17, 2.24.77 NBC
The Pirate tf 11.21, 11.22.78 CBS
Family Tree sr 1.22.83 NBC
The Sky's No Limit tf 2.7.84 CBS

Falcon Crest ep Recriminations 2.22.85 CBS
Falcon Crest ep The Trial 3.15.85 CBS
Falcon Crest ep Devil's Harvest 4.12.85 CBS
Falcon Crest ep The Deadline 4.19.85 CBS
Falcon Crest sr 10.4.85 CBS

ARDEN, EVE
SUPP.:
Masquerade ep Diamonds 1.22.83 ABC
Faerie Tale Theater ep Cinderella 8.14.85 SHO

ARGO, ALLISON*
The Gift tf 12.15.79 CBS
High Ice tf 1.7.80 NBC
WKRP in Cincinnati ep A Family Affair 1.7.80 CBS
Casino tf/pt 8.1.80 ABC
Ladies' Man sr 10.27.80 CBS
The Return of Frank Cannon tf 11.1.80 CBS
An Uncommon Love tf 11.30.83 CBS
The Legmen ep I Shall Be Re-released 2.17.84 NBC

ARGOUD, KARIN*
The ABC Afterschool Special ep Tough Girl 10.28.81 ABC
The Renegades tf/pt 8.11.82 ABC
Quincy, M.E. ep Beyond the Open Door 2.2.83 NBC
Mama's Family sr 1.22.83 NBC
Mama's Family sr ret 9.29.83 NBC

ARLEN, RICHARD
A&C, B.V.:
Wanted: Dead Or Alive ep Rope Law 1.3.59 CBS

ARMSTRONG, BESS*
On Our Own sr 10.9.77 CBS
Getting Married tf 5.17.78 CBS
The Love Boat ep 9.30.78 ABC
How To Pick Up Girls tf 11.3.78 ABC
Sweepstakes ep 2.23.79 NBC
Walking Through the Fire tf 5.15.79 CBS
11th Victim tf 11.6.79 CBS
Barefoot in the Park sp 3.21.82 HBO
This Girl for Hire tf/pt 11.1.83 CBS
Lace tf 2.26, 2.27.84 ABC

ARMSTRONG, KERRY*
Prisoner: Cell Block H sr 1979 NN
Tales from the Darkside ep Slippage 12.22.84 NN
Murder, She Wrote ep Death Takes a Curtain Call 12.16.84 CBS
Dynasty ep The Heiress 5.8.85 ABC
Dynasty ep The Titans 11.13.85 ABC
Dynasty ep The Decision 11.20.85 ABC

ARMSTRONG, LOUIS
A&C, B.V.:
You Are There ep The Emergence of Jazz 9.5.54 CBS

ARNAZ, DESI
A&C, B.V.:
The Danny Thomas Show ep Lucille Ball Upsets the Williams Household 1.5.59 CBS

ARNAZ JR., DESI
A&C, Supp. 1:
The Brady Bunch ep The Possible Dream 2.27.70 ABC
SUPP.:
Automan sr 12.15.83 ABC

ARNAZ, LUCIE
SUPP.:
The Mating Season tf 12.30.80 CBS
Washington Mistress tf 1.13.82 CBS
One More Try pt 8.31.82 CBS
The Lucie Arnaz Show sr 4.2.85 CBS

ARQUETTE, ROSANNA
SUPP.:
The Parade tf 2.29.84 CBS

ASHBROOK, DAPHNE*
Knight Rider ep A Knight in Shining Armor 1.8.84 NBC
Riptide ep Where the Girls Are 10.2.84 NBC
Street Hawk ep Dog Eat Dog 2.1.85 ABC
The A-Team ep Road Games 2.5.85 NBC
Simon and Simon ep 2.14.85 CBS
Our Family Honor sr 9.17.85 ABC

ASHLEY, ELIZABETH*
Harpy tf 3.12.71 CBS
The Face of Fear tf 10.8.71 CBS
When Michael Calls tf 2.5.72 ABC
Second Chance tf/pt 2.8.72 ABC
The Heist tf 11.29.72 ABC
Your Money Or Your Wife tf 12.19.72 CBS
The Magician tf/pt 3.17.73 NBC
One of My Wives Is Missing tf 3.5.76 ABC
Family ep 1.11.77 ABC
The War Between the Tates tf 6.13.77 NBC
Insight ep 4.19.78 NN
Tom and Joann pt 7.5.78 CBS
A Fire in the Sky tf 11.26.78 NBC
Svengali tf 3.9.83 CBS
He's Fired, She's Hired tf 12.18.84 CBS
The Love Boat ep The Perfect Divorce 5.4.85 ABC

Cagney and Lacey ep The Psychic 10.21.85 CBS
The Hitchhiker ep Out of the Night 10.29.85 HBO

ASNER, EDWARD
A&C, Supp. 2:
Naked City ep New York to L.A. 4.19.60 ABC
Route 66 ep The Opponent 6.2.61 CBS
Dr. Kildare ep Shining Image 10.12.61 NBC
Target: The Corruptors ep The Golden Carpet 11.21.61 ABC
Cain's Hundred ep Blues for a Junkman 2.20.62 NBC
Alfred Hitchcock Presents ep What Frightened You, Fred? 5.1.62 NBC
Dr. Kildare ep The Legacy 12.13.62 NBC
The Untouchables ep Search for a Dead Man 1.1.63 ABC
The Eleventh Hour ep My Name Is Judith, I'm Lost, You See 1.16.63 NBC
The Virginian ep Echo of Another Day 3.27.63 NBC
Breaking Point ep Last Summer We Didn't Go Away 9.23.63 ABC
Alfred Hitchcock Presents ep To Catch a Butterfly 9.13.63 NBC
Mr. Novak ep First Year, First Day 9.24.63 NBC
The Nurses ep The Gift 10.17.63 CBS
Ben Casey ep Echo of a Silent Cheer 10.23.63 ABC
Gunsmoke ep Hung High 11.14.64 CBS
Profiles in Courage ep Richard T. Ely 12.6.64 NBC
Mr. Novak ep An Elephant Is Like a Tree 1.12.65 NBC
Profiles in Courage ep Hamilton Fish 3.7.65 NBC
Voyage to the Bottom of the Sea ep The Exile 3.15.65 ABC
Amos Burke, Secret Agent ep Nightmare in the Sun 10.20.65 ABC
A Man Called Shenandoah ep The Verdict 11.1.65 ABC
Please Don't Eat the Daisies ep My Good Friend, What's His Name 1.25.66 NBC
Run For Your Life ep The Committee for the 25th 10.3.66 NBC
The Felony Squad ep The Killer Instinct 12.5.66 ABC
The Girl from UNCLE ep The Double-O-Nothing Affair 3.21.67 NBC
Judd, For the Defense ep The Other Face of the Law 9.22.67 ABC
Here Come the Brides ep The Firemaker 1.15.69 ABC
Medical Center ep The Last Ten Yards 9.24.69 CBS
Here Come the Brides ep The Legend of Big Foot 11.14.69 ABC
Mod Squad ep Should Auld Acquaintance Be Forgot! 3.31.70 ABC
Cade's County ep The Fake 3.26.72 CBS
Hawaii Five-O ep Wooden Model for a Rat 12.11.75 CBS
SUPP.:
A Case of Libel sp 10.83 SHO
Anatomy of an Illness tf 5.15.84 CBS
Off the Rack pt 12.7.84 ABC
Off the Rack sr 3.15.85 ABC
An American Portrait ep Samuel "Golden Rule" Jones 4.17.85 CBS

Tender Is the Night sr 10.27.85 SHO

ASTIN, JOHN
A&C, B.V.:
Peter Loves Mary ep Wilma's Phantom Lover 12.60 NBC
Mrs. G Goes to College ep The Bird 4.62 CBS
Dennis the Menace ep A Quiet Evening Spring 1962 CBS
Hennessy ep Remember Pearl Harbor? Spring 1962 CBS
A&C, Supp. 1:
Get Christie Love ep Our Lady in London 1.29.75 ABC
SUPP.:
The Facts of Life ep Summer of '84 9.26.84 NBC
Diff'rent Strokes ep A Haunting We Will Go 9.29.84 NBC
Murder, She Wrote ep Hooray for Homicide 10.28.84 CBS
Night Court ep Inside Harry Stone 11.29.84 NBC
Simon and Simon ep Revolution #9½ 12.13.84 CBS
Otherworld ep Mansion of the Beast 3.9.85 CBS
Murder, She Wrote ep Joshua Peabody Died Here 10.6.85 CBS
Murder, She Wrote ep A Lady in the Lake 11.10.85 CBS
Mary sr 12.11.85 CBS
Murder, She Wrote ep Sticks and Stones 12.15.85 CBS

ASTIN, MacKENZIE*
Lois Gibb and the Love Canal tf 2.17.82 CBS
Finder of Lost Loves ep Old Friends 11.17.84 ABC
The Facts of Life ep Me and Eleanor (a.k.a. Tootie & Eleanor) 1.2.85 NBC
The Facts of Life ep Jazzbeau 1.16.85 NBC
The Facts of Life ep Two Guys from Appleton 1.23.85 NBC
Hotel ep New Beginnings 1.23.85 ABC
The Facts of Life ep With a Little Help from My Friends 1.30.85 NBC
The Facts of Life ep It's Lovely at the Top 3.27.85 NBC
The Facts of Life ep Grand Opening 9.28.85 NBC
The Facts of Life ep Men for All Seasons 10.19.85 NBC
I Dream of Jeannie: 15 Years Later tf 10.20.85 NBC
The Facts of Life ep Doo Wah 11.2.85 NBC
The Facts of Life ep We Get Letters 11.30.85 NBC

ASTIN, PATTY DUKE (a.k.a. Patty Duke)
SUPP.:
It Takes Two sr 10.14.82 ABC
Something So Right tf 11.30.82 CBS
September Gun tf 10.8.83 CBS
Best Kept Secrets tf 3.26.84 ABC
George Washington ms 4.8, 4.9, 4.10, 4.11.84 CBS
The Love Boat ep What a Drag! 9.22.84 ABC
Hotel ep New Beginnings 1.23.85 ABC
Hail to the Chief sr 4.9.85 ABC

ATWATER, BARRY

A&C, Supp. 2:

Have Gun--Will Travel ep A Reasonable Man 1.1.58 CBS
The Court of Last Resort ep The Jacob Loveless Case 2.21.58 ABC
Goodyear Theater ep Curtain Call 12.22.58 CBS
Bat Masterson ep Trail Pirate 12.31.58 NBC
Black Saddle ep 2.28.59 NBC
Black Saddle ep 5.16.59 NBC
The Loretta Young Theater ep One Beautiful Moment 9.27.59 NBC
The Loretta Young Theater ep Mask of Violence 10.11.59 NBC
Alcoa Presents ep The Day the World Wept 2.9.60 ABC
The Rebel ep Absolution 4.2.60 ABC
Tightrope ep The Hired Guns 5.10.60 CBS
Perry Mason ep The Case of the Waylaid Wolf 2.4.61 CBS
Perry Mason ep The Case of the Prankish Professor 1.7.63 CBS
Empire ep The Four Thumbs Story 1.8.63 ABC
The Outer Limits ep Corpos Earth 11.8.63 ABC
The Kraft Suspense Theater ep The Name of the Game 2.26.63 NBC
The Farmer's Daughter ep Love in the Picket Line 10.23.64 ABC
Voyage to the Bottom of the Sea ep The Buccaneer 2.8.65 ABC
Harry O ep The Mysterious Case of Lester and Dr. Fong 3.18.76 ABC
The Rockford Files ep Hotel of Fear 11.25.77 NBC

AUBERJONOIS, RENE

A&C, Supp. 2:

Love, American Style ep Love and the Spaced-Out Chick 1.19.73 ABC
Harry O ep Anatomy of a Frame 9.11.75 ABC
The Rookies ep 12.9.75 ABC
Rhoda ep Two Little Words: Marriage Counselor 11.76 CBS
Rhoda ep The Ultimatum 1.30.77 CBS
The Rockford Files ep With the French Heel Back, Can the Nehru Jacket Be Far Behind 1.5.79 NBC

SUPP.:

Faerie Tale Theater ep The Tale of the Frog Prince 9.11.82 SHO
Benson sr ret 10.22.82 ABC
Faerie Tale Theater ep Sleeping Beauty 7.7.83 SHO
Benson sr ret 9.16.83 ABC
The Love Boat ep The Love Boat Fall Preview 9.15.84 ABC
Benson sr ret 9.21.84 ABC
Benson sr ret 10.4.85 ABC

AUMONT, JEAN PIERRE

SUPP.:

Hart to Hart ep The Hart of the Matter 2.16.82 ABC
Simon and Simon ep 9.27.84 CBS

AUSTIN, KAREN*
Hart to Hart ep A New Kind of High 11.27.79 ABC
Waikiki tf/pt 4.21.80 ABC
Quincy, M.E. ep The Shadow of Death 2.24.81 NBC
Hill Street Blues ep Blood Money 11.5.81 NBC
A Piano for Mrs. Cimino tf 2.3.82 CBS
Three's Company ep Jack's "10" 2.23.82 ABC
The Quest sr 10.22.82 ABC
Night Court sr 1.4.84 NBC
Celebrity ms 2.12, 2.13, 2.14.84 NBC
London and Davis in New York pt 9.9.84 CBS
St. Elsewhere ep Give the Boy a Hand 1.23.85 NBC
St. Elsewhere ep Any Portrait in a Storm 1.30.85 NBC
Love, Mary tf 10.8.85 CBS
Our Family Honor ep 12.13.85 ABC
A Letter to Three Wives tf 12.16.85 NBC

AUSTIN, TRACY*
Mork and Mindy ep Midas Mork (Tracy's professional acting debut) 4.15.82 ABC
An American Portrait ep Charles Loloma 12.19.85 CBS

AVALON, FRANKIE
A&C, B.V.:
My Sister Eileen ep Ruth Becomes a Success 2.8.61 CBS
SUPP.:
Happy Days ep Poobah Doo Dah 1.26.82 ABC

AXTON, HOYT*
The Bionic Woman ep Road to Nashville 10.20.76 ABC
Flying High ep Great Expectations 12.29.78 CBS
The Dukes of Hazzard ep Good Neighbors Duke 1.2.81 CBS
The Hoyt Axton Show pt 9.28.81 NBC
Seven Brides for Seven Brothers ep 11.3.82 CBS
The Rousters sr 10.1.83 NBC
Faerie Tale Theater ep Goldilocks and the Three Bears 1.9.84 SHO
Domestic Life ep 3.18.84 CBS
Cover Up ep Death in Vogue 9.29.84 CBS
Diff'rent Strokes ep Sam's Father 11.3.84 NBC
Diff'rent Strokes ep A Camping We Will Go 2.23.85 NBC
Steel Collar Man pt 8.7.85 CBS
Trapper John, M.D. ep Game of Hearts 10.6, 10.13.85 CBS
Glitter ep The Runaway 12.26.85 ABC

AYERS-ALLEN, PHYLICIA*
Delvecchio ep Wax Job 10.24.76 CBS
The Cosby Show sr 9.20.84 NBC
The Cosby Show sr ret 9.26.85 NBC
The Love Boat ep A Day in Port 9.28.85 ABC

AYRES, LEAH*
Mother and Me, M.D. pt 6.14.79 NBC
Nine to Five sr 9.29.83 ABC
The Love Boat ep For Bettor or Worse 1.14.84 ABC
Finder of Lost Loves ep Deadly Silence 10.6.84 ABC
The A-Team ep Double Heat 10.23.84 NBC
The Love Boat ep Country Blues 12.8.84 ABC
Hotel ep Identities 3.20.85 ABC
St. Elsewhere ep 12.4.85 NBC
Crazy Like a Fox ep If the Shoe Fits 12.15.85 CBS

AYRES, LEW
A&C, B.V.:
Slattery's People ep The Last Computer 11.19.65 CBS
A&C, Supp. 1:
Hawaii Five-O ep Legacy of Terror 1.1.76 CBS
SUPP.:
Trapper John, M.D. ep Cause for Concern 4.18.82 CBS
Trapper John, M.D. ep Don't Rain on My Charade 9.26.82 CBS
Little House: A New Beginning ep Welcome to Olesonville 10.11.82 NBC
The Devlin Connection ep Claudine 12.11.82 NBC
Quincy, M.E. ep The Law Is a Fool 1.5.83 NBC
Fantasy Island ep Midnight Waltz 2.12.83 ABC
Savage in the Orient pt 6.21.83 CBS
Hotel ep Trials 5.2.84 ABC
Finder of Lost Loves ep Goodbye, Sara 11.3.84 ABC
Lime Street sr 9.28.85 ABC

AVERY, PHYLLIS
A&C, B.V.:
Zane Grey Theater ep The Unrelenting Sky 10.26.56 CBS
Broken Arrow ep The Teacher 11.19.57 ABC
Man With a Camera ep 11.7.58 ABC
Tate ep The Reckoning 8.24.60 NBC
Kraft Suspense Theater ep Are There Any More Out There Like You? 11.7.63 NBC

AZZARA, CANDICE (a.k.a. Candy Azzara)
A&C, Supp. 2:
Rhoda ep Strained Interlude 1.20.75 CBS
Rhoda ep The Jack Story 1.78 CBS
SUPP.:
Trapper John, M.D. ep Call Me Irresponsible 12.21.81 CBS
Million Dollar Infield tf 2.2.82 CBS
Divorce Wars tf 3.1.82 ABC
Diff'rent Strokes ep Have I Got a Girl for You 4.8.82 NBC
The Rainbow Girl (a.k.a. "The Ann Jillian Show") pt 6.4.82 NBC
The Love Boat ep The Arrangement 10.2.82 ABC
Mama Malone ep 3.28.84 CBS

One Day at a Time ep Another Man's Shoes 5.28.84 CBS
E/R ep 12.12.84 CBS
George Burns Comedy Week ep The Smiths 10.9.85 CBS
Remington Steele ep Steele Blushing 10.22.85 NBC
George Burns Comedy Week ep The Borrowing (a.k.a. Kidnappers of the Rich and Famous) 12.25.85 CBS
The New Love, American Style ep A Friendly Christmas 12.25.85 ABC

- B -

BABCOCK, BARBARA
A&C, Supp. 1:
Judd, For the Defense ep Citizens Ritter 11.10.67 ABC
Judd, For the Defense ep To Love and Stand Mute 12.8.67 ABC
Family Affair ep Oh, to Be in England 1.27.69 CBS
SUPP.:
Taxi ep Like Father, Like Son 11.21.81 ABC
McClain's Law ep A Time of Peril 12.4.81 NBC
Best of the West ep Frog's First Gunfight 1.7.82 ABC
Best of the West ep Frog Gets Lucky 1.14.82 ABC
The Big Easy pt 8.15.82 NBC
Memories Never Die tf 12.15.82 CBS
Hill Street Blues sr ret 9.30.82 NBC
Cheers ep Now Pitching: Sam Malone 1.6.83 NBC
Hill Street Blues sr ret 10.13.83 NBC
Quarterback Princess tf 12.3.83 CBS
The Four Seasons sr 1.29.84 CBS
Bliss pt 6.28.84 ABC
Hotel ep Promises 1.9.85 ABC
Murder, She Wrote ep Tough Guys Don't Die 2.24.85 CBS
Crazy Like a Fox ep Fox and Hounds 3.24.85 CBS
Steambath ep 4.8.85 SHO

BACH, CATHERINE
SUPP.:
The Dukes of Hazzard sr ret 9.24.82 CBS
White Water Rebels tf 1.8.83 CBS
The Love Boat ep Putting on the Dog 3.26.83 ABC
The Dukes of Hazzard sr ret 9.23.83 CBS
The Dukes of Hazzard sr ret 9.21.84 CBS

BACKUS, JIM
A&C, B.V.:
The Danny Thomas Show ep The Deerfield Story 4.11.60 CBS
The Brady Bunch ep Ghost Town, U.S.A. 9.22.71 ABC
A&C, Supp. 1:
The Brady Bunch ep The Hustler 3.1.74 ABC

Harry O ep Sound of Trumpets 1.30.75 ABC
SUPP.:
Trapper John, M.D. ep It Only Hurts When I Love 1.16.83 CBS

BADDELEY, HERMIONE
A&C, Supp. 1:
Mr. Novak ep Chin Up, Mr. Novak 2.18.64 NBC
Twelve O'Clock High ep The Trap 3.5.65 ABC
Camp Runamuck sr 9.17.65 NBC
Batman ep The Great Escape 2.1.68, 2.8.68 ABC
A&C, Supp. 2:
Little House on the Prairie ep Castoff 9.12.77 NBC
Little House on the Prairie ep The Handyman 10.3.77 NBC
Little House on the Prairie ep The Lake Kezia Monster 2.12.79 NBC
SUPP.:
The Two of Us ep Brentwood's Mom 2.3.82 CBS
This Girl for Hire tf/pt 11.1.83 CBS
Magnum, P.I. ep 2.23.84 CBS
Shadow Chasers ep The Shadow Chasers (pt/first ep) 11.14.85 ABC
Shadow Chasers ep Parts Unknown 12.12.85 ABC

BADLER, JANE*
One Life to Live sr 1978 ABC
Terror Among Us tf 1.12.81 CBS
V tf/pt 5.1 and 5.2.83 NBC
Mr. Smith ep Mr. Smith Plays Cyrano 11.25.83 NBC
V: The Final Battle ms 5.6, 5.7, 5.8.84 NBC
V: The Series sr 10.26.84 NBC
Covenant pt 8.5.85 ABC
Hotel ep 12.18.85 ABC

BAGGETTA, VINCENT*
Get Christie Love ep For the Family Honor 10.23.74 ABC
Cannon ep Daddy's Little Girl 12.18.74 CBS
Mannix ep A Choice of Victims 12.22.74 CBS
The Rookies ep Take Over 12.30.74 ABC
Starsky and Hutch ep Death Notice 10.15.75 ABC
Kojak ep A Long Way From Times Square 11.30.75 CBS
Jigsaw John ep Plastique 4.19.76 NBC
The Rockford Files ep Drought at Indianhead River 11.5.76 NBC
Delvecchio ep Thicker Than Water 11.7.76 CBS
I Want to Keep My Baby tf 11.19.76 CBS
Switch ep The Four Horsemen 2.13.77 CBS
Westside Medical ep Turnabout 4.7.77 ABC
The Love Boat ep 11.26.77 ABC
Barnaby Jones ep A Ransom in Diamonds 1.12.78 CBS
The Eddie Capra Mysteries sr 9.8.78 NBC
Sweepstakes ep 2.9.79 NBC
Eischied ep Only the Pretty Girls Die 9.21, 9.28.79 NBC

The Chicago Story tf/pt 3.15.81 NBC
The Ordeal of Bill Carney tf 12.23.81 ABC
Chicago Story sr 3.6.82 NBC
Lou Grant ep 4.19.82 CBS
T. J. Hooker ep Walk a Straight Line 11.5.83 ABC
Hill Street Blues ep Ratman and Robbin 1.19.84 NBC
Remington Steele ep Steele Away with Me 1.24.84 NBC
Hill Street Blues ep Nichols from Heaven 1.26.84 NBC
The A-Team ep Bullets and Bikinis 9.18.84 NBC
Hotel ep The Legacy 11.2.84 ABC
Partners in Crime ep Getting in Shape 12.22.84 NBC
MacGruder and Loud ep (pt/first ep) 1.20.85 ABC
Hotel ep New Beginnings 1.23.85 ABC
Murder, She Wrote ep Footnote to Murder 3.10.85 CBS
T. J. Hooker ep The Assassin 11.13.85 CBS
Simon and Simon ep Reunion at Alcatraz 11.14.85 CBS
Doubletake tf 11.24, 11.26.85 CBS
Lady Blue ep 11.30.85 ABC

BAILEY, PEARL*
Trauma Center ep Out of Control 12.8.83 ABC
Silver Spoons ep Lulu's Back in Town 10.7.84 NBC
Silver Spoons ep What's Cookin'? 1.27.85 NBC
An American Portrait ep Bill Sample 1.28.85 CBS
The ABC Afterschool Special ep Cindy Eller: A Modern Fairy Tale 10.9.85 ABC

BAIN, BARBARA
A&C, B.V.:
Harbourmaster ep The Captain's Gun 5.11.58 CBS
Adventures in Paradise ep Nightmare in the Sun 6.19.61 ABC
The Dick Van Dyke Show ep Will You Two Be My Wife 1.16.63 CBS
Empire ep Hidden Asset 3.26.63 ABC
Wagon Train ep The Fenton Canaby Story 12.30.63 ABC
Mr. Novak ep How Does Your Garden Grow? 3.3.64 NBC
SUPP.:
Mickey Spillane's Mike Hammer ep A Death in the Family 11.24.84 CBS
Moonlighting ep My Fair David 10.29.85 ABC

BAIN, CONRAD
A&C, Supp. 2:
N.Y.P.D. ep Shakedown 9.5.67 ABC
SUPP.
Diff'rent Strokes sr ret 10.2.82 NBC
Diff'rent Strokes sr ret 10.1.83 NBC
Diff'rent Strokes sr ret 9.29.84 NBC
The Love Boat ep Unmade for Each Other 1.5.85 ABC
Diff'rent Strokes sr ret 9.25.85 ABC
The Love Boat ep A Day in Port 9.28.85 ABC

BAIO, SCOTT
SUPP.:
Gemini sp 2.82 SHO
Joanie Loves Chachi sr 3.23.82 ABC
Happy Days ep Letting Go 10.12.82 ABC
Joanie Loves Chachi sr ret 10.28.82 ABC
Happy Days ep Who Gives a Hootenanny 11.16.82 ABC
Happy Days ep Going Steady 11.23.83 ABC
Happy Days ep Life's More Important Than Show Business 1.25.83 ABC
Happy Days ep Babysitting 3.1.83 ABC
Happy Days ep Turn Around ... And You're Home 3.15.83 ABC
Happy Days ret to sr (with ep "Because It's There") 9.27.83 ABC
Hotel ep Faith, Hope and Charity 11.23.83 ABC
The CBS Schoolbreak Special ep All the Kids Do It 4.24.84 CBS
Charles in Charge sr 10.3.84 CBS
The Fall Guy ep Femme Fatale 10.10.85 ABC
Alice in Wonderland tf 12.9, 12.10.85 CBS

BAKER, DIANE
SUPP.:
The Blue and The Gray ms 11.14, 11.15, 11.16, 11.17.82 CBS
Fantasy Island ep Saturday's Child 12.10.83 ABC
A Woman of Substance tf 12.5, 12.12.84 OPT

BAKER, JOE DON
A&C, Supp. 1:
Gunsmoke ep Prime of Life 5.7.66 CBS
The Big Valley ep Lightfoot 2.17.69 ABC

BALDING, REBECCA*
The Bionic Woman ep Jaime's Shield 12.15, 12.22.76 ABC
Starsky and Hutch ep Little Girl Lost 12.25.76 ABC
Lou Grant sr 9.20.77 CBS
Deadly Game tf 12.3.77 NBC
The Gathering tf 12.4.77 ABC
Barnaby Jones ep Prime Target 1.19.78 CBS
The Rockford Files ep 1.27.78 NBC
Starsky and Hutch ep Class in Crime 2.15.78 ABC
Soap sr 9.14.78 ABC
Makin' It sr 2.1.79 ABC
The French-Atlantic Affair ms ep 11.18.79 ABC
Supertrain ep 4.28.79 NBC
The Gathering, Part II tf 12.17.79 NBC
Mr. & Mrs. & Mr. pt 9.1.80 CBS
I'm a Big Girl Now ep 1.16.81 ABC
Cagney and Lacey ep 3.7.83 CBS
Matt Houston ep The Woman in White 9.16.83 ABC
Lottery ep New York: Winning Can Be Murder ("I Do, I Don't" segment) 11.18.83 ABC

Gimme a Break ep Herbie 1.5.84 NBC
The Mississippi ep 2.14.84 CBS
Family Ties ep Working at It 5.10.84 NBC
Matt Houston ep Apostle of Death 10.19.84 ABC
The Insiders ep Doctors, Incorporated 10.23.85 ABC
Hotel ep Flashback 11.9.85 ABC
Trapper John, M.D. ep Billboard Barney 12.29.85 CBS

BALDWIN, JUDITH*
The Delphi Bureau tf/pt 3.6.72 ABC
Rescue from Gilligan's Island tf 10.14, 10.21.78 NBC
The Dukes of Hazzard ep Repo Man 2.16.79 CBS
The Castaways on Gilligan's Island tf 5.3.79 NBC
Tales of the Apple Dumpling Gang pt 1.16.82 CBS
The Fall Guy ep Soldiers of Misfortune 2.10.82 ABC
I Was a Mail Order Bride tf 12.14.82
Archie Bunker's Place ep 1.2.83 CBS
The Powers of Matthew Star ep Brain Drain 3.4.83 NBC
Matt Houston ep The Woman in White 9.16.83 ABC
Emerald Point, N.A.S. ep 10.31.83 CBS
E/R ep 10.2.84 CBS

BALIN, INA
SUPP.:
Code Red ep The Little Girl Who Cried Fire 11.22.81 ABC
Hart to Hart ep Hartless Hobby 1.2.82 ABC
Quincy, M.E. ep The Unquiet Grave 4.7.82 NBC
Quincy, M.E. ep Dying for a Drink 11.3.82 NBC
Airwolf ep Flight #093 Is Missing 11.17.84 CBS

BALL, LUCILLE
A&C, B.V.:
The Danny Thomas Show ep Lucille Ball Upsets the Williams Household 1.5.59 CBS
SUPP.:
Stone Pillow tf 11.5.85 CBS

BALSAM, MARTIN
A&C, B.V.:
Suspense ep I, Mike Kenny 3.25.64 CBS
SUPP.:
Quincy, M.E. ep Stolen Tears 3.17.82 NBC
Little Gloria ... Happy at Last tf 10.24, 10.25.82 NBC
I Want to Live tf 5.9.83 ABC
Cold Storage sp 11.11.84 A&E
Space ms 4.14, 4.15, 4.16, 4.17, 4.18.85 CBS
Murder in Space tf 7.28.85 SHO
Grown Ups sp 11.25.85 SHO
Glitter ep The Odd Couple 12.26.85 ABC

BALSAM, TALIA

SUPP.:

Hill Street Blues ep Some Like It Hot Wired 3.18.82 NBC
Chicago Story ep 3.27.82 NBC
Fit for a King pt 6.11.82 ABC
Cagney and Lacey ep 1.24.83 CBS
Family Ties ep Tender Is the Knight 9.28.83 NBC
Calamity Jane tf 3.6.84 CBS
Magnum, P.I. ep 3.15.84 CBS
Nadia tf 6.11.84 OPT
Punky Brewster ep Punky Finds a Home (Part 2) 9.23.84 NBC
Punky Brewster ep Punky Finds a Home (Part 3) 9.30.84 NBC
Consenting Adults tf 2.4.85 ABC
Murder, She Wrote ep Footnote to Murder 3.10.85 CBS

BANCROFT, ANNE

A&C, Supp. 1:

Zane Grey Theater ep In Darkness 11.15.57 CBS

SUPP.:

Marco Polo ms 5.16, 5.17, 5.18, 5.19.82 NBC
That Was the Week That Was pt 4.22.85 ABC

BANNEN, IAN

A&C, B.V.:

The Adventures of Robin Hood ep The May Queen 4.9.56 CBS

BARASH, OLIVIA

SUPP.:

One Day at a Time ep 3.7.83 CBS
Night Court ep Santa Goes Downtown 1.11.84 NBC
Spencer ep 12.8.84 NBC

BARBEAU, ADRIENNE

SUPP.:

Fantasy Island ep Let Them Eat Cake 2.12.83 ABC
Hotel ep Tomorrows 1.11.84 ABC
Seduced tf 3.12.85 CBS
The Twilight Zone ep Teacher's Aide 11.8.85 CBS
Bridge Across Time tf 11.22.85 NBC
Murder, She Wrote ep Jessica Behind Bars 12.1.85 CBS

BARNES, JOANNA

A&C, Supp. 1:

Maverick ep Ghost Rider 10.13.57 ABC
Colt .45 ep Ghost Town 2.21.58 ABC
Maverick ep Lonesome Reunion 9.28.58 ABC
Maverick ep The Burning Sky 2.23.59 ABC
21 Beacon Street sr 7.2.59 NBC
M Squad ep The Twisted Way 1.1.60 NBC
The Man from Blackhawk ep Remember Me Not 9.9.60 ABC
Dante ep One for the Birds 10.3.60 NBC

Adventures in Paradise ep 2.26.60 ABC
Bringing Up Buddy ep Buddy's Transfer 1.61 CBS
Stagecoach West ep The Outcasts 3.7.61 ABC
Laramie ep War Hero 10.2.62 NBC
Have Gun--Will Travel ep Penelope 12.8.62 CBS
The Beverly Hillbillies ep Ellie Starts School 10.16.63 CBS
The Beverly Hillbillies ep The Clampett Look 10.23.63 CBS
Arrest and Trial ep A Circle of Strangers 3.28.64 ABC
The Farmer's Daughter ep The Next Mrs. Morley 4.29.64 ABC
The FBI ep The Prey 12.7.69 ABC
Alias Smith and Jones ep How to Rob a Bank in One Hard Lesson 9.23.71 ABC
Alias Smith and Jones ep Miracle at Santa Marta 12.30.71 ABC
Hawaii Five-O ep Didn't We Meet at a Murder? 2.22.72 CBS
Planet of the Apes ep Up Above the World So High 12.20.74 CBS
SUPP.:
Trapper John, M.D. ep Girl Under Glass 11.23, 11.30.80 CBS
Barney Miller ep Chinatown 2.4, 2.11.82 ABC
Hart to Hart ep Hart's Desire 11.16.82 ABC
Secrets of a Mother and Daughter tf 10.4.83 CBS
Remington Steele ep My Fair Steele 12.6.83 NBC
Trapper John, M.D. ep 3.24.85 CBS

BARNES, SUZANNE*
Angel on My Shoulder tf 5.11.80 ABC
Laverne and Shirley ep The Bardwell Caper 3.17.81 ABC
Hart to Hart ep The Latest Fashion in Murder 5.5.81 ABC
She's in the Army Now tf/pt 5.20.81 ABC
The Renegades ep On the Pad 3.25.83 ABC
The A-Team ep Trouble Brewing 5.7.85 NBC
Who's the Boss? ep Custody 11.5, 11.12.85 ABC
The Fall Guy ep Seavers: Dead or Alive 12.14.85 ABC

BARRIE, BARBARA
A&C, Supp. 1:
The Phil Silvers Show ep Furlough in New York 1956 CBS
The Phil Silvers Show ep The Colonel Breaks Par 1957 CBS
Decoy ep Fall 1957 NN
The Bob Hope Chrysler Theater ep The Eighth Day 12.21.66 NBC
The Mary Tyler Moore Show ep I Love a Piano 12.74 CBS
SUPP.:
Working sp 12.81 SHO
Not Just Another Affair tf 10.2.82 CBS
Tucker's Witch sr 10.6.82 CBS
Reggie sr 8.2.83 ABC
All Together Now pt 6.30.84 NBC
Trapper John, M.D. ep 11.25.84 CBS
Double Trouble sr 12.1.84 NBC
The Execution tf 1.14.85 NBC

BARRY, GENE
SUPP.:
The Love Boat ep She Brought Her Mother Along 3.20.82 ABC

BARRYMORE, DREW*
Bogie tf 3.4.80 CBS
An American Portrait ep Italo Marchiony 12.14.84 CBS
The ABC Weekend Special ep The Adventures of Con Sawyer and Hucklemary Finn 9.7, 9.14.85 ABC
Amazing Stories ep Ghost Train 9.29.85 NBC

BASEHART, RICHARD
A&C, Supp. 1:
Little House on the Prairie ep Troublemaker 2.25.76 NBC
SUPP.:
Knight Rider ep Knight Rider (pt/first ep) 9.26.82 NBC

BASELEON, MICHAEL
A&C, Supp. 2:
Here Come the Brides ep To the Victor 2.27.70 ABC
The High Chaparral ep The Forge of Hate 11.13.70 NBC
The FBI ep Eye of the Needle 1.24.71 ABC
Here Come the Brides ep Land Grant 12.30.71 ABC
Toma ep Stillwater 492 2.1.74 ABC
Toma ep A Time and a Place Unknown 2.8.74 ABC
Cannon ep The Man Who Died Twice 10.15.75 CBS
SUPP.:
The Greatest American Hero ep Dreams 3.17.82 ABC
The A-Team ep Steel 11.29.83 NBC
The Whiz Kids ep Watch Out 1.14.84 CBS
Riptide ep Four Eyes 3.6.84 NBC
The A-Team ep Double Heat 10.23.84 NBC
Hunter ep High Bleacher Man 12.17.84 NBC

BASINGER, KIM
A&C, Supp. 2:
The Six Million Dollar Man ep The Ultimate Imposter 1.2.77 ABC

BATEMAN, JUSTINE*
Family Ties sr 9.22.82 NBC
Family Ties sr ret 9.28.83 NBC
Family Ties sr ret 9.27.84 NBC
Tales from the Darkside ep Mookie and Pookie 11.3.84 NN
One to Grow On ep 11.10.84 NBC
It's Your Move ep Slumber Party 10.31.84 NBC
Glitter ep On Your Toes 12.11.84 ABC
The ABC Afterschool Special ep First the Egg 3.6.85 ABC
Right to Kill tf 5.22.85 ABC
Family Ties Vacation tf 9.23.85 NBC
Family Ties sr ret 9.26.85 NBC

BAUER, JAMIE LYN*
Bronk ep The Deadlier Sex 1.18.76 CBS
Baretta ep Dead Man Out 3.3.76 ABC
The Love Boat ep Too Rich and Too Thin 3.17.84 ABC
Lottery ep Honolulu: 3-2=1 ("Three's a Crowd" segment) 3.29.84 ABC
Fantasy Island ep Lost and Found 4.7.84 ABC
Hotel ep Obsessions 10.31.84 ABC
The Love Boat ep Baby Sister 12.1.84 ABC

BAUMANN, KATHERINE*
The Great American Beauty Contest tf 2.13.73 ABC
Letters from Three Lovers tf 10.3.73 ABC
Death Among Friends tf 5.20.75 NBC
McCloud ep The Shiek of Arami 1.11.76 NBC
Switch ep Come Die with Me 1.27.76 CBS
Flight to Holocaust tf 3.27.77 NBC
Charleston tf 1.15.79 NBC
Trapper John, M.D. ep Girl Under Glass 11.23, 11.30.80 CBS
Enos ep House Cleaners 1.14.81 CBS
B.J. and the Bear ep Who Is B.J.? 4.25.81 NBC
Border Pals pt 8.17.81 ABC
Terror at Alcatraz tf/pt 7.4.82 NBC
Rooster tf/pt 8.19.82 ABC
Simon and Simon ep Sometimes Dreams Come True 12.2.82 CBS
The Fall Guy ep The Winner 12.19.84 ABC
Knight Rider ep Knight Strike 4.5.85 NBC

BAXTER, ANNE
SUPP.:
Hotel sr 9.21.83 ABC
Hotel sr ret 9.26.84 ABC
Hotel sr ret 9.25.85 ABC

BAY, SUSAN*
Matt Helm ep Double Jeopardy 11.22.75 ABC
Look Out World pt 7.27.77 NBC
Alone at Last pt 9.30.80 NBC
Hart to Hart ep What Murder 11.18.80 ABC
Mr. Merlin ep Take My Tonsils 12.9.81 CBS
Family Ties ep Tender Is the Knight 9.28.83 NBC
Remington Steele ep A Steele at Any Price 11.8.83 NBC

BEASLEY, ALLYCE*
King's Crossing ep Triangle 2.6.82 ABC
McClain's Law ep From the Mouths of Babes 3.13.82 NBC
Taxi ep Scenskees from a Marriage 10.28.82 ABC
Remington Steele ep Steele Crazy After All These Years 2.18.83 NBC
One Cooks, the Other Doesn't tf 9.27.83 CBS
Shaping Up ep Baby Be Mine 3.12.84 ABC

Moonlighting pt 3.3.85 ABC
Moonlighting sr 3.5.85 ABC
Moonlighting sr ret 9.24.85 ABC

BEATTY, NED
SUPP.:
Pray TV tf 2.1.82 ABC
A Woman Called Golda ms 4.26, 4.27, 4.28.82 OPT
American Playhouse ep The Ballad of Gregorio Cortez 6.29.82 PBS
Faerie Tale Theater ep Rumplestiltskin 10.16.82 SHO
Kentucky Woman tf 1.11.83 CBS
Robert Kennedy and His Times ms 1.27, 1.28, 1.29, 1.30.84 CBS
Celebrity ms 2.12-2.14.84 NBC
The Last Days of Pompeii ms 5.6-5.8.84 ABC
Murder, She Wrote ep (pt/first ep) 9.30.84 CBS
Alfred Hitchcock Presents ep Incident in a Small Jail (pt ep) 5.12.85 NBC
Wonderworks ep Konrad 10.6.85 PBS
Hostage Flight tf 11.17.85 NBC

BEATTY, WARREN
A&C, B.V.:
The Many Loves of Dobie Gillis ep Caper at the Bijou 10.6.59 CBS
The Many Loves of Dobie Gillis ep The Sweet Singer of Central High 11.10.59 CBS
The Many Loves of Dobie Gillis ep Dobie Gillis, Boy Actor 12.1.59 CBS
The Many Loves of Dobie Gillis ep The Smoke Filled Room 1.12.60 CBS
The Many Loves of Dobie Gillis ep The Fist Fighter 1.19.60 CBS
Alcoa Presents (One Step Beyond) ep The Visitor 5.10.60 ABC
Wagon Train ep The Pearlie Garnet Story 2.24.64 ABC

BEAUMONT, HUGH
A&C, B.V.:
The Tales of Wells Fargo ep Jesse James 7.1.57 NBC

BECK, JOHN*
I Dream of Jeannie ep 12.11.65 NBC
The Mod Squad ep A Seat by the Window 4.15.69 ABC
Mannix ep Color Her Missing 10.4.69 CBS
Love, American Style ep Love and the Roommate 11.17.69 ABC
The Silent Gun tf 12.16.69
Lancer ep Chad 1.20.70 CBS
Gunsmoke ep Kiowa! 2.16.70 CBS
Lancer ep Dream of Falcons 4.7.70 CBS
Bonanza ep 4.12.70 NBC
Mission: Impossible ep The Missile 1.16.71 CBS

Gunsmoke ep The Tycoon 1.25.71 CBS
The Young Lawyers ep The Bradbury War 2.17.71 ABC
Dan August ep The Assassin 4.8.71 ABC
Lock, Stock and Barrel tf/pt 9.24.71 NBC
Nichols sr 9.16.71 NBC
Hawaii Five-O ep Nightmare in Blue 2.5.74 CBS
Sidekicks tf 3.21.74 CBS
The Law tf 10.22.74 NBC
Attack on Terror: The FBI Vs. the Ku Klux Klan tf 2.20, 2.21.75 CBS
Gunsmoke ep 3.10.75 CBS
Call of the Wild tf 5.22.76 NBC
Wheels ms 5.7-5.15.78 NBC
What Really Happened to the Class of '65 ep Reunion in Terror 5.25.78 NBC
The Time Machine tf 11.5.78 NBC
Greatest Heroes of the Bible ep Samson and Delilah 11.14.78 NBC
How the West Was Won ep The Gentleman 3.12.79 ABC
Time Express ep Rodeo 5.10.79 CBS
The Buffalo Soldiers pt 5.26.79 NBC
Mind Over Murder tf 10.23.79 CBS
Flamingo Road tf/pt 5.12.80 NBC
The Great American Traffic Jam tf 10.12.80 NBC
Gridlock tf 10.20.80 NBC
Flamingo Road sr 1.6.81 NBC
Flamingo Road sr ret 11.3.81 NBC
Matt Houston ep 10.24.82 ABC
Fantasy Island ep Candy Kisses 1.15.83 ABC
For Love and Honor ep Old Friends 10.27.83 NBC
Partners in Crime ep Partners in Crime (pt ep) 10.13.84 NBC
Cover Up ep Golden Opportunity 11.3.84 CBS
Finder of Lost Loves ep Portraits 12.1.84 ABC
Murder, She Wrote ep Sudden Death 3.3.85 CBS
The Love Boat ep No Dad of Mine 3.30.85 ABC
Scarecrow and Mrs. King ep Burn Out 4.8.85 CBS
Half Nelson ep Malibu Colony 5.3.85 NBC
Peyton Place: The Next Generation tf 5.13.85 NBC

BECK, KIMBERLY*
The Westwind sr 9.6.75 NBC
Mobile One ep Not By Accident 10.17.75 ABC
Murder in Peyton Place tf 10.3.77 NBC
The Hardy Boys Mysteries ep Acapulco Spies 11.13.77 ABC
Zuma Beach tf 9.27.78 NBC
B.J. and the Bear ep Shine On 2.24.79 NBC
Starting Fresh pt 6.27.79 NBC
Buck Rogers in the 25th Century ep Cruise Ship to the Stars 12.27.79 NBC
Scalpels pt 10.26.80 NBC
Webster ep Green-Eyed Monster 10.28.83 ABC

T. J. Hooker ep Death on the Line 3.3.84 ABC
Hunter ep The Beach Boy 4.6.85 NBC
That Was the Week That Was pt 4.22.85 ABC

BEDELIA, BONNIE
A&C, B.V.:
The High Chaparral ep The Deceivers 11.15.68 NBC
A&C, Supp. 1:
Love Story ep Love Came Laughing 10.3.73 NBC

BEGLEY JR., ED*
Family Flight tf 10.25.72 ABC
Roll Out sr 10.5.73 CBS
Starsky and Hutch ep Murder at Sea 10.2.76 ABC
The New Adventures of Wonder Woman ep Diana's Disappearing Act 2.3.78 CBS
Quincy, M.E. ep No Way to Treat a Body 10.30.78 NBC
Amateur Night at the Dixie Bar and Grill tf 1.18.79 NBC
Elvis tf 2.11.79 ABC
Hot Rod tf 5.25.79 ABC
Charlie's Angels ep Angels on Skates 11.21.79 ABC
A Shining Season tf 12.26.79 CBS
Riker ep Honkeytonk 3.14.81 CBS
Tales of the Apple Dumpling Gang pt 1.16.82 CBS
Rascals and Robbers: The Secret Adventures of Tom Sawyer and Huckleberry Finn tf 2.27.82 CBS
Not Just Another Affair tf 10.2.82 CBS
Voyagers ep Voyagers (first ep) 10.3.82 NBC
St. Elsewhere sr 10.26.82 NBC
Still the Beaver tf/pt 3.19.83 CBS
St. Elsewhere sr ret 10.26.83 NBC
An Uncommon Love tf 11.30.83 CBS
The Love Boat ep Fish Out of Water 3.10.84 ABC
St. Elsewhere sr ret 9.19.84 NBC
St. Elsewhere sr ret 9.18.85 NBC
George Burns Comedy Week ep Christmas Carol II: The Sequel 12.11.85 CBS

BELAFONTE-HARPER, SHARI*
Hart to Hart ep The Latest Fashion in Murder 5.5.81 ABC
Code Red ep My Life Is Yours 1.17.82 ABC
Trapper John, M.D. ep Three on a Mismatch 10.17.82 CBS
Diff'rent Strokes ep The Older Woman 11.13.82 NBC
Hotel sr 9.21.83 ABC
The Love Boat ep Love Is Blind 3.3.84 ABC
Matt Houston ep New Orleans Nightmare 2.8.85 ABC
Hotel sr ret 9.26.84 ABC
Hotel sr ret 9.25.85 ABC
The Midnight Hour tf 11.1.85 ABC

BELFORD, CHRISTINE
A&C, Supp. 2:
Doc Elliot ep Survival 3.27.74 ABC
SUPP.:
Today's FBI ep Surfacing 2.28.82 ABC
The Neighborhood tf 4.25.82 NBC
Dynasty ep The Plea 10.27.82 ABC
Dynasty ep The Wedding 11.10.82 ABC
Silver Spoons ep Evelyn Returns 10.30.82 NBC
Cagney and Lacey ep 11.8.82 CBS
The Greatest American Hero ep 30 Seconds Over Little Tokyo 2.3.83 ABC
Fantasy Island ep Revenge of the Forgotten 2.19.83 ABC
Hart to Hart ep Bahama Bound Harts 2.22.83 ABC
Ace Crawford, Private Eye ep 4.5.83 CBS
It's Not Easy ep (pt/first ep) 9.29.83 ABC
Agatha Christie's "Sparkling Cyanide" tf 11.5.83 CBS
Empire sr 1.4.84 CBS
Silver Spoons ep Uneasy Rider 1.14.84 NBC
Fantasy Island ep To Fly with Eagles 1.21.84 ABC
100 Center Street pt 8.31.84 ABC
Silver Spoons ep The Call of the Wild 10.14.84 NBC
Murder, She Wrote ep We're Off to Kill the Wizard 12.9.84 CBS
Detective in the House ep 4.5.85 CBS
Silver Spoons ep Poor Evelyn 10.6.85 NBC

BEL GEDDES, BARBARA
SUPP.:
Dallas sr ret 10.1.82 CBS
Dallas ret to sr 9.27.84 CBS

BELACK, DORIS*
The Cradle Will Fall tf 5.24.83 CBS
Sessions tf 9.26.83 ABC
Family Ties ep Fabric Smarts 10.25.84 NBC
The Cosby Show ep Father's Day 12.20.84 NBC
Cagney and Lacey ep 1.7.85 CBS
The Golden Girls ep Dorothy's Kid Sister 12.7.85 NBC

BELLAMY, RALPH
A&C, B.V.:
The FBI ep The Death Wind 12.25.66 ABC
SUPP.:
Fantasy Island ep Valerie 1.16.82 ABC
The Winds of War ms 2.6-2.13.83 ABC
Little House: A New Beginning ep 11.3.82 NBC
The Love Boat ep Story of the Century 11.3.84 ABC
The Fourth Wise Man sp 3.30.85 ABC
Space ms 4.14-4.18.85 CBS
Hotel ep 12.18.85 ABC

BELLER, KATHLEEN

A&C, Supp. 2:

Hawaii Five-O ep The Waterfront Steal 11.21.75 CBS
Medical Center ep You Can't Annul My Baby 1.19.76 CBS

SUPP.:

The Blue and the Gray ms 11.14, 11.15, 11.16, 11.17.82 CBS
Dynasty sr (with ep #42: "Kirby") 12.8.82 ABC
Glitter ep An American Princess 9.20.84 ABC
Deadly Messages tf 2.21.85 ABC
Murder, She Wrote ep Funeral at 50 Mile 4.21.85 CBS

BELLWOOD, PAMELA

SUPP.:

Dynasty sr ret 10.27.82 ABC
The Wild Women of Chastity Gulch tf/pt 10.31.82 ABC
Cocaine: One Man's Seduction tf 2.27.83 NBC
Baby Sitter tf 3.6.83 ABC
Dynasty sr ret 9.28.83 ABC
Agatha Christie's "Sparkling Cyanide" tf 11.5.83 CBS
Choices of the Heart tf 12.5.83 NBC
Finder of Lost Loves ep Losing Touch 10.13.84 ABC
Dynasty sr ret 9.26.84 ABC
Dynasty sr ret 9.25.85 ABC

BENADERET, BEA

A&C, B.V.:

I Love Lucy ep Lucy Plays Cupid 1.21.52 CBS
The Life of Riley ep Honeybee's Mother 12.14.56 NBC
Love That Bob ep Bob Meets the Mortons 3.21.57 CBS

BENEDICT, DIRK*

Hawaii Five-O ep 10.24.72 CBS
Chopper One sr 1.17.74 ABC
Journey from Darkness tf 2.25.75 NBC
Charlie's Angels ep Blue Angels 5.4.77 ABC
The Cabot Connection pt 5.10.77 CBS
Cruise Into Terror tf 2.3.78 ABC
Charlie's Angels ep The Jade Trap 3.1.78 ABC
Battlestar Galactica sr 9.17.78 ABC
Galactica 1980 sr 1.27.80 ABC
The Georgia Peaches tf/pt 11.8.80 CBS
The Love Boat ep Captive Audience 12.20.80 ABC
Scruples pt 5.22.81 ABC
Family in Blue pt 6.10.82 CBS
The A-Team sr 1.23.83 NBC
The Love Boat ep Who's Dog Is It Anyway? 3.26.83 ABC
The A-Team sr ret 9.20.83 NBC
The A-Team sr ret 9.18.84 NBC
The A-Team sr ret 9.24.85 NBC
Amazing Stories ep Remote Control Man 12.8.85 NBC

BENNETT, JOAN
SUPP.:
Divorce Wars tf 3.1.82 ABC

BENNY, JACK
A&C, B.V.:
The George Burns and Gracie Allen Show ep Gracie Thinks She's Not Married to George 1953 CBS
The George Burns and Gracie Allen Show ep Gracie Trades Home for Mountain Cabin Fall 1953 CBS
The George Burns and Gracie Allen Show ep Ronnie Gets an Agent 1956 CBS
The George Burns and Gracie Allen Show ep The Home Graduation Spring 1957 CBS
The Danny Thomas Show ep Lose Me in Las Vegas 10.7.57 CBS
Bachelor Father ep Bentley the Homemaker Spring 1958 CBS
The Danny Thomas Show ep Jack Benny Takes Danny's Job 10.6.58 CBS
The Danny Thomas Show ep That Old Devil, Jack Benny 1.11.60 CBS
The Lucy Show ep Lucy and the Celebrities 11.15.71 CBS

BENTON, BARBI
SUPP.:
Matt Houston ep The Purrfect Crime 1.9.83 ABC
Mickey Spillane's Mike Hammer ep Catfight 10.20.84 CBS

BERGAN, JUDITH-MARIE*
Charlie's Angels ep Angels on the Air 11.9.77 ABC
Thou Shalt Not Commit Adultery tf 11.1.78 NBC
The Triangle Factory Fire Scandal tf 1.30.79 NBC
Murder By Natural Causes tf 2.17.79 CBS
The Ordeal of Patty Hearst 3.4.79 ABC
The Son-in-Law pt 10.26.80 NBC
Sizzle tf 11.29.81 ABC
The Two of Us ep Brentwood's Trophy 1.13.82 CBS
Gloria ep 11.7.82 CBS
At Ease ep Maxwell's People 6.3.83 ABC
Oh Madeline ep Mummy Dearest 10.4.83 ABC
Three's Company ep The Odd Couple 12.6.83 ABC
Domestic Life sr 1.4.84 CBS
Hart to Hart ep The Shooting 2.28.84 ABC
The CBS Afternoon Playhouse ep Secret Agent Boy 11.26.82 CBS
Highway to Heaven ep Hotel of Dreams 12.12.84 NBC
Tales from the Darkside ep Effect and Cause 12.7.85 NN

BERGEN, CANDICE
SUPP.:
Hollywood Wives ms 2.17, 2.18, 2.19.85 ABC

Arthur the King tf 4.26.85 CBS
Murder By Reason of Insanity tf 10.1.85 CBS

BERGEN, EDGAR
A&C, B.V.:
December Bride ep 5.58 CBS
Voyage to the Bottom of the Sea ep The Fear Makers 9.28.64 ABC

BERGEN, POLLY
SUPP.:
The Fall of the House of Usher tf 7.25.82 NBC
The Love Boat ep The Spoonmaker Diamond 11.13.82 ABC
The Winds of War ms 2.6-2.13.83 ABC
Fantasy Island ep Lady of the House 2.25.84 ABC
Murder, She Wrote ep School for Scandal 10.20.85 CBS

BERLE, MILTON
A&C, B.V.:
The Danny Thomas Show ep Danny and Milton Quit Show Business 12.7.59 CBS
SUPP.:
The Love Boat ep CPR, I.O.U. 3.12.83 ABC
Diff'rent Strokes ep The Bar Mitzvah Boy 3.17.84 NBC
Gimme a Break ep Grandpa's Secret Life 10.20.84 NBC
Murder, She Wrote ep Broadway Malady 1.13.85 CBS
Fame ep Coco Returns 3.3.85 NN
An American Portrait ep Vladimir Zworykin 4.9.85 CBS
Amazing Stories ep Fine Tuning 11.10.85 NBC

BERLINGER, WARREN
A&C, Supp. 1:
The Goldbergs ep Rosie's Boyfriends 1955 NN
Staccato ep The Angry Young Man 2.25.60 ABC
Gomer Pyle, USMC ep Proxy Poppa Spring 1969 CBS
SUPP.:
Laverne and Shirley ep Lightning Man 3.16.82 ABC
Herbie, the Love Bug ep Calling Dr. Herbie 4.14.82 CBS
Too Close for Comfort ep A Snip in Time 10.21.82 ABC
9 to 5 ep Hard Sell 12.7.82 ABC
Small and Frye sr 3.7.83 CBS
The Other Woman tf 3.22.83 CBS
Charles in Charge ep 1.16.84 CBS
Empire ep 1.18.84 CBS
Trapper John, M.D. ep 1.6.85 CBS
The Jeffersons ep 3.5.85 CBS
Cagney and Lacey ep 3.18.85 CBS
The A-Team ep The Road to Hope 10.29.85 NBC

BERNARD, CRYSTAL*
Gimme a Break ep Hot Muffins 3.11.82 NBC

Happy Days ep Tell Tale Tart 3.16.82 ABC
Dynasty ep The Two Princes 4.28.82 ABC
Dynasty ep Episode 35: Season Finale 5.5.82 ABC
Happy Days sr 9.28.82 ABC
Fantasy Island ep The Devil Stick 3.19.83 ABC
High School, U.S.A. tf/pt 10.16.83 NBC
The Love Boat ep The Bear Essence 11.12.83 ABC
The Master ep State of the Union 2.3.84 NBC
High School, U.S.A. pt 5.26.84 NBC (hour remake of above title)
The Love Boat ep The Odd Tripe 1.12.85 ABC
It's a Living sr 10.85 NN

BERNARDI, HERSCHEL
SUPP.:
Murder, She Wrote ep Capitol Offense 1.6.85 CBS
Hail to the Chief sr 4.9.85 ABC

BERRY, KEN
A&C, Supp. 1:
Mrs. G Goes to College ep Goodbye, Mr. Howell 2.15.62 CBS
The Dick Van Dyke Show ep The Brave and the Backache 2.12.64 CBS
The Dick Van Dyke Show ep My Mother Can Beat Up My Father 9.23.64 CBS
Twelve O'Clock High ep Interlude 11.27.64 ABC
The Andy Griffith Show ep Sam for Town Council 3.11.68 CBS
The Andy Griffith Show ep Opie and Mike 3.18.68 CBS
The Andy Griffith Show ep A Girl for Goober 3.25.68 CBS
The Andy Griffith Show ep Mayberry R.F.D. 4.1.68 CBS
The Brady Bunch ep Kelly's Kids 1.4.74 ABC

BERTINELLI, VALERIE
SUPP.:
One Day at a Time sr ret 10.3.82 CBS
I Was a Mail Order Bride tf 12.14.82 CBS
One Day at a Time sr ret 10.2.83 CBS
The Seduction of Gina tf 1.17.84 CBS
Shattered Vows tf 10.29.84 NBC
Silent Witness tf 10.14.85 NBC

BESCH, BIBI*
Three Times Daley pt 8.3.76 CBS
Police Story ep The Other Side of the Bridge 10.26.76 NBC
Victory at Entebbe tf 12.13.76 ABC
Police Woman ep Sunset 1.18.77 NBC
Police Story ep The Blue Fog 2.1.77 NBC
The Rockford Files ep Beamer's Last Case 9.16.77 NBC
Peter Lundy and the Medicine Hat Stallion tf 11.6.77 NBC
Betrayal tf 11.13.78 NBC
Charlie's Angels ep Game, Set, Death 1.4.78 ABC

The Six Million Dollar Man ep The Madonna Caper 2.6.78 ABC
Tom and Joann pt 7.5.78 CBS
How the West Was Won ep The Widow 2.12.79 ABC
Transplant tf 4.17.79 CBS
Steeltown pt 5.19.79 CBS
Kate Loves a Mystery ep It Goes with the Territory 10.25.79 NBC
Eischied ep The Dancer 11.23.79 NBC
Skag ep The Working Girl 1.31, 2.7.80 NBC
The Plutonium Incident tf 3.11.80 CBS
Secrets of Midland Heights sr 12.6.80 CBS
Hart to Hart ep Murder Takes a Bow 5.19.81 ABC
The Sophisticated Gents tf 9.29, 9.30, 10.1.81 NBC
The ABC Afterschool Special ep Tough Girl 10.28.81 ABC
Death of a Centerfold: The Dorothy Stratton Story tf 11.1.81 NBC
McClain's Law ep (pt/first ep) 11.20.81 NBC
Skyward Christmas pt 12.3.81 NBC
Trapper John, M.D. ep 11.28.82 CBS
The Hamptons sr 7.27.83 ABC
Secrets of a Mother and Daughter tf 10.4.83 CBS
Scarecrow and Mrs. King ep There Goes the Neighborhood 10.10.83 CBS
The Day After tf 11.20.83 ABC
The CBS Schoolbreak Special ep Dead Wrong 1.11.84 CBS
Cagney and Lacey ep 3.19.84 CBS
Trapper John, M.D. ep 5.6.84 CBS
The CBS Schoolbreak Special ep Hear Me Cry 10.16.84 CBS
Who's the Boss? ep Mona Gets Pinned 10.30.84 ABC
Dynasty ep Swept Away 12.12.84 ABC
Partners in Crime ep The Strangler 12.15.84 NBC
Dynasty ep The Will 1.9.85 ABC
Falcon Crest ep Justice for All 3.29.85 CBS
Eye to Eye ep A Crossword Puzzle 4.18.85 ABC
Scene of the Crime ep A Vote for Murder 5.26.85 NBC
Hell Town ep Let My Jennie Go 9.11.85 NBC
Dallas ep Mothers 10.25.85 CBS

BESSELL, TED

A&C, B.V.:

Twelve O'Clock High ep Then Came the Mighty Hunter 9.27.65 ABC

SUPP.:

Hail to the Chief sr 4.9.85 ABC

BEST, JAMES*

Lineup ep San Francisco Playboy 3.4.55 CBS
Lineup ep The Kasino Case 6.17.55 CBS
Trackdown ep The Marple Brothers 10.4.57 CBS
Have Gun--Will Travel ep 11.16.57 CBS
Tombstone Territory ep Guilt of a Town 3.19.58 CBS

Trackdown ep The Mistake 4.18.58 CBS
Alfred Hitchcock Presents ep Life Sentence 4.27.58 CBS
Trackdown ep Sunday's Child 11.21.58 CBS
Wanted: Dead or Alive ep Sheriff of Red Rock 11.29.58 CBS
Rescue 8 ep Trial by Fire 3.11.59 NN
Black Saddle ep Client: Nelson 5.2.59 NBC
The Man and the Challenge ep Maximum Capacity 9.19.59 CBS
Laramie ep The Lawbreakers 10.20.59 NBC
Lineup ep Lonesome as Midnight 11.18.59 CBS
The Texan ep Killer's Road 4.25.60 CBS
Markham ep Sitting Duck 5.15.60 CBS
The Rebel ep Night on a Rainbow 5.29.60 ABC
The Andy Griffith Show ep 10.17.60, 5.15.61 CBS
The Rebel ep Deathwatch 10.23.60 ABC
Michael Shayne, Private Detective ep Strike Out 3.10.61 NBC
The Barbara Stanwyck Theater ep The Choice 4.17.61 NBC
Whispering Smith ep The Hemp Reeger Case 7.17.61 NBC
Surfside Six ep One for the Road 10.2.61 ABC
Laramie ep The Runaway 12.23.62 NBC
The Rifleman ep The Day a Town Slept 4.16.62 ABC
Hawaiian Eye ep Day in the Sun 10.2.62 ABC
G.E. True ep Open Session 1.6.63 CBS
The Gallant Men ep The Warrior 2.23.63 ABC
Gunsmoke ep With a Smile 3.20.63 CBS
Redigo ep Little Angel Blue Eyes 10.29.63 ABC
Ben Casey ep Six Impossible Things Before Breakfast 11.13.63 ABC
Gunsmoke ep The Glory and the Mud 1.4.64 CBS
Combat ep Mail Call 2.4.64 ABC
Temple Houston ep The Case for William Gotch 2.6.64 NBC
Destry ep Go Away, Little Sheba 3.27.64 ABC
Rawhide ep Incident at El Toro 4.9.64 CBS
Death Valley Days ep The Hero of Fort Hallick 1964 NN
Daniel Boone ep The Devil's Four 3.4.65 NBC
Ben Casey ep A Little Fun to Match the Sadness 3.8.65 ABC
Flipper ep The Cry of the Dolphin 4.3.65 NBC
Amos Burke, Secret Agent ep Steam Heat 9.27.65 ABC
Honey West ep A Matter of Wife & Death 10.8.65 ABC
The Virginian ep Letter of the Law 12.22.65 NBC
Perry Mason ep The Case of the Unwelcome Well 4.3.66 CBS
Iron Horse ep High Devil 9.26.66 ABC
The Felony Squad ep Flame Out 10.17.66 ABC
The Green Hornet ep Deadline for Dying 12.2.66 ABC
I Spy ep Lisa 12.7.66 NBC
Hawk ep Blind Man's Bluff 12.29.66 ABC
The Guns of Will Sonnett ep Meeting at Devil's Fork 10.27.67 ABC
Bonanza ep The Price of Salt 2.4.68 NBC
I Spy ep Suitable for Framing 3.25.68 NBC
The Mod Squad ep The Price of Terror 11.26.68 ABC
The Felony Squad ep The Distant Shore 12.20.68 ABC

The Guns of Will Sonnett ep Robber's Roost 1.17.69 ABC
Gunsmoke ep Charlie Noon 11.3.69 CBS
Dan August ep In the Eyes of God 10.21.70 ABC
Run, Simon, Run tf 12.1.70 ABC
Hawkins ep Blood Feud 12.4.73 CBS
Savages tf 9.11.74 ABC
The Runaway Barge tf 3.24.75 NBC
The Savage Bees tf 11.22.76 NBC
The Dukes of Hazzard sr 1.26.79 CBS
The Dukes of Hazzard sr ret 9.21.79 CBS
The Dukes of Hazzard sr ret 10.25.80 CBS
The Dukes of Hazzard sr ret 10.6.81 CBS
Enos ep 12.17.81 CBS
The Dukes of Hazzard sr ret 9.24.82 CBS
The Dukes of Hazzard sr ret 9.23.83 CBS
The Dukes of Hazzard sr ret 9.21.84 CBS

BESWICKE, MARTINE*
Longstreet tf/pt 2.23.71 ABC
Crime Club tf 4.3.75 CBS
Strange New World tf 7.13.75 ABC
Aspen ms 11.5-7.77 NBC
Devil Dog: The Hound of Hell tf 10.31.78 CBS
My Husband Is Missing tf 12.5.78 NBC
The Tenth Month tf 9.16.79 CBS
Hart to Hart ep Murder Is Man's Best Friend 12.9.80 ABC
Quincy, M.E. ep Dear Mummy 1.21.81 NBC
Cassie and Company ep Man Overboard 6.29.82 NBC
The Fall Guy ep Bail and Bond 10.27.82 ABC
Fantasy Island ep Ladies Choice 1.28.84 ABC
Buffalo Bill ep Have Yourself a Very Degrading Christmas 3.21.84 NBC
The Powers of Matthew Star ep Swords and Quests 4.8.84 NBC
Cover Up ep Black Widow 1.5.85 CBS
Cover Up ep Passions 4.6.85 CBS
Falcon Crest ep Ingress & Egress 11.1.85 CBS

BETTGER, LYLE
A&C, B.V.:
The Rifleman ep The Wrong Man 3.1.59 ABC
The Tall Man ep Hard Justice 3.25.61 NBC
Voyage to the Bottom of the Sea ep The Creature 1.1.67 ABC
Daniel Boone ep Delo Jones 3.2.67 NBC
A&C, Supp. 1:
Hawaii Five-O ep The Sunday Torch 10.9.73 CBS
Hawaii Five-O ep Murder--Eyes Only 9.12.75 CBS
Hawaii Five-O ep Let Death Do Us Part 11.18.76 CBS
A&C, Supp. 2:
Hawaii Five-O ep Labyrinth 12.25.79 CBS
Hawaii Five-O ep Woe to Wo Fat 4.5.80 CBS

BIERI, RAMON

A&C, Supp. 1:

Armstrong Circle Theater ep A City Betrayed 11.21.62 CBS
Gunsmoke ep Railroad 11.25.68 CBS
Room 222 ep Choose One: And They Lived (Happily/Unhappily) Ever After 10.21.70 ABC
Gunsmoke ep Alias Festus Haggen 3.6.72 CBS
Cannon ep To Ride a Tiger 2.14.73 CBS
Barnaby Jones ep Death Leap 9.12.73 CBS
The Magician ep The Vanishing Lady 10.9.73 NBC
Chase ep The Game Ball 1.30.74 ABC
The Rockford Files ep Caledonia--It's Worth a Fortune! 12.6.74 NBC
Hawaii Five-O ep Diary of a Gun 3.18.75 CBS
Harry O ep Forbidden City 2.26.76 ABC

A&C, Supp. 2:

Switch ep The Cage 6.25.78 CBS

SUPP.:

Trapper John, M.D. ep 10.3, 10.10.82 CBS
The Fall Guy ep The Backlot Gang (a.k.a. Colt's Outlaws) 11.10.82 ABC
Knight Rider ep The Final Verdict 12.3.82 NBC
Quincy, M.E. ep A Loss for Words 1.26.83 NBC
Matt Houston ep Needle in a Haystack 10.7.83 ABC
The Dukes of Hazzard ep 2.3, 2.10.84 CBS
Highway to Heaven ep Plane Death 1.9.85 NBC
St. Elsewhere ep Slice O'Life 11.6.85 NBC
St. Elsewhere ep Close Encounters 11.20.85 NBC
Murder, She Wrote ep Dead Heat 11.24.85 CBS
St. Elsewhere ep Watch the Skies 11.27.85 NBC
Hunter ep Think Blue 12.14.85 NBC

BIKEL, THEODORE

A&C, B.V.:

Burke's Law ep Who Killed the Surf Board? 9.16.64 ABC

SUPP.:

Trapper John, M.D. ep Russians and Ruses 12.19.82 CBS
Knight Rider ep Chariot of Gold 2.11.83 NBC
Glitter ep On Your Toes 12.11.84 ABC
Hotel ep New Beginnings 1.23.85 ABC
Cover Up ep Rules to Die By 2.2.85 CBS
Dynasty ep Aftermath 9.25.85 ABC
Dynasty ep The Homecoming 10.2.85 ABC
Dynasty ep The Titans 11.13.85 ABC

BILL, TONY

SUPP.:

Washington Mistress tf 1.13.82 CBS
Running Out tf 1.26.83 CBS
Alfred Hitchcock Presents ep Night Caller 11.5.85 NBC

BIRNEY, DAVID
SUPP.:
The Love Boat ep The Gigolo 10.2.82 ABC
St. Elsewhere sr 10.26.82 NBC
St. Elsewhere sr ret 10.26.83 NBC
Master of the Game ms 2.19, 2.20, 2.21.84 CBS
Glitter sr 9.13.84 ABC
The Love Boat Fall Preview Party sp 9.15.84 ABC
An American Portrait ep Jimmie King 1.22.85 CBS
Wonder Works ep Seal Morning 11.3.85 PBS

BIRNEY, MEREDITH BAXTER (a.k.a. Meredith Baxter)
A&C, Supp. 1: (see Baxter, Meredith)
Doc Elliot ep An All Ye Need to Know 10.10.73 ABC
SUPP.:
Family Ties sr 9.22.82 NBC
The Love Boat ep The Gigolo 10.2.82 ABC
Take Your Best Shot tf 10.12.82 CBS
Family Ties sr ret 9.28.83 NBC
Family Ties sr ret 9.27.84 NBC
The Rape of Richard Beck tf 5.27.85 ABC
Family Ties Vacation tf 9.23.85 NBC
Family Ties sr ret 9.26.85 NBC

BISHOP, JOEY
A&C, B.V.:
Richard Diamond ep No Laughing Matter 11.9.59 CBS
SUPP.:
Hardcastle and McCormick ep What's So Funny? 1.21.85 ABC

BIXBY, BILL
A&C, B.V.:
The Danny Thomas Show ep Danny Weaves a Web Fall 1961 CBS
The Many Loves of Dobie Gillis ep The Gigolo 11.7.61 CBS
The Danny Thomas Show ep Danny and Durante 11.27.61 CBS
The Andy Griffith Show ep Bailey's Bad Boy 1.15.62 CBS
SUPP.:
Agatha Christie's "Murder Is Easy" tf 1.2.82 CBS
Goodnight Beantown sr 4.3.83 CBS
Goodnight Beantown sr ret 10.2.83 CBS
International Airport tf/pt 5.25.85 ABC

BLACK, KAREN
SUPP.:
Come Back to the Five and Dime Jimmy Dean, Jimmy Dean sp 6.83 SHO
E/R ep 12.26.84, 1.30.85, 2.6.85 CBS
The Hitchhiker ep Hired Help 3.30.85 HBO

BLACKMAN, HONOR
A&C, B.V.:
The Invisible Man ep Blind Justice 12.30.58 CBS

BLACKMER, SIDNEY

A&C, B.V.:

The Rifleman ep The Sharpshooter 9.30.58 ABC

The Rifleman ep The Safe Guard 1.18.59 ABC

Wanted: Dead Or Alive ep Rope Law 1.3.59 CBS

The Rifleman ep The Photographer 1.27.59 ABC

Daniel Boone ep The Jasper Ledbedder Story 2.2.67 NBC

BLACKMORE, STEPHANIE*

Aspen ms 11.5-11.7.77 NBC

Revenge of the Stepford Wives tf 10.12.80 NBC

Hart to Hart ep Murder in Paradise 1.13.81 ABC

This Is Kate Bennett pt 5.28.82 ABC

Legmen ep Down the Rabbit Hole (a.k.a. A Knight at Casanova's) 1.27.84 NBC

Simon and Simon ep 2.16.84 CBS

Scarecrow and Mrs. King ep 4.23.84 CBS

Mickey Spillane's Mike Hammer: More Than Murder pt 1.26.85 CBS

Crazy Like a Fox ep Fox in Wonderland 3.17.85 CBS

Hunter ep The Last Kill 4.20.85 NBC

Remington Steele ep Forged Steele 11.12.85 NBC

BLAINE, VIVIAN

SUPP.:

Amanda's ep Aunt Sonia 3.24.83 ABC

Murder, She Wrote ep Broadway Malady 1.13.85 CBS

BLAIR, JANET

A&C, B.V.:

Destry ep Stormy Is a Lady 3.6.64 ABC

A&C, Supp. 2:

Switch ep Go for Broke 12.12.77 CBS

SUPP.:

The Love Boat ep Hyde and Seek 10.30.82 ABC

BLAIR, LINDA*

Born Innocent tf 9.10.74 NBC

Sarah T.--Portrait of a Teenage Alcoholic 2.11.75 NBC

Sweet Hostage tf 10.10.75 ABC

Victory at Entebbe tf 12.13.76 ABC

Stranger in Our House tf/pt 10.31.78 NBC

The Love Boat ep Cold Feet 3.20.82 ABC

Fantasy Island ep Shadow Games 1.23.83 ABC

Murder, She Wrote ep Murder Takes the Bus 3.17.85 CBS

BLAKE, AMANDA

SUPP.:

Hart to Hart ep The Wayward Hart 3.8.83 ABC

The Edge of Night ep 6.18-6.29.84 ABC

BLAKE, ROBERT
A&C, B.V.:
Broken Arrow ep Bear Trap 4.29.58 ABC
Black Saddle ep Client: Robinson 2.21.59 NBC
Zane Grey Theater ep Loyalty 4.2.59 CBS
Have Gun--Will Travel ep The Fatalist 9.29.60 CBS
Have Gun--Will Travel ep A Place for Abel Hicks 10.6.63 CBS
Rawhide ep Hostage for Hanging 10.19.65 CBS
SUPP.:
Blood Feud tf 4.25 and 5.2.83 OPT
Joe Dancer: Murder One, Dancer 0 tf/pt 6.5.83 NBC
Hell Town tf/pt 3.6.85 NBC
The Heart of a Champion: The Ray Mancini Story tf 5.1.85 CBS
Hell Town sr 9.11.85 NBC

BLAKELY, SUSAN
SUPP.:
Will There Really Be a Morning? tf 2.22.83 CBS
Hotel ep Obsessions 10.31.84 ABC
The Hitchhiker ep Remembering Melody 11.27.84 HBO
Finder of Lost Loves ep Last Wish 1.5.85 ABC
International Airport tf/pt 5.25.85 ABC
Stingray tf/pt 7.14.85 NBC
The Love Boat ep The Accident 11.2.85 ABC

BLAKLEY, RONEE
SUPP.:
Highway to Heaven ep Song of the Wild West 10.17.84 NBC
Trapper John, M.D. ep 1.17.85 CBS

BLANCHARD, SUSAN
SUPP.:
At Ease ep Prairie Moon Over Texas 3.25.83 ABC
Magnum, P.I. ep Home from the Sea 9.29.83 CBS
The Love Boat ep Soap Gets in Your Eyes 10.20.84 ABC
Falcon Crest ep The Triumvirate 12.14.84 CBS
Murder, She Wrote ep A Lady in the Lake 11.10.85 CBS

BLOCKER, DAN
A&C, B.V.:
Colt. 45 ep A Time to Die 10.25.57 ABC
The Restless Gun ep Jody 11.4.57 NBC

BLONDELL, JOAN
A&C, B.V.:
The Real McCoys ep Aunt Win Arrives 1963 CBS
The Real McCoys ep Aunt Win's Conquest 1963 CBS
Here's Lucy ep The Stunt Man 10.18.65 CBS
A&C, Supp. 1:
Switch ep One of Our Zeppelins Is Missing 2.10.76 CBS

BLOOM, CLAIRE
SUPP.:
Separate Tables sp 3.14.83 HBO
American Playhouse ep The Ghost Writer 3.4.85 PBS
Florence Nightingale tf 4.7.85 NBC
Promises to Keep tf 10.15.85 CBS

BLOOM, LINDSAY*
Starsky and Hutch ep The Vampire 10.30.76 ABC
Switch ep 30,000 Witnesses 12.26.77 CBS
The Dukes of Hazzard ep 10.12.79 CBS
Vegas ep A Christmas Story 12.17.80 ABC
Dallas ep No More Mister Nice Guy 11.7.80 CBS
The Dukes of Hazzard ep Ten Million Dollar Sheriff 11.20.81 CBS
Dallas ep Starting Over 1.15.82 CBS
Dallas ep Denial 1.22.82 CBS
Dallas ep My Father, My Son 2.12.82 CBS
Dallas ep Anniversary 2.19.82 CBS
Dallas ep Adoption 2.26.82 CBS
Strike Force ep Pandora Vector 3.26.82 ABC
Trapper John, M.D. ep 10.2.83 CBS
Mickey Spillane's Mike Hammer: More Than Murder tf/pt 1.26.84 CBS
Mickey Spillane's Mike Hammer sr 1.29.84 CBS
Mickey Spillane's Mike Hammer sr ret 9.29.84 CBS
Bridge Across Time tf 11.22.85 NBC

BLYTH, ANN
SUPP.:
Quincy, M.E. ep Murder on Ice 3.9.83 NBC
Murder, She Wrote ep Reflections of the Mind 11.3.85 CBS

BOCHNER, LLOYD
A&C, Supp. 2:
Ellery Queen ep Castaway on a Nearby Island 4.24.59 NBC
Americans ep The War Between the States 5.11.61 NBC
Thriller ep The Prisoner in the Mirror 5.23.61 NBC
Cain's Hundred ep Inside Track 4.10.62 NBC
Sam Benedict ep Hannigan 9.13.62 NBC
The Eleventh Hour ep There Are Dragons in This Forest 10.10.62 NBC
G.E. True ep Code Name; Christopher 10.21, 10.28,62 CBS
The Dick Powell Show ep Days of Glory 11.13.62 NBC
G.E. True ep Commando 5.19.63 CBS
The Lieutenant ep The War Called Peace 4.11.64 NBC
The Bob Hope Chrysler Theater ep Murder in the First 10.9.64 NBC
Voyage to the Bottom of the Sea ep The Fear Makers 9.28.64 ABC
Perry Mason ep The Case of the Latest Love 12.3.64 CBS

The Bob Hope Chrysler Theater ep The War and Eric Kurtz 3.5.65 NBC
Twelve O'Clock High ep The Cry of Fallen Birds 4.9.65 ABC
For the People ep Seized, Confined and Detained 4.22.65 CBS
Combat ep Evasion 10.19.65 ABC
Twelve O'Clock High ep Show Me a Hero, I'll Show You a Bum 10.25.65 ABC
Voyage to the Bottom of the Sea ep The Deadliest Game 10.31.65 ABC
Branded ep $10,000 for Durango 11.28.65 NBC
Twelve O'Clock High ep Fortress Weisbaden 9.30.66 ABC
The Girl from UNCLE ep The Danish Blue Affair 10.25.66 NBC
The Girl from UNCLE ep The Romany Lie 12.6.66 NBC
The Legend of Custer ep 11.8.67 ABC
The FBI ep The Inside Man 11.30.69 ABC
It Takes a Thief ep Project X 3.23.70 ABC
The Silent Force ep Prosecutor 9.21.70 ABC
The Storefront Lawyers ep 11.18.70 CBS
Hawaii Five-O ep Beautiful Screamer 12.2.70 CBS
The Men from Shiloh ep The Town Killer 3.10.71 NBC
Cannon ep Bitter Legion 9.27.72 CBS
The New Adventures of Perry Mason ep The Case of the Frenzied Feminist 2.16.73 CBS
Switch ep The Cruise Ship Murders 11.11.75 CBS
Hawaii Five-O ep School for Assassins 1.1.80 CBS
Hawaii Five-O ep 3.8.80 CBS
SUPP.:
The Love Boat ep Does Father Know Best? 4.10.82 ABC
Dynasty sr ret 10.27.82 ABC
Matt Houston ep Shark Bait 11.21.82 ABC
Rona Jaffe's "Mazes and Monsters" tf 12.28.82 CBS
Fantasy Island ep Room and Bard 1.29.83 ABC
Matt Houston ep Heritage 9.9.83 ABC
Fantasy Island ep Ladies Choice 1.28.84 ABC
Masquerade ep Winnings 4.6.84 ABC
The A-Team ep Beverly Hills Assault 4.9.85 NBC
Hotel ep Rallying Cry 10.2.85 ABC
Crazy Like a Fox ep If the Shoe Fits 12.15.85 CBS

BOHAY, HEIDI*
Buck Rogers in the 25th Century ep Buck's Duel to the Death 3.20.80 NBC
Here's Boomer ep Boomer and the Musket Cove Treasure 10.4.81 NBC
Quincy, M.E. ep The Golden Hour 11.4.81 NBC
The Child Bride of Short Creek tf 12.7.81 NBC
Teacher's Only ep The Dreyfuss Affair (a.k.a. A Case of Entrapment) 4.21.82 NBC
It Takes Two ep Heartbreak 11.11.82 ABC
Thursday's Child tf 2.1.83 CBS
Grace Kelly tf 2.21.83 ABC

Two Marriages ep The Reunion 8.31.83 ABC
Hotel sr 9.21.83 ABC
The Love Boat ep Three Faces of Love 5.12.84 ABC
Hotel sr ret 9.26.84 ABC
The Love Boat ep Revenge with the Proper Stranger 11.17.84 ABC
Finder of Lost Loves ep Wayward Dreams 1.26.85 ABC
Hotel sr ret 9.25.85 ABC

BOLGER, RAY
SUPP.:
Fantasy Island ep Dancing Lady 10.23.82 ABC
Diff'rent Strokes ep A Haunting We Will Go 9.29.84 NBC

BONADUCE, DANNY
SUPP.:
CHiPs ep The Threat of War: Karate II 3.21.82 NBC

BONET, LISA*
The Cosby Show sr 9.20.84 NBC
The Cosby Show sr ret 9.26.85 NBC
Tales from the Darkside ep The Satanic Piano 11.2.85 NN
The ABC Afterschool Special ep Don't Touch 11.6.85 ABC

BONNER, FRANK*
Fer-De-Lance tf 10.18.74 CBS
Police Woman ep The Pawn Shop 1.20.76 NBC
The Man from Atlantis ep C. W. Hyde 12.13.77 NBC
WKRP in Cincinnati sr 9.18.78 CBS
Rainbow tf 11.6.78 NBC
WKRP in Cincinnati sr ret 11.6.79 CBS
Sex and the Single Parent tf 9.19.79 CBS
WKRP in Cincinnati sr ret 11.1.80 CBS
WKRP in Cincinnati sr ret 10.7.81 CBS
The Love Boat ep Daddy's Little Girl 10.31.81 ABC
Fantasy Island ep Romance Times Three 12.5.81 ABC
The Facts of Life Goes to Paris tf 9.25.82 NBC
Gimme a Break ep The Chief's Gay Evening 11.13.82 NBC
The Love Boat ep Sly As a Fox 1.15.83 ABC
No Man's Land tf 5.27.84 NBC
Newhart ep 2.6.84 CBS
Legmen ep I Shall Be Re-released 2.17.84 NBC
Simon and Simon ep Deep Cover 12.6.84 CBS
Matt Houston ep Death Watch 3.15.85 ABC
Gimme a Break ep Police Mommas 3.23.85 NBC
The Duck Factory ep The Annies 4.26.85 NBC
George Burns Comedy Week ep Home for Dinner 9.25.85 CBS
Scarecrow and Mrs. King sr 10.14.85 CBS
Crazy Like a Fox ep Requiem for a Fox 10.20.85 CBS
Night Court ep 10.24.85 NBC

BONO, SONNY

SUPP.:

Matt Houston ep The Purrfect Crime 1.9.83 ABC

BOOKE, SORRELL

A&C, Supp. 2:

Producer's Showcase ep Mayerling 2.4.57 NBC

Brenner ep The Buff 7.25.59 CBS

Naked City ep The Day It Rained Mink 2.15.61 ABC

Naked City ep A Corpse Ran Down Mulberry Street 10.11.61 ABC

Route 66 ep Voice at the End of the Line 10.19.62 CBS

Naked City ep Beyond This Place There Be Dragons 1.30.63 ABC

The DuPont Show of the Week ep The Legend of Lilah Claire 5.17.63 NBC

Great Adventure ep Escape 4.17.64 CBS

The Bob Hope Chrysler Theater ep Exit from a Plane in Flight 1.22.65 NBC

Twelve O'Clock High ep Faith, Hope and Sgt. Aronson 1.29.65 ABC

Slattery's People ep What's a Swan Song for a Sparrow? 4.16.65 CBS

Dr. Kildare ep With Hellfire and Thunder 10.19.65 NBC

Dr. Kildare ep Daily Flights to Olympus 10.26.65 NBC

The Girl from UNCLE ep The Double-0-Nothing Affair 3.21.67 NBC

Room 222 ep Mr. Bomberg 1.20.71 ABC

The Bob Newhart Show ep Send This Boy to Camp Spring 1976 CBS

SUPP.:

The Dukes of Hazzard sr ret 9.24.82 CBS

The Dukes of Hazzard sr ret 9.23.83 CBS

Alice ep 10.2.83 CBS

The Dukes of Hazzard sr ret 9.21.84 CBS

Newhart ep The Geezers in the Band 11.25.85 CBS

BOONE, DEBBY

SUPP.:

Sins of the Past tf 4.2.84 ABC

BORGNINE, ERNEST

SUPP.:

The Love Boat ep Venetian Love Song 10.2.82 ABC

Magnum, P.I. ep Mr. White Death 11.18.82 CBS

Matt Houston ep Here's Another Fine Mess 3.6.83 ABC

Blood Feud tf 4.25, 5.2.83 OPT

Carpool tf 10.5.83 CBS

Airwolf sr 1.22.84 CBS

The Last Days of Pompeii ms 5.6, 5.7, 5.8.84 ABC

Airwolf sr ret 9.22.84 CBS

The Dirty Dozen: The Next Mission tf/pt 2.4.85 NBC
Airwolf sr ret 9.28.85 CBS
Alice in Wonderland tf 12.9, 12.10.85 CBS

BOSLEY, TOM
A&C, Supp. 2:
Car 54, Where Are You? ep The Star Boarder 2.10.63 NBC
Naked City ep Golden Lady and Girls 5.22.63 ABC
Route 66 ep Soda Pop and Paper Flags 5.31.63 CBS
Route 66 ep Same Picture, Different Frame 10.4.63 CBS
DuPont Show of the Week ep The Gambling Hour 2.23.64 NBC
Dr. Kildare ep All Brides Should Be Beautiful 3.11.65 NBC
Profiles in Courage ep George W. Norris 3.28.65 NBC
The Defenders ep The Bum's Rush 5.6.65 CBS
The Girl from UNCLE ep The Faustus Affair 12.27.66 NBC
The FBI ep Ring of Steel 2.4.68 ABC
The Bill Cosby Show ep The Gumball Incident 2.1.70 NBC
The Most Deadly Game ep Breakdown 10.31.70 ABC
Bewitched ep Samantha's Magic Mirror Spring 71 ABC
Sarge ep Psst! Wanna Buy a Dirty Picture? 9.21.71 NBC
SUPP.:
The Love Boat ep Separate Vacations 3.6.82 ABC
Joanie Loves Chachi ep Chicago 3.23.82 ABC
The Drunkard sp 9.7.82 TEC
Happy Days sr ret 9.28.82 ABC
Happy Days sr ret 9.27.83 ABC
The Love Boat ep Intensive Care 11.19.83 ABC
The Jesse Owens Story tf 7.9, 7.16.84 OPT
Finder of Lost Loves ep Deadly Silence 10.6.84 ABC
Murder, She Wrote ep Deadly Lady 10.7.84 CBS
Murder, She Wrote ep Hit, Run and Homicide 11.25.84 CBS
Murder, She Wrote ep Death Takes a Curtain Call 12.16.84 CBS
Murder, She Wrote ep Murder Takes the Bus 3.17.85 CBS
Private Sessions tf 3.18.85 NBC
The Love Boat ep Picture from the Past 10.12.85 ABC
Murder, She Wrote ep A Lady in the Lake 11.10.85 CBS
Glitter ep Rock 'n' Roll Heaven 12.25.85 ABC

BOTTOMS, JOSEPH
SUPP.:
Side By Side: The True Story of the Osmond Family tf 4.26.82 NBC
I Married Wyatt Earp tf 1.10.83 NBC
The Sins of Dorian Gray tf 5.27.83 ABC
Celebrity ms 2.12, 2.13, 2.14.84 NBC
Time Bomb tf 3.25.84 NBC
Murder, She Wrote ep Murder at the Oasis 4.7.85 CBS
Braker pt 4.28.85 ABC

BOTTOMS, TIMOTHY
SUPP.:
Half Nelson ep Nose Job 4.19.85 NBC

BOXLEITNER, BRUCE
A&C, Supp. 2:
Hawaii Five-O ep We Hang Our Own 10.22.74 CBS
Hawaii Five-O ep And the Horse Jumped Over the Moon 2.18.75 CBS
Hawaii Five-O ep The Capsule Kidnapping 2.16.76 CBS
SUPP.:
Bring 'Em Back Alive sr 9.24.82 CBS
Bare Essence tf/pt 10.4, 10.5.82 CBS
I Married Wyatt Earp tf 1.10.83 NBC
Scarecrow and Mrs. King sr 10.3.83 CBS
Kenny Rogers as the Gambler--The Adventure Continues tf 11.28, 11.29.83 CBS
Scarecrow and Mrs. King sr ret 10.1.84 CBS
Scarecrow and Mrs. King sr ret 9.23.85 CBS

BRADBURY, LANE (a.k.a. Janette Lane Bradbury)
A&C, Supp. 2:
Alias Smith and Jones ep The Day the Amnesty Came Through 11.25.72 ABC
Police Story ep Vice: Twenty-Four Hours 12.5.75 NBC

BRADY, SCOTT
A&C, B.V.:
Studio '57 ep A Case of Blackmail 12.7.54 NN
The David Niven Show ep Maggie Malone 6.9.59 CBS
Gunsmoke ep Danny 10.13.69 CBS
A&C, Supp. 1:
Get Christie Love ep Pawn Ticket for Murder 10.2.74 ABC
Hawaii Five-O ep The Hostage 3.11.75 CBS
The Rockford Files ep Gearjammers 9.26, 10.3.75 NBC
A&C, Supp. 2;
The Rockford Files ep The Trees, the Bees and T. T. Flowers 1.21, 1.28.77 NBC
The Rockford Files ep Local Man Eaten by Newspaper 12.8.78 NBC
SUPP.:
McClain's Law ep Green Light 2.12.82 NBC
Matt Houston ep Killing Isn't Everything 10.24.82 ABC
The Winds of War ms 2.6-2.13.83 ABC
Cagney and Lacey ep 5.9.83 CBS
This Girl for Hire tf/pt 11.1.83 CBS
Simon and Simon ep 11.3.83 CBS
The Whiz Kids ep Altaria 4.28.84 CBS

BRAEDEN, ERIC
A&C, Supp. 2:
Garrison's Gorillas ep The War Diamonds 3.5.68 ABC
Hawaii Five-O ep A Bullet for McGarrett 10.29.69 CBS
Gunsmoke ep The Convict 2.1.71 CBS
Assignment: Vienna ep There Was an Old Woman 1.13.73 ABC

Get Christie Love ep Bullet from the Grave 11.20.74 ABC
Matt Helm ep Panic 12.27.75 ABC
Switch ep Net Loss 9.23.77 CBS
Switch ep Thirty Thousand Witnesses 12.26.77 CBS
SUPP.:
Strike Force ep The John Killer 3.5.82 ABC

BRAND, NEVILLE
A&C, B.V.:
Wagon Train ep The Jeb Whitmore Story 1.13.64 ABC
Wagon Train ep The Zebedee Titus Story 4.20.64 ABC
Daniel Boone ep Tanner 10.5.67 NBC
A&C, Supp. 2:
The Eddie Capra Mysteries ep Murder Plays a Dead Hand 12.22.78 NBC
SUPP.:
Harper Valley ep Grizzly Gap 4.17.82 NBC

BRANDO, JOCELYN
A&C, B.V.:
M Squad ep The Terror of Dark Street 4.24.59 NBC
Riverboat ep The Water of Gorgeous Springs 11.7.60 NBC

BRANIGAN, LAURA*
Automan ep Hot Night 3.12.84 ABC

BRASSELLE, KEEFE
A&C, B.V.:
Science Fiction Theater ep Postcard from Barcelona 11.25.55 NN

BRAY, THOM*
Lou Grant ep Hometown 11.23.81 CBS
Private Benjamin ep For Men Only 1.18.82 CBS
One Day at a Time ep 10.3.82, 10.19.82, 12.19.82 CBS
Remington Steele ep Signed, Steeled and Delivered 10.29.82 NBC
Quincy, M.E. ep A Cry for Help 1.19.83 NBC
Lottery ep Charleston: The Spenders ("Airport Cult" segment) 11.4.83 ABC
An Uncommon Love tf 11.30.83 CBS
Quarterback Princess tf 12.3.83 CBS
Riptide sr 1.3.84 NBC
Anatomy of an Illness tf 5.15.84 CBS
Concrete Beat tf 7.9.84 ABC
Riptide sr ret 10.2.84 NBC
Riptide sr ret 10.1.85 NBC

BRAZZI, ROSSANO
SUPP.:
The Love Boat ep The Gigolo 10.2.82 ABC
Hart to Hart ep Straight Through the Hart 10.4.83 ABC
Christopher Columbus tf 5.19, 5.20.85 CBS

BRECK, PETER*
Highway Patrol ep 1958 NN
77 Sunset Strip ep Lovely Lady, Pity Me 10.17.58 ABC
Have Gun--Will Travel ep The Protege 10.18.58 CBS
The Restless Gun ep The Way Back 12.29.58 NBC
Black Saddle sr 1.10.59 ABC
Black Saddle sr ret 10.2.59 ABC
Maverick ep Destination: Devil's Flat 12.25.60 ABC
Hawaiian Eye ep Baker's Half Dozen 12.28.60 ABC
The Roaring 20s ep Big Town Blues 1.21.61 ABC
Surfside Six ep Thieves Among Honor 1.30.61 ABC
Bronco ep Yankee Tornado 3.13.61 ABC
Maverick ep Triple Indemnity 3.19.61 ABC
Lawman ep Trapped 9.13.61 ABC
The Roaring 20s ep Everybody Loves Benny 11.11.61 ABC
Maverick ep The Maverick Report 3.4.62 ABC
Maverick ep Marshal Maverick 3.11.62 ABC
Hawaiian Eye ep Aloha Cricket 4.18.62 ABC
Maverick ep One of Our Trains Is Missing 4.22.62 ABC
Surfside Six ep Squeeze Play 5.14.62 ABC
77 Sunset Strip ep Nightmare 6.22.62 ABC
The Gallant Men ep Retreat to Concord 10.12.62 ABC
Cheyenne ep Indian Gold 12.21.62 ABC
Gunsmoke ep The Odyssey of Jubal Tanner 5.18.63 CBS
The Outer Limits ep O.B.I.T. 11.4.63 ABC
Mr. Novak ep A Feeling for Friday 11.19.63 NBC
The Virginian ep Rope of Life 3.25.64 NBC
Perry Mason ep The Case of the Antic Angel 4.16.64 CBS
Branded ep The Mission 3.14, 3.21, 3.28.65 NBC
Perry Mason ep The Case of the Gambling Lady 4.8.65 CBS
The Kraft Mystery Theater ep Connery's Hands 7.1.65 NBC
The Big Valley sr 9.14.65 ABC
The Big Valley sr ret 9.12.66 ABC
The Big Valley sr ret 9.11.67 ABC
The Big Valley sr ret 9.23.68 ABC
The Men from Shiloh ep 12.30.70 NBC
Alias Smith and Jones ep The Great Shell Game 2.18.71 ABC
Mission: Impossible ep 12.9.72 CBS
S.W.A.T. ep Murder by Fire 12.6.75 ABC
The Six Million Dollar Man ep To Catch the Eagle 3.6.77 ABC
Black Beauty ms ep 1.31.78 NBC
Vegas ep Second Stanza 12.6.78 ABC
Fantasy Island ep Cowboy 1.22.79 ABC
Cliffhangers: The Secret Empire sr 2.7.79 NBC
The Incredible Hulk ep The Lottery 2.15.80 CBS
The Dukes of Hazzard ep The Hack of Hazzard 4.3.81 CBS
The Fall Guy ep The Human Torch 12.9.81 ABC
Masquerade ep Girls for Sale 12.29.83 ABC
The Fall Guy ep King of the Stuntmen 10.3.85 ABC

BRENNAN, EILEEN

A&C, Supp. 2:
All in the Family ep The Elevator Story 1.1.72 CBS
SUPP.:
Working sp 12.81 SHO
Private Benjamin sr ret 9.28.82 CBS
The Love Boat ep Dutch Treat 9.29.84 ABC
Off the Rack pt 12.7.84 ABC
Off the Rack sr 3.15.85 ABC
The Fourth Wise Man sp 3.30.85 ABC
Answers ep Twinkle, Twinkle sp 4.30.85 A&E

BRENNAN, WALTER
A&C, B.V.:
Alias Smith and Jones ep Twenty-one Days to Tenstrike 1.6.72 ABC
Alias Smith and Jones ep Don't Get Mad, Get Even 2.17.72 ABC

BRENNER, DORI
A&C, Supp. 2:
The Law ep Complaint Amended 3.19.75 NBC
SUPP.:
Hill Street Blues ep Chipped Beef 12.17.81 NBC
Cassie and Company sr 1.29.82 NBC
The CBS Afternoon Playhouse ep Journey to Survival 4.6.82 CBS
At Ease ep Computer Dating 3.28.83 ABC
Obsessed with a Married Woman tf 2.11.85 ABC
Dallas ep Saving Grace 10.18.85 CBS
I Dream of Jeannie: 15 Years Later tf/pt 10.20.85 NBC
Cagney and Lacey ep The Clinic 11.11.85 CBS
Who's the Boss? ep Hunk of the Month 11.19.85 ABC

BRESLIN, PATRICIA (a.k.a. Pat Breslin)
A&C, B.V.:
Tate ep The Return of Jessica Jackson 9.14.60 NBC

BRIDGES, BEAU
A&C, B.V.:
Mr. Novak ep Pay the Two Dollars 11.26.63 NBC
Cimarron Strip ep The Legend of Jud Starr 9.14.67 CBS
SUPP.:
The Kid from Nowhere tf 1.4.82 NBC
Dangerous Company tf 2.9.82 CBS
Witness for the Prosecution tf 12.4.82 CBS
Red Light Sting tf 4.5.84 CBS
Alice in Wonderland tf 12.9, 12.10.85 CBS
Amazing Stories ep Vanessa in the Garden 12.29.85 NBC

BRIDGES, JEFF*
Silent Night, Lonely Night tf 12.16.69 NBC
In Search of America tf 3.23.71 ABC
Faerie Tale Theater ep Rapunzel 2.5.83 SHO

BRIDGES, LLOYD
SUPP.:
Life of the Party: The Story of Beatrice tf 9.29.82 CBS
The Blue and the Gray ms 11.14-11.17.82 CBS
Grace Kelly tf 2.21.83 ABC
Grandpa, Will You Run with Me? sp 4.3.83 NBC
Matt Houston ep Heritage 9.9.83 ABC
George Washington ms 4.8, 4.10, 4.11.84 CBS
The Love Boat Fall Preview Party sp 9.15.84 ABC
Paper Dolls sr 9.23.84 ABC
Alice in Wonderland tf 12.9, 12.10.85 CBS

BRIDGES, TODD*
The Orphan and the Dude pt 7.18.75 ABC
Katherine tf 10.5.75 ABC
Roots ms ep 1.23.77 ABC
Fish sr 2.5.77 ABC
Little House on the Prairie ep The Wisdom of Solomon 3.7.77 NBC
A Killing Affair tf 9.21.77 CBS
The Waltons ep 9.22.77 CBS
Killer on Board tf 10.10.77 NBC
The Love Boat ep Mike and Ike 10.21.78 ABC
Diff'rent Strokes sr 11.3.78 NBC
The Return of Mod Squad tf 5.18.79 ABC
Diff'rent Strokes sr ret 9.21.79 NBC
CHiPs ep CHiPs Goes Roller Disco 9.22.79 NBC
Here's Boomer ep 5.23.80 NBC
CHiPs ep 12.7.80 NBC
Diff'rent Strokes sr ret 11.12.80 NBC
Here's Boomer ep Boomer's Eastside Story 10.11.81 NBC
Diff'rent Strokes sr ret 10.29.81 NBC
Diff'rent Strokes sr ret 10.2.82 NBC
Diff'rent Strokes sr ret 10.1.83 NBC
High School, U.S.A. tf/pt 10.16.83 NBC
Diff'rent Strokes sr ret 9.29.84 NBC
Diff'rent Strokes sr ret 9.27.85 ABC

BRISEBOIS, DANIELLE
SUPP.:
The Love Boat ep The Reluctant Father 11.26.83 ABC
Knots Landing sr 12.1.83 CBS
Hotel ep Reflections 1.4.84 ABC

BRISSETTE, TIFFANY*
Webster ep Too Much Class 11.30.84 ABC
Webster ep The Uh-oh Feeling 1.25.85 ABC
Webster ep Strike Up the Band 2.1.85 ABC
Small Wonder sr 9.85 NN

BRITTANY, MORGAN (a.k.a. Suzanne Cupito)
A&C, Supp. 2:

The Lloyd Bridges Show ep My Child Is Yet a Stranger 9.25.62 CBS
The Lloyd Bridges Show ep The Wonder of Wanda 1.8.63 CBS
Rawhide ep Incident of the Hostages 4.17.63 CBS
Gunsmoke ep Daddy Went Away 5.11.63 CBS
The Richard Boone Show sr 9.24.63 NBC
The Outer Limits ep The Inheritors 11.21.64, 11.28.64 ABC
The Tycoon ep 12.29.64 ABC
Burke's Law ep Who Killed Mother Goose? 1.13.65 ABC
Branded ep Kellie 4.24.66 NBC
The Andy Griffith Show ep Opie's First Love 9.11.67 CBS
Bridget Loves Bernie ep 1972 CBS
SUPP.:
Dallas sr ret 10.1.82 CBS
The Wild Women of Chastity Gulch tf/pt 10.31.82 ABC
The Love Boat ep Sketchy Love 10.30.82 ABC
Fantasy Island ep Operation Breakout 1.15.83 ABC
Dallas sr ret 9.30.83 CBS
The Fall Guy ep Inside/Outside 11.16.83 ABC
The Love Boat ep The Misunderstanding 12.10.83 ABC
Masquerade ep Diamonds 12.22.83 ABC
Hotel ep Prisms 3.14.84 ABC
Glitter sr 9.13.84 ABC
Dallas sr ret 9.28.84 CBS
The Love Boat ep I'll Never Forget What's Her Name 10.27.84 ABC
Murder, She Wrote ep Footnote to Murder 3.10.85 CBS
Half Nelson ep 3.29.85 NBC
The Love Boat ep Ashes to Ashes 3.30.85 ABC
On Top All Over the World pt 4.85 NN
Dallas sr ret 9.27.85 CBS
The New Love, American Style ep Love and the Final Night 12.26.85 ABC

BRODERICK, JAMES*
The Armstrong Circle Theater ep Three Cents Worth of Fear 5.28.57 NBC
The Armstrong Circle Theater ep The Complex Mummy Complex 1.8.58 NBC
Brenner sr 6.6.59 CBS
Great Ghost Tales ep August Heat 8.3.61 CBS
The Defenders ep Storm at Birch Glen 1.27.62 CBS
The U.S. Steel Hour ep Two Black Kings 3.21.62 CBS
The Defenders ep Blood Country 9.22.62 CBS
The Armstrong Circle Theater ep Escape to Nowhere 12.19.62 NBC
The Twilight Zone ep On Thursday We Leave for Home 5.21.63 CBS
Gunsmoke ep My Sister's Keeper 11.2.63 CBS
The Hallmark Hall of Fame ep Abe Lincoln in Illinois 2.3.64 NBC
Gunsmoke ep Doctor's Wife 10.24.64 CBS

The FBI ep Anatomy of a Prison Break 11.27.66 ABC
12 O'Clock High ep Burden of Guilt 12.2.66 ABC
The Fugitive ep Run the Man Down 1.3.67 ABC
ABC Stage '67 ep The Trap of Solid Gold 1.4.67 ABC
N.Y.P.D. ep Shakedown 9.5.67 ABC
Judd, for the Defense ep Runaway 3.14.67 ABC
The Bold Ones: Law Enforcers ep A Thing Not of God 2.1.70 NBC
The Bold Ones: The Doctors ep First--No Ham to the Patient 11.15.70 NBC
Longstreet ep A World of Perfect Complicity 9.23.71 ABC
Nicky's World tf 4.19.74 CBS
Family sr 3.19.76 ABC
Family sr ret 9.28.76 ABC
Family sr ret 9.12.77 ABC
Family sr ret 9.21.78 ABC
Roots: The Next Generation ms 2.18-2.25.79 ABC
Family sr ret 12.24.79 ABC
Family sr ret 6.4.80 ABC
The Shadow Box tf 12.28.80 ABC
American Playhouse ep The Great American Fourth of July and Other Disasters 3.16.82 PBS
Dreams Don't Die tf 5.21.82 ABC

BRODERICK, MATTHEW*
Faerie Tale Theater ep Cinderella 8.14.85 SHO
Master Harold and the Boys sp 11.15.85 PBS

BROLIN, JAMES
A&C, B.V.:
Margie ep 1.18.62 ABC
Twelve O'Clock High ep Rx for a Sick Bird 9.20.65 ABC
The Monroes ep Silent Night, Deadly Night 11.23.66 ABC
The Monroes ep Range War 12.21.66 ABC
The Monroes ep Mask of Death 1.4.67 ABC
SUPP.:
The Ambush Murders tf 1.5.82 CBS
Mae West tf 5.2.82 ABC
White Water Rebels tf 1.8.83 CBS
Cowboy tf 4.30.83 CBS
Hotel sr 9.21.83 ABC
The Love Boat Fall Preview Party sp 9.15.84 ABC
Hotel sr ret 9.26.84 ABC
Hotel sr ret 9.25.85 ABC
Beverly Hills Cowgirl Blues tf/pt 10.5.85 CBS

BRONSON, CHARLES
A&C, B.V.:
Philco Television Playhouse ep Adventure in Java 7.8.54 NBC
Medic ep My Brother Joe 10.25.54 NBC
Lux Video Theater ep A Bell for Adano 2.10.55 NBC

Man Behind the Badge ep The Case of the Invisible Mark 2.19.55 NBC
Stage 7 ep Debt of Honor 2.20.55 CBS
Warner Brothers Presents ep Deep Freeze 5.8.56 ABC
Gunsmoke ep The Killer 5.26.56 CBS
Have Gun--Will Travel ep The Outlaw 9.21.57 CBS
Suspicion ep Doomsday 12.16.57 NBC
Have Gun--Will Travel ep 9.27.58 CBS
The Court of Last Resort ep The Steve Hardlika Case 1.24.58 NBC
Sugarfoot ep Man Wanted 2.18.58 ABC
Tales of Wells Fargo ep Butch Cassidy 10.13.58 NBC
Hennessy ep Hennessy Ala Gunn 10.17.60 CBS
Have Gun--Will Travel ep A Proof of Love 10.14.61 CBS
Have Gun--Will Travel ep Ben Jalisco 11.18.61 CBS
Have Gun--Will Travel ep Brotherhood 1.5.63 CBS
The Travels of Jaimie McPheeters sr 11.17.63 ABC
The Legend of Jesse James ep The Chase 3.7.66 ABC
The FBI ep The Animal 4.17.66 ABC
The Fugitive ep The One That Got Away 1.17.66 ABC
The Virginian ep The Reckoning 9.13.67 NBC
Dundee and the Culhane ep The Cat in the Bag Brief 9.13.67 CBS

BROOKE, HILLARY
A&C, B.V.:
I Love Lucy ep The Fox Hunt 2.6.56 CBS

BROOKS, GERALDINE
A&C, B.V.:
High Chaparral ep The Pride of Revenge 11.19.67 NBC
A&C, Supp. 1:
Baretta ep Runaway Cowboy 10.6.76 ABC

BROOKS, RANDI*
Wizards and Warriors sr 2.26.83 CBS
The Dukes of Hazzard ep 3.11.83 CBS
The Return of the Man from UNCLE: The 15 Years Later Affair 4.5.83 CBS
Mickey Spillane's Mike Hammer: Murder Me, Murder You tf/pt 4.9.83 CBS
Herndon and Me pt 8.26.83 ABC
Simon and Simon ep 12.1.83 CBS
Hardcastle and McCormick ep School for Scandal 1.29.84 ABC
Riptide ep Hatchet Job 1.31.84 NBC
The Rousters ep Snake Eyes 6.30.84 NBC
T. J. Hooker ep Pursuit (a.k.a. Hot Pursuit) 10.27.84 ABC
The Cartier Affair tf 11.4.84 NBC
Who's the Boss? ep A Rash Decision 11.13.84 ABC
Airwolf ep Inn at the End of the Road 1.26.85 CBS
A Bunny's Tale tf 2.25.85 ABC

Knight Rider ep Knight in Retreat 3.29.85 NBC
Double Dare ep Double Negative 4.10.85 CBS

BROPHY, KEVIN*
Lucan tf/pt 5.2.77 ABC
Lucan sr 9.12.77 ABC
The Hardy Boys Mysteries ep The Last Kiss of Summer 10.1, 10.8.77 ABC
Lucan sr ret 11.13.78 ABC
The Yeagers sr 6.1.80 ABC
Trouble in High Timber Country tf/pt 6.27.80 ABC
Trapper John, M.D. ep A Family Affair 2.22.81 CBS
Trapper John, M.D. ep The Peter Pan Syndrome 2.7.82 CBS
Strike Force ep Humiliation 3.19.82 ABC
The Love Boat ep Does Father Know Best? 4.10.82 ABC
Matt Houston ep Whose Party Is This Anyway? 1.23.83 ABC
Trapper John, M.D. ep 11.20.83 CBS
Partners in Crime ep Double Jeopardy 12.29.84 NBC
Scene of the Crime ep Murder on the Rocks 4.28.85 NBC

BROSNAN, PIERCE*
The Manions of America ms 9.30, 10.1, 10.2.82 ABC
Remington Steele sr 10.1.82 NBC
Remington Steele sr ret 9.20.83 NBC
Nancy Astor sr 4.15.84 PBS
Remington Steele sr ret 9.25.84 NBC
Remington Steele sr ret 9.24.85 NBC

BROUGH, CANDI*
More Wild Wild West tf 10.7.80 CBS
B.J. and the Bear sr 9.13.81 NBC
Taxi ep Take My Ex-Wife, Please 2.18.82 ABC
Branagan and Mapes pt 8.11.83 CBS
The Dukes of Hazzard ep 11.25.83 CBS
Happy Days ep Arthur, Arthur 12.6.83 ABC
The Brothers-in-Law pt 4.28.85 ABC

BROUGH, RANDI*
More Wild Wild West tf 10.7.80 CBS
B.J. and the Bear sr 9.13.81 NBC
Taxi ep Take My Ex-Wife, Please 2.18.82 ABC
Branagan and Mapes pt 8.11.83 CBS
The Dukes of Hazzard ep 11.25.83 CBS
Happy Days ep Arthur, Arthur 12.6.83 ABC
The Brothers-in-Law pt 4.28.85 ABC

BROWN, GEORG STANFORD*
Dragnet ep The Big Problem 3.28.68 NBC
Judd, for the Defense ep The Ends of Justice 10.11.68 ABC
Mannix ep Eagles Sometimes Don't Fly 9.27.69 CBS
The Young Lawyers tf 10.28.69 ABC

The Bold Ones: The Lawyers ep The Crowd Pleaser 11.2.69 NBC
Here Come the Brides ep A Bride for Obie Brown 1.9.70 ABC
Ritual of Evil tf 2.23.70 NBC
Medical Center ep The Rebel in White 4.8.70 CBS
The Bold Ones: The Doctors ep Killer on the Loose 10.11.70 NBC
The Bold Ones: The Lawyers ep Cage for a Panther 10.18.70 NBC
The Name of the Game ep The Time Is Now 10.23.70 NBC
Medical Center ep The Man in Hiding 3.3.71 CBS
Mannix ep A Choice of Evils 11.10.71 CBS
Room 222 ep And in This Corner 1.21.72 ABC
Mission: Impossible ep 1.29.72 CBS
The Rookies tf/pt 3.7.72 ABC
The Rookies sr 9.11.72 ABC
The Rookies sr ret 9.10.73 ABC
The Rookies sr ret 9.19.74 ABC
The Rookies sr ret 9.9.75 ABC
Dawn: Portrait of a Teenage Runaway tf 9.27.76 NBC
Roots ms ep 1.29, 1.30.77 ABC
Roots: The Next Generation ms 2.18-2.25.79 ABC
Paris ep 12.14.79 CBS
The Night the City Screamed tf 12.14.80 ABC
Police Squad! ep 3.11.82 ABC
The Kid with the Broken Halo tf/pt 4.5.82 NBC
In Defense of Kids tf 4.6.83 CBS
Cagney and Lacey ep 5.14.84 CBS
The Jesse Owens Story tf 7.9, 7.16.84 OPT

BROWN, PETER*

Cheyenne ep 3.25.59, 4.1.59 ABC
The Lawman sr 10.5.58 ABC
Colt .45 ep Judgment Day 2.2.59 ABC
Sugarfoot ep The Trial of the Canary Kid 9.15.59 ABC
The Lawman sr ret 10.4.59 ABC
The Lawman sr ret 9.18.60 ABC
Maverick ep Hadley's Hunters 9.25.60 ABC
Hawaiian Eye ep Lahana Lady 6.20.62 ABC
77 Sunset Strip ep The Gang's All Here 6.29.62 ABC
Cheyenne ep Pocketful of Stars 11.12.62 ABC
The Gallant Men ep The Bridge 1.16.63 ABC
The Alfred Hitchcock Hour ep Death of a Cop 5.24.63 NBC
Redigo ep The Blooded Bull 10.1.63 ABC
Wagon Train ep The Geneva Balfour Story 1.20.64 ABC
Kraft Suspense Theater ep The Action of the Tiger 2.20.64 NBC
Wagon Train ep Those Who Stay Behind 11.8.64 ABC
The Virginian ep Return a Stranger 11.18.64 NBC
Kraft Suspense Theater ep One Tiger to a Hill 12.3.64 NBC
The Virginian ep We've Lost a Train 4.21.65 NBC
Laredo sr 9.16.65 NBC

Laredo sr ret 9.16.66 NBC
The Virginian ep A Small Taste of Justice 12.20.67 NBC
The Mod Squad ep The Debt 12.30.69 ABC
Hunters Are for Killing tf 3.12.70 CBS
The Most Deadly Game ep War Games 11.28.70 ABC
Dan August ep The Manufactured Man 3.11.71 ABC
Mission: Impossible ep Blind 9.18.71 CBS
O'Hara, United States Treasury ep 11.5.71 CBS
Medical Center ep 2.16.72 CBS
The Bob Newhart Show ep 9.30.72 CBS
The Magician ep The Vanishing Lady 10.9.73 NBC
Police Story ep Love, Mabel 11.26.74 NBC
Marcus Welby, M.D. ep The Covenant 9.30.75 ABC
Matt Helm ep Murder on Ice 10.25.75 ABC
Police Woman ep Above and Beyond 10.31.75 NBC
Streets of San Francisco ep One Last Trick 1.6.77 ABC
Quincy, M.E. ep Main Man 11.11.77 NBC
The New Adventures of Wonder Woman ep Hot Wheels 9.29.78 CBS
Vegas ep The Pageant 11.15.78 ABC
Flying High ep Brides and Grooms 12.15.78 CBS
Salvage tf 1.20.79 ABC
Project U.F.O. ep Sighting 4025: The Spaceship Incident 7.5.79 NBC
Top of the Hill tf 2.80 OPT
The Dukes of Hazzard ep Deputy Daisy 2.1.80 CBS
The Girl, the Gold Watch & Everything pt 5.80 OPT
Fantasy Island ep 1.17.81 ABC
Three Eyes pt 6.27.82 NBC
Magnum, P.I. ep Heal Thyself 12.16.82 CBS
Hart to Hart ep As the Harts Turn 3.1.83 ABC
T. J. Hooker ep Chinatown 10.15.83 ABC
Manimal ep High Stakes 11.4.83 NBC
T. J. Hooker ep Carnal Express 12.31.83 ABC
Simon and Simon ep The Dillinger Print 3.8.84 CBS
The Whiz Kids ep 4.7.84 CBS
The Calendar Girl Murders tf 4.8.84 ABC
Cover Up ep Cover Up (pt) 9.22.84 CBS
The Fall Guy ep The San Francisco Caper 11.21.84 ABC
Riptide ep Peter Pan Is Alive and Well 12.11.84 NBC
Crazy Like a Fox ep Till Death Do Us Part 1.20.85 CBS
Knight Rider ep Knight Behind Bars 12.6.85 NBC

BROWN, ROSCOE LEE

SUPP.:

The High Five pt 7.22.82 NBC
Magnum, P.I. ep Of Sound Mind 1.6.83 CBS

BRULL, PAMELA*

The Secret Empire (segment of Cliffhangers) sr 2.27.79 NBC
Three's Company ep Dying to Meet You 5.5.81 ABC

T. J. Hooker ep The Streets 3.20.82 ABC
T. J. Hooker ep God Bless the Child 3.27.82 ABC
T. J. Hooker ep Blue Murder 12.3.83 ABC
Matt Houston ep Waltz of Death 1.13.84 ABC
Scarecrow and Mrs. King ep A Class Act 12.3.84 CBS
Off the Rack pt 12.7.84 ABC
Off the Rack sr 3.15.85 ABC
The Love Boat ep No More Mr. Nice Guy 11.30.85 ABC

BUCHANAN, EDGAR
A&C, B.V.:
Stagecoach West ep Red Sand 11.22.60 ABC
The Outlaws ep Starfall 11.24, 12.1.60 NBC
Route 66 ep 12.9.68 CBS
Klondike ep The Gold Burro 1.16.61 NBC
Bus Stop ep The Man from Boots Strap 11.26.61 ABC
Thriller ep Till Death Do Us Part 3.12.62 NBC
Stoney Burke ep Fight Night 10.6.62 ABC
The Lloyd Bridges Show ep Just Married 10.16.62 CBS
Wide Country ep Good Old Walt 12.13.62 NBC
The Lloyd Bridges Show ep The Tyrees of Capitol Hill (pilot) 4.9.63 CBS
The Men from Shiloh ep The Legacy of Spencer Flats 1.27.71 NBC

BUCKMAN, TARA*
Kojak ep A Strange Kind of Love 10.9.77 CBS
79 Park Avenue ms 10.16-10.18.77 NBC
Switch ep 12.5.77 CBS
Baretta ep I'll Take You to Lunch 1.18.78 ABC
The Two-Five tf 4.14.78 ABC
Stone tf/pt 8.26.79 ABC
Hart to Hart tf/pt 9.25.79 ABC
Barnaby Jones ep Nightmare in Hawaii 9.27.79 CBS
Quincy, M.E. ep Speed Trap 10.11.79 NBC
Buck Rogers in the 25th Century ep Unchained Woman 11.1.79 NBC
The Man in the Santa Claus Suit tf 12.23.79 NBC
Buck Rogers in the 25th Century ep A Blast for Buck 1.17.80 NBC
Brave New World tf 3.7.80 NBC
Lobo sr 12.30.80 NBC
CHiPs ep Anything But the Truth 11.8.81 NBC
St. Elsewhere ep Bypass 11.9.82 NBC
The Master ep Juggernaut 3.16.84 NBC
The Master ep The Good, the Bad and the Priceless 3.23.84 NBC
Highway to Heaven ep Hotel of Dreams 12.12.84 NBC
T. J. Hooker ep Love Story 2.16.85 ABC

BULIFANT, JOYCE
A&C, Supp. 1:

Gunsmoke ep Uncle Sunday 12.15.62 CBS
Arrest and Trial ep A Roll of the Dice 2.23.64 ABC
SUPP.:
Harper Valley ep The Return of Charlie's Chow Palace 4.24.82 NBC
The Two of Us ep Torch Song 2.17.82 CBS
Charley's Aunt sp 2.6.83 TEC
The Facts of Life ep Student Teacher, Jo 10.5.85 NBC

BUONO, VICTOR
SUPP.:
Two Guys from Muck pt 3.29.82 NBC

BURGHOFF, GARY
SUPP.:
AfterMASH ep Dear Radar 1.16.84 CBS
AfterMASH ep 1.23.84 CBS
W*A*L*T*E*R pt 7.17.84 CBS

BURKE, DELTA*
Charleston tf 1.15.79 NBC
A Last Cry for Help tf 1.19.79 ABC
The Seekers ms 12.3, 12.4.79 OPT
The Chisholms sr 1.19.80 CBS
The Home Front pt 10.9.80 CBS
Filthy Rich sr 8.16.82 CBS
Rooster tf/pt 11.17.82 ABC
The Fall Guy ep The Mighty Myron 11.17.82 ABC
The Love Boat ep Out of My Hair 2.19.83 ABC
Fantasy Island ep The Devil Stick 3.19.83 ABC
Mickey Spillane's Mike Hammer: Murder Me, Murder You tf/pt 4.9.83 CBS
Gun Shy ep 4.19.83 CBS
Johnny Blue pt 9.4.83 CBS
Remington Steele ep Altered Steele 10.11.83 NBC
The Love Boat ep The End Is Near 12.10.83 ABC
Automan ep Unreasonable Facsimile 1.12.84 ABC
Lottery ep Chicago: Another Choice ("Stripper" segment) 3.1.84 ABC
Mickey Spillane's Mike Hammer ep Shots in the Dark 3.8.84 CBS
The Love Boat ep Watching the Master 11.10.84 ABC
First and Ten pt 12.11.84 HBO
T. J. Hooker ep Grand Theft Auto 12.29.84 ABC
Who's the Boss? ep Paint Your Wagon 1.15.85 ABC
First and Ten sr 9.3.85 HBO

BURKE, PAUL
A&C, B.V.:
The Tales of Wells Fargo ep The Killer 12.1.58 NBC
Black Saddle ep Blood Money 12.18.59 ABC
Hotel de Paree ep Sundance and the Long Trek 4.22.60 CBS

Wanted: Dead or Alive ep The Trail 9.21.60 CBS
Twelve O'Clock High ep The Golden Boy Had Nine Black Sheep 9.18.64 ABC
Twelve O'Clock High ep End of the Line 3.12.65 ABC
Twelve O'Clock High sr 9.13.65 ABC
A&C, Supp. 1:
Harry O ep Ballinger's Choice 10.31.74 ABC
A&C, Supp. 2:
Hawaii Five-O ep The Moroville Convent 3.29.80 CBS
SUPP.:
Magnum, P.I. ep 9.30.82 CBS
Dynasty ep La Mirage 12.15.82 ABC
Dynasty ep Acapulco 12.22.82 ABC
Dynasty ep Reunion in Singapore 3.2.83 ABC
Dynasty ep The Dinner 4.6.83 ABC
Dynasty ep The Threat 4.13.83 ABC
Dynasty ep The Bungalow 10.5.83 ABC
Hotel ep Relative Looser 11.2.83 ABC
T. J. Hooker ep Blue Murder 12.3.83 ABC
Fantasy Island ep The Fantasy Island Girl 12.10.83 ABC
The Seduction of Gina tf 1.17.84 CBS
Dynasty ep A Little Girl 2.1.84 ABC
Dynasty ep The Vigil 2.29.84 ABC
Dynasty ep The Engagement 4.25.84 ABC
Santa Barbara sr 9.84 NBC
Finder of Lost Loves ep Deadly Silence 10.6.84 ABC
Dynasty ep Amanda 11.14.84 ABC
Murder, She Wrote ep Murder in the Afternoon 10.13.85 CBS
Magnum, P.I. ep Blood and Honor 12.5.85 CBS

BURKLEY, DENNIS*
The Texas Wheelers ep 9.27.74 ABC
The Law tf 10.22.74 NBC
Starsky and Hutch ep Omaha Tiger 1.28.76 ABC
Family ep 4.13.76 ABC
The Call of the Wild tf 5.22.76 NBC
McCloud ep 10.24.76 NBC
The Rockford Files ep Coulter City Wildcat 11.12.76 NBC
Once an Eagle ms 12.2-12.30.76 NBC
Mary Hartman, Mary Hartman sr 1977 NN
Delta County, U.S.A. tf 5.20.77 ABC
Quincy, M.E. ep No Deadly Secret 9.16.77 NBC
Mad Bull tf 12.21.77 CBS
Maude ep 4.15.78 CBS
Amateur Night at the Dixie Bar and Grill tf 2.17.79 NBC
Charleston tf 1.15.79 NBC
The Rockford Files ep The Return of the Black Shadow 2.17.79 NBC
B.J. and the Bear ep Lobo's Revenge 4.7.79 NBC
B.J. and the Bear ep Lobo 5.5.79 NBC
Hanging In sr 8.8.79 CBS

Mrs. R's Daughter tf 9.19.79 NBC
Young Maverick ep 1.30.80 CBS
The Misadventures of Sheriff Lobo ep 2.5.80 NBC
Ten Speed and Brown Shoe ep The Sixteen Byte Data Chip and the Brown-Eyed Fox 3.9.80 ABC
Sanford sr 3.15.80 NBC
The Dukes of Hazzard ep 9.19.80 CBS
Sanford sr ret 5.29.81 NBC
The Greatest American Hero ep 11.25.81 ABC
Hill Street Blues ep The Belles of St. Mary's 2.17.83 NBC
Amanda's ep The Man Who Came on Wednesday 2.24.83 ABC
Hill Street Blues ep Life in the Minors 2.24.83 NBC
Hill Street Blues ep Eugene's Comedy Empire Strikes Back 3.3.83 NBC
Hill Street Blues ep Spotlight on Rocco 4.28.83 NBC
Knight Rider ep Short Notice 5.6.83 NBC
The Fall Guy ep Baker's Dozen 10.19.83 ABC
Scarecrow and Mrs. King ep Always Look a Gift Horse in the Mouth 11.14.83 CBS
The Mississippi ep 2.7.84 CBS
a.k.a. Pablo ep The Presidential Joke Teller 3.27.84 ABC
Summer Fantasy tf 5.25.84 NBC
The Rousters ep This Town Ain't Big Enough for the Twelve of Us 6.9.84 NBC
E/R ep 10.23.84 CBS
The Dukes of Hazzard ep 1.25.85 CBS
MacGruder and Loud ep The Odds Favor Death 2.5.85 ABC
Brothers-in-Law pt 4.28.85 ABC
Trapper John, M.D. ep Just Around the Coroner 10.27.85 CBS

BURNETT, CAROL
A&C, B.V.:
Gomer Pyle, USMC ep Corporal Carol 9.22.67 CBS
Gomer Pyle, USMC ep Showtime with Sgt Carol Spring 1969 CBS
SUPP.:
Eunice sp 3.15.82 CBS
Life of the Party: The Story of Beatrice tf 9.29.82
Mama's Family ep The Wedding 2.12.83 NBC
Mama's Family ep Positive Thinking 4.30.83 NBC
All My Children ep 4.8-4.19.83 ABC
Between Friends tf 9.15.83 HBO
Magnum, P.I. ep 2.2.84 CBS
An American Portrait ep Belva Lockwood 12.13.84 CBS
The Laundromat sp 4.1.85 HBO

BURNS, GEORGE
A&C, B.V.:
The Bob Cummings Show (Love That Bob) ep Bob Meets the Mortons 3.21.57 CBS
The Bob Cummings Show (Love That Bob) ep Bob Helps Von Zell 6.2.59 CBS

SUPP.:
Two of a Kind tf 10.9.82 CBS
Grandpa, Will You Run with Me? sp hos 4.3.83 NBC
George Burns Comedy Week sr hos 9.18.85 CBS

BURNS, MICHAEL
A&C, B.V.:
Wagon Train ep The Odyssey of Flint McCullough 2.15.61 NBC
The Many Loves of Dobie Gillis ep A Taste for Lobster 6.29.60 CBS
The Big Valley ep A Day of Terror 12.12.66 ABC
Gunsmoke ep Nowhere to Run 1.15.68 CBS

BURR, RAYMOND
SUPP.:
Perry Mason Returns tf 12.1.85 NBC

BURSTYN, ELLEN (a.k.a. Ellen McRae)
A&C, Supp. 1:
I'm Dickens ... He's Fenster ep Harry the Father Image 10.62 ABC
The Many Loves of Dobie Gillis ep A Splinter Off the Old Block 10.24.62 CBS
SUPP.:
Surviving tf 2.10.85 ABC
Into Thin Air tf 10.29.85 CBS

BURTON, KATE*
Ellis Island ms 11.11, 11.13, 11.14.84 CBS
Evergreen ms 2.24, 2.25, 2.26.85 NBC

BURTON, LeVAR
SUPP.:
Trapper John, M.D. ep A Piece of the Action 4.11.82 CBS
Fantasy Island ep Edward 4.9.83 ABC
Emergency Room tf 7.17.83 NN
The Love Boat ep Love Is Blind 3.3.84 ABC
The Jesse Owens Story tf 7.9, 7.16.84 OPT
Breathing Easy sp 11.14.84 PBS
The Midnight Hour tf 11.1.85 ABC

BURTON, RICHARD
SUPP.:
The Fall Guy ep The Reluctant Traveling Companion 11.24.82 ABC
Ellis Island ms 11.11, 11.13, 11.14.84 CBS

BUSEY, GARY
SUPP.:
The Hitchhiker ep W.G.O.D. 11.26.85 HBO

BUTKUS, DICK*
Brian's Song tf 11.30.71 ABC

The Rockford Files ep The No-Cut Contract 1.16.76 NBC
Rich Man, Poor Man ms 2.1-3.15.76 ABC
A Matter of Wife ... and Death tf 4.10.76 NBC
Superdome tf 1.9.78 ABC
Fantasy Island ep Jungle Man 3.8.80 ABC
The Legend of Sleepy Hollow tf 10.31.80 NBC
Magnum, P.I. ep One More Summer 2.11.82 CBS
Cass Malloy pt 7.21.82 CBS
Matt Houston ep Killing Isn't Everything 10.24.82 ABC
Magnum, P.I. ep 10.27.82 CBS
The Greatest American Hero ep The Price Is Right 11.5.82 ABC
Simon and Simon ep Foul Play 12.16.82 CBS
Blue Thunder sr 4.16.84 ABC
Murder, She Wrote ep Sudden Death 3.3.85 CBS
Half Nelson sr 3.29.85 NBC
The Love Boat ep Ace Meets the Champ 10.6.85 ABC

BUTTONS, RED

SUPP.:

The Love Boat ep Discount Romance 3.5.83 ABC
Fantasy Island ep King of Burlesque 3.12.83 ABC
Reunion at Fairborough tf 5.12.85 HBO
Alice in Wonderland tf 12.9, 12.10.85 CBS

BUZZI, RUTH

SUPP.:

Trapper John, M.D. ep 10.17.82 CBS
The CBS Library ep The Incredible Book Escape sp vo 11.25.82 CBS
Gun Shy ep 4.12.83 CBS

BYRNES, EDD (a.k.a. Edward Byrnes)

A&C, Supp. 2:

Colt .45 ep Golden Gun 2.28.58 ABC
Lawman ep The Deputy 10.8.58 ABC
The Alfred Hitchcock Hour ep Final Escape 2.21.64 NBC
Burke's Law ep Who Killed Mr. Colby in Ladies Lingerie? 3.3.65 ABC
Honey West ep Little Green Robin Hood 3.18.60 ABC
The Bob Hope Chrysler Theater ep A Song Called Revenge 3.1.67 NBC
Alias Smith and Jones ep The Ten Days That Shook Kid Curry 11.4.72 ABC

SUPP.:

The Love Boat ep New York A.C. 2.20.82 ABC
Fantasy Island ep The Big Bet 5.1.82 ABC
Quincy, M.E. ep On Dying High 2.9.83 NBC
Simon and Simon ep 2.9.84 CBS

- C -

CAAN, JAMES
A&C, B.V.:
Wide Country ep Cry from the Mountain 1.7.63 NBC
The Kraft Suspense Theater ep The Hand 12.19.63 NBC

CABOT, SEBASTIAN
A&C, B.V.:
Markham ep 42 on a Rope 7.11.59 CBS
Man with a Camera ep Touch Off 1.11.60 ABC

CADORETTE, MARY*
Three's Company ep Cupid Works Overtime 5.15, 5.22.84 ABC
The Love Boat Fall Preview Party sp 9.15.84 ABC
Three's Company ep Friends and Lovers 9.18.84 ABC
Three's a Crowd sr 9.25.84 ABC
The Love Boat ep Made for Each Other 10.19.85 ABC

CAESAR, SID
SUPP.:
Matt Houston ep Recipe for Murder 11.7.82 ABC
Found Money tf 12.19.83 NBC
The Love Boat ep Aunt Emma, I Love You 1.21.84 ABC
Amazing Stories ep Mr. Magic 11.17.85 NBC
Alice in Wonderland tf 12.9, 12.10.85 CBS
Love Is Never Silent tf 12.9.85 NBC
George Burns Comedy Week ep Christmas Carol II: The Sequel 12.11.85 CBS

CALHOUN, RORY
SUPP.:
Hart to Hart ep The Harts at High Noon 11.9.82 ABC
The Blue and the Gray ms 11.14, 11.15, 11.16, 11.17.82 CBS

CALLAN, K*
One Day at a Time ep 2.22.77 CBS
The Four of Us pt 7.18.77 ABC
James at 15 tf/pt 9.15.77 NBC
Rafferty ep 10.24.77 CBS
Rhoda ep 12.25.77 CBS
Kaz ep In a Safe Place 11.26.78 CBS
Visions ep Ladies in Waiting 1.8.79 PBS
Married: The First Year sr 2.28.79 CBS
Ike ms 5.3-5.6.79 ABC
Blind Ambition ms 5.20-5.23.79 CBS
The Waltons ep The Waiting 11.22.79 CBS
Joe's World sr 1.2.80 NBC
Joe's World sr ret 5.10.80 NBC

The Secrets of Midland Heights sr 12.20.80 CBS
This House Possessed tf 2.6.81 ABC
Splendor in the Grass tf 10.26.81 NBC
House Calls ep 1.18.82 CBS
Bosom Buddies ep Kip Off the Old Block 2.11.82 ABC
Police Squad ep The Butler Did It 3.18.82 ABC
Lou Grant ep 5.24.82 CBS
Leadfoot sp 12.82 NN
Private Benjamin ep Captain Lewis, Matchmaker 1.3.83 CBS
Newhart ep 1.17.83 CBS
Knots Landing ep 2.24.83 CBS
Cutter to Houston sr 10.1.83 CBS
AfterMASH ep 1.9.84 CBS
Flight #90: Disaster on the Potomac tf 4.1.84 NBC
E/R ep 11.28.84 CBS
Sara ep Sara's Mom 2.13.85 NBC
Hunter ep Rich Girl 10.19.85 NBC
St. Elsewhere ep Slice O' Life 11.6.85 NBC
St. Elsewhere ep Close Encounters 11.20.85 NBC

CALLAN, MICHAEL
SUPP.:
Hardcastle and McCormick ep Once Again with Vigorish 10.30.83 ABC
Simon and Simon ep 12.15.83 CBS
Last of the Great Survivors tf 1.3.84 CBS
Fantasy Island ep Dark Secret 3.3.84 ABC
The Fall Guy ep Terror U 10.17.84 ABC
E/R ep 10.23.84 CBS
One Life to Live sr 1985 ABC
My Wicked, Wicked Ways ... The Legend of Errol Flynn tf 1.21.85 CBS
T. J. Hooker ep Sanctuary 3.2.85 ABC

CALLAS, CHARLIE
SUPP.:
The Fall Guy ep Ready, Aim ... Die! 12.17.82 ABC
Cagney and Lacey ep 12.17.84 CBS

CALVIN, JOHN*
Cade's County ep Violent Ego 10.24.71 CBS
Winter Kill tf 4.15.74 ABC
The Hatfields and the McCoys tf 1.15.75 ABC
Bronk ep The Fifth Victim 10.19.75 CBS
Kate McShane ep Murder Comes in Little Pills 10.1.75 CBS
The Rookies ep 11.18.75 ABC
Charlie's Angels ep Dirty Business 2.2.77 ABC
Most Wanted ep The Spellbinder 3.7.77 ABC
The Rockford Files ep Crack Back 3.25.77 NBC
The Dark Secret of Harvest Home tf 1.23, 1.24.78 NBC
The Incredible Hulk ep Never Give a Trucker an Even Break 4.28.78 CBS

Kaz ep Which Side You On? 11.5.78 CBS
Barnaby Jones ep Deadly Sanctuary 12.10.78 CBS
Quincy, M.E. ep The Eye of the Needle 4.12.79 NBC
The Last of the Dalton Gang tf 11.20.79 NBC
Beggarman, Thief tf 11.26 and 11.27.79 NBC
From Here to Eternity sr 3.10.80 NBC
Hart to Hart ep Slow Boat to Murder 2.17.81 ABC
Magnum, P.I. ep Wave Goodbye 11.19.81 CBS
Strike Force ep The Predator 12.4.81 ABC
The Ambush Murders tf 1.5.82 CBS
Best of the West ep Elvira's Old Beau 6.7.82 ABC
Tales of the Gold Monkey sr 9.22.82 ABC
Matt Houston ep Who Would Kill Ramona? 10.10.82 ABC
The Devlin Connection ep Arsenic and Old Caviar 12.4.82 NBC
Magnum, P.I. ep Birds of a Feather 3.17.83 CBS
Sitcom pt 10.2.83 HBO
Airwolf ep Airwolf (pt) 1.29.84 CBS
Knight Rider ep Halloween Knight 10.28.84 NBC
Airwolf ep Flight #093 Is Missing 11.17.84 CBS
Mickey Spillane's Mike Hammer ep Firestorm 1.5.85 CBS
The A-Team ep Skins 1.29.85 NBC
Hardcastle and McCormick ep Undercover McCormick 3.11.85 ABC
I Had Three Wives ep 8.14.85 CBS
Hollywood Beat ep No Place to Hide 10.12.85 ABC
Hunter ep Rich Girl 10.19.85 NBC
T. J. Hooker ep Death Is a Four Letter Word 11.6.85 ABC
Scarecrow and Mrs. King ep Reach for the Sky 11.11.85 CBS
Moonlighting ep Portrait of Maddie 11.26.85 ABC
Cheers ep 11.28.85 NBC

CAMPANELLA, JOSEPH

A&C, B.V.:
East Side/West Side ep No Hiding Place 12.2.63 CBS
The Big Valley ep The Martyr 10.17.66 ABC
The Big Valley ep Twin of a Card 3.20.67 ABC
The Fugitive ep The Judgment 8.22.67, 8.29.67 ABC

A&C, Supp. 1:
The Rockford Files ep In Hazard 2.6.76 NBC

SUPP.:
Earthbound sp 1.31, 2.7.82 NBC
My Body, My Child tf 4.12.82 ABC
One Day at a Time ep 9.26.82 CBS
Quincy, M.E. ep Give Me Your Weak 10.27.82 NBC
Matt Houston ep A Novel Way to Die 4.17.83 ABC
Airwolf ep 9.29.84 CBS
Hotel ep Illusions 11.28.84 ABC

CAMPBELL, NICHOLAS*
The Hitchhiker sr 11.23.83 HBO
T. J. Hooker ep Death Strip 3.10.84 ABC

Airwolf ep Inn at the End of the Road 1.26.85 CBS
Airwolf ep Prisoner of Yesterday 2.9.85 CBS
Night Heat ep Obie's Law 2.28.85 CBS
The Insiders sr 9.25.85 ABC
Children of the Night tf 10.26.85 CBS

CAMPBELL, WILLIAM
A&C, B.V.:
Stagecoach West ep Never Walk Alone 4.18.61 ABC
Gunsmoke ep Calvin Strom 12.18.65 CBS

CAMERON, JOANNA
A&C, Supp. 1:
Switch ep Death By Resurrection 12.2.75 CBS

CAMERON, ROD
A&C, B.V.:
Branded ep Barbed Wire 2.13.66 NBC
A&C, Supp. 1:
The Rockford Files ep A Big Deal in the Valley 3.18.76 NBC

CANNON, DYAN (a.k.a. Diane Cannon)
A&C, B.V.:
Wanted: Dead Or Alive ep Vanishing Act 12.26.59 CBS
Johnny Ringo ep Soft Cargo 5.5.60 CBS
The Reporter ep The Man Behind the Badge 11.6.64 CBS
SUPP.:
Having It All tf 10.13.82 ABC
Master of the Game ms 2.19, 2.20, 2.21.84 NBC
Arthur the King tf 4.26.85 CBS
Jenny's War tf 10.28, 11.4.85 OPT

CANNON, J. D.
A&C, Supp. 2:
The U.S. Steel Hour ep Shame on the Devil 12.14.60 CBS
The U.S. Steel Hour ep Operation North Star 12.28.60 CBS
Play of the Week ep A Clearing in the Woods 1.2.61 NN
Play of the Week ep A Cool Wind Over the Living 3.27.61 NN
Naked City ep $C_3H_5(NO_3)^3$ 5.10.61 ABC
The Defenders ep Voice of Death 9.15.62 CBS
Wagon Train ep The Abel Weatherly Story 1.2.63 NBC
The Untouchables ep Man in the Cooler 3.5.63 ABC
Combat ep The Quiet Warrior 3.26.63 ABC
Stoney Burke ep Weapons Man (pilot) 4.8.63 ABC
The Defenders ep Drink Like a Lady 2.29.64 CBS
The Defenders ep Hero of the People 10.8.64 CBS
Rawhide ep Piney 10.9.64 CBS
Gunsmoke ep Chicken 11.28.64 CBS
The Rogues ep The Boston Money Party 12.6.64 NBC
Profiles in Courage ep Sam Houston 12.13.64 NBC
Rawhide ep The Book 1.8.65 CBS

Voyage to the Bottom of the Sea ep The Condemned 4.12.65 ABC
Twelve O'Clock High ep Rx for a Sick Bird 9.20.65 ABC
The FBI ep The Man Who Went Crazy By Mistake 3.6.66 ABC
The FBI ep Flight Plan 3.5.67 ABC
The Fugitive ep The Judgement 8.22.67 and 8.29.67 ABC
The Guns of Will Sonnett ep Find a Sonnett, Kill a Sonnett 12.8.67 ABC
Cimarron Strip ep The Deputy 12.21.67 CBS
The FBI ep Ring of Steel 2.4.68 ABC
Gunsmoke ep MacGraw 12.8.69 CBS
The FBI ep Conspiracy of Corruption 1.11.70 ABC
Alias Smith and Jones ep The Wrong Way to Brimstone 2.4.71 ABC
Alias Smith and Jones ep The Legacy of Charlie O'Rourke 4.22.71 ABC
Alias Smith and Jones ep The Reformation of Harry Briscoe 11.11.71 ABC
Alias Smith and Jones ep The Man That Corrupted Handleyburg 1.22.72 ABC
Alias Smith and Jones ep The Long Chase 9.16.72 ABC
SUPP.:
The Fall Guy ep Soldiers of Misfortune 2.10.82 ABC
Beyond Witch Mountain pt 2.20.82 CBS
Rooster tf/pt 8.19.82 ABC
Fantasy Island ep Cotton Club 2.26.83 ABC
Remington Steele ep Steele in the News 3.4.83 NBC
The Fall Guy ep The Chameleon 4.6.83 ABC
Matt Houston ep The Ghost of Carter Gault 10.28.83 ABC
Remington Steele ep Hounded Steele 5.15.84 NBC
Call to Glory ep Go/No Go 9.24.84 ABC
Call to Glory ep Call It Courage 10.1.84 ABC
Call to Glory ep Cover Sun 10.29.84 ABC
Call to Glory ep A Wind of Change 12.3.84 ABC
Call to Glory ep Moonchild 1.15.85 ABC
Call to Glory ep Just in Time 2.5.85 ABC
Murder, She Wrote ep Funeral at 50 Mile 4.21.85 CBS
Hell Town ep The Pool Game 12.25.85 NBC

CANNON, KATHERINE*
Matt Lincoln ep Lori 11.5.70 ABC
The Young Lawyers ep And the Walls Came Tumbling Down 2.24.71 ABC
Women in Chains tf 1.25.72 ABC
Assignment: Vienna ep Hot Potato 10.19.72 ABC
Can Ellen Be Saved? tf 2.5.74 ABC
Cannon ep The Deadly Trail 10.16.74 CBS
The Streets of San Francisco ep Flags of Terror 10.31.74 ABC
Barnaby Jones ep Dangerous Summer 2.11.75 CBS
Most Wanted ep The White Collar Killer 1.1.77 ABC
Barnaby Jones ep Duet for Danger 3.24.77 CBS

Future Cop ep Girl on the Ledge 4.7.77 ABC
Barnaby Jones ep The Mercenaries 9.22.77 CBS
Lucan ep The Search 12.26.77 ABC
The Black Sheep Squadron ep Wolves in the Sheep Pen 1.4.78 NBC
The Black Sheep Squadron ep Ten'll Get You Five 1.18.78 NBC
The Black Sheep Squadron ep Fighting Angels 3.1.78 NBC
Battlestar Galactica ep The Lost Warrior 10.8.78 ABC
Sword of Justice ep Judgment Day 12.17.78 NBC
B.J. and the Bear ep The Murphy Connection 4.14.79 NBC
The Runaways ep 7.10.79 NBC
The Incredible Hulk ep Metamorphosis 9.21.79 CBS
High Ice tf 1.7.80 NBC
The Contender sr 4.3.80 CBS
High Noon, Part II: The Return of Will Kane tf 11.15.80 CBS
Magnum, P.I. ep Thank Heaven for Little Girls--And Big Ones Too 12.25.80 CBS
CHiPs ep Moonlight 10.18.81 NBC
Father Murphy sr 11.3.81 NBC
Will, G. Gordon Liddy tf 1.10.82 NBC
Father Murphy sr ret 10.26.82 NBC
Magnum, P.I. ep I Do? 2.17.83 CBS
Hotel ep Memories 2.29.84 ABC
Red Light Sting tf 4.5.84 CBS
Mickey Spillane's Mike Hammer ep Back to Back 11.10.84 CBS
Matt Houston ep Deadly Games 12.7.84 ABC
Airwolf ep Fortune Teller 10.19.85 CBS

CANOVA, DIANA
SUPP.:
Foot in the Door sr 3.3.83 CBS
Night Partners tf/pt 10.11.83 CBS
Hotel ep Flashback 11.9.83 ABC
Murder, She Wrote ep Death Casts a Spell 12.30.84 CBS
No Complaints pt 7.24.85 NBC
Trapper John, M.D. ep A Wheel in a Wheel 12.1.85 CBS
The Love Boat ep Heartbreaker 12.7.85 ABC

CAREY, MACDONALD
A&C, B.V.:
Burke's Law ep Who Killed the Surfboard? 9.16.64 ABC
Branded ep The Mission 3.14.65, 3.21.65, 3.28.65
A&C, Supp. 2:
Police Story ep Pressure Point 9.27.77 NBC
SUPP.:
The Days of Our Lives sr role continuing 1982- NBC
Finder of Lost Loves ep Last Wish 1.5.85 ABC

CAREY, MICHELE
A&C, Supp. 2:
Alias Smith and Jones ep A Fistful of Diamonds 3.4.71 ABC

SUPP.:
The Fall Guy ep No Way Out 1.6.82 ABC
Rooster tf/pt 8.19.82 ABC

CARLIN, LYNN
SUPP.:
The Kid from Nowhere tf 1.4.82 NBC
Forbidden Love tf 10.18.82 CBS
A Killer in the Family tf 10.30.83 ABC
Trapper John, M.D. ep Game of Hearts 10.6, 10.13.85 CBS

CARLSON, KAREN*
Night Chase tf 11.20.70 CBS
The Smith Family ep Rumpus Room 11.3.71 ABC
Banyon ep Sally Overman Is Missing 12.1.72 NBC
The Streets of San Francisco ep Legion of the Lost 4.12.73 ABC
Shaft ep The Kidnapping 12.11.73 CBS
Police Woman ep Seven-Eleven 10.4.74 NBC
Movin' On ep Ransom 2.20.75 NBC
Cage Without a Key tf 3.14.75 CBS
Barnaby Jones ep Jeopardy for Two 4.1.75 CBS
The First 36 Hours of Dr. Durant tf 5.13.75 ABC
Matt Helm ep Murder on Ice 10.25.75 ABC
Medical Story ep Woman in White 12.11.75 NBC
S.W.A.T. ep Dragons and Owls 3.6.76 ABC
Starsky and Hutch ep Gillian 10.16.76 ABC
Tail Gunner Joe tf 2.6.77 NBC
Starsky and Hutch ep The Heroes 10.29.77 ABC
It Happened One Christmas tf 12.11.77 ABC
Centennial ms ep 10.1.78 NBC
Buck Rogers in the 25th Century ep Planet of the Slave Girls 9.27.79 NBC
The Incredible Hulk ep Broken Image 1.4.80 CBS
The American Dream sr 4.26.81 ABC
Lou Grant ep Review 2.8.82 CBS
Dangerous Company tf 2.9.82 CBS
T. J. Hooker ep The Streets 3.20.82 ABC
In Love with an Older Woman tf 11.24.82 CBS
The Devlin Connection ep Allison 12.18.82 NBC
Hill Street Blues ep Untitled 1.27.83 NBC
Two Marriages sr 4.23.83 ABC
Lottery ep Portland: Treasure Hunt ("The Election" segment) 10.21.83 ABC
The Yellow Rose ep Hell Hath No Fury 1.14.84 NBC
Two Marriages sr ret 3.8.84 ABC
Finder of Lost Loves ep White Lies 10.20.84 ABC
Hotel ep Identities 3.20.85 ABC
Brotherly Love tf 5.28.85 CBS
Wild Horses tf 11.12.85 CBS

CARLSON, LINDA*
Westside Medical sr 3.15.77 ABC
Kaz sr 9.24.78 CBS
WKRP in Cincinnati ep 11.29.80 CBS
Remington Steele ep Hearts of Steele 1.28.83 NBC
St. Elsewhere ep A Pig Too Far 1.11.84 NBC
The Mississippi ep 3.13.84 CBS
Victims for Victims: The Theresa Saldana Story tf 11.12.84 NBC
Newhart ep 3.11.85 CBS
Scarecrow and Mrs. King ep Vigilante Mothers 5.13.85 CBS
Newhart ep 9.30.85 CBS
Cagney and Lacey ep Entrapment 11.4.85 CBS

CARMEN, JULIE*
Can You Hear the Laughter?: The Story of Freddie Prinze tf 9.11.79 CBS
Lou Grant ep 1.14.80 CBS
Three Hundred Miles for Stephanie tf 1.12.81 NBC
She's in the Army Now tf/pt 5.20.81 ABC
McClain's Law ep Let the Victims Beware 12.11.81 NBC
Fire on the Mountain tf 11.23.81 NBC
Cassie and Company ep Golden Silence 1.29.82 NBC
Cagney and Lacey ep Beyond the Golden Door 4.8.82 CBS
Condo sr 2.10.83 ABC
Remington Steele ep Steele Knuckles and Glass Jaws 11.29.83 NBC
The Fall Guy ep Rabbit's Feet 1.25.84 ABC
T. J. Hooker ep Gang War 5.12.84 ABC
Jessie ep The Lady Killer 9.25.84 ABC
Who's the Boss? ep Angela's First Fight 10.18.84 ABC
Matt Houston ep Caged 10.26.84 ABC
Highway to Heaven ep Hotel of Dreams 12.12.84 NBC
Airwolf ep Prisoner of Yesterday 2.9.85 CBS
The Twilight Zone ep The Wish Bank 10.18.85 CBS
Hollywood Beat ep Baby Blues 10.26.85 ABC
Falcon Crest ep Inconceivable Affairs 12.6.85 CBS
Hotel ep 12.18.85 ABC

CARNE, JUDY
A&C, Supp. 1:
Get Christie Love ep Murder on High C 2.5.75 ABC

CARNEY, ART
SUPP.:
Fame ep A Big Finish 4.15.82 NBC
Terrible Joe Moran tf 3.27.84 CBS
The Last Leaf drama sp 4.84 NN
A Doctor's Story tf 4.23.84 NBC
The Night They Saved Christmas tf 12.13.84 ABC
The Undergrads tf 5.5.85 DIS
Izzy and Moe tf 9.23.85 CBS

Faerie Tale Theater ep The Emperor's New Clothes 10.8.85 SHO
Blue Yonder tf 11.17.85 DIS

CAROLEO, DINA*
Kibbe Hates Finch pt 8.2.65 CBS
Wonder Girl sr 9.73 NN
Magnum, P.I. ep Thank Heaven for Little Girls--And Big Ones Too 12.25.80 CBS
Silver Spoons ep The Most Beautiful Girl in the World 1.8.83 NBC
Outlaw Lady sr 10.83 NN
Three's Company ep She Loves Me, She Loves Me Not 10.4.83 ABC
The Fall Guy ep Pleasure Isle 10.5.83 ABC
Matt Houston ep Target: The Most Beautiful Girls in the World 11.23.83 ABC
Jennifer Slept Here ep Calendar Girl 11.18.83 NBC
Benson ep Unlisted Love 12.2.83 ABC
Velvet pt 8.27.84 ABC
Hardcastle and McCormick ep Never My Love 10.28.84 ABC
The Facts of Life ep Taking a Chance on Love 11.7.84 NBC
Magnum, P.I. ep Dream a Little Dream 11.22.84 CBS
Family Ties ep Don't Kiss Me, I'm Only the Messenger 11.29.84 NBC
Double Trouble ep Do You Believe in Magic? 12.8.84 NBC
Sara ep 27 Candles 1.30.85 NBC
It's Your Move ep A Woman Is Just a Woman 2.9.85 NBC
Otherworld ep I Am Woman, Hear Me Roar 3.2.85 CBS
Remington Steele ep Now You Steele It, Now You Don't 3.5.85 NBC
Crazy Like a Fox ep Fox in 3/4 Time 11.3.85 CBS
My First Swedish Bombshell comedy sp 11.17.85 NN
Punky Brewster ep The Gift 11.24.85 NBC

CARR, DARLEEN
A&C, Supp. 2:
East Side/West Side ep Go Fight City Hall 11.11.63 CBS
The Wonderful World of Disney ep Terror on the Trail 1.29.67 NBC
The Rookies ep The Commitment 10.2.72 ABC
Alias Smith and Jones ep McGuffin 12.9.72 ABC
Manhunter ep The Seventh Man 1.29.75 CBS
SUPP.:
Simon and Simon ep Red Day Blues 3.24.83 CBS
Magnum, P.I. ep 11.3.83 CBS
Blue Thunder ep Arms Race 1.20.84 ABC
Simon and Simon ep Who Killed the 60s? 11.8.84 CBS
V: The Series ep The Rescue 1.25.85 NBC
Crazy Like a Fox ep The Man Who Cried Fox 4.7.85 CBS
Murder, She Wrote ep School for Scandal 10.20.85 CBS
Riptide ep Who Really Watches the Sunset? 11.12.85 NBC

CARRADINE, DAVID
A&C, B.V.:
East Side/West Side ep Go Fight City Hall 11.18.63 CBS
Cimarron Strip ep The Hunted 10.5.67 CBS
SUPP.:
Darkroom ep Partnership 12.25.81 ABC
The Fall Guy ep To the Finish 12.7.83 ABC
Jealousy tf 1.23.84 ABC
Airwolf ep Mind of the Machine 4.7.84 CBS
Partners in Crime ep Paddles Up 10.27.84 NBC
The Fall Guy ep October the 31st 10.31.84 ABC
The Bad Seed tf 2.7.85 ABC
North and South ms 11.3-11.10.85 ABC

CARRADINE, JOHN
A&C, B.V.:
Restless Gun ep More Than Kin 5.26.58 NBC
The Life and Legend of Wyatt Earp ep The Fugitive 1.17.59 ABC
The Rifleman ep The Photographer 1.27.59 ABC
The Rifleman ep The Mindreader 6.30.59 ABC
Gunsmoke ep 9.5.59 CBS
Johnny Ringo ep The Rain Man 11.26.59 CBS
Wanted Dead Or Alive ep Tolliver Bender 2.13.60 CBS
The Beverly Hillbillies ep The Great Jethro Spring 1966 CBS
SUPP.:
Fantasy Island ep The Whistle 1.30.82 ABC
Umbrella Jack drama sp 10.21.84 NN
The Fall Guy ep October the 31st 10.31.84 ABC
Fame ep Leroy and the Kid 10.25.85 NN

CARRADINE, KEITH
SUPP.:
Chiefs ms 11.13, 11.14, 11.15, 11.16.83 CBS
Scorned and Swindled tf 10.9.84 CBS
The Fall Guy ep October the 31st 10.31.84 ABC

CARRADINE, ROBERT*
Kung Fu ep Dark Angel 11.11.72 ABC
Rolling Man tf 10.4.72 ABC
Go Ask Alice tf 1.24.73 ABC
The Hatfields and the McCoys tf 1.15.75 ABC
The Survival of Dana tf 5.29.79 CBS
The Fall Guy ep October the 31st 10.31.84 ABC
The Sun Also Rises tf 12.9, 12.10.84 NBC
Alfred Hitchcock Presents ep Night Fever 10.6.85 NBC

CARROLL, VICTORIA*
The Strangers in 7-A tf 11.14.72 CBS
The Affair tf 11.20.73 ABC
Joe Forrester ep Target: Mexican Syndicate 11.25.75 NBC

Alice ep Sweet Charity 1.14.79 CBS
Murder By Natural Causes tf 2.17.79 CBS
The Incredible Hulk ep Mystery Man 3.2, 3.9.79 CBS
Alice ep 12.2.79 CBS
Freebie and the Bean ep The Seduction of the Bean 12.20.80 CBS
Alice ep 4.5.81 CBS
One Day at a Time ep Plain Favorite 12.20.81 CBS
Mr. Merlin ep The Music in Me 10.28.81 CBS
Dynasty ep Episode 21 1.6.82 ABC
Gimme a Break ep Nell Goes Door to Door 12.11.82 NBC
Small and Frye ep 3.7.83 CBS
At Ease ep The Marriage of the Figaros 4.15.83 ABC
Goodnight Beantown ep 10.2.83 CBS
Benson ep You Can't Give It Away 11.11.83 ABC
Gimme a Break ep Melissa 11.17.83 NBC
Three's Company ep Janet Shapes Up 1.3.84 ABC
W*A*L*T*E*R pt 7.17.84 CBS
Detective in the House ep Whatever Happened to...? 3.15.85 CBS
Murder, She Wrote ep Armed Response 3.31.85 CBS

CARSON, JOHNNY
A&C, B.V.:
Get Smart ep Aboard the Orient Express 12.11.65 NBC
Get Smart ep The King Lives 1.6.68 NBC

CARTER, LYNDA
SUPP.:
Hot Line tf 10.16.82 CBS
Rita Hayworth: The Love Goddess tf 11.2.83 CBS
Partners in Crime sr 9.22.84 NBC

CARTER, NELL
SUPP.:
Gimme a Break sr ret 10.2.82 NBC
Gimme a Break sr ret 9.29.83 NBC
Gimme a Break sr ret 9.29.84 NBC
Gimme a Break sr ret 9.14.85 NBC

CARTWRIGHT, ANGELA*
The Danny Thomas Show sr 10.7.57 CBS
The Danny Thomas Show sr ret 10.58 CBS
The Lucy-Desi Comedy Hour ep Lucy Makes Room for Danny 12.15.58 CBS
The Danny Thomas Show sr ret 10.5.59 CBS
Alfred Hitchcock Presents ep The Scharty-Metterklume Method 6.12.60 CBS
The Danny Thomas Show sr ret 10.3.60 CBS
The Danny Thomas Show sr ret 10.2.61 CBS
The Danny Thomas Show sr ret 10.1.62 CBS

The Danny Thomas Show sr ret 9.30.63 CBS
My Three Sons ep 4.29.65 ABC
Lost in Space sr 9.15.65 CBS
Lost in Space sr ret 9.21.66 CBS
Lost in Space sr ret 9.6.67 CBS
The Danny Thomas Hour ep Make More Room for Daddy 11.6.67 NBC
Make Room for Granddaddy pt 9.14.68 CBS
My Three Sons ep Chip and Debbie 1.18.69 CBS
U.M.C. tf/pt 4.17.65 CBS
Make Room for Granddaddy sr 9.23.70 ABC
Room 222 ep The Nichols Girl 12.22.72 ABC
Logan's Run ep The Collectors 9.23.77 CBS
Scout's Honor tf 9.30.80 NBC
High School, U.S.A. tf/pt 10.16.83 NBC
Airwolf ep Eruption 4.6.85 CBS

CASH, JOHNNY
<u>SUPP.</u>:
Murder in Coweta County tf 2.15.83 CBS
The Baron and the Kid tf 11.21.84 CBS

CASSAVETES, JOHN
<u>A&C, B.V.</u>:
The Bob Hope Chrysler Theater ep Wind Fever 3.2.66 NBC

CASSIDY, DAVID
<u>SUPP.</u>:
Matt Houston ep Joey's Here 12.5.82 ABC
Fantasy Island ep The Song Writer 1.22.83 ABC

CASSIDY, JOANNA
<u>A&C, Supp. 2</u>:
McCoy ep New Dollar Day 1.25.76 NBC
<u>SUPP.</u>:
The Love Boat ep Crazy for You 1.23.82 ABC
Strike Force ep Turnabout 2.26.82 ABC
Lou Grant ep Where's Lou? 9.13.82 CBS
The Devlin Connection ep Lady on the Billboard 10.9.82 NBC
Falcon Crest ep 11.5, 11.12, 11.19.82 CBS
Family Tree sr 1.22.83 NBC
Buffalo Bill sr 6.1.83 NBC
Fantasy Island ep Nurses' Night Out 10.22.83 ABC
Invitation to Hell tf 5.24.84 ABC
Code Name: Foxfire pt ("Slay It Again, Uncle Sam") 1.27.85 NBC
Code Name: Foxfire sr 2.8.85 NBC
Hollywood Wives ms 2.17, 2.18, 2.19.85 ABC

CAST, TRICIA*
The Bad News Bears sr 3.24.79 CBS

Friendships, Secrets and Lies tf 12.3.79 NBC
The Bad News Bears sr ret 6.7.80 CBS
Desperate Lives tf 3.3.82 CBS
The CBS Afternoon Playhouse ep Help Wanted 10.12.82 CBS
Night Partners tf 10.11.83 CBS
It's Your Move sr 9.26.84 NBC
Mr. Belvedere ep What I Did for Love 4.12.85 ABC
Santa Barbara sr Summer 1985 NBC

CATES, PHOEBE*
Baby Sister tf 3.6.83 ABC
Lace ms 2.26, 2.27.84 ABC
Lace II ms 5.5, 5.6.85 ABC

CATTRALL, KIM
SUPP.:
Trapper John, M.D. ep 10.31.82 CBS
Tales of the Gold Monkey ep Naka Jima Kill 3.18.83 ABC
Sins of the Past tf 4.2.84 ABC

CHAKIRIS, GEORGE
SUPP.:
Fantasy Island ep Mata Hari 1.16.82 ABC
CHiPs ep Fox Trap 2.20.83 NBC
Matt Houston ep The Showgirl Murders 3.20.83 ABC
Matt Houston ep Waltz of Death 1.13.84 ABC
Scarecrow and Mrs. King ep Lost and Found 1.16.84 CBS
Hell Town ep Let My Jennie Go 9.11.85 NBC
Dallas ep 11.29.85 CBS

CHAMBERLAIN, RICHARD
A&C, B.V.:
Whispering Smith ep Stain of Justice 6.11.61 NBC
SUPP.:
The Thorn Birds ms 3.27-3.30.83 ABC
Cook and Perry: The Race to the North Pole tf 12.13.83 CBS
Wallenberg: A Hero's Story tf 4.8, 4.9.85 NBC
An American Portrait ep Korczak Ziolkowski 4.18.85 CBS
An American Portrait ep Clifford Beers 4.19.85 CBS

CHANEY, LON
A&C, B.V.:
Wanted: Dead Or Alive ep The Hostage 10.10.59 CBS
Number 13 Demon Street pt 1962 NN

CHANNING, CAROL
SUPP.:
The Love Boat ep My Aunt, the Worrier 2.27.82 ABC
The Love Boat ep My Friend, the Executrix 12.11.82 ABC
Magnum, P.I. ep 10.20.83 CBS
The Love Boat ep Authoress! Authoress! 1.7.84 ABC

The Love Boat ep Soap Star 11.23.85 ABC
Alice in Wonderland tf 12.9, 12.10.85 CBS

CHANNING, STOCKARD
SUPP.:
Not My Kind tf 1.15.85 CBS
An American Portrait ep Sequoya 3.4.85 CBS

CHAO, ROSALIND*
The ABC Afterschool Special ep P.J. and the President's Son 11.10.76 ABC
The Hardy Boys Mysteries ep The Mystery of the Jade Kwan Yin 5.15.77 ABC
How the West Was Won ep China Girl 4.16.79 ABC
The Ultimate Imposter tf/pt 5.12.79 CBS
The Amazing Spider-Man ep The Chinese Web 7.5.79 CBS
The Mysterious Island of Beautiful Women tf 12.1.79 CBS
Almost American pt 4.1.81 NBC
Lobo ep The Roller Disco Karate Caper 4.18.81 NBC
The Harlem Globetrotters on Gilligan's Island tf 5.15.81 NBC
Twirl tf 10.25.81 NBC
One Day at a Time ep Julie's Return (Part 2) 11.5.81 CBS
Moonlight tf/pt 9.14.82 CBS
Bring 'Em Back Alive ep The Reel World of Frank Buck 10.12.82 CBS
Diff'rent Strokes ep A Case of Overexposure 11.20.82 NBC
M*A*S*H ep 2.21, 2.28.83 CBS
Diff'rent Strokes ep Hall Monitor 2.26.83 NBC
Diff'rent Strokes ep Romeo and Juliet 4.30.83 NBC
The Terry Fox Story tf 5.25.83 HBO
AfterMASH sr 9.26.83 CBS
AfterMASH sr ret 9.25.84 CBS
An American Portrait ep Peter Cooper 1.11.85 CBS

CHAPEL, LOYITA*
The Greatest American Hero ep This Is the One the Suit Was Meant for 11.12.82 ABC
Love, Sidney ep One Is Enough 3.28.83 NBC
Cover Up ep Sudden Exposure 10.20.84 CBS
Punky Brewster ep Parents Night 10.28.84 NBC
Punky Brewster ep Gals and Dolls 3.3.85 NBC
Hardcastle and McCormick ep Hardcastle, Hardcastle, Hardcastle & McCormick 2.4.85 ABC
Scene of the Crime ep Murder on the Half Shell 4.28.85 NBC
Punky Brewster ep Miss Adorable 11.25.84 NBC
Simon and Simon ep Quint Is Art 12.5.85 CBS

CHAPMAN, JUDITH*
Barnaby Jones ep The Picture Pirates 12.21.78 CBS
The Paper Chase ep Once More with Feeling 2.27.79 CBS
The Incredible Hulk ep Sideshow 1.25.80 CBS

B.J. and the Bear ep Through the Past Darkly 1.26.80 NBC
Buck Rogers in the 25th Century ep Olympiad 2.7.80 NBC
Beyond Westworld ep Westworld Destroyed 3.5.80 CBS
Nick and the Dobermans pt 4.25.80 NBC
Galactica 1980 ep Starbuck's Great Journey 5.4.80 ABC
Flamingo Road pt 5.12.80 NBC
Flamingo Road ep The Hostages 1.6.81 NBC
Thin Ice tf 2.17.81 CBS
Magnum, P.I. ep The Black Orchid 4.2.81 CBS
The Five of Me tf 5.12.81 CBS
Magnum, P.I. ep Woman on the Beach 10.22.81 CBS
The Fall Guy ep The Rich Get Richer 11.11.81 ABC
Darkroom ep The Rarest of Wines 1.15.82 ABC
McClain's Law ep A Matter of Honor 1.15.82 NBC
The Fall Guy ep Goin' for It 1.27.82 ABC
The Fall Guy ep Three for the Road 4.14.82 ABC
Farrell for the People tf/pt 10.18.82 NBC
Knight Rider ep Inside Out 11.26.82 NBC
The Fall Guy ep Death Boat 2.2.83 ABC
Simon and Simon ep What's in a Gnome? 2.24.83 CBS
The Return of the Man from UNCLE: The 15 Years Later Affair 4.5.83 CBS
Trapper John, M.D. ep 11.6.83 CBS
Remington Steele ep My Fair Steele 12.6.83 NBC
Ryan's Hope sr Summer 1984 ABC

CHARISSE, CYD
SUPP.:
Fantasy Island ep The Big Show 11.12.83 ABC
The Fall Guy ep The Huntress 1.11.84 ABC
Glitter ep Queen of the Soaps 9.27.84 ABC
Murder, She Wrote ep Will No One Weep for Me? 9.29.85 CBS

CHARO
SUPP.:
The Love Boat ep April in Boston 5.1.82 ABC
Fantasy Island ep Charo 2.19.83 ABC
The Love Boat ep I Like to Be in America 2.26.83 ABC
Fantasy Island ep Surrogate Mother 5.19.84 ABC
The Love Boat ep Aerobic April 11.3.84 ABC
The Love Boat ep Forties Fantasy 10.16.85 ABC
The Facts of Life ep Come Back to the Truck Stop Natalie Green, Natalie Green 11.9.85 NBC

CHEEK, MOLLY*
Breaking Up Is Hard to Do tf 9.5, 9.7.79 ABC
The Yeagers sr 6.1.80 ABC
To Find My Son tf 10.6.80 CBS
Mark, I Love You tf 12.10.80 CBS
Chicago Story sr 3.6.82 NBC
St. Elsewhere ep Tweety and Ralph 12.21.82 NBC

The Powers of Matthew Star ep Matthew Star: D.O.A. 1.21.83 NBC
Simon and Simon ep 3.1.84 CBS
Jessie ep Jessie (pt) 9.18.84 ABC
Hardcastle and McCormick ep Never My Love 10.28.84 ABC
Finder of Lost Loves ep Portraits 12.1.84 ABC
T. J. Hooker ep Serial Murders 3.16.85 ABC
A Summer to Remember tf 3.27.85 CBS
No Place Like Home pt 9.6.85 CBS
Family Ties ep The Old College Try 11.7.85 NBC
Hardcastle and McCormick ep Games People Play 11.11.85 ABC

CHER*
Come Back to the Five and Dime Jimmy Dean Jimmy Dean sp 6.83 SHO

CHILES, LINDEN
A&C, Supp. 2:
Gunsmoke ep With a Smile 3.30.61 CBS
Malibu Run ep The Scavenger Adventure 5.31.61 CBS
Perry Mason ep The Case of the Jealous Journalist 6.24.61 CBS
Target: The Corruptors ep The Wrecker 3.2.62 ABC
Perry Mason ep The Case of the Promoter's Pillbox 5.19.62 CBS
Dobie Gillis ep I Was a Spy for the F.O.B. 5.8.63 CBS
Dobie Gillis ep There's a Broken Light for Every Heart on Broadway 5.15.63 CBS
The Eleventh Hour ep Pressure Breakdown 5.15.63 NBC
My Favorite Martian ep 10.6.63 CBS
East Side/West Side ep The Street 2.4.64 CBS
East Side/West Side ep The Passion of the Nickel Player 3.9.64 CBS
East Side/West Side ep Take Side with the Sun 3.16.64 CBS
East Side/West Side ep The Givers 4.13.64 CBS
East Side/West Side ep Here Today 4.27.64 CBS
The Virginian ep Big Image, Little Man 10.28.64 NBC
Medical Center ep The Fallen Image 12.3.69 CBS
Banacek ep Horse of a Slightly Different Color 1.22.74 NBC
SUPP.:
Knight Rider ep Merchants of Death 10.16.83 NBC
Hotel ep Passages 1.18.84 ABC
Falcon Crest ep 2.10.84 CBS
Mickey Spillane's Mike Hammer ep Satin, Cyanide and Arsenic 4.14.84 CBS
Partners in Crime ep Getting in Shape 12.22.84 NBC
Double Dare ep 5.1.85 CBS
Alfred Hitchcock Presents ep The Final Escape 10.27.85 NBC

CIOFFI, CHARLES
A&C, Supp. 2:

Assignment Vienna sr 9.28.72 ABC
Get Christie Love sr 9.11.74 ABC
Hawaii Five-O ep Right Grave, Wrong Body 10.15.74 CBS
Hawaii Five-O ep McGarrett Is Missing 9.19.75 CBS
SUPP.:
Simon and Simon ep Earth to Stacey 2.9.82 CBS
Lou Grant ep 4.12.82 CBS
Taxi ep The Road Not Taken 4.29.82 ABC
Cassie and Company ep A Ring Ain't Always a Circle 8.20.82 NBC
Modesty Blaise pt 9.12.82 ABC
Tucker's Witch ep 11.24.82 CBS
The A-Team ep The Rabbit Who Ate Las Vegas 3.1.83 NBC
Trapper John, M.D. ep 10.9.83 CBS

CIVITA, DIANE*
She Lives tf 9.12.73 ABC
It Couldn't Happen to a Nicer Guy tf 11.19.74 ABC
The Bionic Woman ep Jaime's Shield 12.15, 12.22,76 ABC
The Bionic Woman ep Rancho Outcast 5.6.78 NBC
The Incredible Hulk ep Life and Death 5.12.78 CBS
Voyagers ep Buffalo Bill and Annie Play the Palace 1.9.83 NBC
V ms 5.1 and 5.2.83 NBC
I Want to Live tf 5.9.83 ABC
Hawaiian Heat ep Victims 10.19.84 ABC
Hawaiian Heat ep MIH: Missing in Hawaii 10.26.84 ABC
Kids Don't Tell tf 3.5.85 CBS
The Misfits of Science sr 10.4.85 NBC

CLARK, CANDY*
James Dean tf 2.19.76 NBC
Amateur Night at the Dixie Bar and Grill tf 1.8.79 NBC
Love and Learn pt 8.1.79 NBC
Where Ladies Go tf 3.14.80 ABC
Rodeo Girl tf 9.17.80 CBS
Faerie Tale Theater ep The Tale of the Frog Prince 9.11.82 SHO
Johnny Belinda tf 10.19.82 CBS
Cocaine and Blue Eyes tf 1.2.83 NBC
I Gave at the Office pt 8.15.84 NBC
Magnum, P.I. ep The Hotel Dick 10.17.85 CBS
George Burns Comedy Week ep Boris and Ivan in Las Vegas 11.13.85 CBS

CLARK, DANE
SUPP.:
Fantasy Island ep Image of Celeste 3.20.82 ABC
Matt Houston ep The Visitors 2.27.83 ABC
Quincy ep Murder on Ice 3.9.83 NBC
Mickey Spillane's Mike Hammer ep Negative Image 3.31.84 CBS
Murder, She Wrote ep Death Takes a Curtain Call 12.16.84 CBS
Highway to Heaven ep An Investment in Caring 3.13.85 NBC

CLARK, DORAN*

Too Far to Go tf 3.12.79 NBC
Quincy, M.E. ep The Winning Edge 2.21.80 NBC
The Secrets of Midland Heights sr 12.6.80 CBS
Splendor in the Grass tf 10.26.81 NBC
King's Crossing sr 1.16.82 ABC
The Powers of Matthew Star ep The Racer's Edge 1.28.83 NBC
Tucker's Witch ep Living and Presumed Dead 5.5.83 CBS
Emerald Point, N.A.S. sr 9.26.83 CBS
Prototype tf 12.7.83 CBS
Murder, She Wrote ep Deadly Lady 10.7.84 CBS
Hell Town ep Let My Jennie Go 9.11.85 NBC
Hollywood Beat ep No Place to Hide 10.12.85 ABC
MacGyver ep The Heist 11.3.85 ABC

CLARK, SUSAN

SUPP.:
Webster sr 9.16.83 ABC
Webster sr ret 9.21.84 ABC
Webster sr ret 9.24.85 ABC

CLARKE, MAE

A&C, B.V.:
Broken Arrow ep Attack on Fort Grant 5.21.59 ABC

CLAY, JUANIN*

Thou Shalt Not Commit Adultery tf 11.1.78 NBC
Stunt 7 tf/pt 5.30.79 CBS
Buck Rogers in the 25th Century ep Vegas in Space 10.4.79 NBC
Skag tf/pt 1.6.80 NBC
Buck Rogers in the 25th Century ep A Blast for Buck 1.17.80 NBC
Foul Play ep The Big Bang 1.26.80 ABC
Nero Wolfe ep In the Best of Families 3.6.81 NBC
The Long Summer of George Adams tf 1.18.82 NBC
Father Murphy ep False Blessing 2.2.82 NBC
Father Murphy ep Parable of Amanda 2.9.82 NBC
Robert Kennedy and His Times ms 1.27, 1.28, 1.29, 1.30.84 CBS

CLINGER, DEBRA

SUPP.:
Hart to Hart ep Harts and Palms 2.9.82 ABC

CLOUGH, APRIL*

California Fever sr 9.25.79 CBS
B.J. and the Bear ep Siege 1.19.80 NBC
The Star Maker tf 5.11, 5.12.81 NBC
T. J. Hooker sr 3.18.82 ABC
Flatfoots pt 7.3.82 NBC

I Take These Men tf 1.5.83 CBS
Dallas ep 2.4.83 CBS
The Whiz Kids ep Sabotage 11.9.83 CBS
Three's a Crowd ep The Honeymooners 11.27.84 ABC
Scarecrow and Mrs. King ep Life of the Party 2.18.85 CBS

COATES, PHYLLIS
A&C, B.V.:
Black Saddle ep Client: Davis 1.31.59 NBC
Gunsmoke ep Orval Bass 5.23.64 CBS

COBB, JULIE
SUPP.:
Today's FBI ep Energy Fraud 4.26.82 ABC
Uncommon Valor tf 1.22.83 CBS
The Mississippi ep 3.25.83 CBS
Tucker's Witch ep Living and Presumed Dead 5.5.83 CBS
The Mississippi ep 12.6.83 CBS
Charles in Charge sr 10.3.84 CBS
T. J. Hooker ep To Kill a Cop 10.10.85 CBS
Magnum, P.I. ep Going Home 10.31.85 CBS

COBURN, JAMES
A&C, B.V.:
The Rifleman ep Young Englishman 12.16.58 ABC
Wanted: Dead or Alive ep Reunion for Revenge 1.24.59 CBS
Trackdown ep Hard Lines 3.11.59 CBS
Black Saddle ep Client: Steele 3.21.59 NBC
Wanted: Dead Or Alive ep The Kovack Affair 3.28.59 CBS
Restless Gun ep The Pawn 4.6.59 NBC
Johnny Ringo ep The Arrival 10.1.59 CBS
The Life and Legend of Wyatt Earp ep The Outlaws 11.24.59 ABC
The Life and Legend of Wyatt Earp ep The Clanton's Family Row 12.8.59 ABC
Bat Masterson ep Six Feet of Gold 2.25.60 NBC
Tate ep Home Town 6.8.60 NBC
Wanted: Dead Or Alive ep The Trial 9.21.60 CBS
Zane Grey Theater ep Desert Flight 10.13.60 CBS
SUPP.:
Malibu tf/pt 1.23, 1.24.83 ABC
Faerie Tale Theater ep Pinocchio 5.14.84 SHO
Draw tf 7.15.84 HBO
Sins of the Father tf 1.13.85 NBC

COCO, JAMES
A&C, B.V.:
N.Y.P.D. ep The Witness 11.21.67 ABC
A&C, Supp. 2:
The Eddie Capra Mysteries ep Murder Plays a Dead Hand 12.22.78 NBC

<u>SUPP.:</u>
Matt Houston ep Recipe for Murder 11.7.82 ABC
St. Elsewhere ep Cora and Arnie 11.23.82 NBC
The Love Boat ep Our Son, the Lawyer 1.29.83 ABC
Fantasy Island ep Let Them Eat Cake 2.12.83 ABC
Alice ep 2.12.84 CBS
Mr. Success pt 6.23.84 NBC
The Curious Case of Santa Claus sp 11.20.84 A&E
Murder, She Wrote ep We're Off to Kill the Wizard 12.9.84 CBS
Day to Day Affairs sp 2.4.85 HBO
The Love Boat ep Partners to the End 2.23.85 ABC
Ray Bradbury Theater ep Marionettes, Inc. 5.21.85 HBO
Who's the Boss? ep The Prodigal Father-in-law 10.22.85 ABC
The Twilight Zone ep Playtime 11.15.85 CBS
Who's the Boss? ep The Prodigal Father-in-law Returns 12.3.85 ABC

COLE, DENNIS
<u>SUPP.:</u>
Fantasy Island ep Everybody Goes to Gilley's 11.20.82 ABC
Trapper John, M.D. ep 1.1.83 CBS
Matt Houston ep The Rock and the Hard Place 1.2.83 ABC
Three's Company ep Star Struck 2.15.83 ABC
Cave-in tf 6.19.83 NBC
Automan ep Club Ten 2.2.84 ABC
Fantasy Island ep The Mermaid and the Matchmaker 3.24.84 ABC
The Fall Guy ep The Winner 12.19.84 ABC
Mickey Spillane's Mike Hammer ep Firestorm 1.5.85 CBS
Trapper John, M.D. ep 2.17.85 CBS
The A-Team ep Where Is the Monster When You Need Him? 10.1.85 NBC

COLE, OLIVIA
<u>SUPP.:</u>
Report to Murphy sr 4.5.82 CBS
Something About Amelia tf 1.9.84 ABC
American Playhouse ep Go Tell It on the Mountain 1.14.85 PBS
Murder, She Wrote ep Murder to a Jazz Beat 2.3.85 CBS
North and South ms 11.3-11.10.85 ABC

COLEMAN, DABNEY
<u>A&C, Supp. 2:</u>
The Alfred Hitchcock Hour ep Dear Uncle George 5.10.63 NBC
The Outer Limits ep The Mice 1.6.64 ABC
Ben Casey ep Father Was an Intern 4.1.63 ABC
Alcoa Premiere ep Of Struggle and Flight 3.28.64 NBC
The Alfred Hitchcock Hour ep Isabel 6.5.64 NBC
The Outer Limits ep Wolf 359 11.7.64 ABC
Twelve O'Clock High ep Here's to Courageous Cowards 12.4.64 ABC
The Fugitive ep Nicest Fella You'd Ever Want to Meet 3.19.65 ABC

The Donna Reed Show ep Rally Round the Girls, Boys Fall 1965 ABC
The FBI ep Slow March Up a Steep Hill 10.10.65 ABC
Hazel ep A Haunting We Will Go 11.65 CBS
The Fugitive ep Approach with Care 11.15.66 ABC
The FBI ep The Conspirators 2.5.67 ABC
Room 222 ep Rights of Others 1.12.73 ABC
McMillan and Wife ep After Shock 11.9.75 NBC
Barnaby Jones ep A Taste for Murder 12.4.75 CBS
Switch ep One of Our Zeppelins Is Missing 2.10.76 CBS
SUPP.:
Buffalo Bill sr 6.2.83 NBC

COLEMAN, GARY
SUPP.:
The Kid with the Broken Halo tf/pt 4.5.82 NBC
The Gary Coleman Show sr vo 9.18.82 NBC
Diff'rent Strokes sr ret 10.2.82 NBC
Silver Spoons ep The Great Computer Caper 11.6.82 NBC
The Kid with the 200 I.Q. tf 2.6.83 NBC
Diff'rent Strokes sr ret 10.1.83 NBC
The Fantastic World of D.C. Collins tf 2.10.84 NBC
Diff'rent Strokes sr ret 9.29.84 NBC
Playing with Fire tf 4.14.85 NBC
Diff'rent Strokes sr ret 9.27.85 ABC
Amazing Stories ep Remote Control Man 12.8.85 NBC

COLLINS, GARY
A&C, Supp. 2:
Perry Mason ep The Case of the Fatal Fetish 3.4.65 CBS
Bracken's World ep The Stunt 11.7.69 NBC
Hawaii Five-O ep Dear Enemy 2.17.71 CBS
The Six Million Dollar Man ep Doomsday and Counting 3.1.74 ABC
Barnaby Jones ep Deadly Reunion 2.12.76 CBS
SUPP.:
Fantasy Island ep The Angel's Triangle 11.6.82 ABC
Hotel ep Designs 12.28.83 ABC

COLLINS, JOAN
SUPP.:
Paper Dolls tf/pt 5.24.82 ABC
The Wild Women of Chastity Gulch tf/pt 10.31.82 ABC
Faerie Tale Theater ep Hansel and Gretel 11.20.82 SHO
The Love Boat ep The Captain's Crush 2.19.83 ABC
Dynasty sr ret 10.27.82 ABC
Dynasty sr ret 9.28.83 ABC
The Making of a Male Model tf 10.9.83 ABC
Her Life as a Man tf 3.12.84 NBC
The Love Boat Fall Preview Party sp 9.15.84 ABC
Dynasty sr ret 9.26.84 ABC

The Cartier Affair tf 11.4.84 ABC
Dynasty sr ret 9.25.85 ABC

COMER, ANJANETTE
A&C, Supp. 1:
Perry Mason ep The Case of the Bigamous Spouse 11.14.63 CBS
The Reporter ep A Time to Be Silent 12.4.64 CBS
Harry O ep Shades 10.2.75 ABC
Harry O ep Exercise in Fatality 12.4.75 ABC

CONAWAY, JEFF*
From Sea to Shining Sea drama sp 12.19.74 NN
Movin' On ep Landslide 1.16.75 NBC
Movin' On ep The Long Haul 12.2.75 NBC
Joe Forrester ep The Best Laid Schemes 12.9.75 NBC
Barnaby Jones ep Wipe Out 3.4.76 CBS
Barnaby Jones ep Duet for Danger 3.24.77 CBS
Delta County, U.S.A. tf 5.20.77 ABC
Having Babies ep Sterile Wife 3.28.78 ABC
Taxi sr 9.12.78 NBC
Breaking Up Is Hard to Do tf 9.5 and 9.7.79 ABC
Taxi sr ret 9.11.79 NBC
For the Love of It tf 9.26.80 ABC
Taxi sr ret 11.19.80 NBC
Nashville Grab tf 10.18.81 NBC
Wizards and Warriors sr 2.26.83 CBS
The Making of a Male Model tf 10.9.83 ABC
Mickey Spillane's Mike Hammer ep Shots in the Dark 3.8.84 CBS
Murder, She Wrote ep Birds of a Feather 10.14.84 CBS
The Love Boat ep Heartbreaker 12.7.85 ABC

CONN, DIDI
SUPP.:
Working sp 12.81 SHO
Benson sr ret 10.22.82 ABC
Benson sr ret 9.16.83 ABC
The Love Boat ep Love on Strike 12.17.83 ABC
The ABC Weekend Special ep Bad Cat vo 4.14.84 ABC
Benson sr ret 9.21.84 ABC
Benson sr ret 9.27.85 ABC

CONNELLY, CHRISTOPHER
A&C, Supp. 2:
Alfred Hitchcock Presents ep Starring the Defense 11.15.63 NBC
The Lieutenant ep Alert 12.4.63 NBC
Gunsmoke ep Cool Dawn 5.16.64 CBS
Daniel Boone ep A Bearskin for Jamie Blue 11.27.69 NBC
Mannix ep 11.12.72 CBS
Petrocelli ep The Sleep of Reason 1.15.75 NBC

Petrocelli ep Survival 1.28.76 NBC
Hawaii Five-O ep To Die in Paradise 2.24.77 CBS
SUPP.:
Earthbound sp 1.31, 2.7.82 NBC
Simon and Simon ep Guessing Game 10.21.82 CBS
Bring 'Em Back Alive ep The Shadow Woman of Chung-Tui 1.29.83 CBS
Fantasy Island ep Island of Horrors 4.16.83 ABC
Matt Houston ep China Doll 11.4.83 ABC
The Fall Guy ep Inside, Outside 11.16.83 ABC
Masquerade ep Caribbean Holiday 1.12.84 ABC
Airwolf ep Echoes from the Past 3.3.84 CBS
Airwolf ep HX-1 11.10.84 CBS
The Fall Guy ep San Francisco Caper 11.21.84 ABC
Peyton Place: The Next Generation tf 5.13.85 NBC

CONNORS, CHUCK
A&C, B.V.:
The Rifleman sr ret 9.22.59 ABC
The Rifleman sr ret 9.27.60 ABC
The Rifleman sr ret 10.2.61 ABC
A&C, Supp. 2:
Stone ep Case Number HO-894287: Homicide 1.28.80 ABC
SUPP.:
Best of the West ep Frog Gets Lucky 1.7.82 ABC
The Capture of Grizzly Adams tf 2.21.82 NBC
Fantasy Island ep Sitting Duck 3.6.82 ABC
Matt Houston ep Get Houston 2.20.83 ABC
The Yellow Rose sr 10.2.83 NBC
The Love Boat ep The Hustlers 10.8.83 ABC
An American Portrait ep Edwin Hubble 2.27.85 CBS
Steel Collar Man pt 8.7.85 CBS
Murder, She Wrote ep Joshua Peabody Died Here 10.6.85 CBS
Spenser: For Hire ep Children of a Tempest Storm 10.29.85 ABC

CONNORS, MIKE (a.k.a. Touch Connors and Michael Connors)
A&C, B.V.:
The Rough Riders ep The Wilderness Trace 1.29.59 ABC
Bronco ep School for Cowards 4.21.59 ABC
The Walter Winchell File ep The Steep Hill 12.25.57 ABC
Jefferson Drum ep Simon Pitt 12.11.58 NBC
The Lucy Show ep Lucy and Mannix Held Hostage 10.4.71 CBS
SUPP.:
The Love Boat ep The Spoonmaker Diamond 11.13.82 ABC
The Earthlings pt 7.5.84 CBS
Glitter ep Glitter (pt) 9.13.84 ABC
The Fall Guy ep Private Eyes 10.24.84 ABC

CONRAD, MICHAEL
A&C, Supp. 1:

Harbourmaster ep Spear Gun 10.10.57 CBS
Brenner ep False Witness 6.21.64 CBS
Gunsmoke ep Hung High 11.14.64 CBS
The Reporter ep A Time to Be Silent 12.4.64 CBS
The Dick Van Dyke Show ep Body and Sol 11.24.65 CBS
Gomer Pyle, USMC ep Gomer and the Beast 1.7.66 CBS
The Rockford Files ep The Deep Blue Sleep 10.10.75 NBC
Bronk ep Deception 12.7.75 CBS
A&C, Supp. 2:
Hawaii Five-O ep A Short Walk on the Long Shore 1.2.78 CBS
SUPP.:
Hill Street Blues sr ret 9.30.82 NBC
Hill Street Blues sr ret 10.13.83 NBC

CONRAD, ROBERT
SUPP.:
Will, G. Gordy Liddy tf 1.10.82 NBC
Confessions of a Married Man tf 1.31.83 ABC
Hard Knox tf/pt 1.13.84 NBC
Two Fathers' Justice tf 2.11.85 NBC

CONRAD, WILLIAM
SUPP.:
The Fall Guy ep Private Eyes 10.24.84 ABC
Shocktrauma tf 10.27.82 NN
Murder, She Wrote ep Death Takes a Curtain Call 12.16.84 CBS
In Like Flynn tf/pt 9.14.85 ABC

CONSTANTINE, MICHAEL
A&C, Supp. 2:
Brenner ep Loan Shark 7.4.59 CBS
The Untouchables ep The Nick Moses Story 2.23.61 ABC
The Asphalt Jungle ep The Fighter 6.4.61 ABC
The Detectives ep A Piece of Tomorrow 11.10.61 NBC
Target: The Corruptors ep To Wear a Badge 12.1.61 ABC
Naked City ep Let Me Die Before I Wake 2.14.62 ABC
The Lloyd Bridges Show ep Wheresoever I Enter 9.11.62 CBS
Ben Casey ep The Night That Nothing Happened 10.5.62 ABC
Sam Benedict ep Tears for a Nobody Doll 10.13.62 NBC
The Lloyd Bridges Show ep Scapegoat 1.1.63 CBS
Gunsmoke ep Old York 5.4.63 CBS
Channing ep No Wild Games for Sophie 10.9.63 ABC
The Eleventh Hour ep And Man Created Vanity 10.23.63 NBC
The Greatest Show on Earth ep A Black Dress for Gina 12.17.63 ABC
77 Sunset Strip ep Bonus Baby 12.20.63 ABC
Great Adventure ep Escape 4.17.64 CBS
The Rogues ep The Stefanini Dowry 9.27.64 NBC
Slattery's People ep Remember the Dark Sins of Youth 10.5.64 CBS
Profiles in Courage ep Gov. John M. Slaton 12.20.64 NBC

Profiles in Courage ep Gen. Alexander Wm. Doniphan 1.17.65 NBC
Voyage to the Bottom of the Sea ep Indestructible Man 2.1.65 ABC
The Fugitive ep Everybody Gets Hit in the Mouth Sometime 3.9.65 ABC
The Bob Hope Chrysler Theater ep Memorandum for a Spy 4.2, 4.9.65 NBC
The Fugitive ep A Taste for Tomorrow 4.12.66 ABC
The Dick Van Dyke Show ep You Ought to Be in Pictures 4.27.66 CBS
The Bob Hope Chrysler Theater ep Verdict for a Spy 3.29.67 NBC
The Fugitive ep The Judgment 8.22, 8.29.67 ABC
McMillan and Wife ep The Deadly Cure 1.18.76 NBC
SUPP.:
Quincy, M.E. ep Gentle Into That Good Night 12.6.81 NBC
American Playhouse ep My Palikari 5.4.82 PBS
Lou Grant ep Beachhead 5.24.82 CBS
Benson ep Death in a Funny Position 10.22.82 ABC
Quincy, M.E. ep Give Me Your Weak 10.27.82 NBC
The Powers of Matthew Star ep The Italian Caper 10.29.82 NBC
Amanda's sr 2.10.83 ABC
The Fall Guy ep One Hundred Miles a Gallon 3.9.83 ABC
Matt Houston ep The Beverly Hills Social Club 3.13.83 ABC
The Love Boat ep The Pledge 10.1.83 ABC
Hotel ep Faith, Hope and Charity 11.23.83 ABC
Mickey Spillane's Mike Hammer ep Hot Ice 2.4.84 CBS
Mama's Family ep Harper vs. Harper 3.10.84 NBC
Simon and Simon ep The Disappearance of Harry the Hat 3.29.84 CBS
Masquerade ep Spanish Gambit 4.20.84 ABC
Finder of Lost Loves ep (pt/first ep) 9.22.84 ABC
Remington Steele ep Cast in Steele 12.4.84 NBC
Airwolf ep Prisoner of Yesterday 2.9.85 CBS
MacGyver ep Thief of Budapest 10.13.85 ABC
Highway to Heaven ep The Good Doctor 11.6.85 NBC
Highway to Heaven ep 12.18.85 NBC

CONVERSE, FRANK

A&C, Supp. 1:
The Young Rebels ep Father and I Went Down to Camp 9.20.70 ABC
Alias Smith and Jones ep Bushwack! 10.21.72 ABC
A&C, Supp. 2:
Police Woman ep The Killer Cowboys 2.8.77 NBC
SUPP.:
Nurse ep A Matter of Privacy 1.28.82 CBS
Family Tree sr 1.22.83 NBC
Magnum, P.I. ep The Kona Winds 10.10.85 CBS
The Equalizer ep Back Home 12.18.85 CBS

CONVY, BERT

SUPP.:

It's Not Easy sr 9.29.83 ABC

Love Thy Neighbor tf 5.23.84 ABC

The Love Boat ep What a Drag! 9.22.84 ABC

Murder, She Wrote ep (pt/first ep) 9.30.84 CBS

Hotel ep Fantasies 10.17.84 CBS

COOGAN, JACKIE

A&C, B.V.:

The Andy Griffith Show ep Barney on the Rebound 10.30.61 CBS

Hawaii Five-O ep Face of the Dragon 1.22.69 CBS

Hawaii Five-O ep Which Way Did They Go? 12.24.69 CBS

The Brady Bunch ep Double Parked 3.5.71 ABC

The Brady Bunch ep The Fender Benders 3.10.72 ABC

Alias Smith and Jones ep McGuffin 12.9.72 ABC

Hawaii Five-O ep Little Girl Blue 2.13.73 CBS

COOGAN, RICHARD

A&C, B.V.:

Harbourmaster ep Invisible Island 12.22.57 CBS

Gunsmoke ep Lover Boy 10.5.63 CBS

COOK, ELISHA

A&C, B.V.:

Troubleshooters ep Trapped 11.13.59 NBC

Temple Houston ep Gallows in Galilee 10.31.63 NBC

Wagon Train ep The Ben Engel Story 3.16.64 ABC

Gunsmoke ep Hung High 11.14.64 CBS

The Monroes ep To Break a Colt 1.11.67 ABC

Cimarron Strip ep The Battle of Bloody Stones 10.12.67 CBS

The Ghost and Mrs. Muir ep Not So Desperate Hours 10.30.69 NBC

A&C, Supp. 2:

Switch ep The Four Horsemen 2.13.77 CBS

Baretta ep Think Mink 3.9.77 ABC

SUPP.:

Chicago Story ep Subterranean Blues 5.14.82 NBC

Terror at Alcatraz tf/pt 7.4.82 NBC

Bring 'Em Back Alive ep Wilmer Bass and the Senegeti Kid 11.23.82 CBS

This Girl for Hire tf/pt 11.1.83 CBS

Simon and Simon ep 11.3.83 CBS

Lottery ep New York City: Winning Can Be Murder ("Who Dunit" segment) 11.18.83 ABC

The Whiz Kids ep The Lollipop Gang Strikes Back 2.25.84 CBS

Magnum, P.I. ep 10.18.84 CBS

Off Sides tf 7.6.84 NN

It Came Upon the Midnight Clear tf 12.15.84 NN

Magnum, P.I. ep The Love for Sale Boat 2.14.85 CBS

Night Court ep Married Alive 2.21.85 NBC
Hell Town ep Hell Town Goes Bananas 10.2.85 NBC
The A-Team ep The Road to Hope 10.29.85 NBC
Brothers ep 10.30.85 SHO

COOPER, JACKIE
A&C, B.V.:
Great Adventure ep The Hunley 9.27.63 CBS
Hawaii Five-O ep The Burning Ice 11.9.71 CBS
A&C, Supp. 1:
The Rockford Files ep Claire 1.31.75 NBC
A&C, Supp. 2:
The Rockford Files ep The House on Willis Avenue 2.24.78 NBC

COOPER, MAGGIE*
Lady of the House tf 11.14.78 NBC
And I Alone Survived tf 11.27.78 NBC
Women in White sr 2.8.79 NBC
And Baby Makes Six tf 10.22.79 NBC
The Gift tf 12.15.79 CBS
Death Ray 2000 tf/pt 3.5.81 NBC
Divorce Wars tf 3.1.82 ABC
Gimme a Break ep The Centerfold 1.20 and 1.27.83 NBC
Manimal ep Night of the Beast 12.17.83 NBC
Mickey Spillane's Mike Hammer ep Torch Song 9.29.84 CBS
Airwolf ep 10.26.84 CBS

COPLEY, TERI*
Fantasy Island ep The World's Most Desirable Woman 1.31.81 ABC
The Star Maker tf 5.11 and 5.12.81 NBC
Fly Away Home tf/pt 9.18.81 ABC
We Got It Made sr 9.8.83 NBC
Glitter ep Glitter (pt) 9.13.84 ABC
The Love Boat ep Dutch Treat 9.29.84 ABC
I Married a Centerfold tf 11.11.84 NBC
Gus Brown and Midnight Brewster tf/pt 6.2.85 NBC

CORBETT, GLENN
A&C, B.V.:
Twelve O'Clock High ep The Men and the Boys 10.2.64 ABC
Alias Smith and Jones ep 21 Days to Tenstrike 1.6.72 ABC
Alias Smith and Jones ep Bushwack! 10.21.72
A&C, Supp. 2:
The Rockford Files ep The Battle Ax and the Exploding Cigar 1.12.79 NBC
SUPP.:
Simon and Simon ep 12.8.83 CBS
Dallas ep 10.21.83 CBS
Manimal ep Night of the Scorpion 10.21.83 NBC

CORBETT, GRETCHEN

A&C, Supp. 2:

N.Y.P.D. ep The Case of the Shady Lady 11.19.68 ABC
Kojak ep Conspiracy of Fear 12.19.73 CBS
Switch ep Come Watch Me Die (a.k.a. Come Die with Me) 1.27.76 CBS
Marcus Welby, M.D. ep Vanity Case 4.27.76, 5.4.76, 5.11.76 ABC

SUPP.:

One Day at a Time ep Plain Farewell 12.20.81 CBS
Trapper John, M.D. ep Victims 1.10.82 CBS
Million Dollar Infield tf 2.2.82 CBS
Today's FBI ep Deep Cover 2.7.82 ABC
Cheers ep Diane's Perfect Date 2.10.83 NBC
The Mississippi ep 11.1.83 CBS
Magnum, P.I. ep The Cook 12.8.83 CBS
Things Are Looking Up pt 6.29.84 CBS
Otherworld sr 1.26.85 CBS
North Beach and Rawhide tf 11.12, 11.13.85 CBS

CORBY, ELLEN*

Big Town ep The Harbor Story 10.11.54 NBC
Alfred Hitchcock Presents ep Trigger by a Leash 10.16.55 CBS
The Life and Legend of Wyatt Earp ep Shootin' Woman 1.1.57 ABC
The Adventures of Rin Tin Tin ep Stagecoach Sally 4.19.57 ABC
Trackdown ep The House 3.21.58 CBS
The Restless Gun ep Suffragette 3.24.58 NBC
Alfred Hitchcock Presents ep Bull in a China Shop 3.30.58 CBS
Trackdown ep Killer Take All 9.5.58 CBS
Trackdown ep The Setup 9.26.58 CBS
Rescue 8 ep The Crack-Up 12.58 NN
Trackdown ep The Kid 12.12.58 CBS
The Texan ep The Lord Will Provide 12.29.58 CBS
Trackdown ep McCallin's Daughter 1.2.59 CBS
Trackdown ep Stranger in Town 3.25.59 CBS
Trackdown ep False Witness 4.8.59 CBS
Trackdown ep The Vote 5.6.59 CBS
Trackdown ep Tossup 5.20.59 CBS
Lineup ep The Chloroform Murder Case 5.22.59 CBS
Richard Diamond, Private Detective ep Marked for Murder 12.14.59 CBS
Bonanza ep The Gunmen 1.23.60 NBC
Wagon Train ep Wagons Ho! 9.28.60 NBC
G.E. Theater ep The Graduation Dress 10.30.60 CBS
The Tab Hunter Show ep The Invitation 4.3.61 NBC
The Roaring 20s ep Scandal Sheet 4.22.61 ABC
Frontier Circus ep Dr. Sam 10.26.61 CBS
The Rifleman ep The High Country 12.18.61 ABC
Follow the Sun ep Mele Kalikimaka to You 12.24.61 ABC

Saints and Sinners ep The Year Joan Crawford Won the Oscar 1.21.63 NBC
Bonanza ep The Hayburner 2.17.63 NBC
Ben Casey ep A Woods Full of Question Marks 10.26.64 ABC
The Virginian ep All Nice and Legal 11.15.64 NBC
Daniel Boone ep The Hostages 1.7.65 NBC
The Baileys of Balboa ep 1.14.65 CBS
The Addams Family ep Mother Lurch Visits the Addams Family 1.15.65 ABC
The Farmer's Daughter ep The Woman Behind the Man 4.2.65 ABC
Tammy ep 10.8.65 ABC
Hazel ep The Hold Out 10.18.65 CBS
The FBI ep The Forests of the Night 1.2.66 ABC
Honey West ep Come to Me, My Litigation Baby 2.18.66 ABC
The Fugitive ep The Sharp Edge of Chivalry 10.4.66 ABC
Laredo ep The Sweet Gang 11.4.66 NBC
The Invaders ep Beachhead 1.10.67 ABC
The Girl from UNCLE ep The Moulin Ruse Affair 1.17.67 NBC
Mr. Terrific ep 2.6.67 CBS
Please Don't Eat the Daisies ep 3.4.67 NBC
The FBI ep The Satellite 4.2.67 ABC
The Big Valley ep A Noose Is Waiting 11.13.67 ABC
Accidental Family ep 11.24.67 NBC
The Felony Squad ep Nightmare on a Dead End Street 2.19.68 ABC
The Guns of Will Sonnett ep Pariah 10.18.68 ABC
Hawaii Five-O ep Yesterday Died and Tomorrow Won't Be Born 11.7.68 CBS
Adam-12 ep Log 122 12.21.68 NBC
Lancer ep Zee 9.30.69 CBS
Adam-12 ep Log 22: Pig Is a Three Letter Word 10.11.69 NBC
Bracken's World ep Murder Off Camera 9.25.70 NBC
The Bill Cosby Show ep The Old Man in 4-C 10.11.70 NBC
The FBI ep The Savage Wilderness 10.18.70 ABC
Dan August ep The Worst Crime 2.11.71 ABC
Adam-12 ep Log 56: Vice Versa 3.11.71 NBC
The D.A. ep The People vs. Drake 9.17.71 NBC
A Tattered Web tf 9.24.71 CBS
The Homecoming tf/pt 12.19.71 CBS
The Waltons sr 9.14.72 CBS
Night Gallery ep Fright Night 10.15.72 NBC
The Waltons sr ret 9.13.73 CBS
Tenafly ep Joyride to Nowhere 10.10.73 NBC
The Story of Pretty Boy Floyd tf 5.7.74 ABC
The Waltons sr ret 9.12.74 CBS
The Waltons sr ret 9.11.75 CBS
The Waltons sr ret 9.23.76 CBS
The Waltons sr ret 9.11.77 CBS
The Waltons sr ret 9.21.78 CBS
The Waltons sr ret 9.20.79 CBS

The Waltons sr ret 11.20.80 CBS
A Wedding on Waltons Mountain tf 2.22.82 NBC
A Day for Thanks on Waltons Mountain tf 11.22.82 NBC
The Mississippi ep 12.13.83 CBS

CORD, ALEX (a.k.a. Alex Viespi)
A&C, B.V.:
Ben Casey ep Pavane for a Gentle Lady 11.20.61 ABC
Cain's Hundred ep Take a Number 1.9.62 NBC
Naked City ep Make It $50 and Love to Nona 11.14.62 ABC
East Side/West Side ep If Your Grandmother Had Wheels 3.2.64 CBS
Route 66 ep Where There's a Will, There's a Way 3.6, 3.13.64 CBS
The Bob Hope Chrysler Theater ep The Lady Is My Wife 2.1.67 NBC
The Scorpio Letters tf 2.19.67 ABC
Night Gallery ep Keep in Touch, We'll Think of Something 11.24.71 NBC
Gunsmoke ep The Sodbusters 11.20.72 CBS
Mission: Impossible ep Crack-Up 12.9.72 CBS
A&C, Supp. 1:
Genesis II tf 3.23.73 CBS
The FBI ep Night of the Long Knives 3.25.73 ABC
Police Story ep Line of Fire 12.18.73 NBC
Police Story ep To Steal a Million 2.4.75 NBC
Police Story ep The Losing Game 9.30.75 NBC
Matt Helm ep Murder on Ice 10.25.75 ABC
Joe Forrester ep Squeeze Play 2.9.76 NBC
Police Story ep Officer Dooley 3.5.76 NBC
The Quest ep The Buffalo Hunters 9.29.76 NBC
Police Woman ep Tennis Bum 11.30.76 NBC
The Six Million Dollar Man ep Task Force 12.19.76 ABC
SUPP.:
Fantasy Island ep Eternal Flame 3.5.83 ABC
Fantasy Island ep The High Cost of Loving 1.21.84 ABC
Airwolf sr 1.22.84 CBS
Airwolf sr ret 9.22.84 CBS
Hotel ep Flesh and Blood 10.10.84 ABC
Airwolf sr ret 9.28.85 CBS

CORNELL, LYDIA
SUPP.:
The Love Boat ep The Irresistible Man 2.6.82 ABC
Fantasy Island ep The Big Bet 5.1.82 ABC
Too Close for Comfort sr ret 10.14.82 ABC
Too Close for Comfort sr ret 10.83 NN
The Love Boat ep Lotions of Love 10.8.83 ABC
The Dukes of Hazzard ep 2.3, 2.10.84 CBS
Knight Rider ep Speed Demons 2.12.84 NBC
Hotel ep Trials 5.2.84 ABC

The Love Boat ep Doc's Slump 9.22.84 ABC
Too Close for Comfort sr ret 10.84 NN
Too Close for Comfort sr ret 10.85 NN

COSBY, BILL
SUPP.:
The Fat Albert Easter Special sp vo 4.3.82 CBS
The Cosby Show sr 9.20.84 NBC
The Cosby Show sr ret 9.26.85 NBC

COTTEN, JOSEPH
SUPP.:
The Love Boat ep Aunt Hilly 3.14.82 ABC

COX, RONNY
SUPP.:
Two of a Kind tf 10.9.82 CBS
The Jesse Owens Story tf 7.9, 7.16.84 NN
Spencer sr 12.1.84 NBC

CRAIG, YVONNE
A&C, Supp. 1:
The Many Loves of Dobie Gillis ep Dobie's Navy Blues Fall 1959 CBS
Man with a Camera ep Hot Ice Cream 1.25.60 ABC
The Many Loves of Dobie Gillis ep The Flying Millicans 2.2.60 CBS
Hennessy ep Scarlet Woman in White Spring 1960 CBS
The Detectives ep Quiet Night 1.27.61 ABC
Dobie Gillis ep Like Mother, Like Daughter, Like Wow 5.2.61 CBS
Malibu Run ep The Rainbow Adventure 4.26.61 CBS
The Jim Backus Show--Hot Off the Wire ep Dora's Vacation Spring 1961 NN
Follow the Sun ep A Ghost in Her Gazebo 3.18.62 ABC
Dobie Gillis ep Sweet Smell of Success 4.24.62 CBS
The New Breed ep Hail, Hail, the Gang's All Here 4.24.62 ABC
Mrs. G. Goes to College ep Mrs. G's Private Telephone Spring 1962 CBS
Laramie ep The Long Road Back 10.23.62 NBC
Wide Country ep Bravest Man in the World 12.6.62 NBC
Dobie Gillis ep Flow Gently, Sweet Money 11.21.62 CBS
Channing ep My Son, the All-American 4.8.64 ABC
Wagon Train ep The Link Cheney Story 4.13.64 ABC
Voyage to the Bottom of the Sea ep Turn Back the Clock 10.26.64 ABC
Dr. Kildare ep A Day to Remember 12.2.64 NBC
The Man from UNCLE ep The Brain Killer Affair 3.8.65 NBC
The Big Valley ep The Invaders 12.29.65 ABC
The Six Million Dollar Man ep The Infiltrators 2.6.77 ABC

CRAWFORD, BRODERICK

A&C, B.V.:

The Rough Riders ep The Plot to Assassinate President Jackson 2.5.59 ABC

Burke's Law ep Who Killed Avery Lord? 3.6.64 ABC

Cimarron Strip ep The Blue Moon Train 2.15.68 CBS

Alias Smith and Jones ep The Man Who Broke the Bank at Red Gap 1.20.72 ABC

A&C, Supp. 1:

Harry O ep Forty Reasons to Kill 12.5.74 ABC

Little House on the Prairie ep The Hunters 12.20.76 NBC

SUPP.:

Simon and Simon ep Rough Rider Rides Again 11.18.82 CBS

CRAWFORD, JOHNNY

A&C, B.V.:

The Restless Gun ep Gratitude 6.16.58 NBC

The Rifleman sr ret 9.29.59 ABC

The Rifleman sr ret 9.27.60 ABC

Hawaii Five-O ep By the Numbers 12.12.68 CBS

The Big Valley ep The Other Face of Justice 3.31.69 ABC

CRENNA, RICHARD

SUPP.:

The Day the Bubble Burst tf 2.7.82 NBC

It Takes Two sr 10.14.82 ABC

London and Davis in New York pt 9.9.84 CBS

The Rape of Richard Beck tf 5.27.85 ABC

Doubletake tf 11.24, 11.26.85 CBS

CRISTAL, LINDA

SUPP.:

The Love Boat ep The Duel 3.14.82 ABC

CROSBY, BING

A&C, B.V.:

The Bob Hope Chrysler Theater ep Fantastic Stomach 11.16.66 NBC

CROSBY, CATHY LEE

A&C, Supp. 2:

Hawaii Five-O ep The Kahuna 12.18.79 CBS

SUPP.:

The Fall Guy ep No Way Out 1.6.82 ABC

World War III tf 1.31, 2.1.82 NBC

Hotel ep Flashback 11.9.83 ABC

Hardcastle and McCormick ep The Homecoming 3.4, 3.11.84 ABC

An American Portrait ep Althea Gibson 12.10.84 CBS

The Love Boat ep The Captain Wears Pantyhose 2.16.85 ABC

Finder of Lost Loves ep Tricks 2.23.85 ABC

CROSBY, MARY

SUPP.:

The Big Easy pt 8.15.82 NBC
The Fall Guy ep Ready, Aim ... Die! 12.17.82 ABC
Confessions of a Married Man tf 1.31.83 ABC
The Fall Guy ep Strange Bedfellows 2.23.83 ABC
Hotel ep The Wedding 2.22.84 ABC
The Love Boat ep The Experiment 3.6.82 ABC
The Love Boat ep Fish Out of Water 3.10.84 ABC
The Fall Guy ep Undersea Odyssey 3.21.84 ABC
Cover Up ep Cover Up (pt) 9.22.84 CBS
Finder of Lost Loves ep Yesterday's Child 9.29.84 ABC
Glitter ep On Your Toes 12.11.84 ABC
Hollywood Wives ms 2.17, 2.18, 2.19.85 ABC
Hotel ep Distortions 2.27.85 ABC
Hotel ep 12.4.85 ABC
Final Jeopardy tf 12.8.85 NBC

CROSS, MURPHY*

Torn Between Two Lovers tf 5.2.79 CBS
Scruples ms 2.25, 2.26, 2.27, 2.28.80 CBS
Phyl and Mikhy sr 5.26.80 CBS
The Love Boat ep From Here to Maternity 1.17.81 ABC
Happy Endings tf 3.1.83 CBS
Taxi ep Louie and the Blind Girl 4.6.83 NBC
Taxi ep The Shloogel 9.30.82 NBC
Cheers ep The Coach Returns to Action 11.25.82 NBC
Riptide ep #1 with a Bullet 3.20.84 NBC
Night Court ep Bull's Baby 3.28.84 NBC
Sara ep Dueling Lawyers 2.13.85 NBC
Knots Landing ep The Emperor's Clothes 2.21.85 CBS
Maximum Security sr 3.9.85 HBO

CROTHERS, SCATMAN

A&C, Supp. 1:

Bewitched ep Three Men and a Witch on a Horse Spring 1972 ABC
Griff ep Isolate and Destroy 12.22.73 ABC
Toma ep The Street 5.3.74 ABC
Petrocelli ep 1.13.76 NBC

SUPP.:

The Love Boat ep Isaac's History Lesson 1.28.78 ABC
Charlie's Angels ep Angels in Vegas 9.13.78 ABC
Flying High ep The Marcy Connection 10.13.78 CBS
Vegas ep The Usurper 9.26.79 ABC
Magnum, P.I. ep Least We Forget 2.12.81 CBS
The Harlem Globetrotters on Gilligan's Island tf 5.15.81 NBC
Working sp 12.81 SHO
One of the Boys sr 1.23.82 NBC
Benson ep In the Red 3.26.82 ABC
Banjo, the Woodpile Car sp vo 5.1.82 ABC

It Takes Two ep Death Penalty 10.28.82 ABC
Missing Children: A Mother's Story tf 12.1.82 CBS
Grandpa, Will You Run with Me? sp 4.3.83 NBC
Casablanca sr 4.10.83 NBC
Taxi ep A Grand Gesture 5.25.83 ABC
Hotel ep Confrontations 11.16.83 ABC
We Got It Made ep Mickey Makes the Grade 3.10.84 NBC
The Love Boat ep Santa, Santa, Santa 12.15.84 ABC
Pryor's Place ep 12.15.84 CBS
Matt Houston ep Death Trap 1.18.85 ABC

CROWLEY, PATRICIA (a.k.a. Pat Crowley)
A&C, B.V.:
Wanted: Dead Or Alive ep 1.31.59 CBS
Alias Smith and Jones ep The Miracle at Santa Maria 12.30.71 ABC
A&C, Supp. 2:
The Eddie Capra Mysteries ep The Two Million Dollar Stowaway 12.6.78 NBC
The Rockford Files ep Guilt 1.19.79 NBC
Hawaii Five-O ep Woe to Wo Fat 4.5.80 CBS
SUPP.:
The Love Boat ep Return of the Captain's Lady 2.6.82 ABC
Fantasy Island ep The Fantasy Island Girl 12.10.83 ABC
Hotel ep Crossroads 1.30.85 ABC
International Airport tf/pt 5.25.85 ABC

CULEA, MELINDA*
Dear Teacher pt 7.17.81 NBC
Whacked Out pt 9.26.81 NBC
The Rules of Marriage tf 5.10, 5.11.82 CBS
The ABC Afterschool Special ep Sometimes I Don't Love My Mother 10.13.82 ABC
Gavilan ep The Hydra 11.30.82 NBC
The A-Team sr 1.23.83 NBC
The A-Team sr ret 9.20.83 NBC
Fantasy Island ep Hooker's Holiday 10.15.83 ABC
Glitter sr 9.27.84 ABC
Hotel ep Outsiders 11.21.84 ABC
The New Love, American Style ep Love and Dear Penelope 12.25.85 ABC

CULP, ROBERT
A&C, B.V.:
Johnny Ringo ep Cave-in 6.30.60 CBS
The Westerner ep Line Camp 12.9.60 NBC
The Bob Hope Chrysler Theater ep Slow Fade to Black 3.27.64 NBC
SUPP.:
Thou Shalt Not Kill tf 4.12.82 NBC
The Greatest American Hero sr ret 10.29.82 ABC

Hardcastle and McCormick ep School for Scandal 1.29.84 ABC
Her Life as a Man tf 3.12.84 NBC
No Man's Land tf 5.27.84 NBC
The Brothers-in-Law pt 4.28.85 ABC
The Key to Rebecca tf 4.29, 5.6.85 OPT

CUMBUKA, JI-TU*
Brian's Song tf 11.30.71 ABC
Chase ep The Game Ball 1.30.74 NBC
Get Christie Love ep Emperor at Death Street 9.25.74 ABC
The Dream Makers tf 1.7.75 NBC
The Blue Knight tf/pt 5.9.75 CBS
S.W.A.T. ep Any Second Now 3.13.76 ABC
Police Story ep Trash Detail, Front and Center 11.16.76 NBC
Roots ms 1.23-1.30.77 ABC
Last of the Good Guys tf 3.7.78 CBS
Mandrake tf/pt 1.24.79 NBC
The Nightingale pt 5.19.79 NBC
Ebony, Ivory and Jade tf/pt 8.3.79 CBS
A Man Called Sloane sr 9.22.79 NBC
Flesh and Blood tf 10.14, 10.16.79 CBS
Death Ray 2000 tf/pt 3.5.81 NBC
The Quest ep His Majesty, I Presume 11.12.82 ABC
Hardcastle and McCormick ep The Crystal Duck 10.2.83 ABC
The Cracker Brothers pt 9.14.84 NBC
MacGruder and Loud ep The Inside Man 1.29.85 ABC
The Dukes of Hazzard ep 2.8.85 CBS
Knight Rider ep Ten Wheel Trouble 3.24.85 NBC
The A-Team ep The Heart of Rock and Roll 11.5.85 NBC

CUMMINGS, BOB
A&C, B.V.:
The Beverly Hillbillies ep The Race for Queen Spring 1964 CBS
Here Come the Brides ep The She-Bear 1.30.70 ABC
Bewitched ep Samantha and the Troll 2.71 ABC

CUMMINGS, QUINN
A&C, Supp. 2:
Baretta ep The Dream 5.4.78 ABC
SUPP.:
The CBS Library ep The Incredible Book Escape 11.25.82 CBS
Grandpa, Will You Run with Me? sp 4.3.83 NBC
Remington Steele ep Elegy in Steele 2.21.84 NBC
Hail to the Chief sr 4.9.85 ABC

CURTIN, JANE*
What Really Happened to the Class of '65 ep The Class Hustler 12.15.77 NBC
The Coneheads pt vo 10.14.83 NBC
Bedrooms comedy sp 2.14.84 HBO
Kate and Allie sr 3.19.84 CBS

Kate and Allie sr ret 10.8.84 CBS
Kate and Allie sr ret 9.30.85 CBS

CURTIS, JAMIE LEE
SUPP.:
Callahan pt 9.9.82 ABC
Money on the Side tf 9.29.82 ABC
Tall Tales ep Annie Oakley 12.20.85 SHO

CURTIS, TONY
SUPP.:
Portrait of a Showgirl tf 5.4.82 CBS
The Fall Guy ep Eight Ball 2.9.83 ABC
Half Nelson ep 3.29.85 NBC

- D -

D'ABRBANVILLE, PATTI*
Once an Eagle ms 12.2-12.30.76 NBC
The Eddie Capra Mysteries ep Where There's Smoke 9.22.78 NBC
Barnaby Jones ep Run to Death 1.3.80 CBS
Charlie's Angels ep Angels of the Deep 12.7.80 ABC
Darkroom ep Guillotine 1.8.82 ABC
Murder, She Wrote ep Hit, Run and Homicide 11.25.84 CBS
Miami Vice ep Back in the World 12.6.85 NBC

DAHL, ARLENE
SUPP.:
The Love Boat ep Love Below Decks 12.10.83 ABC

DALY, JAMES
A&C, B.V.:
Twelve O'Clock High ep Falling Star 1.3.66 ABC
The Fugitive ep Running Scared 2.22.66 ABC

DALY, TYNE
A&C, Supp. 2:
CBS Playhouse ep Sadbird sp 12.1.69 CBS
The New People ep The Horizon 1.12.70 ABC
Medical Center ep Moment of Decision 1.14.70 CBS
Lucas Tanner ep 3.12.75 NBC
SUPP.:
Magnum, P.I. ep The Jororo Kill 1.7.82 CBS
Quincy, M.E. ep For Love of Joshua 2.3.81 NBC
Magnum, P.I. ep 1.7.83 CBS
Your Place or Mine tf 3.2.83 CBS
Cagney and Lacey sr 3.25.82 CBS

Cagney and Lacey sr ret 10.25.82 CBS
The Mississippi ep 10.25.83 CBS
Cagney and Lacey sr ret 3.19.84 CBS
Cagney and Lacey sr ret 10.15.84 CBS
Cagney and Lacey sr ret 9.30.85 CBS

DAMON, CATHRYN
SUPP.:
Not in Front of the Children tf 10.26.82 CBS
Fantasy Island ep Let Them Eat Cake 2.12.83 ABC
Who Will Love My Children? tf 2.14.83 ABC
Simon and Simon ep 1.12.84 CBS
Webster sr (with ep "Moving On") 11.2.84 ABC
Murder, She Wrote ep It's a Dog's Life 11.4.84 CBS
Webster sr ret 9.27.85 ABC

DAMON, STUART*
The Champions sr 5.26.68 NBC
The Adventurer sr 9.72 NN
Melody of Hate (a.k.a. Nightmare for a Nightingale) sp 9.30.75 ABC
General Hospital sr 1979 ABC
Fantasies tf 1.18.82 ABC
Fantasy Island ep The Case Against Mr. Roarke 2.6.82 ABC
Fantasy Island ep Second Time Around 11.19.83 ABC
Hotel ep 12.11.85 ABC

DANA, BILL
A&C, Supp. 2:
The Phil Silvers Show ep Hollywood 1.3.56 CBS
The Danny Thomas Show ep The Dog Walkers Spring 1961 CBS
The Danny Thomas Show ep For Every Man There's a Woman Fall 1961 CBS
The Danny Thomas Show ep Jose's Protege Spring 1962 CBS
The Bill Dana Show sr ret 9.20.64 NBC
Get Smart ep Supersonic Boom 10.28.67 NBC
Get Smart ep Ice Station Siegfried 12.69 NBC
Switch ep Gaffing the Skim 11.16.76 CBS
SUPP.:
Fantasy Island ep La Liberadora 11.7.81 ABC
Too Close for Comfort ep Rafkin's Bum 11.24.81 ABC
Too Close for Comfort ep A Matter of Degree 3.23.82 ABC
No Soap Radio sr 4.15.82 ABC
Zorro and Son sr 4.6.83 CBS
The Facts of Life ep It's Lonely at the Top 3.27.85 NBC

D'ANGELO, BEVERLY*
Captains and the Kings ms 9.30-11.11.76 NBC
Faerie Tale Theater ep Sleeping Beauty 7.7.83 SHO
A Streetcar Named Desire tf 3.14.84 ABC
Doubletake tf 11.24, 11.26.85 CBS

DANIELS, WILLIAM

A&C, Supp. 1:

Brenner ep Man in the Middle 8.15.59 CBS

East Side/West Side ep I Before E 10.20.63 CBS

For the People ep Any Benevolent Purpose 5.9.65 CBS

Toma ep Stillwater 492 2.1.74 ABC

Toma ep A Time and a Place Unknown 2.8.74 ABC

The Rockford Files ep The Italian Bird Fiasco 2.13.76 NBC

The Rockford Files ep So Help Me God 11.19.76 NBC

SUPP.:

Hart to Hart ep Hartless Hobby 1.12.82 ABC

Rehearsal for Murder tf 5.26.82 CBS

Rooster tf/pt 8.19.82 ABC

Drop Out Father tf 9.27.82 CBS

Knight Rider sr (vo) 9.26.82 NBC

St. Elsewhere sr 10.26.82 NBC

Knight Rider sr ret (vo) 10.2.83 NBC

St. Elsewhere sr ret 10.26.83 NBC

St. Elsewhere sr ret 9.19.84 NBC

Knight Rider sr ret (vo) 9.30.84 NBC

St. Elsewhere sr ret 9.18.85 NBC

Knight Rider sr ret (vo) 9.20.85 NBC

DANNER, BLYTHE

SUPP.:

Inside the Third Reich tf 5.9, 5.10.82 ABC

In Defense of Kids tf 4.6.83 CBS

St. Elsewhere ep The Women 3.28.84 NBC

Helen Keller: The Miracle Continues tf 4.23.84 OPT

Guilty Conscience tf 4.2.85 CBS

DANNING, SYBIL*

Vegas ep Set Up 3.25.81 ABC

Simon and Simon ep 12.15.83 CBS

The Fall Guy ep Prisoner 10.10.84 ABC

V: The Series ep Visitor's Choice 11.23.84 NBC

The Hitchhiker ep Face to Face 12.11.84 HBO

Street Hawk ep Street Hawk (pt) 1.25.85 ABC

DANSON, TED*

Kate Loves a Mystery ep Love on Instant Replay 10.18.79 NBC

The Women's Room tf 9.14.80 ABC

Once Upon a Spy tf/pt 9.19.80 ABC

Our Family Business tf/pt 9.20.81 ABC

Taxi ep The Unkindest Cut 2.25.82 ABC

Tucker's Witch ep The Good Witch of Laurel Canyon 10.6.82 CBS

Cowboy tf 4.30.83 CBS

Allison Sidney Harrison pt 8.19.83 NBC

Cheers sr 9.30.82 NBC

Cheers sr ret 9.29.83 NBC

Quarterback Princess tf 12.3.83 CBS
Cheers sr ret 9.27.84 NBC
An American Portrait ep 11.9.84 CBS
Cheers sr ret 9.26.85 NBC

DANTON, RAY
A&C, B.V.:
Trackdown ep Sweetwater, Texas 11.8.57 CBS
Perry Mason ep The Case of the Loquacious Liar 12.3.60 CBS
The Dick Powell Show ep The Hook 3.6.62 NBC
Hawaii Five-O ep Cloth of Gold 2.8.72 CBS
A&C, Supp. 1:
Toma ep Pound of Flesh 4.19.74 ABC
The Rockford Files ep Chicken Little Is a Little Chicken 11.14.75 NBC
Switch ep Big Deal in Paradise 2.24.76 CBS

DANZA, TONY*
Taxi sr 9.12.78 ABC
Taxi sr ret 9.11.79 ABC
Taxi sr ret 11.19.80 ABC
Taxi sr ret 10.22.81 ABC
Taxi sr ret 9.30.82 NBC
The Love Boat Fall Preview Party sp 9.15.84 ABC
Who's the Boss? sr 9.20.84 ABC
Who's the Boss? sr ret 9.24.85 ABC

DANZIGER, MAIA
SUPP.:
My Body, My Child tf 4.12.82 ABC
Kate and Allie ep Pirates 11.26.84 CBS

DARBY, KIM
SUPP.:
Fantasy Island ep A Genie Named Joe 2.13.82 ABC
The Capture of Grizzly Adams tf 2.21.82 NBC
The Love Boat ep Father, Dear Father 12.4.82 ABC
Trapper John, M.D. ep Pasts Imperfect 2.20.83 CBS
Close Ties drama sp 3.6.83 TEC
Summer Girl tf 4.12.83 CBS
Trapper John, M.D. ep 1.15.84 CBS
E/R ep 11.7.84 CBS
Hotel ep Ideals 12.12.84 ABC
Murder, She Wrote ep We're Off to Kill the Wizard 12.9.84 CBS
First Steps tf 3.19.85 CBS
Embassy tf 4.21.85 NBC
Scarecrow and Mrs. King ep Over the Limit 10.7.85 CBS

DARDEN, SEVERN
A&C, Supp. 2:
Honey West ep Little Green Robin Hood 3.18.66 ABC

Alias Smith and Jones ep Never Trust an Honest Man 4.15.71 ABC
Harry O ep The Acolyte 10.16.75 ABC
SUPP.:
Star of the Family ep The Critic 10.7.82 ABC
Cheers ep Homicidal Ham 10.27.83 NBC
Me and Mom ep The Murder Game 5.10.85 ABC
George Burns Comedy Week ep The Assignment 10.30.85 CBS

DARREN, JAMES
SUPP.:
Fantasy Island ep Sweet Suzi Swann 3.6.82 ABC
T.J. Hooker ep King of the Hill 10.2.82 ABC
One Day at a Time ep 1.23.83 CBS
T.J. Hooker ep Lady in Blue 5.7.83 ABC
T.J. Hooker sr 10.1.83 ABC
T.J. Hooker sr ret 9.25.85 CBS

DARROW, HENRY
A&C, Supp. 2:
Daniel Boone ep Take the Southbound Stage 4.6.67 NBC
Mod Squad ep No More Oak Leaves for Ernie Holland 2.1.71 ABC
Hawaii Five-O ep No Bottles ... No Cans ... No People 9.21.71 CBS
Man and the City ep Handwriting on the Wall 10.27.71 ABC
The Bold Ones: The Doctors ep The Night Crawler 1.6.73 NBC
Kojak ep Before the Devil Knows 2.27.74 CBS
Harry O sr 9.12.74 (to 12.26.74) ABC
Harry O ep Elegy for a Cop 2.27.75 ABC
Hawaii Five-O ep Loose Ends Get Hit 1.8.76 CBS
The Six Million Dollar Man ep Vulture of the Andes 11.21.76 ABC
Police Woman ep The Inside Connection 11.22.77 NBC
SUPP.:
American Playhouse ep Sequin 1.26.82 PBS
Quincy, M.E. ep Into the Murdering Mind 2.10.82 NBC
Cassie and Company ep One Thief Too Many 6.15.82 NBC
Born to the Wind sr 8.19.82 NBC
Benson ep What a Revoltin' Development 10.29.82 ABC
T.J. Hooker ep A Cry for Help 11.27.82 ABC
Hart to Hart ep Chamber of Lost Harts 2.1.83 ABC
Tales of the Gold Monkey ep Last Chance Louie 3.11.83 ABC
Dallas ep 3.25.83 CBS
Zorro and Son sr 4.6.83 CBS
Scarecrow and Mrs. King ep If Thoughts Could Kill 10.17.83 CBS
Jennifer Slept Here ep Trading Faces 12.2.83 NBC
Scarecrow and Mrs. King ep Remembrance of Things Past 1.9.84 CBS

The Fall Guy ep Rabbit's Feet 1.25.84 ABC
Airwolf ep One Way Express 2.18.84 CBS
100 Center Street pt 8.31.84 ABC
Cover Up ep Sudden Exposure 10.20.84 CBS
Me and Mom ep Davie 4.19.85 ABC
Me and Mom ep The Murder Game 5.10.85 ABC
Magnum, P.I. ep Paniolo 11.7.85 CBS

DAVALOS, ELYSSA*
The ABC Afterschool Special ep Dear Lovey Hart (I Am Desperate) 5.19.76 ABC
Charlie's Angels ep The Mexican Connection 9.29.76 ABC
Good Against Evil tf 5.22.77 ABC
Wild and Wooly tf 2.20.78 ABC
How the West Was Won ep Hillary 2.26.79 ABC
Vegas ep Doubtful Target 3.7.79 ABC
Hawaii Five-O ep The Moroville Convent 10.18.79 CBS
Vegas ep No Way to Treat a Victim 2.18.81 ABC
Riker ep Honkey Tonk 3.14.81 CBS
Code Red ep A Saved Life 11.1.81 ABC
Code Red ep Death of a Fireman 11.8.81 ABC
Matt Houston ep The Hunted 4.24.83 ABC
Matt Houston ep Needle in a Haystack 10.7.83 ABC
Knight Rider ep Blind Spot 10.23.83 NBC
Mickey Spillane's Mike Hammer ep The Perfect 20 4.7.84 CBS
Riptide ep Something Fishy 5.22.84 NBC
Scarecrow and Mrs. King ep Over the Limit 10.7.85 CBS

DAVID, THAYER
A&C, Supp. 1:
The Wild Wild West ep The Night of the Spanish Curse 1.3.69 CBS
Kojak ep Close Cover Before Killing 1.5.75 CBS
The Rockford Files ep Say Goodbye to Jennifer 2.7.75 NBC
Harry O ep Shades 10.2.75 ABC
Switch ep The Twelfth Commandment 9.28.76 CBS
Hawaii Five-O ep Double Exposure 12.2.76 CBS

DAVIDSON, JOHN
A&C, B.V.:
Daniel Boone ep Perilous Passage 1.15.70 NBC
SUPP.:
Hotel ep Deceptions 11.30.83 ABC
Fantasy Island ep The Imposter 3.17.84 ABC
Hotel ep Vantage Point 12.5.84 ABC
The Love Boat ep Girl of the Midnight Sun 2.2.85 ABC
Scene of the Crime ep Murder on the Rocks 4.29.85 NBC
Goodbye Charlie pt 6.4.85 ABC

DAVIS, BETTE
SUPP.:
A Piano for Mrs. Cimino tf 2.3.82 CBS

Little Gloria ... Happy at Last tf 10.24, 10.25.82 NBC
Hotel ep Hotel (pt) 9.21.83 ABC
Right of Way tf 11.21.83 HBO
Murder with Mirrors tf 2.20.85 CBS

DAVIS, GAIL
A&C, B.V.:
The Andy Griffith Show ep The Perfect Female 11.27.61 CBS

DAVIS, GEENA*
Buffalo Bill sr 6.1.83 NBC
Knight Rider ep Kitt the Cat 11.6.83 NBC
Fantasy Island ep Don Juan's Last Affair 4.14.84 ABC
Riptide ep Raiders of the Lost Sub 5.15.84 NBC
Family Ties ep Help Wanted 12.6.84 NBC
Family Ties ep Karen II, Alex 0 12.13.84 NBC
Sara sr 1.23.85 NBC
Day to Day Affairs comedy sp 2.4.85 HBO
Remington Steele ep Steele in the Chips 3.19.85 NBC
George Burns Comedy Week ep Dream, Dream, Dream 11.6.85 NBC

DAVIS, JIM
A&C, Supp. 2:
The Tales of Wells Fargo ep Two Cartridges 9.16.57 NBC
December Bride ep Stan Loses His Nerve 3.59 CBS
Markham ep The Snowman 9.1.60 CBS
Tall Man ep The Lonely Star 10.8.60 NBC
Wagon Train ep The Candy O'Hara Story 12.7.60 NBC
The Outlaws ep The Brothers 5.11.61 NBC
Gunsmoke ep The Imposter 5.13.61 CBS
Malibu Run ep The Diana Adventure 6.7.61 CBS
Have Gun--Will Travel ep Treasure 12.29.62 CBS
The Donna Reed Show ep Pioneer Woman 2.63 ABC
Laramie ep The Dispossessed 2.19.63 NBC
Laramie ep Trapped 5.14.63 NBC
Wagon Train ep The Melanie Craig Story 2.17.64 NBC
Alcoa Premiere ep Jeeney Ray 3.14.64 CBS
The Donna Reed Show ep Indoor Outing 4.8.65 ABC
Branded ep One Way Out 4.18.65 NBC
Branded ep Salute the Soldier Briefly 10.24.65 NBC
Gunsmoke ep The Raid 1.22, 1.29.66 CBS
Gunsmoke ep Treasure of John Walking Fox 4.16.66 CBS
Gunsmoke ep Mission 10.8.66 CBS
Daniel Boone ep River Passage 12.15.66 NBC
Daniel Boone ep The Ordeal of Israel Boone 9.21.67 NBC
Cimarron Strip ep The Search 11.9.67 CBS
The Guns of Will Sonnett ep The Warriors 3.1.68 ABC
The High Chaparral ep New Hostess in Town 3.20.70 NBC
Gunsmoke ep McCabe 11.30.70 CBS
The Men from Shiloh ep The Politician 1.13.71 NBC

Gunsmoke ep Murdock 2.8.71 CBS
The Sixth Sense ep Echo of a Distant Scream 4.1.72 ABC
Banacek ep If Max Is So Smart, Why Doesn't He Tell Us Where He Is? 11.7.73 NBC

DAVIS, PATTI (a.k.a. Patricia Davis)
SUPP.:
Here's Boomer ep Boomer and Miss 21st Century 9.20.81 NBC
Vegas ep Love Affair 11.26.81 ABC
Hart to Hart ep To Coin a Hart 5.11.82 ABC
Simon and Simon ep Design for Killing 2.10.83 CBS
Trapper John, M.D. ep 10.16.83 CBS
Simon and Simon ep 2.10.84 CBS
Rituals ep 10.24, 10.25.84 NN
Simon and Simon ep Marlowe, Come Home 2.28.85 CBS

DAVIS, PHYLLIS
SUPP.:
Fantasy Island ep Mata Hari 1.16.82 ABC
The Love Boat ep Love Ain't Legal 2.6.82 ABC
Knight Rider ep Knight Rider (pt) 9.26.82 NBC
Matt Houston ep Killing Isn't Everything 10.24.82 ABC
The Wild Women of Chastity Gulch tf/pt 11.20.82 ABC
Fantasy Island ep Castaways 11.26.83 ABC
Hotel ep Mistaken Identities 2.1.84 ABC
Fantasy Island ep Final Adieu 4.14.84 ABC
The Love Boat ep All the Congressmen's Women 5.12.84 ABC
Mr. Mom pt 11.30.84 ABC
Finder of Lost Loves ep Tricks 2.23.85 ABC
Magnum, P.I. ep The Hotel Dick 10.17.85 CBS

DAVIS JR., SAMMY
A&C, B.V.:
The Courtship of Eddie's Father ep A Little Help from My Friend 2.72 ABC
SUPP.:
Fantasy Island ep Edward 4.9.83 ABC
The Jeffersons ep 1.1.84 CBS
Fantasy Island ep Bojangles and the Dancer 5.12.84 ABC
Alice in Wonderland tf 12.9 and 12.10.85 CBS

DAVIS, VIVEKA*
V ms 5.1, 5.2.83 NBC
The Mississippi ep 10.25.83 CBS
V: The Final Battle ms 5.6, 5.7, 5.8.84 NBC
E/R ep 12.12.84 CBS
Not My Kid tf 1.15.85 CBS
Under One Roof ep Crazy Girl 4.20.85 NBC

DAWBER, PAM
SUPP.:
Mork and Mindy sr ret 4.15.82 ABC

Mork and Mindy sr (cartoon) vo 9.25.82 ABC
Remembrance of Love tf 12.6.82 NBC
Through Naked Eyes tf 12.11.83 ABC
Last of the Great Survivors tf 1.3.84 CBS
This Wife for Hire tf/pt 3.18.85 ABC
An American Portrait ep William Henry Jackson 3.22.85 CBS
Wild Horses tf 11.12.85 CBS
The Twilight Zone ep But Can She Type? 12.20.85 CBS

DAY, LARAINE
A&C, B.V.:
Burke's Law ep Who Killed Billy Joe? 11.8.63 ABC
Wagon Train ep The Cassie Vance Story 12.23.63 ABC
SUPP.:
Airwolf ep Eruption 4.6.85 CBS
Hotel ep Second Offense 10.16.85 ABC

DEAN, JAMES
A&C, B.V.:
Tales of Tomorrow ep The Evil Within 5.1.53 ABC

DEAN, JIMMY
A&C, B.V.:
Daniel Boone ep The Flaming Rocks 2.1.68 NBC

DEARDEN, ROBIN*
Magic Mongo sr 9.10.77 ABC
David Cassidy--Man Undercover ep Baby Makes Three 11.9.78 NBC
B.J. and the Bear ep Gasolhol 11.24.79 NBC
To Race the Wind tf 3.12.80 CBS
Trouble in High Timber Country tf/pt 6.27.80 ABC
Fugitive Family tf 10.1.80 CBS
Magnum, P.I. ep No Need to Know 1.8.81 CBS
The Incredible Hulk ep Danny 5.15.81 CBS
Happy Days ep The Other Guy 11.10.81 ABC
Love, Sidney ep The Torch 3.17.82 NBC
Magnum, P.I. ep The Elmo Ziller Story 3.25.82 CBS
T.J. Hooker ep Big Foot 10.9.82 ABC
Knight Rider ep Give Me Liberty or Give Me Death 1.21.83 NBC
The Cradle Will Fall tf 5.24.83 CBS
The A-Team ep The Taxi Cab Wars 11.1.83 NBC
Masquerade ep Spanish Gambit 4.20.84 ABC
The Earthlings pt 7.5.84 ABC
Highway to Heaven ep One Winged Angels 1.16.85 NBC
Knight Rider ep Buyout 2.10.85 NBC

DeBANZIE, LOIS*
One of the Boys ep Too Much to Lose 2.20.82 NBC
Remington Steele ep Steele's Gold 3.22.83 NBC
Cheers ep Showdown 3.31.83 NBC

The Return of the Man from UNCLE: The 15 Years Later Affair tf 4.5.83 CBS
Lottery ep New York City: Winning Can Be Murder ("Whodunit" segment) 11.18.83 ABC
Newhart ep The Stratford Wives 11.7.83 CBS
Mr. Smith ep Mr. Smith Loses a Friend 11.18.83 NBC
Family Ties ep Baby Boy Doe 3.8.84 NBC
Ernie Kovacs: Between the Laughter tf 5.14.84 ABC
Punky Brewster ep Bye Bye My 11.11.84 NBC
Amos tf 9.29.85 CBS

DeBENNING, BURR
SUPP.:
Father Murphy ep 11.3.81 NBC
McClain's Law ep Portrait of a Playmate 12.18.81 NBC
Magnum, P.I. ep The Jororo Kill 1.7.82 CBS
The Fall Guy ep Goin' for It 1.27.82 ABC
Simon and Simon ep Tanks for the Memories 3.16.82 CBS
Father Murphy ep Matthew and Elizabeth 3.28.82 NBC
Father Murphy ep The First Miracle 4.4, 4.11.82 NBC
The Fall Guy ep Manhunter 1.19.83 ABC
Hotel ep Flashback 11.9.83 ABC
Father Murphy ep Blood Right 12.21.82 NBC
Father Murphy ep The Rockets' Red Glare 4.15.83 NBC
Mickey Spillane's Mike Hammer ep 3.8.84 NBC
Riptide ep Catch of the Day 10.23.84 NBC
Hollywood Beat ep Across the Line 10.26.85 ABC
Hollywood Beat ep 11.2.85 ABC
Highway to Heaven ep The Monster 12.4, 12.11.85 NBC

DeCAMP, ROSEMARY
A&C, B.V.:
Ensign O'Toole ep Operation Swindle 7.14.63 NBC
Here Come the Brides ep The Crimpers 3.5.69 ABC
A&C, Supp. 1:
The Rockford Files ep Gear Jammers 9.26.75, 10.3.75 NBC

DeCARLO, YVONNE
SUPP.:
Murder, She Wrote ep Jessica Behind Bars 12.1.85 CBS

DEE, RUBY
SUPP.:
An American Portrait ep Arthur Mitchell 11.26.84 CBS
American Playhouse ep Go Tell It on the Mountain 1.14.85 PBS
The Atlanta Child Murders tf 2.10, 2.12.85 CBS

DEE, SANDRA
SUPP.:
Fantasy Island ep A Date with Burt 3.5.83 ABC

DeFORE, DON
SUPP.:
Matt Houston ep The Beverly Hills Social Club 3.13.83 ABC

DeHAVEN, GLORIA
A&C, B.V.:
Johnny Ringo ep Love Affair 12.17.59 CBS
A&C, Supp. 2:
Police Story ep A Chance to Live 5.28.78 NBC
The Eddie Capra Mysteries ep The Two Million Dollar Stowaway 12.8.78 NBC
SUPP.:
Fantasy Island ep My Man Friday 10.16.82 ABC
Hart to Hart ep Rich and Hartless 11.23.82 ABC
Falcon Crest ep 1.28.83 CBS
The Love Boat ep Don't Leave Home Without It 10.15.83 ABC
Ryan's Hope sr Summer 1984 ABC
Off Sides tf 7.6.84 NBC

de HAVILLAND, OLIVIA
SUPP.:
Agatha Christie's "Murder Is Easy" tf 1.2.82 CBS
The Love Boat ep Aunt Hilly 3.14.82 ABC
The Royal Romance of Charles and Diana tf 9.20.82 CBS

DEHNER, JOHN*
Frontier ep Georgia Gold 6.10.56 NBC
Tales of the 77th Bengal Lancers ep Relentless Man 3.3.57 ABC
Cheyenne ep The Broken Pledge 6.4.57 ABC
Gunsmoke ep Crack-Up 9.14.57 CBS
Have Gun--Will Travel ep High Wire 11.2.57 CBS
Zorro ep The Fall of Monasterio 1.2.58 ABC
The Restless Gun ep The Coward 1.6.58 NBC
The Restless Gun ep Quiet City 2.3.58 NBC
Ellery Queen ep Ten Days Wonder 10.10.58 NBC
Perry Mason ep The Case of the Sardonic Sergeant 10.11.58 CBS
Maverick ep Shady Deal at Sunny Acres 11.23.58 ABC
Black Saddle ep Client: Robinson 2.21.59 ABC
Wanted: Dead or Alive ep Angels of Vengeance 4.18.59 CBS
The David Niven Theater ep The Twist of the Key 3.12.59 CBS
The Restless Gun ep The Hill of Death 6.22.59 NBC
The Tales of Wells Fargo ep Young Jim Hardie 9.7.59 NBC
The Rifleman ep The Blowout 10.13.59 ABC
Bat Masterson ep Wanted--Dead 10.15.59 NBC
The Alaskans ep 10.18.59 ABC
The Alaskans ep Big Deal 11.8.59 ABC
The Twilight Zone ep The Lonely 11.13.59 CBS
Wanted: Dead or Alive ep Twelve Hours to Crazy Horse 11.21.59 CBS

Philip Marlowe ep The Temple of Love 11.24.59 ABC
The Rifleman ep The Baby Sitter 12.15.59 ABC
Wichita Town ep Death Watch 12.16.59 NBC
Law of the Plainsman ep Clear Title 12.17.59 NBC
The Alaskans ep Remember the Maine 12.20.59 ABC
Laramie ep Company Man 2.9.60 NBC
Rawhide ep Incident at Sulphur Creek 3.11.60 CBS
The Roaring 20s sr 10.15.60 ABC
The Westerner ep Brown 10.21.60 NBC
Gunsmoke ep The Badge 11.12.60 CBS
The Zane Grey Theater ep So Young This Savage Land 11.21.60 CBS
The Tales of Wells Fargo ep Jeff Davis's Treasure 12.5.60 NBC
The Rebel ep The Scalp Hunter 12.11.60 ABC
Stagecoach West ep Image of a Man 1.13.61 ABC
The Rebel ep Jerkwater 1.22.61 ABC
Bat Masterson ep The Prescott Campaign 2.2.61 NBC
Stagecoach West ep The Root of Evil 2.28.61 ABC
Rawhide ep Incident of the New Start 3.3.61 CBS
The Rifleman ep The Prisoner 3.14.61 ABC
Stagecoach West ep The Butcher 3.28.61 ABC
Maverick ep The Devil's Necklace 4.23.61 ABC
The Untouchables ep The Nero Rankin Story 5.11.61 ABC
Malibu Run ep The Stakeout Adventure 5.24.61 CBS
The Tales of Wells Fargo ep A Quiet Little Town 6.5.61 NBC
The Roaring 20s sr ret 10.7.61 ABC
Checkmate ep The Heat of Passion 10.18.61 CBS
77 Sunset Strip ep The Unremembered 10.27.61 ABC
Gunsmoke ep The Squaw 11.11.61 CBS
The Twilight Zone ep The Jungle 12.1.61 CBS
Surfside Six ep A Slight Case of Chivalry 12.18.61 ABC
Hawaiian Eye ep A Scent of Whales 3.7.62 ABC
Maverick ep Marshal Maverick 3.11.62 ABC
77 Sunset Strip ep The Disappearance 4.7.62 ABC
Gunsmoke ep Root Down 10.6.62 CBS
Empire ep Ride to a Fall 10.16.62 ABC
The Gallant Men ep One Moderately, Peaceful Sunday 11.2.62 ABC
Stoney Burke ep King of the Hill 1.21.63 ABC
Rawhide ep Incident at Judgement Day 2.8.63 CBS
Gunsmoke ep Ash 2.16.63 CBS
The Virginian ep Echo of Another Day 3.27.63 NBC
77 Sunset Strip ep Reunion at Balboa 4.12.63 ABC
The Virginian ep To Make This Place Remember 9.25.63 NBC
Temple Houston ep Enough Rope 12.19.63 NBC
The Greatest Show on Earth ep Where the Wire Ends 1.7.64 ABC
Combat ep The General and the Sergeant 1.14.64 ABC
Bonanza ep The Gentleman from New Orleans 2.2.64 NBC
Rawhide ep Incident of the Swindler 2.20.64 CBS
Great Adventure ep Plague 2.28.64 CBS

Temple Houston ep The Gun That Swept the West 3.5.64 NBC
Gunsmoke ep Homecoming 3.28.64 CBS
East Side/West Side ep The Givers 4.13.64 CBS
The Twilight Zone ep Mr. Garrity and the Graves 5.8.64 CBS
The Rogues ep The Personal Touch 9.13.64 NBC
The Baileys of Balboa sr 9.23.64 CBS
Gunsmoke ep The Pariah 4.17.65 CBS
Branded ep One Way Out 4.18.65 NBC
The Virginian sr 9.15.65 NBC
Hogan's Heroes ep The Late Inspector General 10.8.65 CBS
The Wild Wild West ep The Night of the Casual Killer 10.15.65 CBS
A Man Called Shenandoah ep The Young Outlaw 12.27.65 ABC
The Big Valley ep Invaders 12.29.65 ABC
The Wild Wild West ep The Night of the Steel Assassin 1.7.66 CBS
Voyage to the Bottom of the Sea ep The Manfish 3.6.66 ABC
Jericho ep Wall to Wall Kaput 10.27.66 CBS
Run for Your Life ep Edge of the Volcano 10.31.66 NBC
Hogan's Heroes ep 11.18, 11.25.66 CBS
T.H.E. Cat ep King of Limpets 12.9.66 NBC
The Road West ep Power of Fear 12.26.66 NBC
The Monroes ep Gun Bound 1.25.67 ABC
Winchester '67 tf 3.14.67 NBC
Judd, for the Defense ep A Civil Case of Murder 9.29.67 ABC
The Man from UNCLE ep The Prince of Darkness Affair 10.2, 10.9.67 NBC
Tarzan ep Jai's Amnesia 12.15.67 NBC
Gunsmoke ep Dead Man's Law 1.8.68 CBS
The Flying Nun ep 3.21.68 ABC
The Outcasts ep Take Your Lover in the Ring 10.28.68 ABC
Something for a Lonely Man tf 11.26.68 NBC
Ironside ep Officer Mike 12.12.68 NBC
Mannix ep Only Giants Can Play 1.18.69 CBS
Judd, for the Defense ep The Holy Ground 2.14, 2.21.69 ABC
The High Chaparral ep Surtee 2.28.69 NBC
The High Chaparral ep The Legacy 11.28.69 NBC
Then Came Bronson ep The Gleam of the Eagle Mind 1.21.70 NBC
Land of the Giants ep The Deadly Dart 2.1.70 ABC
Quarantined tf 2.24.70 NBC
The Silent Force ep The Judge 10.19.70 ABC
The Immortal ep White Horse, Steel Horse 11.5.70 ABC
My Wives Jane pt 8.1.71 CBS
The Doris Day Show sr 9.13.71 CBS
The Doris Day Show sr ret 9.11.72 CBS
The New Temperatures Rising sr 9.25.73 ABC
Columbo ep Swan Song 3.3.74 NBC
The Magician ep Illusion of the Cat's Eye 3.25.74 NBC
Honky Tonk tf 4.1.74 NBC

Petrocelli ep Once Upon a Victim 1.29.75 NBC
The Night Stalker ep The Knightly Murders 3.7.75 ABC
The Big Ripoff tf 3.11.75 NBC
Switch ep Story from Behind 9.30.75 CBS
S.W.A.T. ep Pressure Cooker 11.15.75 ABC
Movin' On ep Please Don't Talk to the Driver 11.25.75 NBC
Ellery Queen ep Adventure of the Blunt Instrument 12.18.75 NBC
The Barbary Coast ep The Day Cable Was Hanged 12.26.75 ABC
Columbo ep Last Salute to the Commodore 5.2.76 NBC
The New Adventures of Joshua Cabe tf/pt 5.29.76 ABC
The Rockford Files ep There's One in Every Port 1.7.77 NBC
How the West Was Won ms 2.6-2.14.77 ABC
Danger in Paradise tf/pt 5.12.77 NBC
Big Hawaii sr 9.21.77 NBC
Greatest Heroes of the Bible ep David and Goliath 11.19.78 NBC
Quincy, M.E. ep Physician, Heal Thyself 2.22.79 NBC
Young Maverick sr 11.28.79 CBS
Hawaii Five-O ep 3.22.80 CBS
Enos sr 11.12.80 CBS
Bare Essence sr 2.15.83 NBC
Hardcastle and McCormick ep Surprise at Seagull Beach 2.4.85 ABC

DeLISLE, CHRISTINE*
Wild and Woolly tf/pt 2.20.78 ABC
Colorado C.I. pt 5.26.78 CBS
Beach Patrol tf/pt 4.30.79 ABC
A Man Called Sloane ep Night of the Wizard 9.22.79 NBC
The Incredible Hulk ep Equinox 3.21.80 CBS
CHiPs ep Wheels of Justice 12.21.80 NBC
Simon and Simon ep Guessing Game 10.21.82 CBS
Wizards and Warriors ep The Kidnap 3.5.83 CBS
Knight Rider ep Speed Demons 2.12.84 NBC

DENNEHY, BRIAN
SUPP.:
Star of the Family sr 9.30.82 ABC
I Take These Men tf 1.5.83 CBS
Blood Feud tf 4.25 and 5.2.83 OPT
The Mississippi ep 3.13.84 CBS
Cagney and Lacey ep 4.23.84 CBS
Off Sides tf 7.6.84 NBC
Hunter ep Hunter (pt) 9.18.84 NBC
Private Sessions ms 2.24, 2.25, 2.26.85 NBC
Tall Tales ep Annie Oakley 12.20.85 SHO

DENNING, RICHARD
A&C, B.V.:
Cheyenne ep The Black Hawk War 1.24.56 ABC
A&C, Supp. 1:

McCloud ep Cowboy in Paradise 1.20.74 NBC
A&C, Supp. 2:
Hawaii Five-O ep A Capitol Crime 2.17.77 CBS
Hawaii Five-O ep Blood Money Is Hard to Wash 3.3.77 CBS
Hawaii Five-O ep Up the Rebels 9.15.77 CBS

DENNIS, SANDY
SUPP.:
The Execution tf 1.4.85 NBC
The Love Boat ep Out of the Blue 12.7.85 ABC
Alfred Hitchcock Presents ep Arthur 12.15.85 NBC

DENNISON, RACHEL*
9 to 5 sr 3.25.82 ABC
9 to 5 sr ret 9.29.83 ABC

DENVER, BOB
SUPP.:
The Love Boat ep A Dress to Remember 5.8.82 ABC
The Invisible Woman tf/pt 2.13.83 NBC
Fantasy Island ep Love Island 5.14.83 ABC
High School, U.S.A. tf/pt 10.16.83 NBC

DERN, BRUCE
A&C, B.V.:
Branded ep The Wolfers 1.9.66 NBC
SUPP.:
Space ms 4.14, 4.15, 4.16, 4.17, 4.18.85 CBS
Tough Love tf 10.13.85 ABC

DEVANE, WILLIAM
SUPP.:
The Big Easy pt 8.15.82 NBC
Jane Doe tf 3.12.83 CBS
Knots Landing sr 9.28.83 CBS
Knots Landing sr ret 10.4.84 CBS
With Intent to Kill tf 10.24.84 CBS
Knots Landing sr ret 9.26.85 CBS

DeVITO, DANNY*
Starsky and Hutch ep The Collector 12.3.77 ABC
Police Woman ep Death Game 12.21.77 NBC
Taxi sr 9.12.78 ABC
Taxi sr ret 9.11.79 ABC
Taxi sr ret 11.19.80 ABC
Taxi sr ret 10.22.81 ABC
Taxi sr ret 9.30.82 NBC
The CBS Afterschool Special ep All the Kids Do It 4.24.84 CBS
The Ratings Game tf 12.15.84 TMC

DEWHURST, COLLEEN

SUPP.:

Quincy, M.E. ep For Love of Joshua 2.3.82 NBC
You Can't Take It with You comedy sp 5.84 SHO
Finder of Lost Loves ep Echoes 10.27.84 ABC
The Glitter Dome tf 11.18.84 HBO
The Love Boat ep The Death and Life of Sir Albert Demerest 11.24.84 ABC
A.D. ms 3.31, 4.1, 4.2, 4.3, 4.4.85 ABC

DeWINDT, SHEILA*

Baretta ep The Bundle 5.18.78 ABC
Eischied ep Only the Pretty Girls Die 9.21, 9.28.79 NBC
Quincy, M.E. ep TKO 3.13.80 NBC
B.J. and the Bear sr 9.13.81 NBC
McClain's Law ep A Time of Peril 12.4.81 NBC
The New Odd Couple ep That Was No Lady 11.19.82 ABC
The Jeffersons ep 12.12.82 CBS
The Powers of Matthew Star ep Brain Drain 3.4.83 NBC
Webster ep Dreamland 3.9.84 ABC

DeWITT, JOYCE

A&C, Supp. 2:

Baretta ep Sharper Than a Serpent's Tooth 12.17.75 ABC

SUPP.:

Three's Company sr ret 9.28.82 ABC
Three's Company sr ret 9.27.83 ABC
Saturday's the Place comedy sp 9.14.84 CBS
Finder of Lost Loves ep Portraits 12.1.84 ABC

DEY, SUSAN

A&C, Supp. 1:

Hawaii Five-O ep Target? The Lady 10.3.75 CBS

SUPP.:

The Gift of Life tf 3.26.82 CBS
Malibu tf/pt 1.23, 1.24.83 ABC
Emerald Point, N.A.S. sr 9.26.83 CBS
Sunset Limousine tf 10.12.83 CBS

DeYOUNG, CLIFF

SUPP.:

Invasion of Privacy tf 1.12.83 CBS
This Girl for Hire tf/pt 11.1.83 CBS
The Awakening of Candra tf 12.16.83 CBS
Master of the Game ms 12.19, 12.20, 12.21.84 CBS
Deadly Intentions tf 5.19, 5.20.85 ABC
Tall Tales ep Annie Oakley 12.20.85 SHO

DHIEGH, KHIGH

A&C, Supp. 1:

Hawaii Five-O tf 9.20.68 CBS

Hawaii Five-O ep Forty Feet High and It Kills! 10.8.69 CBS
Hawaii Five-O ep A Bullet for McGarrett 10.29.69 CBS
Hawaii Five-O ep F.O.B. in Honolulu 1.27.71, 2.3.71
Hawaii Five-O ep The Jinn Who Clears the Way 12.5.72 CBS
Hawaii Five-O ep Presenting ... In the Center Ring--Murder 12.10.74 CBS
Hawaii Five-O ep Murder--Eyes Only 9.12.75 CBS
Hawaii Five-O ep Nine Dragons 9.30.76 CBS
A&C, Supp. 2:
Hawaii Five-O ep Woe to Wo Fat 4.5.80 CBS
SUPP.:
Matt Houston ep Return to Nam 11.2.84 ABC

DIAMOND, SELMA*
Too Close for Comfort ep The Return of Rafkin 5.12.81 ABC
Too Close for Comfort ep Tenants, Anyone? 12.22.81 ABC
Archie Bunker's Place ep 1.16.82 CBS
Too Close for Comfort ep Brotherly Hate 2.2.82 ABC
Too Close for Comfort ep Break Out the Pampers 9.30.82 ABC
Too Close for Comfort ep Mr. Christmas 12.16.82 ABC
9 to 5 ep The Phantom 5.10.83 ABC
Alice ep 5.22.83 CBS
Trapper John, M.D. ep 10.30.83 CBS
Night Court sr 1.4.84 NBC
Night Court sr ret 9.27.84 NBC
The New Jetsons sr (vo) 9.85 NN

DICKINSON, ANGIE
A&C, B.V.:
Broken Arrow ep The Conspirators 12.18.56 ABC
Restless Gun ep Imposter for a Day 2.17.58 NBC
Colt .45 ep The Deserters 3.28.58 ABC
Man with a Camera ep Close Up on Violence 10.31.58 ABC
SUPP.:
Cassie and Company sr 1.29.82 NBC
One Shoe Makes It Murder tf 11.6.82 CBS
Jealousy tf 1.23.84 ABC
A Touch of Scandal tf 11.27.84 CBS
Hollywood Wives ms 2.17, 2.18, 2.19.85 ABC

DILLMAN, BRADFORD
SUPP.:
King's Crosing sr 1.6.82 ABC
The Legend of Walks Far Woman tf 5.30.82 NBC
Matt Houston ep Stop the Presses 10.3.82 ABC
Falcon Crest ep 10.8.82, 12.17.82, 2.25.83, 3.4.83 CBS
Hotel ep Prisms 3.14.84 ABC
Dynasty ep The Verdict 11.7.84 ABC

Dynasty ep Amanda 11.14.84 ABC
Murder, She Wrote ep Murder to a Jazz Beat 2.3.85 CBS
Hotel ep Lost and Found 2.13.85 ABC
Covenant pt 8.5.85 ABC

DIXON, DONNA
SUPP.:
No Man's Land tf 5.27.84 NBC
Hawaiian Heat ep Andy's Mom 11.23.84 ABC
Berringer's ep Hidden Agenda 3.2.85 NBC
Berringer's ep Maelstrom 3.9.85 NBC

DOBSON, KEVIN
SUPP.:
The CBS Afternoon Playhouse ep Help Wanted 10.12.82 CBS
Knots Landing sr 9.29.83 CBS
Knots Landing sr ret 10.4.84 CBS
Sweet Revenge tf 10.31.84 CBS
Knots Landing sr ret 9.26.85 CBS

DONAHUE, ELINOR
A&C, B.V.:
The George Burns and Gracie Allen Show ep The Newlywed 4.2.56 CBS
The Flying Nun ep My Sister, My Sister Spring 1968 ABC
SUPP.:
The Dukes of Hazzard ep Sound of Music--Hazzard Style 1.8.82 CBS
High School, U.S.A. tf/pt 10.16.83 NBC
Hotel ep Deceptions 11.30.83 ABC
Happy Days ep School Dazed 7.12.84 ABC
The Days of Our Lives sr 10.12.84 NBC
The CBS Schoolbreak Special ep Hear Me Cry 10.16.84 CBS

DONAHUE, TROY
SUPP.:
Matt Houston ep Joey's Here 12.5.82 ABC
Malibu tf/pt 1.23, 1.24.83 ABC

DONNELL, JEFF
A&C, Supp. 1:
Matt Helm sr 9.20.75 ABC
Police Story ep Face for a Shadow 11.7.75 NBC

DOUGLAS, KIRK
SUPP.:
Remembrance of Love tf 12.6.82 NBC
Draw tf 7.15.84 HBO
Amos tf 9.29.85 CBS

DOUGLASS, ROBYN*
The Clone Master tf 9.14.78 NBC
The Girls in the Office tf 2.2.79 ABC
Galactica 1980 sr 1.27.80 ABC
Trapper John, M.D. ep Second Sight 4.5.81 CBS
Golden Gate tf 9.25.81 ABC
Her Life as a Man tf 3.12.84 NBC
Mickey Spillane's Mike Hammer: More Than Murder tf/pt 1.26.85 CBS
Stingray tf/pt 7.14.85 NBC

DOYLE, DAVID
A&C, Supp. 2:
Car 54, Where Are You? ep A Star Is Born in the Bronx 11.25.62 NBC
Car 54, Where Are You? ep The Loves of Sylvia Schnauser 3.30.63 NBC
The Defenders ep The 700-year-old Gang 10.1.64 CBS
For the People ep Dangerous to the Public Peace and Safety 3.21.65 CBS
Storefront Lawyers ep 11.18.70 CBS
McCoy ep Bless the Big Fish 10.5.75 NBC
Police Story ep Vice: Twenty-Four Hours 12.5.75 NBC
SUPP.:
The Love Boat ep The Same Wavelength 10.23.82 ABC
The Blue and the Gray ms 11.14, 11.15, 11.16, 11.17.82 CBS
Fantasy Island ep Naughty Marietta 1.8.83 ABC
Wait Till Your Mother Gets Home tf 1.17.83 NBC
The Invisible Woman tf/pt 2.13.83 NBC
The Love Boat ep Don't Take My Wife, Please 11.26.83 ABC
The Fall Guy ep Wheels 12.21.83 ABC
The Love Boat ep Partners to the End 2.23.85 ABC
Murder, She Wrote ep Sudden Death 3.3.85 CBS

DRAKE, CHARLES
A&C, B.V.:
Wagon Train ep The Sam Livingston Story 6.15.60 NBC
Daniel Boone ep Heroes Welcome 2.22.68 NBC
A&C, Supp. 1:
Harry O ep Mortal Sin 10.3.74 ABC
Switch ep Mistresses, Murder and Millions 12.23.75 CBS

DRAKE, TOM
A&C, B.V.:
Gunsmoke ep Ring of Darkness 12.1.69 CBS
A&C, Supp. 2:
The Eddie Capra Mysteries ep Where There's Smoke 9.22.78 NBC

DRURY, JAMES
A&C, B.V.:

Cameo Theater ep The Grown Ones 7.24.55 NBC
Broken Arrow ep Power 4.22.58 ABC
Alfred Hitchcock Presents ep The Right Kind of House 3.9.58 CBS
Lawman ep Power 4.22.58 ABC
The Rifleman ep The Marshal 10.21.58 ABC
Lawman ep The Gang 3.29.59 ABC
Black Saddle ep Client: Neal Adams 5.9.59 NBC
Wagon Train ep The Bleymeier Story 11.16.60 NBC
Alias Smith and Jones ep The Long Chase 9.16.72 ABC

DRYER, FRED*
The Star Maker tf 5.11, 5.12.81 NBC
The Kid from Nowhere tf 1.4.82 NBC
Force Seven pt 5.23.82 NBC
Something So Right tf 11.30.82 CBS
A Girl's Life pt 8.4.83 NBC
Cheers ep Old Flames 11.17.83 NBC
Cheers ep Sam at Eleven 12.30.83 NBC
The Fantastic World of D.C. Collins tf 10.10.84 NBC
Hart to Hart ep Slam Dunk 3.6.84 ABC
Hunter sr 9.18.84 NBC
Hunter sr ret 3.23.85 NBC
Hunter sr ret 9.21.85 NBC

DuBOIS, JA'NET*
Shaft ep The Killing 10.30.73 CBS
The Blue Knight ms 11.11-11.16.73 NBC
Kojak ep Loser Take All 12.22.74 CBS
Caribe ep Flowers of Death 3.24.75 ABC
Good Times sr 9.21.77 CBS
Good Times sr ret 9.16.78 CBS
Roots: The Next Generation ms 2.18-2.25.79 ABC
Good Times sr ret 5.23.79 CBS
The Love Boat ep Matchmaker, Matchmaker 1.26.80 ABC
Hellinger's Law pt 3.10.81 CBS
The Parkers pt 3.25.81 NBC
The Sophisticated Gents tf 9.29, 9.30, 10.1.81 NBC
The Big Easy pt 8.15.82 NBC
The Tom Swift and Linda Craig Mystery Hour pt 7.3.83 ABC
Spencer ep Spencer (pt) 12.1.84 NBC
Crazy Like a Fox ep Some Day My Prints Will Come 12.1.85 CBS

DuBOIS, MARTA*
Magnum, P.I. ep Memories Are Forever 11.5.81 CBS
Trapper John, M.D. ep Cooperative Care 11.15.81 CBS
McClain's Law ep To Save the Queen 1.8.83 NBC
Shannon ep 4.14.82 CBS
Voyagers ep Agents of Satan 10.31.82 NBC
Grace Kelly tf 2.21.83 ABC

Hardcastle and McCormick ep The Black Widow 10.16.83 ABC
Matt Houston ep The Crying Clown 11.25.83 ABC
Trapper John, M.D. ep 1.8.84 CBS
Riptide ep Double Your Pleasure 4.3.84 NBC
Hawaiian Heat ep Hawaiian Heat (pt) 9.14.84 ABC
The A-Team ep The Bend in the River 9.25.84 NBC
MacGruder and Loud ep The Odds Favor Death 2.5.85 ABC
Generation tf 5.24.85 ABC

DUFF, HOWARD
A&C, B.V.:
Bus Stop ep Door Without a Key 3.4.62 ABC
Burke's Law ep Who Killed Billy Joe? 11.8.63 ABC
A&C, Supp. 2:
The Rockford Files ep There's One in Every Port 1.7.77 NBC
Switch ep Who Killed Lila Craig? 1.6.78 CBS
SUPP.:
The Wild Women of Chastity Gulch tf/pt 10.31.82 ABC
The Love Boat ep The Tomorrow Lady 12.4.82 ABC
St. Elsewhere ep Addiction 5.3.83 NBC
This Girl for Hire tf/pt 11.1.83 CBS
Hotel ep Lifelines 5.9.84 ABC
Murder, She Wrote ep Deadly Lady 10.7.84 CBS
Knots Landing sr (with ep Message in a Bottle) 12.13.84 CBS
Hotel ep Anniversary 2.20.85 ABC
Detective in the House ep Down and Out 3.29.85 CBS
Scarecrow and Mrs. King ep Tail of the Dancing Weasel 10.14.85 CBS
Love on the Run tf 10.21.85 NBC

DUFFY, JULIA*
Love of Life sr 1978 CBS
Lou Grant ep 1.12.81 CBS
Irene pt 8.19.81 NBC
Cheers ep Any Friend of Diane's 11.4.82 NBC
Newhart ep What Is This Thing Called Lust? 1.31.83 CBS
Wizards and Warriors sr 2.26.83 CBS
Simon and Simon ep Room 3502 3.10.83 CBS
Voyagers ep Jack's Back 7.10.83 NBC
Newhart sr 10.17.83 CBS
Newhart sr ret 10.15.84 CBS
The Love Boat ep The Last Heist 11.10.84 ABC
Children in the Crossfire tf 12.3.84 NBC
Hotel ep Hearts and Minds 5.8.85 ABC
Newhart sr ret 9.30.85 CBS

DUFFY, PATRICK
A&C, Supp. 2:
Switch ep The Walking Bomb 1.6.76 CBS
SUPP.:
Dallas sr ret 10.1.82 CBS

Cry for the Strangers tf 12.11.82 CBS
Dallas sr ret 9.30.83 CBS
Dallas sr ret 9.28.84 CBS
Dallas sr ret 9.27.85 CBS
George Burns Comedy Week ep Dream, Dream, Dream 11.6.85 CBS
Alice in Wonderland tf 12.9, 12.10.85 CBS

DUGGAN, ANDREW
A&C, Supp. 2:
Medic ep The Good Samaritan 5.21.56 NBC
Cheyenne ep The Bounty Killer 10.23.56 ABC
Cheyenne ep Land Beyond the Law 1.15.57 ABC
Wire Service ep Confirm Or Deny 5.27.57 ABC
Colt .45 ep The Peacemaker 10.18.57 ABC
Tombstone Territory ep The Epitaph 2.26.58 ABC
Jefferson Drum ep The Cheater 5.23.58 NBC
Cheyenne ep The Angry Sky 6.17.58 ABC
Suspicion ep Eye for Eye 6.23.58 NBC
Tombstone Territory ep Outlaw's Badge 8.6.58 ABC
Colt .45 ep Judgment Day 2.22.59 ABC
77 Sunset Strip ep Mr. Paradise 5.22.59 ABC
Dow Hour of Great Mysteries ep The Cat and the Canary 9.27.60 NBC
77 Sunset Strip ep The Hamlet Caper 1.6.61 ABC
Lawman ep Marked Man 1.22.61 ABC
Maverick ep The Ice Man 1.29.61 ABC
Cheyenne ep The Frightened Town 3.20.61 ABC
77 Sunset Strip ep The Celluloid Cowboy 4.28.61 ABC
77 Sunset Strip ep The Baker Street Caper 3.16.62 ABC
77 Sunset Strip ep Upbeat 6.15.62 ABC
The Dakotas ep Red Sky Over Bismark 1.14.63 ABC
The Travels of Jaimie McPheeters ep Day of the Golden Fleece 10.6.63 ABC
The Lieutenant ep In the Highest Tradition 2.29.64 NBC
Arrest and Trial ep The Black Flower 3.1.64 ABC
Great Adventure ep Kentucky's Bloody Ground 4.10.64 CBS
Greatest Show on Earth ep This Train Doesn't Stop Till It Gets There 4.14.64 ABC
The Bob Hope Chrysler Theater ep The Command 5.22.64 NBC
The DuPont Show of the Week ep Ambassador at Large 6.16.64 NBC
The Alfred Hitchcock Hour ep The McGregor Affair 11.23.64 NBC
Slattery's People ep Do the Ignorant Sleep in Pure White Beds? 11.30.64 CBS
Gunsmoke ep Bad Lady from Brookline 4.24.65 CBS
The Fugitive ep The End Is But the Beginning 1.5.65 ABC
The Big Valley ep Forty Rifles 9.22.65 ABC
Twelve O'Clock High sr 9.65 ABC
The Fugitive ep Shadow of the Swan 2.5.66 ABC

The FBI ep A Bomb That Walked Like a Man 5.1.66 ABC
F Troop ep The New G.I. Spring 1966 ABC
Twelve O'Clock High sr ret 9.66 ABC
The Bob Hope Chrysler Theater ep The 8th Day 12.21.66 NBC
The FBI ep A Question of Guilt 1.22.67 ABC
The Big Valley ep The Haunted Gun 2.6.67 ABC
Cimarron Strip ep The Battleground 9.28.67 CBS
The FBI ep The Traitor 10.15.67 ABC
Cimarron Strip ep The Roarer 11.2.67 CBS
Cimarron Strip ep Without Honor 2.29.68 CBS
Medical Center ep Undercurrent 9.23.70 CBS
Hawaii Five-O ep The Ransom 1.20.71 CBS
Barnaby Jones ep Foul Play 3.31.74 CBS
Switch ep Fade-out 10.14.77 CBS
The Eddie Capra Mysteries ep And the Sea Shall Give Up Her Dead 10.20.78 NBC
Hawaii Five-O ep Use a Gun, Go to Hell 11.29.79 CBS
SUPP.:
The Winds of War ms 2.6-2.13.83 ABC
Hart to Hart ep Bahama Bound Harts 2.22.83 ABC
Hardcastle and McCormick ep The Georgia Street Motors 2.5.84 ABC
Falcon Crest ep Strangers 10.12.84 CBS
Falcon Crest ep The Outcasts 10.19.84 CBS
Matt Houston ep Company Secrets 2.15.85 ABC
Highway to Heaven ep An Investment in Caring 3.13.85 NBC
Glitter ep Fathers and Children 12.20.85 ABC

DUNAWAY, FAYE
SUPP.:
The Country Girl drama sp 5.82 SHO
Ellis Island ms 11.11-11.14.84 CBS
Christopher Columbus tf 5.19 and 5.20.85 CBS
Agatha Christie's "Thirteen at Dinner" tf 10.19.85 CBS
Supergirl--The Making of the Movie sp hos 12.29.85 ABC

DUNNE, DOMINIQUE
SUPP.:
Hart to Hart ep Hart, Line and Sinker 12.27.81 ABC
Fame ep Street Kid 2.25.82 NBC
St. Elsewhere ep (pt/first ep) 10.26.82 NBC
The Quest ep He Stole-A My Art 11.5.82 ABC
Hill Street Blues ep Requiem for a Hairbag 11.18.82 NBC

DURNING, CHARLES
A&C, Supp. 2:
N.Y.P.D. ep Old Gangsters Never Die 10.17.67 ABC
The High Chaparral ep The Reluctant Deputy 3.6.70 NBC
Barnaby Jones ep The Deadly Conspiracy 9.19.75 CBS
Hawaii Five-O ep Retire in Sunny Hawaii ... Forever 11.7.75 CBS

SUPP.:
American Playhouse ep Working 4.13.82 PBS
Mr. Roberts drama sp 3.19.84 NBC
Side By Side pt 7.6.84 ABC
P.O.P. pt 8.29.84 NBC
Eye to Eye sr 3.21.85 ABC
Death of a Salesman tf 9.15.85 CBS
Amazing Stories ep Guilt Trip 12.1.85 NBC

DURYEA, DAN
A&C, B.V.:
Wagon Train ep The Bleymeier Story 11.16.60 NBC
Bewitched ep The Magic Cabin 1.66 ABC
The Bob Hope Chrysler Theater ep Massacre at Fort Phil Kearney 10.26.66 NBC
Monroes ep Gold River 12.14.66 ABC

DUSAY, MARJ*
The Wild Wild West ep The Night of the Turncoat 12.1.67 CBS
Cimarron Strip ep 12.1.67 CBS
Bonanza ep Commitment at Angeles 4.7.68 NBC
Star Trek ep Spock's Brain 9.20.68 NBC
The Wild Wild West ep The Night of the Krakan 11.1.68 CBS
Hawaii Five-O ep The 24 Karat Kill 11.14.68 CBS
The Felony Squad ep Conspiracy of Power 1.10.69, 1.17.69 ABC
Bonanza ep A Ride in the Sun 5.11.69 NBC
Daniel Boone ep Benvenuto ... Who? 10.9.69 NBC
Hawaii Five-O ep The Singapore File 11.19.69 CBS
The Mod Squad ep The Debt 12.30.69 ABC
McCloud ep Who Says You Can't Make Friends in New York City? 9.16.70 NBC
The Most Deadly Game ep Little David 10.10.70 ABC
McCloud ep Man from Taos 10.21.70 NBC
The FBI ep The Impersonator 11.12.70 ABC
The Mod Squad ep The Judas Trap 12.8.70 ABC
The Bold Ones: The Lawyers ep The Loneliest Racket 10.20.70 NBC
The Immortal ep 1.17.71 ABC
Mannix ep A Gathering of Ghosts 2.6.71 CBS
Alias Smith and Jones ep 4.15.71 ABC
The FBI ep Superstition Rock 11.28.71 ABC
Cannon ep Bold Cats and Sudden Death 9.13.72 CBS
Love, American Style ep Love and the Penal Code 9.17.71 ABC
The FBI ep The Wizard 11.12.72 ABC
Climb An Angry Mountain tf 12.23.72 NBC
The FBI ep The Big Job 9.16.73 ABC
Cannon ep Murder by Proxy 10.10.73 CBS
Barnaby Jones ep The Killing Defense 12.2.73 CBS
Mannix ep Mask for a Charade 3.3.74 CBS
Manhunter ep The Doomsday Gang 10.23.74 CBS
The Streets of San Francisco ep Murder by Proxy 10.23.75 ABC

Petrocelli ep Terror by the Book 12.10.75 NBC
Most Wanted tf/pt 3.21.76 ABC
The Bionic Woman ep In This Corner, Jaime Sommers 9.29.76 ABC
Police Story ep Two Frogs on a Mongoose 10.12.76 NBC
The Fantastic Journey ep Beyond the Mountain 2.17.77 NBC
The Hardy Boys Mysteries ep The Disappearing Floor 3.6.77 ABC
Murder in Peyton Place tf 10.3.77 NBC
Barnaby Jones ep Final Judgment 1.26.78 CBS
Sorority '62 pt 1.78 NN
Wheels ms 5.7-5.15.78 NBC
Quincy, M.E. ep No Way to Treat a Body 11.30.78 NBC
Cliffhangers: Stop Susan Williams sr 2.27.79 NBC
The Child Stealer tf 3.9.79 ABC
The Paradise Connection tf 9.17.79 CBS
The Murder That Wouldn't Die tf/pt 3.9.80 NBC
Bret Maverick ep The Yellow Rose 12.22.81 NBC
The Facts of Life ep A Friend in Deed 11.18.81 NBC
Bret Maverick ep Faith, Hope and Charity 4.13, 4.20.82 NBC
Tucker's Witch ep The Curse of the Tolric Death Mask 10.27.82 CBS
The Devlin Connection ep Of Nuns and Other Black Birds 11.13.82 NBC
Square Pegs ep 11.29.82 CBS
Capitol sr 1983 CBS
At Ease ep Computer Dating 3.18.83 ABC
Hart to Hart ep Too Close to Hart 5.3.83 ABC
E/R ep 10.30.84, 11.13.84 CBS
The Facts of Life ep Sisters 3.20.85 NBC
The Facts of Life ep Mother and Daughter 10.26.85 NBC
The Facts of Life ep A Baby for Christmas 12.14.85 NBC

DUSENBERRY, ANN*
Captains and the Kings ms 9.30-11.11.76 NBC
McCloud ep It Was the Fight Before Christmas 12.26.76 NBC
Stonestreet: Who Killed the Centerfold Model? tf/pt 1.16.77 NBC
The Man in the Iron Mask tf/pt 1.17.77 NBC
The Possessed tf 5.1.77 NBC
Eight Is Enough ep 3.22.78 ABC
Little Women tf/pt 10.2, 10.3.78 NBC
Desperate Women tf 10.25.78 NBC
Little Women sr 2.8.79 NBC
The Secret War of Jackie's Girls tf/pt 11.29.80 NBC
Elvis and the Beauty Queen tf 3.1.81 NBC
Killjoy tf 10.22.81 CBS
Magnum, P.I. ep Italian Ice 2.4.82 CBS
Trapper John, M.D. ep Medicine Man 2.21.82 CBS
Seven Brides for Seven Brothers ep 10.6.82 CBS
Family Tree sr 1.22.83 NBC

Confessions of a Married Man tf 1.31.83 ABC
Close Ties drama sp 3.6.83 TEC
Remington Steele ep My Fair Steele 12.6.83 NBC
Simon and Simon ep 12.12.83 CBS
Emerald Point, N.A.S. ep 1.16.84 CBS
He's Not Your Son tf 10.3.84 CBS
Fraud Squad pt 5.17.85 ABC

DUSSAULT, NANCY
A&C, Supp. 2:
The Hallmark Hall of Fame ep A Punt, a Pass and a Prayer 11.20.68 NBC
SUPP.:
Too Close for Comfort sr ret 10.14.82 ABC
Too Close for Comfort sr ret 10.83 NN
The Love Boat ep The Spoonmaker Diamond 11.13.83 ABC
Too Close for Comfort sr ret 10.84 NN
Too Close for Comfort sr ret 10.85 NN

DUVALL, SHELLY
SUPP.:
Faerie Tale Theater sr hos 9.11.82 SHO
Faerie Tale Theater ep Rumpelstiltskin 10.16.82 SHO
Faerie Tale Theater ep Rapunzel 2.5.83 SHO
Faerie Tale Theater sr ret 2.5.83 SHO
Faerie Tale Theater sr ret 4.16.84 SHO
The Secret World of the Very Young sp 9.12.84 CBS
Faerie Tale Theater sr ret 2.12.85 SHO
Tall Tales sr hos 12.20.85 SHO

DZUNDZA, GEORGE
SUPP.:
The Face of Rage tf 3.20.83 ABC
The Lost Honor of Kathryn Beck tf 1.24.84 CBS
When She Says No tf 1.30.84 ABC
The CBS Schoolbreak Special ep All the Kids Do It 4.24.84 CBS
The Rape of Richard Beck tf 5.27.85 ABC
Brotherly Love tf 5.28.85 CBS
The Execution of Raymond Graham drama sp 11.17.85 ABC

- E -

EASTERBROOK, LESLIE*
Aloha Paradise ep 4.15.81 ABC
Laverne and Shirley sr 10.31.81 ABC
The Love Boat ep Kleinschmidt 11.17.81 ABC
Laverne and Shirley sr ret 10.12.82 ABC
The Devlin Connection ep The Absolute Monarch of Ward C

10.30.82 NBC
Fantasy Island ep The Perfect Gentleman 10.30.82 ABC
Ace Crawford, Private Eye ep 3.29.83 CBS
The Love Boat ep The Prize Winner 12.3.83 ABC
The Dukes of Hazzard ep 3.23.84 CBS
Domestic Life ep 3.25.84 CBS
His and Hers pt 5.15.84 CBS
Glitter ep High-Energy Workout 9.20.84 ABC
First and Ten pt 12.11.84 HBO

EASTWOOD, CLINT
A&C, B.V.:
West Point ep White Fury 3.1.57 ABC
Wagon Train ep The Charles Avery Story 11.13.57 NBC
Maverick ep Duel at Sundown 2.1.59 ABC
Rawhide sr ret 9.18.59 CBS
Rawhide sr ret 9.30.60 CBS

EBSEN, BONNIE
A&C, Supp. 2:
The Hardy Boys ep The Haunted House 1.30.77 ABC

EBSEN, BUDDY
A&C, B.V.:
The Tales of Wells Fargo ep Dead Man's Street 4.18.60 NBC
Riverboat ep The Water of Gorgeous Springs 11.7.60 NBC
Hawaii Five-O ep 3,000 Crooked Miles in Honolulu 10.5.71 CBS
Alias Smith and Jones ep What's In It for Mia 2.24.72 ABC
SUPP.:
Hardcastle and McCormick ep Killer B's 11.6.83 ABC
The Love Boat Fall Preview Party sp 9.15.84 ABC
Matt Houston sr 9.21.84 ABC
Finder of Lost Loves ep Old Friends 11.17.84 ABC

EDELMAN, HERB
A&C, Supp. 2:
The Reporter ep How Much for a Prince? 10.9.64 CBS
The Doctors and the Nurses ep The Witnesses 4.27.65 CBS
That Girl ep 11.3.66 ABC
Hey, Landlord! ep The Long, Hot Bus 10.30.66 NBC
Occasional Wife ep 11.22.66 NBC
It's About Time ep The Stone Age Diplomats Spring 1967 CBS
The Girl from UNCLE ep The Furnace Flats Affair 2.21.67 NBC
The Bob Hope Chrysler Theater ep A Song Called Revenge 3.1.67 NBC
The Flying Nun ep Ah Love, Could You and I Conspire? 10.67 ABC
The Bill Cosby Show ep Tobacco Road 2.71 NBC
Police Story ep The Long Ball 2.13.76 NBC
Kojak ep The Pride and the Princess 11.28.76 CBS
SUPP.:

Matt Houston ep Stop the Presses 10.3.82 ABC
9 to 5 sr 10.5.82 ABC
Shooting Stars tf/pt 7.28.83 ABC
Matt Houston ep The Crying Clown 11.25.83 ABC
Trapper John, M.D. ep 1.15.84 CBS
The Love Boat ep Shop Ahoy 2.4.84 ABC
Matt Houston ep Vanished 9.28.84 ABC
Murder, She Wrote ep Murder, She Wrote (pt) 9.30.84 CBS
Cagney and Lacey ep 12.10.84 CBS
St. Elsewhere ep Saving Face 1.16.85 NBC
St. Elsewhere ep Red, White, Black and Blue 2.13.85 NBC
Highway to Heaven ep A Song for Jason 9.18, 9.25.85 NBC
The Golden Girls ep Guess Who's Coming to the Wedding? 9.21.85 NBC
Picking Up the Pieces tf 10.22.85 CBS
Hardcastle and McCormick ep Games People Play 11.11.85 ABC
The Golden Girls ep The Return of Dorothy's Ex 11.30.85 NBC
Cagney and Lacey ep Power 12.16.85 CBS
Crazy Like a Fox ep Year of the Fox 12.29.85 CBS

EDEN, BARBARA
A&C, B.V.:
I Love Lucy ep Country Club Dance 4.22.57 CBS
Bachelor Father ep Bentley and the Revolting Housekeeper Fall 1957 CBS
The Andy Griffith Show ep The Manicurist 1.22.62 CBS
SUPP.:
I Dream of Jeannie: 15 Years Later tf/pt 10.20.85 NBC

EDWARDS, GAIL*
Barnaby Jones ep Girl on the Road 10.25.79 CBS
It's a Living sr 10.30.80 ABC
Blinded By the Light tf 12.16.80 CBS
Making a Living sr 10.24.81 ABC
M*A*S*H ep That's Show Biz 10.26.81 CBS
Knight Rider ep Nobody Does It Better 4.29.83 NBC
Buffalo Bill ep The Interview 1.12.84 NBC
Jennifer Slept Here ep The Tutor Who Came to Dinner 5.5.84 NBC
Benson ep Double Date 11.23.84 ABC
Three's a Crowd ep 1.15.85 ABC
Just Married pt 5.10.85 ABC
J.O.E. and the Colonel tf/pt 9.11.85 ABC
Amazing Stories ep Ghost Train 9.29.85 NBC
It's a Living sr ret 9.29.85 NN

EDWARDS, PADDI*
Rape and Marriage: The Rideout Case tf 10.30.80 CBS
Trapper John, M.D. ep Candy Doctor 3.21.82 CBS
Life of the Party: The Story of Beatrice tf 9.29.82 CBS
Newhart ep 1.3.83 CBS

Wait Till Your Mother Gets Home! tf 1.17.83 NBC
One Cooks, the Other Doesn't tf 9.27.83 CBS
Scarecrow and Mrs. King ep 4.23.84 CBS
Charlie and Company ep 11.6.85 CBS

EDWARDS, VINCE
SUPP.:
Knight Rider ep Knight Rider (pt) 9.26.82 NBC
Cover Up ep Nothing to Lose 10.27.84 CBS
Our Family Honor ep The Mark of Cain 11.29.85 ABC
Our Family Honor ep 12.6.85 ABC

EGGAR, SAMANTHA
SUPP.:
Darkroom ep Exit Line 1.15.82 ABC
Hart to Hart ep Long Lost Love 11.22.83 ABC
Murder, She Wrote ep Hooray for Homicide 10.28.84 CBS
Magnum, P.I. ep Fragments 11.1.84 CBS
Finder of Lost Loves ep Wayward Dreams 1.26.85 ABC
George Burns Comedy Week ep Christmas Carol II: The Sequel 12.11.85 CBS
Hotel ep 12.25.85 ABC

EILBACHER, CYNTHIA (a.k.a. Cindy Eilbacher)
A&C, Supp. 2:
Many Happy Returns ep 11.18.64 CBS
Laredo ep Rendezvous at Arillo 10.7.65 NBC
Please Don't Eat the Daisies ep 10.29.66 NBC
Shazam ep 9.20.75 CBS
SUPP.:
Otherworld sp Paradise Lost 2.9.85 CBS

EILBACHER, LISA
A&C, Supp. 2:
The Streets of San Francisco ep Dead or Alive 10.21.76 ABC
SUPP.:
Simon and Simon ep Earth to Stacey 2.9.82 CBS
Simon and Simon ep Sometimes Dreams Come True 12.2.82 CBS
The Winds of War tf 2.6-2.13.83 ABC
Ryan's Four sr 4.6.83 ABC
Feel the Heat pt 8.5.83 ABC
Me and Mom sr 4.5.85 ABC

EILBER, JANET*
This Is Kate Bennett tf/pt 5.28.82 ABC
Two Marriages sr 8.31.83 ABC
Two Marriages sr ret 3.8.84 ABC
The Best Times sr 4.19.85 NBC

EISENMANN, IKE
SUPP.:
Dreams Don't Die tf 5.21.82 ABC

T.J. Hooker ep The Fast Lane 1.8.83 ABC
Voyagers ep Sneak Attack 2.20.83 NBC
Scene of the Crime ep Education in Murder 4.14.85 NBC
Buchanan High School sr 10.85 NN

EKLAND, BRITT
<u>SUPP.</u>:
The Love Boat ep Safety Last 1.2.82 ABC
Fantasy Island ep Wuthering Heights 1.9.82 ABC
Matt Houston ep Deadly Fashion 10.17.82 ABC
Fantasy Island ep The Sisters 5.14.83 ABC
The Fall Guy ep Always Say Always 2.22.84 ABC
Simon and Simon ep Love and/or Marriage 10.3.85 CBS

ELAM, JACK
<u>A&C, Supp. 2</u>:
The Tales of Wells Fargo ep The Hijackers 6.17.57 NBC
Restless Gun ep Hornita's Town 2.10.58 NBC
Lawman ep The Deputy 10.5.58 ABC
The Rifleman ep Duel of Honor 11.11.58 ABC
Tombstone Territory ep Day of the Amnesty 4.3.59 ABC
Have Gun--Will Travel ep Hunt the Man Down 4.25.59 CBS
Lawman ep The Senator 5.17.59 ABC
The Rifleman ep Tension 10.27.59 ABC
Richard Diamond ep One Dead Cast 12.28.59 CBS
Tightrope ep Broken Rope 1.12.60 CBS
Gunsmoke ep Where'd They Go? 3.12.60 CBS
The Rifleman ep Shotgun Man 4.12.60 ABC
Sugarfoot ep Toothy Thompson 1.16.61 ABC
Klondike ep Queen of the Klondike 1.30.61 NBC
Gunsmoke ep Love Thy Neighbor 1.28.61 CBS
Gunslinger ep The Hostage Fort 2.16.61 CBS
Sugarfoot ep Angel 3.6.61 ABC
Americans ep The Go 4.3.61 NBC
The Rebel ep Helping Hand 4.30.61 ABC
Lawman ep The Four 10.1.61 ABC
Have Gun--Will Travel ep One, Two, Three 2.17.62 ABC
Ben Casey ep The Night That Nothing Happened 10.8.62 ABC
Cheyenne ep A Man Called Ragan (pilot for "The Dakotas") 4.23.62 ABC
The Dakotas sr 1.7.63 ABC
Gunsmoke ep Orval Ball 5.23.64 CBS
Cheyenne ep The Durango Brothers 9.14.62 ABC
Laramie ep Gun Duel 12.25.62 NBC
Gunsmoke ep Help Me, Kitty 11.7.64 CBS
F Troop ep Dirge for the Scourge 10.19.65 ABC
Gunsmoke ep Clayton Thaddeus Greenwood 10.2.65 CBS
Gunsmoke ep Malachi 11.13.65 CBS
Gunsmoke ep My Father, My Son 4.23.66 CBS
Hondo ep The Rebel Hat 12.29.67 ABC
Cimarron Strip ep Big Jessie 2.8.68 CBS

Gunsmoke ep The First People 2.19.68 CBS
The High Chaparral ep North to Tucson 11.8.68 NBC
Gunsmoke ep The Sisters 12.29.69 CBS
Gunsmoke ep Murdock 2.8.71 CBS
Alias Smith and Jones ep Bad Night in Big Butte 3.2.72 ABC
SUPP.:
Sawyer and Finn pt 4.22.83 NBC
Scrooge's Rock 'n' Roll Christmas sp 12.2.84 NN
Detective in the House sr 3.15.85 CBS

ELCAR, DANA
A&C, Supp. 2:
Naked City ep Strike a Statue 5.16.62 ABC
DuPont Show of the Week ep Big Deal in Laredo 10.7.62 NBC
The Doctors and the Nurses ep The Black Candles 11.22.62 CBS
Naked City ep A Man Without a Skin 2.6.63 ABC
Car 54, Where Are You? ep The Star Boarder 2.10.63 NBC
The Defenders ep The Captive 10.22.63 CBS
The Hallmark Hall of Fame ep The Patriots 11.15.63 NBC
The Nurses ep To Spend, to Give, to Want 12.12.63 CBS
The Defenders ep All the Silent Voices 2.1.64 CBS
The Doctors and the Nurses ep The Suspect 9.29.64, 10.6.64 CBS
The Patty Duke Show ep The Best Date in Town 12.9.64 ABC
The Defenders ep The Objector 2.11.65 CBS
The Doctors and the Nurses ep The Unweeded Garden 5.11.65 CBS
Hawk ep Thanks for the Honeymoon 9.22.66 ABC
N.Y.P.D. ep Shakedown 9.5.67 ABC
Judd, For the Defense ep Weep the Hunter Home 11.8.68 ABC
Get Smart ep And Baby Makes Four 11.69 NBC
Hawaii Five-O ep 2.25.70, 3.4.70 CBS
The Storefront Lawyers ep The Electric Kid 10.7.70 CBS
Room 222 ep The Lincoln Story 10.7.70 ABC
Alias Smith and Jones ep Stagecoach 7 3.11.71 ABC
Sarge ep John Michael O'Flaherty Presents the Eleven O'Clock War 11.2.71 NBC
Ironside ep The Savage Sentry 9.21.72 NBC
Alias Smith and Jones ep Only Three to a Bed 1.13.73 ABC
Baretta sr 1.17.75 ABC
The Rockford Files ep The Great Blue Lake Land and Development Company 10.17.75 NBC
The Six Million Dollar Man ep Nightmare in the Sky 9.26.76 ABC
Police Story ep Trial Board 1.4.77 NBC
SUPP.:
Washington Mistress tf 1.13.82 CBS
Code Red ep My Life Is Yours 1.17.82 ABC
The Day the Bubble Burst tf 2.7.82 NBC
Falcon Crest ep The Candidate 2.26.82 CBS
Falcon Crest ep Heir Apparent 3.19.82 CBS

Herbie, the Love Bug ep Calling Dr. Herbie 4.14.82 CBS
Teachers Only ep The Make-up Test 5.12.82 NBC
Forbidden Love tf 10.18.82 CBS
Inspector Perez pt 1.8.83 NBC
Newhart ep 1.17.83 CBS
Trapper John, M.D. ep Pasts Imperfect 2.20.83 CBS
Voyagers ep Sneak Attack 2.20.83 NBC
I Want to Live tf 5.9.83 ABC
Small and Frye ep 6.8.83 CBS
Seven Brides for Seven Brothers ep 9.22.83 CBS
Knight Rider ep Merchants of Death 10.16.83 NBC
Hart to Hart ep Pandora Has Wings 10.25.83 ABC
Quarterback Princess tf 12.3.83 CBS
Hardcastle and McCormick ep The Georgia Street Motors 2.5.84 ABC
Matt Houston ep Death Match 2.24.84 ABC
The Fall Guy ep Terror U 10.17.84 ABC
The A-Team ep Double Heat 10.23.84 NBC
Scarecrow and Mrs. King ep Spiderweb 1.14.85 CBS
Hill Street Blues ep Washington Deceased 2.7.85 NBC
Riptide ep Arrivederci Baby 5.17.85 NBC
MacGyver ep (pt/first ep) 9.29.85 ABC
Tough Love tf 10.13.85 ABC
MacGyver ep 12.15.85 ABC
Trapper John, M.D. ep Billboard Barney 12.29.85 CBS

ELSON, ANDREA*
The Whiz Kids sr 10.5.83 CBS
Simon and Simon ep 10.27.83 CBS
Silver Spoons ep Promises, Promises 9.22.85 NBC

ELVIRA see PETERSON, Cassandra

ELY, RON
SUPP.:
Fantasy Island ep Save Sherlock Holmes 2.6.82 ABC
The Love Boat ep Live It Up 2.20.82 ABC
The Love Boat ep Off-Course Romance 2.19.83 ABC
Fantasy Island ep A Date with Burt 3.5.83 ABC
Matt Helm ep A Deadly Parlay 4.10.83 ABC
Hotel ep Charades 10.19.83 ABC
Fantasy Island ep Ambitious Lady 1.7.84 ABC

ENGEL, GEORGIA
SUPP.:
The Love Boat ep Meet the Author 3.27.82 ABC
Fantasy Island ep Touch and Go 3.19.83 ABC
Jennifer Slept Here sr 10.21.83 NBC

ERICKSON, LEIF
A&C, B.V.:
Branded ep Barbed Wire 2.13.66 NBC

The Bob Hope Chrysler Theater ep Guilty or Not Guilty 3.9.66 NBC
Harry O ep The Admiral's Lady 9.19.74 ABC
Movin' On ep The Old South Will Rise Again 1.6.76 NBC
SUPP.:
Savage in the Orient pt 6.21.83 CBS
Fantasy Island ep Goin' On Home 1.7.84 ABC

ERICSON, DEVON
SUPP.:
Knight Rider ep Deadly Maneuvers 10.1.82 NBC
The A-Team ep West Coast Turnaround 4.5.83 NBC
Hotel ep Memories 2.29.84 ABC
The Mystic Warrior tf 5.20, 5.21.84 ABC
The Love Boat ep Don't Get Mad, Get Even 11.17.84 ABC
Airwolf ep Dambreakers 3.16.85 CBS
Hunter ep Guilty 4.13.85 NBC
Trapper John, M.D. ep Just Around the Coroner 10.27.85 CBS
Airwolf ep Kingdom Come 11.2.85 CBS

ERICSON, JOHN
SUPP.:
One Day at a Time ep Meow, Meow 3.28.82 CBS
Knight Rider ep The Topaz Connection 1.28.83 NBC
The A-Team ep Till Death Do Us Part 4.19.83 NBC
Robert Kennedy and His Times ms 1.27-1.30.84 CBS
Automan ep Death By Design 4.2.84 ABC
Airwolf ep Fallen Angel 11.3.84 CBS
Detective in the House ep Whatever Happened to...? 3.15.85 CBS

ESTRADA, ERIK
A&C, Supp. 2:
Hawaii Five-O ep Engaged to Be Buried 2.27.73 CBS
Baretta ep Dead Man Out 3.3.76 ABC
SUPP.:
CHiPs sr ret 10.1.82 NBC
Honeyboy tf 10.17.82 NBC
Grandpa, Will You Run with Me? sp 4.3.83 NBC

EVANS, LINDA
A&C, Supp. 2:
The Adventures of Ozzie and Harriet ep 1961 ABC
The Eleventh Hour ep Where Ignorant Armies Clash By Night 3.22.63 NBC
The Lieutenant ep The Two-Star Grant 10.5.63 NBC
Wagon Train ep 2.14.65 ABC
SUPP.:
The Love Boat ep The Role Model 11.13.82 ABC
Dynasty sr ret 10.27.82 ABC
Dynasty sr ret 9.28.83 ABC

The Love Boat ep Dear Roberta 10.1.83 ABC
Kenny Rogers as the Gambler: The Adventure Continues 11.28, 11.29.83 CBS
The Love Boat Fall Preview Party sp 9.15.84 ABC
Dynasty sr ret 9.26.84 ABC
Dynasty sr ret 9.15.85 ABC

EVERETT, CHAD
SUPP.:
Malibu tf/pt 1.23, 1.24.83 ABC
The Rousters sr 10.1.83 NBC
The Rousters sr ret 6.9.84 NBC

EVERS, JASON
A&C, Supp. 1:
Perry Mason ep The Case of the Difficult Detour 3.25.61 CBS
Gunsmoke ep Reprisal 3.10.62 CBS
Tales of Wells Fargo ep Remember the Yazoo 4.14.62 NBC
Gunsmoke ep 10.20.62 CBS
Channing sr 9.18.63 ABC
Gunsmoke ep Cornelia Conrad 6.7.64 CBS
Gunsmoke ep Innocence 12.12.64 CBS
Branded ep The Test 2.7.65 NBC
The Big Valley ep The Odyssey of Jubal Tanner 10.13.65 ABC
The FBI ep The Problem of the Honorable Wife 10.31.65 ABC
The FBI ep Flight to Harbin 2.27.66 ABC
The Big Valley ep Death Town 10.28.68 ABC
Hawaii Five-O ep All the King's Horses 11.26.69 CBS
Hawaii Five-O ep Cloth of Gold 2.8.72 CBS
Switch ep Come Die with Me 1.27.76 CBS
A&C, Supp. 2:
The Rockford Files ep Requiem for a Funny Box 11.4.77 NBC
Hawaii Five-O ep Good Help Is Hard to Find 11.1.79 CBS
SUPP.:
The Fall Guy ep Spaced Out 2.16.83 ABC
Small and Frye ep 3.14.83 CBS
T.J. Hooker ep Hot Property 2.25.84 ABC
Knight Rider ep Halloween Knight 10.28.84 NBC
Scarecrow and Mrs. King ep Charity Begins at Home 10.29.84 CBS
The A-Team ep Road Games 2.5.85 NBC
Murder, She Wrote ep My Johnnie Lies Over the Ocean 2.10.85 CBS

EVIGAN, GREG
SUPP.:
Fame ep Relationships 1.6.83 NBC
Masquerade sr 12.22.83 ABC
The Yellow Rose ep Debt of Honor 3.17.84 NBC
Scene of the Crime pt 9.30.84 NBC
Private Sessions tf 3.18.85 NBC

EWELL, TOM
SUPP.:
Trapper John, M.D. ep 11.28.82 CBS

- F -

FABARES, SHELLEY
A&C, B.V.:
The Donna Reed Show ep The Daughter Complex 10.64 ABC
A&C, Supp. 1:
The Rockford Files ep Caledonia--It's Worth a Fortune! 12.6.74 NBC
SUPP.:
One Day at a Time ep The Not So Silent Partner 1.10.82 CBS
One Day at a Time ep 2.7.82 CBS
One Day at a Time ep Meow, Meow 3.28.82 CBS
One Day at a Time ep Orville and Family Strike Back 5.2.82 CBS
One Day at a Time sr 10.24.82 CBS
The Love Boat ep Sly as a Fox 1.15.83 ABC
Matt Houston ep The Visitors 2.27.83 ABC
The ABC Afterschool Special ep The Celebrity and the Arcade Kid 11.9.83 ABC
Memorial Day tf 11.27.83 CBS
One Day at a Time sr ret 12.25.83 CBS
His and Hers pt 5.15.84 CBS
The Love Boat ep Her Honor, the Mayor 1.26.85 ABC
An American Portrait ep Dr. Ernest Burgess 3.7.85 CBS
Suburban Beat pt 8.17.85 NBC
Wonderworks ep The Canterville Ghost 11.17.85 PBS

FABRAY, NANETTE
SUPP.:
One Day at a Time ep 1.17.82, 2.7.82, 5.9.82, 5.16.82 CBS
One Day at a Time sr 10.3.82 CBS
Hotel ep Charades 10.19.83 ABC

FAIRBANKS JR., DOUGLAS
SUPP.:
An American Portrait ep Frank C. Laubach 2.1.85 CBS

FAIRCHILD, MORGAN
A&C, Supp. 2:
Switch ep Downshift 9.30.77 CBS
SUPP.:
Magnum, P.I. ep 10.7.82 CBS
Simon and Simon ep 10.7.82 CBS
Honeyboy tf 10.17.82 NBC

Time Bomb tf 3.25.84 NBC
The Zany Adventures of Robin Hood tf 5.22.84 CBS
The Love Boat Fall Preview Party sp 9.15.84 ABC
Paper Dolls sr 9.23.84 ABC
Falcon Crest sr 10.4.85 CBS
North and South ms 11.3-11.11.85 ABC

FALK, PETER
A&C, B.V.:
Have Gun--Will Travel ep The Poker Friend 11.12.60 CBS
The DuPont Show of the Week ep A Sound of Hunting 5.24.62 NBC

FARACY, STEPHANIE*
Laverne and Shirley ep The Dancing Contest Fall 1976 ABC
Bumpers pt 5.16.77 NBC
The Fighting Nightingales pt 1.16.78 CBS
The Last Resort sr 9.19.79 CBS
Visions ep It's the Willingness 1.19.80 PBS
Trapper John, M.D. ep Have I Got a Girl for You 2.1.81 CBS
Stephanie pt 9.8.81 CBS
Private Benjamin ep Judy's Cousin 1.10.83 CBS
The Thorn Birds ms 3.27, 3.28, 3.29, 3.30.83 ABC
Goodnight, Beantown sr 10.2.83 CBS
Carpool tf 10.5.83 CBS
Fantasy Island ep The Other Man--Mr. Roarke 10.8.83 ABC
Mama Malone ep 3.14.84 CBS
The Love Boat ep Honey Beats the Odds 10.13.84 ABC
Eye to Eye sr 3.21.85 ABC
Space ms 4.14, 4.15, 4.16, 4.17, 4.18.85 CBS
Goldie and the Bears pt 5.26.85 ABC

FARENTINO, JAMES
A&C, B.V.:
Alfred Hitchcock Presents ep Black Curtain 11.15.62 CBS
SUPP.:
Something So Right tf 11.30.82 CBS
The Cradle Will Fall tf 5.24.83 CBS
License to Kill tf 1.10.84 CBS
Blue Thunder sr 4.16.84 ABC
A Summer to Remember tf 3.27.85 CBS
Mary sr 12.11.85 CBS

FARGAS, ANTONIO
SUPP.:
The Ambush Murders tf 1.5.82 CBS
Paper Dolls tf/pt 5.24.82 ABC
Hardcastle and McCormick ep Once Again with Vigorish 10.30.83 ABC
A Good Sport tf 2.8.84 CBS

FARR, JAMIE

A&C, Supp. 1:

The Dick Van Dyke Show ep Sally and the Lab Technician 10.17.61 CBS

The Dick Van Dyke Show ep Washington Vs. the Bunny 10.24.61 CBS

The Dick Van Dyke Show ep Sally Is a Girl 12.19.61 CBS

Gomer Pyle, USMC ep Gomer Pyle, P.O.W. 12.24.65 CBS

The Andy Griffith Show ep The Gypsies 2.21.66 CBS

Toma ep Indictment 4.26.74 ABC

SUPP.:

M*A*S*H sr ret 10.25.82 CBS

AfterMASH sr 9.26.83 CBS

AfterMASH sr ret 9.25.84 CBS

The Love Boat ep Youth Takes a Holiday 10.15.83 ABC

For Love or Money tf 11.20.84 CBS

The New Love, American Style ep Love and the Second Honeymoon 12.23.85 ABC

FARRELL, MIKE

SUPP.:

Prime Suspect tf 1.10.82 CBS

M*A*S*H sr ret 10.25.82 CBS

Memorial Day tf 11.27.83 CBS

Choices of the Heart tf 12.5.83 NBC

An American Portrait ep David Rothenberg 10.23.84 CBS

Private Sessions tf/pt 3.18.85 NBC

FARRELL, SHARON

A&C, B.V.:

Arrest and Trial ep Onward and Upward 1.19.64 ABC

Wagon Train ep The Pearlie Garnet Story 2.24.64 ABC

Gunsmoke ep Scott Free 5.2.64 CBS

Burke's Law ep Who Killed The Surf Board? 9.16.64 ABC

A&C, Supp. 1:

Chase ep Remote Control 2.27.74 NBC

Harry O ep For the Love of Money 1.16.75 ABC

The Six Million Dollar Man ep Stranger in Broken Fork 3.30.75 ABC

A&C, Supp. 2:

Switch ep Butterfly Mourning 2.6.77 CBS

Hawaii Five-O ep A Capitol Crime 2.17.77 CBS

SUPP.:

Hart to Hart ep Harts at High Noon 11.9.82 ABC

Small and Frye ep 3.21.83 CBS

The Mississippi ep 11.22.83 CBS

Rituals sr 9.84 NN

FAWCETT, FARRAH (a.k.a. Farrah Fawcett-Majors)

A&C, Supp. 1:

I Dream of Jeannie ep See You in C-U-B-A 11.69 NBC

I Dream of Jeannie ep My Sister, the Homemaker 12.8.69 NBC
The Flying Nun ep Armando and the Pool Table 1.70 ABC
The Girl with Something Extra ep How Green Was Las Vegas 10.73 NBC
Apple's Way ep The First Love 10.13.74 CBS
Harry O ep APB Harry Orwell 11.6.75 ABC
SUPP.:
Red Light Sting tf 4.5.84 CBS
The Burning Bed tf 10.8.84 NBC

FEE, MELINDA*
Caribe ep The Assassin 5.5.75 ABC
The Invisible Man tf/pt 5.6.75 NBC
The Invisible Man sr 9.8.75 NBC
Quincy, M.E. ep An Unfriendly Romance 4.29.77 NBC
The Bionic Woman ep Fem Bots in Las Vegas 9.24, 10.1.77 NBC
Dallas ep The Return of Ellie's Brother 1.7.79 CBS
The Aliens Are Coming tf/pt 3.2.80 NBC
Vegas ep A Christmas Story 12.17.80 NBC
Flamingo Road ep The Election 2.10.81 NBC
Casablanca ep The Cashier and the Belly Dancer 8.27.83 NBC
Knight Rider ep Custom Knight 11.13.83 NBC
A Good Sport tf 2.8.84 CBS
Three's a Crowd ep The Happy Couple 10.9.84 ABC

FELDON, BARBARA
SUPP.:
The ABC Afterschool Special ep The Unforgivable Secret 2.10.82 ABC

FELDSHUH, TOVAH
SUPP.:
Airwolf ep Fight Like a Dove 3.10.84 CBS
The Love Boat ep Call Me a Doctor 10.6.84 ABC
The Equalizer ep Desperately 12.4.85 CBS

FELL, NORMAN
A&C, Supp. 2:
Perry Mason ep The Case of the Mythical Monkeys 2.27.60 CBS
The Tom Ewell Show ep 12.27.60 CBS
The Tab Hunter Show ep Me and My Shadow 2.19.61 NBC
Peter Gunn ep A Kill and a Half 2.20.61 NBC
Malibu Run ep The Rainbow Adventure 4.26.61 CBS
Checkmate ep Hot Wind in a Cold Town 6.10.61 CBS
87th Precinct sr 9.25.61 NBC
Cain's Hundred ep Final Judgment 12.19.61 NBC
The Eleventh Hour ep Five Moments Out of Time 3.6.63 NBC
The Lloyd Bridges Show ep Gym in January 3.11.63 CBS
Mystery Theater ep Go Look at Roses 9.11.63 NBC
The Lieutenant ep Cool of the Evening 9.21.63 NBC
Kraft Suspense Theater ep 10.10, 10.17.63 NBC

East Side/West Side ep Not Bad for Openers 11.18.63 CBS
Alfred Hitchcock Presents ep The Dividing Wall 12.10.63 CBS
Ben Casey ep I'll Get on My Icefloe and Wave Goodbye 1.8.64 ABC
The Defenders ep Moment of Truth 3.21.64 CBS
Suspense ep I, Bradford Charles 4.8.64 CBS
Ben Casey ep Where Does the Boomerang Go? 1.16.65 ABC
The Fugitive ep May God Have Mercy 3.16.65 ABC
Mr. Novak ep And Then I Wrote 4.20.65 NBC
Dr. Kildare ep A Reverence of Life 4.29.65 NBC
Dr. Kildare ep Farmers and Daughters 11.22.65 NBC
Dr. Kildare ep A Gift of Love 11.29.65 NBC
The FBI ep All the Streets Are Silent 11.28.65 ABC
Dr. Kildare ep Going Home 11.30.65 NBC
The Fugitive ep Stranger in the Mirror 12.7.65 ABC
Twelve O'Clock High ep The All-American 10.28.66 ABC
Bewitched ep I'd Rather Twitch Than Fight 11.66 ABC
The Bob Hope Chrysler Theater ep Dear Deductible 11.9.66 NBC
The FBI ep The Mercenary 4.29.68 ABC
Judd, For the Defense ep Sound of the Plastic Axe 10.25.68 ABC
The Name of the Game ep A Hard Case of the Blues 9.26.69 NBC
Switch ep Gaffing the Skim 11.16.76 CBS
Police Story ep One of Our Cops Is Missing 3.1.77 NBC
SUPP.:
Teachers Only sr 4.4.82 NBC
Matt Houston ep Joey's Here 12.5.82 ABC
Uncommon Valor tf 1.22.83 CBS
Teachers Only sr ret 2.12.83 NBC
The Jesse Owens Story tf 7.9, 7.16.84 NN
Murder, She Wrote ep Dead Heat 11.24.85 CBS
Crazy Like a Fox ep Some Day My Prints Will Come 12.1.85 CBS
Simon and Simon ep Facets 12.26.85 CBS

FENMORE, TANYA*
Tucker's Witch ep The Good Witch of Laurel Canyon 10.6.82 CBS
Love, Sidney ep Show Biz Names 4.4.83 NBC
Family Ties ep Batter Up 11.30.83 NBC
Mama's Family ep Mama's Birthday 3.17.84 NBC
Newhart ep 1.14.85 CBS
Trapper John, M.D. ep 2.3.85 CBS
Tales from the Darkside ep The Trouble with Mary Jane 11.23.85 NN

FERDIN, PAMELYN*
The John Forsythe Show sr 9.13.65 NBC
Star Trek ep And the Children Shall Be Saved 10.11.68 NBC

The High Chaparral ep No Bugles, No Women 3.14.69 NBC
The High Chaparral ep For the Love of Carlos 4.4.69 NBC
Daughter of the Mind tf 12.9.69 ABC
The Forgotten Man tf 9.14.71 ABC
Marcus Welby, M.D. ep A Portrait of Debbie 9.21.71 ABC
Lassie sr 10.6.71 NN
The Odd Couple ep 12.1.77 ABC
The Odd Couple ep 2.11.72 ABC
The Delphi Bureau tf/pt 3.6.72 ABC
The Paul Lynde Show sr 9.13.72 ABC
Marcus Welby, M.D. ep The Tall Tree 11.6.73 ABC
Love Story ep Mirabelle's Summer 11.7.73 NBC
A Tree Grows in Brooklyn tf/pt 3.27.74 NBC
Apple's Way ep The Flag 11.17.74 CBS
Miles to Go Before I Sleep tf 1.8.75 CBS
CHiPs ep 1.12.75 NBC
Baretta ep The Runaway 2.16.77 ABC
Space Academy sr 9.10.77 CBS
Space Academy sr ret 9.16.78 CBS
Vegas ep Serve, Volley and Kill 12.20.78 ABC
Project UFO ep Sighting 4026 12.28.78 NBC
240-Robert ep 240-Robert (pt) 8.28.79 ABC

FERRER, JOSE
SUPP.:
Quincy, M.E. ep Ghost of a Chance 10.6.82 NBC
Another World sr 1.83 NBC
Blood Feud 4.25, 5.2.83 OPT
This Girl for Hire tf/pt 11.1.83 CBS
Fantasy Island ep Random Choices 12.3.83 ABC
Hotel ep Passages 1.18.84 ABC
Samson and Delilah tf 4.1.84 ABC
George Washington ms 4.8, 4.9, 4.10, 4.11.84 CBS
Murder, She Wrote ep Death Casts a Spell 12.30.84 CBS
Hitler's SS: Portrait in Evil tf 2.17.85 NBC
Newhart ep 2.25.85 CBS
Seduced tf 3.12.85 CBS
Covenant tf/pt 8.5.85 NBC
The Love Boat ep The Art Lover 10.19.85 ABC
Newhart ep Lock, Stock and Noodlehead 11.11.85 CBS

FERRER, MEL
SUPP.:
Falcon Crest ep Ultimate Answers 4.9, 4.16.82 CBS
Falcon Crest sr 10.8.82 CBS
One Shoe Makes It Murder tf 11.6.82 CBS
Hotel ep Resolutions 10.24.84 ABC
Finder of Lost Loves ep Forgotten Melodies 12.22.84 ABC
Seduced tf 3.12.85 CBS
Murder, She Wrote ep Will No One Weep for Me? 9.29.85 CBS
The Love Boat ep The Villa 11.2.85 ABC

Glitter ep 12.18.85 ABC
Hotel ep 12.18.85 ABC

FERRIGNO, LOU*
The Incredible Hulk tf/pt 11.4.77 CBS
The Incredible Hulk sr 3.10.78 CBS
The Incredible Hulk sr ret 9.22.78 CBS
The Incredible Hulk sr ret 9.21.79 CBS
The Incredible Hulk sr ret 11.7.80 CBS
The Fall Guy ep License to Kill 1.13, 1.20.82 ABC
Trauma Center sr 9.22.83 ABC
The Fall Guy ep Trauma 9.28.83 ABC
Matt Houston ep Blood Ties 3.2.84 ABC
Mickey Spillane's Mike Hammer ep Catfight 10.20.84 CBS
Night Court ep The Battling Bailiff 2.7.85 NBC

FIELDS, KIM*
Baby, I'm Back pt 10.22.77 CBS
Baby, I'm Back sr 1.30.78 CBS
Good Times ep 12.13.78 CBS
The Facts of Life sr 8.24.79 NBC
The Facts of Life sr ret 3.12.80 NBC
The Facts of Life sr ret 11.19.80 NBC
The Facts of Life sr ret 10.28.81 NBC
Diff'rent Strokes ep First Day Blues 11.5.81 NBC
Diff'rent Strokes ep The Team 11.19.81 NBC
The Facts of Life Goes to Paris tf 9.25.82 NBC
The Facts of Life sr ret 10.6.82 NBC
The Facts of Life sr ret 9.21.83 NBC
The Facts of Life sr ret 9.26.84 NBC
Pryor's Place ep 12.1.84 CBS
The Facts of Life sr ret 9.14.85 NBC

FISHER, CARRIE*
Come Back, Little Sheba tf 12.31.77 NBC
Leave Yesterday Behind tf 5.14.78 ABC
Laverne and Shirley ep The Playboy Show 11.9.82 ABC
Classic Creatures: Return of the Jedi sp hos 11.21.83 CBS
Frankenstein sp 6.84 SHO
Faerie Tale Theater ep Thumbelina 6.11.84 SHO
George Burns Comedy Week ep The Couch 10.16.85 CBS

FISHER, GAIL
<u>SUPP.</u>:
Knight Rider ep Short Notice 5.6.83 NBC

FITZGERALD, GERALDINE
<u>A&C, B.V.</u>:
Alfred Hitchcock Presents ep A Woman's Help 3.28.61 NBC
<u>SUPP.</u>:
Dixie: Changing Habits tf 2.16.83 CBS

Kennedy ms 11.20-11.22.83 NBC
Oh Madeline ep My Mother the Carnal 1.31.84 ABC
St. Elsewhere ep Attack 2.22.84 NBC
Trapper John, M.D. ep 3.3.85 CBS
Cagney and Lacey ep 3.11.85 CBS
Do You Remember Love? tf 5.21.85 CBS
The Hitchhiker ep W.G.O.D. 11.26.85 HBO

FLANAGAN, FIONNUALA
A&C, Supp. 2:
Police Story ep The Company Man 12.19.75 NBC
Movin' On ep Love, Death, and Laura Brown 12.23.75 NBC
Kojak ep The Condemned 1.11.77 CBS
SUPP.:
Benson ep Sweet Irish Rose 2.12.82 ABC
Voyagers ep The Voyagers of the Titanic 2.27.83 NBC
Through Naked Eyes tf 12.11.83 ABC
Simon and Simon ep 1.5.84 CBS
Scorned and Swindled tf 10.9.84 CBS
The Ewok Adventure tf 11.25.84 ABC
Riptide ep Peter Pan Is Alive and Well 12.11.84 NBC
Cagney and Lacey ep The Clinic 11.11.85 CBS

FLYNN, MIRIAM*
Maggie sr 10.24.81 ABC
Mr. Success pt 6.23.84 NBC
Night Court ep The Computer Kid 11.1.84 NBC
Silver Spoons ep 'Twas the Night Before Christmas 12.16.84 NBC
Webster ep The Uh-oh Feeling 1.25.85 ABC
Riptide ep Robin and Marian 12.3.85 NBC

FOCH, NINA
SUPP.:
Trapper John, M.D. ep 1.8.84 CBS
Shadow Chasers sr 11.14.85 ABC

FOLLOWS, MEGAN*
The Baxters sr 9.79 NN
The Mating Season tf 12.30.80 CBS
Jo's Cousins pt 4.14.82 NBC
Domestic Life sr 1.4.84 CBS
Wonderworks ep Jen's Place 1.21.85 PBS
Hockey Night tf 4.1.85 HBO

FONDA, JANE
SUPP.:
9 to 5 ep The Security Guard 10.12.82 ABC
The Dollmaker tf 5.13.84 ABC
An American Portrait ep Maggie Kuhn 2.11.85 CBS

FONDA, PETER
SUPP.:
A Reason to Live tf 1.7.85 NBC

FONTAINE, JOAN
SUPP.:
Bare Essence ep Hour Four 3.1.83 NBC
An American Portrait ep George Catlin 2.22.85 CBS

FORAN, DICK
A&C, B.V.:
Father Knows Best ep Carnival 1956 NBC
Richard Diamond ep The Adjuster 12.7.59 CBS
Wanted: Dead or Alive ep The Choice 12.14.60 CBS
Gunsmoke ep With a Smile 3.30.63 CBS

FORD, CONSTANCE
A&C, B.V.:
Wanted: Dead or Alive ep The Last Retreat 1.11.61 CBS
Gunsmoke ep Wagon Girls 4.7.62 CBS

FORD, WALLACE
A&C, B.V.:
The Andy Griffith Show ep Aunt Bee's Romance 10.19.64 CBS

FORREST, STEVE
A&C, B.V.:
The High Chaparral ep The Guns of Johnny Rondo 2.6.70 NBC
Alias Smith and Jones ep 21 Days to Tenstrike 1.6.72 ABC
SUPP.:
Hotline tf 10.16.82 CBS
Malibu tf 1.23, 1.24.83 ABC
Finder of Lost Loves ep (pt/first ep) 9.22.84 ABC
Hollywood Wives ms 2.17, 2.18, 2.19.85 ABC
Hotel ep The Wedding 2.22.85 ABC

FORSLUND, CONSTANCE
SUPP.:
Making a Living ep Strange Bedfellows 6.4.82 ABC
The Love Boat ep Abbey's Maiden Voyage 2.26.83 ABC
Magnum, P.I. ep Home from the Sea 9.29.83 ABC
The Love Boat ep The Hustlers 10.8.83 ABC
Murder, She Wrote ep Footnote to Murder 3.10.85 CBS

FORSYTH, ROSEMARY
A&C, B.V.:
Mr. Broadway ep Smelling Like a Rose 11.28.64 CBS
SUPP.:
T.J. Hooker ep The Fast Lane 1.8.83 ABC
Fantasy Island ep The Song Writer 1.22.83 ABC
Magnum, P.I. ep 3.10.83 CBS

Simon and Simon ep 10.20.83 CBS
Murder, She Wrote ep My Johnnie Lies Over the Ocean 2.10.85 CBS
Dallas ep 2.1.85, 3.15.85 CBS
Simon and Simon ep Reunion at Alcatraz 11.14.85 CBS

FORSYTHE, JOHN

A&C, B.V.:

Kraft Suspense Theater ep The Sweet Taste of Vengeance 4.30.64 NBC

A&C, Supp. 2:

Switch ep Death Tong 1.9.78 CBS

SUPP.:

The Mysterious Two tf/pt 5.31.82 NBC
Dynasty sr ret 10.27.82 ABC
Dynasty sr ret 9.28.83 ABC
The Love Boat ep The Pledge 10.1.83 ABC
The Love Boat Fall Preview Party sp 9.15.84 ABC
Dynasty sr ret 9.26.84 ABC
Dynasty sr ret 9.25.85 ABC
Dynasty II: The Colbys ep Family Album 12.5.85 ABC

FOSTER, JODIE

A&C, Supp. 1:

Daniel Boone ep Israel and Love 5.7.70 NBC

FOSTER, MEG

A&C, Supp. 2:

Here Come the Brides ep Two Worlds 2.20.70 ABC
Mod Squad ep Who Are the Keepers, Who Are the Inmates? 10.6.70 ABC
Men at Law ep Hostage 2.24.71 CBS
Hawaii Five-O ep Double Exposure 12.2.76 CBS

SUPP.:

Cagney and Lacey sr 3.25.82 CBS
Cagney and Lacey sr ret 10.25.82 CBS
Desperate Intruder tf 7.31.83 NN
The Best Kept Secrets tf 3.26.84 ABC
The Twilight Zone ep Dreams for Sale 10.4.85 CBS
Murder, She Wrote ep Joshua Peabody Died Here 10.6.85 CBS

FOX, MICHAEL J.*

Palmerstown, U.S.A. sr 3.17.81 CBS
Trapper John, M.D. ep Brain Child 5.17.81 CBS
Teachers Only ep The Make-up Test 5.12.82 NBC
Family Ties sr 9.22.82 NBC
The Love Boat ep He Ain't Heavy 2.26.83 ABC
Family Ties sr ret 9.28.83 NBC
High School, U.S.A. tf/pt 10.16.83 NBC
Night Court ep Santa Goes Downtown 1.11.84 NBC
Family Ties sr ret 9.27.84 NBC

Time Travel: Fact, Fiction & Fantasy sp hos-nar 7.85 NN
Family Ties Vacation tf 9.23.85 NBC
Family Ties sr ret 9.26.85 NBC

FOXWORTH, ROBERT
A&C, Supp. 1:
Hawaii Five-O ep The Listener 1.16.73 CBS
Marcus Welby, M.D. ep The Fruitfulness of Mrs. Steffie Rhodes 9.16.75 ABC
Marcus Welby, M.D. ep The Media Factor 12.2.75 ABC
SUPP.:
Falcon Crest sr 12.4.81 CBS
Falcon Crest sr ret 10.1.82 CBS
Falcon Crest sr ret 9.30.83 CBS
Falcon Crest sr ret 9.28.84 CBS
Falcon Crest sr ret 10.4.85 CBS

FRANCIOSA, ANTHONY
SUPP.:
Masquerade ep The French Connection 3.30.84 ABC
The Love Boat Fall Preview Party sp 9.15.84 ABC
Finder of Lost Loves sr 9.22.84 ABC

FRANCIS, ANNE
A&C, B.V.:
The Reporter ep Hideout 10.2.64 CBS
A&C, Supp. 2:
The Eddie Capra Mysteries ep How Do I Kill Thee? 11.3.78 NBC
SUPP.:
CHiPs ep In the Best of Families 2.21.82 NBC
Rona Jaffe's "Mazes and Monsters" tf 12.28.82 CBS
O'Malley pt 1.8.83 NBC
Charley's Aunt comedy sp 2.6.83 TEC
Simon and Simon ep The Shadow of Sam Penny 11.3.83 CBS
Trapper John, M.D. ep 12.4.83 CBS
Riptide ep Riptide (pt) 1.3.84 NBC
Riptide ep The Mean Green Love Machine 2.7.84 NBC
Riptide ep Diamonds Are for Never 2.21.84 NBC
Murder, She Wrote ep Murder, She Wrote (pt) 9.30.84 CBS
Partners in Crime ep Getting in Shape 11.22.84 NBC
The Love Boat ep Noel's Christmas Carol 12.5.84 ABC
Crazy Like a Fox ep Premium for Murder 1.13.85 CBS
Hardcastle and McCormick ep The Long Ago Girl 2.11.85 ABC
Finder of Lost Loves ep Connections 4.13.85 ABC

FRANCIS, GENIE*
General Hospital sr 1978 ABC
Fantasy Island ep Daddy's Little Girl 1.30.82 ABC
Bare Essence ms 10.4, 10.5.82 CBS
Bare Essence sr 2.8.83 NBC

Murder, She Wrote ep Birds of a Feather 10.14.84 CBS
Hotel ep Outsiders 11.21.84 ABC
North and South ms 11.3-11.10.85 ABC
Glitter ep The Matriarch 12.19.85 ABC

FRANCIS, IVOR
A&C, Supp. 1:
Search ep The Mattson Papers 2.28.73 NBC
A&C, Supp. 2:
The Eddie Capra Mysteries ep Who Killed Charles Pendragon? 9.8.78 NBC

FRANCISCUS, JAMES
A&C, B.V.:
The Rifleman ep The Legacy 12.8.59 ABC

FRANK, CHARLES*
The Silence tf 11.6.75 NBC
Three for the Road ep 11.23.75 CBS
Police Woman ep The Melting Point of Ice 1.6.76 NBC
Barney Miller ep 2.19.76 ABC
Panache tf 5.15.76 ABC
Laverne and Shirley ep 10.5.76 ABC
Barnaby Jones ep The Fatal Drive 10.28.76 CBS
The New, Original Wonder Woman ep The Feminum Mystique 11.6, 11.8.76 ABC
Hawaii Five-O ep Practical Jokes Can Kill You 5.5.77 CBS
Riding High pt 8.25.77 NBC
Rafferty ep Brothers and Sons 9.12.77 CBS
The Love Boat ep The Goldenagers 10.8.77 ABC
Barnaby Jones ep The Captives 11.10.77 CBS
Columbo ep Try and Catch Me 11.21.77 NBC
What Really Happened to the Class of '65 ep Everybody's Girl 12.8.77 NBC
Tarantulas: The Deadly Cargo tf 12.28.77 CBS
Annie Flynn pt 1.21.78 CBS
Ski Lift to Death tf 3.3.78 CBS
Go West Young Girl tf/pt 4.27.78 ABC
The New Maverick tf/pt 7.3.78 ABC
A Guide for the Married Man tf 10.13.78 ABC
The Chisholms ms 3.29-4.19.79 CBS
Young Maverick sr 11.28.79 CBS
Filthy Rich sr 8.16.82 CBS
Emerald Point, N.A.S. sr 9.26.83 CBS
The Love Boat ep Soap Gets in Your Eyes 10.20.84 ABC
Covenant tf/pt 8.5.85 NBC
Murder, She Wrote ep A Lady in the Lake 11.10.85 CBS
The Love Boat ep The Iron Man 11.23.85 ABC
A Letter to Three Wives tf 12.16.85 NBC
Glitter ep Fathers and Children 12.20.85 ABC

FRANKLIN, BONNIE
A&C, Supp. 1:
A Christmas Carol sp 12.23.54 CBS
Karen ep 2.22.65 NBC
Gidget ep Too Many Cooks 12.29.65 ABC
SUPP.:
One Day at a Time sr ret 10.3.82 CBS
Your Place or Mine tf 3.2.83 CBS
One Day at a Time sr ret 10.2.83 CBS

FRANN, MARY*
Search ep Operation Iceman 10.25.72 NBC
Cannon ep 2.7.73 CBS
The Rockford Files ep Country Gambit 1.24.75 NBC
The Fantastic Journey ep Funhouse 3.31.77 NBC
The Rockford Files ep A Fast Count 12.1.78 NBC
The Incredible Hulk ep Stop the Presses 11.24.79 CBS
Stone ep The Man in the Full Toledo 2.4.80 ABC
Portrait of an Escort tf 10.8.80 CBS
First Time, Second Time pt 10.25.80 CBS
Darkroom ep Closed Circuit 11.27.81 ABC
King's Crossing sr 1.16.82 ABC
Newhart sr 10.25.82 CBS
Newhart sr ret 10.17.83 CBS
Hotel ep Flesh and Blood 10.10.84 ABC
Newhart sr ret 10.15.84 CBS
Gidget's Summer Reunion tf/pt 6.85 NN
Newhart sr ret 9.30.85 CBS

FRANZ, ARTHUR
A&C, B.V.:
Mr. Novak ep With a Hammer in His Hand, Lord, Lord! 9.29.64 NBC
The Fugitive ep Landscaping with Running Figures 11.16.65, 11.23.65 ABC
A&C, Supp. 2:
The Waltons ep The Seashore 1.20.77 CBS

FREEMAN, DEENA
SUPP.:
Deadly Lessons tf 3.7.83 ABC
The Powers of Matthew Star ep Road Rebels 3.25.83 NBC
Newhart ep 12.3.84 CBS
Crazy Like a Fox ep Requiem for a Fox 10.20.85 CBS

FRENCH, VICTOR*
Temple Houston ep Letter of the Law 10.3.63 NBC
No Time for Sergeants ep The $100,000 Canteen 11.30.64 ABC
The Wild Wild West ep The Night of a Thousand Eyes 10.22.65 CBS
Ben Casey ep The Man from Quasilia 11.29.65 ABC

Gunsmoke ep Wishbone 2.19.66 CBS
Gunsmoke ep Prime of Life 5.7.66 CBS
The Hero sr 9.8.66 NBC
Gunsmoke ep Saturday Night 1.7.67 CBS
Tarzan ep A Pride of Assassins 1.27.67 NBC
Iron Horse ep Decision at Sundown 2.27.67 ABC
Gunsmoke ep Vengeance 10.2, 10.9.67 CBS
Gunsmoke ep Major Glory 10.30.67 CBS
Cimarron Strip ep Till the End of the Night 11.16.67 CBS
The FBI ep False Witness 12.10.67 ABC
Bonanza ep The Burning Sky 1.28.68 NBC
Gunsmoke ep Hill Girl 1.29.68 CBS
Mission: Impossible ep Trial by Fury 3.10.68 CBS
Gunsmoke ep Uncle Feeney 10.14.68 CBS
Gunsmoke ep O'Quillian 10.28.68 CBS
Daniel Boone ep Love and Equity 3.31.69 NBC
The FBI ep Moment of Truth 3.30.69 ABC
Bonanza ep Meena 11.16.69 NBC
Cutter's Trail tf 2.10.70 CBS
Gunsmoke ep Kiowa! 2.16.70 CBS
Mannix ep Figures in a Landscape 10.10.70 CBS
Dan August ep When the Shooting Dies 11.25.70 ABC
Bonanza ep An Earthquake Called Callahan 4.11.71 NBC
Longstreet ep One in the Reality Column 9.30.71 ABC
Gunsmoke ep Trafton 10.25.71 CBS
Gunsmoke ep Phoebe 2.21.72 CBS
Gunsmoke ep The Drummer 10.9.72 CBS
O'Hara, United States Treasury ep 11.21.71 CBS
The Streets of San Francisco ep Deathwatch 1.13.73 ABC
Gunsmoke ep This Golden Land 3.5.73 CBS
Kung Fu ep The Ancient Warrior 5.3.73 ABC
The Rookies ep The Deadly Case 9.24.73 ABC
Gunsmoke ep Matt's Love Story 9.24.73 CBS
The FBI ep Town of Terror 10.28.73 ABC
Mannix ep The Dark Hours 1.20.74 CBS
Little House on the Prairie tf/pt 3.20.74 NBC
Gunsmoke ep Tarnished Badge 11.11.74 CBS
The Tribe tf 12.11.74 ABC
Gunsmoke ep The Sharecroppers 3.31.75 CBS
Little House on the Prairie ep Mr. Edwards' Homecoming 10.2.74 NBC
Little House on the Prairie ep Ma's Holiday 11.6.74 NBC
Little House on the Prairie ep The Lord Is My Shepherd 12.8.74 NBC
Little House on the Prairie ep Plague 1.29.75 NBC
Little House on the Prairie ep To See the World 3.5.75 NBC
Carter Country sr 9.15.77 ABC
Carter Country sr ret 5.2.78 ABC
Amateur Night at the Dixie Bar and Grill tf 1.8.79 NBC
Little House on the Prairie ep The Return of Mr. Edwards 11.5.79 NBC

The Golden Moment: An Olympic Love Story tf 5.25, 5.26.80 NBC
Pony Express pt 9.3.80 CBS
Little House: A New Beginning sr 9.27.82 NBC
Little House: Look Back to Yesterday tf 12.12.83 NBC
Little House: The Last Farewell tf 2.6.84 NBC
Little House: Bless All the Dear Children tf 12.17.84 NBC
Highway to Heaven sr 9.19.84 NBC
Highway to Heaven sr ret 9.18.85 NBC

FRYE, SOLEIL MOON*
Missing Children: A Mother's Story tf 12.1.82 CBS
Who Will Love My Children? tf 2.14.83 ABC
Ernie Kovacs: Between the Laughter 5.14.84 ABC
Invitation to Hell tf 5.24.84 ABC
Punky Brewster sr 9.16.84 NBC
Diff'rent Strokes ep Sam's New Pal 2.2.85 NBC
Back to Next Saturday sp 9.12.85 NBC
Punky Brewster sr (animated) vo 9.14.85 NBC
Punky Brewster sr (live action) ret 9.15.85 NBC

FULLER, PENNY*
Women in Chains tf 1.25.72 ABC
Applause sp 3.15.73 CBS
Love, American Style ep Love and the Teller's Tale 9.14.73 ABC
The Six Million Dollar Man ep Population Zero 1.18.74 ABC
Barnaby Jones ep 1.20.74 CBS
Ann in Blue pt 8.8.74 ABC
Barnaby Jones ep Poisoned Pigeon 3.25.75 CBS
Movin' On ep Woman of Steel 1.27.76 NBC
McNaughton's Daughter ep The Smashed Lady 3.31.76 NBC
Ebony, Ivory and Jade tf/pt 8.3.79 CBS
Trapper John, M.D. ep One for My Baby 11.18.79 CBS
Trapper John, M.D. ep Have I Got a Girl for You 2.1.81 CBS
A Piano for Mrs. Cimino tf 2.3.82 CBS
Lois Gibbs and the Love Canal tf 2.17.82 CBS
Newhart ep The Senator's Wife Was Indiscreet 12.27.82 CBS
Simon and Simon ep Design for Killing 2.10.83 CBS
Your Place or Mine tf 3.2.83 CBS
Intimate Agony tf 3.21.83 ABC
One Day at a Time ep 11.6.83 CBS
The Love Boat ep Julie and the Bachelors 11.19.83 ABC
Newhart ep 12.27.83 CBS
License to Kill tf 1.10.84 CBS
Simon and Simon ep 2.10.84 CBS
Cat on a Hot Tin Roof drama sp 8.19.84 SHO
MacGruder and Loud ep The Violation 1.22.85 ABC
The Duck Factory ep The Duck Stops Here 7.4.85 NBC
The Love Boat ep Joint Custody 10.5.85 ABC

FULLER, ROBERT
A&C, B.V.:
Restless Gun ep Peligrosso 12.29.58 NBC
The Life and Legend of Wyatt Earp ep The Judas Goat 3.31.59 ABC
Lawman ep The Friend 6.28.59 ABC
Court-Martial ep 11.16.66 ABC
SUPP.:
The Love Boat ep Her Honor, the Mayor 1.26.85 ABC
Matt Houston ep New Orleans Nightmare 2.8.85 ABC

FULTON, WENDY*
Knight Rider ep Plush Ride 10.22.82 NBC
Voyagers ep An Arrow Pointing East 12.12.82 NBC
V: The Series ep The Littlest Dragon 2.22.85 NBC
The A-Team ep Bounty 4.2.85 NBC

FUNICELLO, ANNETTE
A&C, Supp. 2:
The Danny Thomas Show ep Girl from Italy 3.2.59 CBS
The Danny Thomas Show ep Frankie Laine Sings for Gina 3.9.59 CBS
The Danny Thomas Show ep Gina's First Date 1959 CBS
The Danny Thomas Show ep The Latin Lover 1959 CBS
The Danny Thomas Show ep Gina for President 1959 CBS
The Greatest Show on Earth ep Rosetta 3.24.64 ABC
Burke's Law ep Who Killed the Strangler? 1.6.65 ABC
SUPP.:
The Love Boat ep New York A.C. 2.20.82 ABC
Lots of Luck tf 2.3.85 DIS

- G -

GABOR, EVA
A&C, B.V.:
The Ann Sothern Show ep The Royal Visit Spring 1961 CBS
The Beverly Hillbillies ep The Thanksgiving Story 11.68 CBS
SUPP.:
The Love Boat ep Mothers Don't Do That 5.15.82 ABC
Hart to Hart ep With This Hart, I Thee Wed 10.12.82 ABC
Hotel ep Prisms 3.14.84 ABC

GABOR, ZSA ZSA
A&C, B.V.:
Love That Bob ep Grandpa Meets Zsa Zsa 10.4.56 CBS
The Life of Riley ep Foreign Intrigue 1957 NBC
The Danny Thomas Show ep Kathy and the Glamour Girl 10.31.60 CBS

F Troop ep Play, Gypsy, Play 3.1.66 ABC
SUPP.:
Knots Landing ep Svengali 10.21.82 CBS
California Girls tf 3.24.85 ABC

GAIL, MAX
SUPP.:
The Whiz Kids sr 10.5.83 CBS
The Comedy Factory ep Harry and the Kids 7.5.85 ABC
The Other Lover tf 9.24.85 CBS
Babe sp 10.15.85 ESPN
Trapper John, M.D. ep Billboard Barney 12.29.85 CBS

GALLOWAY, DON
A&C, Supp. 1:
Tom, Dick, and Mary sr 10.5.64 NBC
Get Christie Love ep A High Fashion Heist 3.12.75 ABC
A&C, Supp. 2:
Vegas ep Love, Laugh or Die 10.18.79 ABC
SUPP.:
Knight Rider ep The Long Way Home 2.25.83 NBC
Hotel ep Prisms 3.14.84 ABC
Fantasy Island ep The Ideal Woman 5.19.84 NBC
The Fall Guy ep High Orbit 2.6.85 ABC
Scarecrow and Mrs. King ep Odds on a Dead Pigeon 2.25.85 CBS
Crazy Like a Fox ep 3.10.85 CBS

GAM, RITA
A&C, B.V.:
Voyage to the Bottom of the Sea ep The Midst of Silence 10.5.64 ABC
Family Affair ep Beware the Other Woman 11.66 CBS

GANZEL, TERESA*
Three's Company ep Lies My Roommate Told Me 11.10.81 ABC
Teachers Only sr 2.12.83 NBC
Pumpboys and Dinettes on Television pt 8.15.83 NBC
The Duck Factory sr 4.12.84 NBC
Hotel ep Transitions 11.14.84 ABC
The Love Boat ep Ace Takes the First 1.12.85 ABC
Remington Steele ep Steele Trying 5.7.85 NBC
Dirty Work pt 6.6.85 NBC
Three's a Crowd ep Deeds of Trust 2.19.85 ABC
Shadow Chasers ep Parts Unknown 12.12.85 ABC

GARAS, KAZ
A&C, Supp. 1:
Hawaii Five-O ep Twenty-four Karat Kill 11.14.68 CBS
Hawaii Five-O ep The Joker's Wild, Man, Wild 12.17.69 CBS
The High Chaparral ep Sangre 2.26.71 NBC

Griff ep Don't Call Us, We'll Call You 10.20.73 ABC
Cannon ep The Melted Man 11.12.75 CBS
A&C, Supp. 2:
Hawaii Five-O ep Voice of Terror 12.4.79 CBS
SUPP.:
The Powers of Matthew Star ep Daredevil 1.14.82 NBC
The Dukes of Hazzard ep Bad Day in Hazzard 3.5.82 CBS
The Phoenix ep Presence of Evil 4.9.82 ABC
Massarati and the Brain tf/pt 8.26.82 ABC
Hart to Hart ep The Harts at High Noon 11.9.82 ABC
Seven Brides for Seven Brothers ep 12.22.82 CBS
The Dukes of Hazzard ep 2.24.84 CBS
The Master ep Rogues 4.20.84 NBC
Scarecrow and Mrs. King ep Double Agent 10.15.84 CBS
Partners in Crime ep Fashioned for Murder 12.8.84 NBC
The A-Team ep Road Games 2.5.85 NBC

GARDINER, REGINALD
A&C, B.V.:
Burke's Law ep Who Killed Who IV? 4.3.64 ABC
Bewitched ep I Get Your Nanny, You Get My Goat 12.14.67 ABC

GARDNER, AVA
SUPP.:
Knots Landing ep The Deluge 2.28.84 CBS
Knots Landing ep A Piece of the Pie 3.7.85 CBS
A.D. ms 3.31, 4.1, 4.2, 4.3, 4.4.85 NBC
Knots Landing ep Four No Trump 4.11.85 CBS
Knots Landing ep A Price to Pay 5.2.85 CBS
Knots Landing ep One Day in a Row 5.9.85 CBS
Knots Landing ep Vulnerable 5.16.85 CBS
The Long Hot Summer tf 10.6, 10.7.85 NBC

GARLAND, BEVERLY
A&C, B.V.:
Trackdown ep Hard Lines 3.11.59 CBS
Wanted: Dead or Alive ep Prison Trail 5.14.60 CBS
A&C, Supp. 1:
The New Adventures of Perry Mason ep 9.23.73 CBS
Switch ep The Argonaut Special 10.12.76 CBS
SUPP.:
Magnum, P.I. ep Three Minus Two 4.1.82 CBS
Remington Steele ep Thou Shalt Not Steele 11.5.82 NBC
Matt Houston ep The Good Doctor 12.12.82 ABC
Remington Steele ep Sting of Steele 4.5.83 NBC
Scarecrow and Mrs. King sr 10.3.83 CBS
This Girl for Hire tf/pt 11.1.83 CBS
Scarecrow and Mrs. King sr ret 10.1.84 CBS
Hotel ep New Beginnings 1.23.85 ABC
Scarecrow and Mrs. King sr ret 9.23.85 CBS

GARNER, JAMES
SUPP.:
The Long Summer of George Adams tf 1.18.82 NBC
The Glitter Dome tf 11.18.84 HBO
Heartsounds tf 9.30.84 ABC
Space ms 4.14, 4.15, 4.16, 4.17, 4.18.85 CBS

GARNER, PEGGY ANN
A&C, B.V.:
The Big Valley ep The Prize 12.16.68 ABC

GARR, TERI
A&C, Supp. 1:
The Andy Griffith Show ep The Wedding 3.4.68 CBS
SUPP.:
Prime Suspect tf 1.20.82 CBS
Faerie Tale Theater ep The Tale of the Frog Prince 9.11.82 SHO
John Steinbeck's "The Winter of Our Discontent" tf 12.6.83 CBS
To Catch a King tf 2.12.84 HBO

GARRETT, JOY*
Charlie's Angels ep Little Angels of the Night 2.22.78 ABC
Quincy, M.E. ep The Heart of the Matter 3.3.78 NBC
The Hoyt Axton Show pt 9.28.81 NBC
Callie and Son tf 10.13.81 CBS
Born to Be Sold tf 11.2.81 NBC
Cassie and Company ep Replay 2.12.82 NBC
Too Close for Comfort ep A Policeman's Wife Is Not a Happy One 5.4.82 ABC
Hotline tf 10.16.82 CBS
The Dukes of Hazzard ep 12.12.82 CBS
Archie Bunker's Place ep 1.2.83 CBS
Three's Company ep Star Struck 2.15.83 ABC
Remington Steele ep High Flying Steele 1.17.84 NBC
Magnum, P.I. ep 5.3.84 CBS
The Young and the Restless sr 5.30.84 CBS

GARSON, GREER
SUPP.:
The Love Boat ep The Tomorrow Lady 12.4.82 ABC

GARVER, KATHY
A&C, B.V.:
The Travels of Jaimie McPheeters ep Day of the Pawnees 12.22.63, 12.29.63 ABC
Mr. Novak ep Sparrow on the Wire 1.21.64 NBC

GAUTIER, DICK
SUPP.:
Fantasy Island ep Forget-Me-Not 4.10.82 ABC

Quincy, M.E. ep A Cry for Help 1.19.83 NBC
Zorro and Son ep 5.4.83 CBS
Alice ep 10.16.83 CBS
Masquerade ep Diamonds 12.22.83 ABC
Goodnight Beantown ep 1.1.84 CBS
Fantasy Island ep Mrs. Brandell's Favorites 2.25.84 ABC
Murder, She Wrote ep Birds of a Feather 10.14.84 CBS
Knight Rider ep The Chameleon 12.30.84 NBC
Alice ep 1.15.85 CBS
This Wife for Hire tf/pt 3.18.85 ABC

GAYNES, GEORGE*
The Six Million Dollar Man ep Nuclear Alert 9.13.74 ABC
Trilogy of Terror tf 3.4.75 ABC
Woman of the Year tf 7.28.76 CBS
Captains and the Kings ms 9.30-11.11.76 NBC
Delvecchio ep Hot Spell 11.14.76 CBS
Washington: Behind Closed Doors ms 9.6, 9.7, 9.8, 9.9, 9.10, 9.11.77 ABC
The Girl in the Empty Grave tf 9.20.77 NBC
Breaking Up Is Hard to Do tf 9.5, 9.7.79 ABC
Scruples ms 2.25, 2.26, 2.27, 2.28.80 CBS
Evita Peron tf 2.23, 2.24.81 NBC
Quincy, M.E. ep The Unquiet Grave 4.7.82 NBC
The ABC Afterschool Special ep Mom's on Strike 11.14.84 ABC
Punky Brewster sr 9.16.84 NBC
It Came Upon the Midnight Clear tf 12.15.84 NN
Punky Brewster sr (animated) vo 9.14.85 NBC
Punky Brewster sr (live action) ret 9.15.85 NBC

GAZZARA, BEN
SUPP.:
A Question of Honor tf 4.28.82 CBS
Hollywood's Most Sensational Mysteries sp hos 2.4.84 NBC
An Early Frost tf 11.11.85 NBC
A Letter to Three Wives tf 12.16.85 NBC

GEER, ELLEN*
The Jimmy Stewart Show sr 1.19.71 NBC
Ghost Story ep Bad Connection 10.6.72 NBC
The Waltons ep 11.9.72 CBS
The New Perry Mason ep The Case of the Deadly Deeds 10.21.73 CBS
The New Land ep The Word Is: Growth 9.21.74 ABC
Babe tf 10.23.75 CBS
Barnaby Jones ep Beware the Dog 11.21.75 CBS
Delvecchio ep The Silent Prey 10.31.76 CBS
Westside Medical ep Pressure Cook 8.25.77 ABC
The Trial of Lee Harvey Oswald tf 9.30, 10.2.77 ABC
Night Cries tf 1.29.78 ABC
Fantasy Island ep 12.2.78 ABC

Dallas ep Whatever Happened to Baby John? 3.23, 3.30.79 CBS
Barnaby Jones ep Man on Fire 9.20.79 CBS
Paris ep Once More for Free 12.11.79 CBS
A Shining Season tf 12.26.79 CBS
My Kidnapper, My Love tf 12.8.80 NBC
The Princess and the Cabbie tf 11.3.81 CBS
Quincy, M.E. ep For Love of Joshua 2.3.81 NBC
Code Red ep No Escape 3.21.82 ABC
Quincy, M.E. ep Ghost of a Chance 10.6.82 NBC
Deadly Lessons tf 3.7.83 ABC
Voyagers ep Destiny's Choice 3.13.83 NBC
I Want to Live tf 5.9.83 ABC
Call to Glory ep Call It Courage 10.1.84 ABC
Buchanan High School ep The Star Player 12.27.85 NN

GEESON, JUDY
SUPP.:
Murder, She Wrote ep Paint Me a Murder 2.17.85 CBS

GEORGE, CHRISTOPHER
A&C, Supp. 2:
The FBI ep Return to Power 2.15.70 ABC
Police Story ep The Executioner 10.29.74 NBC
SUPP.:
Fantasy Island ep Valerie 1.16.82 ABC

GEORGE, LYNDA DAY (a.k.a. Lynda Day)
A&C, Supp. 1:
Hawk ep Game with a Dead End 9.29.66 ABC
Good Morning World ep For My Daughter's Hand You'd Get My Foot 1968 CBS
Here Come the Brides ep Two Women 4.3.70 ABC
Petrocelli ep By Reason of Madness 9.25.74 NBC
Switch ep Two on the Run 3.27.77 CBS
SUPP.:
Benson ep Death in a Funny Position 10.22.82 ABC
Masquerade ep Girls for Sale 12.29.83 ABC
Fantasy Island ep Games People Play 1.14.84 ABC
Hardcastle and McCormick ep Too Rich and Too Thin 1.14.85 ABC
Murder, She Wrote ep My Johnnie Lies Over the Ocean 2.10.85 CBS

GERARD, GIL
A&C, Supp. 2:
Little House on the Prairie ep The Handyman 10.3.77 NBC
SUPP.:
Washington Mistress tf 1.13.82 CBS
Not Just Another Affair tf 10.2.82 CBS
Hear No Evil tf/pt 11.20.82 CBS
Johnny Blue pt 9.4.83 CBS

For Love or Money tf 11.20.84 CBS
Stormin' Home tf 4.5.85 CBS
International Airport tf/pt 5.25.85 ABC

GERRITSEN, LISA
A&C, Supp. 1:
Family Affair ep A Diller, a Dollar 3.69 CBS
Gunsmoke ep Sam McTavish, M.D. 10.5.70 CBS
Harry O ep Ballinger's Choice 10.31.74 ABC

GERTZ, JAMI*
Square Pegs sr 9.27.82 CBS
For Members Only pt 7.11.83 CBS
The Facts of Life ep Advanced Placement 11.2.83 NBC
The Facts of Life ep All or Nothing 1.11.84 NBC
The Facts of Life ep A Star at Langley 2.15.84 NBC
Family Ties ep Double Date 2.16.84 NBC
Dreams sr 10.3.84 CBS

GETTY, ESTELLE*
One of the Boys ep Don't Bank On It 4.17.82 NBC
Cagney and Lacey ep 4.30.84 CBS
No Man's Land tf 5.27.84 NBC
Hotel ep Intimate Strangers 9.26.84 ABC
Newhart ep 5.27.85 CBS
The Golden Girls sr 9.14.85 NBC
Copacabana tf 12.3.85 CBS

GHOSTLEY, ALICE
SUPP.:
Come Blow Your Horn sp 11.81 SHO
Gimme a Break ep Love Thy Neighbor 12.18.82 NBC
We Got It Made ep The Fight 2.25.84 NBC
Trapper John, M.D. ep 3.11.84 CBS
Mama Malone ep 6.16.84 CBS
Tales from the Darkside ep Anniversary Dinner 2.2.85 NN
Highway to Heaven ep Cindy 10.23.85 NBC
Stir Crazy ep 12.24.85 CBS

GIAMBALVO, LOUIS*
Escape tf 2.20.80 CBS
Reward tf 5.23.80 ABC
Alcatraz: The Whole Shocking Story tf 11.5, 11.6.80 NBC
Hill Street Blues ep Can World War Three Be an Attitude? 1.24.81 NBC
Hill Street Blues ep Dressed to Kill 1.31.81 NBC
The Gangster Chronicles sr 2.21.81 NBC
The White Shadow ep 3.2.81 CBS
Riker ep Busted Cop 4.11.81 CBS
Fly Away Home tf/pt 9.18.81 ABC
The Ambush Murders tf 1.5.82 CBS

Barney Miller ep Examination Day 1.14.82 ABC
Marian Rose White tf 1.19.82 CBS
Chicago Story ep 4.3.82 NBC
Chicago Story ep Vendetta 4.24.82 NBC
Mae West tf 5.2.82 ABC
The Devlin Connection sr 10.2.82 NBC
9 to 5 ep Temporarily Disconnected 11.30.82 ABC
Hart to Hart ep As the Harts Turn 3.1.83 ABC
Goodnight Beantown ep 4.17.83 CBS
St. Elsewhere ep Baron Von Munchausen 4.19.83 NBC
Oh Madeline sr 9.27.83 ABC
Hill Street Blues ep The Russians Are Coming 12.15.83 NBC
Remington Steele ep Second Base Steele 10.23.84 NBC
Simon and Simon ep Yes, Virginia, There Is a Liberace 12.20.84 CBS
The A-Team ep Trouble Brewing 5.17.85 NBC
Dirty Work pt 6.6.85 CBS

GIBB, ANDY*
Something's Afoot sp 12.82 SHO
Gimme a Break ep The Groupie 9.29.83 NBC
Punky Brewster ep Miss Adorable 11.25.84 NBC
Punky Brewster ep Play It Again, Punky 1.13.85 NBC

GIBB, CYNTHIA*
Fame sr 10.84 NN
Fame sr ret 10.85 NN

GIBBS, MARLA*
The Jeffersons sr 9.79 CBS
The Jeffersons sr ret 10.80 CBS
Checking In sr 4.9.81 CBS
The Jeffersons sr ret 10.4.81 CBS
The Love Boat ep Isaac and the Marriage Counselor 10.24.81 ABC
The Jeffersons sr ret 10.2.83 CBS
The Jeffersons sr ret 10.14.84 CBS
Pryor's Place ep 10.27.84, 11.3.84, 11.24.84 CBS
227 sr 9.14.85 NBC

GIBSON, HENRY
A&C, Supp. 1:
The Beverly Hillbillies ep A Man for Elly Spring 1964 CBS
F Troop ep The Return of Wrongo Starr Spring 1967 ABC
Bewitched ep Samantha's French Pastry Fall 1968 ABC
Get Christie Love ep Murder on High C 2.5.75 ABC
SUPP.:
Trapper John, M.D. ep Candy Doctor 3.21.82 CBS
Magnum, P.I. ep Mixed Doubles 12.2.82 CBS
Simon and Simon ep Fowl Play 12.16.82 CBS

The Love Boat ep The Christmas Presence 12.18.82 ABC
Quincy, M.E. ep Murder on Ice 3.9.83 NBC
Small and Frye ep 3.14.83 CBS
Masquerade ep Spanish Gambit 4.20.84 ABC
High School, U.S.A. pt 5.26.84 NBC
Cover Up ep The Million Dollar Face 10.6.84 CBS
The Fall Guy ep Terror U 10.17.84 ABC
Mickey Spillane's Mike Hammer ep Deadly Prey 11.10.84 CBS

GIELGUD, SIR JOHN
SUPP.:
The Hunchback of Notre Dame tf 2.4.82 CBS
Inside the Third Reich tf 5.9, 5.10.82 ABC
Marco Polo ms 5.16-5.19.82 NBC
The Scarlet and the Black tf 2.2.83 CBS
The Master of Ballantrae tf 1.31.84 CBS
The Far Pavillions ms 4.22, 4.23, 4.24.84 HBO
Camille tf 12.11.84 CBS
Romance on the Orient Express tf 3.4.85 NBC

GIFTOS, ELAINE
SUPP.:
Trapper John, M.D. ep Ladies in Waiting 1.31.82 CBS
Games Mother Never Taught You tf 11.27.82 CBS
Three's Company ep An Affair to Forget 11.30.82 ABC
Magnum, P.I. ep Mixed Doubles 12.2.82 CBS
Trapper John, M.D. ep 1.1.83 CBS
Matt Houston ep The Centerfold Murders 9.30.83 ABC
Trapper John, M.D. ep 1.1.84 CBS
Knight Rider ep Custom Made Killer 1.6.85 NBC
Murder, She Wrote ep Broadway Malady 1.13.85 CBS

GILBERT, MELISSA
SUPP.:
Little House: A New Beginning sr 9.27.82 NBC
Choices of the Heart tf 12.5.83 NBC
Little House: Look Back to Yesterday tf 12.12.83 NBC
Little House: The Last Farewell tf 2.6.84 NBC
Family Secrets tf 5.13.84 NBC
Little House: Bless All the Dear Children tf 12.17.84 NBC
Faerie Tale Theater ep The Snow Queen 3.11.85 SHO

GILFORD, JACK
A&C, B.V.:
Ghost and Mrs. Muir ep Uncle Arnold the Magnificent 11.9.68 ABC
SUPP.:
The Love Boat ep A Honeymoon for Horace 10.23.82 ABC
Trapper John, M.D. ep Getting to Know You 12.12.82 CBS
Happy tf 10.26.83 CBS
Mama's Family ep Aunt Gert Rides Again 12.1.83 NBC
The Duck Factory sr 4.12.84 NBC

Night Court ep An Old Flame 1.24.85 NBC
Day to Day Affairs sp 2.4.85 HBO
Hostage Flight tf 11.17.85 NBC
George Burns Comedy Week ep The Funniest Guy in the World 12.4.85 CBS

GING, JACK
A&C, B.V.:
M Squad ep The Baited Hook 5.8.59 NBC
Bat Masterson ep Dead Men Don't Pay Debts 11.19.59 NBC
Perry Mason ep The Case of the Slandered Submarine 5.17.60 CBS
The Six Million Dollar Man ep Kill Oscar 10.31.76 ABC
Kojak ep Cry for the Kids 10.23.77
SUPP.:
The Winds of War ms 2.6-2.13.83 ABC
Riptide sr 1.3.84 NBC
Riptide sr ret 10.2.84 NBC
Riptide sr ret 10.1.85 (role until 12.10.85) NBC

GINGOLD, HERMIONE
SUPP.:
The ABC Afterschool Special ep Amy and the Angel 9.22.82 ABC

GINTY, ROBERT*
Nakia ep The Sand Trap 10.5.74 ABC
The Turning Point of Jim Malloy tf/pt 4.12.75 NBC
Police Woman ep Glitter with a Bullet 11.18.75 NBC
The Courage and the Passion tf 5.27.78 NBC
The Paper Chase sr 9.12.78 CBS
Eischied ep Who Is the Missing Woman? 11.30.79 NBC
The Big Stuffed Dog sp 2.8.80 NBC
Quincy, M.E. ep The Night Killer 11.26.80 NBC
Quincy, M.E. ep Give Me Your Weak 10.27.82 NBC
I Want to Live tf 5.9.83 ABC
Gavilan ep Best Friend Money Can Buy 12.21.82 NBC
Simon and Simon ep Psyched Out 1.13.83 CBS
Simon and Simon ep The Club Murder Vacation 1.27.83 CBS
Simon and Simon ep It's Only a Game 2.3.83 CBS
Knight Rider ep Nobody Does It Better 4.29.83 NBC
Hawaiian Heat sr 9.14.84 ABC
The Love Boat Fall Preview Party sp 9.15.84 ABC

GISH, LILLIAN
SUPP.:
Hobson's Choice tf 12.21.83 CBS
An American Portrait ep Anna Mary Robertson 3.20.85 CBS

GLASER, PAUL MICHAEL
A&C, Supp. 1:

The Streets of San Francisco ep Bitter Wine 12.23.72 ABC
Toma ep The Street 5.3.74 ABC
The Rockford Files ep Find Me If You Can 11.1.74 NBC

GLEASON, JACKIE
A&C, B.V.:
The Bob Hope Chrysler Theater ep Fantastic Stomach 11.16.66 NBC
SUPP.:
Izzy and Moe tf 9.23.85 CBS

GLESS, SHARON
SUPP.:
House Calls sr (with ep Fun with Doc and Jane) 1.4.82 CBS
Palms Precinct pt 1.8.82 NBC
Cagney and Lacey sr 10.25.82 CBS
Hobson's Choice tf 12.21.83 CBS
The Sky's No Limit tf 2.7.84 CBS
Cagney and Lacey sr ret 3.19.84 CBS
Cagney and Lacey sr ret 10.15.84 CBS
An American Portrait ep Bonnie Prudden 12.3.84 CBS
Letting Go tf 5.11.85 ABC
Cagney and Lacey sr ret 9.30.85 CBS

GODSHALL, LIBERTY*
Human Feelings tf/pt 10.16.78 NBC
Barnaby Jones ep Temptation 4.19.79 CBS
Buck Rogers in the 25th Century ep Planet of the Amazon Women 11.8.79 NBC
B.J. and the Bear ep S.T.U.N.T. 3.31.81 NBC
Simon and Simon ep Love, Christy 12.1.81 CBS
The James Boys pt 6.25.82 NBC
9 to 5 ep Power Failure 12.14.82 ABC
Special Bulletin tf 3.20.83 NBC
Hardcastle and McCormick ep Third Down and Twenty Years to Life 1.1.84 ABC
The A-Team ep Chopping Spree 2.14.84 NBC

GOLD, MISSY*
Captains and the Kings ms 9.30-11.11.76 NBC
The Nancy Drew Mysteries ep Will the Real Santa Claus...? 12.18.77 ABC
Little Mo tf 9.5.78 NBC
Ishi: The Last of His Tribe tf 12.20.78 NBC
Benson sr 9.13.79 ABC
Twirl tf 10.25.81 NBC
Benson sr ret 11.6.81 ABC
Benson sr ret 10.22.82 ABC
Benson sr ret 9.16.83 ABC
The Love Boat Fall Preview Party sp 9.15.84 ABC

Benson sr ret 9.21.84 ABC
Trapper John, M.D. ep 10.21.84 CBS
Benson sr ret 10.4.85 ABC

GOLD, TRACEY*
Captains and the Kings ms 9.30-11.11.76 NBC
The Dark Secret of Harvest Home tf 1.23, 1.24.78 NBC
Night Cries tf 1.29.78 ABC
Little Mo tf 9.5.78 NBC
The Incredible Journey of Dr. Meg Laurel 1.2.79 CBS
Jennifer: A Woman's Story tf 3.5.79 NBC
The Child Stealer tf 3.9.79 ABC
CHiPs ep Drive, Lady, Drive 11.10.79 NBC
Marilyn: The Untold Story tf 9.28.80 ABC
Trapper John, M.D. ep Girl Under Glass 11.23, 11.30.80 CBS
The CBS Afternoon Playhouse ep I Think I'm Having a Baby 3.3.81 CBS
A Few Days in Weasel Creek tf 10.21.81 CBS
The CBS Library ep A Tale of Four Wishes 11.8.81 CBS
Beyond Witch Mountain pt 2.20.82 CBS
The Phoenix ep The Fire Within 4.16.82 ABC
Father Murphy ep 11.19.82 NBC
Another Woman's Child tf 1.19.83 CBS
Thursday's Child tf 2.1.83 CBS
Who Will Love My Children? tf 2.14.83 ABC
Goodnight, Beantown sr 4.3.83 CBS
Goodnight, Beantown sr ret 10.2.83 CBS
The ABC Afterschool Special ep The Hand-Me-Down Kid 10.5.83 ABC
Fantasy Island ep Second Time Around 11.19.83 ABC
Trapper John, M.D. ep 1.29.84 CBS
A Reason to Live tf 1.7.85 NBC
Lots of Luck tf 2.3.85 DIS
Benson ep Katie's Cousin 3.22.85 ABC
Growing Pains sr 9.24.85 ABC

GOLONKA, ARLENE
A&C, Supp. 1:
Car 54, Where Are You? ep The White Elephant 1.6.63 NBC
The Andy Griffith Show ep Howard's Main Event 10.16.67 CBS
The Andy Griffith Show ep Howard and Millie 11.27.67 CBS
Chase ep Vacation for a President 2.6.74 NBC
The Rockford Files ep The Gang at Dan's Drive-in 1.13.78 NBC
SUPP.:
Fantasy Island ep A Very Strange Affair 1.2.82 ABC
The Love Boat ep Good Neighbors 1.9.82 ABC
Gimme a Break ep Brother Ed and the Hooker 2.24.82 NBC
Gimme a Break ep Eddie Gets Married 10.9.82 NBC
The CBS Afternoon Playhouse ep Help Wanted 10.12.82 CBS
The Best of Times pt 8.29.83 CBS

Simon and Simon ep 10.27.83 CBS
Benson ep Unlisted Love 12.2.83 ABC
The New Love, American Style ep Love and the Second Honeymoon 12.23.85 ABC

GOODFRIEND, LYNDA*
Blansky's Beauties sr 2.12.77 ABC
Legs pt 5.19.78 ABC
Who's Watching the Kids? sr 9.22.78 NBC
Happy Days sr 9.11.79 ABC
Happy Days sr ret 11.11.80 ABC
The Love Boat ep The Girl Next Door 1.3.81 ABC
Happy Days sr ret 10.6.81 ABC
Fantasy Island ep Dancing Lady 10.23.82 ABC
The Love Boat ep The Bad Luck Cabin 5.7.83 ABC
Happy Days ep Welcome Home 10.25, 11.1.83 ABC

GOODMAN, DODY
SUPP.:
Just Our Luck ep Uncle Harry 10.25.83 ABC
One Life to Live sr 4.19.84 ABC
Punky Brewster ep Parents Night 10.28.84 NBC
Punky Brewster ep My Aged Valentine 2.10.85 NBC
I Dream of Jeannie: 15 Years Later tf/pt 10.20.85 NBC

GORSHIN, FRANK
A&C, Supp. 1:
Navy Log ep Amscray 2.13.57 ABC
Hennessy ep Hennessy Meets Honeyboy 10.5.59 CBS
The Law and Mr. Jones ep One for the Money 2.24.61 ABC
Combat ep The Medal 1.8.63 ABC
Naked City ep Beyond This Place There Be Dreams 1.30.63 ABC
Combat ep The Hell Machine 3.30.65 ABC
Batman ep A Riddle a Day Keeps the Riddler Away 2.66 ABC
Batman ep Death in Slow Motion 4.27.66, 4.28.66 ABC
Batman ep Ring Around the Riddler 1.21.67 ABC
The Men from Shiloh ep Follow the Leader 12.2.70 NBC
SUPP.:
The Fall Guy ep Losers Weepers 9.19.84 ABC

GORTNER, MARJOE*
The Marcus-Nelson Murders tf 3.8.73 CBS
Pray for the Wildcats tf 1.23.74 ABC
The Gun and the Pulpit tf/pt 4.3.74 ABC
Mayday at 40,000 Feet tf 11.12.76 CBS
Fantasy Island ep Something Borrowed, Something Blue 2.14.81 ABC
Fantasy Island ep Revenge of the Forgotten 2.19.83 ABC
The A-Team ep Recipe for Heavy Bread 9.27.83 NBC
T.J. Hooker ep Slay Ride 12.17.83 ABC

Street Hawk ep The Adjustor 1.18.85 ABC
Otherworld ep Village of the Motorpigs 2.23.85 CBS
Airwolf ep Dambreakers 3.16.85 CBS
T.J. Hooker ep Lag Time 3.23.85 ABC
Half Nelson ep Beverly Hills Princess 5.10.85 NBC

GOSSETT, LOU (a.k.a. Louis Gossett and Louis Gossett Jr.)
A&C, Supp. 1:
Alias Smith and Jones ep The Bounty Hunter 12.9.71 ABC
Harry O ep Shades 10.2.75 ABC
The Six Million Dollar Man ep Clark Templeton O'Flaherty 12.14.75 ABC
The Rockford Files ep Foul on the First Play 3.12.76 NBC
A&C, Supp. 2:
The Rockford Files ep Just Another Polish Wedding 2.18.77 NBC
SUPP.:
Benny's Place tf 5.31.82 ABC
The Powers of Matthew Star sr 12.24.82 NBC
Sadat tf 10.31, 11.7.83 OPT
The Guardian tf 10.84 HBO

GOULD, ELLIOTT*
Once Upon a Mattress sp 6.3.64 CBS
Come Blow Your Horn sp 11.81 SHO
The Rules of Marriage tf 5.10, 5.11.82 CBS
Faerie Tale Theater ep Jack and the Beanstalk 9.8.83 SHO
E/R sr 9.16.84 CBS
An American Portrait ep Moe Berg 4.4.85 CBS
George Burns Comedy Week ep The Assignment 10.30.85 CBS

GOULD, HAROLD*
Follow the Sun ep Another Part of the Jungle 10.29.61 ABC
Cain's Hundred ep Markdown on a Man 10.11.61 NBC
Route 66 ep Go Read the River 3.16.62 CBS
The Donna Reed Show ep Rebel with a Cause 11.8.62 ABC
It's a Man's World ep The Long Short Cut 12.17.62 NBC
Empire ep Stopover on the Way to the Moon 1.1.63 ABC
Dennis the Menace ep 4.21.63 CBS
The Lieutenant ep The Two-Star Giant 10.5.63 NBC
The Twilight Zone ep Probe Seven, Over and Out 11.29.63 CBS
The Twilight Zone ep The Bewitchin' Pool 6.19.64 CBS
The Man from UNCLE ep The Double Affair 11.17.64 NBC
Kentucky Jones ep 11.21.64 NBC
Dr. Kildare ep Please Let My Baby Live 1.28.65 NBC
The Farmer's Daughter ep The Oscar Hummingbird Story 1.28.65 ABC
The Jack Benny Program ep 2.19.65 CBS
Hazel ep George's Man Friday 3.18.65 NBC
12 O'Clock High ep The Threat 3.19.65 ABC

The Virginian ep Farewell to Honesty 3.24.65 NBC
The Fugitive ep Wings of an Angel 9.14.65 ABC
The Long, Hot Summer ep 9.16.65 ABC
The Virginian ep Day of the Scorpion 9.22.65 NBC
The FBI ep Slow March Up a Steep Hill 10.10.65 ABC
The Farmer's Daughter ep 10.18.65 ABC
Convoy ep No More Souvenirs 11.26.65 NBC
The FBI ep The Man Who Went Mad by Mistake 3.6.66 ABC
Love on a Rooftop ep 11.4.66 ABC
Get Smart ep 11.26.66 NBC
The Green Hornet ep May the Best Man Lose 12.23.66 ABC
The FBI ep The Courier 1.15.67 ABC
The Invaders ep The Experiment 1.17.67 ABC
The Fugitive ep Concrete Evidence 1.24.67 ABC
Run for Your Life ep The Assassin 2.27.67 NBC
The Felony Squad ep The Savage Streets 4.3.67 ABC
The Big Valley ep Cage of Eagles 4.14.67 ABC
He and She sr 9.6.67 CBS
The Wild Wild West ep The Night of the Bubbling Death 9.8.67 CBS
Judd, for the Defense ep Shadow of a Killer 10.6.67 ABC
The Invaders ep The Trial 10.10.67 ABC
The Flying Nun ep 11.9.67 ABC
Garrison's Gorillas ep Friendly Enemies 11.21.67 ABC
The FBI ep The Daughter 1.14.68 ABC
Daniel Boone ep The Imposter 1.18.68 NBC
The Big Valley ep The Challenge 3.18.68 ABC
The Flying Nun ep 10.10.68 ABC
Judd, for the Defense ep Weep the Hunter Home 11.8.68 ABC
Lancer ep The Last Train for Charlie Poe 11.26.68 CBS
The Wild Wild West ep The Night of the Avaricious Actuary 12.6.68 CBS
The FBI ep The Butcher 12.8.68 ABC
I Dream of Jeannie ep House for Sale 2.3.69 NBC
The Big Valley ep The Royal Road 3.3.69 ABC
Under the Yum Yum Tree pt 9.2.69 ABC
Mission: Impossible ep 9.28.69 CBS
Here Come the Brides ep Break the Bank of Tacoma 1.16.70 ABC
Lancer ep Dream of Falcons 4.7.70 CBS
The High Chaparral ep A Good Sound Profit 10.30.70 NBC
The FBI ep The Stalking Horse 1.10.71 ABC
Ransom for a Dead Man tf/pt 3.11.71 NBC
Cannon ep A Lonely Place to Die 11.16.71 CBS
A Death of Innocence tf 11.26.71 CBS
The Mod Squad ep The Loser 11.30.71 ABC
The FBI ep The Test 2.20.72 ABC
Love, American Style ep Love and the Happy Days pt 2.25.72 ABC
The Mary Tyler Moore Show ep 10.3.72 CBS
The Delphi Bureau ep The Man Upstairs/The Man Downstairs Project 10.26.72 ABC

Mannix ep One Step to Midnight 11.12.72 CBS
Hawaii Five-O ep V for Vashon 11.14, 11.21, 11.28.72 CBS
The Streets of San Francisco ep The Takers 12.2.72 ABC
Cannon ep The Prisoners 2.21.73 CBS
Murdock's Gang tf/pt 3.20.73 CBS
Bachelor at Law pt 6.5.73 CBS
The Partridge Family ep Classical Music 9.29.73 ABC
Ironside ep The Armageddon Gang 10.11.73 NBC
Lotsa Luck ep 10.15.73 NBC
Chase ep John Doe Bucks 1.16.74 NBC
Conflicts ep Double Solitaire 1.21.74 PBS
Judgement: The Trial of Ethel and Julius Rosenberg tf 1.28.74 ABC
The Streets of San Francisco ep Death and the Favored Few 3.14.74 ABC
Rhoda sr 9.9.74 CBS
Gunsmoke ep The Guns of Cibola Blanca 9.23, 9.30.74 CBS
Police Story ep Fathers and Sons 10.1.74 NBC
Petrocelli ep Death in High Places 10.23.74 NBC
Petrocelli ep Mirror Mirror on the Wall 11.6.74 NBC
The Bob Crane Show ep 3.13.75 NBC
Cannon ep Tomorrow Ends at Noon 3.19.75 CBS
Medical Story tf/pt 9.4.75 NBC
Hawaii Five-O ep The Case Against McGarrett 10.17.75 CBS
The Rookies ep 10.28.75 ABC
Medical Story ep The Quality of Mercy 1.8.76 NBC
Flannery and Quilt pt 2.1.76 CBS
Police Story ep Eamon Kinsella Royce 2.20.76 NBC
How to Break Up a Happy Divorce tf 10.6.76 NBC
Never Con a Killer tf/pt 12.6.76 ABC
Police Story ep The Blue Fog 2.1.77 NBC
The Feather and Father Gang sr 3.7.77 ABC
Washington: Behind Closed Doors ms 9.6-9.11.77 ABC
Family ep Acts of Love 9.20.77 ABC
Soap ep 11.15, 11.22.77 ABC
The Hallmark Hall of Fame ep Have I Got a Christmas for You 12.16.77 NBC
The Love Boat ep 1.21.78 ABC
Rhoda ep 1.29.78, 11.11.78 CBS
Watts Made Out of Thread sp 10.1.78 NN
Grandpa Goes to Washington ep 10.24.78 NBC
The Rockford Files ep The Return of Richie Brockelman 3.3.79 NBC
Sergeant T.K. Yu pt 4.19.79 NBC
The Misadventures of Sheriff Lobo ep 10.9.79 NBC
Better Late Than Never tf 10.17.79 NBC
Lou Grant ep 10.29.79 CBS
11th Victim tf 11.6.79 CBS
Aunt Mary tf 12.5.79 CBS
The Man in the Santa Claus Suit tf 12.23.79 NBC
Kenny Rogers as the Gambler tf 4.8.80 CBS

Moviola: The Scarlet O'Hara War tf 5.19.80 NBC
Moviola: The Silent Lovers tf 5.20.80 NBC
Charlie's Angels ep He Married an Angel 1.31.81 ABC
Park Place sr 4.9.81 CBS
Born to Be Sold tf 11.2.81 NBC
Help Wanted: Male tf 1.16.82 CBS
Foot in the Door sr 3.28.83 CBS
Kenny Rogers as the Gambler: The Adventure Continues tf 11.28, 11.29.83 CBS
Red Light Sting tf 4.5.84 CBS
Webster ep The Great Walnutto 10.12.84 ABC
Finder of Lost Loves ep Echoes 10.27.84 ABC
Under One Roof sr 3.23.85 NBC
The Fourth Wiseman sp 3.30.85 ABC
No Complaints pt 7.24.85 NBC
The Golden Girls ep Rose the Prud 9.28.85 NBC
Trapper John, M.D. ep Just Around the Coroner 11.10.85 CBS

GOULET, ROBERT
SUPP.:
Fantasy Island ep Image of Celeste 3.20.82 ABC
Matt Houston ep The Showgirl Murders 3.20.83 ABC
Glitter ep Illusions 12.25.84 ABC
Murder, She Wrote ep Paint Me a Murder 2.17.85 CBS

GRAFF, ILENE*
Super Train sr 2.7.79 NBC
Beulah Land ms 10.7-10.9.80 NBC
Heaven on Earth pt 4.12.81 NBC
Lewis and Clark sr 10.30.81 NBC
Mork and Mindy ep Gotta Run 5.6.82 ABC
Remington Steele ep Steele Belted 11.12.82 NBC
Charley's Aunt sp 2.6.83 TEC
Three's Company ep The Apartment 3.22.83 ABC
13 Thirteenth Avenue pt 8.15.83 CBS
The Earthlings pt 7.5.84 ABC
Mr. Belvedere sr 3.15.85 ABC
Mr. Belvedere sr ret 9.27.85 ABC

GRANDY, FRED
SUPP.:
The Love Boat sr ret 10.2.82 ABC
Matt Houston ep The Showgirl Murders 3.20.83 ABC
The Love Boat sr ret 10.1.83 ABC
Cagney and Lacey ep 3.19.84 CBS
The Love Boat sr ret 9.22.84 ABC
The Love Boat sr ret 9.28.85 ABC

GRANGER, FARLEY
SUPP.:
Tales from the Darkside ep Pain Killer 10.84 NN

The Love Boat ep A Matter of Taste 12.8.84 ABC
The Love Boat ep Call Me Grandma 5.4.85 ABC

GRANGER, STEWART
SUPP.:
The Fall Guy ep Manhunter 1.19.83 ABC
Hotel ep Blackout 9.28.83 ABC
Murder, She Wrote ep Paint Me a Murder 2.17.85 CBS

GRANT, FAYE*
The Greatest American Hero sr 3.25.81 ABC
Home Room pt 8.10.81 ABC
Senior Trip tf 12.30.81 CBS
The Incredible Hulk ep 5.5.82 CBS
Voyagers ep The Voyagers 10.3.82 NBC
The Devlin Connection ep The Corpse in the Chronicle 10.23.82 NBC
Tales of the Gold Monkey ep Last Chance Louie 3.11.83 ABC
V ms 5.1, 5.2.83 NBC
V: The Final Battle ms 5.6-5.8.84 NBC
V: The Series sr 10.26.84 NBC

GRANT, LEE
SUPP.:
Thou Shalt Not Kill tf/pt 4.12.82 NBC
Bare Essence ms 10.4, 10.5.82 CBS
Plaza Suite sp 12.31.82 HBO
Will There Really Be a Morning? tf 2.22.83 CBS
One Day at a Time ep 2.12.84 CBS
Mussolini: The Untold Story ms 11.24, 11.25, 11.26.85 NBC

GRAVES, PETER
A&C, B.V.:
Cimarron City ep The Unaccounted 1.3.59 NBC
SUPP.:
Fantasy Island ep The Sailor 1.2.82 ABC
The Winds of War ms 2.6-2.13.83 ABC
Fantasy Island ep Nurses' Night Out 10.22.83 ABC
Murder, She Wrote ep Lovers and Other Killers 11.18.84 CBS

GRAY, ERIN
SUPP.:
Born Beautiful tf 11.1.82 NBC
The Fall Guy ep License to Kill 1.13, 1.20.82 ABC
Simon and Simon ep Matchmaker 3.9.82 CBS
Fantasy Island ep Face of Love 3.20.82 ABC
Silver Spoons sr 9.25.82 NBC
Silver Spoons sr ret 10.15.83 NBC
Silver Spoons sr ret 9.23.84 NBC
Code of Vengeance tf/pt 6.30.85 NBC
Silver Spoons sr ret 9.15.85 NBC

GRAY, LINDA
SUPP.:
Dallas sr ret 10.1.82 CBS
Not in Front of the Children tf 10.26.82 CBS
Dallas sr ret 9.30.83 CBS
Beauty and the Beast sp vo 11.25.83 CBS
Dallas sr ret 9.28.84 CBS
Dallas sr ret 9.27.85 CBS

GREENE, LORNE
A&C, B.V.:
You Are There ep The Fall of Parnell 6.13.54 CBS
SUPP.:
Police Squad! ep A Substantial Gift 3.4.82 ABC
The Love Boat ep Love Will Find a Way 11.20.82 ABC
Highway to Heaven ep The Smile in the Third Row 11.20.85 NBC

GREGG, JULIE*
Cannon ep Target in the Mirror 10.3.73 CBS

GREGORY, JAMES
A&C, Supp. 2:
The Web ep All the Way to the Moon 10.3.51 CBS
Armstrong Circle Theater ep Transfusion 3.31.53 NBC
Danger ep Last Stop Before Albany 5.5.53 CBS
Danger ep Surface Treason 6.30.53 CBS
Armstrong Circle Theater ep The Old Man's Gold 1.26.54 NBC
Danger ep Fall Guy 2.16.54 CBS
Danger ep Outlaw's Boots 5.11.54 CBS
Danger ep Knife in the Dark 12.7.54 CBS
Playwrights '56 ep The Heart's a Forgotten Hotel 10.25.55 NBC
Alfred Hitchcock Presents ep The Perfect Crime 10.20.57 CBS
Pursuit ep The House at Malibu 11.26.58 CBS
Laramie ep Man of God 12.1.59 NBC
The June Allyson Show ep I Hit and Run 1.20.60 CBS
Alcoa Theater ep Head to Head 2.22.60 CBS
Wagon Train ep The Ricky and Laura Bell Story 2.24.60 NBC
Checkmate ep Hour of the Execution 1.21.61 CBS
Thriller ep The Meriwether File 2.14.61 NBC
The Loretta Young Show ep Those at the Top 5.7.61 NBC
Lawless Years sr ret 5.12.61 NBC
Frontier Circus ep The Depths of Fear 10.5.61 CBS
The New Breed ep Prime Target 10.10.61 ABC
Target: The Corruptors ep The Malignant Hearts 3.5.62 ABC
Empire ep When the Gods Laugh 12.18.62 ABC
Laramie ep The Sometime Gambler 3.19.63 NBC
The Defenders ep All the Silent Voices 2.1.64 CBS
The Lieutenant ep Capp's Lady 2.8.64 NBC
Ben Casey ep There Once Was a Man in the Land of Uz 1.23.64 ABC

Breaking Point ep Glass Flowers Never Drop Petals 3.23.64 ABC
Rawhide ep Incident of the Peyote Cup 5.14.64 CBS
Gunsmoke ep The New Society 5.22.65 CBS
The Wild Wild West ep The Night of the Inferno 9.17.65 CBS
The FBI ep To Feed My Enemy 10.24.65 ABC
Gunsmoke ep Judge Calvin Strom 12.18.65 CBS
F Troop ep Lt. O'Rourke, Front and Center Fall 1966 ABC
The Fugitive ep Wine Is a Traitor 11.1.66 ABC
F Troop ep Carpetbagging, Anyone? Spring 1967 ABC
Cimarron Strip ep The Hunted 10.5.67 CBS
Gunsmoke ep The Victim 1.1.68 CBS
The High Chaparral ep The Hair Hunter 3.10.68 NBC
Judd, For the Defense ep The Death Farm 11.1.68 ABC
Bracken's World ep Day for Night 3.20.70 NBC
Headmaster ep 11.18.70 CBS
The Paul Lynde Show sr 9.13.72 ABC
Columbo ep The Most Crucial Game 11.5.72 NBC
Police Story ep The Witness 3.11.75 NBC
SUPP.:
Quincy, M.E. ep The Last of Leadbottom 4.18.82 NBC
Wait Till Your Mother Gets Home tf 1.17.83 NBC

GREGORY, NATALIE*
Matt Houston ep The Ghost of Carter Gault 10.28.83 ABC
Two Marriages ep Commitment 4.5.84 ABC
Cagney and Lacey ep Child Witness 10.15.84 CBS
Magnum, P.I. ep Blind Justice 11.8.84 CBS
Kids Don't Tell tf 1.15.85 CBS
Robert Kennedy and His Times ms 1.27, 1.28, 1.29, 1.30.85 CBS
Alice in Wonderland tf 12.9, 12.10.85 CBS

GRIER, ROSEY
SUPP.:
The Jeffersons ep 11.20.83 CBS

GRIFFETH, SIMONE*
Only with Married Men tf 12.4.74 ABC
Starsky and Hutch tf/pt 4.30.75 ABC
The Six Million Dollar Man ep Dark Side of the Moon 11.6, 11.13.77 ABC
Black Beauty ms 1.31-2.4.78 NBC
Quincy, M.E. ep Ashes to Ashes 2.10.78 NBC
The Incredible Hulk ep The Hulk Breaks Las Vegas 4.21.78 CBS
The American Girls ep The Beautiful People Jungle 9.30.78 CBS
The Next Step Beyond ep Key to Understanding 1.79 NN
Mandrake tf/pt 1.24.79 NBC
Hawaii Five-O ep A Very Personal Affair 3.15.79 CBS

The Second Time Around pt 7.24.79 ABC
Tenspeed and Brown Shoe ep Tenspeed and Brown Show (pt) 1.27.80 ABC
When the Whistle Blows ep 3.28.80 ABC
Hart to Hart ep Cruise at Your Own Risk 4.8.80 ABC
Fighting Back tf 12.7.80 ABC
Ladies' Man sr 10.27.80 CBS
The Greatest American Hero ep Reseda Rose 4.15.81 ABC
Nero Wolfe ep Sweet Revenge 4.28.81 NBC
Today's FBI ep Career Move 12.6.81 ABC
Report to Murphy ep Girl Most Likely 4.12.82 CBS
Bret Maverick ep Faith, Hope and Charity 4.13, 4.20.82 NBC
Gavilan ep A Drop in the Ocean 12.7.82 NBC
Amanda's sr 2.10.83 ABC
Buffalo Bill ep 6.8.83 NBC
Hart to Hart ep Love Game 11.8.83 ABC
T.J. Hooker ep Undercover Affair 12.10.83 ABC
Mickey Spillane's Mike Hammer ep Deadly Reunion 1.12.85 CBS
Riptide ep Wipe Out 10.1.85 NBC
Magnum, P.I. ep Blood and Honor 12.5.85 CBS
Crazy Like a Fox ep Is There a Fox in the House? 12.22.85 CBS

GRIFFITH, ANDY
SUPP.:
For Lovers Only tf/pt 10.15.82 ABC
Fantasy Island ep Legend 10.30.82 ABC
Murder in Coweta County tf 2.15.83 CBS
The Demon Murder Case tf 3.6.83 NBC
Fatal Vision tf 11.18, 11.19.84 NBC
Hotel ep Illusions 11.28.84 ABC
The Love Boat ep Hidden Treasure 10.12.85 ABC
Crime of Innocence tf 10.27.85 NBC

GRIMES, TAMMY
SUPP.:
The CBS Library ep The Incredible Book Escape vo 11.25.82 CBS
An Invasion of Privacy tf 1.12.83 CBS
St. Elsewhere ep Playing God 9.26.84 NBC
Royal Match pt 8.2.85 CBS

GRIZZARD, GEORGE
SUPP.:
American Playhouse ep The Shady Hill Kidnapping 1.12.82 PBS
Trapper John, M.D. ep 1.8.84 CBS
Robert Kennedy and His Times ms 1.27, 1.28, 1.29, 1.30.84 CBS
Embassy tf 4.21.85 NBC
Midas Valley tf 6.27.85 ABC
Spenser: For Hire ep The Choice 10.4.85 ABC

GRODIN, CHARLES
A&C, Supp. 2:
The Young Marrieds sr 10.5.64 ABC
The Trials of O'Brien ep Picture Me a Murder 11.27.65 CBS
The Felony Squad ep A Penny Game, A Two-Bit Murder 12.19.66 ABC
The FBI ep Sky on Fire 2.26.67 ABC
The Guns of Will Sonnett ep A Bell for Will Sonnett 9.15.67 ABC
The Big Valley ep The Good Thieves 1.1.67 ABC
N.Y.P.D. ep Money Man 10.10.67 ABC
SUPP.:
Love, Sex ... and Marriage sp 5.11.83 ABC
Grown Ups sp 11.25.85 SHO

GROH, DAVID
SUPP.:
Today's FBI ep Bank Job 3.7.82 ABC
The CBS Children's Mystery Theater ep The Zertigo Diamond Caper 9.28.82 CBS
Matt Houston ep The Visitors 2.27.83 ABC
General Hospital sr 5.83 ABC
The Whiz Kids ep Watch Out 1.14.84 CBS
Hotel ep Hearts and Minds 5.8.85 ABC
Murder She Wrote ep Murder Digs Deep 12.29.85 CBS

GROSS, MICHAEL*
A Girl Named Sooner tf 6.18.75 NBC
FDR: The Last Year tf 5.15.80 NBC
Dream House tf 11.28.81 CBS
The Neighborhood tf 4.25.82 NBC
Family Ties sr 9.22.82 NBC
Little Gloria ... Happy at Last tf 10.24, 10.25.82 NBC
Family Ties sr ret 9.28.83 NBC
Cook and Perry: The Race to the Pole tf 12.13.83 CBS
Summer Fantasy tf 5.25.84 NBC
Family Ties sr ret 9.27.84 NBC
Finder of Lost Loves ep Last Wish 1.5.85 ABC
Family Ties Vacation tf 9.23.85 NBC
Family Ties sr ret 9.26.85 NBC
A Letter to Three Wives tf 12.16.85 NBC

GUARDINO, HARRY
A&C, B.V.:
Johnny Staccato ep Murder in Hi Fi 11.5.59 NBC
Twelve O'Clock High ep The Slaughter Pen 1.10.66 ABC
Hawaii Five-O ep Murder--Eyes Only 9.12.75 CBS
A&C, Supp. 2:
Hawaii Five-O ep A Lion in the Streets 10.4.79 CBS
SUPP.:
Lovers and Other Strangers pt 7.22.83 ABC

Murder, She Wrote ep Birds of a Feather 10.14.84 CBS
Hotel ep Resolutions 10.24.84 ABC
Jessie ep King of the Streets 10.30.84 ABC
On Our Way pt 6.29.85 CBS

GUILLAUME, ROBERT
SUPP.:
Purlie sp 10.81 SHO
The Kid with the Broken Halo tf/pt 4.5.82 NBC
Benson sr ret 10.22.82 ABC
The Kid with the 100 I.Q. tf 2.6.83 ABC
Benson sr ret 9.16.83 ABC
The Love Boat Fall Preview Party sp 9.15.84 ABC
Benson sr ret 9.21.84 ABC
Benson sr ret 10.4.85 ABC
North and South ms 11.3-11.20.85 ABC

GULAGER, CLU
A&C, Supp. 1:
Black Saddle ep Client: Meade 1.17.59 NBC
Wanted: Dead or Alive ep Crossroads 4.11.59 CBS
Lawless Years ep The Immigrant 4.23.59 NBC
Wagon Train ep The Stagecoach Story 9.3.59 NBC
Alfred Hitchcock Presents ep Appointment at Eleven 10.11.59 CBS
Law of the Plainsman ep The Hostiles 10.22.59 NBC
Wagon Train ep The Clarence Mullins Story 5.1.63 NBC
Wagon Train ep The Sam Spicer Story 10.28.63 NBC
Wagon Train ep The Ben Engel Story 3.16.64 ABC
Hawaii Five-O ep Fools Die Twice 10.17.72 CBS
Hawaii Five-O ep Assault on the Palace 10.7.76 CBS
SUPP.:
Quincy, M.E. ep For Love of Joshua 2.3.82 NBC
The Fall Guy ep Hell on Wheels 12.8.82 ABC
Living Proof: The Hank Williams Jr. Story tf 3.7.83 NBC
The Fall Guy ep Trauma (a.k.a. Notes About Courage) 9.28.83 ABC
The Master ep Max 1.20.84 NBC
Masquerade ep Oil 1.26.84 ABC
The Yellow Rose ep Villa's Gold 5.5.84 NBC
Cover Up ep Sudden Exposure 10.20.84 CBS
Street Hawk ep Fire on the Wing 2.8.85 ABC
Knight Rider ep Buyout 2.10.85 NBC
The Fall Guy ep The Last Chance Platoon 10.24.85 ABC
Bridge Across Time tf 11.22.85 NBC
Murder, She Wrote ep Dead Heat 11.24.85 CBS
Riptide ep Requiem for Icarus 12.10.85 NBC

GUNN, MOSES
A&C, Supp. 2:
The FBI ep Eye of the Storm 1.5.69 ABC

Kung Fu ep The Stone 4.12.74 ABC
Switch ep Heritage of Death 4.3.77 CBS
SUPP.:
Father Murphy sr ret 10.26.82 NBC
Highway to Heaven ep Popcorn, Peanuts and Crackerjacks 11.13.85 NBC

GWYNNE, FRED
SUPP.:
American Playhouse ep Sense and Humor: Any Friend of Nicholas Nickleby Is a Friend of Mine 2.9.82 PBS

- H -

HACK, SHELLEY
SUPP.:
Close Ties sp 3.6.83 TEC
Cutter to Houston sr 10.1.83 CBS
Trackdown: Finding the Goodbar Killer tf 10.15.83 CBS
Found Money tf 12.19.83 NBC

HACKETT, BUDDY
SUPP.:
The Fall Guy ep The Adventures of Ozzie and Harold 2.3.82 ABC
The Fall Guy ep The Further Adventures of Ozzie and Harold 1.26.83 ABC

HACKETT, JOAN
A&C, B.V.:
Daniel Boone ep A Pinch of Salt 5.1.69 NBC
Alias Smith and Jones ep The Legacy of Charlie O'Rourke 4.22.71 ABC
SUPP.:
A Girl's Life pt 8.4.83 NBC

HADDOCK, JULIE ANN
SUPP.:
Boone ep 9.26.83 NBC
Boone ep Banjo 10.10.83 NBC
Under One Roof ep Wayne's Nose Job 5.11.85 NBC

HADEN, SARA
A&C, B.V.:
Perry Mason ep The Case of the Romantic Rogue 2.14.59 CBS
Bonanza ep The Jury 12.30.62 NBC
Breaking Point ep The Gnu, Now Almost Extinct 12.9.63 ABC

HAGGERTY, DAN

SUPP.:

The Capture of Grizzly Adams tf 2.21.82 NBC

The Love Boat ep The World's Greatest Kisser 11.26.83 ABC

HAGMAN, LARRY

A&C, B.V.:

Harbourmaster ep The Captain's Gun 5.11.58 CBS

The Defenders ep The Noose 4.27.63 CBS

A&C, Supp. 1:

Police Story ep Glamour Boy 10.29.74 NBC

Harry O ep One for the Road 9.18.75 ABC

A&C, Supp. 2:

The Rockford Files ep Forced Retirement 12.9.77 NBC

SUPP.:

Dallas sr ret 10.1.82 CBS

Knots Landing ep 10.7.82 CBS

Deadly Encounter tf 12.18.82 CBS

Dallas sr ret 9.30.83 CBS

Dallas sr ret 9.28.84 CBS

Dallas sr ret 9.27.85 CBS

HAID, CHARLES

SUPP.:

Divorce Wars tf 3.1.82 ABC

American Playhouse ep Working 4.13.82 PBS

Hill Street Blues sr ret 9.30.82 NBC

Hill Street Blues sr ret 10.13.83 NBC

Hill Street Blues sr ret 9.27.84 NBC

Children in the Crossfire tf 12.3.84 NBC

Code of Vengeance tf/pt 6.30.85 NBC

Hill Street Blues sr ret 9.26.85 NBC

HALL, KEVIN PETER*

Rona Jaffe's "Mazes and Monsters" tf 12.28.82 CBS

E/R ep 11.21.84 CBS

The Dukes of Hazzard ep 2.8.85 CBS

The Misfits of Science sr 10.4.85 NBC

HALOP, BILLY

A&C, B.V.:

Richard Diamond ep 4.19.59 CBS

Gunsmoke ep Stranger in Town 11.20.67 CBS

Gomer Pyle, USMC ep A Dog Is a Dog Is a Dog 1.68 CBS

HALOP, FLORENCE

A&C, B.V.:

The Dick Van Dyke Show ep The Ugliest Dog in the World 10.6.65 CBS

Captain Nice ep The Man with Three Blue Eyes 2.20.67 NBC

SUPP.:
St. Elsewhere ep Dr. Wyler, I Presume 12.19.84 NBC
St. Elsewhere ep Whistle Wyler Works 1.2.85 NBC
St. Elsewhere ep Saving Face 1.16.85 NBC
St. Elsewhere ep Any Portrait in a Storm 1.30.85 NBC
St. Elsewhere ep Red, White, Black and Blue 2.13.85 NBC
St. Elsewhere ep Murder, She Rote (cq) 2.27.85 NBC
St. Elsewhere ep Tears of a Clown 3.13.85 NBC
Anything for Love pt 8.7.85 NBC
Night Court sr (with ep Hello, Goodbye) 9.26.85 NBC

HAMEL, VERONICA
A&C, Supp. 2:
Joe Forrester ep Fashion Mart 12.16.75 NBC
Kojak ep A House of Prayer, a Den of Thieves 12.21.75 CBS
The Rockford Files ep A Big Deal in the Valley 3.19.76 NBC
Switch ep Round Up the Usual Suspects 3.23.76 CBS
The Rockford Files ep Return to the 38th Parallel 12.10.76 NBC
The Eddie Capra Mysteries ep The Intimate Friends of Jenny Wilde 11.10.78 NBC
SUPP.:
Hill Street Blues sr ret 9.30.82 NBC
Sessions tf 9.26.83 ABC
Hill Street Blues sr ret 10.13.83 NBC
Hill Street Blues sr ret 9.27.84 NBC
The Duck Factory ep The Annies 4.26.85 NBC
Hill Street Blues sr ret 9.26.85 NBC
Kane and Abel ms 11.17, 11.18, 11.19.85 CBS

HAMILL, DOROTHY*
Fantasy Island ep Naughty Marietta 1.8.83 ABC
Diff'rent Strokes ep Family on Ice 2.19.83 NBC
Grandpa, Will You Run with Me? sp 4.3.83 NBC

HAMILL, MARK
A&C, Supp. 2:
Headmaster ep 10.30.70 CBS
Manhunter ep The Lodester Ambush 12.4.74 CBS
Medical Center ep You Can't Annul My Baby 1.9.76 CBS
Streets of San Francisco ep Innocent No More 2.24.77 ABC
Eight Is Enough sr 3.15.77 ABC

HAMILTON, ALEXA*
The Greatest American Hero ep Saturday on Sunset Boulevard 4.8.81 ABC
CHiPs ep The Killer Indy 10.25.81 NBC
Bosom Buddies ep The Way Kip and Henry Were 3.4.82 ABC
Tucker's Witch ep The Good Witch of Laurel Canyon 10.6.82 CBS
Gavilan ep Sarah and the Buzz 10.26.82 NBC
Voyagers ep The Day the Rebels Took Lincoln 11.21.82 NBC

The Quest ep Escape from a Velvet Box 11.19.82 NBC
The Invisible Woman tf/pt 2.13.83 NBC
Trapper John, M.D. ep 3.20.83 CBS
Tales of the Gold Monkey ep Morning Becomes Matuka 6.1.83 ABC
Legmen ep 2.3.84 NBC
Knight Rider ep A Good Knight's Work 3.4.84 NBC
Hardcastle and McCormick ep Really Neat Cars and Guys with a Sense of Humor 3.25.84 ABC
Happy Days ep The Spirit Is Willing 4.24.84 ABC
Hail to the Chief sr 4.9.85 ABC
Beverly Hills Cowgirl Blues tf/pt 10.5.85 CBS

HAMILTON, GEORGE
A&C, B.V.:
The Adventures of Rin Tin Tin ep The Misfit Marshal 1.9.59 ABC
Bus Stop ep The Opposite Virtues 2.18.62 ABC
SUPP.:
Malibu tf/pt 1.23, 1.24.83 ABC
Poor Richard pt 1.21.84 CBS
Two Fathers' Justice tf 2.11.85 NBC

HAMILTON, LINDA*
Reunion tf 10.14.80 CBS
Rape and Marriage: The Rideout Case 10.30.80 CBS
King's Crossing sr 1.16.82 ABC
Country Gold tf 11.23.82 CBS
Wishman pt 6.23.83 ABC
Secrets of a Mother and Daughter tf 10.4.83 CBS
Hill Street Blues ep Untitled 1.26.84 NBC
Hill Street Blues ep Grace Under Pressure 2.2.84 NBC
Hill Street Blues ep The Other Side of Oneness 2.9.84 NBC
Hill Street Blues ep Parting Is Such Sweet Sorrow 2.16.84 NBC

HAMILTON, MARGARET
SUPP.:
Lou Grant ep Review 2.8.82 CBS

HAMILTON, NEIL
A&C, B.V.:
Zorro ep Spark of Revenge 2.19.59 ABC
Bourbon Street Beat ep The House of Lidezan 2.22.60 ABC
Bachelor Father ep Kelly's Engagement Spring 1962 CBS

HAMMOND, NICHOLAS*
Mr. and Mrs. Bo Jo Jones tf 11.16.71 ABC
Owen Marshall, Counselor at Law ep A Killer with a Badge 10.12.72 ABC
The Waltons ep The Townie 3.8.73 CBS
Gunsmoke ep Women for Sale 9.10, 9.17.73 CBS

Outrage! tf 11.28.73 ABC
Conflict ep Double Solitaire 1.21.74 PBS
Dirty Sally ep 4.19.74 CBS
Lucas Tanner ep Thirteen Going on Twenty 10.2.74 NBC
Gunsmoke ep Thirty a Month and Found 10.7.74 CBS
Petrocelli ep Blood Money 2.11.76 NBC
Law of the Land tf 4.29.76 NBC
Family ep 11.30.76 ABC
The Fantastic Journey ep The Innocent Prey 6.17.77 NBC
Spider-Man tf/pt 9.14.77 CBS
The Oregon Trail ep The Army Deserter 10.19.77 NBC
Eight Is Enough ep 12.14.77 ABC
Logan's Run ep Judas Goat 12.19.77 CBS
The Nancy Drew Mysteries ep The Lady on Thursday at 10 1.1.78 ABC
The Amazing Spider-Man sr 4.5.78 CBS
The Amazing Spider-Man sr ret 9.5.78 CBS
Super Train ep Where Have You Been, Billy Boy? 5.5.79 NBC
The Martian Chronicles ms 1.27-1.29.80 NBC
The Home Front pt 10.9.80 CBS
The Manions of America ms 9.30, 10.1,10.2.81 ABC
Adventures of Pollyana pt 4.10.82 CBS
Magnum, P.I. ep 11.11.82 CBS
Dallas ep 11.12.82 CBS
Two Marriages ep Legacy 3.22.84 ABC
Crazy Like a Fox ep Till Death Do Us Part 1.20.85 CBS
Murder, She Wrote ep Murder in the Afternoon 10.13.85 CBS

HANKS, TOM*
The Love Boat ep Friends and Lovers? 10.25.80 ABC
Bosom Buddies sr 11.27.80 ABC
Bosom Buddies sr ret 10.8.81 ABC
Taxi ep The Road Not Taken 4.29.82 ABC
Happy Days ep A Little Case of Revenge 11.9.82 ABC
Rona Jaffe's "Mazes and Monsters" tf 12.28.82 CBS
Family Ties ep The Fugitive 1.19.83 NBC
Family Ties ep Say Uncle 1.26.84 NBC
Saturday Night Live hos 12.14.85 NBC

HANLEY, BRIDGET
SUPP.:
Simon and Simon ep Rough Rider Rides Again 11.18.82 CBS
Malibu tf/pt 1.23, 1.24.83 ABC
Love Sidney ep Show Biz Mamas 4.4.83 NBC
Mama's Family ep The Mama Who Came to Dinner 12.22.83 NBC

HARDIN, MELORA*
Thunder sr 9.10.77 NBC
Quincy, M.E. ep Speed Trap 10.11.79 NBC
Haywire tf 5.14.80 CBS
Quincy, M.E. ep Next Stop Nowhere 12.1.82 NBC

Family Tree sr 1.22.83 NBC
Two Marriages sr 4.23.83 ABC
Magnum, P.I. ep Luther Gillis File #521 10.6.83 CBS
Little House: Look Back to Yesterday tf 12.12.83 NBC
Two Marriages ep Choices 3.8.84 ABC
Two Marriages ep Friendships 3.15.84 ABC
Mama Malone ep 4.25.84 CBS
The Best Times sr 4.19.85 NBC

HAREWOOD, DORIAN*
Foster and Laurie tf 11.13.75 CBS
Panic in Echo Park tf 6.23.77 NBC
Siege tf 4.26.78 CBS
Roots: The Next Generation ms 2.18-2.25.79 ABC
An American Christmas Carol tf 12.16.79 ABC
High Ice tf 1.7.80 NBC
Beulah Land ms 10.7, 10.8, 10.9.80 NBC
Strike Force sr 11.13.81 ABC
The Ambush Murders tf 1.5.82 CBS
I, Desire tf 11.15.82 ABC
Matt Houston ep The Rock and the Hard Place 1.2.83 ABC
Trauma Center sr 9.22.83 ABC
The Jesse Owens Story tf 7.9, 7.16.84 NN
Glitter sr 9.27.84 ABC
Hotel ep Passports 4.10.85 ABC
Dirty Work pt 6.6.85 CBS

HARMON, DEBORAH*
The Ted Knight Show sr 4.8.78 CBS
Comedy of Horrors pt 9.1.81 CBS
M*A*S*H ep 10.25.82 CBS
The Facts of Life ep Teacher's Pet 1.26.83 NBC
Used Cars pt 5.15.84 CBS
My Wicked, Wicked Ways.... The Legend of Errol Flynn tf 1.21.85 CBS
George Burns Comedy Week ep Death Benefits 10.2.85 CBS

HARMON, JOY*
Gidget sr 9.15.65 ABC
Bewitched ep Divided He Falls 4.66 ABC
Mr. Roberts ep Carry Me Back to Cococe Island Spring 1966 NBC
20th Century Follies pt 2.16.72 ABC

HARMON, MARK
SUPP.:
Intimate Agony tf 3.21.83 ABC
St. Elsewhere sr 10.26.83 NBC
The Love Boat ep Set Up For Romance 11.19.83 ABC
St. Elsewhere sr ret 9.19.84 NBC
St. Elsewhere sr ret 9.18.85 NBC

HARPER, TESS*
Kentucky Woman tf 1.11.83 CBS
Starflight: The Plane That Couldn't Land tf 2.27.83 ABC
Chiefs ms 11.13-11.16.83 CBS
Celebrity ms 2.12-2.14.84 NBC
George Burns Comedy Week ep The Smiths 10.9.85 CBS
Promises to Keep tf 10.15.85 CBS

HARPER, VALERIE
SUPP.:
Farrell for the People tf/pt 10.18.82 NBC
Don't Go to Sleep tf 12.10.82 ABC
An Invasion of Privacy tf 1.12.83 CBS
The Execution tf 1.14.85 NBC

HARRINGTON, PAT (a.k.a. Pat Harrington Jr.)
A&C, Supp. 2:
Grindl ep Grindl, Girl WAC 3.15.64 NBC
Mr. Novak ep There's a Penguin in My Garden 4.6.65 NBC
Hank ep 2.4.66 NBC
F Troop ep Spy, Counterspy, Counter Counterspy Spring 1966 ABC
Captain Nice ep The Week They Stole Payday 4.3.67 NBC
Here Come the Brides ep Debt of Honor 1.23.70 ABC
The New Andy Griffith Show ep 2.12.71 CBS
The Girl With Something Extra ep John and Sally and Fred and Linda 10.73 NBC
SUPP.:
Between Two Brothers tf 3.9.82 CBS
One Day at a Time sr ret 10.3.82 CBS
One Day at a Time sr ret 10.2.83 CBS
The Love Boat ep Dutch Treat 9.29.84 ABC
Glitter ep Mr. Television 12.18.84 ABC
Who's the Boss? ep Guess Who's Coming Forever? 1.29.85 ABC
Murder, She Wrote ep Footnote to Murder 3.10.85 CBS
The Comedy Factory ep Max and Me 7.12.85 ABC
Crazy Like a Fox ep Eye in the Sky 10.6.85 CBS

HARRIS, JO ANN
A&C, Supp. 2:
The High Chaparral ep The Little Thieves 12.26.69 NBC
Medical Center ep The Professional 3.11.70 CBS
The Men from Shiloh ep Jenny 9.30.70 NBC
Hawaii Five-O ep And the Horse Jumped Over the Moon 2.18.75 CBS
SUPP.:
Laverne and Shirley ep Short on Time 2.8.83 ABC
The Duck Factory ep The Children's Half-Hour 6.27.85 NBC

HARRIS, JULIE
SUPP.:

Knots Landing sr ret 9.30.82 CBS
Knots Landing sr ret 9.29.83 CBS
Knots Landing sr ret 10.4.84 CBS
Knots Landing sr ret 9.26.85 CBS

HARRISON, GREGORY
SUPP.:
Trapper John, M.D. sr ret 9.26.82 CBS
The Fighter tf 2.19.83 CBS
The Hasty Heart sp 9.83 SHO
Trapper John, M.D. sr ret 10.2.83 CBS
Trapper John, M.D. sr ret 9.30.84 CBS
Seduced tf 3.12.85 CBS
Trapper John, M.D. sr ret 9.29.85 CBS

HARRISON, JENILEE
SUPP.:
Fantasy Island ep Natchez Bound 11.6.82 ABC
The Love Boat ep Here Comes the Bride ... Maybe 1.15.83 ABC
Malibu tf/pt 1.23, 1.24.83 ABC
Bring 'Em Back Alive ep The Shadow Woman of Chung-Tui 1.29.83 CBS
Fantasy Island ep Games People Play 1.14.84 ABC
The Love Boat ep The Baby Makers 3.3.84 ABC
Mickey Spillane's Mike Hammer ep Shots in the Dark 3.8.84 CBS
Dallas sr 10.19.84 CBS
Dallas sr ret 9.27.85 CBS

HARRISON, REX
SUPP.:
Heartbreak House sp 4.16.85 SHO

HART, MARY*
Hollywood Wives ms 2.17, 2.18, 2.19.85 ABC

HARTLEY, MARIETTE
A&C, Supp. 2:
Stoney Burke ep Bandwagon 12.14.62 ABC
Gunsmoke ep Cutter's Girl 2.21.63 CBS
Ben Casey ep For I Will Plait Thy Hair With Gold 3.25.63 ABC
Breaking Point ep The Bull Roarer 10.21.63 NBC
The Travels of Jaimie McPheeters ep Day of the Misfits 12.15.63 ABC
Channing ep The Last Testament of Buddy Crown 12.18.63 ABC
Breaking Point ep No Squares in My Family Circle 2.10.64 ABC
Gunsmoke ep Chicken 11.28.64 CBS
He and She ep 11.15.67 CBS
Cimarron Strip ep Big Jessie 2.8.68 CBS
Gunsmoke ep Phoenix 9.20.71 CBS
SUPP.:

Drop-Out Father tf 9.27.82 CBS
M.A.D.D.: Mothers Against Drunk Drivers tf 3.4.83 NBC
Goodnight Beantown sr 4.3.83 CBS
Goodnight Beantown sr ret 10.2.83 CBS
The Love Boat ep The Captain and the Geisha 11.5.83 ABC
Silence of the Heart tf 10.30.84 CBS

HARTMAN, LISA
SUPP.:
T. J. Hooker ep The Witness 4.10.82 ABC
Scared Silly pt 9.2.82 ABC
Knots Landing sr 10.21.82 CBS
High Performance sr 3.2.83 ABC
Knots Landing return to sr 11.3.83 CBS
Knots Landing sr ret 10.4.84 CBS
Knots Landing sr ret 9.26.85 CBS
Beverly Hills Cowgirl Blues tf/pt 10.5.85 CBS

HASKELL, PETER
A&C, Supp. 1:
The Outer Limits ep Wolf 359 11.7.64 ABC
The Man from UNCLE ep The Mad, Mad Tea Party Affair 2.1.65 NBC
Twelve O'Clock High ep POW 4.23.65 and 4.30.65 ABC
The Big Valley ep The Fallen Hawk 3.2.66 ABC
The Big Valley ep Bounty on a Barkley 2.26.68 ABC
The Big Valley ep The Prize 12.16.68 ABC
The Interns ep The Guardian 3.5.71 CBS
Hawaii Five-O ep The Flip Side Is Death 12.18.73 CBS
SUPP.:
Father Murphy ep Outrageous Fortune 11.2.82 NBC
Ryan's Hope sr 1984 ABC
The A-Team ep The Heart of Rock and Roll 11.5.85 NBC

HASSELHOFF, DAVID*
The Young and the Restless sr 1975 CBS
Pleasure Cove tf/pt 1.3.79 NBC
The Love Boat ep September Song 4.19.80 ABC
The Love Boat ep Humpty Dumpty 2.7.81 ABC
Knight Rider sr 9.26.82 NBC
Knight Rider sr ret 10.2.83 NBC
Diff'rent Strokes ep Hooray for Hollywood 2.18.84 NBC
Knight Rider sr ret 9.30.84 NBC
The Cartier Affair tf 11.4.84 ABC
Knight Rider sr ret 9.20.85 NBC
Bridge Across Time tf 11.22.85 NBC

HASSO, SIGNE
SUPP.:
The Fall Guy ep October the 31st 10.31.84 ABC

HATCH, RICHARD*
The Sixth Sense ep Gallows in the Wind 12.16.72 ABC
Room 222 ep The Quitter 2.25.72 ABC
Hawaii Five-O ep The Child Stealers 1.2.73 CBS
Crime Club tf 3.6.73 CBS
The Rookies ep Lots of Trees and a Running Stream 12.3.73 ABC
F. Scott Fitzgerald and "The Last of the Belles" tf 1.7.74 ABC
Nakia ep The Dream 11.23.74 ABC
Medical Center ep Three on a Tightrope 11.25.74 CBS
The Hatfields and the McCoys tf 1.15.75 ABC
Hawaii Five-O ep A Study in Rage 2.11.75 CBS
Hawaii Five-O ep The Waterfront Story 11.21.75 CBS
The Waltons ep The Estrangement 12.4.75 CBS
Cannon ep The Star 12.10.75 CBS
Addie and the King of Hearts pt 1.25.76 CBS
Deadman's Curve tf 2.3.78 CBS
Ring of Passion tf 2.4.78 NBC
What Really Happened to the Class of '65 ep Mr. Potential 2.23.78 NBC
Battlestar Galactica sr 9.17.78 ABC
The Nightengales pt 5.19.79 NBC
The Hustler of Muscle Beach tf/pt 5.16.80 ABC
The Love Boat ep Too Many Dads 11.20.82 ABC
Prisoners of the Lost Universe tf/pt 8.15.83 SHO
Hotel ep Blackout 9.28.83 ABC
Dynasty ep The Secret 11.21.84 ABC
Dynasty ep Domestic Interest 11.28.84 ABC
Dynasty ep Swept Away 12.12.84 ABC
Cover Up ep The Assassin 1.26.85 CBS
T. J. Hooker ep Trackdown 1.26.85 ABC
The Love Boat ep The Perfect Arrangement 2.23.85 ABC
Riptide ep Wipe Out 10.1.85 NBC
The Love Boat ep Mermaid and the Cop 11.30.85 ABC
Hotel ep 12.25.85 ABC

HAUSER, WINGS*
Movin' On ep The Big Switch 1.20.76 NBC
Magnum, P.I. ep Wave Goodbye 11.19.81 CBS
Jessie ep Flesh Wounds 10.9.84 ABC
Sweet Revenge tf 10.31.84 CBS
Hunter ep Dead or Alive 11.30.84 NBC
The A-Team ep The Big Squeeze 1.15.85 NBC
Hardcastle and McCormick ep You Don't Hear the One That Gets You 2.18.85 ABC
Airwolf ep Airwolf II 10.5.85 CBS
Murder, She Wrote ep Reflections in the Mind 11.3.85 CBS
The A-Team ep Blood, Sweat and Cheers 11.19.85 NBC

HAYES, HELEN
A&C, Supp. 1:

Hawaii Five-O Retire in Sunny Hawaii ... Forever 11.7.75 CBS

SUPP.:

Glitter ep The Tribute 10.11.84 ABC

Murder with Mirrors tf 2.20.85 CBS

HAYES, MARGARET

A&C, B.V.:

The Life and Legend of Wyatt Earp ep The Double Life of Dora Hand 9.18.56 ABC

Tombstone Territory ep Cave-in 3.26.58 ABC

HAYNES, LLOYD

SUPP.:

Simon and Simon ep Psyched Out 1.13.83 CBS

Hotel ep Lifeline 5.9.84 ABC

HAYS, ROBERT

SUPP.:

The Day the Bubble Burst tf 2.7.82 NBC

The Fall of the House of Usher tf 7.25.82 NBC

Mr. Roberts [live] sp 3.19.84 NBC

HEASLEY, MARLA*

The A-Team ep A Battle in Bel Air 1.10.84 NBC

The A-Team ep Pure Poison 1.31.84 NBC

The A-Team ep A Desert Out There 2.7.84 NBC

The A-Team ep Curtain Call 5.15.84 NBC

The A-Team ep The Bend in the River 9.25.84 NBC

The Love Boat ep Ace Takes a Holiday 2.9.85 ABC

HEATHERTON, JOEY

A&C, B.V.:

Breaking Point ep I, the Dancer 4.20.64 ABC

HECHT, GINA*

Hizzoner sr 5.10.79 NBC

Mork and Mindy sr 11.13.80 ABC

Mork and Mindy sr ret 10.8.81 ABC

Trapper John, M.D. ep Angel of Mercy 1.17.82 CBS

St. Elsewhere ep Tears of a Clown 3.13.85 NBC

Rockhopper pt 7.9.85 CBS

Hollywood Beat ep No Place to Hide 12.12.85 ABC

HECKART, EILEEN

SUPP.:

Gloria ep 2.13.82 CBS

Games Mother Never Taught You tf 11.27.82 CBS

Trauma Center sr 9.22.83 ABC

Trapper John, M.D. ep 2.12.84 CBS

Partners in Crime sr 9.22.84 NBC

Highway to Heaven ep An Investment in Caring 3.13.85 NBC
The Recovery Room pt 7.16.85 CBS

HEDISON, DAVID
SUPP.:
Hart to Hart ep Hart of Diamonds 2.2.82 ABC
The Fall Guy ep Snow Job 3.3.82 ABC
T. J. Hooker ep (pt/first ep) 3.13.82 ABC
The Love Boat ep April in Boston 5.1.82 ABC
The Love Boat ep The Role Model 11.13.82 ABC
Fantasy Island ep Face of Fire 11.20.82 ABC
Amanda's ep Amanda's By the Sea 2.10.83 ABC
Dynasty ep The Downstairs Bride 3.16.83 ABC
Dynasty ep The Vote 3.23.83 ABC
Kenny Rogers as the Gambler: The Adventure Continues tf 11.28, 11.29.83 CBS
Fantasy Island ep Final Adieu 4.14.84 ABC
Partners in Crime ep Fantasyland 11.24.84 NBC
The Fall Guy ep Her Bodyguard 1.9.85 ABC
Simon and Simon ep Simon Without Simon 1.24.85 CBS
The Love Boat ep Her Honor, the Mayor 1.26.85 ABC
Hotel ep Distortions 2.27.85 ABC
Knight Rider ep Knight in Retreat 3.29.85 NBC
Crazy Like a Fox ep Eye in the Sky 10.6.85 CBS
The A-Team ep Mind Games 11.26.85 NBC
Trapper John, M.D. ep The Second Best Man 12.15.85 CBS

HEDREN, TIPPI
SUPP.:
Hart to Hart ep Hunted Hart 1.4.83 ABC
Tales from the Darkside ep Mookie and Pookie 11.3.84 NN
Alfred Hitchcock Presents ep Man from the South (pt ep) 5.12.85 NBC

HELLER, RANDEE*
Husbands and Wives pt 7.18.77 CBS
Husbands, Wives & Lovers sr 3.10.78 CBS
True Grit: A Further Adventure tf/pt 5.19.78 ABC
And Your Name is Jonah tf 1.28.79 CBS
Soap sr 2.1.79 ABC
Super Train ep 3.14.79 NBC
Can You Hear the Laughter?: The Story of Freddie Prinze tf 9.11.79 CBS
240-Robert ep Songwriter 9.20.79 ABC
The White Shadow ep The Stripper 1.29.80 CBS
Number 96 sr 12.10.80 NBC
Quincy, M.E. ep D.U.I. 12.2.81 NBC
Today's FBI ep Woman's Story 1.17.82 ABC
Amanda's ep Last of the Red Hot Brothers 5.5.83 ABC
Oh Madeline ep Ladies Night Out 2.21.84 ABC
Mama Malone sr 3.7.84 CBS

Oh Madeline ep A Little Fight Music 3.13.84 ABC
Obsessed with a Married Woman tf 2.11.85 NBC
Fame ep A Place to Belong 10.13.85 NN
Hunter ep Killer in a Halloween Mask 10.26.85 NBC
Growing Pains ep Superdad 10.29.85 ABC
Night Court ep 12.19.85 NBC

HELMOND, KATHERINE

SUPP.:

World War III tf 1.31.82, 2.1.82 ABC
Fit for a King pt 6.11.82 ABC
For Lovers Only tf 10.15.82 ABC
Rosie: The Rosemary Clooney Story tf 12.8.82 CBS
Faerie Tale Theater ep Jack and the Beanstalk 9.8.83 SHO
Benson ep God, I Need This Job 9.30.83 ABC
Fantasy Island ep The Big Switch 10.15.83 ABC
Not in Front of the Kids pt 6.16.84 ABC
Side by Side pt 7.6.84 ABC
The Love Boat Fall Preview Party sp 9.15.84 ABC
Who's the Boss? sr 9.20.84 ABC
Who's the Boss? sr ret 9.24.85 ABC

HENDERSON, FLORENCE

SUPP.:

Fantasy Island ep The Sailor 1.2.82 ABC
Alice ep 10.30.83 CBS
Fantasy Island ep My Mommy the Swinger 12.3.83 ABC
The Love Boat ep The Return of Annabelle 4.30.84 ABC
Finder of Lost Loves ep Forgotten Melodies 12.22.84 ABC
The Love Boat ep The Runaway 2.23.85 CBS
Cover Up ep Healthy, Wealthy and Dead 2.2.85 CBS
The New Love, American Style ep Love and the Piano Teacher 12.26.85 ABC

HENDLER, LAURI

SUPP.:

Gimme a Break sr ret 10.2.82 NBC
Gimme a Break sr ret 9.29.83 NBC
High School U.S.A. tf/pt 10.16.83 NBC
Gimme a Break sr ret 9.29.84 NBC
Gimme a Break sr ret 9.14.85 NBC

HENNER, MARILU

SUPP.:

Taxi sr ret 9.30.82 NBC
Mr. Roberts live sp 3.19.84 NBC
Stark tf 4.10.85 CBS
Alfred Hitchcock Presents ep Method Actor 11.10.85 NBC
Grown Ups sp 11.25.85 SHO

HENSLEY, PAMELA

A&C, Supp. 2:

Toma ep The Contract on Alex Cordeen 3.8.74 ABC
Switch ep The Legend of the Macunas 10.21.77 CBS
SUPP.:
Matt Houston sr 9.26.82 ABC
Fantasy Island ep My Man Friday 10.16.82 ABC
Matt Houston sr ret 9.9.83 ABC
Hotel ep Passages 1.18.84 ABC
The Love Boat ep Polly's Poker Palace 2.4.84 ABC
The Love Boat Fall Preview Party sp 9.15.84 ABC
Matt Houston sr ret 9.21.84 ABC

HENTELOFF, ALEX*
Ironside ep Class of '57 12.16.71 NBC
Love, American Style ep 1.7.72 ABC
McCloud ep Fifth Man in a String Quartet 2.2.72 NBC
M*A*S*H ep 2.4.73 CBS
Partners in Crime tf 3.24.73 NBC
Kung Fu ep Cry of the Night Beast 10.19.74 ABC
Apple's Way ep The Outsider 12.15.74 CBS
The Last Survivors tf 3.4.75 NBC
Barnaby Jones ep Poisoned Pigeon 3.25.75 CBS
Cannon ep Search and Destroy 4.2.75 CBS
The Invisible Man tf/pt 5.6.75 NBC
The First 36 Hours of Dr. Durant tf/pt 5.13.75 ABC
Three for the Road ep 9.28.75 CBS
Jeremiah of Jacob's Neck pt 8.13.76 CBS
Charlie's Angels ep The Night of the Strangler 10.13.76 ABC
The Black Sheep Squadron ep Last Mission Over Sangai 2.8.77 NBC
Barnaby Jones ep Duet for Dying 2.17.77 CBS
Code Name Diamond Head tf/pt 5.3.77 NBC
The Betty White Show sr 9.12.77 CBS
Escapade pt 5.19.78 CBS
The Bastard/Kent Family Chronicles tf 5.22, 5.23.78 OPT
The New Adventures of Heidi tf 12.13.78 NBC
Quincy, M.E. ep House of No Return 1.11.79 NBC
B.J. and the Bear ep Lobo's Revenge 4.7.79 NBC
A Man Called Sloane ep The Venus Microbe 10.27.79 NBC
Vegas ep Dan Tanna Is Dead 11.21.79 ABC
The Misadventures of Sheriff Lobo ep 1.29.80 NBC
Barnaby Jones ep Deadline for Murder 3.27.80 CBS
Angie ep 9.4.80 ABC
Lou Grant ep Goop 11.24.80 CBS
Enos ep Horse Cops 1.28.81 CBS
Enos ep Head Hunter 2.11.81 CBS
Strike Force ep The Hollow Man 12.25.81 ABC
Victims tf 1.11.82 NBC
Simon and Simon ep Matchmakers 3.9.82 CBS
Barney Miller ep Altercation 4.9.82 ABC
Trapper John, M.D. ep Russians and Ruses 12.19.82 CBS
Matt Houston ep The Visitors 2.27.83 ABC

Hart to Hart ep As the Harts Turn 3.1.83 ABC
Knots Landing ep 3.3.83 CBS
Lottery ep Charleston: The Spenders ("The Lumberyard" segment) 11.4.83 ABC
Simon and Simon ep 11.10.83 CBS
The ABC Weekend Special ep The Dog Days of Arthur Cane 2.18, 2.25.84 ABC
Night Court ep Bull's Baby 3.28.84 NBC
Red Light Sting tf 4.5.84 CBS
Dynasty ep The Check 4.11.84 ABC
Knight Rider ep Ice Bandits 10.7.84 NBC
Simon and Simon ep Enter the Jaguar 1.17.85 CBS
MacGruder and Loud ep The Violation 1.22.85 ABC
Cover Up ep Healthy, Wealthy and Dead 2.23.85 CBS
The Insiders ep The Insiders (pt) 9.25.85 ABC
Hill Street Blues ep An Oy for an Oy 11.14.85 NBC
Simon and Simon ep Facets 12.26.85 CBS

HERMAN, PEE WEE see REUBENS, Paul

HERSHEY, BARBARA
SUPP.:
Working sp 12.81 SHO
American Playhouse ep Weekend 4.20.82 PBS
Faerie Tale Theater ep The Nightingale 5.10.83 SHO
My Wicked, Wicked Ways.... The Legend of Errol Flynn 1.21.85 CBS
Alfred Hitchcock Presents ep Wake Me When I'm Dead (a.k.a. Murder Me Twice) 10.20.85 NBC

HESSEMAN, HOWARD
SUPP.:
Victims tf 1.11.82 NBC
One Shoe Makes It Murder tf 11.6.82 CBS
One Day at a Time sr 11.7.82 CBS
9 to 5 ep Home Is Where the Heart Is 11.9.82 ABC
Love, Sidney ep The Shrink 5.30.83 NBC
One Day at a Time sr ret 10.2.83 CBS
Mr. Roberts live sp 3.19.84 NBC
The Best Kept Secrets tf 3.26.84 ABC
Silence of the Heart tf 10.30.84 CBS
Murder, She Wrote ep Will No One Weep for Me? 9.29.85 CBS
George Burns Comedy Week ep The Honeybunnies 11.27.85 CBS

HESTON, CHARLTON
SUPP.:
An American Portrait ep Gutzon Borglum 3.28.85 CBS
Dynasty ep The Californians 10.9.85 ABC
Dynasty ep The Man 10.16.85 ABC
Dynasty ep 11.13.85 ABC
Dynasty II: The Colbys sr 11.20.85 ABC

HEWITT, CHRISTOPHER*
Hart to Hart ep Vintage Harts 3.23.82 ABC
Massarati and the Brain tf/pt 8.26.82 ABC
Fantasy Island sr 10.8.83 ABC
E/R ep 11.21.84 CBS
Mr. Belvedere sr 3.15.85 ABC
Mr. Belvedere sr ret 9.27.85 ABC

HICKMAN, DWAYNE
SUPP.:
High School, U.S.A. tf/pt 10.6.83 NBC

HICKS, CATHERINE*
Love for Rent tf 11.11.79 ABC
To Race the Wind tf 3.12.80 CBS
Marilyn: The Untold Story tf 9.28.80 ABC
Jacqueline Susann's Valley of the Dolls 1981 tf/pt 10.19, 10.20.81 CBS
Tucker's Witch sr 10.6.82 CBS
Happy Endings tf 3.1.83 CBS

HIGGINS, JOEL
SUPP.:
Bare Essence ms 10.4, 10.5.82 CBS
Silver Spoons sr 9.25.82 NBC
Silver Spoons sr ret 10.15.83 NBC
First Affair tf 10.25.83 CBS
Silver Spoons sr ret 9.23.84 NBC
Silver Spoons sr ret 9.15.85 NBC

HILL, ARTHUR
SUPP.:
Tomorrow's Child tf 3.22.82 ABC
Intimate Agony tf 3.21.83 ABC
Prototype tf 12.7.83 CBS
The Love Boat Fall Preview Party sp 9.15.84 ABC
Glitter sr 9.13.84 ABC
Murder, She Wrote ep Murder, She Wrote (pt) 9.30.84 CBS
Murder in Space tf 7.28.85 SHO

HILL, DANA
SUPP.:
The Fall Guy ep Child's Play 3.24.82 ABC
The Member of the Wedding live sp 12.20.82 NBC
Magnum, P.I. ep Basket Case 2.3.83 CBS
The Fall Guy ep P.S. I Love You 3.16.83 ABC
Branagan and Mapes pt 8.1.83 CBS
The CBS Schoolbreak Special ep Welcome Home, Jellybean 3.27.84 CBS
Faerie Tale Theater ep The Boy Who Left Home to Find Out About the Shivers 10.14.84 SHO
Silence of the Heart tf 10.30.84 CBS

HILLERMAN, JOHN
Simon and Simon ep 10.7.82 CBS
Magnum, P.I. sr ret 10.7.82 CBS
Little Gloria ... Happy at Last 10.24, 10.25.82 NBC
Magnum, P.I. sr ret 9.29.83 CBS
The Love Boat ep The Last Case 12.17.83 ABC
Magnum, P.I. sr ret 9.27.84 CBS
An American Portrait ep Mary Kawena Pukui 11.1.84 CBS
Magnum, P.I. sr ret 9.26.85 CBS

HINGLE, PAT
SUPP.:
Hart to Hart ep From the Depths of My Hart 1.5.82 ABC
Washington Mistress tf 1.13.82 CBS
The Fighter tf 2.19.83 CBS
St. Elsewhere ep Brothers 3.15.83 NBC
Simon and Simon ep 12.8.83 CBS
The Yellow Rose ep Beyond Vengeance 4.21.84 NBC
Magnum, P.I. ep 10.18.84 CBS
Trapper John, M.D. ep 1.13.85 CBS
American Playhouse ep Noon Wine 1.21.85 PBS
The Lady from Yesterday tf 5.7.85 CBS
The Rape of Richard Beck tf 5.27.85 ABC
Amazing Stories ep Santa '85 12.15.85 NBC

HIRSCH, JUDD
SUPP.:
Taxi sr ret 9.30.82 NBC
An American Portrait ep Joshua Albook 12.21.84 CBS
Detective in the House sr 3.15.85 CBS
First Steps tf 3.19.85 CBS
Brotherly Love tf 5.28.85 CBS

HOBBS, HEATHER*
The Dark Side of Terror tf 4.3.79 CBS
Taxi ep On the Job 5.7.81 ABC
Jacqueline Bouvier Kennedy tf 10.14.81 ABC
King's Crossing ep Keepers of the Ring 1.16.82 ABC
Cass Malloy pt 7.21.82 CBS
Having It All tf 10.13.82 ABC
Cagney and Lacey ep 12.31.84 CBS

HOFFMAN, DUSTIN
SUPP.:
Death of a Salesman tf 9.15.85 CBS

HOGAN, TERRY "HULK"*
Goldie and the Bears pt 5.26.85 ABC
Hulk Hogan's Rock 'n' Wrestling sr 9.14.85 CBS
The A-Team ep Body Slam 11.12.85 NBC

HOLBROOK, HAL
SUPP.:
Celebrity ms 2.12-2.14.84 NBC
George Washington ms 4.8, 4.9, 4.10, 4.11.84 CBS
The Three Wishes of Billy Grier tf 11.1.84 ABC
North and South ms 11.3-11.10.85 ABC
Behind Enemy Lines tf/pt 12.29.85 NBC

HOLDEN, REBECCA*
Hart to Hart ep Which Way Freeway? 1.29.80 ABC
House Calls ep 1.29.80 CBS
Magnum, P.I. ep Missing in Action 2.5.81 CBS
Enos ep The Moonshiners 4.1.81 CBS
Hot W.A.C.S. pt 6.1.81 ABC
Private Benjamin ep 2.15.82 CBS
Too Close for Comfort ep Seventh Month Blues 3.2.82 ABC
Quincy, M.E. ep The Last of Leadbottom 4.28.82 NBC
T. J. Hooker ep Second Chance 9.25.82 ABC
Johnny Blue pt 9.4.83 CBS
Matt Houston ep Heritage 9.9.83 ABC
Knight Rider sr 10.1.83 NBC
The Master ep Failure to Communicate 5.4.84 NBC
The Love Boat ep Doc's Slump 9.22.84 ABC
Hollywood Beat ep Girls, Girls, Girls 11.30.85 ABC

HOLDRIDGE, CHERYL*
The Mickey Mouse Club sr 10.3.55 (through 9.25.59) ABC
Leave It to Beaver ep Wally's Pug Nose 2.5.59 ABC
Archie untelecast pt (filmed in 1961)
Leave It to Beaver ep Teacher's Daughter 1.7.61 ABC
Bringing Up Buddy ep Buddy and the Teenager Spring 1961 CBS
The Adventures of Ozzie and Harriet ep Ricky Grades a Test Fall 1961 ABC
The Rifleman ep A Young Man's Fancy 2.5.62 ABC
Leave It to Beaver ep Wally's Dinner Date 9.27.62 ABC
Leave It to Beaver ep The Mustache 1.3.63 ABC
The Dick Van Dyke Show ep The Third One from the Left 1.1.64 CBS
Bewitched ep The Girl Reporter Fall 1964 ABC

HOLLIDAY, POLLY
SUPP.:
American Playhouse ep The Shady Hill Kidnapping 1.12.82 PBS
Missing Children: A Mother's Story tf 12.1.82 CBS
Private Benjamin ep The Replacement 1.3.83 CBS
Private Benjamin ep Judy's Cousin 1.10.83 CBS
The Gift of Love: A Christmas Story tf 12.20.83 CBS
Lots of Luck tf 2.3.85 DIS
Stir Crazy ep Stir Crazy (pt) 9.18.85 CBS
Wonder Works ep Konrad 10.6.85 PBS

HOLLIMAN, EARL
SUPP.:
Country Gold tf 11.23.82 CBS
The Thorn Birds ms 3.27, 3.28, 3.29, 3.30.83 ABC

HOLM, CELESTE
SUPP.:
American Playhouse ep The Shady Hill Kidnapping 1.12.82 PBS
Trapper John, M.D. ep Cause for Concern 4.18.82 CBS
Trapper John, M.D. ep Don't Rain on My Charade 9.26.82 CBS
This Girl for Hire tf/pt 11.1.83 CBS
The Love Boat ep Bet On It 1.14.84 ABC
The Love Boat Fall Preview Party sp 9.15.84 ABC
Jessie sr 9.18.84 ABC
Matt Houston ep Company Secrets 2.15.85 ABC

HOLMES, JENNIFER*
Barnaby Jones ep Homecoming for a Dead Man 11.8.79 CBS
The $5.20 an Hour Dream tf 1.26.80 CBS
Quincy, M.E. ep The Winning Edge 2.21.80 NBC
Here's Boomer ep The Prince and Boomer 10.18.81 NBC
Bosom Buddies ep Other Than That, She's a Wonderful Person 12.25.81 ABC
Lou Grant ep Friends 12.28.81 CBS
Falcon Crest ep Dark Journey 1.29.82 CBS
Newhart sr 10.25.82 CBS
Simon and Simon ep Art for Arthur's Sake 10.28.82 CBS
Voyagers ep Agents of Satan 10.31.82 NBC
Thursday's Child tf 2.1.83 CBS
Hobson's Choice tf 12.21.83 CBS
The Fall Guy ep Olympic Quest 2.11.84 ABC
Samson and Delilah tf 4.1.84 ABC
Hawaiian Heat ep Wave of Controversy 9.28.84 ABC
The Love Boat ep Ace Meets the Champ 10.6.84 ABC
Webster ep Runaway 1.11.85 ABC
The Fall Guy ep The Skip Family Robinson 3.13.85 ABC
The Misfits of Science sr 10.4.85 NBC

HOPE, BOB
A&C, B.V.:
The Danny Thomas Show ep Bob and Danny Become Directors 1.26.59 CBS
The Danny Thomas Show ep Tonoose the Liar Fall 1960 CBS
The Danny Thomas Show ep Danny and Bob Get Away from It All 4.2.62 CBS

HOPKINS, ANTHONY
SUPP.:
The Hunchback of Notre Dame tf 2.4.82 CBS
A Married Man tf 5.23, 5.30.84 NN
Hollywood Wives ms 2.17-2.19.85 ABC

Guilty Conscience tf 4.2.85 CBS
Arch of Triumph tf 5.29.85 CBS

HOPKINS, BO
SUPP.:
Fantasy Island ep The Spoilers 5.8.82 ABC
Matt Houston ep The Beverly Hills Social Club 3.13.83 ABC
Ghost Dancing tf 5.30.83 ABC
The A-Team ep Pure-Dee Poison 1.31.84 NBC
Hotel ep Encores 3.7.84 ABC
Murder, She Wrote ep Armed Response 3.31.85 CBS
Scarecrow and Mrs. King ep J. Edgar's Ghost 11.18.85 CBS
An American Portrait ep Bill W 1.1.85 CBS

HOPKINS, TELMA*
Roots: The Next Generation ms 2.18-2.25.79 ABC
Marie pt 12.1.79 ABC
Bosom Buddies sr 11.27.80 ABC
The Kid with the Broken Halo tf/pt 4.5.82 NBC
The New Odd Couple ep Frances Moves In 11.12.82 ABC
The Love Boat ep The Senior Citizens 1.22.83 ABC
Gimme a Break ep Nell's Friend 12.1.83 NBC
Gimme a Break ep James Returns 1.12.84 NBC
Gimme a Break ep Valentine 2.9.84 NBC
Gimme a Break ep Big Apple 2.16.84 NBC
Gimme a Break ep Katie's College 3.15.84 NBC
Gimme a Break ep Class of '84 5.3.84 NBC
Fantasy Island ep Bojangles and the Dancer 5.12.84 ABC
The Love Boat ep Ashes to Ashes 3.30.85 ABC
Gimme a Break sr 11.3.84 NBC
Gimme a Break sr ret 9.14.85 NBC

HORAN, BARBRA*
B.J. and the Bear sr 9.13.81 NBC
Hart to Hart ep Murder Up Their Sleeve 10.27.81 ABC
CHiPs ep Bright Flashes 1.17.82 NBC
House Calls ep 1.25.82 CBS
The Fall Guy ep Guess Who's Coming to Win? 3.17.82 ABC
Gavilan ep Best Friend Money Can Buy 12.21.82 NBC
The Dukes of Hazzard ep 1.14.83 CBS
High Performance ep Deadly Performance 3.23.83 ABC
Bring 'Em Back Alive ep 5.31.83 CBS
Automan ep Club Ten 2.2.84 ABC
The Rousters ep Slade vs. Slade 6.23.84 NBC
Charles in Charge ep 11.21.84 CBS
The Love Boat ep The Death and Life of Sir Albert Demerest 11.24.84 ABC
Mickey Spillane's Mike Hammer ep Dead Man's Run 12.29.84 CBS
Remington Steele ep Gourmet Steele 1.8.85 NBC
T. J. Hooker ep The Bribe 2.9.85 ABC

Crazy Like a Fox ep Suitable for Framing 3.31.85 CBS
Hardcastle and McCormick ep Faster Heart 9.30.85 ABC

HORSLEY, LEE*
Nero Wolfe sr 1.16.81 NBC
Matt Houston sr 9.26.82 ABC
The Wild Women of Chastity Gulch tf/pt 10.31.82 ABC
Matt Houston sr ret 9.9.83 ABC
The Love Boat ep My Two Dumplings 10.1.83 ABC
The Love Boat Fall Preview Party sp 9.15.84 ABC
Matt Houston sr ret 9.21.84 ABC
When Dreams Come True tf 5.28.85 ABC
Agatha Christie's "Thirteen at Dinner" tf 10.19.85 CBS

HOULIHAN, KERI*
Simon and Simon ep Thin Air 12.30.82 CBS
Lovers and Other Strangers pt 7.22.83 ABC
V: The Series ep A Reflection in Terror 12.21.84 NBC
Sam pt 6.11.85 ABC
Murder: By Reason of Insanity tf 10.1.85 CBS
Who's the Boss? ep Hunk of the Month 11.19.85 ABC

HOUSEMAN, JOHN
A&C, Supp. 2:
Hazard's People pt 4.9.76 CBS
SUPP.:
Mork and Mindy ep Mork, Mindy and Mearth Meet Milt 2.18.82 ABC
Marco Polo ms 5.16-5.19.82 NBC
Silver Spoons ep Grandfather Stratton 10.9.82 NBC
Silver Spoons ep Honor Thy Father 11.20.82 NBC
The Winds of War ms 2.6-2.13.83 ABC
Silver Spoons ep The Empire Strikes Out 2.26.83 NBC
Silver Spoons ep A Hunting We Will Go 11.12.83 NBC
Silver Spoons ep Driver Ed 11.26.83 NBC
Silver Spoons ep Happy Birthday 12.10.83 NBC
The Paper Chase: The Second Year sr 5.22.84 SHO
Silver Spoons ep I Won't Dance 10.21.84 NBC
Silver Spoons ep The Trouble with Grandfather 11.4.84 NBC
Silver Spoons ep What's Cookin'? 1.27.85 NBC
Silver Spoons ep Marry Me, Marry Me 2.3, 2.10.85 NBC
A.D. ms 3.31-4.4.85 NBC
The Paper Chase: The Third Year sr 5.11.85 SHO
Silver Spoons ep One Strike and You're Out 11.10.85 NBC
Silver Spoons ep 12.8.85 NBC

HOWARD, D. D.*
Trapper John, M.D. ep 1.2.83 CBS
Shooting Stars tf/pt 7.28.83 ABC
Trapper John, M.D. ep 11.20.83 CBS
Remington Steele ep Steele Eligible 1.10.84 NBC

Riptide ep Four Eyes 3.6.84 NBC
Night Court ep Bull's Baby 3.28.84 NBC
The A-Team ep Showdown 11.20.84 NBC
Hunter ep High Bleacher Man 12.7.84 NBC
Knight Rider ep Many Happy Returns 11.15.85 NBC

HOWARD, KEN
SUPP.:
Victims tf 1.11.82 NBC
The Country Girl sp 5.82 SHO
Rage of Angels tf 2.20, 2.21.83 NBC
The Thorn Birds ms 3.27, 3.28, 3.29, 3.30.83 ABC
It's Not Easy sr 9.29.83 ABC
Hotel ep Passages 1.18.84 ABC
He's Not Your Son tf 10.3.84 CBS
Glitter ep Glitter 9.13.84 ABC
Murder, She Wrote ep Murder at the Oasis 4.7.85 CBS

HOWARD, RON (a.k.a. Ronny Howard)
A&C, B.V.:
Dennis the Menace ep The Fishing Trip 1959 CBS
Dennis the Menace ep Dennis Haunts a House 1959 CBS
The Many Loves of Dobie Gillis ep Dobie's Birthday Party 12.15.59 CBS
Dennis the Menace ep The Fishing Trip Fall 1959 CBS
Johnny Ringo ep The Accused 10.15.59 CBS
The Many Loves of Dobie Gillis ep Room at the Bottom 2.9.60 CBS
The Danny Thomas Show ep Danny Meets Andy Griffith 2.15.60 CBS
The Many Loves of Dobie Gillis ep Where There's a Will 5.10.60 CBS
Gomer Pyle, USMC ep Opie Joins the Marines 3.18.66 CBS
SUPP.:
Happy Days ep Welcome Home 10.25.83, 11.1.83 ABC

HOWARD, SUSAN
A&C, Supp. 1:
Here Come the Brides ep Wives for Wakando 1.22.69 ABC
Griff ep The Framing of Billy the Kid 9.29.73 ABC
The Rockford Files ep Feeding Frenzy 10.15.76 NBC
SUPP.:
Dallas sr ret 10.1.82 CBS
Dallas sr ret 9.30.83 CBS
Dallas sr ret 9.28.84 CBS
Dallas sr ret 9.27.85 CBS

HOWARD, TREVOR
SUPP.:
Inside the Third Reich tf 5.9, 5.10.82 ABC
Deadly Game sp 7.23.82 HBO
George Washington ms 4.8, 4.9, 4.10, 4.11.84 CBS

HOWLAND, BETH
SUPP.:
American Playhouse ep Working 4.13.82 PBS
Alice sr ret 10.6.82 CBS
Simon and Simon ep Pirate's Key 1.20.83 CBS
The Love Boat ep The Real Thing 4.30.83 ABC
Alice sr ret 10.2.83 CBS
The Love Boat ep Prisoner of Love 10.15.83 ABC
Alice sr ret 10.14.84 CBS
The Comedy Factory ep It Takes Two 8.2.85 ABC

HUBLEY, SEASON
SUPP.:
Agatha Christie "A Caribbean Mystery" tf 10.22.83 CBS
London and Davis in New York pt 9.9.84 CBS
The Three Wishes of Billy Grier tf 11.1.84 CBS
The Key to Rebecca tf 4.29, 5.6.85 NN
The Twilight Zone ep Little Boy Lost 10.18.85 CBS
Alfred Hitchcock Presents ep Final Escape 10.27.85 NBC

HUDDLESTON, DAVID
A&C, Supp. 2:
Then Came Bronson ep Your Love Is Like a Demolition Derby in My Heart 11.16.69 NBC
Room 222 ep Hip Hip Hooray 2.17.71 ABC
SUPP.:
Computercide tf 8.1.82 NBC
The ABC Afterschool Special ep Amy and the Angel 9.22.82 ABC
Trapper John, M.D. ep 10.3, 10.10.82 CBS
The Fall Guy ep Win One for the Gipper 1.5.83 ABC
M.A.D.D.: Mothers Against Drunk Drivers tf 3.14.83 NBC
Finnegan Begin Again tf 2.24.85 HBO

HUDSON, ROCK
SUPP.:
World War III tf 1.31, 2.1.82 ABC
The Devlin Connection sr 10.2.82 NBC
The Vegas Strip War tf 11.25.84 NBC
Dynasty ep The Holiday Spirit 12.19.84 ABC
Dynasty ep The Avenger 1.2.85 ABC
Dynasty ep The Treasure 1.16.85 ABC
Dynasty ep Foreign Relations 1.23.85 ABC
Dynasty ep The Ball 2.6.85 ABC
Dynasty ep Circumstantial Evidence 2.13.85 ABC
Dynasty ep The Crash 3.20.85 ABC
An American Portrait ep Jerrold Petrofsky 3.21.85 CBS
Dynasty ep Reconciliation 3.27.85 ABC

HUGHES, BARNARD
SUPP.:

Little Gloria ... Happy at Last tf 10.24, 10.25.82 NBC
Agatha Christie's "A Caribbean Mystery" tf 10.22.83 CBS
Hotel ep Passages 1.18.84 ABC
The Sky's No Limit tf 2.7.84 CBS

HULL, HENRY
A&C, B.V.:
Trackdown ep Three Legged Fox 12.5.58 CBS
Restless Gun ep Dead Man's Hand 3.16.59 NBC

HUNNICUTT, GAYLE
SUPP.:
Philip Marlowe--Private Eye ep Finger Man 4.26.84 HBO
Lime Street ep Swiss Watch--and Wait 11.2.85 ABC

HUNT, HELEN
SUPP.:
Desperate Lives tf 3.3.82 CBS
Gimme a Break ep An Unconventional Couple 4.1.82 NBC
American Playhouse ep Weekend 4.20.82 PBS
It Takes Two sr 10.14.82 ABC
Bill On His Own tf 11.9.83 CBS
Quarterback Princess tf 12.3.83 CBS
Choices of the Heart tf 12.5.83 NBC
St. Elsewhere ep Playing God 9.19, 9.26.84 NBC
Sweet Revenge tf 10.31.84 CBS
St. Elsewhere ep Homecoming 12.15.84 NBC
St. Elsewhere ep Tears of a Clown 3.13.85 NBC
Highway to Heaven ep Thoroughbreds 5.1, 5.8.85 NBC

HUNTER, KIM
SUPP.:
Scene of the Crime pt ep (Story 1) 9.30.84 NBC
Private Sessions tf/pt 3.18.85 NBC

HUNTER, TAB
A&C, B.V.:
Love That Bob ep The Letter 1.5.56 CBS
SUPP.:
The Fall Guy ep P.S. I Love You 3.16.83 ABC
Just Our Luck ep (pt/first ep) 9.20.83 ABC
The Fall Guy ep Bite of the Wasp 1.18.84 ABC
Masquerade ep Spying Down to Mexico 4.27.85 ABC

HUSSEY, OLIVIA
SUPP.:
Ivanhoe tf 2.23.82 CBS
The Last Days of Pompeii ms 5.6, 5.7, 5.8.84 ABC
The Corsican Brothers tf 2.5.85 CBS
Murder, She Wrote ep Sing a Song of Murder 10.27.85 CBS

HUTTON, LAUREN
<u>SUPP.</u>:
Starflight: The Plane That Couldn't Land tf 2.27.83 ABC
The Cradle Will Fall tf 5.24.83 CBS
Scandal Sheet tf 1.21.85 ABC
Faerie Tale Theater ep The Snow Queen 3.11.85 SHO

HYDE-WHITE, WILFRID
<u>A&C, B.V.</u>:
The Bob Hope Chrysler Theater ep Wind Fever 3.2.66 NBC
<u>A&C, Supp. 1</u>:
Get Christie Love ep Our Lady in London 1.29.75 ABC
<u>SUPP.</u>:
Filthy Rich ep 6.15.83 CBS

HYER, MARTHA
<u>A&C, B.V.</u>:
The Lone Ranger ep The Man Who Came Back 1.5.50 ABC
Burke's Law ep Who Killed April? 1.31.64 ABC

HYLAND, DIANA
<u>A&C, B.V.</u>:
The Kraft Suspense Theater ep The Sweet Taste of Vengeance 4.30.64 NBC
<u>A&C, Supp. 1</u>:
Harry O ep The Confetti People 1.23.75 ABC

HYLANDS, SCOTT
<u>A&C, Supp. 1</u>:
Griff ep Marked for Murder 10.27.73 ABC
Harry O ep The Confetti People 1.23.75 ABC
<u>A&C, Supp. 2</u>:
Police Story ep Pressure Point 9.27.77 NBC

- I -

IMPERT, MARGIE*
Cannon ep The Iceman 10.1.75 CBS
Spencer's Pilots pt 4.9.76 CBS
Spencer's Pilots sr 9.17.76 CBS
The Rockford Files ep Forced Retirement 12.9.77 NBC
Barnaby Jones ep Echo of a Distant Battle 1.11.79 CBS
Crisis in Mid-Air tf 2.13.79 CBS
A Christmas for Boomer pt 12.6.79 NBC
The Incredible Hulk ep Behind the Wheel 11.9.79 CBS
Lou Grant ep 2.18.80 CBS
Magnum, P.I. ep Mr. White Death 11.18.82 CBS
Trauma Center ep Breakthrough 10.13.83 ABC

A Doctor's Story tf 4.23.84 NBC
Magnum, P.I. ep Blind Justice 11.8.84 CBS
Magnum, P.I. ep Ms. Jones 3.7.85 CBS
Highway to Heaven ep The Monster 12.4, 12.11.85 NBC

INGELS, MARTY
A&C, B.V.:
Hennessy ep The Specialist 1.23.61 CBS
The Ann Sothern Show ep Always April 2.23.61 CBS
Hennessy ep The Patient Vanishes Spring 1961 CBS
The Dick Van Dyke Show ep Oh How We Met on the Night That We Danced 10.31.61 CBS
The Dick Van Dyke Show ep Sol and the Sponsor 4.11.62 CBS
The Addams Family ep Cat Addams 3.11.66 ABC
Good Morning World ep Knits to You, Sir 9.5.67 CBS

IRELAND, JOHN
SUPP.:
Cassie and Company sr 1.29.82 NBC
Hardcastle and McCormick ep The Homecoming 3.4, 3.11.84 ABC
Mickey Spillane's Mike Hammer ep A Death in the Family 11.24.84 CBS
Airwolf ep Santini's Millions 2.2.85 CBS
The Fall Guy ep The Skip Family Robinson 3.13.85 ABC
The Hitchhiker ep A Time for Rifles 2.26.85 HBO

IRENE, GEORGI*
Barbara Mandrell and the Mandrell Sisters sr 1.18.80 NBC
Barbara Mandrell and the Mandrell Sisters sr ret 4.17.82 NBC
Silver Spoons ep Hospital 11.12.83 NBC
Silver Spoons ep A Summer's Romance 3.10, 3.17.84 NBC
The Get Along Gang sr vo 9.15.84 CBS
The Get Along Gang sr vo ret 9.14.85 CBS

IRVING, AMY*
Police Woman ep The Hit 12.9.75 NBC
James Dean tf 2.19.76 NBC
James A. Michener's "Dynasty" tf/pt 3.13.76 NBC
Panache tf 5.15.76 ABC
Once an Eagle ms 12.2.76-1.13.77 NBC
The Far Pavilions ms 4.22, 4.23, 4.24.84 HBO
Heartbreak House sp 4.16.85 SHO
Amazing Stories ep Ghost Train 9.29.85 NBC

IVES, BURL
SUPP.:
The Ewok Adventure tf nar 11.25.84 ABC

- J -

JACKSON, ANNE
SUPP.:
A Woman Called Golda ms 4.26, 4.27, 4.28.82 OPT
An American Portrait ep Rachel Carson 2.25.85 CBS
The Equalizer ep The Confrontation Day 10.23.85 CBS
The Facts of Life ep We Get Letters 11.30.85 NBC

JACKSON, JANET*
Good Times sr 9.16.78 CBS
Good Times sr ret 5.23.79 CBS
Diff'rent Strokes ep Growing Up 10.29.81 NBC
Diff'rent Strokes ep Jilted 1.21.82 NBC
Diff'rent Strokes ep The Car 2.25.82 NBC
Diff'rent Strokes ep The Music Man (a.k.a. Music Show) 5.6.82 NBC
Diff'rent Strokes ep Short But Sweet 5.13.82 NBC
Diff'rent Strokes ep In the Swim 10.9.82 NBC
Diff'rent Strokes ep The Older Woman 11.13.82 NBC
Fame sr 10.84 NN
The Love Boat ep Too Many Isaacs 2.2.85 ABC
Fame sr ret 10.85 NN

JACKSON, KATE
SUPP.:
Listen to Your Heart tf 1.4.83 CBS
Scarecrow and Mrs. King sr 10.3.83 CBS
Scarecrow and Mrs. King sr ret 10.1.84 CBS
Scarecrow and Mrs. King sr ret 9.23.85 CBS

JACKSON, MALLIE*
Evita Perone tf 2.23-2.24.81 NBC
The ABC Afterschool Special ep Daddy, I'm Their Mama Now 3.3.82 ABC
Kudzu pt 8.13.83 CBS
Lottery ep Los Angeles: Market Battle 9.16.83 ABC
The Best Kept Secrets tf 3.26.84 ABC
Sins of the Past tf 4.2.84 ABC

JACKSON, SHERRY
A&C, B.V.:
The Rifleman ep The Sister 11.25.58 ABC
The Many Loves of Dobie Gillis ep The Prettiest Collateral in Town 4.12.60 CBS
Riverboat ep The Water of Gorgeous Springs 11.7.60 NBC
Gunsmoke ep Lacey 1.13.62 CBS
Wagon Train ep The Geneva Balfour Story 1.20.64 ABC
Gomer Pyle, USMC ep Sgt. Carter Gets a Dear John Letter 2.5.62 CBS

Branded ep Barbed Wire 2.13.66 NBC
A&C, Supp. 1:
Chase ep $35 Will Fly You to the Moon 1.23.74 NBC
The Rockford Files ep The Real Easy Red Dog 10.31.75 NBC
Switch ep The $100,000 Ruble Rumble 12.21.76 CBS

JACOBI, LOU
SUPP.:
Love, Sidney ep Sidney's Hero 12.11.82 NBC
Tales from the Darkside ep Pain Killer 10.13.84 NN
Too Close for Comfort ep The Proposal 11.17.84 NN
Cagney and Lacey ep 1.7.85 CBS
Joanna pt 4.30.85 ABC

JACOBS, RACHEL*
The Love Boat ep April the Ninny 1.17.81 ABC
The Kid with the Broken Halo tf/pt 4.5.82 NBC
The Invisible Woman tf/pt 2.13.83 NBC
It's Not Easy sr 9.29.83 ABC
Silver Spoons ep The Secret Life of Ricky Stratton 3.24.85 NBC

JAECKEL, RICHARD
A&C, B.V.:
Behind Closed Doors ep The Germany Story 1.8.59 NBC
Trackdown ep The Protector 4.1.59 CBS
SUPP.:
McClain's Law ep What Patrick Doesn't Know 2.5.82 NBC
King's Crossing ep Home Front 2.27.82 ABC
Cassie and Company ep A Friend in Need 7.6.82 NBC
Matt Houston ep The Rock and the Hard Place 1.2.83 ABC
Fantasy Island ep Operation Breakout 1.15.83 ABC
At Ease sr 3.4.83 ABC
Dallas ep 11.11, 11.18.83 CBS
The Awakening of Candra tf 12.16.83 CBS
The Love Boat ep Bet On It 1.14.84 ABC
Masquerade ep Spanish Gambit 4.20.84 ABC
Cover Up ep Murder Off Shore 1.12.85 CBS
The Dirty Dozen: The Next Mission tf/pt 2.4.85 NBC
Spenser: For Hire sr 9.20.85 ABC

JAMES, JOHN*
Dynasty sr 1.12.81 ABC
Dynasty sr ret 11.4.81 ABC
The Love Boat ep The Experiment 3.6.82 ABC
Fantasy Island ep The Big Bet 5.1.82 ABC
The Love Boat ep The Arrangement 10.2.82 ABC
Dynasty sr ret 10.27.82 ABC
Dynasty sr ret 9.28.83 ABC
The Love Boat Fall Preview Party sp 9.15.84 ABC
Finder of Lost Loves ep Yesterday's Child 9.29.84 ABC

He's Not Your Son tf 10.31.84 ABC
Dynasty sr ret 9.26.84 ABC
Dynasty sr ret 9.25.85 ABC
Dynasty II: The Colbys sr 11.20.85 ABC

JANIS, CONRAD
SUPP.:
Trapper John, M.D. ep 1.30.83 CBS
Murder, She Wrote ep Death Casts a Spell 12.30.84 CBS
Remington Steele ep Stronger Than Steele 1.15.85 NBC
George Burns Comedy Week ep Christmas Carol II: The Sequel 12.11.85 CBS

JANSSEN, DAVID
A&C, B.V.:
Zane Grey Theater ep Trial By Fear 1.10.58 CBS
Alcoa Theater ep Decoy Duck 6.30.58 CBS

JARESS, JILL*
The Seekers tf 12.3-12.4.79 OPT
Taxi ep The Road Not Taken 5.6.82 NBC
Honeyboy tf 10.17.82 NBC
Trapper John, M.D. ep Primetime 3.13.83 CBS
Scarecrow and Mrs. King ep If Thoughts Could Kill 10.17.83 CBS
Me and Mom ep The Murder Game 5.10.85 ABC

JARRETT, RENNE
A&C, Supp. 2:
Then Came Bronson ep Sybil 12.31.69 NBC
The High Chaparral ep The Lieutenant 2.27.70 NBC
Medical Center ep The Combatants 3.18.70 CBS

JEFFREYS, ANNE
A&C, B.V.:
Love That Bob ep Bob and the Pediatrician 6.9.59 CBS
Love That Bob ep Bob Gets Hypnotized 6.16.59 CBS
SUPP.:
Mr. Merlin ep 3.15.82 CBS
Falcon Crest ep 12.10.82 CBS
Fantasy Island ep I'm a Country Girl 12.11.82 ABC
Falcon Crest ep 1.7, 1.14, 1.21, 1.28, 2.4.83 CBS
Matt Houston ep Here's Another Fine Mess 3.6.83 ABC
Hotel ep Tomorrows 1.11.84 ABC
The Love Boat Fall Preview Party sp 9.15.84 ABC
Finder of Lost Loves sr 9.22.84 ABC

JENS, SALOME
SUPP.:
Quincy, M.E. ep Dead Stop 12.23.81 NBC
Tomorrow's Child tf 3.22.82 ABC

Trapper John, M.D. ep The One and Only 5.16.82 CBS
Uncommon Valor tf 1.22.83 CBS
Grace Kelly tf 2.21.83 ABC
A Killer in the Family tf 10.30.83 NBC
Playing with Fire tf 4.14.85 NBC

JILLIAN, ANN
A&C, Supp. 2:
Ben Casey ep It's Getting Dark ... And We Are Lost 12.18.63 ABC
Hazel ep Who's in Charge Here? 9.13.65 CBS
Hazel ep How to Lose 30 Pounds in 30 Minutes 9.27.65 CBS
Hazel ep Hazel Needs a Car 11.1.65 CBS
SUPP.:
Mae West tf 5.2.82 ABC
The Rainbow Girl (a.k.a. The Ann Jillian Show) pt 6.4.82 NBC
Malibu tf/pt 1.23, 1.24.83 ABC
Jennifer Slept Here sr 10.21.83 NBC
Girls of the White Orchid tf 11.28.83 NBC
Ellis Island ms 11.12-11.14.84 CBS
This Wife for Hire tf/pt 3.18.85 ABC
It's a Living sr ret 9.29.85 NN
Alice in Wonderland tf 12.9, 12.10.85 CBS

JOHNSON, ANNE-MARIE*
High School, U.S.A. pt 5.26.84 NBC
Diff'rent Strokes ep Undercover Cover 10.20.84 NBC
Double Trouble ep O Come All Ye Faithful 12.22.84 NBC
Double Trouble ep Two Girls for Every Boy 1.26.85 NBC
Double Trouble ep The Write Stuff 2.2.85 NBC
Double Trouble ep Commercial Break 2.9.85 NBC
Double Trouble ep Old Movies 2.16.85 NBC
Double Trouble ep September Song 2.23.85 NBC
Double Trouble ep Where's Poppa? 3.30.85 NBC
Double Trouble ep Man for Margo 4.27.85 NBC
What's Happening Now?! sr 9.85 NN
Hill Street Blues sr 9.26.85 NBC

JOHNSON, ARTE
A&C, Supp. 2:
Hennessy ep Harvey's Pad Spring 1961 CBS
Hennessy ep Aunt Sarah 10.30.61 CBS
The Andy Griffith Show ep Andy and Barney in the Big City 3.26.62 CBS
The Greatest Show on Earth ep Man in a Hole 2.18.64 ABC
The Donna Reed Show ep Is There a Small Hotel? 2.66 ABC
I Dream of Jeannie ep The Biggest Star in Hollywood 2.24.69 NBC
Get Christie Love ep Murder on Hich C 2.5.75 ABC
SUPP.:
Tales of the Apple Dumpling Gang pt 1.16.82 CBS

The Love Boat ep Marrying for Money 5.15.82 ABC
The CBS Library ep The Incredible Book Escape vo 11.25.82 CBS
Fame ep Relationships 1.13.83 NBC
The Love Boat ep Sly as a Fox 1.15.83 ABC
Making of a Male Model tf 10.9.83 ABC
Hotel ep The Offer 12.7.83 ABC
Trapper John, M.D. ep 1.8.84 CBS
The Love Boat ep A Rose Is Not a Rose 3.17.84 ABC
Glitter sr 9.13.84 ABC
The Love Boat ep What a Drag! 9.22.84 ABC
Airwolf ep Severance Pay 3.23.85 CBS
Alice in Wonderland tf 12.9, 12.10.85 CBS
The A-Team ep Uncle Buckle-Up 12.17.85 NBC

JOHNSON, DON*
Kung Fu ep The Spirit Helper 11.8.73 ABC
The Rookies ep The Teacher 2.4.74 ABC
Law of the Land tf 4.29.76 NBC
The Streets of San Francisco ep Hot Dog 12.9.76 ABC
The City tf 1.12.77 NBC
Cover Girls tf/pt 5.18.77 NBC
Big Hawaii ep Gandy 9.21.77 NBC
Police Story ep Pressure Point 9.27.77 NBC
Cover Girls tf/pt 5.18.77 NBC
Ski Lift to Death tf 3.3.78 CBS
The Two-Five tf 4.14.78 ABC
The American Girls ep A Crash Course in Survival 10.21.78 CBS
Katie: Portrait of a Centerfold tf 10.23.78 NBC
First You Cry tf 11.8.78 CBS
What Really Happened to the Class of '65 ep The Class Crusader 1.12.78 NBC
Amateur Night at the Dixie Bar and Grill tf 1.8.79 NBC
The Rebels tf 5.14, 5.21.79 OPT
From Here to Eternity sr 3.10.80 NBC
Beulah Land ms 10.7-10.9.80 NBC
Revenge of the Stepford Wives tf 10.12.80 NBC
Elvis and the Beauty Queen tf 3.1.81 NBC
The Two Lives of Carol Litner tf 10.14.81 CBS
Six Pack pt 7.24.83 NBC
Matt Houston ep The Woman in White 9.16.83 ABC
The Mississippi ep 11.15.83 CBS
Miami Vice sr 9.16.84 NBC
Miami Vice sr ret 9.27.85 NBC
The Long, Hot Summer tf 10.6, 10.7.85 NBC

JOHNSON, JANET LOUISE (a.k.a. Janet Julian)*
Alias Smith and Jones ep Only Three to a Bed 1.13.73 ABC
The Nancy Drew Mysteries sr 2.12.78 ABC
B.J. and the Bear ep Shine On 2.24.79 NBC

B.J. and the Bear sr (with ep Snow White and the Seven Lady Truckers) 9.29.79 NBC
California Fever ep 11.6.79 CBS
240-Robert ep Earthquake 11.19.79 ABC
Enos ep The Hostage 2.18.81 CBS
Key Tortuga pt 9.11.81 CBS
Today's FBI ep Bank Job 3.7.82 ABC
The Fall Guy ep Hell on Wheels 12.8.82 ABC
Simon and Simon ep Design for Killing 2.10.83 CBS
Simon and Simon ep 2.10.84 CBS
Knight Rider ep Ice Bandits 10.7.84 NBC

JOHNSON, LYNN HOLLY*
CHiPs ep Fallout 12.19.82 NBC
Matt Houston ep A Deadly Parlay 4.10.83 ABC
Trapper John, M.D. ep 10.2.83 CBS
Mickey Spillane's Mike Hammer: More Than Murder tf/pt 1.26.85 CBS

JOHNSON, VAN
SUPP.:
One Day at a Time ep 2.7.82 CBS
The Love Boat ep The Musical 2.27.82 ABC
Fantasy Island ep Charo 2.19.83 ABC
Glitter ep Glitter (pt) 9.13.84 ABC
Murder, She Wrote ep Hit, Run and Homicide 11.15.84 CBS

JONES, CAROLYN
SUPP.:
Fantasy Island ep Daddy's Little Girl 1.30.82 ABC
Capitol sr 3.29.82 CBS

JONES, DEAN
SUPP.:
Herbie, The Love Bug sr 3.17.82 CBS
The Love Boat ep Julie and the Producer 5.5.84 ABC
Murder, She Wrote ep It's a Dog's Life 11.4.84 CBS

JONES, HENRY
A&C, B.V.:
Father Knows Best ep Margaret's Other Family 2.58 NBC
Hawk ep Ullysses and the Republic 11.17.66 ABC
Here Come the Brides ep Mr. and Mrs. J. Bolt 3.12.69 ABC
Alias Smith and Jones ep The Day They Hanged Kid Curry 9.16.71 ABC
SUPP.:
The Love Boat ep Familiar Faces 1.9.82 ABC
The Dukes of Hazzard ep Pin the Tail on the Dukes 1.22.82 CBS
McClain's Law ep Takeover 2.26.82 NBC
Filthy Rich ep 8.23.82 CBS

Gun Shy sr 3.15.83 CBS
Scene of the Crime pt (ep Story 1) 9.30.84 NBC
Code Name: Foxfire pt (ep "Slay It Again, Uncle Sam") 1.27.85 NBC
Code Name: Foxfire sr 2.8.85 NBC
Falcon Crest ep Echoes 10.25.85 CBS
Cagney and Lacey ep Entrapment 11.4.85 CBS

JONES, JAMES EARL
SUPP.:
The ABC Afterschool Special ep Amy and the Angel 9.22.82 ABC
The Vegas Strip War tf 11.25.84 NBC
The Atlanta Child Murders tf 2.10.85 CBS
Me and Mom sr 4.5.85 ABC

JONES, L. Q.*
Cheyenne sr 9.23.55 (through 6.5.56) ABC
Perry Mason ep The Case of the Lonely Heiress 2.1.58 CBS
Black Saddle ep 4.11.59 NBC
Tightrope ep The Frame 9.22.59 CBS
Two Faces West ep The Lost Man 1960 NN
Two Faces West ep The Noose 1960 NN
Johnny Ringo ep Four Came Quietly 1.28.60 CBS
The Rebel ep The Earl of Durango 6.12.60 ABC
Klondike sr 10.10.60 NBC
The Rebel ep Explosion 11.27.60 ABC
The Detectives ep Kinfolk 1.20.61 ABC
The Life and Legend of Wyatt Earp ep Casey and the Clowns 2.21.61 ABC
Americans ep The Coward 5.8.61 NBC
Laramie ep The Replacement 3.27.62 NBC
The Lawman ep The Bride 4.1.62 ABC
Ben Casey ep The Fireman Who Raised Rabbits 11.28.62 ABC
Wagon Train ep Charlie Wooster--Outlaw 2.20.63 NBC
Empire ep The Convention 5.14.63 ABC
Gunsmoke ep Tobe 10.19.63 CBS
The Virginian ep Run Quiet 11.13.63 NBC
Rawhide ep Incident at Gila Flats 1.3.64 CBS
Rawhide ep The Race 9.25.64 CBS
Gunsmoke ep Jonah Hutchinson 12.5.64 CBS
Slattery's People ep How Do You Fall in Love with a Town? 1.22.65 CBS
Gunsmoke ep Dry Run to Nowhere 4.3.65 CBS
My Favorite Martian ep 11.21.65 CBS
A Man Called Shenandoah ep Rope's End 1.17.66 ABC
The Big Valley ep By Force and Violence 3.30.66 ABC
The Big Valley ep Court-Martial 3.6.67 ABC
The Big Valley ep Showdown in Limbo 3.27.67 ABC
The Virginian ep Lady of the House 4.5.67 NBC
The Big Valley ep Ambush 9.18.67 ABC

Cimarron Strip ep The Search 11.9.67 CBS
Hondo ep Hondo and the Death Drive 12.1.67 ABC
The Big Valley ep Fall of a Hero 2.5.68 ABC
Hawaii-Five-O ep King of the Hill 1.8.69 CBS
Gunsmoke ep The Good Samaritans 3.10.69 CBS
Lancer ep Blind Man's Bluff 9.23.69 CBS
Gunsmoke ep Albert 2.9.70 CBS
Gunsmoke ep The Gun 11.9.70 CBS
The FBI ep Dynasty of Hate 10.10.71 ABC
Cannon ep Fool's Gold 10.19.71 CBS
Alias Smith and Jones ep Stagecoach Seven 3.11.71 ABC
Cade's County ep Delegate at Large 11.21.71 CBS
The Bravos tf 1.9.72 ABC
Gunsmoke ep Tara 1.17.72 CBS
Fireball Foreward tf 3.5.72 ABC
The Delphi Bureau ep The Man Upstairs/The Man Downstairs Project 10.26.72 ABC
The Bold Ones: The Doctors ep A Purge of Madness 12.5.72 NBC
Alias Smith and Jones ep McGuffin 12.9.72 ABC
Ironside ep The Caller 1.25.73 NBC
Kung Fu ep An Eye for an Eye 1.25.73 ABC
Assignment: Vienna ep A Deadly Shade of Green 1.27.73 ABC
Cannon ep The Perfect Alibi 10.31.73 CBS
The Magician ep The Illusion of the Curious Counterfeit 1.14, 1.21.74 NBC
Mrs. Sundance tf 1.15.74 ABC
Manhunter tf/pt 2.26.74 CBS
The Strange and Deadly Occurrence tf 9.24.74 NBC
Attack on Terror: The FBI vs. the Ku Klux Klan tf 2.20, 2.21.75 CBS
Kung Fu ep The Last Raid 4.5.75 ABC
Matt Helm ep Deadly Breed 11.8.75 ABC
Movin' On ep The Big Switch 1.20.76 NBC
Banjo Hackett: Roamin' Free tf 5.30.76 NBC
Charlie's Angels ep Bullseye 12.1.76 ABC
McCloud ep 1.23.77 NBC
Rafferty ep The Burning Man 11.21.77 CBS
CHiPs ep 1.12.78 NBC
Standing Tall tf 1.21.78 NBC
Charlie's Angels ep Angels in the Backfield 1.25.78 ABC
Columbo ep The Conspirators 5.13.78 NBC
Colorado C.I. pt 5.26.78 CBS
The Sacketts tf 5.15, 5.16,79 CBS
The Buffalo Soldiers pt 5.26.79 NBC
The Runaways ep They'll Never Forgive Me 7.24.79 NBC
The Incredible Hulk ep Jake 11.2.79 CBS
Charlie's Angels ep Angel Hunt 12.5.79 ABC
Wild Times tf 1.24, 1.31.80 NN
Charlie's Angels ep An Angel's Trail 2.27.80 ABC
Enos ep Blue Flu 12.10.80 CBS

Walking Tall ep The Hit Man 2.7.81 NBC
Riker ep Honkeytonk 3.14.81 CBS
The Dukes of Hazzard ep Sound of Music--Hazzard Style 1.8.82 CBS
The Fall Guy ep Colt's Outlaws (a.k.a. The Backlot Gang) 11.10.82 ABC
Matt Houston ep The Monster 1.6.84 ABC

JONES, MARILYN*
11th Victim tf 11.6.79 CBS
B.J. and the Bear ep Mary Ellen 11.17.79 NBC
Lou Grant ep Harassment 9.29.80 CBS
King's Crossing sr 1.16.82 ABC
I, Desire tf 11.15.82 ABC
Remington Steele ep Steele Among the Living 2.25.83 NBC
It's Not Easy ep Teacher's Pets 10.27.83 ABC
Hardcastle and McCormick ep Whatever Happened to Guts? 11.4.84 ABC
Magnum, P.I. ep Murder 101 11.15.84 CBS
V: The Series ep The Return 3.22.85 NBC
Hardcastle and McCormick ep Really Neat Cars and Guys with a Sense of Humor 3.25.85 ABC
Do You Remember Love? tf 5.21.85 CBS
Tales from the Darkside ep Uras Minor 11.30.85 NN

JONES, MICKEY*
The Dream Makers tf 1.7.75 NBC
See How She Runs tf 2.1.78 CBS
Lacey and the Mississippi Queen tf/pt 5.17.78 NBC
The Incredible Hulk ep Ricky 10.6.78 CBS
Charlie's Angels ep Angels Go Trucking 9.19.79 ABC
The Dukes of Hazzard ep Granny Annie 11.23.79 CBS
Stand By Your Man tf 5.13.81 CBS
Hart to Hart ep Rhinestone Harts 12.1.81 ABC
Flamingo Road ep The Powers That Be 12.15.81 NBC
Johnny Belinda tf 10.19.82 CBS
Hear No Evil tf/pt 11.20.82 CBS
Living Proof: The Hank Williams Jr. Story 3.7.83 NBC
AfterMASH ep 12.12.83 CBS
The Master ep State of the Union 2.3.84 NBC
V: The Final Battle ms 5.6, 5.7, 5.8.84 NBC
Jessie ep The Long Fuse 10.16.84 ABC
V: The Series ep A Reflection in Terror 12.21.84 NBC
Alice ep 1.29, 2.5.85 CBS
The Misfits of Science ep 10.4.85 NBC

JONES, SHIRLEY
A&C, B.V.:
The Danny Thomas Show ep Shirley Makes Good 2.16.59 CBS
SUPP.:
The Adventures of Pollyana pt 4.10.82 CBS
The Love Boat ep The Dean and the Flunkie 2.5.83 ABC

JONES, TOMMY LEE
SUPP.:
The Rainmaker sp 10.22.82 SHO
Cat on a Hot Tin Roof sp 8.19.84 SHO
This Park Is Mine tf 10.6.85 HBO

JORY, VICTOR
A&C, B.V.:
Wanted: Dead or Alive ep The Legend 3.7.59 CBS
F Troop ep Indian Fever Fall 1966 ABC
A&C, Supp. 1:
Marcus Welby, M.D. ep Tomorrow May Never Come 9.9.75 ABC
A&C, Supp. 2:
The Rockford Files ep The Attractive Nuisance 1.6.78 NBC

JOURDAN, LOUIS
SUPP.:
Hotel ep Prisms 3.14.84 ABC
The First Olympics: Athens 1896 tf 5.20, 5.21.84 NBC
Cover Up ep Cover Up (pt) 9.22.84 CBS

JOYCE, ELAINE
A&C, Supp. 1:
The Andy Griffith Show ep Helen, the Authoress 2.27.67 CBS
Here Come the Brides ep Man of the Family 10.16.67 ABC
Hawaii Five-O ep Just Lucky, I Guess 10.15.69 CBS
Hawaii Five-O ep Oldest Profession, Latest Price 10.14.76 CBS
SUPP.:
The Love Boat ep The Groupies 11.6.82 ABC
Magnum, P.I. ep Of Sound Mind 1.6.83 CBS
Hart to Hart ep A Lighter Hart 5.10.83 ABC
Allison Sidney Harrison pt 8.19.83 NBC
We Got It Made ep Mickey's Mom 10.27.83 NBC
Hotel ep Faith, Hope and Charity 11.23.83 ABC
The Love Boat ep The World's Greatest Kisser 11.26.83 ABC
Fantasy Island ep Outrageous Mr. Smith 3.3.84 ABC
Simon and Simon ep The Disappearance of Harry the Hat 3.29.84 CBS
Masquerade ep The French Connection 3.20.84 ABC
Murder, She Wrote ep Death Casts a Spell 12.30.84 CBS
Simon and Simon ep Enchalada Express 10.24.85 CBS

JULIAN, JANET see JOHNSON, Janet Louise

JUMP, GORDON
A&C, Supp. 2:
Chase ep $35 Will Fly You to the Moon 1.23.74 NBC
Switch ep Stung from Behind 9.30.75 CBS
The Rockford Files ep Big Deal in the Valley 3.19.76 NBC
SUPP.:
For Lovers Only tf 10.15.82 ABC

Diff'rent Strokes ep The Bicycle Man 2.5, 2.12.83 NBC
The Love Boat ep Putting on the Dog 3.26.83 ABC
Great Day pt 11.19.83 CBS
Second Edition pt 7.17.84 NBC
The Love Boat ep Aerobic April 11.3.84 ABC
The CBS Children's Mystery Theater ep The Dirkin Detective Agency 1.25.85 CBS
Night Court ep World War III 5.2.85 NBC
Amazing Stories ep Guilt Trip 12.1.85 NBC

- K -

KACZMAREK, JANE*
St. Elsewhere ep Graveyard 1.18.82 NBC
For Lovers Only tf/pt 10.15.82 ABC
St. Elsewhere ep Release 2.1.83 NBC
St. Elsewhere ep Family History 2.8.83 NBC
Something About Amelia tf 1.9.84 ABC
Hill Street Blues ep Grace Under Pressure 2.2.84 NBC
Hill Street Blues ep The Other Side of Oneness 2.9.84 NBC
Hill Street Blues ep Parting Is Such Sweet Sorrow 2.16.84 NBC
Hill Street Blues ep The Count of Monty Tasco 3.8.84 NBC
Hill Street Blues ep Untitled 3.15.84 NBC
Flight #90: Disaster on the Potomac tf 4.1.84 NBC
Paper Chase: The Second Year sr 4.15.83 SHO
Remington Steele ep Altered Steele 10.11.83 NBC
Scarecrow and Mrs. King ep Always Look a Gift Horse in the Mouth 11.14.83 CBS
The Last Leaf drama sp 4.84 NN
Crazy Like a Fox ep Crazy Like a Fox (pt) 12.30.84 CBS
Hometown sr 8.22.85 CBS

KAHAN, JUDY
SUPP.:
Newhart ep Some Are Born Writers, Others Have Writers Thrust Upon Them 12.13.82 CBS

KANALY, STEVE*
Chase ep Sizzling Stones 12.18.73 NBC
Police Story ep Trial Board 1.4.77 NBC
Hawaii Five-O ep The Sleeper 9.28.78 CBS
Time Express ep Death 5.17.79 CBS
Dallas sr 9.21.79 CBS
Charlie's Angels ep Avenging Angels 9.26.79 ABC
Dallas sr ret 11.7.80 CBS
Dallas sr ret 10.9.81 CBS
Dallas sr ret 10.1.82 CBS
Fantasy Island ep Beautiful Skeptic 11.27.82 ABC

Fantasy Island ep Revenge of the Forgotten 2.19.83 ABC
The Love Boat ep The Real Thing 4.30.83 ABC
Dallas sr ret 9.30.83 CBS
Hotel ep Mistaken Identities 2.1.84 ABC
Dallas sr ret 9.28.84 CBS
Scene of the Crime pt (Story 1) 9.30.84 NBC
Hotel ep Love and Honor 1.16.85 ABC
Dallas sr ret 9.27.85 CBS

KANE, CAROL*
The Felony Squad ep Epitaph for a Cop 2.26.68 ABC
American Parade ep We the Women (sp) 3.17.74 CBS
Visions ep Fans of the Kosko Show 10.23.78 PBS
American Short Story ep The Greatest Man in the World 2.18.80 PBS
Taxi ep Simka Returns 2.4.82 ABC
Taxi ep The Shloogel 9.30.82 NBC
Taxi ep Scenskees from a Marriage 10.28.82 NBC
Taxi ep Alex the Gofer 11.11.82 NBC
Laverne and Shirley ep Jinxed 11.30.82 ABC
Taxi ep Elaine and the Monk 12.2.82 NBC
Taxi ep Get Me Through the Holidays 12.16.82 NBC
Taxi ep Louie Moves Uptown 1.22.83 NBC
Taxi ep Alex's Old Buddy 1.29.83 NBC
Taxi ep Celebration of Taxi 3.23.83 NBC
Taxi ep Louie and the Blind Girl 4.6.83 NBC
Taxi ep Arnie Meets the Kids 4.13.83 NBC
Taxi ep Jim's Mario's 5.18.83 NBC
Taxi ep A Grand Gesture 5.25.83 NBC
Taxi ep Simka's Monthlies 6.15.83 NBC
Faerie Tale Theater ep Sleeping Beauty 7.7.83 SHO
Burning Rage tf 9.21.84 CBS
Cheers ep A Ditch in Time 12.20.84 NBC
Crazy Like a Fox ep Bum Tip 2.24.85 CBS
Tales from the Darkside ep Snip, Snip 2.9.85 NN

KAPLAN, GABE
SUPP.:
Murder, She Wrote ep Birds of a Feather 10.14.84 CBS
Wonder Works ep The Hoboken Chicken Emergency 11.19.84 PBS

KAPLAN, MARVIN
A&C, B.V.:
The Danny Thomas Show ep The Honeymoon Flashback 10.14.57 CBS
M Squad ep A Gun for Mother's Day 4.12.60 NBC
Gidget ep Don't Defrost the Alligator 4.21.66 ABC
Gomer Pyle, USMC ep The Carriage Waits 2.68 CBS
I Dream of Jeannie ep One of Our Hotels Is Growing 1.70 NBC
SUPP.:

Alice sr ret 10.6.82 CBS
Alice sr ret 10.2.83 CBS
The ABC Weekend Special ep Bad Cat vo 4.14.84 ABC
Alice sr ret 10.14.84 CBS

KARABATSOS, RON*
Cheers ep The Tortelli Tart 10.14.82 NBC
Hear No Evil tf/pt 11.20.82 CBS
Blood Feud tf 4.25, 5.2.83 OPT
Legs tf 5.2.83 ABC
Missing Pieces tf 5.14.83 CBS
Dreams sr 10.3.84 CBS
Family Ties ep Birth of a Keaton 1.24, 1.31.85 NBC
Diff'rent Strokes ep Blue Collar Drummond 3.9.85 NBC
Double Dare ep 4.24.85 CBS
Joanna pt 4.30.85 ABC
Double Dare ep 5.15.85 CBS
Brotherly Love tf 5.28.85 CBS
Our Family Honor sr 9.17.85 ABC

KARLEN, JOHN*
The Detectives ep Strangers in the House 5.4.62 ABC
The Patriots sp 11.15.63 NBC
Dark Shadows sr 6.27.66 ABC
Hawk ep The Longleaf Chronicles 9.15.66 ABC
N.Y.P.D. ep Murder for Infinity 11.7.67 ABC
Night of Terror tf 10.10.72 ABC
Cool Million tf/pt 10.16.72 NBC
The Sixth Sense ep Through a Flame, Darkly 11.4.72 ABC
The Mod Squad ep Belinda--End of Little Miss Bubble Gum 12.7.72 ABC
Medical Center ep 1.10.73 CBS
Frankenstein tf 1.16, 1.17.73 ABC
The Police Story tf/pt 3.20.73 NBC
The Picture of Dorian Gray tf 4.23, 4.24.73 ABC
The Magician ep The Vanishing Lady 10.9.73 NBC
Shirts/Skins tf 10.9.73 ABC
Melvin Purvis: G-Man tf/pt 4.9.74 ABC
Doc Elliot ep The Pharmacist 5.1.74 ABC
Mannix ep Quartet for Blunt Instrument 2.23.75 CBS
Trilogy of Terror tf 3.4.75 ABC
Delancey Street: The Crisis Within tf/pt 4.19.75 NBC
The Streets of San Francisco ep Poisoned Snow 9.11.75 ABC
Joe Forrester ep The Witness 9.16.75 NBC
Kansas City Massacre tf 9.19.75 ABC
Medical Center ep No Hiding Place 9.19.75 CBS
Mobile One ep 12.1.75 ABC
Hawaii Five-O ep Is This Any Way to Run Paradise? 1.15.76 CBS
The Waltons ep The Baptism 10.14.76 CBS
The Streets of San Francisco ep No Minor Vices 11.4.76 ABC

Serpico ep Rapid Fire 12.10.76 NBC
Most Wanted ep The White Collar Killer 1.1.77 ABC
Dog and Cat ep Live Bait 3.19.77 ABC
The ABC Short Story Special ep My Dear Uncle Sherlock 4.16.77 ABC
The Feather and Father Gang ep Welcome Home, Vinnie 6.18.77 ABC
Charlie's Angels ep Angel Baby 11.16.77 ABC
The Nancy Drew Mysteries ep The Lady on Thursday at 10 1.1.78 ABC
Kojak ep The Captain's Brother's Wife 2.4.78 CBS
Colorado C.I. pt 5.26.78 CBS
The Rockford Files ep Rosenthal and Gilda Stern Are Dead 9.29.78 NBC
Barnaby Jones ep Hitchhike to Terror 10.19.78 CBS
Quincy, M.E. ep Semper-Fidelis 3.15.79 NBC
Kaz ep The Battered Bride 4.11.79 CBS
The Return of the Mod Squad tf/pt 5.18.79 ABC
Sword of Justice ep Blackjack 7.11.79 NBC
Quincy, M.E. ep Hot Ice 10.18.79 NBC
Lou Grant ep 11.5.79 CBS
The Last of the Dalton Gang tf 11.20.79 NBC
The Long Days of Summer tf/pt 5.23.80 ABC
Vegas ep The Day the Gambling Stopped 6.18.80 ABC
Quincy, M.E. ep Dear Mummy 1.21.81 NBC
Vegas ep Out of Sight 3.18.81 ABC
Trapper John, M.D. ep A Case of the Crazies 3.29.81 CBS
American Dream tf/pt 4.26.81 ABC
Hill Street Blues ep The Spy Who Came in from Delgado 1.21.82 NBC
Strike Force ep Shark 2.19.82 ABC
King's Crossing ep Home Front 2.27.82 ABC
Cagney and Lacey sr 3.25.82 CBS
Cagney and Lacey sr ret 10.25.82 CBS
Rosie: The Rosemary Clooney Story tf 12.8.82 CBS
The Winds of War ms 2.6-2.13.83 ABC
Branagan and Mapes pt 8.1.83 CBS
Bay City Blues ep Bay City Blues (pt) 10.25.83 NBC
Bay City Blues ep I Never Swang for My Father 11.15.83 NBC
Cagney and Lacey sr ret 3.19.84 CBS
Cagney and Lacey sr ret 10.15.84 CBS
Cagney and Lacey sr ret 9.30.85 CBS
Hostage Flight tf 11.17.85 NBC

KARRON, RICHARD*
Mad Bull tf 12.21.77 CBS
Starsky and Hutch ep Golden Angel 1.16.79 ABC
Charlie's Angels ep Angels on the Street 11.7.79 ABC
Good Time Harry sr 7.19.80 NBC
Teachers Only sr 4.4.82 NBC
Star of the Family ep Spring Is in the Air 11.1.82 ABC

Teachers Only sr ret 2.12.83 NBC
The New Odd Couple ep The Perils of Pauline 5.13.83 ABC
Webster ep Happy Un-Birthday 9.23.83 ABC
Dempsey tf 9.28.83 CBS
Webster ep Second Time Around 11.4.83 ABC
Webster sr 9.21.84 ABC
Charlie and Company sr 9.18.85 CBS

KASZNAR, KURT
A&C, B.V.:
Ellery Queen ep Revolution 1.16.59 NBC
The Reporter ep Hideout 10.2.64 CBS
The Lucy Show ep Lucy and the Group Encounter 12.18.72 CBS

KATT, WILLIAM
A&C, Supp. 2:
The Rookies ep The Old Neighborhood 11.25.74 ABC
Kojak ep 10.26.75 CBS
SUPP.:
The Rainmaker sp 10.22.82 SHO
The Greatest American Hero sr ret 10.29.82 ABC
Pippin sp 4.83 SHO
Faerie Tale Theater ep Thumbelina 6.11.84 SHO
Perry Mason Returns tf 12.1.85 NBC

KAY, DIANNE*
Starsky and Hutch ep The Psychic 1.15.77 ABC
Eight Is Enough sr 8.10.77 (through 8.29.81) ABC
Flamingo Road tf/pt 5.12.80 NBC
Nashville Grab tf 10.18.81 NBC
Fantasy Island ep Night of the Tormented Soul 12.5.81 ABC
Darkroom ep Who's There? 1.15.82 ABC
Portrait of a Showgirl tf 5.4.82 CBS
Cass Malloy pt 7.21.82 CBS
Trapper John, M.D. ep Baby on the Line 1.9.83 CBS
Reggie sr 8.2.83 ABC
Hotel ep The Offer 12.7.83 ABC
Simon and Simon ep 2.9.84 CBS
Fantasy Island ep Dick Turpin's Last Ride 4.7.84 ABC
The Love Boat ep Tugs of the Heart 10.20.84 ABC

KAYE, CAREN*
Alice ep 1976 CBS
The Mary Tyler Moore Show ep What's Wrong with Swimming? 10.16.76 CBS
Rhoda ep 12.20.76 CBS
Blansky's Beauties sr 2.12.77 ABC
The Natural Look pt 7.6.77 NBC
The Betty White Show sr 9.12.77 CBS
The Love Boat ep The Business of Love 5.13.78 ABC

Fantasy Island ep 5.15.78 ABC
Legs pt 5.19.78 ABC
Who's Watching the Kids? sr 9.22.78 NBC
Starsky and Hutch ep The Groupie 11.28.78 ABC
The Love Boat ep 9.15.79 ABC
The Misadventures of Sheriff Lobo ep 9.18.79 NBC
Help Wanted: Male tf 1.16.82 CBS
The Love Boat ep Marrying for Money 5.15.82 ABC
Remington Steele ep Hearts of Steele 1.28.83 NBC
The Love Boat ep The Maid Cleans Up 3.12.83 ABC
Hardcastle and McCormick ep Goin' Nowhere Fast 10.9.83 ABC
Empire sr 1.4.84 CBS
Matt Houston ep The Bikini Murders 2.3.84 ABC
Side By Side pt 7.6.84 ABC
It's Your Move sr 9.26.84 NBC
Hotel ep Detours 11.7.84 ABC
Finder of Lost Loves ep From the Heart 2.9.85 ABC
Poison Ivy tf/pt 2.10.85 NBC
The Love Boat ep Couples 10.19.85 ABC
Simon and Simon ep Reunion at Alcatraz 11.14.85 CBS
The New Love, American Style ep How to Pick Up a Man 12.31.85 ABC

KAYE, DANNY
SUPP.:
The Twilight Zone ep Paladin of the Lost Hour 11.8.85 CBS

KAZAN, LAINIE
SUPP.:
Too Close for Comfort ep Family Business 5.5.83 ABC
Sunset Limousine tf 10.12.83 CBS
The Jerk, Too tf/pt 1.6.84 NBC
Faerie Tale Theater ep Pinocchio 5.15.84 SHO
Obsessive Love tf 10.29.84 CBS
The ABC Weekend Special ep The Adventures of a Two-Minute Werewolf 3.2.85 ABC
The Paper Chase: The Third Year sr 5.11.85 SHO

KEACH, STACY
A&C, B.V.:
Colt .45 ep Last Chance 12.6.57 ABC
Navy Log ep The Brothers of Kapsan 1.2.58 ABC
How to Marry a Millionaire ep The New Lease Fall 1958 NN
Markham ep 2.11.60 CBS
Get Smart ep 10.1.66 NBC
SUPP.:
The Blue and the Gray ms 11.14, 11.15, 11.16, 11.17.82 CBS
Wait Until Dark sp 12.29.82 HBO
Mickey Spillane's Mike Hammer: Murder Me, Murder You tf/pt 4.9.83 CBS
Princess Daisy tf 11.6, 11.7.83 NBC

Mickey Spillane's Mike Hammer: More Than Murder tf/pt 1.26.84 CBS
Mickey Spillane's Mike Hammer sr 1.29.84 CBS
Mickey Spillane's Mike Hammer sr ret 9.29.84 CBS
An American Portrait ep Edwin Drake 11.16.84 CBS

KEANE, JAMES*
Intimate Strangers tf 11.11.77 ABC
Sunshine Christmas tf 12.12.77 NBC
Night Cries tf 1.29.78 ABC
The Paper Chase sr 9.9.78 CBS
Ike ms 5.3-5.6.79 ABC
Hart to Hart ep Harts Under Glass 11.24.81 ABC
The Ambush Murders tf 1.5.82 CBS
Pray TV tf 2.1.82 ABC
In Security pt 7.7.82 CBS
St. Elsewhere ep Legionnaires I 12.7.82 NBC
The Paper Chase: The Second Year sr 5.22.84 SHO
The Paper Chase: The Third Year sr 5.1.85 SHO

KEANE, KERRIE*
Shocktrauma tf 10.27.82 NN
Trapper John, M.D. ep 11.27.83 CBS
The Yellow Rose sr (with ep A Question of Love) 12.10.83 NBC
Flight #90: Disaster on the Potomac tf 4.1.84 NBC
Hot Pursuit sr 9.22.84 NBC
Matt Houston ep Killing Time 2.22.85 ABC
A Death in California tf 5.12, 5.13.85 ABC
Dirty Work pt 6.6.85 CBS
Perry Mason Returns tf 12.1.85 NBC

KEE CHEUNG, GEORGE*
Hart to Hart ep The Man with the Jade Eyes 12.11.79 ABC
Trapper John, M.D. ep 3.2.80 CBS
The Six O'Clock Follies sr 4.24.80 NBC
Magnum, P.I. ep Never Play with a China Doll 12.18.80 CBS
Cagney and Lacey ep Pop Used to Work Chinatown 4.1.82 CBS
Bring 'Em Back Alive sr 9.24.82 CBS
Archie Bunker's Place ep 1.9.83 CBS
Johnny Blue pt 9.4.83 CBS
Hart to Hart ep Year of the Dog 12.13.83 ABC
Manimal ep Breath of the Dragon 12.10.83 NBC
Mickey Spillane's Mike Hammer ep Hot Ice 2.4.84 CBS
Simon and Simon ep 3.1.84 CBS
Matt Houston ep Wanted Man 9.21.84 ABC
T. J. Hooker ep Night Vigil 10.13.84 ABC
MacGyver ep The Golden Triangle 10.6.85 ABC
Airwolf ep The Deadly Circle 11.30.85 CBS

KEEL, HOWARD
SUPP.:
Fantasy Island ep Nancy and the Thunderbirds 5.1.82 ABC

Dallas sr 10.1.82 CBS
Dallas sr ret 9.30.83 CBS
Dallas sr ret 9.28.84 CBS
Dallas sr ret 9.27.85 CBS

KEITH, BRIAN
A&C, B.V.:
Ellery Queen ep The Hinnlity Story 1.9.59 NBC
The Kraft Suspense Theater ep A Cause of Anger 3.19.64 NBC
SUPP.:
Hardcastle and McCormick sr 9.18.83 ABC
Hardcastle and McCormick sr ret 9.23.84 ABC
Murder, She Wrote ep (pt/first ep) 9.30.84 CBS
Hardcastle and McCormick sr ret 9.23.85 ABC

KELLERMAN, SALLY
A&C, B.V.:
Bachelor Father ep Kelly and the College Man Spring 1960 NBC
The Bob Hope Chrysler Theater ep Slow Fade to Black 3.27.64 NBC
Hawaii Five-O ep The Big Kahuna 3.19.69 CBS
SUPP.:
Murder Among Friends sp 4.82 SHO
For Lovers Only tf 10.15.82 ABC
Faerie Tale Theater ep Sleeping Beauty 7.7.83 SHO
Dempsey tf 9.28.83 CBS
September Gun tf 10.8.83 CBS
The CBS Children's Mystery Theater ep Dirkham Detective Agency 1.25.84 CBS
Hotel ep Lifelines 5.9.84 ABC

KELLERMAN, SUSAN*
Taxi ep The Road Not Taken 5.6.82 NBC
The Wild Women of Chastity Gulch tf/pt 10.31.82 ABC
Remington Steele ep Hearts of Steele 1.28.83 NBC
Dixie: Changing Habits tf 2.16.83 CBS
The Fighter tf 2.19.83 CBS
Knight Rider ep Knightmares 12.11.83 NBC
The Jeffersons ep 2.12.84 CBS
At Your Service pt 8.1.84 NBC
Cagney and Lacey ep 2.18.85 CBS

KELLY, GENE
SUPP.:
The Love Boat ep The Hong Kong Affair 2.4.84 ABC
North and South ms 11.3-11.10.85 ABC

KELLY, JACK
A&C, B.V.:
Wagon Train ep The Fenton Canaby Story 10.30.63 ABC
The High Chaparral ep The Doctor from Dodge 1.29.67 NBC

A&C, Supp. 1:
Chase ep Out of Gas? 2.20.74 NBC
Toma ep Joey the Weep 3.22.74 ABC
Hawaii Five-O ep Let Death Do Us Part 11.18.76 CBS
A&C, Supp. 2:
The Rockford Files ep The Becker Connection 2.11.77 NBC
The Rockford Files ep Beamer's Last Case 9.16.77 NBC
SUPP.:
Palms Precinct pt 1.8.82 NBC
The Master ep Kunoichi 4.6.84 NBC

KELLY, ROZ
SUPP.:
Fantasy Island ep Roller Derby Dolls 12.4.82 ABC
Trapper John, M.D. ep 3.6.83 CBS
Trapper John, M.D. ep Prime Time 3.13.83 CBS

KELSEY, LINDA
A&C, Supp. 2:
The Rockford Files ep The Dexter Crisis 11.15.74 NBC
Harry O ep Mayday 10.23.75 ABC
SUPP.:
His Mistress tf 10.21.84 NBC
Murder, She Wrote ep Capitol Offense 1.6.85 CBS
St. Elsewhere ep Haunted 10.16.85 NBC
Murder, She Wrote ep Jessica Behind Bars 12.1.85 CBS

KEMP, SALLY*
Apple's Way ep The Musician 2.17.74 CBS
Planet Earth tf 4.23.74 ABC
Get Christie Love ep Murder on High C 2.5.75 ABC
Get Christie Love ep From Paris With Love 3.5.75 ABC
Kojak ep No Immunity for Murder 11.23.75 CBS
Roots ms 1.23-1.30.77 ABC
A Death in Canaan tf 3.1.78 CBS
The Millionaire tf/pt 12.19.78 CBS
Strangers: The Story of a Mother and Daughter tf 5.13.79 CBS
The Lazarus Syndrome ep Malpractice 10.2.79 ABC
Kate Loves a Mystery ep Feelings Can Be Murder 12.6.79 NBC
Paris ep 1.1.80 CBS
The Hoyt Axton Show pt 9.28.81 NBC
Twirl tf 10.25.81 NBC
The ABC Afterschool Special ep Tough Girl 10.28.81 ABC
Isabel's Choice tf 12.16.81 CBS
Teachers Only ep Diana, Substitute Mother 4.14.82 NBC
Cassie and Company ep A Friend in Need 7.6.82 NBC
Dynasty ep Kirby 12.8.82 ABC
Dynasty ep Fathers and Sons 3.9.83 ABC
Dynasty ep The Threat 4.13.83 ABC
Dynasty ep The Cabin 4.20.83 ABC

Carpool tf 10.5.83 CBS
Hart to Hart ep Meanwhile Back at the Ranch 5.22.84 ABC
Simon and Simon ep The Third Eye 10.17.85 CBS

KENNEDY, GEORGE
A&C, B.V.:
The Phil Silvers Show ep Bilko Retires from Gambling 1958 CBS
The Phil Silvers Show ep Bilko's Vacation 1958 CBS
The Phil Silvers Show ep Bilko's Secret Mission 1958 CBS
The Phil Silvers Show ep Bilko's Small Car 1959 CBS
Cheyenne ep The Prisoner of Moon Mesa 11.16.59 ABC
Gunsmoke ep The Blacksmith ep 9.17.60 CBS
Have Gun--Will Travel ep A Head of Hair 9.24.60 CBS
Have Gun--Will Travel ep The Legacy 12.10.60 CBS
Klondike ep Swing on Your Partner 1.9.61 NBC
Gunsmoke ep Kitty Shot 2.11.61 CBS
Gunsmoke ep Big Man 3.25.61 CBS
Have Gun--Will Travel ep The Road 5.27.61 CBS
Have Gun--Will Travel ep The Vigil 9.16.61 CBS
Have Gun--Will Travel ep A Proof of Love 10.14.61 CBS
Have Gun--Will Travel ep Don't Shoot the Piano Player 3.10.62 CBS
Gunsmoke ep The Boys 5.26.62 CBS
The Andy Griffith Show ep The Big House 5.6.63 CBS
Gunsmoke ep Crooked Mile 10.3.64 CBS
Gunsmoke ep Cool Dawn 5.16.64 CBS
The Rogues ep The Computer Goes West 12.13.64 NBC
Daniel Boone ep A Rope for Mingo 12.2.65 NBC
Gunsmoke ep Harvest 3.26.66 CBS
Tarzan ep Thief Catcher 9.29.67 NBC
SUPP.:
Bliss pt 6.28.84 ABC
The Love Boat ep Stolen Years 9.29.84 ABC
Half Nelson ep 3.29.85 NBC
International Airport tf/pt 5.25.85 ABC

KENNEDY, JAYNE
SUPP.:
The Love Boat ep The Very Temporary Secretary 2.12.83 ABC
Diff'rent Strokes ep The Moonlighter 11.26.83 NBC
Benson ep Let's Get Physical 10.12.84 ABC

KENNEDY, MIMI
SUPP.:
Robert Kennedy and His Times ms 1.27, 1.28, 1.29, 1.30.84 CBS
Spencer sr 12.1.84 NBC
Night Court ep Married Alive 2.21.85 NBC
Under One Roof sr 3.23.85 NBC

KENIN, ALEXA*
The ABC Afterschool Special ep The Amazing Cosmic Awareness

of Duffy Moon 2.4.76 ABC
The ABC Afterschool Special ep Me and Dad's New Wife 2.18.76 ABC
The Word ms 11.12, 11.13, 11.14, 11.15.78 CBS
Co-ed Fever pt 2.4.79 CBS
The ABC Afterschool Special ep Make Believe Marriage 2.14.79 ABC
A Perfect Match tf 10.5.80 CBS
Word of Honor tf 1.6.81 CBS
The Facts of Life ep New York, New York 3.3.82 NBC
A Piano for Mrs. Cimino tf 2.3.83 CBS
The Mississippi ep 4.1.83 CBS
Princess Daisy tf 11.6, 11.7.83 NBC

KERCHEVAL, KEN*
Get Christie Love ep Market for Murder 9.11.74 ABC
Judge Horton and the Scottsboro Boys tf 4.22.76 NBC
Rafferty ep Death Out of a Blue Sky 12.5.77 CBS
Devil Dog: The Hound of Hell tf 10.31.78 CBS
Starsky and Hutch ep Targets Without a Badge 3.6, 3.11.79 ABC
Too Far to Go tf 3.12.79 NBC
Walking Through the Fire tf 5.15.79 CBS
Dallas sr 11.7.80 CBS
The Love Boat ep Two for Julie 3.14.81 ABC
Trapper John, M.D. ep That Old Gang of Mine 10.4.81 CBS
Dallas sr ret 10.9.81 ABC
The Patricia Neal Story tf 12.8.81 CBS
The Demon Murder Case tf 3.6.83 NBC
Dallas sr ret 9.30.83 CBS
Hotel ep Flashback 11.9.83 ABC
Calamity Jane tf 3.6.84 CBS
Dallas sr ret 9.28.84 CBS
The Love Boat ep Revenge with the Proper Stranger 11.17.84 ABC
Dallas sr ret 9.27.85 CBS
Glitter ep Fathers and Children 12.20.85 ABC

KERNS, JOANNA*
Switch ep Playoff 7.23.78 CBS
Marriage Is Alive and Well tf 1.25.80 NBC
CHiPs ep Dead Man's Riddle 5.10.81 NBC
Fitz and Bones ep Difficult Lesson 11.14.81 NBC
A Wedding on Waltons Mountain tf 2.22.82 NBC
Magnum, P.I. ep The Last Page 3.4.82 CBS
Mother's Day on Waltons Mountain tf 5.9.82 NBC
Star of the Family ep Spring Is in the Air 11.11.82 ABC
Laverne and Shirley ep The Fashion Show 12.7.82 ABC
Magnum, P.I. ep Birds of a Feather 3.17.83 CBS
Ryan's 4 ep 4.13.83 ABC
V ms 5.1, 5.2.83 NBC

The A-Team ep A Nice Place to Visit 5.10.83 NBC
Three's Company ep Jack Be Quick 9.27.83 ABC
The Whiz Kids ep Fatal Error 10.12.83 CBS
The Four Seasons sr 1.29.84 CBS
Hill Street Blues ep Hair Apparent 5.13.84 NBC
The Return of Marcus Welby, M.D. tf/pt 2.22.85 ABC
Street Hawk ep Hot Target 3.1.85 ABC
Hunter ep (pt/first ep) 9.18.84 NBC
A Bunny's Tale tf 2.25.85 ABC
The Rape of Richard Beck tf 5.27.85 ABC
Growing Pains sr 9.24.85 ABC

KERR, DEBORAH
SUPP.:
A Woman of Substance tf 12.5, 12.12.84 NN
Reunion at Fairborough tf 5.12.85 HBO

KERR, JOHN
A&C, B.V.:
Twelve O'Clock High ep An Act of War 12.25.64 ABC
The High Chaparral ep Sudden Country 11.5.67 NBC
Columbo ep Dead Weight 10.27.71 NBC
A&C, Supp. 1:
Alias Smith and Jones ep Only Three to a Bed 1.13.73 ABC
Toma ep Indictment 4.26.74 ABC
Switch ep Death By Resurrection 12.2.75 CBS

KERWIN, BRIAN*
Logan's Run ep The Innocent 10.10.77 CBS
The Greatest Thing That Almost Happened tf 10.26.77 CBS
A Real American Hero tf 12.9.78 CBS
The Chisholms ms 3.29-4.19.79 CBS
The Paradise Connection tf 9.15.79 CBS
The Misadventures of Sheriff Lobo sr 9.18.79 NBC
Power tf 1.14, 1.15.80 NBC
Lobo sr 12.30.80 NBC
The Love Boat ep The Incredible Hunk 10.24.81 ABC
The James Boys pt 6.25.82 NBC
The Blue and the Gray ms 11.14, 11.15, 11.16, 11.17.82 CBS
Miss All-American Beauty tf 12.29.82 CBS
Seven Brides for Seven Brothers ep 3.2.83 CBS
Intimate Agony tf 3.21.83 ABC
Simon and Simon ep Manna from Heaven 10.25.84 CBS
Wet Gold tf 10.28.84 ABC
Highway to Heaven ep Hotel of Dreams 12.12.84 NBC
Murder, She Wrote ep Death Casts a Spell 12.30.84 CBS

KERWIN, LANCE
SUPP.:
Trapper John, M.D. ep "42" 1.3.82 CBS
The CBS Afternoon Playhouse ep The Shooting 6.1.82 CBS

A Killer in the Family tf 10.30.83 ABC
Trapper John, M.D. ep 2.24.85 CBS
Faerie Tale Theater ep Snow Queen 3.11.85 SHO
The Fourth Wise Man sp 3.30.85 ABC

KEYES, EVELYN
SUPP.:
The Love Boat ep Lotions of Love 10.8.83 ABC
Murder, She Wrote ep Sticks and Stones 12.15.85 CBS

KIDDER, MARGOT
SUPP.:
Pygmalion sp 7.83 SHO
The Glitter Dome tf 11.18.84 HBO
The Hitchhiker ep Night Shift 10.15.85 HBO
Picking Up the Pieces tf 10.22.85 CBS

KILEY, RICHARD
SUPP.:
Pray TV tf 2.1.82 ABC
The Thorn Birds ms 3.27, 3.28, 3.29, 3.30.83 ABC
George Washington ms 4.8, 4.9, 4.10, 4.11.84 CBS
Hotel ep Promises 1.9.85 ABC
Do You Remember Love? tf 5.21.85 CBS
Wonder Works ep The Canterville Ghost 11.17.85 PBS

KILPATRICK, LINCOLN*
The Mask of Sheba tf 3.9.70 NBC
Baretta ep The Fire Man 10.8.75 ABC
Just Another Old Sweet Song tf 9.14.76 CBS
The Moneychangers ms 12.4-12.19.76 NBC
Kojak ep Mouse 1.21.78 CBS
King ms 2.12, 2.13, 2.14.78 NBC
Dr. Scorpion tf/pt 2.24.78 ABC
Buck Rogers in the 25th Century ep Space Vampire 1.3.80 NBC
The Greatest American Hero ep A Chicken in Every Pot 2.17.82 ABC
Lou Grant ep Victims 8.30.82 CBS
The Devlin Connection ep Claudine 12.11.82 NBC
Hill Street Blues ep Untitled 2.10.83 NBC
Matt Houston sr 9.9.83 ABC
Matt Houston sr ret 9.21.84 ABC
Trapper John, M.D. ep Prisoner 9.30.84 CBS

KIMMELL, DANA*
Midnight Offerings tf 2.27.81 ABC
The Return of the Beverly Hillbillies tf 10.6.81 CBS
Code Red ep The Little Girl Who Cried Fire 11.22.81 ABC
Diff'rent Strokes ep The Ski Weekend 11.26.81 NBC
The Facts of Life ep New York, New York 3.3.82 NBC
Hart to Hart ep A Christmas Hart 12.21.82 ABC

Fame ep Love Is the Question 1.27.83 NBC
Diff'rent Strokes ep Coming of Age 12.3.83 NBC
Hart to Hart ep Silent Dance 1.31.84 ABC
Hollywood Beat ep Baby Blues 10.26.85 ABC

KING, PERRY*
Cannon ep Blood Money 2.6.74 CBS
Foster and Laurie tf/pt 11.13.75 CBS
Captains and the Kings ms 9.30-11.11.76 NBC
Aspen ms 11.5, 11.6, 11.7.77 NBC
The Cracker Factory tf 3.16.79 ABC
Love's Savage Fury tf 5.20.79 ABC
The Last Convertible ms 9.24, 9.25, 9.26.79 NBC
City in Fear tf 3.30.80 ABC
Inmates: A Love Story tf 2.13.81 ABC
Golden Gate tf 9.25.81 ABC
The Quest sr 10.22.82 ABC
The Hasty Heart sp 9.83 SHO
Riptide sr 1.3.84 NBC
Helen Keller: The Miracle Continues tf 4.2, 4.3.84 OPT
Riptide sr ret 10.2.84 NBC
Riptide sr ret 10.1.85 NBC

KINSKI, CLAUS*
Faerie Tale Theater ep Beauty and the Beast 8.13.84 SHO
The Hitchhiker ep Love Sounds 11.13.84 HBO

KIRKCONNELL, CLARE*
The Paper Chase: The Third Year sr 5.11.85 SHO
The Fall Guy ep A Fistful of Lire 10.17.85 ABC
T.J. Hooker ep Funny Money 11.27.85 CBS

KIRKLAND, SALLY
A&C, Supp. 2:
Petrocelli ep Too Many Alibis 12.24.75 NBC
SUPP.:
Lou Grant ep Law 4.12.82 CBS
Falcon Crest ep 12.9.83 CBS

KISER, TERRY*
The Doctors (afternoon soap) sr 1967 NBC
N.Y.P.D. ep The Love Hustle 12.31.68 ABC
Change at 125th Street pt 3.28.74 CBS
Doctors' Hospital ep Sleepless and Pale Eyelids 9.24.75 NBC
Baretta ep Nobody in a Nothing Place 10.1.75 ABC
Marcus Welby, M.D. ep Calculated Risk 11.11.75 ABC
Switch ep The Walking Bomb 1.6.76 CBS
The Six Million Dollar Man ep Love Song for Tanya 2.15.76 ABC
Barnaby Jones ep The Eyes of Terror 3.11.76 CBS
City of Angels ep Palm Springs Answer 3.23.76 NBC
Jigsaw John ep Eclipse 3.29.76 NBC

Jigsaw John ep The Executioner 4.5.76 NBC
The Bionic Woman ep Mirror Image 5.19.76 ABC
Captains and the Kings ms 9.30-11.11.76 NBC
The Gemini Man ep Run, Sam, Run 10.28.76 NBC
Benny and Barney: Las Vegas Undercover tf/pt 1.9.77 NBC
Delvecchio ep Dying Can Be a Pleasure 1.23.77 CBS
Hawaii Five-O ep Blood Money Is Hard to Wash 3.3.77 CBS
The Nancy Drew Mysteries ep The Mystery of the Solid Gold Kicker 5.22.77 ABC
Bay City Amusement Company pt 7.28.77 NBC
Maude ep 1.28.78 CBS
The Cops and Robin tf/pt 3.28.78 NBC
All in the Family ep 2.19.78 CBS
Roller Girls sr 4.2.78 NBC
The Last Ride of the Dalton Gang tf 11.20.79 NBC
WKRP in Cincinnati ep Venus Rising 3.10.80 CBS
Enos ep Once and Fur All 3.11.81 CBS
The Fall Guy ep The Rich Get Richer 11.18.81 ABC
Bosom Buddies ep Cablevision 12.18.81 ABC
Prime Suspect tf 1.20.82 CBS
Three's Company ep A Friend in Need 2.16.82 ABC
Cassie and Company ep Fade Out 7.30.82 NBC
The Fall Guy ep A Piece of Cake 12.1.82 ABC
It Takes Two ep Anniversary 1.13.83 ABC
Hill Street Blues ep The Belles of St. Mary's 2.17.83 NBC
Hill Street Blues ep Life in the Minors 2.24.83 NBC
CHiPs ep Fox Trap 2.20.83 NBC
Starflight: The Plane That Couldn't Land tf 2.27.83 ABC
Your Place or Mine tf 3.2.83 CBS
Tucker's Witch ep The Rock Star Murders 4.14.83 CBS
Manimal ep 9.30.83 NBC
The Rousters ep The Carnival That Ate Sladetown 10.15.83 NBC
Diff'rent Strokes ep Rashomoon II 10.22.83 NBC
The Fall Guy ep Dirty Laundry 11.9.83 ABC
Hardcastle and McCormick ep Hot Shoes 12.18.83 ABC
Night Court ep The Former Harry Stone 1.18.84 NBC
Automan ep Renegade Run 3.5.84 ABC
Night Court ep Harry and the Rock Star 3.21.84 NBC
Scarecrow and Mrs. King ep Fearless Dotty 4.26.84 CBS
Cover Up ep (pt/first ep) 9.22.84 CBS
E/R ep 10.16.84 CBS
Night Court ep Pick a Number 10.25.84 NBC
Night Court ep Last Madam in New York (a.k.a. Harry and the Madam) 11.22.84 NBC
Hail to the Chief ep Hail to the Chief #4 4.23.85 ABC
The Fall Guy ep Split Image 2.27.85 ABC
Half Nelson ep 3.29.85 NBC
Murder, She Wrote ep Murder in the Afternoon 10.13.85 CBS
Trapper John, M.D. ep Friends and Lovers 11.3.85 CBS

KLINE, RICHARD*
Serpico ep The Indian 10.8.76 NBC
The Mary Tyler Moore Show ep Mary Gets a Lawyer 11.13.76 CBS
Three's Company sr 3.15.77 ABC
Three's Company sr ret 9.13.77 ABC
Three's Company sr ret 9.12.78 ABC
Three's Company sr ret 9.11.79 ABC
The Love Boat ep My Boyfriend's Back 10.6.79 ABC
Three's Company sr ret 10.28.80 ABC
Three's Company sr ret 10.6.81 ABC
Three's Company sr ret 9.28.82 ABC
The Love Boat ep Paroled to Love 1.8.83 ABC
Three's Company sr ret 9.27.83 ABC
Fantasy Island ep The Other Man--Mr. Roarke 10.8.83 ABC
His and Hers pt 5.15.84 CBS
The Love Boat ep I'll Never Forget What's Her Name 10.27.84 ABC
Glitter ep Illusions 12.25.84 ABC
Three's a Crowd ep Deeds of Trust 2.19.85 ABC
Under One Roof ep Doris and the Tutor 4.13.85 NBC
The Comedy Factory ep The Second Time Around 7.26.85 ABC
It's a Living sr 11.3.85 NN
The New Love, American Style ep Love and the Final Night 12.26.85 ABC

KLOUS, PATRICIA (a.k.a. Pat Klous)*
Flying High tf/pt 8.28.78 CBS
Flying High sr 9.29.78 CBS
Fantasy Island ep 5.5.79 ABC
The Dukes of Hazzard ep The People's Choice 11.30.79 CBS
Terror Among Us tf 1.12.81 CBS
The Love Boat ep The Lone Arranger 1.17.81 ABC
Fantasy Island ep A Night in a Harem 11.14.81 ABC
The Love Boat ep The Irresistible Man 2.6.82 ABC
Johnny Blue pt 9.4.83 CBS
The Love Boat ep My Two Dumplings 10.1.83 ABC
Fantasy Island ep Nurses' Night Out 10.22.83 ABC
Hotel ep Deceptions 11.30.83 ABC
Matt Houston ep Waltz of Death 1.13.84 ABC
Matt Houston ep On the Run 3.30.84 ABC
The Love Boat sr (with ep The Crew's Cruise Director) 9.22.84 ABC
The Love Boat sr ret 9.28.85 ABC

KLUGMAN, JACK
A&C, B.V.:
Rocky King, Detective ep 5.23.54 DuMont
Suspicion ep Diary for Death 11.4.57 NBC
Suspicion ep The Dark Stairway 12.23.57 NBC
SUPP.:

Quincy, M.E. sr ret 9.29.82 NBC
The Love Boat ep There'll Be Some Changes Made 2.2.85 ABC

KNIGHT, GLADYS*
The Jeffersons ep 2.20.83 CBS
Benson ep Too Pooped to Pip 1.6.84 ABC
Charlie and Company sr 9.18.85 CBS

KNIGHT, SHIRLEY
A&C, B.V.:
Bronco ep The Baron of Broken Lance 1.13.59 ABC
The Big Valley ep The Iron Box 11.28.66 ABC
SUPP.:
Nurse ep A Necessary End 5.14.82 CBS
With Intent to Kill tf 10.24.84 CBS
Spenser: For Hire ep Internal Affairs 12.17.85 NBC

KNIGHT, TED
A&C, Supp. 2:
How to Marry a Millionaire ep A Call to Arms 1958 NN
The Donna Reed Show ep April Fool 4.1.59 ABC
Peter Gunn ep Crisscross 9.28.59 NBC
Alfred Hitchcock Presents ep Party Line 5.29.60 CBS
Dr. Kildare ep Immunity 10.5.61 NBC
Twelve O'Clock High ep Storm at Twilight 11.22.65 ABC
The Eleventh Hour ep Which Men Will Die? 1.2.63 NBC
The Untouchables ep The Speculator 1.15.63 ABC
Sam Benedict ep Season for Vengeance 3.30.63 NBC
Combat ep Weep No More 3.17.64 ABC
Kraft Suspense Theater ep Once Upon a Starry Night 4.2.64 NBC
The FBI ep An Elephant Is Like a Rope 12.5.65 ABC
Gomer Pyle, USMC ep Gomer, the Would-be Hero 4.66 CBS
Combat ep The Brothers 10.4.66 ABC
Gomer Pyle ep 4.15.66 CBS
The FBI ep The Assassin 10.9.66 ABC
The Fugitive ep Second Light 10.25.66 ABC
Get Smart ep Pussycat Galore 4.1.67 NBC
Garrison's Gorillas ep The War Diamonds 3.5.68 ABC
The Outsider ep Tell It Like It Was ... And You're Dead 12.4.68 NBC
SUPP.:
The Love Boat ep Pride of the Pacific 3.6.82 ABC
Too Close for Comfort sr ret 10.14.82 ABC
Too Close for Comfort sr ret 10.83 NN
The Love Boat ep The Lottery Winners 11.5.83 ABC
Saturday's the Place sp 9.14.84 CBS
Too Close for Comfort sr ret 10.84 NN
Too Close for Comfort sr ret 10.85 NN

KNOTTS, DON
A&C, B.V.:

Love That Bob ep Bob and Schultzy at Sea 1958 NBC
The Many Loves of Dobie Gillis ep Rock-A-Bye Dobie 7.5.60 CBS
The Andy Griffith Show ep The Return of Barney Fife 1.10.66 CBS
The Andy Griffith Show ep The Legend of Barney Fife 1.17.66 CBS
The Andy Griffith Show ep A Visit to Barney Fife 1.16.67 CBS
The Andy Griffith Show ep Barney Comes to Mayberry 1.23.67 CBS
The Andy Griffith Show ep Barney Hosts a Summit Meeting 1.29.68 CBS
SUPP.:
Three's Company sr ret 9.28.82 ABC
Three's Company sr ret 9.27.83 ABC
George Burns Comedy Week ep Disaster at Buzz Creek 10.23.85 CBS

KOPELL, BERNIE
A&C, B.V.:
Alfred Hitchcock Presents ep Goodbye George 12.13.63 CBS
The Beverly Hillbillies ep The Movie Starlet 1.13.65 CBS
The Farmer's Daughter ep Anyone for Spindling? Spring 1966 ABC
The Hero ep I Have a Friend 12.66 NBC
The Bob Newhart Show ep I Want to Be Alone Fall 1972 ABC
Harry O ep For the Love of Money 1.16.75 ABC
Switch ep Ain't Nobody Here Named Barney 1.13.76 CBS
Switch ep Gaffing the Skim 11.16.76 CBS
SUPP.:
The Love Boat sr ret 10.2.82 ABC
Fantasy Island ep The Devil Stick 3.19.83 ABC
The Love Boat sr ret 10.1.83 ABC
Legmen ep Apple Dan's Last Stand 2.3.84 NBC
The Love Boat sr ret 9.22.84 ABC
Half Nelson ep 3.29.85 NBC
The Love Boat sr ret 9.28.85 ABC

KOPINS, KAREN*
Riptide ep Riptide (pt) 1.3.84 NBC
T. J. Hooker ep Target: Hooker 11.17.84 ABC
Knight Rider ep Dead of Knight 12.2.84 NBC
The Love Boat ep Getting Started 2.16.85 ABC
Heart Beat pt 8.14.85 NBC
Amazing Stories ep The Mission 11.3.85 NBC

KOTTO, YAPHET
SUPP.:
Fantasy Island ep Cotton Club 2.26.83 ABC
The A-Team ep The Out-of-Towners 3.22.83 NBC
For Love and Honor sr 9.23.83 NBC

Harpy tf 10.26.83 CBS
Playing with Fire tf 4.14.85 NBC
Badge of the Assassin tf 11.2.85 CBS
Alfred Hitchcock Presents ep You Gotta Have Luck 12.8.85 NBC

KOVE, MARTIN*
Switch ep The Deadly Missiles Caper 10.7.75 CBS
Kingston: The Power Play tf/pt 9.15.76 NBC
Captains and the Kings ms 9.30-11.11.76 NBC
The Streets of San Francisco ep The Drop 10.28.76 ABC
The Rockford Files ep 4.1.77 NBC
The Nancy Drew Mysteries ep The Mystery of the Solid Gold Kicker 5.22.77 ABC
We've Got Each Other sr 10.1.77 CBS
The Incredible Hulk ep Final Round 3.10.78 CBS
Barnaby Jones ep Nest of Scorpions 10.26.78 CBS
Starsky and Hutch ep Birds of a Feather 1.30.79 ABC
Quincy, M.E. ep Death's Challenge 3.29.79 NBC
Barnaby Jones ep Girl on the Road 10.25.79 CBS
A Man Called Sloane ep Lady Bug 12.8.79 NBC
Tenspeed and Brown Shoe ep Savage Says: What Are Friends For? 3.2.80 ABC
Trouble in High Timber Country tf/pt 6.27.80 ABC
Cagney and Lacey sr 3.25.82 CBS
Cagney and Lacey sr ret 10.25.82 CBS
Cry for the Strangers tf 12.11.82 CBS
Cagney and Lacey sr ret 3.19.84 CBS
Cagney and Lacey sr ret 10.15.84 CBS
Murder, She Wrote ep Armed Response 3.31.85 CBS
Cagney and Lacey sr ret 9.30.85 CBS
The Twilight Zone ep Opening Day 11.29.85 CBS

KRAMER, STEPFANIE*
The Runaways ep Dreams of My Father 7.3.79 NBC
Vegas ep Sudden Death 11.19.80 ABC
Trapper John, M.D. ep Straight and Narrow 1.11.81 CBS
Bosom Buddies ep All You Need Is Love 12.18.81 ABC
The Devlin Connection ep Ring of Kings, Ring of Thieves 11.27.82 NBC
Knots Landing ep 4.8.82 CBS
High Performance ep Along Came a Spider 3.2.83 ABC
We Got It Made sr 9.8.83 NBC
The Dukes of Hazzard ep 2.3, 2.10.84 CBS
Riptide ep Four Eyes 3.6.84 NBC
Mickey Spillane's Mike Hammer ep Satin, Cyanide and Arsenic 4.14.84 CBS
Hunter sr 9.18.84 NBC
The A-Team Fire 10.2.84 NBC
Hunter sr ret 3.23.85 NBC
Hunter sr ret 9.21.85 NBC
Bridge Across Time tf 11.22.85 NBC

KURTZ, SWOOSIE
SUPP.:
Love, Sidney sr ret 9.15.82 NBC
Fifth of July sp 10.14.82 SHO
Agatha Christie's "A Caribbean Mystery" tf 10.22.83 CBS
Guilty Conscience tf 4.2.85 CBS
A Time to Live tf 10.28.85 NBC

KURTZMAN, KATY
SUPP.:
Allison Sidney Harrison pt 8.19.83 NBC
The CBS Schoolbreak Special ep Student Court 4.23.85 CBS

KWAN, NANCY
SUPP.:
The Last Ninja tf 7.7.83 ABC
Trapper John, M.D. ep 3.4.84 CBS
Partners in Crime ep Duke 10.20.84 NBC
Blade in Hong Kong tf/pt 5.15.85 CBS

- L -

LADD, CHERYL
A&C, Supp. 2:
Police Story ep Prime Rib 4.5.77 NBC
SUPP.:
Kentucky Woman tf 1.11.83 CBS
Grace Kelly tf 2.21.83 ABC
The Hasty Heart sp 9.83 SHO
Romance on the Orient Express tf 3.4.85 NBC
A Death in California tf 5.12, 5.13.85 ABC

LADD, DIANE
A&C, Supp. 2:
Hazel ep George's 32nd Cousin 11.63 NBC
Daniel Boone ep Seminole Territory 1.13.66 NBC
Gunsmoke ep The Favor 3.11.67 CBS
SUPP.:
Desperate Lives tf 3.3.82 CBS
Grace Kelly tf 2.21.83 ABC
Faerie Tale Theater ep Little Red Riding Hood 11.10.83 SHO
The Love Boat ep The Crew's Cruise Director 9.22.84 ABC
I Married a Centerfold tf 11.11.84 NBC
The Love Boat ep A Day in Port 9.28.85 ABC
Crime of Innocence tf 10.27.85 NBC

LADD, MARGARET*
A Time for Us sr 12.28.64 ABC

Quincy, M.E. ep A Deadly Silence 2.7.80 NBC
Quincy, M.E. ep Cover Up 2.7.80 NBC
Falcon Crest sr 12.4.81 CBS
Falcon Crest sr ret 10.1.82 CBS
Falcon Crest sr ret 9.30.83 CBS
Falcon Crest sr ret 9.28.84 CBS
Falcon Crest sr ret 10.4.85 CBS

LAINE, FRANKIE
A&C, B.V.:
The Danny Thomas Show ep Frankie Laine Sings for Gina 3.9.59 CBS
Bachelor Father ep A Party for Peter Fall 1961 ABC

LAMAS, LORENZO
SUPP.:
Falcon Crest sr ret 10.1.82 CBS
The Love Boat ep Julie's Tycoon 11.13.82 ABC
Fantasy Island ep Naughty Marietta 1.8.83 ABC
Falcon Crest sr ret 9.30.83 CBS
Hotel ep The Offer 12.7.83 ABC
Falcon Crest sr ret 9.28.84 CBS
An American Portrait ep Paul Gonzales 1.18.85 CBS
Falcon Crest sr ret 10.4.85 CBS

LAMB, GIL
A&C, B.V.:
My Little Margie ep Daughter-in-Law 1954 NBC
Camp Runamuck ep Air Conditioner Spring 1966 NBC
The Man from UNCLE ep The Apple-a-Day Affair 3.24.67 NBC
The Andy Griffith Show ep Sam for Town Council 3.11.68 CBS

LAMBERT, ZOHRA
SUPP.:
Airwolf ep Echoes from the Past 3.3.84 CBS
Izzy and Moe tf 9.23.85 CBS

LAMOUR, DOROTHY
SUPP.:
Hart to Hart ep Max's Waltz 1.17.84 ABC
Remington Steele ep Cast in Steele 12.4.84 NBC

LANCASTER, BURT
SUPP.:
Scandal Sheet tf 1.21.85 ABC

LANDAU, MARTIN
A&C, B.V.:
Lawman ep The Outcast 11.2.58 ABC
Lawless Years ep Lucky Silva 8.13.59 NBC
Wanted: Dead Or Alive ep The Monsters 1.16.60 CBS

Johnny Ringo ep The Derelict 5.25.60 CBS
The Rifleman ep The Vaqueros 10.2.61 ABC
The Tall Man ep The Black Robe 5.5.62 NBC
SUPP.:
The Fall of the House of Usher tf 7.25.82 NBC
Matt Houston ep The Hunted 4.24.83 ABC
Hotel ep Confrontations 11.16.83 ABC
Buffalo Bill ep Company, Ink 1.19.84 NBC
Murder, She Wrote ep Birds of a Feather 10.14.84 CBS
The Twilight Zone ep The Beacon 12.6.85 CBS

LANDERS, AUDREY
SUPP.:
Fit for a King pt 6.11.82 ABC
Dallas sr ret 10.1.82 CBS
Fantasy Island ep The Tallowed Image 1.29.83 ABC
Dallas sr ret 9.30.83 CBS
Fantasy Island ep The Fantasy Island Girl 12.10.83 ABC
The Hitchhiker ep Split Decision 12.14.83 HBO
The Love Boat ep Mother Comes First 1.25.84 ABC
Fantasy Island ep Deuces Are Wild 5.12.84 ABC
Dallas sr ret 9.28.84 CBS
The Dukes of Hazzard ep 10.19.84 CBS
Dallas sr ret 9.27.85 CBS
The Love Boat ep All for One 11.2.85 ABC

LANDERS, JUDY
SUPP.:
The Love Boat ep His Girls Fridays 2.13.82 ABC
The Fall Guy ep Three for the Road 4.14.82 ABC
That's TV pt 4.18.82 NBC
The Love Boat ep Substitute Lover 5.15.82 ABC
Madame's Place sr 9.82 NN
Knight Rider ep Forget Me Not 12.17.82 NBC
The Love Boat ep The Maid Cleans Up 3.12.83 ABC
The Hitchhiker ep Split Decision 12.14.83 HBO
Night Court ep The Former Harry Stone 1.18.84 NBC
Lottery ep Chicago: Another Chance ("Bradshaw" segment) 3.1.84 ABC
Fantasy Island ep Deuces Are Wild 5.12.84 ABC
Knight Rider ep Knight Strike 4.5.85 NBC
The Comedy Factory ep Four in Love 7.19.85 ABC
The A-Team ep Where Is the Monster When You Need Him? 10.1.85 NBC
The Love Boat ep All for One 11.2.85 ABC

LANDON, MICHAEL
A&C, B.V.:
The Adventures of Jim Bowie ep Deputy Sheriff 9.28.56 ABC
Goodyear Theater ep The Giant Step 4.28.58 CBS
Alcoa Theater ep Johnny Risk (pilot) 6.16.58 CBS

Wanted: Dead Or Alive ep The Martin Poster 9.6.58 CBS
Tombstone Territory ep The Rose of Rio Bravo 9.17.58 ABC
The Rifleman ep End of a Young Gun 10.14.58 ABC
Wanted: Dead or Alive ep The Legend 3.7.59 CBS
Tombstone Territory ep The Man from Brewster 4.24.59 ABC
The Rifleman ep The Murderer 6.30.59 ABC
SUPP.:
Love Is Forever tf 4.3.83 NBC
Little House: Look Back to Yesterday tf 12.12.83 NBC
Little House: The Last Farewell tf 2.6.84 NBC
Highway to Heaven sr 9.19.84 NBC
Highway to Heaven sr ret 9.18.85 NBC

LANE, ABBE
SUPP.:
Hart to Hart ep Straight Through the Hart 10.4.83 ABC
Amazing Stories ep Guilt Trip 12.1.85 NBC

LANGDON, SUE ANE
A&C, Supp. 2:
Bourbon Street Beat ep The Light Touch of Terror 12.7.59 ABC
Surfside 6 ep Local Girl 10.31.60 ABC
The Outlaws ep Culley 2.16.61 NBC
Surfside 6 ep The Bhoyo and the Blonde 5.16.61 ABC
The Joey Bishop Show ep The Bachelor 10.25.61 NBC
Room for One More ep The Girl from Sweden 2.17.62 ABC
The Detectives ep A Barrel Full of Monkeys 10.27.61 ABC
Gunsmoke ep Catawomper 2.10.62 CBS
Thriller ep Cousin Tundifer 2.19.62 NBC
The Dick Van Dyke Show ep One Angry Man 3.7.62 CBS
Follow the Sun ep The Inhuman Equater 3.11.62 ABC
The Andy Griffith Show ep Three's a Crowd 4.9.62 CBS
77 Sunset Strip ep The Fumble 12.13.63 ABC
No Time for Sergeants ep The Velvet Wiggle 5.3.65 ABC
Perry Mason ep The Case of the Avenging Angel 3.13.66 CBS
SUPP.:
Three's Company ep Urban Playboy 2.9.82 ABC
Happy Days ep All I Want for Christmas 12.14.82 ABC
Hart to Hart ep Bahama Bound Harts 2.22.83 ABC

LANGE, HOPE
SUPP.:
Matt Houston ep Recipe for Murder 11.7.82 ABC
Fantasy Island ep The Winning Ticket 1.8.83 ABC
Finder of Lost Loves ep (pt/first ep) 9.22.84 ABC
Private Sessions tf/pt 3.18.85 NBC

LANKFORD, KIM*
Police Woman ep Task Force: Cop Killer 3.2, 3.9.76 NBC
The Love Boat ep Chimpanzeeshines 1.14.78 ABC
The Waverly Wonders sr 9.22.78 NBC

Knots Landing sr 12.27.79 CBS
Knots Landing sr ret 11.20.80 CBS
Terror Among Us tf 1.12.81 CBS
Knots Landing sr ret 9.30.81 CBS
Three Eyes pt 6.27.82 NBC
Knots Landing sr ret 9.30.82 CBS
Fantasy Island ep Roller Derby Dolls 12.4.82 ABC
Knots Landing sr ret 9.29.83 CBS
Fantasy Island ep Ladies Choice 1.28.84 ABC
Finder of Lost Loves ep White Lies 10.20.84 ABC
Cheers ep Sam Turns the Other Cheek 11.1.84 NBC
The Love Boat ep Noel's Christmas Carol 12.15.84 ABC
The Hitchhiker ep A Time for Rifles 2.26.85 HBO

LANSBURY, ANGELA
SUPP.:
Sweeney Todd sp 9.12.82 TEC
Little Gloria ... Happy at Last tf 10.24, 10.25.82 NBC
The Gift of Love: A Christmas Story sp 12.20.83 CBS
Lace ms 2.26, 2.27.84 ABC
A Talent for Murder sp 3.26.84 SHO
The First Olympics: Athens 1896 tf 5.20, 5.21.84 NBC
Murder, She Wrote sr 9.30.84 CBS
Murder, She Wrote sr ret 9.29.85 CBS

LANSING, ROBERT
A&C, B.V.:
The Donna Reed Show ep Donna Meets Roberta 5.3.62 ABC
The DuPont Show of the Week ep A Sound of Hunting 5.20.62 NBC
Wagon Train ep The Geneva Belfour Story 1.20.64 ABC
Channing ep Wave Goodbye to Our Fair-Haired Boy 3.18.64 ABC
The Monroes ep Manhunt 3.1.67 ABC
SUPP.:
Simon and Simon ep Shadow of Sam Penny 11.3.83 CBS
Automan sr 12.15.83 ABC
The Equalizer sr 9.18.85 CBS
Simon and Simon ep Reunion at Alcatraz 11.14.85 CBS

LARCH, JOHN*
You Are There ep Benedict Arnold's Plot Against West Point 1.1.56 CBS
The Web ep Last Chance 9.1.57 CBS
The Restless Gun ep The Shooting of Jett King 10.28.57 NBC
You Are There ep 11.6.57 CBS
Gunsmoke ep Fingered 11.23.57 CBS
The Restless Gun ep Hornita's Town 2.10.58 NBC
Jefferson Drum ep The Bounty Man 4.25.58 ABC
The Texan ep Law of the Gun 9.29.58 CBS
The Restless Gun ep Thunder Valley 10.13.58 NBC

Wanted: Dead or Alive ep Die by the Gun 12.6.58 CBS
Black Saddle ep Client: Northrup 3.14.59 NBC
Gunsmoke ep The Constable 5.30.59 CBS
Yancy Derringer ep Two Tickets to Promontory 6.4.59 CBS
Bonanza ep The Newcomers 9.26.59 NBC
The Troubleshooters ep Gino 10.23.59 NBC
Wichita Town ep Drifting 10.28.59 NBC
Gunsmoke ep The Boots 11.14.59 CBS
Tales of Wells Fargo ep End of a Legend 11.23.59 NBC
The Loretta Young Show ep Christmas Stopover 12.20.59 NBC
Laramie ep Day of Reckoning 1.19.60 NBC
Johnny Ringo ep The Liars 2.4.60 CBS
Gunsmoke ep Jailbait Janet 2.27.60 CBS
Goodyear Theater ep The Proud Earth 5.23.60 CBS
Route 66 ep The Strengthening Angels 11.4.60 CBS
The Deputy ep The Higher Law 11.12.60 NBC
Gunsmoke ep Long Hours, Short Pay 4.29.61 CBS
Gunsmoke ep All That 10.28.61 CBS
Tales of Wells Fargo ep A Killing in Calico 12.16.61 NBC
The Untouchables ep Hammerlock 12.21.61 ABC
Ben Casey ep And If I Die 1.1.62 ABC
Laramie ep The Confederate Express 1.30.62 NBC
Naked City ep Today the Man Who Kills Aunts Is Coming 3.7.62 ABC
Route 66 ep Go Read the River 3.16.62 CBS
Wagon Train ep The Baylor Crowfoot Story 3.21.62 NBC
Stoney Burke ep Gold Plated Maverick 1.7.63 ABC
Dr. Kildare ep A Trip to Niagara 2.21.63 NBC
Arrest and Trial sr 9.15.63 ABC
The Fugitive ep Man on a String 9.29.64 ABC
Slattery's People ep Is Democracy Too Expensive? 2.26.65 CBS
Convoy sr 9.17.65 NBC
The FBI ep The Price of Death 9.18.66 ABC
The Felony Squad ep The Broken Badge 9.26.66 ABC
The Fugitive ep The Other Side of the Coin 1.10.67 ABC
The Invaders ep Genesis 2.7.67 ABC
Ironside ep The Leaf in the Forest 9.21.67 NBC
The Man from UNCLE ep The Man from THRUSH Affair 12.4.67 NBC
Daniel Boone ep Chief Mingo 12.7.67 NBC
Judd, for the Defense ep The Living Victim 12.15.67 ABC
The Virginian ep The Good-Hearted Badman 2.7.68 NBC
The Felony Squad ep The Deadly Abductors 2.12.68 ABC
Hawaii Five-O ep Yesterday Died and Tomorrow Won't Be Born 11.7.68 CBS
The Young Lawyers ep A Simple Thing Called Justice 9.28.70 ABC
Alias Smith and Jones ep The Girl in Boxcar Number 3 2.11.71 ABC
The City tf 5.17.71 ABC
Owen Marshall, Counselor at Law ep Shadow of a Name 10.8.71 ABC

Nanny and the Professor ep 12.13.71 ABC
The Smith Family ep Class of '46 12.8.71 ABC
Cannon ep A Deadly Quiet Town 2.15.72 CBS
O'Hara, United States Treasury ep 3.3.72 CBS
The FBI ep The Outcast 12.17.72 ABC
Cannon ep To Ride a Tiger 2.14.73 CBS
Madigan ep The Park Avenue Beat 2.28.73 NBC
Police Story ep Requiem for an Informer 10.9.73 NBC
Owen Marshall, Counselor at Law ep The Camerons Are a Special Clan 10.24.73 ABC
The Streets of San Francisco ep Inferno 2.14.74 ABC
Winterkill tf 4.15.74 ABC
The Chadwick Family tf 4.17.74 ABC
Bad Ronald tf 10.23.74 ABC
The Desperate Miles tf 3.5.75 ABC
Ellery Queen tf/pt 3.23.75 NBC
Bronk ep Bargain in Blood 11.16.75 CBS
Future Cop tf/pt 5.1.76 ABC
Charlie's Angels ep Angel Trap 1.5.77 ABC
The Feather and Father Gang ep Sun, Sand and Death 3.14.77 ABC
Kingston: Confidential ep The Cult 7.13.77 NBC
The Critical List tf 9.11, 9.12.78 NBC
Lucan ep Nightmare 11.13.78 ABC
Quincy, M.E. ep Aftermath 2.7.79 NBC
Lou Grant ep Hollywood 12.17.79 CBS
Little House on the Prairie ep A New Beginning 10.6.80 NBC
Vegas ep Deadly Blessing 12.10.80 ABC
The Dukes of Hazzard ep Good Neighbors Duke 1.2.81 CBS
Dynasty sr 1.12.81 ABC

LARKEN, SHEILA*
Marcus Welby, M.D. tf/pt 3.26.69 ABC
The Storefront Lawyers sr 9.16.70 CBS
Sarge ep 10.12.71 NBC
Owen Marshall, Counselor at Law ep Journey Through Limbo 10.12.72 ABC
Cannon ep Memo from a Dead Man 9.19.73 CBS
Police Story ep The Ripper 2.12.74 NBC
Barnaby Jones ep Trap Play 1.7.75 CBS
Police Story ep Sniper 2.11.75 NBC
Sarah T.--Portrait of a Teenage Alcoholic tf 2.11.75 NBC
Attack on Terror: The FBI vs. the Ku Klux Klan tf 2.20, 2.21.75 CBS
Medical Story ep The Right to Die 9.11.75 NBC
Joe Forrester ep The Witness 9.16.75 NBC
Starsky and Hutch ep Terror on the Docks 11.26.75 ABC
The Blue Knight ep The Candy Man 2.4.76 CBS
Barnaby Jones ep The Eyes of Terror 3.11.76 CBS
Barnaby Jones ep Sister of Death 1.6.77 CBS
Tales of the Unexpected ep No Way Out 8.24.77 NBC

The Incredible Hulk ep The Waterfront Story 5.31.78 CBS
Dallas ep John Ewing III 9.21, 9.28.79 CBS
Trapper John, M.D. ep 12.9.79 CBS
Lou Grant ep 3.17.80 CBS
The Incredible Hulk ep Nine Hours 4.4.80 CBS
The Other Victim tf 11.4.81 CBS
Little House: A New Beginning ep 1.10.82 NBC
McClain's Law ep What Patrick Doesn't Know 2.5.82 NBC
Quincy, M.E. ep Sleeping Dogs 11.17.82 NBC
Trapper John, M.D. ep Forget Me Not 1.30.83 CBS
Cave-In tf 6.19.83 NBC
Simon and Simon ep 2.23.84 CBS
The Midnight Hour tf 11.1.85 ABC

LARROQUETTE, JOHN*
Doctor's Hospital ep My Cup Runneth Over 1.12.75 NBC
Black Sheep Squadron sr 9.21.76 NBC
The 416th pt 8.25.79 CBS
Bare Essence ms 10.4, 10.5.82 CBS
9 to 5 ep Dick Doesn't Live Here Anymore 10.26.82 ABC
The Last Ninja tf/pt 7.7.83 ABC
Night Court sr 1.14.84 NBC
Night Court sr ret 9.27.84 NBC
Night Court sr ret 9.26.85 NBC
Hello Sucker! sp 10.11.85 SHO

LASSER, LOUISE
SUPP.:
Taxi ep Take My Ex-Wife, Please 2.18.82 ABC
Taxi ep Get Me Through the Holidays 12.16.82 NBC
Laverne and Shirley ep The Monastery Show 1.4.83 ABC
St. Elsewhere ep In Sickness and Health 2.8.84 NBC
Bedrooms comedy sp 2.14.84 HBO
St. Elsewhere ep Cramming 5.2.84 NBC

LASSICK, SYDNEY*
Serpico tf/pt 4.26.76 NBC
The Man from Atlantis ep Hawk of Mu 10.18.77 NBC
Baretta ep Who Can Make the Sun Shine? 11.30.77 ABC
Hawaii Five-O ep A Stranger in His Grave 3.23.78 CBS
Kaz ep Which Side You On? 11.5.78 CBS
The Cracker Factory tf 3.16.79 ABC
Damien: The Leper Priest tf 10.27.80 NBC
Murder One, Dancer 0 tf/pt 6.5.83 NBC
Simon and Simon ep 10.6.83 CBS
Matt Houston ep Needle in a Haystack 10.7.83 CBS
Night Court ep Pick a Number 10.25.84 NBC
Mickey Spillane's Mike Hammer ep Back to Back 11.10.84 CBS
Amazing Stories ep Remote Control Man 12.8.85 NBC

LATHAM, LOUISE

A&C, Supp. 2:

The Rogues ep The Laughing Lady of Luxor 2.21.65 NBC
Perry Mason ep The Case of the Careless Killer 3.25.65 CBS
Family Affair ep One in Love with Buffy 2.13.67 CBS
The Fugitive ep The Judgement 8.22.67, 8.29.67 ABC
Family Affair ep Family Reunion 1.1.68 CBS
Gunsmoke ep Hawk 10.20.69 CBS
Gunsmoke ep Roots of Fear 12.15.69 CBS
Gunsmoke ep Gentry's Law 10.12.70 CBS

SUPP.:

Pray TV tf 2.1.82 ABC
Lois Gibbs and the Love Canal tf 2.17.82 CBS
Obsessive Love tf 10.2.84 CBS
Love Lives On tf 4.1.85 ABC
Tough Love tf 10.13.85 ABC

LAUREN, TAMMY

SUPP.:

The Facts of Life ep Runaway 2.24.82 NBC
The Kid with the Broken Halo tf/pt 4.5.82 NBC
CHiPs ep Brat Patrol 2.27.83 NBC
M.A.D.D.: Mothers Against Drunk Drivers tf 3.14.83 NBC
Things Are Looking Up pt 6.29.84 CBS
E/R ep 9.16.84 CBS
Playing with Fire tf 4.14.85 NBC
The Best Times sr 4.19.85 NBC
Crime of Innocence tf 10.27.85 NBC

LAURIE, PIPER

SUPP.:

Mae West tf 5.2.82 ABC
The Thorn Birds ms 3.27, 3.28, 3.29, 3.30.83 ABC
St. Elsewhere ep Ties That Bind 10.26.83 NBC
St. Elsewhere ep Lust et Veritas 11.2.83 NBC
St. Elsewhere ep Newheart 11.9.83 NBC
Hotel ep Illusions 11.28.84 ABC
Murder, She Wrote ep Murder at the Oasis 4.7.85 CBS
Love, Mary tf 10.8.85 CBS
Tough Love tf 10.13.85 ABC
Tender Is the Night sr 10.27.85 SHO
The Twilight Zone ep The Burning Man 11.15.85 CBS

LAVIN, LINDA

SUPP.:

Alice sr ret 10.6.82 CBS
Another Woman's Child tf 1.19.83 CBS
Alice sr ret 12.2.83 CBS
Alice sr ret 10.14.84 CBS

LAWFORD, PETER

SUPP.:

Fantasy Island ep Save Sherlock Holmes 2.6.82 ABC

Matt Houston ep Joey's Here 12.5.82 ABC

LAWRENCE, CAROL

SUPP.:

Matt Houston ep Deadly Fashion 10.17.82 ABC

Archie Bunker's Place ep 2.20.83 CBS

Murder, She Wrote ep Birds of a Feather 10.14.84 CBS

Simon and Simon ep 11.15.84 CBS

Hotel ep Fallen Idols 1.2.85 ABC

LAWRENCE, VICKI*

The Eddie Capra Mysteries ep Murder on the Flip Side 10.6.78 NBC

The Love Boat ep The Congressman Was Indiscreet 1.28.78 ABC

The Love Boat ep Rent a Romeo 1.26.80 ABC

The Love Boat ep Love with a Skinny Stranger 4.11.81 ABC

Laverne and Shirley ep Out, Out Damned Plout 5.5.81 ABC

Fantasy Island ep Funny Man 2.20.82 ABC

Eunice sp 3.15.82 CBS

The Love Boat ep Paroled to Love 1.8.83 ABC

Laverne and Shirley ep The Baby Show 1.18.83 ABC

Mama's Family sr 1.22.83 NBC

Mama's Family sr ret 9.29.83 NBC

Murder, She Wrote ep My Johnnie Lies Over the Ocean 2.10.85 CBS

Anything for Love pt 8.7.85 NBC

The Love Boat ep Couples 10.19.85 ABC

LAZENBY, GEORGE*

Cover Girls tf/pt 5.18.77 NBC

An Evening in Byzantium ms 8.14, 8.15.78 OPT

Hawaii Five-O ep The Year of the Horse 4.5.79 CBS

B.J. and the Bear ep B.J.'s Sweethearts 12.1.79 NBC

The Return of the Man from UNCLE: The 15 Years Later Affair tf/pt 4.5.83 CBS

Hotel ep Tomorrows 1.1.84 ABC

The Master ep Hostages 2.17.84 NBC

Rituals sr 9.84 NN

Cover Up ep Jack of Spades 3.30.85 CBS

LEACHMAN, CLORIS

A&C, B.V.:

Wanted: Dead or Alive ep The Medicine Man 11.23.60 CBS

A&C, Supp. 2:

The Mary Tyler Moore Show ep 5.77 CBS

SUPP.:

Perfectly Frank sp 1.82 SHO

Twigs sp 11.7.82 TEC

Miss All-American Beauty tf 12.29.82 CBS
The ABC Afterschool Special ep The Woman Who Willed a Miracle 2.9.83 ABC
Dixie: Changing Habits tf 2.16.83 CBS
The Demon Murder Case tf 3.6.83 NBC
Ernie Kovacs: Between the Laughter tf 5.14.84 ABC
The Love Boat ep Stolen Years 9.29.84 ABC
An American Portrait ep Helen Hunt Jackson 1.7.85 CBS
Deadly Intentions tf 5.19, 5.20.85 ABC
American Playhouse ep Breakfast with Les and Bess 8.28.85 PBS
Blind Alleys sp 9.4.85 MM
The Love Boat ep Hidden Treasures 10.12.85 ABC
Love Is Never Silent tf 12.9.85 NBC

LEARNED, MICHAEL
SUPP.:
Mother's Day on Waltons Mountain tf 5.9.82 NBC
The Parade tf 2.29.84 CBS
St. Elsewhere ep Playing God 9.19, 9.26.84 NBC

LEARY, BRIANNE
SUPP.:
Private Benjamin ep The Track Meet 11.1.82 CBS
Archie Bunker's Place ep 11.28.82 CBS
No Soap Radio ep (pt/first ep) 4.15.82 ABC
The Love Boat ep A Dress to Remember 5.8.82 ABC
The Astronauts pt 8.11.82 CBS
Voyagers ep Sneak Attack 2.20.83 NBC
Amanda's ep I Ain't Got No Body 3.3.83 ABC
Just Our Luck ep (pt/first ep) 9.20.83 ABC
Hawaiian Heat ep Yanks vs. Cubs 11.2.84 ABC
Night Court ep 10.7.85 NBC

LeBEAUF, SONDRA*
The Cosby Show ep Bonjour Sondra 11.22.84 NBC
The Cosby Show ep Clair's Case 2.21.85 NBC
The Cosby Show ep The Younger Woman 3.14.85 NBC
The Cosby Show sr 9.26.85 NBC

LEDERER, SUZANNE*
Judge Horton and the Scottsboro Boys tf 4.22.76 NBC
Eischied sr 9.21.79 NBC
Power tf 11.14, 11.15.80 NBC
Today's FBI ep Kidnap 4.4.82 ABC
Hunter ep High Bleacher Man 12.7.84 NBC
St. Elsewhere ep Fathers and Sons 9.25.85 NBC
St. Elsewhere ep Haunted 10.16.85 NBC
Trapper John, M.D. ep Just Around the Coroner 11.10.85 CBS

LEE, CHRISTOPHER

SUPP.:

Massarati and the Brain tf/pt 8.26.82 ABC

Charles and Diana: A Royal Love Story 9.17.82 ABC

The Far Pavilions ms 4.22, 4.23, 4.24.84 HBO

Faerie Tale Theater ep The Boy Who Left Home to Find Out About the Shivers 9.17.84 SHO

LEE, JONNA*

Lottery ep Houston: Duffy's Choice ("Duffy's Tale" segment) 11.25.83 ABC

Quarterback Princess tf 12.3.83 CBS

Jessie ep Trick of Fate 11.13.84 ABC

Otherworld sr 1.26.85 CBS

Scene of the Crime ep Education in Murder 4.14.85 NBC

The Midnight Hour tf 11.1.85 ABC

Hardcastle and McCormick ep You're 16, You're Beautiful and You're His!! 11.18.85 ABC

LEE, MICHELE

A&C, Supp. 2:

Dobie Gillis ep Crazy Legs Gillis 12.26.61 CBS

Alias Smith and Jones ep Bad Night in Big Butte 3.2.72 ABC

SUPP.:

The Love Boat ep Separate Vacations 3.6.82 ABC

Knots Landing sr ret 9.30.82 CBS

Knots Landing sr ret 9.29.83 CBS

Knots Landing sr ret 10.4.84 CBS

An American Portrait ep Leo Baekeland 1.17.85 CBS

Knots Landing sr ret 9.26.85 CBS

A Letter to Three Wives tf 12.16.85 NBC

LEMBECK, HARVEY

SUPP.:

Mork and Mindy ep Pajama Game II 1.7.82 ABC

LEMBECK, MICHAEL

A&C, Supp. 2:

Room 222 ep Cry Uncle 1.11.74 ABC

SUPP.:

Darkroom ep Who's There? 1.15.82 ABC

Goodbye Doesn't Mean Forever pt 5.28.82 NBC

One Day at a Time sr ret 10.3.82 CBS

Fantasy Island ep Extraordinary Miss Jones 4.9.83 ABC

One Day at a Time sr ret 10.2.83 CBS

The Love Boat ep Long Time No See 11.12.83 ABC

Fantasy Island ep Skin Deep 1.28.84 ABC

Foley Square sr 12.11.85 CBS

Crazy Like a Fox ep Is There a Fox in the House? 12.22.85 CBS

LEEDS, ELISSA*
The Guiding Light sr 1973 CBS
Charlie's Angels ep Teen Angels 2.28.79 ABC
Dorothy sr 8.8.79 CBS
Blue Jeans pt 7.26.80 ABC
Vegas ep The Andreas Addiction 12.24.80 ABC
Fantasy Island ep Portrait of Solange 2.28.81 ABC
Earthbound sp 1.31, 2.7.82 NBC
Baby Makes Five ep Jennie's Old Flame 4.29.83 ABC
My Wicked, Wicked Ways.... The Legend of Errol Flynn tf 1.21.85 CBS

LeGAULT, LANCE (a.k.a. W. L. LeGault)*
Pioneer Woman tf 12.19.73 ABC
Police Woman ep Requiem for Bored Housewives 11.29.74 NBC
This Is the West That Was tf 12.17.74 NBC
The Barbary Coast ep Jesse Who? 9.22.75 ABC
Police Woman ep Farewell, Mary Jane 11.4.75 NBC
Police Woman ep Bondage 3.1.77 NBC
Logan's Run ep Judas Goat 12.19.77 CBS
Nowhere to Run tf 1.16.78 NBC
The Busters pt 5.28.78 CBS
The Incredible Hulk ep The Antowick Horror 9.29.78 CBS
The New Adventures of Wonder Woman ep Hot Wheels 9.29.78 CBS
Battlestar Galactica ep The Lost Warrior 10.8.78 ABC
Donner Pass: The Road to Survival tf 10.24.78 NBC
Captain America tf/pt 1.19.79 CBS
Battlestar Galactica ep The Man with Nine Lives 1.28.79 ABC
How the West Was Won ep The Gentleman 3.12.79 ABC
B.J. and the Bear ep Lobo's Revenge 4.7.79 NBC
Undercover with the KKK tf 10.23.79 NBC
The French Atlantic Affair ms 11.15, 11.16, 11.17, 11.18.79 ABC
The Afternoon Playhouse ep The Year of the Gentle Tiger 11.23.79 CBS
Power tf 1.14, 1.15.80 NBC
Kenny Rogers as the Gambler tf 4.8.80 CBS
Reward tf 5.23.80 ABC
Buck Rogers in the 25th Century ep Time of the Hawk 1.15.81 NBC
Magnum, P.I. ep Missing in Action 2.5.81 CBS
Walking Tall ep 4.18.81 NBC
Magnum, P.I. ep Memories Are Forever 11.5.81 CBS
Dynasty ep Episode 19 12.16.81 ABC
Dynasty ep Episode 24 1.27.82 ABC
McClain's Law ep Use of Deadly Force 2.19.82 NBC
Simon and Simon ep Tanks for the Memories 3.16.82 CBS
Dynasty ep Episode 31 3.24.82 ABC
Dynasty ep Episode 32: The Fragment 4.7.82 ABC
Knight Rider ep Knight Rider (pt) 9.26.82 NBC

Magnum, P.I. ep 9.30.82 CBS
Voyagers ep Old Hickory and the Pirate 11.28.82 NBC
T. J. Hooker ep The Hostages 3.5.83 ABC
The A-Team ep When You Comin' Home, Range Rider? 10.25.83 NBC
The A-Team ep Labor Pains 11.8.83 NBC
The A-Team ep There's Always a Catch 11.15.83 NBC
The A-Team ep The White Ballot 12.6.83 NBC
Knight Rider ep A Knight in Shining Armor 1.8.84 NBC
The A-Team ep The Battle of Bel Air 1.10.84 NBC
The A-Team ep Say It with Bullets 1.17.84 NBC
Automan ep Death By Design 4.2.84 ABC
Airwolf ep To Snare a Wolf 4.14.84 CBS
The A-Team ep Curtain Call 5.15.84 NBC
Airwolf ep Sweet Britches 9.22.84 CBS
Partners in Crime ep Paddles Up 10.27.84 NBC
Call to Glory ep Realities 11.12.84 ABC
The A-Team ep The Island 11.13.84 NBC
The A-Team ep Breakout 12.18.84 NBC
The A-Team ep Road Games 2.5.85 NBC
Magnum, P.I. ep Ms. Jones 3.7.85 CBS
The A-Team ep Bounty 4.2.85 NBC
The A-Team ep Incident at Crystal Lake 5.14.85 NBC
Super Sunday sr vo 10.85 NN
Magnum, P.I. ep 10.11.85 CBS
The A-Team ep Blood, Sweat and Cheers 11.19.85 NBC
The A-Team ep The Road to Hope 10.29.85 NBC
The A-Team ep Body Slam 11.12.85 NBC
Simon and Simon ep Down Home Country Blues 11.21.85 CBS

LEIBMAN, RON
<u>SUPP.</u>:
Side By Side pt 7.6.84 ABC
An American Portrait ep John Coleman 1.14.85 CBS
Day to Day Affairs sp 2.4.85 HBO

LEIGH, JANET
<u>SUPP.</u>:
Matt Houston ep Who Killed Ramona? 10.10.82 ABC
Fantasy Island ep Thanks a Million 12.4.82 ABC
The Love Boat ep Unmade for Each Other 1.5.85 ABC
On Our Way pt 6.29.85 CBS

LEIGH, JENNIFER JASON*
Angel City tf 11.12.80 CBS
The Waltons ep The Pursuit 1.1.81 CBS
The CBS Afternoon Playhouse ep I Think I'm Having a Baby 3.3.81 CBS
The Killing of Randy Webster tf 3.11.81 CBS
The Best Little Girl in the World tf 5.11.81 ABC
Trapper John, M.D. ep The One and Only 5.16.82 CBS

The First Time tf 11.8.82 ABC
The ABC Afterschool Special ep Have You Ever Been Ashamed of Your Parents? 3.16.83 ABC
The Girls of the White Orchid tf 11.28.83 NBC

LEMMON, CHRIS*
Mirror, Mirror tf 10.10.79 NBC
Too Close for Comfort ep Where There's a Will 12.1.81 ABC
Uncommon Valor tf 1.22.83 CBS
9 to 5 ep When Violet Goes Blue 2.22.83 ABC
The Outlaws tf 7.9.84 ABC
An American Portrait ep Linn Yann 4.1.85 CBS

LENZ, KAY
SUPP.:
Insight ep Matchpoint 1.1.83 NN
Prisoners of the Lost Universe tf/pt 8.15.83 SHO
Hotel ep Reflections 1.4.84 ABC
Simon and Simon ep Blood Lines 1.19.84 CBS
The Whiz Kids ep Amen to Amen-Re 1.28.84 CBS
Magnum, P.I. ep 2.23.84 CBS
Cagney and Lacey ep 4.16.84 CBS
The Fall Guy ep Losers Weepers 9.19.84 ABC
Matt Houston ep Stolen 12.21.84 ABC
Simon and Simon ep Almost Foolproof 1.3.85 CBS
Finder of Lost Loves ep Last Wish 1.5.85 ABC
Murder, She Wrote ep Armed Response 3.31.85 CBS
Scene of the Crime ep A Very Practical Joke 4.28.85 NBC
MacGyver ep Last Stand 11.17.85 ABC
Riptide ep Still Goin' Steady 11.19.85 NBC

LENZ, RICK
A&C, Supp. 2:
The Streets of San Francisco ep One Last Trick 1.6.77 ABC
SUPP.:
T. J. Hooker ep God Bless the Child 3.27.82 ABC
Lou Grant ep Blacklist 4.5.82 CBS
Silver Spoons ep The Best Christmas Ever 12.18.82 NBC
Simon and Simon ep Pirate's Key 1.20.83 CBS
Automan ep The Biggest Game in Town 1.26.84 ABC
Airwolf ep 2.11.84 CBS
Magnum, P.I. ep Tran Quoc Jones 11.29.84 CBS
Simon and Simon ep Mummy Talks 2.21.85 CBS
Malice in Wonderland tf 5.12.85 CBS

LERMAN, APRIL*
The CBS Afternoon Playhouse ep Revenge of the Nerd 4.19.83 CBS
Charles in Charge sr 10.3.84 CBS

LETHIN, LORI*
A Man Called Sloane ep Architect of Evil 12.15.79 NBC

The Dukes of Hazzard ep Southern Comforts 3.21.80 CBS
Freebie and the Bean ep 12.6.80 CBS
Palmerstown, U.S.A. ep 3.17.81 CBS
The ABC Theater for Young Americans ep The Wave 10.4.81 ABC
Goliath Awaits tf 11.16, 11.17.81 OPT
Intimate Agony tf 3.21.83 ABC
The Day After tf 11.20.83 ABC
The Mississippi ep 11.29.83 CBS
The Master ep Out-of-Time Step 1.27.84 NBC
The A-Team ep Harder Than It Looks 2.21.84 NBC
E/R ep 11.14.84 CBS
For Love or Money tf 11.20.84 CBS
Brotherly Love tf 5.28.85 CBS
Crazy Like a Fox ep Desert Fox 11.10.85 CBS
The Insiders ep Gun Runners 11.13.85 ABC

LEWIS, CATHY
A&C, B.V.:
The Danny Thomas Show ep Kathy's Career 1.59 CBS
Ensign O'Toole ep Operation Re-enlistment Spring 1963 NBC
The Adventures of Jonny Quest vo ep Terror Island 2.25.65 ABC

LEWIS, EMMANUEL*
Webster sr 9.16.83 ABC
Secret World of the Very Young sp 9.12.84 NBC
The Love Boat Fall Preview Party sp 9.15.84 ABC
Webster sr ret 9.21.84 ABC
The Love Boat ep Only the Good Die Young 10.13.84 ABC
Webster sr ret 9.27.85 ABC
Lost in London tf 11.20.85 CBS

LIGHT, JUDITH*
Kojak ep Monkey on a String 2.15.77 CBS
Intimate Agony tf 3.21.83 ABC
St. Elsewhere ep Dog Day Hospital 3.22.83 NBC
Family Ties ep Not an Affair to Remember 11.2.83 NBC
The Mississippi ep 3.13.84 CBS
The Love Boat Fall Preview sp 9.15.84 ABC
Who's the Boss? sr 9.20.84 ABC
Who's the Boss? sr ret 9.24.85 ABC

LINDEN, HAL
SUPP.:
Starflight: The Plane That Couldn't Land tf 2.27.83 ABC
The Other Woman tf 3.22.83 CBS
Second Edition pt 7.17.84 CBS
I Do! I Do! sp 1.8.85 A&E
My Wicked, Wicked Ways.... The Legend of Errol Flynn tf 1.21.85 CBS

LINDFORS, VIVECA
SUPP.:
Divorce Wars tf 3.1.82 ABC
Inside the Third Reich tf 5.9, 5.10.82 ABC
Trapper John, M.D. ep 3.18.84 CBS
A Doctor's Story tf 4.23.84 NBC
Glitter ep On Your Toes 12.11.84 ABC

LINDGREN, LISA*
Alice ep Give My Regards to Broadway 4.4.82 CBS
Joanie Loves Chachi ep College Days 4.13.82 ABC
Seven Brides for Seven Brothers ep Man Without a Pass 12.15.82 CBS
CHiPs ep Fast Company 3.20.83 NBC
Simon and Simon ep 1.12.84 CBS

LINKER, AMY*
A Time for Miracles tf 12.21.80 ABC
Lewis and Clark sr 10.29.81 NBC
Square Pegs sr 9.27.82 CBS
Mr. T sr vo 9.17.83 NBC
Fantasy Island ep Saturday's Child 12.10.83 ABC
Two Marriages ep Reflections 4.15.84 ABC
E/R ep 11.13.84 CBS

LINVILLE, LARRY
A&C, Supp. 1:
Here Come the Brides ep The Bank of Tacomo 1.16.70 ABC
Men at Law ep Let the Dier Beware 3.17.71 CBS
A&C, Supp. 2:
The Rockford Files ep The Deadly Maze 12.23.77 NBC
SUPP.:
Fantasy Island ep A Genie Named Joe 3.13.82 ABC
Herbie, the Love Bug sr 3.17.82 CBS
Night Partners tf 10.11.83 CBS
Paper Dolls sr 9.25.84 ABC
Murder, She Wrote ep Murder Takes the Bus 3.17.85 CBS
Detective in the House ep Guilt By Association 4.12.85 CBS
Airwolf ep And a Child Shall Lead 10.12.85 CBS
Riptide ep Does Not Compute 10.29.85 NBC

LIPTON, PEGGY
A&C, Supp. 1:
The Bob Hope Chrysler Theater ep A Song Called Revenge 3.1.67 NBC

LITHGOW, JOHN*
Mom, the Wolfman and Me tf 10.20.80 OPT
Not in Front of the Children tf 10.26.82 CBS
The Day After tf 11.20.83 ABC

Faerie Tale Theater ep Goldilocks and the Three Bears 1.9.84 SHO
The Glitter Dome tf 11.18.84 HBO

LITTLE, CLEAVON
A&C, Supp. 2:
The Rockford Files ep Sticks and Stones Will Break Your Bones But Waterbury Will Bury You 1.14.77 NBC
SUPP.:
The ABC Afterschool Special ep The Color of Friendship 11.11.81 ABC
One of the Boys ep Don't Bank On It 4.10.82 NBC
Simon and Simon ep Red Day Blues 3.24.83 CBS
The Fall Guy ep The Chase 4.13.83 ABC
Now We're Cookin' pt 4.19.83 CBS

LLOYD, CHRISTOPHER*
The Adams Chronicles sr 1.20.76 PBS
Lacey and the Mississippi Queen tf/pt 4.17.78 NBC
The Word ms 11.12-11.15.78 CBS
Barney Miller ep Open House 2.15.79 ABC
Stunt Seven tf/pt 5.30.79 CBS
Taxi sr 9.11.79 ABC
Visions ep It's the Willingness 1.19.80 PBS
Semi Tough ep 6.19.80 ABC
Taxi sr ret 11.19.80 ABC
Freebie and the Bean ep The Seduction of the Bean 12.20.80 CBS
Best of the West ep The Calico Kid 9.10.81 ABC
Best of the West ep The Calico Kid Returns 10.1.81 ABC
Taxi sr ret 10.8.81 ABC
Best of the West ep The Calico Kid Goes to School 1.14.82 ABC
American Playhouse ep Pilgrim, Farewell 3.23.82 PBS
Money on the Side tf 9.29.82 CBS
Taxi sr ret 9.30.82 NBC
September Gun tf 10.8.83 CBS
Cheers ep I'll Be Seeing You 5.3, 5.10.84 NBC
Old Friends pt 7.12.84 ABC
The Cowboy and the Ballerina tf 10.23.84 CBS
Street Hawk ep Street Hawk (pt) 1.4.85 ABC

LLOYD, KATHLEEN*
Owen Marshall, Counselor at Law tf/pt 9.12.71 ABC
Medical Center ep Terror 1.26.72 CBS
Incident on a Dark Street tf 1.13.73 NBC
The Rookies ep Solomon's Dilemma 1.27.85 ABC
Harry O ep Silent Kill 2.6.75 ABC
Police Woman ep Nothing Left to Lose 2.14.75 NBC
Harry O ep Elegy for a Cop 2.27.75 ABC
Lacey and the Mississippi Queen tf/pt 5.17.78 NBC

Hart to Hart ep You Made Me Kill You 10.23.79 ABC
High Midnight tf 11.27.79 CBS
Kate Loves a Mystery ep Feelings Can Be Murder 12.6.79 NBC
Trapper John, M.D. ep Big Bomb 1.6.80 CBS
Make Me an Offer tf 1.11.80 ABC
The White Shadow ep Gonna Fly Now 2.5.80 CBS
The Incredible Hulk ep On the Line 4.11.80 CBS
The Jayne Mansfield Story tf 10.29.80 CBS
The Choice tf 2.10.81 CBS
The Gangster Chronicles sr 2.21.81 NBC
Trapper John, M.D. ep A Case of the Crazies 3.29.81 CBS
Shannon ep Beating the Prime 12.2.81 CBS
Simon and Simon ep Guessing Game 10.21.82 CBS
Hill Street Blues ep Stan the Man 11.4.82 NBC
Hill Street Blues ep Requiem for a Hairbag 11.18.82 NBC
Magnum, P.I. ep Almost Home 12.9.82 CBS
Hill Street Blues ep Spotlight on Rico 4.28.83 NBC
Shooting Stars tf/pt 7.28.83 ABC
Trauma Center ep Trail's End 11.10.83 ABC
Lottery ep Minneapolis: Six Months Down ("Pi Lota Gamma" segment) 4.5.84 ABC
Magnum, P.I. ep 10.20.83, 1.26.84, 3.15.84 CBS
Airwolf ep To Snare a Wolf 4.14.84 CBS
Call to Glory ep Call to Glory (pt) 8.13.84 ABC
Magnum, P.I. ep Blind Justice 11.8.84 CBS
Sins of the Father tf 1.13.85 NBC
Call to Glory ep Images 1.22.85 ABC
Magnum, P.I. ep Compulsion 1.24.85 CBS
Magnum, P.I. ep The Love for Sale Boat 2.14.85 CBS
Trapper John, M.D. ep 3.10.85 CBS
Magnum, P.I. ep The Man from Marseille 3.14.85 CBS
Magnum, P.I. ep A Pretty Good Dancing Chicken 4.4.85 CBS

LOCANE, AMY*
Spencer sr 12.1.84 NBC
Out of Time sp 1.29.85 NBC
Under One Roof sr 3.23.85 NBC

LOCKE, ROSANNA*
CHiPs ep Brat Patrol 2.27.83 NBC
CHiPs ep Return of the Brat Patrol 5.8.83 NBC
The Best of Times pt 8.29.83 CBS
T. J. Hooker ep Death Is a Four Letter Word 11.6.85 CBS

LOCKE, SONDRA*
Amazing Stories ep Vanessa in the Garden 12.29.85 NBC

LOCKHART, ANNE
A&C, Supp. 2:
Get Christie Love ep Bullet from the Grave 11.20.74 ABC
The Eddie Capra Mysteries ep Breakdown to Murder 12.1.78 NBC

SUPP.:
Magnum, P.I. ep Lest We Forget 2.12.81 CBS
Darkroom ep Exit Line 12.25.81 ABC
The Fall Guy ep Snow Job 3.3.82 ABC
Knight Rider ep Good Day at White Rock 10.8.82 NBC
Magnum, P.I. ep Flashback 11.4.82 CBS
Tales of the Gold Monkey ep The Lady and the Tiger 12.8.82 ABC
Voyagers ep Merry Christmas, Bogg 12.19.82 NBC
Simon and Simon ep What's in a Gnome? 2.24.83 CBS
Knight Rider ep Return to Cadiz 10.30.83 NBC
The Fall Guy ep Inside, Outside 11.16.83 ABC
T. J. Hooker ep Hot Property 2.25.84 ABC
Automan ep Death by Design 4.2.84 ABC
Lottery ep Minneapolis: Six Months Down 4.5.84 ABC
Scene of the Crime ep The Babysitter 9.30.84 NBC
Murder, She Wrote ep Deadly Lady 10.7.84 CBS
Washingtoon pt 10.15.84 SHO
Airwolf ep Random Target 12.8.84 CBS
Simon and Simon ep Yes Virginia, There Is a Liberace 12.20.84 CBS
Gidget's Summer Reunion tf/pt 6.85 NN
George Burns Comedy Week ep Home for Dinner 9.25.85 CBS
Murder, She Wrote ep Will No One Weep for Me? 9.19.85 CBS
Divorce Court ep Meechum vs. Meechum 11.25.85 NN
The New Love, American Style ep Love and the Caterer 12.24.85 ABC

LOCKHART, JUNE
A&C, B.V.:
Wagon Train ep The Ricky and Laura Bell Story 2.24.60 NBC
The Beverly Hillbillies ep The Thanksgiving Story 11.68 CBS
SUPP.:
Falcon Crest ep Dark Journey 1.29.82 CBS
The Capture of Grizzly Adams tf 2.21.82 NBC
Knots Landing ep Encounters 10.14.82 CBS
The Greatest American Hero ep The Newlywed Game 1.6.83 ABC
Quincy, M.E. ep Quincy's Wedding 2.23.83 NBC
The Whiz Kids ep Maid in America 2.4.84 CBS
The Night They Saved Christmas tf 12.13.84 ABC
Detective in the House ep Down and Out 3.29.85 CBS
Murder, She Wrote ep School for Scandal 10.20.85 CBS

LOCKLEAR, HEATHER*
240-Robert ep Hostages 3.21.81 ABC
Dynasty sr 11.11.81 ABC
The Fall Guy ep Scavenger Hunt 5.5.82 ABC
T. J. Hooker sr 9.25.82 ABC
Matt Houston ep Stop the Presses 10.3.82 ABC
Fantasy Island ep I'm a Country Girl 12.11.82 ABC
Dynasty ep Samantha 1.12.83 ABC

Dynasty ep Danny 1.19.83 ABC
The Fall Guy ep Just a Small Circle of Friends 5.4.83 ABC
T. J. Hooker sr ret 10.1.83 ABC
Hotel ep Choices 10.5.83 ABC
The Love Boat ep Youth Takes a Holiday 10.15.83 ABC
Dynasty ep The Check 4.11.84 ABC
Dynasty ep The Engagement 4.25.84 ABC
Dynasty ep New Lady in Town 5.2.84 ABC
Dynasty ep Nightmare 5.9.84 ABC
The Love Boat Fall Preview Party sp 9.15.84 ABC
Dynasty ret to sr 9.26.84 ABC
T. J. Hooker sr ret 10.6.84 ABC
Dynasty sr ret 9.25.85 ABC
T. J. Hooker sr ret 9.25.85 CBS

LOCKWOOD, GARY
A&C, B.V.:
Twelve O'Clock High ep The Idol Hater 10.4.65 ABC
A&C, Supp. 2:
The Streets of San Francisco ep Monkey Is Back 1.13.77 ABC
Hawaii Five-O ep School for Assassins 1.1.80 CBS
SUPP.:
The Fall Guy ep Scavenger Hunt 5.5.82 ABC
Matt Houston ep The Good Doctor 12.12.82 ABC
Hart to Hart ep Emily, By Hart 1.11.83 ABC
Emergency Room tf 7.17.83 NN
T. J. Hooker ep The Snow Game 1.14.84 ABC
Simon and Simon ep 2.9.84 CBS
Matt Houston ep On the Run 3.30.84 ABC
Cover Up ep The Million Dollar Face 10.6.84 CBS
Finder of Lost Loves ep Wayward Dreams 1.26.85 ABC
Simon and Simon ep 2.14.85 CBS
Half Nelson ep 3.29.85 NBC
T. J. Hooker ep To Kill a Cop 10.10.85 CBS

LOGGIA, ROBERT
A&C, Supp. 1:
Wagon Train ep The Jose and Marcia Moran Story 5.27.59 NBC
Desilu Playhouse ep Come Back to Sorrento 11.6.59 CBS
Alcoa Presents ep The Hand 12.29.59 ABC
Overland Trail ep Mission to Mexico 4.24.60 ABC
Alfred Hitchcock Presents ep The Money 11.29.60 CBS
Naked City ep The Fingers of Henri Tourelli 10.18.61 ABC
The Defenders ep Perjury 12.2.61 CBS
Alcoa Premiere ep The End of the World 12.17.61 CBS
Alfred Hitchcock Presents ep The Case of M.J.H. 1.23.62 CBS
The Untouchables ep Take Over 3.1.62 ABC
The Dick Powell Show ep The Hook 3.6.62 NBC
The DuPont Show of the Week ep The Interrogator 9.23.62 NBC
The Defenders ep Eye of Fear 2.23.63 CBS
Rawhide ep Incident of the Comanchero 3.22.63 CBS

Ben Casey ep Justice to a Microbe 9.18.63 ABC
Alfred Hitchcock Presents ep You'll Be the Death of Me 10.18.63 CBS
The Eleventh Hour ep Bronze Locust 11.6.63 NBC
Route 66 ep I'm Here to Kill a King 11.29.63 CBS
Breaking Point ep The Summer House 3.16.64 ABC
Kraft Suspense Theatre ep The Robrioz Ring 5.28.64 NBC
Kraft Suspense Theatre ep A Cruel and Unusual Night 6.4.64 NBC
Ben Casey ep The Wild, Wild, Wild Waltzing World 12.14.64 ABC
Gunsmoke ep Chief Joseph 1.30.65 CBS
Combat ep The Tree of Maras 3.16.65 ABC
The Alfred Hitchcock Hour ep The World's Oldest Motive 4.12.65 NBC
Kraft Suspense Theatre ep Jungle of Fear 4.22.65 NBC
The Trials of O'Brien ep Goodbye and Keep Cool 10.23.65 CBS
Voyage to the Bottom of the Sea ep Graveyard of Fear 1.30.66 ABC
T.H.E. Cat sr 9.16.66 NBC
The Legend of Custer ep Suspicion 10.18.67 ABC
The High Chaparral ep The Deceivers 11.15.68 NBC
The Big Valley ep The Profit and the Lost 12.2.68 ABC
The High Chaparral ep The Forge of Hate 11.13.70 NBC
The FBI ep The Deadly Pact 11.8.70 ABC
Harry O ep One for the Road 9.18.75 ABC
Cannon ep Snap Shot 2.11.76 CBS
Police Woman ep Wednesday's Child 2.3.76 NBC
S.W.A.T. ep Any Second Now 3.13.76 ABC

A&C, Supp. 2:

Switch ep The Snitch 1.16.77 CBS
Police Woman ep Shadow of Doubt 2.1.77 NBC
The Rockford Files ep Beamer's Last Case 9.16.77 NBC
The Rockford Files ep Rosenthal and Gilda Stern Are Dead 9.29.78 NBC
The Eddie Capra Mysteries ep How Do I Kill Thee? 11.3.78 NBC

SUPP.:

A Woman Called Golda ms 4.26, 4.27, 4.28.82 OPT
Emerald Point, N.A.S. sr 9.26.83 CBS
A Touch of Scandal tf 11.27.84 CBS
Matt Houston ep Return to Nam 11.2.84 ABC
Matt Houston ep Escape from Nam 11.9.84 ABC
Murder, She Wrote ep Death Casts a Spell 12.30.84 CBS
Streets of Justice tf 11.10.85 NBC

LOLLOBRIGIDA, GINA

SUPP.:

Falcon Crest ep The Intruder 11.9.84 CBS
Falcon Crest ep Pain and Pleasure 11.16.84 CBS
Falcon Crest ep The Trump Card 11.23.84 CBS
Falcon Crest ep Tarantella 11.30.84 CBS

Falcon Crest ep Going Once, Going Twice 12.7.84 CBS
Deceptions tf 5.26, 5.27.85 NBC

LONDON, JULIE
A&C, B.V.:
The Man from UNCLE ep The Prince of Darkness Affair 10.2.67, 10.9.67 NBC
The Big Valley ep They Call Her Delilah 9.30.68 ABC

LONG, RICHARD
A&C, B.V.:
Ellery Queen ep Bury Me Deep 1.2.59 NBC

LONG, SHELLEY*
The Cracker Factory tf 3.16.79 ABC
The Dooley Brothers pt 7.31.79 CBS
Trapper John, M.D. ep The Shattered Image 10.28.79 CBS
The Promise of Love tf 11.11.80 CBS
The Princess and the Cabbie tf 11.3.81 CBS
Cheers sr 9.30.82 NBC
Cheers sr ret 9.29.83 NBC
Cheers sr ret 9.27.84 NBC
Cheers sr ret 9.26.85 NBC

LONGAKER, RACHEL
SUPP.:
Kate and Allie ep 10.22.84 CBS

LONGO, TONY*
Fantasy Island ep 11.14.81 ABC
Private Benjamin ep Undercover Judy 12.7.81 CBS
Laverne and Shirley ep Rocky Ragu 1.26.82 ABC
Alice ep My Mother, the Landlord 5.16.82 CBS
CHiPs ep Force Seven 5.23.82 NBC
The Fall Guy ep Win One for the Gipper 1.5.83 ABC
Simon and Simon ep Psyched Out 1.13.83 CBS
Alice ep 2.28.83, 3.28.83 CBS
Herndon and Me pt 8.26.83 ABC
The Best of Times pt 8.29.83 CBS
Alice ep 10.2.83 CBS
Just Our Luck ep No Holds Barred 11.22.83 ABC
We Got It Made ep The Fight 2.25.84 NBC
Alice ep 4.15.84 CBS
E/R ep 9.18.84 CBS
The Facts of Life ep A Slice of Life 10.3.84 NBC
Simon and Simon ep Revolution #9½ 12.13.84 CBS
Hardcastle and McCormick ep There Goes the Neighborhood 1.7.85 ABC
The CBS Schoolbreak Special ep Ace Hits the Big Time 3.18.85 CBS
Just Married pt 5.10.85 ABC

First and Ten sr 9.3.85 HBO
Hell Town sr 9.11.85 NBC

LONOW, CLAUDIA*
Knots Landing sr 12.27.79 CBS
Knots Landing sr ret 11.12.80 CBS
Knots Landing sr ret 11.12.81 CBS
Knots Landing sr ret 9.30.82 CBS
Fantasy Island ep The Perfect Gentleman 10.30.82 ABC
The Love Boat ep The Zinging Valentine 2.12.83 ABC
Knots Landing sr ret 9.29.83 CBS
Knots Landing sr ret 10.4.84 CBS
Knots Landing sr ret 9.26.85 CBS
The New Love, American Style ep Love and the Maid of Honor 12.23.85 ABC

LORD, JACK
A&C, B.V.:
Playhouse 90 ep Lone Woman 12.26.57 CBS
The Loretta Young Show ep Marriage Crisis 2.15.59 NBC
Rawhide ep Incident of the Calico Gun 4.24.59 CBS
Naked City ep The Human Trap 11.30.60 ABC
The Invaders ep Vikor 2.14.67 ABC

LORRE, PETER
A&C, B.V.:
Mrs. G Goes to College ep First Test 10.11.61 CBS

LOUANNE*
The Long Days of Summer tf/pt 5.23.80 ABC
The Last Song tf 10.23.80 CBS
Mork and Mindy ep P.S. 2001 12.17.81 ABC
The Love Boat ep Father, Dear Father 12.4.82 ABC
Seven Brides for Seven Brothers ep 3.9.83 CBS
Missing Pieces tf 5.14.83 CBS
Two Marriages sr 8.31.83 ABC
Two Marriages sr ret 3.8.84 ABC

LOUISE, TINA
A&C, B.V.:
Burke's Law ep Who Killed Billy Joe? 11.8.63 ABC
SUPP.:
Matt Houston ep The Kidnapping 11.28.82 ABC
Knight Rider ep The Topaz Connection 1.28.83 NBC
Rituals sr 9.84 NN

LOY, MYRNA
SUPP.:
Love, Sidney ep Sidney and the Actress 6.16.82 NBC

LUCCI, SUSAN*
All My Children sr 1970 ABC

The Love Boat ep The Auditor 11.6.82 ABC
Fantasy Island ep Queen of the Soaps 1.22.83 ABC
Invitation to Hell tf 5.24.84 ABC
The Fall Guy ep Stranger Than Fiction 9.26.84 ABC

LUCKINBILL, LAURENCE
SUPP.:
One More Try pt 8.31.82 CBS
Murder, She Wrote ep A Lady in the Lake 11.10.85 CBS

LUFT, LORNA*
McCloud ep Park Avenue Pirates 9.21.75 NBC
Murder, She Wrote ep Broadway Malady 1.13.85 CBS
Trapper John, M.D. sr 10.6.85 CBS
The Twilight Zone ep Children's Zoo 10.11.85 CBS

LUKE, KEYE
SUPP.:
Remington Steele ep You're Steele the One for Me 11.26.82 NBC
Cocaine and Blue Eyes tf/pt 1.2.83 NBC
Falcon Crest ep 2.11.83, 3.4.83 CBS
Magnum, P.I. ep 40 Years from Sand Island 2.24.83 CBS
Alvin and the Chipmunks sr vo 9.17.83 NBC
The A-Team ep The Maltese Cow 12.13.83 NBC
Mickey Spillane's Mike Hammer ep Hot Ice 2.4.84 CBS
Trapper John, M.D. ep 10.29.84 CBS
Street Hawk ep Chinatown Memories 2.15.85 ABC
MacGyver ep The Golden Triangle 10.6.85 ABC
Crazy Like a Fox ep Requiem for a Fox 10.20.85 CBS

LUNA, BARBARA
SUPP.:
Fantasy Island ep Operation Breakout 1.15.83 ABC
T. J. Hooker ep Outcall 2.2.85 ABC

LUPINO, IDA
A&C, B.V.:
Burke's Law ep Who Killed Billy Joe? 11.8.63 ABC
Family Affair ep The Return of Maudie 10.15.70 CBS
Alias Smith and Jones ep What's in It for Mia? 2.24.72 ABC
A&C, Supp. 1:
Switch ep Stung from Behind 9.30.75 CBS

LUPTON, JOHN
A&C, B.V.:
I Married Joan ep 1954 NBC
Wanted: Dead or Alive ep Secret Ballot 2.14.59 CBS
Black Saddle ep Client: Peter Warren 10.30.59 ABC
Gunsmoke ep Ben Tolliver's Stand 11.26.60 CBS
Wagon Train ep The Trace McCloud Story 3.2.64 ABC
Slattery's People ep Does Nero Still at Ringside Sit? 2.5.65 CBS

Family Affair ep Our Friend Stanley 11.67 CBS
Hawaii Five-O ep Dear Enemy 2.17.71 CBS
A&C, Supp. 1:
Harry O ep APB Harry Orwell 11.6.75 ABC
A&C, Supp. 2:
The Rockford Files ep The Competitive Edge 2.10.78 NBC

LUZ, FRANC*
Remington Steele ep Steele Eligible 1.10.84 NBC
Ryan's Hope sr 1984 ABC
Hometown sr 8.22.85 CBS
Kate and Allie ep Allie's Affair 11.11.85 CBS

LYMAN, DOROTHY*
All My Children sr 1977 ABC
Mama's Family sr 1.22.83 NBC
Mama's Family sr ret 9.29.83 NBC
Summer Fantasy tf 5.25.84 NBC
Tales from the Darkside ep In the Cards 1.26.85 NN
Hearts Island pt 8.31.85 NBC

LYNCH, RICHARD*
Jigsaw tf 3.26.72 ABC
Starsky and Hutch tf/pt 4.30.75 ABC
Bronk ep Target: Unknown 2.8.76 CBS
Switch ep The 12th Commandment 9.28.76 CBS
Serpico ep Every Man Pays His Dues 10.29.76 NBC
Police Woman ep Solitaire 2.22.77 NBC
Roger and Harry tf/pt 5.2.77 ABC
Good Against Evil tf 5.22.77 NBC
The Streets of San Francisco ep Time Out 6.16.77 ABC
Dog and Cat tf/pt 7.22.77 ABC
The Bionic Woman ep Out of Body 3.4.78 NBC
Starsky and Hutch ep Quadromania 5.10.78 ABC
Battlestar Galactica ep Gun on the Ice Planet 10.22, 10.29.78 ABC
Vegas ep Kill Dan Tanna 1.10.79 ABC
Starsky and Hutch ep Starsky vs. Hutch 5.8.79 ABC
Buck Rogers in the 25th Century ep Vegas in Space 10.4.79 NBC
Vampire tf 10.7.79 ABC
A Man Called Sloane ep Masquerade of Terror 10.13.79 NBC
Charlie's Angels ep Angels on the Street 11.7.79 ABC
Buck Rogers in the 25th Century ep A Blast for Buck 1.17.80 NBC
Galactica 1980 sr 1.27.80 ABC
Alcatraz: The Whole Shocking Story tf 11.5, 11.6.80 NBC
Vegas ep Dead Ringer 4.29.81 ABC
Sizzle tf 11.29.81 ABC
McClain's Law ep Sign of the Beast 1.22, 1.29.82 NBC
The Phoenix sr 3.26.82 ABC

White Water Rebels tf 1.8.83 CBS
The Last Ninja tf/pt 7.7.83 ABC
T. J. Hooker ep Carnal Express 12.31.83 ABC
The Fall Guy ep Pleasure Isle 10.5.83 ABC
Manimal ep Illusion 10.14.83 NBC
Blue Thunder ep Second Thunder 1.6.84 ABC
Automan ep Renegade Run 3.5.84 ABC
The Fall Guy ep Stranger Than Fiction 9.26.84 ABC
Matt Houston ep Apostle of Death 10.19.84 ABC
Cover Up ep Murder in Malibu 12.1.84 CBS
The A-Team ep Hot Styles 12.11.84 NBC
Partners in Crime ep Double Jeopardy 12.29.84 NBC
MacGruder and Loud ep The Odds Favor Death 2.5.85 ABC
Scarecrow and Mrs. King ep You Only Die Twice 4.1.85 CBS
Airwolf ep The Horn of Plenty 9.28.85 CBS
Riptide ep The Curse of the Mary Aberdeen 12.9.85 NBC

LYNDE, PAUL
A&C, B.V.:
The Hallmark Hall of Fame ep The Good Fairy 2.5.56 NBC
The Phil Silvers Show ep Bilko's Big Woman Hunt 1958 CBS
The Munsters ep Rock-a-Bye Munster Fall 1964 CBS
Gidget ep Take a Lesson 3.10.66 ABC
F Troop ep The Singing Mountie 9.8.66 ABC

LYNLEY, CAROL
A&C, B.V.:
The Big Valley ep Hell Hath No Fury 11.18.68 ABC
A&C, Supp. 2:
Hawaii Five-O ep Angel in Blue 3.9.78 CBS
SUPP.:
Fantasy Island ep King Arthur in Mr. Roarke's Court 1.23.82 ABC
Fantasy Island ep The Angel's Triangle 11.6.82 ABC
The Fall Guy ep Pleasure Isle 10.5.83 ABC
Hotel ep Faith, Hope and Charity 11.23.83 ABC
Fantasy Island ep Lost and Found 4.7.84 ABC
Finder of Lost Loves ep Forgotten Melodies 12.22.84 ABC

LYNN, LORETTA*
Fantasy Island ep I'm a Country Girl 12.11.84 ABC

- M -

McADAM, HEATHER*
Salvage 1 ep Hard Water 11.11.79 ABC
Fantasy Island ep 1.26.80 ABC
Off the Minnesota Strip tf 5.5.80 ABC

Walking Tall sr 1.17.81 NBC
The ABC Weekend Special ep Mayday! Mayday! 1.24, 1.31.81 ABC
Freedom tf 5.18.81 ABC
The CBS Afternoon Playhouse ep Just Pals 9.14.82 CBS
Father Murphy ep The Reluctant Runaway 11.23.82 NBC
Starflight: The Plane That Couldn't Land tf 2.27.83 ABC
The Facts of Life ep A Royal Pain 1.5.83 NBC
The Facts of Life ep Help from Home 4.6.83 NBC
The Facts of Life ep Graduation 5.4.83 NBC
St. Elsewhere ep Bypass 11.9.85 NBC

MacARTHUR, JAMES
A&C, B.V.:
Arrest and Trial ep A Shield Is for Hiding Behind 1.6.63 ABC
SUPP.:
The Love Boat ep I Don't Play Anymore 1.23.82 ABC
Murder, She Wrote ep Hooray for Homicide 10.28.84 CBS
The Love Boat ep Vicki's Gentleman Caller 2.23.85 ABC

McBROOM, AMANDA*
The Magician ep The Manhunter 10.2.73 NBC
Love, American Style ep Love and the Stutter 10.5.73 ABC
Cannon ep Dead Lady's Tears 11.7.73 CBS
Police Story ep Captain Hook 12.3.74 NBC
Big Shamus, Little Shamus ep (pt) 9.29.79 CBS
M*A*S*H ep That's Show Biz 10.26.81 CBS
The Powers of Matthew Star ep Experiment 11.26.82 NBC
Remington Steele ep Steele in Circulation 4.12.83 NBC
Cover Up ep Sudden Exposure 10.20.84 CBS
Magnum, P.I. ep Let Me Hear the Music 2.21.85 CBS

McCALLUM, DAVID
SUPP.:
Strike Force ep 1.15.82 ABC
Hart to Hart ep Hunted Harts 1.4.83 ABC
The Return of the Man from UNCLE: The 15 Years Later Affair tf/pt 4.5.83 CBS
The Master ep Hostages 2.17.84 NBC
Behind Enemy Lines tf/pt 12.29.85 NBC

McCARTHY, KEVIN
A&C, B.V.:
Amos Burke, Secret Agent ep Terror in a Tiny Town 1.5.66, 1.12.66 ABC
The FBI ep Counter-Stroke 10.1.67 ABC
The Guns of Will Sonnett ep Ride the Man Down 11.17.67 ABC
Garrison's Gorillas ep The Expendables 12.26.67 ABC
A&C, Supp. 1:
Love Story ep The Youngest Lovers 12.19.73 NBC
Theater in America ep June Moon 1.30.74 PBS

Hawaii Five-O ep The Last of the Great Paperhangers 11.4.76 CBS
SUPP.:
Rosie: The Rosemary Clooney Story tf 12.8.82 CBS
Amanda's sr (with ep Last of the Red Hot Brothers) 5.5.83 ABC
The Making of a Male Model tf 10.9.83 ABC
The Love Boat ep One Last Time 10.22.83 ABC
Bay City Blues ep I Never Swang for My Father 11.15.83 NBC
Fantasy Island ep The Sweet Life 1.14.84 ABC
Invitation to Hell tf 5.24.84 ABC
The Rousters ep Slade vs. Slade 6.23.84 NBC
Dynasty ep Fallon 10.17.84 ABC
Dynasty ep The Rescue 10.24.84 ABC
Murder, She Wrote ep Armed Response 3.31.85 CBS
Deadly Intentions tf 5.19, 5.20.85 ABC
Scarecrow and Mrs. King ep Over the Limit 10.7.85 CBS
Hotel ep Second Offense 10.16.85 ABC
The Midnight Hour tf 11.1.85 ABC

McCASHIN, CONSTANCE*
Special Olympics tf 2.22.78 CBS
The Many Loves of Arthur pt 5.23.78 NBC
Daddy, I Don't Like It Like This tf 7.12.78 CBS
Family ep 10.12.78 ABC
Married: The First Year sr 2.28.79 CBS
The Two Worlds of Jennie Logan tf 10.31.79 CBS
Knots Landing sr 12.27.79 CBS
Knots Landing sr ret 11.20.80 CBS
Knots Landing sr ret 9.30.81 CBS
Knots Landing sr ret 10.4.82 CBS
Knots Landing sr ret 9.29.83 CBS
Hotel ep Designs 12.28.83 ABC
Love Thy Neighbor tf 5.23.84 ABC
Knots Landing sr ret 10.4.84 CBS
Obsessive Love tf 10.2.84 CBS
Knots Landing sr ret 9.26.85 CBS
Love on the Run tf 10.21.85 NBC

McCASLIN, MAYLO*
The Home Front pt 10.9.80 CBS
The Kid Super Power Hour with Shazam sr 9.12.81 NBC
The Powers of Matthew Star ep The Powers of Matthew Star (pt) 9.17.82 NBC
Riptide ep Hatchet Job 1.31.84 NBC
Blue Thunder ep God Child 3.23.84 ABC
Hunter ep A Long Way from L.A. 10.2.84 NBC
Hardcastle and McCormick ep It Coulda Been Worse, She Coulda Been a Welder 12.2.84 ABC
The A-Team ep Beverly Hills Assault 4.9.85 NBC

McCLANAHAN, RUE
SUPP.:
The Day the Bubble Burst tf 2.7.82 NBC
Newhart ep The Way We Thought We Were 1.10.83 CBS
The Love Boat ep His Girls Friday 2.12.82 ABC
Trapper John, M.D. ep John's Other Life 5.2.82 CBS
Fantasy Island ep The Final Road 10.23.82 ABC
Mama's Family sr 1.22.83 NBC
Small and Frye ep 6.1.83 CBS
Mama's Family sr ret 9.29.83 NBC
The Love Boat ep How Do I Love Thee? 1.7.84 ABC
Alice ep 10.14.84 CBS
Gimme a Break ep Grandpa's Secret Life 10.20.84 NBC
The Love Boat ep Paying the Piper 12.1.84 ABC
Charles in Charge ep Grandma's Visit 12.9.84 CBS
Crazy Like a Fox ep Turn of the Century-Fox 1.6.85 CBS
Charles in Charge ep Grandma Returns 1.30.85 CBS
Murder, She Wrote ep Murder Takes the Bus 3.17.85 CBS
The Golden Girls sr 9.14.85 NBC

McCLURE, DOUG
SUPP.:
The Fall Guy ep Scavenger Hunt 5.5.82 ABC
Fantasy Island ep The Angels Triangle 11.6.82 ABC
Manimal ep Night of the Scorpion 10.21.83 NBC
The Fall Guy ep Cool Hand Colt 1.4.84 ABC
Scarecrow and Mrs. King ep Remembrance of Things Past 1.9.84 CBS
Fantasy Island ep To Fly with Eagles 1.21.84 ABC
Hardcastle and McCormick ep School for Scandal 1.29.84 ABC
Simon and Simon ep 3.1.84 CBS
The Master ep Failure to Communicate 5.4.84 NBC
Cover Up ep Cover Up (pt) 9.22.84 CBS
The Fall Guy ep October the 31st 10.31.84 ABC
Magnum, P.I. ep Paniolo 11.7.85 CBS
The Fall Guy ep October the 32nd 12.7.85 ABC
Airwolf ep Half-Pint 12.21.85 CBS

MacCORKINDALE, SIMON*
The Dukes of Hazzard ep The Duke of Duke 1.4.80 CBS
Scalpels pt 10.26.80 NBC
The Manions of America ms 9.30-10.2.81 ABC
Fantasy Island ep Cyrano 10.24.81 ABC
Hart to Hart ep Million Dollar Harts 10.19.82 ABC
Dynasty ep The Will 11.17.82 ABC
Falcon's Gold (a.k.a. Robbers of the Sacred Mountain) tf/pt 12.18.82 SHO
Manimal sr 9.30.83 NBC
Falcon Crest sr 9.28.84 CBS
Obsessive Love tf 10.2.84 CBS
Matt Houston ep Eye Witness 10.12.84 ABC
Falcon Crest sr ret 10.4.85 CBS

McCORMACK, PATRICIA
SUPP.:
Dallas ep The Prodigal 12.18.81 CBS
Dallas ep Anniversary 2.12.82 CBS
Magnum, P.I. ep Foiled Again 11.11.82 CBS
Night Partners tf/pt 10.11.83 CBS
Hotel ep The Wedding 2.22.84 ABC
Invitation to Hell tf 5.24.84 ABC
Remington Steele ep Second Base Steele 10.23.84 NBC
Partners in Crime ep Fashioned in Murder 12.8.84 NBC
Answers ep Good Time sp 4.30.85 A&E

McCORMICK, MAUREEN
A&C, Supp. 2:
The Farmer's Daughter ep Why Don't They Ever Pick Me? 3.65 ABC
Camp Runamuck ep Tomboy 1.66 NBC
I Dream of Jeannie ep My Master, the Doctor 2.5.66 NBC
SUPP.:
The Love Boat ep The Christmas Presence 12.18.82 ABC
Fantasy Island ep The Sisters 5.14.83 ABC

McDOWALL, RODDY
SUPP.:
Mae West tf 5.28.82 ABC
Tales of the Gold Monkey sr 9.29.82 ABC
Fantasy Island ep Natchez Bound 11.6.82 ABC
Small and Frye ep 6.1.83 CBS
This Girl for Hire tf/pt 11.1.83 CBS
The Zany Adventures of Robin Hood tf 5.22.84 CBS
London and Davis in New York pt 9.9.84 CBS
Hotel ep Intimate Strangers 9.26.84 ABC
Hollywood Wives ms 2.17-2.19.85 ABC
Alice in Wonderland tf 12.9, 12.10.85 CBS
Murder, She Wrote ep School for Scandal 10.20.85 CBS

McEACHIN, JAMES
SUPP.:
McClain's Law ep Portrait of a Playmate 12.18.81 NBC
Honeyboy tf 10.17.82 NBC
T. J. Hooker ep The Decoy 1.22.83 ABC
Murder, She Wrote ep Sudden Death 3.3.85 CBS
Hill Street Blues ep Fathers and Huns 10.31.85 NBC

McGAVIN, DARREN
A&C, B.V.:
Cimarron Strip ep The Legend of Jud Starr 9.14.67 CBS
SUPP.:
Small and Frye sr 3.7.83 CBS
The Return of Marcus Welby, M.D. tf/pt 5.16.84 ABC
The Baron and the Kid tf 11.21.84 CBS

My Wicked, Wicked Ways.... The Legend of Errol Flynn tf 1.21.85 CBS
The Hitchhiker ep Night Shift 10.15.85 HBO
Tales from the Darkside ep Distant Signals 11.16.85 NN

McGEEHAN, MARY KATE*
240-Robert ep First Loss 3.14.81 ABC
Voyagers ep Worlds Apart 11.7.82 NBC
Fantasy Island ep The Ideal Woman 5.19.84 ABC
The Love Boat ep The Wager 11.3.84 ABC
Hotel ep Illusions 11.28.84 ABC
Finder of Lost Loves ep Aftershocks 2.16.85 ABC
Highway to Heaven ep An Investment in Caring 3.13.85 NBC
Murder, She Wrote ep School for Scandal 10.20.85 CBS
Magnum, P.I. ep Paniolo 11.7.85 CBS

McGOOHAN, PATRICK
SUPP.:
American Playhouse ep Three Sovereigns for Sarah 5.29, 6.3, 6.10.85 PBS
Jamaica Inn tf 6.3.85 NN

MacGRAW, ALI*
The Winds of War ms 2.6-2.13.83 ABC
China Rose tf 10.18.83 CBS
Dynasty ep Foreign Relations 1.23.85 ABC
Dynsty ep The Ball 2.6.85 ABC
Dynasty ep Circumstantial Evidence 2.13.85 ABC
Dynasty ep The Collapse 2.20.85 ABC
Dynasty ep Life and Death 2.27.85 ABC
Dynasty ep The Crash 3.20.85 ABC
Dynasty ep Reconciliation 3.27.85 ABC
Dynasty ep Kidnapped 4.10.85 ABC
Dynasty ep The Heiress 5.8.85 ABC

McGRAW, CHARLES
A&C, Supp. 1:
The Life and Legend of Wyatt Earp ep The Scout 3.1.60 ABC
Dante ep Hunter with a Badge 3.20.61 NBC
The Man from UNCLE ep The Survival School Affair 11.20.67 NBC

McGUIRE, DOROTHY
SUPP.:
The Love Boat ep Love Will Find a Way 11.20.82 ABC
Ghost Dancing tf 5.30.83 ABC
Fantasy Island ep Second Time Around 11.19.83 ABC
The Love Boat ep Story of the Century 11.3.84 ABC
Amos tf 9.29.85 CBS
Glitter ep 12.19.85 ABC
Between the Darkness and the Dawn tf 12.23.85 NBC

McINTIRE, JOHN

A&C, B.V.:

Father Knows Best ep Bud, the Carpenter 11.58 NBC
Cimarron City ep Chinese Invasion 3.21.59 NBC
Wanted: Dead Or Alive ep Crossroads 4.11.59 CBS
Daniel Boone ep The Thanksgiving Story 11.25.65 NBC
Slattery's People ep Color Him Red 11.26.65 CBS

SUPP.:

Lone Star pt 7.31.83 NBC
Hotel ep Flashback 11.9.83 ABC
The Cowboy and the Ballerina tf 10.23.84 CBS
Night Court ep Dan's Parents 1.10.85 NBC
Diff'rent Strokes ep 1.19.85 NBC

McKECHNIE, DONNA*

Cheers ep Sam's Women 10.7.82 NBC
Family Ties ep To Snatch a Keith 12.21.83 NBC
Hardcastle and McCormick ep Angie's Choice 12.2.84 ABC
MacGruder and Loud ep MacGruder and Loud (pt) 1.20.85 ABC

McKENZIE, PATCH*

Get Christie Love ep Highway to Murder 10.30.74 ABC
Charlie's Angels ep Angels in the Backfield 1.25.78 ABC
Young Maverick ep 1.16.80 CBS
Nightside pt 6.8.80 ABC
Charlie's Angels ep Hula Angels 1.11.81 ABC
Heaven on Earth pt 4.12.81 NBC
Magnum, P.I. ep Ghost Writer 12.24.81 CBS
Knight Rider ep Big Iron 5.27.84 NBC
E/R ep 9.16.84, 10.0.84 CBS
E/R ep 1.30.85, 2.6.85 CBS
Falcon Crest ep Retribution 2.8.85 CBS
Shadow Chasers ep Amazing Grace 11.28.85 ABC

McKEON, NANCY

A&C, Supp. 2:

Stone tf/pt 8.26.79 ABC

SUPP.:

The Facts of Life Goes to Paris tf 9.25.82 NBC
The Facts of Life sr ret 10.6.82 NBC
Dusty pt 9.21.83 NBC
The Facts of Life sr ret 9.21.83 NBC
High School, U.S.A. tf/pt 10.16.83 NBC
The Facts of Life sr ret 9.26.84 NBC
Poison Ivy tf/pt 2.10.85 NBC
The Facts of Life sr ret 9.14.85 NBC
This Child Is Mine tf 11.14.85 NBC

MacLACHLAN, JANET

A&C, Supp. 1:

Alfred Hitchcock Hour ep Completely Foolproof 9.19.64 NBC

Alfred Hitchcock Hour ep The Monkey's Paw: A Retelling 4.19.65 NBC
The Girl from UNCLE ep The UFO Affair 1.3.67 NBC
I Spy ep Laya 9.25.67 NBC
The Bob Hope Chrysler Theater ep Kicks 10.13.65 NBC
The Interns ep The Manly Art 3.2.71 CBS
Longstreet ep Elegy in Brass 10.14.71 ABC
Love Story ep The Glow of Dying Embers 12.26.73 NBC
Griff ep Fugitive from Fear 1.5.74 ABC
The Rockford Files ep The Deep Blue Sleep 10.10.75 NBC
A&C, Supp. 2:
All in the Family ep The Family Next Door 3.18.79 CBS
SUPP.:
The Kid from Nowhere tf 1.4.82 NBC
Cagney and Lacey ep 12.6.82 CBS
Thursday's Child tf 2.1.83 CBS
Cagney and Lacey ep 3.14.83 CBS
Fantasy Island ep Edward 4.9.83 CBS
Trapper John, M.D. ep 1.20.85 CBS
Cagney and Lacey ep 3.18.85 CBS
Tough Love tf 10.13.85 ABC
Punky Brewster ep The Search 11.10.85 NBC
Murder, She Wrote ep Jessica Behind Bars 12.1.85 CBS

MacLEOD, GAVIN
A&C, Supp. 2:
The Whirlybirds ep Baby Face Killer 1957 NN
The Walter Winchell File ep The Walkout 2.28.58 ABC
Father Knows Best ep Bud, the Carpenter Fall 1958 NBC
Peter Gunn ep The Kill 9.22.58 NBC
Dan Raven ep Tinge of Red 12.16.60 NBC
Perry Mason ep The Case of the Crumbling Grandfather 5.27.61 CBS
Cain's Hundred ep Crime and Commitment 9.19.61 NBC
Cain's Hundred ep Rules of Guidance 9.26.61 NBC
The Investigators ep Style of Living 11.9.61 CBS
Straightaway ep The Heist 11.10.61 ABC
The Dick Van Dyke Show ep Empress Carlotta's Necklace 12.12.61 CBS
The DuPont Show of the Week ep The World's Greatest Robbery 4.29.62 NBC
The Dick Van Dyke Show ep Romance, Roses and Rye Bread 10.28.64 CBS
The Munsters ep Sleeping Cutie 12.10.64 CBS
The Andy Griffith Show ep TV or Not TV 3.1.65 CBS
The Andy Griffith Show ep The Taylors in Hollywood 11.1.65 CBS
Gomer Pyle, USMC ep Dance, Marine, Dance 1.8.65 CBS
The Andy Griffith Show ep 11.1.65 CBS
Perry Mason ep The Case of the Runaway Racer 11.14.65 CBS
Hogan's Heroes ep 1.21.66 CBS

Ben Casey ep Then Suddenly, Panic! 3.12.66 ABC
Combat ep The Masquers 2.14.67 ABC
Garrison's Gorillas ep Black Market 11.28.67 ABC
The Flying Nun ep A Star Is Reborn 1.69 ABC
SUPP.:
The Love Boat sr ret 10.2.82 ABC
The Love Boat sr ret 9.17.83 ABC
The Love Boat sr ret 9.22.84 ABC
Hotel ep Fallen Idols 1.2.85 ABC
The Love Boat sr ret 9.28.85 ABC

McMAHON, ED*
Here's Lucy ep Lucy Meets Johnny Carson 12.1.69 CBS
The Kid from Left Field tf 9.30.79 NBC
The Golden Moment: An Olympic Love Story tf 5.25, 5.26.80 NBC
Gridlock tf 10.2.80 NBC
The Star Maker tf 5.11, 5.12.81 NBC

McNAIR, BARBARA
SUPP.:
The Jeffersons ep 4.1.84 CBS
Glitter sr 9.13.84 ABC
Airwolf ep Dambreakers 3.16.85 CBS
Hell Town ep 12.25.85 NBC

McNAIR, HEATHER*
Automan sr 12.15.83 ABC
Legmen ep Still Alone at Five 3.9.84 NBC
Cover Up ep Harper-Gate 10.13.84 CBS
Cover Up ep Nothing to Lose 10.27.84 CBS

McNALLY, STEPHEN
A&C, B.V.:
The Big Valley ep Hide the Children 12.19.66 ABC
A&C, Supp. 1:
The Rockford Files ep Exit Prentiss Carr 10.4.74 NBC
Get Christie Love ep Death on Delivery 10.9.74 ABC
Switch ep The Deadly Missiles Caper 10.7.75 CBS

MACNEE, PATRICK
A&C, Supp. 1:
Suspicion ep The Voice in the Night 5.26.58 NBC
Suspicion ep Depth of Three-Hundred 10.26.58 NBC
Northwest Passage ep The Redcoat 12.14.58 NBC
Black Saddle ep Client: McQueen 1.24.59 NBC
Markham ep The Counterfeit Stamps 7.25.59 CBS
Alias Smith and Jones ep The Man Who Murdered Himself 3.18.71 ABC
SUPP.:
Rehearsal for Murder tf 5.26.82 CBS

Gavilan sr 10.26.82 NBC
The Return of the Man from UNCLE: The 15 Years Later Affair tf/pt 4.5.83 CBS
Empire sr 1.4.84 CBS
Magnum, P.I. ep 3.8.84 CBS
Hart to Hart ep Meanwhile, Back at the Ranch 5.22.84 ABC
The Love Boat ep The Last Heist 11.10.84 ABC
Hotel ep Hearts and Minds 5.8.85 ABC
Lime Street ep The Mystery of Flight 401 9.28.85 ABC
Lime Street sr 10.5.85 ABC
Murder, She Wrote ep Sing a Song of Murder 10.27.85 CBS

McNICHOL, KRISTY
<u>SUPP.</u>:
Love, Mary tf 10.8.85 CBS

MacNICHOL, PETER*
Faerie Tale Theater ep The Boy Who Left Home to Find Out About the Shivers 10.14.84 SHO

McPHERSON, PATRICIA*
Knight Rider sr (with ep Deadly Maneuvers) 10.1.82
Knight Rider ret to sr (with ep Knight of the Drones) 9.30.84 NBC
Knight Rider sr ret 9.20.85 NBC

McRANEY, GERALD*
Gunsmoke ep Kitty's Love Affair 10.22.73 CBS
Cannon ep Photo Finish 1.2.74 CBS
The FBI Story: The FBI vs. Alvin Karpis, Public Enemy tf 11.8.74 CBS
Barnaby Jones ep Mystery Cycle 11.12.74 CBS
The Rockford Files ep Sleight of Hand 1.17.75 NBC
Mannix ep Edge of the Web 2.2.75 CBS
Gunsmoke ep Hard Labor 2.24.75 CBS
Petrocelli ep Shadow of Fear 9.10.75 NBC
The Streets of San Francisco ep Deadly Silence 10.16.75 ABC
Petrocelli ep Terror on Wheels 11.5.75 NBC
Barnaby Jones ep Dangerous Gambit 2.26.76 CBS
Police Woman ep Task Force: Cop Killer 3.2, 3.9.76 NBC
The Blue Knight ep Upward Mobility 10.13.76 CBS
The Streets of San Francisco ep Hot Dog 12.9.76 ABC
Hawaii Five-O ep Target--A Cop 12.23.76 CBS
The Six Million Dollar Man ep To Catch the Eagle 3.6.77 ABC
Switch ep Heritage of Death 3.27.77 CBS
The Incredible Hulk: A Death in the Family tf/pt 11.22.77 CBS
The Rockford Files ep Hotel of Fear 11.22.77 NBC
Baretta ep Why Me? 1.11.78 ABC
Logan's Run ep Turnabout 1.30.78 CBS
The Incredible Hulk ep Ricky 10.6.78 CBS
The Jordan Chance tf/pt 12.12.78 CBS

Women in White sr 2.8.79 NBC
The Incredible Hulk ep The Disciple 3.16.79 CBS
240-Robert ep Bank Job 10.1.79 ABC
The Aliens Are Coming tf/pt 3.2.80 NBC
The Incredible Hulk ep Death Mask 3.14.80 CBS
Where the Ladies Go tf 3.14.80 ABC
Rape and Marriage: The Rideout Case tf 10.30.80 CBS
Simon and Simon sr 11.24.81 CBS
Simon and Simon sr ret 11.4.82 CBS
Memories Never Die tf 12.15.82 CBS
Magnum, P.I. ep 9.29.83 CBS
Simon and Simon sr ret 9.29.83 CBS
The Haunting Passion tf 10.24.83 NBC
The City Killer tf 10.28.84 NBC
Simon and Simon sr ret 10.3.85 CBS

McVEY, PATRICK
A&C, B.V.:
Restless Gun ep Strange Family in Town 1.20.58 NBC
Lawman ep Wanted 11.16.58 ABC
Wanted: Dead Or Alive ep Bounty for a Bride 4.4.59 CBS
The Rifleman ep The Hawk 4.14.59 ABC
Black Saddle ep Client: Nelson 5.2.59 NBC
Gunsmoke ep Quint's Indian 3.1.63 CBS

McWILLIAMS, CAROLINE
SUPP.:
The Day the Bubble Burst tf 2.7.82 NBC
The Gift of Life tf 3.16.82 CBS
Cass Malloy pt 7.21.82 CBS
Hill Street Blues ep Untitled 1.26.84 NBC
Shattered Vows tf 10.29.84 NBC
Hill Street Blues ep Untitled 11.28.84 NBC
Maximum Security ep Cottage Nine 3.9.85 HBO
Into Thin Air tf 10.29.85 CBS

MACY, BILL
SUPP.:
The Day the Bubble Burst tf 2.7.82 NBC
The Love Boat ep A Match Made in Heaven 10.20.84 ABC
Riptide ep Games People Play 1.8.85 NBC
Masquerade ep Spying Down to Rio 4.27.85 ABC
Eye to Eye ep The Crossword Puzzle 4.18.85 ABC
Highway to Heaven ep Cindy 10.23.85 NBC
Hardcastle and McCormick ep Games People Play 11.11.85 ABC
Tales from the Darkside ep Lifebomb 12.14.85 NN

MAHARIS, GEORGE
A&C, B.V.:
Brenner ep Word of Honor 7.11.59 CBS
A&C, Supp. 2:

Switch ep The Legend of the Macunas 10.21.77 CBS
SUPP.:
Fantasy Island ep Sweet Suzi Swann 3.6.82 ABC
Matt Houston ep The Bikini Murders 2.3.84 ABC
The Master ep The Good, the Bad and the Priceless 3.23.84 NBC

MAISNIK, KATHY*
Star of the Family sr 9.30.82 ABC
CHiPs ep Return of the Brat Patrol 5.8.83 NBC
Hollywood's Most Sensational Mysteries sp 2.2.84 NBC
Remington Steele ep Breath of Steele 11.27.84 NBC

MAJORS, LEE
SUPP.:
The Fall Guy sr ret 10.27.82 ABC
Starflight: The Plane That Couldn't Land tf 2.27.83 ABC
The Fall Guy sr ret 9.21.83 ABC
Trauma Center ep Notes About Courage 9.29.83 ABC
The Love Boat ep Dear Roberta 10.1.83 ABC
The Fall Guy sr ret 9.19.84 ABC
The Cowboy and the Ballerina tf 10.23.84 CBS
The Fall Guy sr ret 9.26.85 ABC

MAKO
A&C, Supp. 1:
The Lloyd Bridges Show ep Yankee Stay Here 11.13.62 CBS
Gidget ep The War Between Men, Women and Gidget 11.65 ABC
F Troop ep From Karate with Love 1.5.67 ABC
The Big Valley ep Rimfire 2.19.68 ABC
Hawaii Five-O ep Legacy of Terror 1.1.76 CBS

MALDEN, KARL
SUPP.:
Fatal Vision tf 11.18, 11.19.84 NBC
With Intent to Kill tf 10.24.84 CBS
Alice in Wonderland tf 12.9, 12.10.85 CBS

MALONE, DOROTHY
A&C, B.V.:
Arrest and Trial ep Modus Operandi 3.15.64 ABC
SUPP.:
Matt Houston ep Shark Bait 11.21.82 ABC
He's Not Your Son tf 10.3.84 CBS
Peyton Place: The Next Generation tf/pt 5.13.85 NBC

MALONE, NANCY
A&C, Supp. 2:
The Armstrong Circle Theater ep For Worse 7.15.52 NBC
Robert Montgomery Presents ep There's No Need to Shout

6.20.55 NBC
Robert Montgomery Presents ep Sturdevant's Daughters 5.27.57 NBC
Great Adventure ep the Story of Nathan Hale 10.25.63 CBS
Dr. Kildare ep The Exploiters 10.31.63 NBC
The Fugitive ep Bloodline 2.11.64 ABC
The Andy Griffith Show ep A Girl for Goober 3.25.68 CBS
McMillan and Wife ep Greed 2.15.76 NBC
Switch ep Three Blind Mice 8.6.78 CBS
SUPP.:
Scene of the Crime ep Murder on the Rocks 4.28.85 NBC

MANDAN, ROBERT
A&C, Supp. 2:
The Rockford Files ep Where's Houston? 2.20.76 NBC
Marcus Welby, M.D. ep Vanity Case 4.27.76, 5.4.76, 5.11.76 ABC
Police Story ep Hard Rock Brown 2.15.77 NBC
SUPP.:
Fantasy Island ep King Arthur in Mr. Roarke's Court 1.23.82 ABC
Too Close for Comfort ep Brotherly Hate 2.2.82 ABC
Private Benjamin ep I Wonder Who's Blackballing Her Now? 2.1.82 CBS
The Love Boat ep Love Ain't Legal 2.6.82 ABC
Private Benjamin ep When It's Hot, It's Hot 3.1.82 CBS
Private Benjamin ep Reds and Blues 3.15.82 CBS
Private Benjamin ep Profiles in Courage 4.5.82 CBS
Private Benjamin ep Smash 4.12.82 CBS
Private Benjamin ep Me, Me, Me 4.19.82 CBS
Private Benjamin ep The Real Thing 4.26.82 CBS
Private Benjamin sr 9.28.82 CBS
The Love Boat ep The Anniversary Gift 10.16.82 ABC
In Love with an Older Woman tf 11.24.82 CBS
For Members Only tf 7.11.83 CBS
Trapper John, M.D. ep 10.16.83 CBS
Three's Company ep Cupid Works Overtime 5.15, 5.22.84 ABC
The Outlaws tf/pt 7.9.84 ABC
The Love Boat Fall Preview Party sp 9.15.84 ABC
Three's a Crowd sr 9.25.84 ABC

MANDRELL, BARBARA*
Murder in Music City tf 1.16.79 NBC
The Concrete Cowboys tf/pt 10.17.79 CBS
Country Gold tf 11.23.82 CBS
Burning Rage tf 9.21.84 CBS

MANDRELL, IRLENE*
The Love Boat ep Vicki Swings 11.14.81 ABC
The Love Boat ep Instinct 1.5.85 ABC

MANHOFF, DINAH*
Visions ep The Great Cherub Knitwear Strike 11.25.76 PBS
Raid on Entebbe tf 1.9.77 NBC
Night Terror tf 2.7.77 NBC
The Possessed tf 5.1.77 NBC
Lou Grant ep Bomb 3.26.79 CBS
For Ladies Only tf 11.9.81 ABC
A Matter of Sex tf 1.16.84 NBC
The Seduction of Gina tf 1.23.84 ABC
Celebrity ms 2.12-2.14.84 NBC
Flight #90: Disaster on the Potomac 4.1.84 NBC
Night Court ep The Nun 9.27.84 NBC
Cagney and Lacey ep 11.12.84 CBS
Hot Pursuit ep Gillian 11.24.84 NBC

MANILOW, BARRY*
Copacabana tf 12.3.85 CBS

MANTOOTH, RANDOLPH*
Split Second to an Epitaph tf 9.26.68 NBC
Vanished tf 3.8, 3.9.71 NBC
Marriage: Year One tf 10.15.71 NBC
The Bold Ones: The Lawyers ep The Strange Secret of Yermo Bill 10.17.71 NBC
Sarge ep The Combatants 11.30.71 NBC
McCloud ep The Disposal Man 12.29.71 NBC
The Bravos tf 1.9.72 ABC
Emergency tf/pt 1.15.72 NBC
Emergency sr 1.22.72 (through 12.31.78) NBC
Emergency Plus Four sr vo 9.8.73 NBC
Owen Marshall, Counselor at Law ep The Destruction of Keith Ryder 3.30.74 ABC
Testimony of Two Men ms 5.1-5.3.78 OPT
Operation Petticoat sr 9.18.78 ABC
Project UFO ep Sighting 4018: The Pipeline Incident 10.5.78 NBC
Vegas ep Serve, Volley and Kill 12.20.78 ABC
Emergency sr ret 6.26.79 NBC
The Seekers ms 12.3, 12.4.79 OPT
The Love Boat ep 12.7.79 ABC
Fantasy Island ep The Unkillable 4.16.81 ABC
The Fall Guy ep To the Finish 12.7.83 ABC
Dallas ep 10.19.84 CBS
The Fall Guy ep The Winner 12.19.84 ABC
Scene of the Crime ep Memory Game 4.14.85 NBC
Bridge Across Time tf 11.22.85 NBC
Murder, She Wrote ep Murder Digs Deep 12.29.85 CBS

MARCHAND, NANCY
SUPP.:
Grandpa, Will You Run with Me? sp 4.2.83 NBC

Agatha Christie's "Sparkling Cyanide" tf 11.5.83 CBS
Cheers ep Diane Meets Mom 11.22.84 NBC

MARCOVICCI, ANDREA
SUPP.:
The Phoenix ep One of Them 4.2.82 ABC
Voyagers ep Cleo and the Babe 10.17.82 NBC
Taxi ep Louie's Revenge 11.18.82 NBC
Packin' It In tf 2.7.83 CBS
Scarecrow and Mrs. King ep Lost and Found 1.16.84 CBS
Trapper John, M.D. ep 3.4.84 CBS
Spraggue tf/pt 6.29.84 ABC
Trapper John, M.D. ep Game of Hearts 10.6, 10.13.85 CBS
Trapper John, M.D. ep Billboard Barney 12.29.85 CBS

MARGOLIN, JANET
A&C, B.V.:
East Side/West Side ep You Can't Beat the System 10.7.63 CBS
Arrest and Trial ep A Circle of Strangers 3.8.64 ABC
Owen Marshall, Counselor at Law ep The Forest and the Trees 10.7.71 ABC

MARGOLIN, STUART
A&C, Supp. 1:
Mrs. G Goes to College ep Lonely Sunday Fall 1961 CBS
Mrs. G Goes to College ep High Finance Spring 1962 CBS
Ensign O'Toole ep Operation Impersonation 11.62 NBC
The Lieutenant ep A Very Private Affair 10.12.63 NBC
The Alfred Hitchcock Hour ep The Monkey's Paw: A Retelling 4.19.65 NBC
Branded ep A Taste of Poison 5.2.65 NBC
SUPP.:
The CBS Children's Mystery Theater ep Dirkham Detective Agency 1.25.83 CBS
The Fall Guy ep The Molly Sue 3.2.83 ABC
Magnum, P.I. ep Legacy from a Friend 3.10.83 CBS
Magnum, P.I. ep 3.31.83 CBS
Mr. Smith ep Mr. Smith Goes to Washington 9.23.83 NBC
A Killer in the Family tf 10.30.83 ABC
The Glitter Dome tf 11.18.84 HBO
Hill Street Blues ep Hacket to Pieces 10.3.85 NBC
Hill Street Blues ep Seoul on Ice 10.17.85 NBC

MARKHAM, MONTE
A&C, Supp. 1:
Bracken's World ep A Perfect Piece of Casting 1.30.70 NBC
Here Come the Brides ep Something to Get Hung About 10.21.71 ABC
Hawaii Five-O ep Wednesday, Ladies Free 12.14.71 CBS
Hawaii Five-O ep Here Today ... Gone Tonight 1.23.73 CBS
Hawaii Five-O ep School for Assassins 1.1.80 CBS

SUPP.:
The Fall Guy ep License to Kill 1.13, 1.20.82 ABC
Fantasy Island ep Mata Hari 1.16.82 ABC
Bret Maverick ep The Vulture Also Rises 3.16.82 NBC
Fantasy Island ep Face of Love 3.20.82 ABC
Drop-Out Father tf 9.27.82 CBS
Hotline tf 10.16.82 CBS
Simon and Simon ep Psyched Out 1.13.83 CBS
The Love Boat ep Off-Course Romance 2.19.83 ABC
Fantasy Island ep Nurses' Night Out 10.22.83 ABC
Hotel ep Designs 12.28.83 ABC
The A-Team ep Say It with Bullets 1.17.84 NBC
Rituals sr 9.84 NN
Finder of Lost Loves ep (pt/first ep) 9.22.84 ABC

MARS, KENNETH (a.k.a. Ken Mars)
A&C, Supp. 1:
Harry O ep Coinage of the Realm 10.10.74 ABC
Barnaby Jones ep Honeymoon with Death 10.17.75 CBS
Harry O ep Tender Killing Care 10.30.75 ABC
SUPP.:
Magnum, P.I. ep The Woman on the Beach 10.22.81 CBS
Private Benjamin ep A Bath for Benjamin 12.28.81 CBS
Simon and Simon ep The Dead Letter File 1.5.82 CBS
Alice ep Mel Wins by a Nose 3.21.82 CBS
Tucker's Witch ep Terminal Case 11.3.82 CBS
Trapper John, M.D. ep 11.28.82 CBS
Cagney and Lacey ep 3.2.83 CBS
Small and Frye ep 6.1.83 CBS
The Rules of Marriage tf 5.10, 5.11.83 CBS
The Mississippi ep 11.1.83 CBS
The Whiz Kids ep The Lollipop Gang Strikes Back 2.25.84 CBS
Trapper John, M.D. ep 3.25.84 CBS
Call to Glory ep A Wind from the East 10.8.84 ABC
Hardcastle and McCormick ep Too Rich and Too Thin 1.14.85 ABC
Murder, She Wrote ep Footnote to Murder 3.10.85 CBS
The Duck Factory ep You Always Love the One You Hurt 6.20.85 NBC
Remington Steele ep Steele Blushing 10.22.85 NBC

MARSH, JEAN*
The Moon and Sixpence sp 10.30.59 NBC
I Spy ep The War Lord 2.1.67 NBC
Jane Eyre tf 3.24.71 NBC
The Waltons ep The Hiding Place 3.3.77 CBS
Hawaii Five-O ep The Miracle Man 11.23.78 CBS
Hawaii Five-O ep Image of Fear 11.8.79 CBS
Momma the Detective (a.k.a. See China and Die) pt 1.9.80 NBC
Goliath Awaits tf 11.16, 11.17.81 OPT
9 to 5 sr 3.25.82 ABC

9 to 5 sr ret 9.29.83 ABC
The Love Boat ep The Emperor's Fortune 11.5.83 ABC
Master of the Game ms 2.19-2.21.84 CBS
Tales from the Darkside ep Answer Me 12.2.84 NN
The Corsican Brothers tf 2.5.85 CBS

MARSHALL, E. G.
SUPP.:
The Phoenix ep In Search of Mira 3.26.82 ABC
Nurse ep Father 4.23.82 CBS
Eleanor, First Lady of the World tf 5.12.82 CBS
Falcon Crest ep 10.1.82 CBS
Kennedy ms 11.20-11.22.83 NBC
John Steinbeck's "The Winter of Our Discontent" tf 12.6.83 CBS

MARSHALL, PENNY
SUPP.:
Laverne and Shirley sr ret 10.12.82 ABC
Love Thy Neighbor tf 5.23.84 ABC
Challenge of a Lifetime tf 2.14.85 ABC

MARTA, LYNNE
A&C, Supp. 1:
Dan August ep The Soldier 12.2.70 ABC
Cannon ep Girl in the Electric Coffin 10.26.71 CBS
The Man and the City ep The Handwriting on the Door 10.27.71 ABC
The Rookies ep 10.16.72 ABC
Gunsmoke ep Homecoming 1.8.73 CBS
Cannon ep 3.21.73 CBS
Genesis II tf/pt 3.23.73 CBS
Barnaby Jones ep Divorce--Murderer's Style 10.28.73 CBS
Kojak ep 18 Hours of Fear 2.20.74 CBS
Manhunter ep The Baby-Faced Killers 9.25.74 CBS
Barnaby Jones ep Forfeit by Death 10.15.74 CBS
Adams of Eagle Lake ep 1.10.75 ABC
Caribe ep The Survivor 3.3.75 ABC
Starsky and Hutch ep The Bait 11.5.75 ABC
Medical Center ep The High Cost of Winning 12.15.75 CBS
The Streets of San Francisco ep Clown of Death 2.26.76 ABC
City of Angels ep Say Goodbye to Yesterday 4.4.76 NBC
Starsky and Hutch ep Murder at Sea 10.2.76 ABC
SUPP.:
Barnaby Jones ep Duet for Dying 2.17.77 CBS
In the Glitter Palace tf 2.27.77 NBC
Once an Eagle ms 12.2-1.13.77 NBC
The Rockford Files ep Heartaches of a Fool 9.22.78 NBC
The Rockford Files ep The Girl in the Bay City Boy's Club 12.22.78 NBC
Vegas ep The Macho Murders 11.28.79 ABC
Trapper John, M.D. ep 2.10.80 CBS

Charlie's Angels ep One Love ... Two Angels 4.30, 5.7.80 ABC
Homeward Bound tf 11.19.80 CBS
Vegas ep No Way to Treat a Lady 3.18.81 ABC
Trapper John, M.D. ep Maybe Baby 3.7.82 CBS
Matt Houston ep Fear for Tomorrow 4.3.83 ABC
Goodnight Beantown ep 11.6.83 CBS

MARTIN, DEAN PAUL*
The Love Boat ep Father in the Cradle 1.28.84 ABC
The Misfits of Science sr 10.4.85 NBC

MARTIN, DEWEY
A&C, B.V.:
Zane Grey Theater ep Stagecoach to Yuma 5.5.60 CBS
Burke's Law ep Who Killed the Surf Board? 9.16.64 ABC
A&C, Supp. 1:
Petrocelli ep Terror By the Book 12.10.75 NBC

MARTIN, LORI*
National Velvet sr 9.18.60 NBC
National Velvet sr ret 9.18.61 NBC
The Donna Reed Show ep All Women Are Dangerous 1963 ABC
Leave It to Beaver ep Beaver Sees America 6.6.63 ABC
The Breaking Point ep Tides of Darkness 3.2.64 ABC
Slattery's People ep Question: Do the Ignorant Sleep in Pure White Beds? 11.30.64 CBS
My Three Sons ep Robbie's Double Life Fall 1965 CBS
Please Don't Eat the Daisies ep Professor, Please! Spring 1966 NBC
Weekend pt 9.9.67 NBC

MARTIN, MARY
SUPP.:
The Love Boat ep So Help Me Hannah 3.12.83 ABC
Hardcastle and McCormick ep Hardcastle, Hardcastle, Hardcastle and McCormick 1.24.85 ABC

MARTIN, PAMELA SUE
SUPP.:
Dynasty sr ret 10.27.82 ABC
Dynasty sr ret 9.28.83 ABC

MARTIN, ROSS
A&C, Supp. 2:
The Web ep The Hunted 1.17.54 CBS
The Ann Sothern Show ep The Big Gamble 1958 CBS
M Squad ep Contraband 12.19.58 NBC
Richard Diamond ep 2.15.59 CBS
Naked City ep Ten Cent Dreams 3.10.59 ABC
Richard Diamond ep The Bookie 10.19.59 CBS
The Danny Thomas Show ep 1.13.64 CBS

SUPP.:
I Married Wyatt Earp tf 1.10.83 NBC

MARTINEZ, A*
The Outcasts ep A Time of Darkness 3.24.69 ABC
Ironside ep The Machismo Bag 11.13.69 NBC
Hunters Are for Killing tf 3.12.70 CBS
Adam-12 ep Log 114: The Hero 3.28.70 NBC
The Storefront Lawyers sr 9.16.70 CBS
Bonanza ep Gideon, the Good 10.18.70 NBC
The Smith Family ep Chicano 2.3.71 ABC
The Bold Ones: The Lawyers ep Justice Is a Sometime Thing 12.12.71 NBC
Probe tf/pt 2.12.72 NBC
The Sixth Sense ep Echo of a Distant Scream 4.1.72 ABC
The Streets of San Francisco ep Hall of Mirrors 11.4.72 ABC
Hawaii Five-O ep A Bullet for El Diablo 11.13.73 CBS
The Cowboys sr 2.6.74 ABC
Nakia ep The Non-Person 9.21.74 ABC
Kung Fu ep My Brother, My Executioner 10.12.74 ABC
Movin' On ep Cowhands 10.24.74 NBC
The Streets of San Francisco ep False Witness 1.9.75 ABC
The Abduction of St. Anne tf 1.21.75 ABC
McCloud ep Sharks! 2.23.75 NBC
Kung Fu ep Full Circle 3.8.75 ABC
Mrs. R: Death Among Friends tf/pt 5.20.75 NBC
Petrocelli ep The Gamblers 11.12.75 NBC
Barnaby Jones ep Shadow of Guilt 2.5.76 CBS
Mallory: Circumstantial Evidence tf/pt 2.8.76 NBC
The Streets of San Francisco ep Superstar 3.4.76 ABC
The Streets of San Francisco ep Alien Country 3.11.76 ABC
Columbo ep A Matter of Honor 2.1.76 NBC
The Nancy Drew Mysteries ep The Mystery of the Fallen Angel 4.17.77 ABC
Exo-Man tf/pt 6.18.77 NBC
All in the Family ep Archie's Bitter Pill Fall 1977 CBS
Baretta ep Por Nada 11.23.77 ABC
Police Woman ep The Buttercup Killer 12.13.77 NBC
What Really Happened to the Class of '65 ep The Class Hustler 12.15.77 NBC
Barnaby Jones ep Deadly Homecoming 12.22.77 CBS
Centennial sr 10.1.78 NBC
Quincy, M.E. ep Walk Softly Through the Night 2.1.79 NBC
The Incredible Hulk ep Kindred Spirits 4.6.79 CBS
B. J. and the Bear ep The Murphy Connection 4.17.79 NBC
Barnaby Jones ep Cry for Vengeance 12.27.79 CBS
Quincy, M.E. ep No Way to Treat a Patient 4.30.80 NBC
Roughnecks ms 7.15, 7.16.80 NN
The White Shadow ep 3.2.81 CBS
Fantasy Island ep Paquito's Birthday 5.23.81 ABC
American Playhouse ep Sequin 1.26.82 PBS

Cassie and Company sr 1.29.82 NBC
Falcon Crest ep Victims 2.5.82 CBS
Born to the Wind sr 8.19.82 NBC
Hart to Hart ep Straight Through the Hart 10.4.83 ABC
The Whiz Kids sr (with ep Fatal Error) 10.12.83 CBS
Remington Steele ep High Flying Steele 1.17.84 NBC
The Yellow Rose ep Chains of Fear 3.24.84 NBC
Santa Barbara sr 7.30.84 NBC

MARVIN, LEE
A&C, B.V.:
Route 66 ep Sheba 1.6.61 CBS
The Barbara Stanwyck Theater ep Confession 2.20.61 NBC
SUPP.:
The Dirty Dozen: The Next Mission tf/pt 2.4.85 NBC

MARX, GROUCHO
A&C, B.V.:
I Dream of Jeannie ep Greatest Invention in the World 1.67 NBC

MASAK, RON
A&C, Supp. 1:
The Flying Nun ep Where There's a Will Fall 1968 ABC
Bewitched ep Samantha's Power Failure Spring 1969 ABC
Police Story ep Little Boy Lost 11.28.73 NBC
A&C, Supp. 2:
The Rockford Files ep Forced Retirement 12.9.77 NBC
The Eddie Capra Mysteries ep The Two Million Dollar Stowaway 12.8.78 NBC
SUPP.:
World War III tf 1.31, 2.1.82 NBC
The Neighborhood tf 4.25.82 NBC
Goodnight Beantown ep 1.8.84 CBS
Masquerade ep Sleeper 4.13.84 ABC
E/R ep 11.21.84 CBS
Diff'rent Strokes ep Sam's New Pal 2.2.85 NBC
Murder, She Wrote ep Footnote to Murder 3.10.85 CBS
Remington Steele ep Forged Steele 11.12.85 NBC

MASON, JAMES
SUPP.:
Ivanhoe tf 2.25.82 CBS
George Washington ms 4.8,4.10,4.11.84 CBS
A.D. ms 3.31-4.4.85 NBC

MASON, MARLYN
A&C, Supp. 2:
The Lieutenant ep Instant Wedding 11.9.63 NBC
The Eleventh Hour ep To Love Is to Live 4.15.64 NBC
Burke's Law ep Who Killed Jason Shaw? 1.3.64 ABC
Destry ep The Infernal Triangle (a.k.a. The Infernal Machine)

5.1.64 ABC
The Rogues ep The Project Man 11.1.64 NBC
Ben Casey ep Run for Your Lives, Dr. Golanos Practices Here 10.4.65 ABC
Ben Casey ep Francini? Who Is Francini? 10.25.65 ABC
Gomer Pyle ep A Groom for Sgt. Carter's Sister 12.65 CBS
Perry Mason ep The Case of the Final Fadeout 5.22.66 CBS
The FBI ep The Escape 10.2.66 ABC
Twelve O'Clock High ep Fighter Pilot 11.11.66 ABC
The Fugitive ep Goodbye, My Love 2.28.67 ABC
Captain Nice ep May I Have the Last Dance Spring 1967 NBC
Hey, Landlord! ep Same Time, Same Station, Same Girl 1.67 NBC
Bracken's World ep The Chase Sequence 12.26.69 NBC
Ghost Story ep Elegy for a Vampire 12.1.72 NBC
Caribe ep The Mercenary 3.10.75 ABC
SUPP.:
Boone ep The Front Line 8.4.84 NBC
Scarecrow and Mrs. King ep Ship of Spies 1.7.85 CBS

MASON, PAMELA
SUPP.:
My Wicked, Wicked Ways.... The Legend of Errol Flynn tf 1.21.85 CBS

MASSEY, RAYMOND
A&C, B.V.:
The Girl from UNCLE ep The Faustus Affair 12.27.66 NBC

MATHERS, JERRY
SUPP.:
Still the Beaver tf/pt 3.19.83 CBS
Still the Beaver sr Fall 1984 DIS

MATHIAS, DARIAN*
Please Stand By sr 9.78 NN
Love, Natalie pt 7.11.80 NBC
The Facts of Life ep The Source 10.6.81 NBC
Open All Night ep First Love 1.2.82 ABC
Joanie Loves Chachi ep No Nudes Is Good Nudes 10.28.83 ABC
One Day at a Time ep Another Man's Shoes 5.28.84 CBS
My Wicked, Wicked Ways.... The Legend of Errol Flynn tf 1.21.85 CBS

MATHIS, JOHNNY*
Oh Madeline ep Chances Are 11.29.83 ABC
Ryan's Hope ep Week of July 1, 1985 ABC

MATTSON, ROBIN*
The Secret Night Caller tf 2.18.75 NBC
The Hardy Boys Mysteries ep The Strange Fate of Flight 608

11.6.77 ABC
Superdome tf 1.9.78 ABC
What Really Happened to the Class of '65 ep The Class Clown 1.26.78 NBC
Doctors' Private Lives sr 3.20.78 ABC
Operation Runaway ep Melinda and the Pinball Wizard 5.4.78 NBC
Are You in the House Alone? tf 9.20.78 CBS
The Incredible Hulk ep Ricky 10.6.78 CBS
Barnaby Jones ep Hitchhike to Terror 10.19.78 CBS
Sword of Justice ep The Girl on the Edge 10.28.78 NBC
Captain America tf/pt 1.19.79 CBS
Hot Rod tf 5.25.79 ABC
Mirror, Mirror tf 10.10.79 NBC
Charlie's Angels ep Of Ghosts and Angels 1.20.80 ABC
Battles: The Murder That Wouldn't Die tf/pt 3.9.80 NBC
The Dukes of Hazzard ep Carnival of Thrills 9.16.80 CBS
Fantasies tf 1.18.82 ABC
Fantasy Island ep Awakening of Love 3.17.84 ABC
Ryans Hope sr Winter-Spring 1985 ABC

MATUSZAK, JOHN*
The Dukes of Hazzard ep 10.19.84 CBS
The Fall Guy ep Catastrophe 1.2.85 ABC
Stir Crazy ep Stir Crazy (pt) 9.18.85 CBS
Hollywood Beat sr 9.21.85 ABC

MAXWELL, MARILYN
A&C, B.V.:
Wagon Train ep The Pearlie Garnet Story 2.24.64 ABC
Branded ep Price of a Name 5.23.65 NBC

MAYO, VIRGINIA
SUPP.:
Murder, She Wrote ep Hooray for Homicide 10.28.84 CBS
Remington Steele ep Cast in Steele 12.4.84 NBC

MEADOWS, AUDREY
SUPP.:
Too Close for Comfort ep My Unfavorite Uncle 2.23.82 ABC
The Close for Comfort sr 10.14.82 ABC
The Love Boat ep Novelties 3.17.84 ABC
Hotel ep Pathways 10.30.85 ABC

MEADOWS, JAYNE
SUPP.:
Miss All-American Beauty tf 12.29.82 CBS
Matt Houston ep The Beverly Woods Social Club 3.13.83 ABC
Fantasy Island ep What's the Matter with Kids? 4.16.83 ABC
It's Not Easy sr 9.29.83 ABC
Hotel ep Detours 11.7.84
Alice in Wonderland tf 12.9, 12.10.85 CBS

MEADOWS, KRISTEN*
The Fall Guy ep The Molly Sue 3.2.83 ABC
The A-Team ep Diamonds 'n Dust 9.20.83 NBC
Lottery ep New York City: Winning Can Be Murder ("I Do, I Don't" segment) 11.18.83 ABC
T. J. Hooker ep A Matter of Passion 11.26.83 ABC
Riptide ep Conflict of Interest 1.10.84 NBC
Automan ep The Biggest Game in Town 1.26.84 ABC
Sins of the Past tf 4.2.84 ABC
Glitter sr 9.13.84 ABC
The Fall Guy ep Losers Weepers 9.19.84 ABC
Simon and Simon ep Simon Without Simon 1.24, 1.31.85 CBS
Street Hawk ep Fire on the Wing 2.8.85 ABC
Double Dare ep 5.1.85 CBS
The A-Team ep Incident at Crystal Lake 5.14.85 NBC

MEARA, ANNE
SUPP.:
The Other Woman tf 3.22.83 CBS
The Love Boat ep We, the Jury 4.2.83 ABC

MEDINA, PATRICIA
A&C, B.V.:
Branded ep Yellow for Courage 2.20.66 NBC

MEEKER, RALPH
A&C, B.V.:
Wanted: Dead Or Alive ep Reunion for Revenge 1.24.59 CBS
Suspense ep I, Lloyd Denson 5.27.64 CBS
The High Chaparral ep The Pride of Revenge 11.19.67 NBC
A&C, Supp. 1:
Toma ep The Friends of Danny Beecher 3.29.74 ABC
Harry O ep Exercise in Fatality 12.4.75 ABC
A&C, Supp. 2:
The Eddie Capra Mysteries ep Murder Plays a Dead Hand 12.22.78 NBC

MENZIES, HEATHER
A&C, Supp. 2:
The Farmer's Daughter ep Like Father, Like Son 12.64 ABC
The High Chaparral ep The Little Thieves 12.26.69 NBC
Alias Smith and Jones ep The Girl in Box Car #3 2.11.71 ABC
SUPP.:
Gavilan ep Pirates 11.9.82 NBC
T. J. Hooker ep A Kind of Rage 12.1.84 ABC

MERCER, MARIAN
SUPP.:
9 to 5 ep The Loveware Party 9.28.82 ABC
Life of the Party: The Story of Beatrice tf 9.29.82 CBS
Foot in the Door sr 3.28.83 CBS

Ace Crawford, Private Eye ep 4.12.83 CBS
St. Elsewhere ep Lust et Veritas 11.2.83 NBC
St. Elsewhere ep Newheart 11.9.83 NBC
St. Elsewhere ep Qui Transtulit Sustinet 11.16.83 NBC
St. Elsewhere ep All About Eve 12.14.83 NBC
The Love Boat ep Mother Comes First 2.25.84 ABC
Benson ep Made in Hong Kong 11.2, 11.9.84 ABC
It's a Living sr ret 9.29.85 NN

MEREDITH, BURGESS
SUPP.:
Archie Bunker's Place ep Gloria Comes Home 2.28.82 CBS
Puff and the Incredible Mr. Nobody sp vo 5.17.82 CBS
Gloria sr 10.3.82 CBS
Faerie Tale Theater ep Thumbelina 6.11.84 SHO
Glitter ep The Tribute 10.11.84 ABC
Wet Gold tf 10.28.84 ABC

MERIWETHER, LEE
A&C, Supp. 2:
Bringing Up Buddy ep Buddy in the Amazon 4.61 CBS
Dr. Kildare ep Vote of Confidence 12.26.63 NBC
The Bob Hope Chrysler Theater ep Double Jeopardy 1.8.65 NBC
The Jack Benny Program ep 1.8.65 CBS
Hazel ep How to Lose Thirty Pounds in Thirty Minutes 9.27.65 CBS
Perry Mason ep The Case of the Cheating Chancellor 10.3.65 CBS
Twelve O'Clock High ep The Idolater 10.4.65 ABC
F Troop ep O'Rourke vs. O'Reilly 11.65 ABC
Twelve O'Clock High ep The Outsider 1.31.66 ABC
The Fugitive ep Not with a Whimper 1.4.66 ABC
Batman ep King Tut's Coup 3.8.67, 3.9.67 ABC
Family Affair ep First Love 9.67 CBS
Kojak ep Nursemaid 10.20.74 CBS
SUPP.:
The Love Boat ep The Captain's Portrait 1.9.82 ABC
Fantasy Island ep The Butler's Affair 11.12.83 ABC
The Love Boat ep Father in the Cradle 1.28.84 ABC
Finder of Lost Loves ep Portraits 12.1.84 ABC
Hotel ep 12.25.85 ABC
Glitter ep The Rivals 12.26.85 ABC

MERMAN, ETHEL
SUPP.:
The Love Boat ep The Musical 2.27.82 ABC

MERRILL, DINA
A&C, Supp. 1:
Switch ep Kiss of Death 11.25.75 CBS

Hawaii Five-O ep Nine Dragons 9.30.76 CBS
SUPP.:
Hotel ep The Wedding 2.22.84 ABC
Hot Pursuit sr 9.22.84 NBC

METRANO, ART
SUPP.:
Masquerade ep Winnings 4.6.84 ABC
Punky Brewster ep Take Me to the Ballgame 10.21.84 NBC
The A-Team ep Uncle Buckle-Up 12.17.85 NBC

METTEY, LYNNETTE
SUPP.:
Simon and Simon ep Double Entry 3.2.82 CBS
Simon and Simon ep Matchmakers 3.9.82 CBS
Terror at Alcatraz tf/pt 7.24.82 NBC
Simon and Simon ep The List 2.17.83 CBS
Silence of the Heart tf 10.30.84 CBS
Simon and Simon ep Our Fair City 11.29.84 CBS
Trapper John, M.D. ep 2.24.85 CBS

MEYERS, ARI*
Running Out tf 1.26.83 CBS
License to Kill tf 1.10.84 CBS
Kate and Allie sr 3.19.84 CBS
Kate and Allie sr ret 10.8.84 CBS
Kids Don't Tell tf 3.5.85 CBS
Kate and Allie sr ret 9.30.85 CBS
Picking Up the Pieces tf 10.22.85 CBS

MICHAELSEN, KARI
SUPP.:
Gimme a Break sr ret 10.2.82 NBC
Fantasy Island ep The Perfect Gentleman 10.30.82 ABC
The Kid with the 200 I.Q. tf 2.6.83 NBC
The ABC Afterschool Special ep Have You Ever Been Ashamed of Your Parents? 3.16.83 ABC
Gimme a Break sr ret 9.29.83 NBC
Hart to Hart ep Twist Your Hart 12.20.83 ABC
Gimme a Break sr ret 9.29.84 NBC
Gimme a Break sr ret 9.14.85 NBC

MICHAELSEN, MELISSA
SUPP.:
Code Red ep Wildfire 1.10.82 ABC

MILANO, ALYSSA*
Who's the Boss? sr 9.20.84 ABC
Who's the Boss? sr ret 9.24.85 ABC

MILES, VERA

SUPP.:

The Love Boat ep The Girl Who Stood Still 2.13.82 ABC
Rona Jaffe's "Mazes and Monsters" tf 12.28.82 CBS
Little House: A New Beginning ep The Last Summer 2.21.83 NBC
Trapper John, M.D. ep 3.13.83 CBS
Travis McGee tf 5.18.83 ABC
The Love Boat ep The Hustlers 10.8.83 ABC
Hotel ep The Wedding 2.22.84 ABC
Helen Keller: The Miracle Continues tf 4.23.84 OPT
Finder of Lost Loves ep Deadly Silence 10.6.84 ABC
Matt Houston ep High Fashion Murders 11.16.84 ABC
The Love Boat ep Baby Sister 12.1.84 ABC
Hotel ep New Beginnings 1.23.85 ABC
International Airport tf/pt 5.25.85 ABC
Hotel ep Imperfect Union 10.9.85 ABC
Crazy Like a Fox ep Requiem for a Fox 10.20.85 CBS
Murder, She Wrote ep Jessica Behind Bars 12.1.85 CBS

MILLAND, RAY

SUPP.:

Hart to Hart ep My Hart Belongs to Daddy 1.19.82 ABC
The Royal Romance of Charles and Diana tf 9.20.82 CBS
Starflight: The Plane That Couldn't Land tf 2.27.83 ABC
Cave-In tf 6.19.83 NBC
Hart to Hart ep Long Lost Love 11.22.83 ABC

MILLER, DENISE

SUPP.:

The Love Boat ep The Girl Who Stood Still 2.13.82 ABC
The Love Boat ep The Victims 11.27.82 ABC
Knight Rider ep Custom KITT 11.13.83 NBC
Private Sessions tf/pt 3.18.85 NBC

MILLER, DENNY (a.k.a. Scott Miller and Denny Scott Miller)

A&C, Supp. 2:

Northwest Passage ep Flight at the River 12.21.58 NBC
Have Gun--Will Travel ep Saturday Night 10.8.60 CBS
The Rebel ep Explosion 11.27.60 ABC
The Rifleman ep The Promoter 12.6.60 ABC
Hong Kong ep Night Cry 1.25.61 ABC
Wagon Train ep Weight of Command 1.25.61 NBC
The Deputy ep Brother in Arms 4.15.61 NBC
Wagon Train sr 4.26.61 NBC
Wagon Train sr ret 9.27.61 NBC
Wagon Train sr ret 9.19.62 NBC
Wagon Train sr ret 9.16.63 NBC
The Girl from UNCLE ep The Atlantis Affair 11.15.66 NBC
The Fugitive ep Approach with Care 11.15.66 ABC
Gilligan's Island ep Our Vines Have Tender Apes 1.67 CBS

I Spy ep Anyplace I Hang Myself Is Home 1.15.68 NBC
Hawaii Five-O ep Pray Love Remember, Pray Love Remember 1.1.69 CBS
The Men from Shiloh ep The Politician 1.13.71 NBC
Stone ep But Can She Type? 1.21.80 ABC
SUPP.:
Magnum, P.I. ep Three Minus Two 4.1.82 CBS
Today's FBI ep Energy Fraud 4.26.82 ABC
The Fall Guy ep Mighty Myron 11.17.82 ABC
Voyagers ep An Arrow Pointing East 12.12.82 NBC
Simon and Simon ep Design for Killing 2.10.83 CBS
Matt Houston ep A Novel Way to Die 4.17.83 ABC
V ms 5.1, 5.2.83 NBC
Shooting Stars tf/pt 7.28.83 ABC
Magnum, P.I. ep 12.1.83 CBS
Simon and Simon ep 2.10.84 CBS
Dallas ep 3.23.84, 4.6.84, 4.13.84, 5.4.84, 5.11.84 CBS
Hart to Hart ep Meanwhile, Back at the Ranch 5.22.84 ABC
Knight Rider ep The Rotten Apples 11.1.84 NBC
The Fall Guy ep Dead Bounty 11.14.84 ABC
Matt Houston ep Blood Money 11.30.84 ABC
Mickey Spillane's Mike Hammer: More Than Murder tf/pt 1.26.85 CBS
Detective in the House ep Whatever Happened to.... 3.15.85 CBS

MILLER, LARA JILL
SUPP.:
Gimme a Break sr ret 10.2.82 NBC
Gimme a Break sr ret 9.29.83 NBC
Gimme a Break sr ret 9.29.84 NBC
Gimme a Break sr ret 9.14.85 NBC

MILLS, ALLEY*
Kaz ep They've Taken Our Daughter 3.21.79 CBS
The Associates sr 9.23.79 ABC
Rape and Marriage: The Rideout Case tf 10.30.80 CBS
A Matter of Life and Death tf 1.13.81 CBS
Lou Grant ep Search 2.9.81 CBS
Hill Street Blues ep Zen and the Art of Law Enforcement 2.18.82 NBC
Hill Street Blues ep Personal Foul 3.25.82 NBC
Making the Grade sr 4.5.82 CBS
Hill Street Blues ep Invasion of the Third World Mutant Body Snatchers 5.13.82 NBC
The Other Woman tf 3.22.83 CBS
Newhart ep Sprained Dreams 11.3.83 CBS
Prototype tf 12.7.83 CBS
Poor Richard pt 1.21.84 CBS
Second Edition pt 7.17.84 CBS
The Atlanta Child Murders tf 2.10, 2.12.85 CBS

MILLS, DONNA

A&C, Supp. 1:

The Good Life sr 9.18.71 NBC

Owen Marshall, Counselor at Law ep The Triangle 12.30.71 ABC

Hawaii Five-O ep Murder--Eyes Only 9.12.75 CBS

SUPP.:

Bare Essence ms 10.4, 10.5.82 CBS

Knots Landing sr ret 10.4.82 CBS

Knots Landing sr ret 9.29.83 CBS

He's Not Your Son tf 10.3.84 CBS

Knots Landing sr ret 10.4.84 CBS

Knots Landing sr ret 9.26.85 CBS

Alice in Wonderland tf 12.9, 12.10.85 CBS

MILLS, HAYLEY

SUPP.:

The Love Boat ep The Perfect Divorce 5.4.85 ABC

MILLS, JOHN

SUPP.:

A Woman of Substance tf 11.26.84 OPT

Murder with Mirrors tf 2.20.85 CBS

Dempsey and Makepeace ep Make Peace Not War 12.14.85 NN

MILLS, JULIET

A&C, Supp. 1:

The Bob Hope Chrysler Theater ep Don't Wait for Tomorrow 4.19.67 NBC

Harry O ep Ballinger's Choice 10.31.74 ABC

Hawaii Five-O ep Terminator with Extensive Prejudice 9.26.75 CBS

A&C, Supp. 2:

Switch ep Coronado Circle 7.2.78 CBS

SUPP.:

Hart to Hart ep Downhill to Death 12.29.82 ABC

Fantasy Island ep Surrogate Mother 5.19.84 ABC

The Love Boat ep A Match Made in Heaven 10.20.84 ABC

Dynasty ep The Secret 11.21.84 ABC

Dynasty ep The Holiday Spirit 12.19.84 ABC

Hotel ep Fallen Idols 1.2.85 ABC

MILNER, MARTIN

SUPP.:

Masquerade ep Winnings 4.6.85 ABC

Airwolf ep Severance Pay 3.23.85 CBS

Murder, She Wrote ep Reflections in the Mind 11.3.85 CBS

MIMIEUX, YVETTE

SUPP.:

Forbidden Love tf 10.18.82 CBS

Night Partners tf/pt 10.11.83 CBS
The Love Boat ep The Hong Kong Affair 2.4.84 ABC
Obsessive Love tf 10.2.84 CBS
Lime Street ep Old Pilots Never Die 10.19.85 ABC

MINEO, SAL
A&C, B.V.:
The DuPont Show of the Week ep A Sound of Hunting 5.20.62 NBC
The Kraft Suspense Theater ep The World I Want 10.1.64 NBC
Combat ep The Hard Way Back 10.20.64 NBC
Hawaii Five-O ep Tiger By the Tail 10.10.72 CBS
A&C, Supp. 1:
Griff ep Marked for Murder 10.27.73 ABC
Hawaii Five-O ep Hit Gun for Sale 2.25.75 CBS
Harry O ep Elegy for a Cop 2.27.75 ABC

MINNELLI, LIZA*
The Dangerous Christmas of Red Riding Hood sp 11.28.65 ABC
Are You Now or Have You Ever Been? sp 8.80 SHO
Faerie Tale Theater ep The Princess and the Pea 4.16.84 SHO
A Time to Live tf 10.28.85 NBC

MR. T (a.k.a. Lawrence Tero)*
Silver Spoons ep Me and Mr. T 10.2.82 NBC
The A-Team sr 1.23.83 NBC
Mr. T sr vo 9.17.83 NBC
The A-Team sr ret 9.20.83 NBC
Diff'rent Strokes ep Mr. T and mr. t 10.1.83 NBC
Secret World of the Very Young sp 9.12.84 CBS
The A-Team sr ret 9.18.84 NBC
The Toughest Man in the World tf 11.7.84 CBS
The A-Team sr ret 9.24.85 NBC

MITCHELL, CAMERON
SUPP.:
Matt Houston ep The Good Doctor 12.12.82 ABC
Seven Brides for Seven Brothers ep 12.15.82 CBS
Kenny Rogers as the Gambler: The Adventure Continues tf 1.28, 1.29.83 CBS
Knight Rider ep Diamonds Aren't a Girl's Best Friend 1.15.84 NBC
Empire ep 2.1.84 CBS
Hardcastle and McCormick ep The Homecoming 3.4, 3.11.84 ABC
Partners in Crime ep Duke 10.20.84 NBC
The Fall Guy ep Private Eyes 10.24.84 ABC
Murder, She Wrote ep Murder to a Jazz Beat 2.3.85 CBS

MITCHUM, CHRISTOPHER*
Flight to Holocaust tf 3.27.77 NBC
A Rumor of War tf 9.24, 9.25.80 CBS

Magnum, P.I. ep 2.23.84 CBS
Promises to Keep tf 10.15.85 CBS

MITCHUM, ROBERT
SUPP.:
One Shoe Makes It Murder tf 11.6.82 CBS
The Winds of War ms 2.6-2.13.83 ABC
A Killer in the Family tf 10.30.83 ABC
The Hearst-Davies Affair tf 1.14.85 ABC
Reunion at Fairborough tf 5.12.85 HBO
Promises to Keep tf 10.15.85 CBS
North and South ms 11.3-11.10.85 ABC

MOBLEY, MARY ANN
A&C, Supp. 2:
Perry Mason ep The Case of the Blonde Bonanza 12.17.64 CBS
The Smothers Brothers Show ep The Ghost Is Clear 2.18.66 CBS
The Sixth Sense ep Shadow in the Wall 4.15.72 ABC
The Sixth Sense ep Five Women Weeping 12.9.72 ABC
SUPP.:
Fantasy Island ep Nancy and the Thunderbirds 5.1.82 ABC
Matt Houston ep The Yacht Club Murders 1.16.83 ABC
Fantasy Island ep Ambitious Lady 1.7.84 ABC
Hotel ep Ideals 12.12.84 ABC
The Love Boat ep The Odd Triple 1.12.85 ABC
Diff'rent Strokes sr 9.27.85 ABC

MODEAN, JAYNE*
Me and Ducky pt 6.21.79 NBC
Trauma Center sr 9.22.83 ABC
The Fall Guy ep Notes About Courage (a.k.a. Trauma) 9.28.83 ABC
Street Hawk ep Street Hawk (pt) 1.4.85 ABC

MOFFAT, DONALD*
Hawaii Five-O ep And a Time to Die 9.16.70 CBS
Mission: Impossible ep 10.9.71 CBS
Bonanza ep Face of Fear 11.14.71 NBC
Night Gallery ep Pickman's Model 12.1.71 NBC
The Devil and Miss Sarah tf 12.4.71 ABC
Ironside ep Shadow Soldiers 12.21.72 NBC
Mannix ep All the Dead Were Strangers 12.16.73 CBS
The Snoop Sisters ep Corpse and Robbers 12.19.73 NBC
Gunsmoke ep The Foundling 2.11.74 CBS
Ironside ep Close to the Heart 2.28.74 NBC
The New Land sr 9.14.74 ABC
The Six Million Dollar Man ep The Bionic Criminal 11.9.75 ABC
The Call of the Wild tf 5.22.76 NBC
The Waltons ep John's Crossroads 1.20.77 CBS
Code R ep 2.11.77 CBS

Family ep 3.8.77 ABC
Eleanor and Franklin: The White House Years tf 3.13.77 ABC
Exo-Man tf/pt 6.18.77 NBC
Logan's Run sr 9.16.77 CBS
The Last Hurrah tf 11.16.77 NBC
The Fitzpatricks ep The Sacrament 11.29.77 CBS
Mary White tf 11.18.77 ABC
Theater in America ep Tartuffe 5.31.78 PBS
Sergeant Matlovich vs. the U.S. Air Force tf 8.21.78 NBC
The Word ms 11.12-11.15.78 CBS
The Gift of Love tf 12.8.78 ABC
Family ep 1.4.79 ABC
Strangers: The Story of a Mother and Daughter tf 5.13.79 CBS
Ebony, Ivory and Jade tf/pt 8.3.79 CBS
Mrs. R's Daughter tf 9.19.79 NBC
The Chisholms sr 2.2.80 CBS
The Long Days of Summer tf/pt 5.23.80 ABC
Jacqueline Bouvier Kennedy tf 10.14.81 ABC
Dallas ep 12.31.82 CBS
Dallas ep 1.4.83 CBS
Who Will Love My Children? tf 2.14.83 ABC
Through Naked Eyes tf 12.11.83 ABC
License to Kill tf 1.10.84 CBS
Murder, She Wrote ep Murder at 50 Mile 4.21.85 CBS

MOFFAT, KITTY*
The A-Team ep The Rabbit Who Ate Las Vegas 3.1.83 NBC
Boone sr 9.26.83 NBC
Fantasy Island ep Random Choices 12.3.83 ABC
Hawaiian Heat ep Ice Cream Man 9.21.84 ABC
Knight Rider ep Knight in Disgrace 11.18.84 NBC
The Dukes of Hazzard ep 1.11.85 CBS
The Love Boat ep Don't Call Me Gopher 1.26.85 ABC
International Airport tf/pt 5.25.85 ABC
Simon and Simon ep The Skull of Nostradamus 10.31.85 CBS
Glitter ep Illusions 12.25.85 ABC

MOLL, RICHARD*
How the West Was Won ep The Enemy 2.5.79 ABC
The Jericho Mile tf 3.18.79 ABC
The Archer--Fugitive from the Empire tf/pt 4.12.81 NBC
Best of the West ep The Prisoner 9.17.81 ABC
Code Red ep Dark Fire 11.15.81 ABC
Laverne and Shirley ep The Defiant One 11.17.81 ABC
T. J. Hooker ep Hooker's War 4.3.82 ABC
Here's Boomer ep Camitville Boomer 6.3.82 NBC
9 to 5 ep Movin' On 3.22.83 ABC
The Dukes of Hazzard ep 3.25.83 CBS
Alice ep 6.19.83 CBS
Just Our Luck ep Uncle Harry 10.25.83 ABC

The Dukes of Hazzard ep 11.4.83 CBS
Night Court sr 1.4.84 NBC
The Dukes of Hazzard ep 5.11.84 CBS
Night Court sr ret 9.27.84 NBC
Night Court sr ret 9.26.85 NBC

MONTALBAN, RICARDO
A&C, B.V.:
Cain's Hundred ep A Creature Lurks in Ambush 4.17.62 ABC
Daniel Boone ep The Symbol 12.29.66 NBC
SUPP.:
Fantasy Island sr ret 10.16.82 ABC
Fantasy Island sr ret 10.8.83 ABC
An American Portrait ep Gabriel Navarete 4.10.85 CBS
Dynasty II: The Colbys sr 11.20.85 ABC

MONTGOMERY, BELINDA J.
A&C, Supp. 2:
Medical Center ep Twenty-Four Hours 12.17.69 CBS
Matt Lincoln ep Nina 10.8.70 ABC
SUPP.:
Simon and Simon ep Ashes to Ashes and None Too Soon 1.19.82 CBS
Dynasty ep The Baby 3.3.82 ABC
Dynasty ep Mother and Son 3.17.82 ABC
CHiPs ep Trained for Trouble 4.4.82 NBC
Bare Essence ms 10.4, 10.5.82 CBS
Uncommon Valor tf 1.22.83 CBS
Simon and Simon ep 10.20.83 CBS
T. J. Hooker ep Walk a Straight Line 11.5.83 ABC
The Whiz Kids ep Watch Out 1.14.84 CBS
Blue Thunder ep Payload 3.9.84 ABC
Lottery ep Miami: Sharing 3.15.84 ABC
Miami Vice ep Miami Vice (pt) 9.16.84 NBC
Simon and Simon ep 10.11.84 CBS
Miami Vice ep Hit List 10.12.84 NBC
Magnum, P.I. ep 10.18.84 CBS
Simon and Simon ep Manna from Heaven 10.25.84 CBS
Miami Vice ep Calderone's Demise 10.26.84 NBC
T. J. Hooker ep The Surrogate 1.12.85 ABC
Murder, She Wrote ep My Johnnie Lies Over the Ocean 2.10.85 CBS
Crazy Like a Fox ep Wanted Dead or Alive 2.17.85 CBS
Riptide ep Girls Night Out 2.19.85 NBC
Hitchhiker ep Man at the Window 3.3.85 HBO
Street Hawk ep Murder Is a Novel Idea 3.8.85 ABC
The Love Boat ep The Iron Man 11.23.85 ABC

MONTGOMERY, ELIZABETH
SUPP.:
The Rules of Marriage tf 5.10, 5.11.82 CBS

Missing Pieces tf 5.14.83 CBS
Second Sight: A Love Story tf 3.13.84 CBS
Amos tf 9.29.85 CBS
Between the Darkness and the Dawn tf 12.23.85 NBC

MOODY, LYNNE*
S.W.A.T. ep Any Second Now 3.13.76 ABC
Nightmare in Badham County tf 11.5.76 ABC
Roots ms 1.23-1.30.77 ABC
Quincy, M.E. ep A Blow to the Heart 9.23.77 NBC
Charleston tf 1.15.79 NBC
Roots: The Next Generation ms 2.18-2.25.79 ABC
Tenspeed and Brown Shoe ep The 16 Byte Data Chip and the Brown-Eyed Fox 3.9.80 ABC
Lou Grant ep 1.12.81 CBS
A Matter of Life and Death tf 1.13.81 CBS
The Oklahoma City Dolls tf 1.23.81 ABC
Goldie and the Boxer Go to Hollywood tf 2.19.81 NBC
The White Shadow ep 3.9.81 CBS
Fly Away Home tf/pt 9.18.81 ABC
Strike Force ep Victims 10.27.81 ABC
Lou Grant ep Risk 11.30.81 CBS
Trapper John, M.D. ep Tis the Season 12.20.81 CBS
The Jeffersons ep A Small Victory 1.31.82 CBS
T. J. Hooker ep (pt ep) 3.13.82 ABC
The Love Boat ep Pal-I-Mony-O-Mine 4.10.82 ABC
Magnum, P.I. ep Black on White 10.28.82 CBS
Hill Street Blues ep Requiem for a Hairbag 11.18.82 NBC
Hill Street Blues ep A Hair of the Dog 11.25.82 NBC
Hill Street Blues ep The Phantom of the Hill 12.2.82 NBC
Wait Till Your Mother Gets Home! tf 1.17.83 NBC
Benson ep Love in a Funny Phase 3.31.83 ABC
Now We're Cookin' pt 4.19.83 CBS
Agatha Christie's "A Caribbean Mystery" tf 10.22.83 CBS
Just Our Luck ep Wedding Bells Shablues 12.6.83 ABC
Hill Street Blues ep Ratman and Bobbin 1.12.84 NBC
T. J. Hooker ep Death on the Line 3.3.84 ABC
E/R sr 9.16.84 CBS
The Toughest Man in the World tf 11.7.84 CBS
The Atlanta Child Murders tf 2.10.85 CBS
Lost in London tf 11.20.85 CBS
Hollywood Beat ep Across the Line 11.26.85 ABC

MOODY, RON
SUPP.:
Hart to Hart ep Two Harts Are Better Than One 9.27.83 ABC
Highway to Heaven ep Divine Madness 11.7.84 ABC
Murder, She Wrote ep Paint Me a Murder 2.17.85 CBS

MOORE, MARY TYLER
A&C, B.V.:
Bachelor Father ep Bentley and the Big Board Fall 1960 NBC

Wanted: Dead Or Alive ep The Twain Shall Meet 10.19.60 CBS
Thriller ep The Fatal Impulse 11.29.60 NBC
The Aquanauts ep 1.25.61 CBS
Straightaway ep Sounds of Fury 2.7.62 ABC
Thriller ep Men of Mystery 4.2.62 NBC
SUPP.:
Heart Sounds tf 9.30.84 ABC
Finnegan Begin Again tf 2.24.85 HBO
Mary sr 12.11.85 CBS

MOORE, MELBA*
Flamingo Road tf/pt 5.12.80 NBC
Ellis Island ms 11.11-11.14.84 CBS
American Playhouse ep Charlotte Forten's Mission 2.25.85 PBS

MOORE, TERRY
SUPP.:
Matt Houston ep A Novel Way to Die 4.17.83 ABC
Knight Rider ep KITT the Cat 11.6.83 NBC
Fantasy Island ep The Butler's Affair 11.12.83 ABC
The Love Boat ep A Matter of Taste 12.8.84 ABC

MORAN, ERIN
A&C, Supp. 1:
Death Valley Days ep The Tenderfoot 1969 NN
Death Valley Days ep Billy the Kid 1969 NN
Family Affair ep There Goes New York 2.71 CBS
Gunsmoke ep Lijah 11.8.71 CBS
Gunsmoke ep P.S. Murry Christmas 12.27.71 CBS
SUPP.:
Joanie Loves Chachi sr 3.23.82 ABC
Happy Days ep Letting Go 10.12.82 ABC
Joanie Loves Chachi sr ret 10.28.82 ABC
Happy Days ep Who Gives a Hootenanny 11.16.82 ABC
Happy Days ep There's No Business Like No Business 12.7.82 ABC
Happy Days ep Life Is More Important Than Show Business 1.25.83 ABC
Happy Days ep Baby Sitting 3.1.83 ABC
Happy Days ep Turn Around and You're Home 3.15.83 ABC
Happy Days ret to sr (with ep Because It's There) 9.27.83 ABC
The Love Boat ep My Two Dumplings 10.1.83 ABC
Glitter ep The Paternity Suit 9.27.84 ABC
The Love Boat ep The Counterfeit Couple 1.12.85 ABC
The Love Boat ep Forties Fantasy 11.16.85 ABC
The New Love, American Style ep Love and New Year's Eve 12.27.85 ABC

MORENO, RITA
SUPP.:
The CBS Library ep Orphans, Waifs and Wards 11.26.81 CBS

Working sp 12.81 SHO
9 to 5 sr 3.25.82 ABC
Portrait of a Showgirl tf 5.4.82 CBS
9 to 5 sr ret 9.29.83 ABC
The Love Boat ep The Lottery Winners 11.5.83 ABC

MORGAN, HARRY
SUPP.:
M*A*S*H sr ret 10.25.82 CBS
AfterMASH sr 9.26.83 CBS
Agatha Christie's "Sparkling Cyanide" tf 11.5.83 CBS
AfterMASH sr ret 9.25.84 CBS
The Love Boat ep The Racer's Edge 11.2.85 ABC

MORIARTY, MICHAEL*
A Summer Without Boys tf 12.4.73 ABC
The Glass Menagerie tf 12.16.73 ABC
The Deadliest Season tf 3.16.77 CBS
Holocaust ms 4.16-19.78 NBC
The Winds of Kitty Hawk tf 12.17.78 NBC
NBC Theater ep Too Far to Go 3.12.79 NBC
The Sound of Murder sp 7.82 SHO

MORITA, PAT (a.k.a. Noriyuki "Pat" Morita)
A&C, Supp. 1:
The Bill Cosby Show ep Power of the Trees 2.28.71 NBC
Hawaii Five-O ep Tricks Are Not Treats 10.23.73 CBS
SUPP.:
Lou Grant ep Recovery 3.8.82 CBS
Happy Days ep Empty Nest 10.19.82 ABC
Happy Days ep A Little Case of Revenge 11.9.82 ABC
Happy Days ep Who Gives a Hootenanny 11.16.82 ABC
Happy Days ep Such a Nice Girl 11.30.82 ABC
Happy Days ep There's No Business Like No Business 12.7.82 ABC
Happy Days ep All I Want for Christmas 12.14.82 ABC
Happy Days ep I Am Not at Liberty 2.8.83 ABC
Happy Days ep Turn Around ... And You're Home 3.15.83 ABC
Happy Days ep Because It's There 9.27.83 ABC
The Vegas Strip War tf 11.25.84 NBC
Blind Alleys sp 9.4.85 MM
Amos tf 9.29.85 CBS
Alice in Wonderland tf 12.9, 12.10.85 CBS

MORLEY, ROBERT
SUPP.:
Deadly Game sp 7.23.82 HBO
Alice in Wonderland tf 12.9, 12.10.85 CBS

MORRIS, GARRETT*
The ABC Weekend Special ep The Seven Wishes of Joanna Peabody 9.9.78 ABC
Diff'rent Strokes ep Santa's Helper 12.18.82 NBC
At Your Service pt 8.1.84 NBC
Hill Street Blues ep Davenport in a Storm 1.31.85 NBC
It's Your Move sr (with ep Eli's Song) 2.2.85 NBC
Murder, She Wrote ep Murder to a Jazz Beat 2.3.85 CBS
The Twilight Zone ep Dealer's Choice 11.15.85 CBS
Scarecrow and Mrs. King ep The Wrong Way Home 12.2.85 CBS

MORRIS, GREG
A&C, B.V.:
Alfred Hitchcock Presents ep Forecast: Low Clouds and Coastal Fog 1.18.63 CBS
Channing ep A Patron Saint for the Cargo Cult 11.13.63 ABC
A&C, Supp. 2:
The Eddie Capra Mysteries ep The Intimate Friends of Jenny Wilde 11.10.78 NBC
SUPP.:
The Fall Guy ep P.S. I Love You 3.16.83 ABC
The Jeffersons ep 10.2, 10.3, 10.9.83 CBS
T. J. Hooker ep Exercise in Murder 1.28.84 ABC
The Jesse Owens Story tf 7.9, 7.16.84 NN
Murder, She Wrote ep Lovers and Other Killers 11.18.84 CBS
George Burns Comedy Week ep Home for Dinner 9.25.85 CBS

MORRIS, WAYNE
A&C, B.V.:
Lawman ep The Master 12.28.58 ABC
Wanted: Dead Or Alive ep Secret Ballot 2.14.59 CBS

MORROW, VIC
A&C, Supp. 2:
Alfred Hitchcock Presents ep A Little Sleep 6.16.57 CBS
The Rifleman ep The Angry Gun 12.23.58 ABC
Naked City ep The Shield 2.3.59 ABC
The Lawless Years ep The Nick Joseph Story 4.16.59 NBC
The Line-Up ep My Son Is a Stranger 10.14.59 CBS
Wichita Town ep They Won't Hang Jimmy Relson 10.12.59 NBC
The Rifleman ep Letter of the Law 12.1.59 ABC
Johnny Ringo ep Kid with a Gun 12.24.59 CBS
The Line-Up ep Vengeful Knife 12.16.59 CBS
The Outlaws ep Ballad for a Badman 10.6.60 NBC
The Outlaws ep Beat the Drum Slowly 10.20.60 NBC
The Untouchables ep The Tommy Karpelas Story 12.29.60 ABC
The Law and Mr. Jones ep 3.24.61 ABC
The Outlaws ep The Avenger 4.13.61 NBC
The Lawless Years ep Little Augie 7.21.61 NBC
Target: The Corruptors ep Pier 60 10.6.61 ABC
The Tall Man ep Time of Foreshadowing 11.25.61 NBC

The Outlaws ep No Work on Friday 11.30.61 NBC
The Untouchables ep The Maggie Storm Show 3.29.62 ABC
Suspense ep I, Buck Larsen 4.15.64 CBS
The Alfred Hitchcock Hour ep A Little Sleep 6.16.64 NBC
The Immortal ep The Rainbow Butcher 10.22.70 ABC
Dan August ep The Union Forever 11.11.70 ABC
The FBI ep Center of Peril 1.17.71 ABC
Owen Marshall, Counselor at Law ep Eight Cents Worth of Protection 1.13.72 ABC
The Evil Touch ep Murder Is for the Birds 11.11.73 NN
SUPP.:
Fantasy Island ep The Challenge 2.13.82 ABC

MORSE, ROBERT
SUPP.:
One Day at a Time ep 11.6.83 CBS
Murder, She Wrote ep Broadway Malady 1.13.85 CBS
Day to Day Affairs sp 2.4.85 HBO
Trapper John, M.D. ep 3.17.85 CBS
The Twilight Zone ep Ye Gods 10.25.85 CBS
The New Love, American Style ep Gotta Dance 12.24.85 ABC

MOSCHITTA, JOHN (a.k.a. John Moschitta Jr.)*
Madame's Place sr 9.82 NN
Matt Houston ep Here's Another Fine Mess 3.6.83 ABC
Matt Houston ep The Showgirl Murders 3.20.83 ABC
Zorro and Son sr 4.6.83 CBS
Matt Houston ep A Novel Way to Die 4.17.83 ABC
The A-Team ep Hot Styles 12.11.84 NBC
Spencer ep Spencer Joins the Army 12.21.84 NBC

MOSES, WILLIAM R. (a.k.a. Billy Moses)*
Falcon Crest sr 12.4.81 CBS
Fantasy Island ep The Final Round 10.23.82 ABC
Falcon Crest sr ret 10.1.82 CBS
The Love Boat ep The Dean and the Flunkee 2.5.83 ABC
Falcon Crest sr ret 9.30.83 CBS
Falcon Crest sr ret 9.28.84 CBS
Finder of Lost Loves ep (pt/first ep) 9.22.84 ABC
The Love Boat ep Revenge with the Proper Stranger 11.17.84 ABC
Falcon Crest sr ret 10.4.85 CBS

MOULTRIE, EMILY*
Going Bananas sr 9.15.84 NBC
Highway to Heaven ep Catch a Falling Star 11.14.84 NBC
No Complaints pt 7.17.85 NBC
The Twilight Zone ep Shadow Man 11.29.85 CBS

MUELLERLEILE, MARIANNE*
Magnum, P.I. ep From Moscow to Maui 10.29.81 CBS

The Greatest American Hero ep Hog Wild 11.25.81 ABC
I'd Rather Be Calm pt 8.24.82 CBS
Gimme a Break ep Porko's II 11.6.82 NBC
The Jeffersons ep 12.26.82 CBS
Archie Bunker's Place ep 1.2.83 CBS
One Day at a Time ep 3.28.84 CBS
Knots Landing ep Lead Me to the Altar 1.31.85 CBS

MULDAUR, DIANA
SUPP.:
Terror at Alcatraz tf/pt 7.4.82 NBC
Hart to Hart ep Harts on the Scent 2.15.83 ABC
Too Good to Be True pt 8.5.83 ABC
Hart to Hart ep Harts on the Run 1.3.84 ABC
The Master ep Juggernaut 3.16.84 NBC
Murder, She Wrote ep Footnote to Murder 3.10.85 CBS

MULGREW, KATE
SUPP.:
Jessie ep McLaughlin's Flame 10.23.84 ABC
Ryan's Hope ret to sr Summer 1985 ABC

MULHARE, EDWARD
A&C, B.V.:
The Adventures of Robin Hood ep The Imposters 11.5.56 CBS
The Adventures of Robin Hood ep The Ransom 11.12.56 CBS
The Farmer's Daughter ep Katy and the Prince 2.64 ABC
Daniel Boone ep The Ben Franklin Encounter 3.18.65 NBC
Twelve O'Clock High ep Duel at Mont Sainte Marie 12.23.66 ABC
The Legend of Custer ep The Gauntlet 12.20.67 ABC
SUPP.:
Knight Rider sr 9.26.82 NBC
Matt Houston ep Whose Party Is This Anyway? 1.23.83 ABC
Knight Rider sr ret 10.2.83 NBC
Knight Rider sr ret 9.30.84 NBC
Knight Rider sr ret 9.20.85 NBC

MULLAVEY, GREG
SUPP.:
Hart to Hart ep My Hart Belongs to Daddy 1.19.82 ABC
This Is Kate Bennett tf/pt 5.28.82 ABC
Cagney and Lacey ep 5.2.83 CBS
The Whiz Kids ep Deadly Access 10.26.83 CBS
Magnum, P.I. ep 12.1.83 CBS
Automan ep Murder, Take One 3.19.84 ABC
Simon and Simon ep Corpus Delecti 3.22.84 CBS
Rituals sr 9.84 NN
Hardcastle and McCormick ep D-Day 10.14.84 ABC
The Fall Guy ep 9.26.85 ABC
Hill Street Blues ep Seoul on Ice 10.17.85 NBC

MULLIGAN, RICHARD*
The Hero sr 9.8.66 NBC
The Rat Patrol ep The Take Me to Your Leader Raid 3.20.67 ABC
Mannix ep Beyond the Shadow of a Dream 11.4.67 CBS
Gunsmoke ep 12.18.67 CBS
The Most Deadly Game ep Witches' Sabbath 10.17.70 ABC
The Partridge Family ep Why Did the Music Stop? 1.28.71 ABC
Bonanza ep Kingdom of Fear 4.4.71 NBC
Bonanza ep Don't Cry, My Son 10.31.71 NBC
The Hallmark Hall of Fame ep Harvey 3.22.72 NBC
Ghost Story ep House of Evil 11.10.72 NBC
Diana ep 9.10, 10.8, 10.29.73 NBC
The Partridge Family ep 11.3.73 ABC
Police Surgeon ep 1.18.74 NN
Medical Story ep The Right to Die 9.11.75 NBC
Little House on the Prairie ep Four Eyes 9.17.75 NBC
Matt Helm ep Dead Men Talk 9.20.75 ABC
Kate McShane ep Who Will Bless Thy Daughter Norah? 10.8.75 CBS
Doctors' Hospital ep The Loneliest Night 11.19.75 NBC
Little House on the Prairie ep Soldier's Return 3.24.76 NBC
Switch ep The Argonaut Special 10.12.76 CBS
Charlie's Angels ep The Killing Kind 10.13.76 ABC
Gibbsville ep Saturday Night 11.18.76 NBC
Hunter ep Mirror Image 2.25.77 CBS
Kingston: Confidential ep Triple Exposure 4.13.77 NBC
Dog and Cat ep Brother Death 4.16.77 ABC
Soap sr 9.13.77 ABC
The Love Boat ep Ex Plus Y 10.8.77 ABC
Having Babies III tf/pt 3.3.78 ABC
Soap sr ret 9.14.78 ABC
The Love Boat ep 10.14.78 ABC
Sweepstakes ep 2.2.79 NBC
Greatest Heroes of the Bible ep The Story of the Ten Commandments 5.8.79 NBC
Soap sr ret 9.13.79 ABC
Soap sr ret 10.29.80 ABC
Reggie sr 8.2.83 ABC
Malibu tf 1.23, 1.24.83 ABC
Jealousy tf 1.23.84 ABC
The Twilight Zone ep Night of the Meek 12.20.85 CBS

MURPHY, BEN
SUPP.:
Trapper John, M.D. ep Medicine Man 2.21.82 CBS
Uncommon Valor tf 1.22.83 CBS
Fantasy Island ep Operation Breakout 1.15.83 ABC
The Winds of War ms 2.6-2.13.83 ABC
The Love Boat ep The Maid Cleans Up 3.12.83 ABC
Matt Houston ep The Beverly Woods Social Club 3.13.83 ABC

The Cradle Will Fall tf 5.24.83 CBS
Lottery sr 9.3.83 ABC
The Love Boat ep Polly's Poker Palace 2.4.84 ABC
Finder of Lost Loves ep Losing Touch 10.13.84 ABC
Hotel ep Fantasies 10.17.84 ABC
The Love Boat ep The Wager 11.3.84 ABC
MacGruder and Loud ep On the Wire 2.12.85 ABC
Gidget's Summer Reunion tf/pt 6.85 NN
Scarecrow and Mrs. King ep A Lovely Little Affair 9.23.85 CBS
Murder, She Wrote ep Reflections in the Mind 11.3.85 CBS

MURRAY, DON
SUPP.:
Thursday's Child tf 2.1.83 CBS
Branagan and Mapes pt 8.1.83 CBS
Quarterback Princess tf 12.3.83 CBS
License to Kill tf 1.10.84 CBS
A Touch of Scandal tf 11.27.84 CBS

MUSANTE, TONY
SUPP.:
Review Mirror tf 11.26.84 NBC
MacGruder and Loud ep MacGruder and Loud (pt) 1.20.85 ABC

- N -

NATWICK, MILDRED
SUPP.:
Maid in America tf 9.22.82 CBS
Hardcastle and McCormick ep Hardcastle, Hardcastle, Hardcastle and McCormick 2.4.85 ABC

NAUD, MELINDA
SUPP.:
The Dukes of Hazzard ep The Law and Jesse Duke 3.26.82 CBS
A Day for Thanks on Waltons Mountain tf 11.22.82 NBC
Happy Days ep Going Steady 11.23.82 ABC
The Cracker Brothers pt 9.14.84 NBC

NAVIN JR, JOHN P.*
The Facts of Life ep The Academy 3.31.82 NBC
Cheers ep Give Me a Ring Sometime 9.30.82 NBC
The Facts of Life ep Academy II 12.8.82 NBC
Silver Spoons ep Twelve Angry Kids 1.15.83 NBC
Jennifer Slept Here sr 10.21.83 NBC
Double Trouble ep Bad Chemistry 4.25.84 NBC
The Toughest Man in the World tf 11.7.84 CBS

NEAL, PATRICIA
SUPP.:
Glitter ep Glitter (pt) 9.13.84 ABC
Shattered Vows tf 10.29.84 NBC

NELKIN, STACEY*
The Paper Chase ep The Man Who Would Be King 9.26.78 CBS
The Waltons ep The Calling 9.28.78 CBS
Like Mom, Like Me tf 10.22.78 CBS
The Chisholms ms 3.29-4.19.79 CBS
The Last Convertible ms 9.24-9.26.79 NBC
Children of Divorce tf 11.24.80 NBC
Trapper John, M.D. ep A Family Affair 2.22.81 CBS
The Adventures of Pollyana pt 4.10.82 CBS
Sunset Limousine tf 10.12.83 CBS
The Jerk, Too tf/pt 1.6.84 NBC
T.L.C. pt 8.8.84 NBC
Simon and Simon ep Deep Cover 12.6.84 CBS
Finder of Lost Loves ep Aftershocks 2.16.85 ABC
The Fall Guy ep Femme Fatale 10.10.85 ABC
Murder, She Wrote ep Reflections in the Mind 11.3.85 CBS
The Insiders ep After the Fox 11.6.85 ABC

NELSON, BARRY
SUPP.:
Magnum, P.I. ep Double Jeopardy 2.25.82 CBS
Fantasy Island ep Extraordinary Miss Jones 4.9.83 ABC

NELSON, DAVID
SUPP.:
High School, U.S.A. tf/pt 10.16.83 NBC

NELSON, ED
A&C, Supp. 2:
M Squad ep The Phantom Raiders 11.7.58 NBC
Alfred Hitchcock Presents ep The Morning After 1.11.59 CBS
Have Gun--Will Travel ep Hunt the Man Down 4.25.59 CBS
Have Gun--Will Travel ep Homecoming 5.16.59 CBS
Black Saddle ep Client: Varden 5.30.59 NBC
Black Saddle ep Client: Peter Warren 10.30.59 NBC
Gunsmoke ep Miguel's Daughter 11.28.59 CBS
Johnny Ringo ep The Assassins 2.18.60 CBS
Johnny Ringo ep Border Town 3.17.60 CBS
Riverboat ep The Quick Noose 4.11.60 NBC
M Squad ep A Gun for Mother's Day 4.12.60 NBC
The Rebel ep Johnny Yuma at Appamattox 9.18.60 ABC
The Rebel ep Run, Killer, Run 10.30.60 ABC
Zane Grey Theater ep Ransom 11.17.60 CBS
The Rifleman ep Dead Cold Cash 11.22.60 ABC
The Life and Legend of Wyatt Earp ep The Too Perfect Crime 12.6.60 ABC

The Rifleman ep The Illustrator 12.13.60 ABC
The Rebel ep The Guard 1.8.61 ABC
Checkmate ep Between Two Guns 2.11.61 CBS
Surfside 6 ep Invitation to a Party 3.27.61 ABC
Thriller ep A Good Imagination 5.2.61 NBC
Laramie ep Bitter Glory 5.2.61 NBC
Have Gun--Will Travel ep My Brother's Keeper 5.6.61 CBS
Bat Masterson ep The Fatal Gambit 5.21.61 NBC
The Rifleman ep First Wages 10.9.61 ABC
Tales of Wells Fargo ep A Field of Honor 11.18.61 NBC
Perry Mason ep The Case of the Left-Handed Liar 11.25.61 CBS
Thriller ep Dialogue with Death 12.4.61 NBC
The Defenders ep Escort 12.15.61 CBS
The Detectives ep Crossed Wires 1.19.62 ABC
87th Precinct ep A Bullet for Katie 2.12.62 NBC
Gunsmoke ep The Prisoner 5.19.62 CBS
The Tall Man ep G.P. 5.19.62 NBC
Checkmate ep Side By Side 6.13.62 CBS
Wide Country ep Who Killed Eddie Gorman? 10.11.62 NBC
Rawhide ep Incident of the Reluctant Bridegroom 11.30.62 CBS
Stoney Burke ep Five By Eight 12.10.62 ABC
Gunsmoke ep Uncle Sunday 12.15.62 CBS
Saints and Sinners ep The Homecoming Bit 1.7.63 NBC
Alfred Hitchcock Presents ep I'll Be the Judge, I'll Be the Jury 2.15.63 CBS
The Dakotas ep Walk Through the Badlands 3.18.63 ABC
The Gallant Men ep The Crucible 3.23.63 ABC
The Eleventh Hour ep Everybody Knows You've Left Me 4.10.63 NBC
Wagon Train ep The Bleecker Story 12.9.63 ABC
Redigo ep Hostage Hero Hiding 12.10.63 ABC
The Fugitive ep The Girl from Little Egypt 12.14.63 ABC
The Fugitive ep Flight from the Final Demon 3.10.64 ABC
Gunsmoke ep Father Love 3.14.64 CBS
Arrest and Trial ep He Ran for His Life 4.5.64 ABC
The Alfred Hitchcock Hour ep Triumph 12.14.64 NBC
The Sixth Sense ep Two Hour Streets 9.16.72 ABC
Kung Fu ep The Third Man 4.26.73 ABC
Get Christie Love ep I'm Your New Neighbor 4.4.75 ABC
The Rockford Files ep Lions, Tigers, Monkeys and Dogs 10.12.79 NBC

SUPP.:

Bret Maverick ep Dateline: Sweetwater 1.12.82 NBC
Help Wanted: Male tf 1.16.82 CBS
Matt Houston ep Get Houston 2.20.83 ABC
The Fall Guy ep The Chase 4.13.83 ABC
Finder of Lost Loves ep Echoes 10.27.84 ABC
Murder, She Wrote ep Murder to a Jazz Beat 2.3.85 CBS
Peyton Place: The Next Generation tf/pt 5.13.85 NBC

NELSON, HARRIET
SUPP.:
The First Time tf 11.8.82 ABC
The Kid with the 200 I.Q. tf 2.6.83 NBC

NELSON, RICK
SUPP.:
Fathers and Sons pt 6.16.85 NBC

NELSON, TRACY*
The Adventures of Ozzie and Harriet ep Christmas with the Nelsons 12.66 ABC
Square Pegs sr 9.27.82 CBS
Hotel ep Blackout 9.28.83 ABC
Family Ties ep Ladies' Man 2.2.84 NBC
Glitter sr 9.13.84 ABC
The Love Boat ep The Runaway 2.9.85 ABC

NETTLETON, LOIS
A&C, B.V.:
Brenner ep One of Our Own 8.8.59 CBS
Gunsmoke ep Nina's Revenge 12.16.61 CBS
Twelve O'Clock High ep Show Me a Hero, I'll Show You a Bum 10.25.65 ABC
Daniel Boone ep The Bait 11.7.68 NBC
A&C, Supp. 1:
Hawaii Five-O ep Sing a Song of Suspense 10.31.75 CBS
SUPP.:
Trapper John, M.D. ep Three on a Mismatch 10.17.82 CBS
Murder, She Wrote ep Lovers and Other Killers 11.18.84 CBS
Glitter ep A Minor Miracle 12.18.84 ABC
Finder of Lost Loves ep From the Heart 2.9.85 ABC
Hotel ep Lost and Found 2.13.85 ABC
Brass tf/pt 9.11.85 CBS

NEVINS, CLAUDETTE
A&C, Supp. 2:
Harry O ep Street Games 3.13.75 ABC
Switch ep The Lady from Liechtenstein 11.23.76, 11.30.76 CBS
Switch ep Formula for Murder 8.20.78 CBS
SUPP.:
Cassie and Company ep Gorky's Army 2.19.82 NBC
Police Squad! ep Testimony of Evil 4.8.82 ABC
One Day at a Time ep 9.26.82 CBS
Take Your Best Shot tf 10.12.82 CBS
Magnum, P.I. ep Mixed Doubles 12.2.82 CBS
Don't Go to Sleep tf 12.10.82 ABC
One Day at a Time ep 10.16.83 CBS
The Mississippi ep 1.24.84 CBS

NEWMAN, LARAINE*
Laverne and Shirley ep Death Row 11.16, 11.23.82 ABC

St. Elsewhere ep Legionnaire's II 12.14.82 NBC
Her Life as a Man tf 3.12.84 NBC
This Wife for Hire tf 3.18.85 ABC
George Burns Comedy Week ep The Honeybunnies 11.27.85 CBS

NEWMAR, JULIE*
The Phil Silvers Show ep The Colonel's Maid 1958 CBS
My Living Doll sr 9.27.64 CBS
Batman ep The Purr-fect Crime 3.16.66 ABC
Batman ep Better Luck Next Time 3.24.66 ABC
Batman ep Hot Off the Griddle 9.14.66 ABC
Batman ep The Cat and the Fiddle 9.15.66 ABC
Batman ep The Cat's Meow 12.14.66 ABC
Batman ep The Bat's Kow Tow 12.15.66 ABC
Batman ep The Sandman Cometh 12.28.66 ABC
Batman ep The Cat Woman Goeth 12.29.66 ABC
Batman ep That Darn Cat Woman 1.19.67 ABC
Batman ep Scat, Darn Cat Woman 1.25.67 ABC
Batman ep Cat Woman Goes to College 2.22.67 ABC
Batman ep Batman Displays His Knowledge 2.23.67 ABC
McCloud: Who Killed Miss U.S.A.? tf/pt 2.17.70 NBC
The Feminist and the Fuzz tf 1.26.71 ABC
A Very Missing Person tf 3.4.72 ABC
Columbo ep Double Shock 3.25.73 NBC
McMillan and Wife ep Aftershock 11.9.75 NBC
The Bionic Woman ep Black Magic 11.10.76 ABC
Mystery of the Week ep The Black Box Murders 4.13.77 ABC
Terraces tf 6.27.77 NBC
Jason of Star Command ep 10.20.79 CBS
The Love Boat ep 10.20.79 ABC
Buck Rogers in the 25th Century ep Flight of the War Witch 3.27, 4.3.80 NBC
The Love Boat ep Haven't I Seen You? 4.5.80 ABC
Jason of Star Command ep 9.7.80 CBS
The Powers of Matthew Star ep The Triangle 11.19.82 NBC
CHiPs ep This Year's Riot 11.28.82 NBC
Fantasy Island ep King of Burlesque 3.12.83 ABC
Hart to Hart ep A Change of Hart 3.22.83 ABC
High School, U.S.A. pt 5.26.84 NBC

NICHOLAS, DENISE
SUPP.:
The Love Boat ep Pal-I-Mony-O-Mine 4.10.82 ABC
One Day at a Time ep 11.27.82 CBS
One Day at a Time ep 12.4.83 CBS
Magnum, P.I. ep 5.3.84 CBS

NICHOLSON, JACK
A&C, B.V.:
Sea Hunt ep 1960 NN

The Barbara Stanwyck Theater ep The Mink Coat 9.19.60 NBC
Bronco ep The Equalizer 12.18.61 ABC
The Andy Griffith Show ep Opie Finds a Baby 11.21.66 CBS
The Andy Griffith Show ep Aunt Bee the Juror 10.23.67 CBS

NIELSEN, LESLIE

A&C, B.V.:
Stage 13 ep Never Murder Your Grandfather 5.10.50 CBS
The Clock ep Prescription for Death 9.8.50 CBS
Robert Montgomery Presents The Lucky Strike Theater ep The Philadelphia Story 12.4.50 NBC
The Web ep You Killed Elizabeth 1.24.51 CBS
Starlight Theater ep The Magic Wire 2.2.51 CBS
The Armstrong Circle Theater ep Lover's Leap 6.5.51 NBC
The Web ep After the Fact 1.9.52 CBS
The Armstrong Circle Theater ep Candle in a Bottle 5.12.53 NBC
Danger ep The Psychological Error 12.29.53 CBS
Alfred Hitchcock Presents ep Ambition 7.4.61 CBS
Daniel Boone ep Mountain of the Dead 12.17.64 NBC
Peyton Place sr 1965 ABC
Run for Your Life ep The Last Safari 4.25.66 NBC
Cimarron Strip ep The Beast That Walks Like a Man 11.30.67 CBS
Hawaii Five-O ep We Hang Our Own 10.22.74 CBS
SUPP.:
Police Squad! sr 3.4.82 ABC
Murder Among Friends sp 4.8.82 SHO
Cave-In tf 6.19.83 NBC
Shaping Up sr 3.12.84 ABC
Hotel ep Crossroads 1.30.85 ABC
Murder, She Wrote ep My Johnnie Lies Over the Ocean 2.10.85 CBS
Finder of Lost Loves ep Aftershocks 2.16.85 ABC
Blade in Hong Kong tf/pt 5.15.85 CBS
The Ray Bradbury Theater ep Marionettes, Inc. 5.21.85 HBO
227 ep A Letter to the President 11.9.85 NBC

NIMOY, LEONARD

A&C, B.V.:
Colt .45 ep Night of Decision 6.28.59 ABC
Wagon Train ep The Estaban Zamora Story 10.21.59 NBC
Wagon Train ep The Maggie Hamilton Story 4.6.60 NBC
Gunsmoke ep I Call Him Wonder 3.26.63 CBS
Profiles in Courage ep Richard T. Ely 12.6.64 NBC
SUPP.:
A Woman Called Golda ms 4.26-4.28.82 OPT
Marco Polo ms 5.16-5.19.82 NBC
Vincent drama sp 11.6.84 A&E
The Sun Also Rises tf 12.9, 12.10.84 NBC

NOBLE, TRISHA

SUPP.:

Hart to Hart ep In the Hart of the Night 11.30.82 ABC
Casablanca ep Why Am I Killing? 4.10.83 NBC
Oh Madeline ep The Book of Love 11.1.83 ABC
Matt Houston ep Butterfly 11.18.83 ABC
T. J. Hooker ep Carnal Express 12.31.83 ABC

NOLAN, JEANETTE

A&C, Supp. 2:

You Are There ep The Last Day of an English Queen 9.18.55 CBS
Alfred Hitchcock Presents ep The Right Kind of Horse 3.9.58 CBS
Alfred Hitchcock Presents ep The Morning After 1.11.59 CBS
Tales of Wells Fargo ep The Tired Gun 3.30.59 NBC
Tales of Wells Fargo ep The Daltons 5.25.59 NBC
Restless Gun ep The Sweet Sisters 3.23.59 NBC
Lawman ep The Souvenir 4.5.59 ABC
The Rough Riders ep Paradise Gap 4.16.59 ABC
Black Saddle ep Client: Jessup 4.18.59 NBC
Richard Diamond ep 6.14.59 CBS
The Troubleshooters ep Trouble at Elbow Bend 9.25.59 NBC
Bourbon Street Beat ep Woman in the River 10.26.59 ABC
Have Gun--Will Travel ep The Tender Gun 11.22.60 CBS
Wanted: Dead Or Alive ep Witch Woman 12.28.60 CBS
Gunsmoke ep Love Thy Neighbor 1.28.61 CBS
Guestward Ho! ep Hawkeye's First Love 2.61 ABC
The Outlaws ep The Avengers 4.13.61 NBC
Thriller ep Parasite Mansion 4.25.61 NBC
Thriller ep La Strega 1.15.62 NBC
Have Gun--Will Travel ep The Trap 3.3.62 CBS
87th Precinct ep Idol in the Dust 4.2.62 NBC
Ben Casey ep When You See an Evil Man 5.28.62 ABC
Saints and Sinners ep Daddy's Girl 11.12.62 NBC
Hawaiian Eye ep Go Steady with Danger 1.1.63 ABC
The Virginian ep Mountain of the Sun 4.17.63 NBC
Combat ep Infant of Prague 4.14.64 ABC
The Eleventh Hour ep To Love Is to Live 4.15.64 NBC
Dr. Kildare ep A Sense of Tempo 5.13.64 NBC
Dr. Kildare ep The Hand That Hurts, the Hand That Heals 10.8.64 NBC
Gunsmoke ep Aunt Thede 12.29.64 CBS
The Man from UNCLE ep The Gazebo in the Maze Affair 4.5.65 NBC
The Farmer's Daughter ep 12.4.65 ABC
Amos Burke, Secret Agent ep A Little Gift from Cairo 12.22.65 ABC
The High Chaparral ep A Time of Flight 9.21.66 NBC
F Troop ep A Fort's Best Friend Is Not a Mother Fall 1966 ABC
Here Come the Brides ep The Last Winter 3.27.70 ABC

Gunsmoke ep Pike 3.1.71, 3.8.71 CBS
The Sixth Sense ep Shadow in the Wall 4.15.72 ABC
SUPP.:
Strike Force ep Sharks 2.19.82 ABC
Fantasy Island ep Funny Man 2.20.82 ABC
T. J. Hooker ep The Empty Gun 10.16.82 ABC
The Wild Women of Chastity Gulch tf/pt 10.31.82 ABC
Matt Houston ep The Good Doctor 12.12.82 ABC
Quincy, M.E. ep Quincy's Wedding 2.16, 2.23.83 NBC
Hotel ep Flashback 11.9.83 ABC
Trapper John, M.D. ep 10.21.84 CBS
Cover Up ep Nothing to Lose 10.27.84 CBS
Night Court ep Dan's Parents 1.10.85 NBC
Hell Town ep Hell Town Goes Bananas 10.2.85 NBC
The Golden Girls ep Blanche and the Younger Man 11.16.85 NBC

NOLAN, KATHLEEN (a.k.a. Kathy Nolan)
A&C, B.V.:
Broken Arrow ep The Rescue 1.8.57 ABC
Tombstone Territory ep Rose of the Rio Bravo 9.17.58 ABC
Gunsmoke ep Call Me Dodie 9.22.62 CBS
A&C, Supp. 2:
The Rockford Files ep New Life, Old Dragons 2.25.77 NBC

NOLAN, LLOYD
SUPP.:
Archie Bunker's Place ep 1.4, 1.11.81 CBS
Adams House pt 7.14.83 CBS
Remington Steele ep Cast in Steele 12.4.84 NBC
It Came Upon the Midnight Clear tf 12.15.84 NN
Murder She Wrote ep Murder in the Afternoon 10.13.85 CBS

NOLTE, NICK*
Griff ep The Framing of Billy the Kid 9.29.73 ABC
Medical Center ep Impasse 10.1.73 CBS
Cannon ep Arena of Fear 12.9.73 CBS
The Streets of San Francisco ep Crossfire 1.31.74 ABC
Emergency! ep 2.2.74 NBC
The Rookies ep The Teacher 2.4.74 ABC
Barnaby Jones ep Dark Legacy 3.3.74 CBS
Medical Center ep 3.11.74 CBS
Toma ep The Conspirators 3.29.74 ABC
Chopper One ep 4.11.74 ABC
Winter Kill tf 4.15.74 ABC
The California Kid tf 9.25.74 ABC
Death Sentence tf 10.2.74 ABC
Gunsmoke ep 11.11.74 CBS
Barnaby Jones ep Trap Play 1.7.75 CBS
The Runaway Barge tf/pt 3.24.75 NBC
Adams of Eagle Lake sr 8.23.75 ABC
Rich Man, Poor Man ms 2.1-3.15.76 ABC

NORRIS, CHRISTOPHER*
Mr. and Mrs. Bo Jo Jones tf 11.16.71 ABC
The Great American Beauty Contest tf 2.13.73 ABC
Senior Year tf 3.22.74 CBS
The Hatfields and the McCoys tf 1.15.75 ABC
Police Story ep Odyssey of Death 1.9, 1.16.76 NBC
Mayday at 40,000 Feet tf 11.12.76 CBS
The New, Original Wonder Woman ep Wonder Woman in Hollywood 2.16.77 ABC
Lady of the House tf 11.14.78 NBC
Suddenly, Love tf 12.4.78 NBC
Trapper John, M.D. sr 9.23.79 CBS
The Love Boat ep The Caller 5.3.80 ABC
Gridlock tf 10.2.80 NBC
Trapper John, M.D. sr ret 11.23.80 CBS
Trapper John, M.D. sr ret 10.4.81 CBS
The Love Boat ep The Incredible Hunk 10.24.81 ABC
Trapper John, M.D. sr ret 9.26.82 CBS
The Love Boat ep Arrivederci Gopher 10.2.82 ABC
Trapper John, M.D. sr ret 10.2.83 CBS
Hotel ep Charades 10.19.83 ABC
The Love Boat ep Girl of the Midnight Sun 2.2.85 ABC
Trapper John, M.D. sr ret 9.30.84 CBS
Finder of Lost Loves ep Losing Touch 10.13.84 ABC
Trapper John, M.D. sr ret 10.6.85 CBS

NORTH, SHEREE
A&C, B.V.:
Here Come the Brides ep A Card to Play 10.23.68 ABC
Alias Smith and Jones ep The Man That Corrupted Hadleyburg 1.27.72 ABC
A&C, Supp. 2:
Switch ep The Hemlein Heist 2.27.77 CBS
Baretta ep Big Bad Charlie 3.30.77 ABC
SUPP.:
Gemini sp 2.82 SHO
Legs tf 5.2.83 ABC
Bay City Blues sr 10.25.83 NBC
Magnum, P.I. ep The Return of Luther Gillis 2.16.84 CBS
Scorned and Swindled tf 10.9.84 CBS
Trapper John, M.D. ep 3.10.85 CBS
The Golden Girls ep Transplant 10.5.85 NBC

NOVACK, SHELLEY
A&C, Supp. 1:
The Name of the Game ep Breakout to a Fast Buck 3.14.69 NBC
Ironside ep L'chayim 12.4.69 NBC
Gunsmoke ep Stark 9.28.70 CBS
The Mod Squad ep The Sands of Anger 10.26.71 ABC
The D.A. ep The People vs. Boley 1.7.72 NBC
Hawaii Five-O ep Small Witness, Large Crime 1.28.75 CBS

A&C, Supp. 2:
Hawaii Five-O ep Ready, Aim.... 1.20.70 CBS
Police Story ep Stigma 11.9.77 NBC

NUYEN, FRANCE
SUPP.:
Trapper John, M.D. ep It Only Hurts When I Love 1.16.83 CBS
Automan ep Ships in the Night 12.29.83 ABC
Jealousy tf 1.23.84 ABC
Magnum, P.I. ep Torah, Torah, Torah 3.28.85 CBS
Midas Valley tf/pt 6.27.85 ABC
Crazy Like a Fox ep Year of the Fox 12.29.85 CBS

- O -

OAKES, RANDI
A&C, Supp. 2:
Switch ep The Cold War Con 12.9.75 CBS
Switch ep Who Killed Lila Craig? 1.16.78 CBS
SUPP.:
The Love Boat ep Honey Bee Mine 10.16.82 ABC
Fantasy Island ep Eternal Flame 3.5.83 ABC
Lovers and Other Strangers pt 7.22.83 ABC
The Love Boat ep The Bear Essence 11.12.83 ABC
Fantasy Island ep Lady of the House 2.25.84 ABC
Masquerade ep Winnings 4.6.84 ABC
Glitter ep A Day at the Beach 12.27.85 ABC

OAKLAND, SIMON
A&C, Supp. 2:
Have Gun--Will Travel ep The Statue of San Sebastian 6.14.58 CBS
Black Saddle ep Client: Mowrey 3.28.59 NBC
Brenner ep Small Talk 8.1.59 CBS
Gunsmoke ep Miguel's Daughter 11.28.59 CBS
Brenner ep Small Take 8.1.59 CBS
Tightrope ep The Cracking Point 10.6.59 CBS
Perry Mason ep The Case of the Frantic Flyer 1.9.60 CBS
Sugarfoot ep Every Man a Hero 2.23.60 ABC
Adventures in Paradise ep Beached 5.2.60 ABC
Wagon Train ep The Countess Baranof Story 5.11.60 NBC
G.E. Theater ep Image of a Doctor 2.26.61 CBS
The Outlaws ep The Bell 3.9.61 NBC
Adventures in Paradise ep Wild Mangoes 5.8.61 ABC
Follow the Sun ep Conspiracy of Silence 12.10.61 ABC
The Untouchables ep Canada Run 1.4.62 ABC
Tales of Wells Fargo ep Portrait of Teresa 2.10.62 NBC

The Untouchables ep Downfall 5.3.62 ABC
Ben Casey ep When You See an Evil Man 5.28.62 ABC
The Nurses ep The Prisoner 11.8.62 CBS
Saints and Sinners ep Judith Was a Lady 12.3.62 NBC
Wagon Train ep The Donna Fuller Story 12.19.62 NBC
The Defenders ep Kill or Be Killed 1.5.63 CBS
The Untouchables ep The Jazz Man 4.30.63 ABC
Rawhide ep Incident of the Traveling Man 10.17.63 CBS
The Bob Hope Chrysler Theater ep Four Kings 11.1.63 NBC
East Side/West Side ep Where's Harry? 12.9.63 CBS
The Defenders ep The Sixth Alarm 5.23.64 CBS
Mr. Novak ep With a Hammer in His Hand, Lord, Lord! 9.29.64 NBC
Mr. Broadway ep Try to Find a Spy 10.10.64 CBS
The Reporter ep Vote for Murder 12.18.64 CBS
Profiles in Courage ep Gen. Alexander Wm. Doniphan 1.17.65 NBC
The Rogues ep The Bartered MacBride 2.28.65 NBC
Profiles in Courage ep Edmund G. Ross 3.21.65 NBC
Combat ep The Old Men 11.16.65 ABC
Gunsmoke ep The Hostage 12.4.65 CBS
Cimarron Strip ep 11.30.67 CBS
The Felony Squad ep No Sad Songs for Charlie 12.25.67 ABC
Judd, For the Defense ep Square House 3.1.68 ABC
The Mod Squad ep Confrontation! 11.11.69 ABC
Medical Center ep Runaway 1.21.70 CBS
The Young Lawyers ep A Busload of Bishops 11.30.70 ABC
Ironside ep Lesson in Terror 3.18.71 NBC
Hawaii Five-O ep Didn't We Meet at a Murder? 2.2.72 CBS
Police Story ep The Jar 12.14.76, 12.21.76 NBC
SUPP.:
Bret Maverick ep A Horse of Another Color 1.5.82 NBC
Quincy, M.E. ep Bitter Pill 1.6.82 NBC
CHiPs ep Alarmed 2.14.82 NBC
Lou Grant ep Obituary 3.22.82 CBS
Quincy, M.E. ep Give Me Your Weak 10.27.82 NBC
Tucker's Witch ep Living and Presumed Dead 5.5.83 CBS

OATES, WARREN
A&C, B.V.:
The Rifleman ep The Marshal 10.21.58 ABC
The Adventures of Rin Tin Tin ep The Epidemic 11.21.58 ABC
Wanted: Dead or Alive ep Die by the Gun 12.6.58 CBS
Trackdown ep Bad Judgment 1.28.59 CBS
Wanted: Dead Or Alive ep The Legend 3.7.59 CBS
Trackdown ep Fear 3.18.59 CBS
Black Saddle ep Client: Steele 3.21.59 NBC
Wanted: Dead Or Alive ep Amos Carter 5.9.59 CBS
The Rifleman ep Blood Lines 10.6.59 ABC
Wanted: Dead Or Alive ep Angela 1.9.60 CBS
Sugarfoot ep Every Man a Hero 2.23.60 ABC

The Rifleman ep The Prodigal 4.26.60 ABC
Johnny Ringo ep Single Debt 5.12.60 CBS
Gunsmoke ep Small Water 9.24.60 CBS
The Westerner ep Jeff 9.30.60 NBC
Have Gun--Will Travel ep The Poker Friend 11.12.60 CBS
Wanted: Dead Or Alive ep The Last Retreat 1.11.61 CBS
Gunsmoke ep Love Thy Neighbor 1.28.61 CBS
The Lawless Years ep Artie Moon 8.25.61 NBC
Gunsmoke ep The Do-Cadder 1.6.62 CBS
The Big Valley ep The Murdered Party 11.17.65 ABC
The Big Valley ep The Great Safe Robbery 11.21.66 ABC
Cimarron Strip ep Nobody 12.7.67 CBS

O'BRIAN, HUGH
SUPP.:
Bush Doctor sp 1.82 NN
Fantasy Island ep Wuthering Heights 1.9.82 ABC
The Love Boat ep Saving Grace 5.11.82 ABC
Matt Houston ep The Kidnapping 11.28.83 ABC

O'BRIEN, MARGARET
SUPP.:
Hotel ep The Offer 12.7.83 ABC

O'BRIEN, PAT
SUPP.:
Happy Days ep Grandma Nussbaum 1.19.82 ABC

O'CONNELL, ARTHUR
A&C, B.V.:
Father Knows Best ep Hard Luck Leo Spring 1959 CBS
The Big Valley ep The Odyssey of Jubal Tanner 10.13.65 ABC
Alias Smith and Jones ep Bad Night in Big Butte 3.2.72 ABC

O'CONNELL, TAAFFE*
Baretta ep Pay or Die 1.28.76 ABC
Blansky's Beauties sr 2.12.77 ABC
The New Adventures of Wonder Woman ep A Date with Doomsday 3.10.79 CBS
The Incredible Hulk ep Darkside 12.5.80 CBS
Laverne and Shirley ep Helmut Weekend 3.2.82 ABC
Archie Bunker's Place ep 9.26.82 CBS
Three's Company ep Jack's Double Date 3.1.83 ABC
Knight Rider ep Halloween Knight 10.28.84 NBC

O'CONNOR, CARROLL
SUPP.:
Brass tf 9.11.85 CBS

O'CONNOR, DONALD
SUPP.:
Fantasy Island ep Save Sherlock Holmes 2.6.82 ABC

Simon and Simon ep 9.29.83 CBS
Hotel ep The Offer 12.7.83 ABC
The Love Boat ep Paying the Piper 12.1.84 ABC
Alice in Wonderland tf 12.9, 12.10.85 CBS

O'CONNOR, GLYNNIS
A&C, Supp. 2:
Harry O ep Mister Five and Dime 1.8.76 ABC
SUPP.:
The Fighter tf 2.19.83 CBS
Why Me? tf 3.12.84 ABC
Sins of the Father tf 1.13.85 NBC

O'CONNOR, TIM
A&C, Supp. 2:
Play of the Week ep The White Steed 11.23.59 NN
Moment of Fear ep If I Should Die 8.19.60 NBC
Alfred Hitchcock Presents ep What Really Happened 1.11.63 CBS
The Defenders ep The Traitor 2.16.63 CBS
The Fugitive ep Ticket to Alaska 11.12.63 ABC
Great Adventure ep The Treasure Train of Jefferson Davis 11.15.63 CBS
East Side/West Side ep The $5.98 Dress 1.13.64 CBS
The Fugitive ep Taps for a Dead War 3.17.64 ABC
Gunsmoke ep Blue Heaven 9.26.64 CBS
The Defenders ep May Day! May Day! 4.18.64 CBS
Twelve O'Clock High ep Decision 11.6.64 ABC
The Fugitive ep The Cage 11.24.64 ABC
Profiles in Courage ep Gen. Alexander Wm. Doniphan 1.17.65 NBC
The FBI ep The Satellite 4.2.67 ABC
Judd, For the Defense ep Kingdom of the Blind 2.9.68 ABC
Medical Center ep His Brother's Keeper 4.1.70 CBS
Gunsmoke ep The Witness 11.23.70 CBS
San Francisco International Airport ep Supersonic Transport 11.25.70 NBC
Doc Elliot ep Things That Might Have Been 4.3.74 ABC
Manhunter ep The Ma Gentry Gang 9.11.74 CBS
Get Christie Love ep Downbeat for a Dead Man 11.13.74 ABC
The Six Million Dollar Man ep The Deadly Test 10.19.75 ABC
Police Woman ep The Human Rights of Tiki Man 2.1.78 NBC
SUPP.:
The Dukes of Hazzard ep Bad Day in Hazzard 3.5.82 CBS
Dynasty ep The Party 2.24.82 ABC
Dynasty ep The Fragment 4.7.82 ABC
Dynasty ep The Plea 10.27.82 ABC
Deadly Encounters tf 12.18.82 CBS
High Performance ep Deadly Performance 3.23.83 ABC
Matt Houston ep Fear for Tomorrow 4.3.83 ABC
Knight Rider ep Brother's Keeper 10.9.83 NBC

The Mississippi ep 11.22.83 CBS
The A-Team ep Not So Friendly Persuasion 5.8.84 NBC
MacGruder and Loud ep Sanctuary 3.12.85 ABC
Peyton Place: The Next Generation tf/pt 5.13.85 NBC
Hardcastle and McCormick ep Conventional Warfare 12.9.85 ABC

OH, SOON-TECK*
Hawaii Five-O tf/pt 9.20.68 CBS
The Reluctant Heroes tf 11.23.71 ABC
Kung Fu ep Sun and Cloud Shadow 2.22.73 ABC
The Magician ep The Illusion of the Lost Dragon 2.18.74 NBC
Rex Harrison's Short Stories of Love pt ep Epicac 5.1.74 NBC
Judge Dee and the Monastery Murders tf/pt 12.29.74 ABC
Hawaii Five-O ep The Defector 10.24.75 CBS
The Black Sheep Squadron ep Poor Little Lambs 2.22.77 NBC
Logan's Run ep Crypt 11.7.77 CBS
The Black Sheep Squadron ep Divine Wind 12.14.77 NBC
Hawaii Five-O ep The Silk Trap 2.9.78 CBS
How the West Was Won ep China Girl 4.16.79 ABC
Stunt Seven tf/pt 5.30.79 CBS
Happiness is a Warm Clue (a.k.a. The Return of Charlie Chan) tf/pt 7.17.79 ABC
Hawaii Five-O ep Image of Fear 11.8.79 CBS
Diff'rent Strokes ep Return of the Gooch 6.25.80 NBC
Charlie's Angels ep Angels of the Deep 12.7.80 ABC
Charlie's Angels ep Waikiki Angels 1.4.81 ABC
East of Eden ms 2.8-2.11.81 ABC
Magnum, P.I. ep Memories Are Forever 11.5.81 CBS
The Letter tf 5.3.82 ABC
Marco Polo ms 5.16-5.19.82 NBC
Cassie and Company ep There Went the Bride 7.20.82 NBC
The CBS Children's Mystery Theater ep The Zertigo Diamond Caper 9.28.82 CBS
Bring 'Em Back Alive ep The Warlord 10.26.82 CBS
M*A*S*H ep 11.8.82 CBS
Quincy, M.E. ep Sword of Honor, Blade of Death 12.15.82 NBC
The Greatest American Hero ep 30 Seconds Over Little Tokyo 2.3.83 ABC
Magnum, P.I. ep Birds of a Feather 3.17.83 CBS
Girls of the White Orchid tf 11.28.83 NBC
Hart to Hart ep Year of the Dog 12.13.83 ABC
The Master ep Out-of-Time Step 1.27.84 NBC
The Fall Guy ep Always Say Always 2.22.84 ABC
Matt Houston ep Return to Nam 11.2.84 ABC
Matt Houston ep Escape from Nam 11.9.84 ABC
Airwolf ep Once a Hero 11.24.84 CBS
Magnum, P.I. ep 12.13.84 CBS
Airwolf ep The American Dream 1.12.85 CBS
T. J. Hooker ep Outcall 2.2.85 ABC
Hill Street Blues ep Hacked to Pieces 10.3.85 NBC
Hill Street Blues ep In the Belly of the Bus 10.24.85 NBC

O'HARA, JENNY
SUPP.:
Simon and Simon ep Trapadoors 12.8.81 CBS
Bret Maverick ep The Mayflower Women's Historical Society 2.2.82 NBC
Quincy, M.E. ep Deadly Protection 5.5.82 NBC
Another Woman's Child tf 1.19.83 CBS
Trapper John, M.D. ep 1.30.83 CBS
Remington Steele ep Steele in the News 3.4.83 NBC
The Mississippi ep 10.11.83 CBS
Trapper John, M.D. ep 1.21.84 CBS
V: The Final Battle ms 5.6-5.8.84 NBC
Our Family Honor ep 12.6.85 ABC

O'HERLIHY, DAN
SUPP.:
Trapper John, M.D. ep Danny 1.24.82 CBS
The Whiz Kids sr (with ep Maid in America) 2.4.84 CBS
Murder, She Wrote ep It's a Dog's Life 11.4.84 CBS

OLIVER, SUSAN
A&C, B.V.:
Father Knows Best ep Country Cousin 3.58 NBC
The Andy Griffith Show ep Prisoner of Love 2.10.64 CBS
Gomer Pyle, USMC ep A Date with Miss Camp Henderson 3.25.66 CBS
Alias Smith and Jones ep Journey from San Juan 4.8.71 ABC
A&C, Supp. 2:
The Streets of San Francisco ep Hang Tough 2.17.77 ABC
SUPP.:
Tomorrow's Child tf 3.22.82 ABC
Magnum, P.I. ep Let Me Hear the Music 2.21.85 CBS
Murder, She Wrote ep Armed Response 3.31.85 CBS
International Airport tf/pt 5.25.85 ABC
Murder, She Wrote ep Jessica Behind Bars 12.1.85 CBS

OLIVIER, SIR LAURENCE
SUPP.:
A Talent for Murder sp 1.84 SHO

OLKEWICZ, WALTER*
The Last Resort sr 9.19.79 CBS
Flesh and Blood tf 10.14, 10.16.79 CBS
Enola Gay tf 11.23.80 NBC
Alice ep 1.18.81 CBS
Comedy of Horrors pt 9.1.81 CBS
Barney Miller ep The Clown 1.21.82 ABC
Making a Living ep Falling in Love Again 2.19.82 ABC
The Blue and the Gray ms 11.14-11.17.82 CBS
The Executioner's Song tf 11.28, 11.29.82 NBC
Wizards and Warriors sr 2.26.83 CBS

Taxi ep Jim's Mario's 5.18.83 NBC
Travis McGee tf 5.18.83 ABC
Cheers ep They Called Me Mayday 12.1.83 NBC
The Love Boat ep Julie's Blind Date 12.3.83 ABC
Calamity Jane tf 3.6.84 CBS
Family Ties ep Working at It 5.10.84 NBC
The Duck Factory ep The Children's Half-Hour 6.27.84 NBC
Partners in Crime sr 9.29.84 NBC
Newhart ep 3.4.85 CBS
Trapper John, M.D. ep 5.5.85 CBS
I Had Three Wives sr 8.14.85 CBS
Hollywood Beat ep The Long Weekend 11.16.85 ABC
The A-Team ep There Goes the Neighborhood 12.3.85 NBC
Riptide ep Robin and Marion 12.3.85 NBC

O'LOUGHLIN, GERALD S.
A&C, Supp. 2:
The U.S. Steel Hour ep The Two Worlds of Charlie Gordon 2.22.61 CBS
The Asphalt Jungle ep The Fighter 6.4.61 ABC
Ben Casey ep Of All Save Pain Bereft 11.12.62 ABC
The Defenders ep Kill or Be Killed 1.5.63 CBS
Alcoa Premiere ep Of Struggle and Flight 3.28.63 CBS
Dr. Kildare ep Speak Not in Angry Whispers 5.14.64 NBC
Twelve O'Clock High ep Here's to Courageous Cowards 12.4.64 ABC
Gunsmoke ep 20 Miles from Dodge 4.10.65 CBS
The FBI ep Ordeal 11.6.66 ABC
Cimarron Strip ep The Sound of a Drum 2.1.68 CBS
The Felony Squad ep Nightmare on a Dead-End Street 2.19.68 ABC
Judd, For the Defense ep A Swim with Sharks 12.20.68 ABC
Then Came Bronson ep The Mary R 3.25.70 NBC
The FBI ep The Fatal Imposter 1.4.70 ABC
The Young Lawyers ep The Russell Incident 11.9.70 ABC
Room 222 ep The Quitter 1.25.72 ABC
SUPP.:
Trapper John, M.D. ep Angel of Mercy 1.17.82 CBS
Quincy, M.E. ep Trial By Fire 1.27.82 NBC
Code Red ep Riddle in the Flames 3.14.82 ABC
The Blue and the Gray ms 11.14-11.17.82 CBS
M*A*S*H ep 11.29.82 CBS
Quincy, M.E. ep A Loss for Words 1.26.83 NBC
Simon and Simon ep Room 3502 3.10.83 CBS
Matt Houston ep A Deadly Parlay 4.10.83 ABC
The Powers of Matthew Star ep Starr Knight 4.15.83 NBC
Automan sr 12.15.83 ABC
London and Davis in New York pt 9.9.84 CBS
Cover Up ep Harper Gate 10.13.84 CBS
Riptide ep The Orange Grove 10.16.84 NBC
Murder, She Wrote ep Tough Guys Don't Die 2.24.85 CBS

Highway to Heaven ep The Brightest Star 3.6.85 NBC
Brothers-in-Law tf/pt 4.28.85 ABC

OLSON, JAMES*
Mannix ep The Odds Against Donald Jordan 3.1.69 CBS
Ironside ep Contract: Kill Ironside 9.21.71 NBC
Paper Man tf 11.12.71 CBS
The Bold Ones: The Lawyers ep The Letter of the Law 12.26.71 NBC
McCloud ep 12.29.71 NBC
Hawaii Five-O ep Bait Once, Bait Twice 1.4.72 CBS
Cannon ep 2.8.72 CBS
Columbo ep Etude in Black 9.17.72 NBC
The Streets of San Francisco ep The First Day of Forever 9.30.72 ABC
Gunsmoke ep The Fugitives 10.23.72 CBS
Bonanza ep Ambush at Rio Lobo 10.24.72 NBC
The Rookies ep The Good Die Young 11.13.72 ABC
Jigsaw ep To Stalk the Night 11.30.72 ABC
Incident on a Dark Street tf 1.13.73 NBC
Barnaby Jones ep Catch Me If You Can 10.21.73 CBS
The Rookies ep Justice for Jill Danko 10.22.73 ABC
McMillan and Wife ep Free Fall to Terror 11.11.73 NBC
Police Story ep Man on a Rack 12.11.73 NBC
The FBI ep The Betrayal 2.3.74 ABC
Marcus Welby, M.D. ep Angela's Nightmare 2.5.74 ABC
Manhunter tf/pt 2.26.74 CBS
A Tree Grows in Brooklyn tf/pt 3.27.74 NBC
The New Land ep The Word Is: Persistence 9.14.74 ABC
Hawaii Five-O ep Hawaiian Nightmare 9.17.74 CBS
The Sex Symbol tf 9.17.74 ABC
Movin' On ep Grit 9.26.74 NBC
Mannix ep Game Plan 9.29.74 CBS
The New Land ep The Word Is: Alternative 10.12.74 ABC
Kung Fu ep The Devil's Champion 11.1.74 ABC
Harry O ep Material Witness 11.14.74 ABC
The Missiles of October tf 12.18.74 ABC
The Family Nobody Wanted tf 2.19.75 ABC
The Streets of San Francisco ep Asylum 2.20.75 ABC
Someone I Touched tf 2.26.75 ABC
Caribe ep One Second to Doom 4.14.75 ABC
Man on the Outside tf 6.29.75 ABC
Strange New World tf 7.13.75 ABC
Maude ep The Election 10.6.75 CBS
Cannon ep And Down Will Come Baby 11.19.75 CBS
Law and Order tf 5.6.76 NBC
Barnaby Jones ep Blood Vengeance 10.7.76 CBS
The Streets of San Francisco ep No Minor Vices 11.4.76 ABC
The New, Original Wonder Woman ep The Last of the Two Dollar Bills 1.8.77 ABC
Most Wanted ep The Ritual Killer 2.12.77 ABC

The Spell tf 2.20.77 NBC
The Bionic Woman ep Fem Bots in Las Vegas 9.24, 10.1.77 NBC
The Hallmark Hall of Fame ep The Court-Martial of George Armstrong Custer 12.1.77 NBC
Operation Runaway ep Operation Runaway (pt) 4.27.78 NBC
Hawaii Five-O ep A Distant Thunder 11.9.78 CBS
Project UFO ep Sighting 4022: The Island Incident 11.30.78 NBC
The Misadventures of Sheriff Lobo ep 11.6.79 NBC
Little House on the Prairie ep The Faith Healer 11.19.79 NBC
Hawaii Five-O ep Labyrinth 12.25.79 CBS
Moviola: The Silent Lovers tf 5.20.80 NBC
The Yeagers ep 6.8.80 ABC
Cave-In tf 6.19.83 NBC
The Parade tf 2.29.84 CBS
Matt Houston ep Vanished 9.28.84 ABC
Hawaiian Heat ep The Island 10.12.84 ABC
North Beach and Rawhide tf 11.12, 11.13.85 CBS

O'NEAL, PATRICK
SUPP.:
Nurse ep To Life 1.7.82 CBS
Help Wanted: Male tf 1.16.82 CBS
Fantasies tf 1.18.62 ABC
Emerald Point, N.A.S. sr 9.26.83 CBS
Spraggue tf/pt 6.29.84 ABC
Murder, She Wrote ep Broadway Malady 1.13.85 CBS
Perry Mason Returns tf 12.1.85 NBC

O'NEAL, TATUM*
Faerie Tale Theater ep Goldilocks and the Three Bears 1.9.84 SHO

O'NEAL, TRICIA*
Ellery Queen ep The Adventure of the Wary Witness 1.25.76 NBC
Serpico ep The Indian 10.8.76 NBC
Delvecchio ep A Madness Within 2.20, 2.27.77 CBS
Charlie Cobb: Nice Night for a Hanging tf/pt 6.9.77 NBC
Mary Jane Harper Cried Last Night tf 10.5.77 CBS
Columbo ep How to Dial a Murder 4.15.78 NBC
Are You in the House Alone? tf 9.20.78 CBS
The Eddie Capra Mysteries ep Who Killed Lloyd Wesley Gordon? 9.29.78 NBC
Hawaii Five-O ep The Bark and the Bite 9.28.79 CBS
The Kid from Left Field tf 9.30.79 NBC
Hawaii Five-O ep Labyrinth 12.25.79 CBS
Brave New World tf 3.7.80 NBC
The Fall Guy ep Charlie 10.6.81 ABC
Jacqueline Susann's Valley of the Dolls, 1981 tf/pt 10.19, 10.20.81 CBS
Palms Precinct pt 1.8.82 NBC

Hart to Hart ep The Harts Strike Out 5.4.82 ABC
The Powers of Matthew Star ep Mother 11.26.82 NBC
Voyagers ep Old Hickory and the Pirate 11.28.82 NBC
Simon and Simon ep It's Only a Game 2.3.83 CBS
The A-Team ep Black Day at Bad Rock 2.22.83 NBC
The Mississippi ep 9.27.83 CBS
The Fall Guy ep The Last Drive 10.26.83 ABC
The Whiz Kids ep Deadly Access 10.26.83 CBS
Hardcastle and McCormick ep Once Again with Vigorish 10.30.83 ABC
Lottery ep New York City: Winning Can Be Murder ("Whodunit" segment) 11.18.83 ABC
The A-Team ep Deadly Maneuvers 2.28.84 NBC
Murder, She Wrote ep Murder She Wrote (pt) 9.30.84 CBS
Riptide ep Catch of the Day 10.23.84 NBC
Scarecrow and Mrs. King ep A Little Sex, a Little Scandal 2.4.85 CBS
Murder, She Wrote ep Murder in the Afternoon 10.13.85 CBS
Airwolf ep Annie Oakley 11.16.85 CBS

O'NEILL, JENNIFER*
Love's Savage Fury tf 5.20.79 ABC
The Other Victim tf 11.4.81 CBS
Bare Essence sr 2.8.83 NBC
Cover Up sr 9.22.84 CBS
Chase tf/pt 11.23.85 CBS

OPATOSHU, DAVID
A&C, B.V.:
Brenner ep The Vigilantes 5.31.64 CBS
A&C, Supp. 1:
S.W.A.T. ep Running Man 1.24.76 ABC
A&C, Supp. 2:
The Six Million Dollar Man ep Danny's Inferno 1.23.77 ABC
Police Woman ep The Young and the Fair 1.25.78 NBC
SUPP.:
Hardcastle and McCormick ep D-Day 10.14.85 ABC

O'ROURKE, HEATHER*
Happy Days sr 9.28.82 ABC
CHiPs ep Funhouse 3.13.83 NBC
Webster ep Katherine's Swan Song 10.7.83 ABC
Webster ep Second Time Around 11.4.83 ABC
Webster ep Travis 11.11.83 ABC
Finder of Lost Loves ep Yesterday's Child 9.29.84 ABC
Surviving tf 2.10.85 ABC

OSMOND, MARIE
SUPP.:
Walt Disney ... One Man's Dream sp 12.12.81 CBS
Side by Side: The True Story of the Osmond Family tf 4.26.82 NBC

Rooster tf/pt 8.19.82 ABC
The Love Boat ep The Arrangement 10.2.82 ABC
I Married Wyatt Earp tf 1.10.83 NBC
Rose-Petal Place pt vo 4.85 NN

O'SULLIVAN, MAUREEN
SUPP.:
Mornings at Seven sp 9.82 SHO
All My Children sr 4.21.83-5.10.83 ABC

O'TOOLE, ANNETTE
A&C, Supp. 2:
Gunsmoke ep The Witness 11.23.70 CBS
Mod Squad ep A Bummer for R.J. 1.19.71 ABC
SUPP.:
Best Legs in the 8th Grade comedy sp 10.7.84 HBO
Alfred Hitchcock Presents pt ep An Unlocked Window 5.12.85 NBC
Secret World of the Very Young sp 9.12.85 CBS
Copacabana tf 12.3.85 CBS
American Playhouse ep Bridge to Terabithia 12.15.85 PBS

O'TOOLE, PETER
SUPP.:
Pygmalion sp 7.83 SHO

OXENBERG, CATHERINE*
The Royal Romance of Charles and Diana tf 9.20.82 CBS
Cover Up ep Cover Up (pt) 9.22.84 CBS
The Love Boat ep The Present 11.24.84 ABC
Dynasty sr (with ep Amanda) 11.14.84 ABC
Dynasty sr ret 9.25.85 ABC

- P -

PAGE, GERALDINE
SUPP.:
The Blue and the Gray ms 11.14-11.17.82 CBS
The Parade tf 2.29.84 CBS
The Dollmaker tf 5.13.84 ABC
The Hitchhiker ep W.G.O.D. 11.26.85 HBO

PAIGE, JANIS
SUPP.:
Too Close for Comfort ep The Last Weekend 2.16.82 ABC
Flamingo Road ep The Powers That Be 12.15.82 NBC
Matt Houston ep The Purrfect Crime 1.9.83 ABC
St. Elsewhere ep Permission 2.15.83 NBC

Gun Shy ep 3.22.83 CBS
The Other Woman tf 3.22.83 CBS
Baby Makes Five sr 4.1.83 ABC
No Man's Land tf 5.27.84 NBC
Rockhopper pt 7.9.85 CBS
Trapper John, M.D. ep Game of Hearts 10.6, 10.13.85 CBS

PALANCE, JACK
SUPP.:
The Love Boat Fall Preview Party sp 9.15.84 ABC

PALMER, BETSY
SUPP.:
The Love Boat ep She Brought Her Mother Along 3.20.82 ABC
Maggie ep Maggie the Poet 5.21.82 ABC
Murder, She Wrote ep Sticks and Stones 12.15.85 CBS

PALMER, LILLI
SUPP.:
The Love Boat ep My Mother, My Chaperone 11.24.84 ABC

PANKIN, STUART*
The San Pedro Bums tf/pt 5.13.77 ABC
The San Pedro Beach Bums sr 9.19.77 ABC
B.J. and the Bear ep Wheels of Fortune 4.21.79 NBC
Valentine Magic on Love Island tf/pt 2.15.80 NBC
House Calls ep 1.26.81 CBS
CHiPs ep Ponch's Angels 2.28.81 NBC
Here's Boomer ep Boomer and the Musket Cove Treasure 10.4.81 NBC
Benson ep Stress 12.18.81 ABC
Earthbound sp 1.31, 2.7.82 NBC
Strike Force ep Pandora Vector 3.26.82 ABC
The Powers of Matthew Star ep Accused 9.24.82 NBC
It Takes Two ep Hello, I Must Be Going 11.18.82 ABC
Not Necessarily the News sr 1.3.83 HBO
Trapper John, M.D. ep Forget Me Not 1.30.83 CBS
Mickey Spillane's Mike Hammer ep Shots in the Dark 3.8.84 CBS
Matt Houston ep Cash and Carry 3.23.84 ABC
Trapper John, M.D. ep 2.24.85 CBS
It's a Living ep Sonny's Big Chance 10.27.85 NN
Night Court ep 11.28.85 NBC

PARKER, ELEANOR
SUPP.:
The Love Boat ep A Dress to Remember 5.8.82 ABC
Fantasy Island ep Nurses' Night Out 10.22.83 ABC
Hotel ep The Offer 12.7.83 ABC
Finder of Lost Loves ep A Gift 12.8.84 ABC

PARKER, FESS
A&C, B.V.:
Annie Oakley ep Annie and the Texas Sandman 5.8.54 NN
Burke's Law ep Who Killed Who IV? 4.3.64 ABC

PARKER, JAMISON*
Women at West Point tf 2.27.79 CBS
Anatomy of a Seduction tf 5.8.79 CBS
The Gathering, Part II tf 12.17.79 NBC
Hart to Hart ep A Question of Innocence 1.15.80 ABC
The Promise of Love tf 11.11.80 CBS
Callie and Son tf 10.13.81 CBS
Simon and Simon sr 11.24.81 CBS
Simon and Simon sr ret 10.7.82 CBS
Simon and Simon sr ret 9.29.83 CBS
Agatha Christie's "A Caribbean Mystery" tf 10.22.83 CBS
The Whiz Kids ep Deadly Access 10.26.83 CBS
Simon and Simon sr ret 9.27.84 CBS
Simon and Simon sr ret 10.3.85 CBS

PARKER, LARA
SUPP.:
Rooster tf/pt 8.19.82 ABC
Remington Steele ep Steele Threads 12.13.83 NBC

PARKER, SARAH JESSICA*
My Body, My Child tf 4.12.82 ABC
Square Pegs sr 9.27.82 CBS
The ABC Afterschool Special ep The Almost Royal Family 10.24.84 ABC
Going for the Gold: The Bill Johnson Story tf 5.8.85 CBS

PARKINS, BARBARA
SUPP.:
Uncommon Valor tf 1.22.83 CBS
Hotel ep Faith, Hope and Charity 11.23.83 ABC
To Catch a King tf 2.12.84 HBO
The Calendar Girl Murders tf 4.8.84 ABC
Peyton Place: The Next Generation tf/pt 5.13.85 NBC

PARKS, MICHAEL
A&C, B.V.:
The Zane Grey Theater ep Ransom 11.17.60 CBS
Gunsmoke ep The Boys 5.26.62 CBS
Channing ep An Obelisk for Benny 10.2.63 ABC
Arrest and Trial ep We May Be Better Strangers 12.1.63 ABC
A&C, Supp. 1:
Get Christie Love ep My Son, the Murderer 2.12.75 ABC
SUPP.:
Chase tf/pt 11.23.85 CBS

PARSONS, ESTELLE
SUPP.:
American Playhouse ep Sense of Humor: Come Along with Me 2.16.82 PBS

PATTERSON, ELIZABETH
A&C, B.V.:
I Love Lucy ep No Children Allowed 4.20.53 CBS
I Love Lucy ep Lucy's Last Birthday 5.11.53 CBS
I Love Lucy ep Too Many Crooks 11.30.53 CBS
I Love Lucy ep The Business Manager 10.4.54 CBS
I Love Lucy ep Ricky's Movie Offer 11.8.54 CBS
I Love Lucy ep California, Here We Come 1.10.55 CBS
I Love Lucy ep Homecoming 11.7.55 CBS
I Love Lucy ep Bon Voyage 1.16.56 CBS
I Love Lucy ep Little Ricky Learns to Play the Drums 10.8.56 CBS
The Adventures of Jim Bowie ep A Fortune for Madame 10.18.57 ABC
Dan Raven ep The Empty Frame 11.4.60 NBC

PATTERSON, LORNA
SUPP.:
Private Benjamin sr ret 9.28.82 CBS
Hawaiian Heat ep Yanks vs. the Cubs 11.2.84 ABC
The Imposter tf 11.8.84 ABC

PATTERSON, NEVA
A&C, B.V.:
The Hallmark Hall of Fame ep Hamlet 4.26.53 NBC
For the People ep Between Candor and Shame 3.7.65 CBS
The Rockford Files ep Just by Accident 2.28.75 NBC
SUPP.:
The Rules of Marriage tf 5.10, 5.11.82 CBS
Something So Right tf 11.30.82 CBS
Cagney and Lacey ep 3.21.83 CBS
V ms 5.1, 5.2.83 NBC
V: The Final Battle ms 5.6-5.8.84 NBC
Webster ep Good Grief 10.25.85 ABC

PAULSEN, ALBERT*
Combat! ep Forgotten Front 10.2.62 ABC
Combat! ep Escape to Nowhere 11.20.62 ABC
G.E. True ep The Wrong Nickel 12.16.62 CBS
The Gallant Men ep Operation Secret 2.16.63 ABC
The Lloyd Bridges Show ep Freedom Is for Those Who Want It 4.30.63 CBS
G.E. True ep Heyerich 5.5, 5.12.63 CBS
77 Sunset Strip ep Our Man in Switzerland 5.24.63 ABC
77 Sunset Strip ep Never to Have Loved 6.14.63 ABC
The Bob Hope Chrysler Theater ep One Day in the Life of Ivan

Denisovich 11.8.63 NBC
Combat! ep The Pillbox 1.7.64 ABC
The Man from UNCLE ep The Terbuf Affair 12.29.64 NBC
Twelve O'Clock High ep The Clash 2.12.65 ABC
The Bob Hope Chrysler Theater ep Memorandum for a Spy 4.2, 4.9.65 NBC
The Kraft Suspense Theater ep The Safe House 5.20.65 NBC
I Spy ep The Loser 10.20.65 NBC
Twelve O'Clock High ep Runaway in the Dark 11.1.65 ABC
Amos Burke, Secret Agent ep Whatever Happened to Adriana, and Why Won't She Stay Dead? 12.1.65 ABC
The Trials of O'Brien ep The Ten-Foot, Six-Inch Pole 1.14.66 CBS
The FBI ep The Sacrifice 1.16.66 ABC
Combat! ep Retribution 1.18.66 ABC
The Rat Patrol ep The Life Against Death Raid 9.19.66 ABC
Jericho ep A Jug of Wine, a Loaf of Bread--and POW! 9.22.66 CBS
Mission: Impossible ep The Butcher of the Balkans 9.24.66 CBS
Run for Your Life ep The Word Would Be Goodbye 4.27.67 NBC
Mission: Impossible ep 9.24.67 CBS
N.Y.P.D. ep The Patriots 1.2.68 ABC
The Man from UNCLE ep The Seven Wonders of the World Affair 1.8, 1.15.68 NBC
The Rat Patrol ep The Field of Death Raid 2.12.68 ABC
Mission: Impossible ep 12.15.68 CBS
The Name of the Game ep The Revolutionary 12.29.68 NBC
Hawaii Five-O ep Just Lucky, I Guess 9.24.69 CBS
Mission: Impossible ep 3.1.70 CBS
A World Apart sr 3.30.70 ABC
Hawaii Five-O ep The Guarnerius Caper 10.14.70 CBS
Mission: Impossible ep 12.12.70 CBS
The Silent Force ep The Octopus 12.21.70 ABC
Hawaii Five-O ep Nine, Ten, You're Dead 11.30.71 CBS
Mission: Impossible ep 1.18.72 CBS
Search ep Let Us Prey 1.3.73 NBC
Hollywood Television Theater ep Carola 2.5.73 PBS
Griff ep Prey 10.27.73 ABC
Police Story ep Cop in the Middle 1.29.74 NBC
Search for the Gods tf 3.9.75 ABC
Night Stalker ep Sentry 3.28.75 ABC
One of Our Own tf 5.5.75 NBC
Doctors' Hospital sr 9.10.75 NBC
Starsky and Hutch ep Shootout 12.17.75 ABC
Louis Armstrong--Country Style tf 1.25.76 ABC
Joe Forrester ep The Invaders 2.23.76 NBC
Switch ep Quicker Than the Eye 11.9.76 CBS
Charlie's Angels ep Angels on a String 1.9.77 ABC
Kojak ep Monkey on a String 2.15.77 CBS
The Gypsy Warriors pt 5.12.78 CBS

The New Adventures of Wonder Woman ep One of Our Teen Idols Is Missing 9.22.78 CBS
Cliffhangers: Stop Susan Williams sr 2.27.79 NBC
Trapper John, M.D. ep The Surrogate 12.23.79 CBS
Galactica 1980 ep Galactica Discovers Earth 2.3, 2.10.80 ABC
Hawaii Five-O ep 3.8.80 CBS
Side Show tf 6.5.81 NBC
Manimal ep Night of the Scorpion 10.21.83 NBC
Automan ep Murder MTV 3.12.84 ABC
Airwolf ep Crossover 10.26.85 CBS

PAYNE, JULIE*
Friendships, Secrets, and Lies tf 12.3.79 NBC
Hart to Hart ep Harts and Fraud 5.18.82 ABC
Wizards and Warriors sr 2.26.83 CBS
The Duck Factory sr 4.12.84 NBC
E/R ep 12.12.84 CBS
Joanna pt 4.30.85 ABC
George Burns Comedy Week ep The Dynamite Girl 9.18.85 CBS
The Twilight Zone ep The Wish Bank 11.18.85 CBS

PEAKER, E. J.
A&C, Supp. 1:
Good Morning World ep The Lady and the Pussycat 3.19.68 CBS
Get Christie Love ep My Son, the Murderer 2.12.75 ABC
The Rockford Files ep Just by Accident 2.28.75 NBC

PECK, GREGORY
SUPP.:
The Blue and the Gray ms 11.14-11.17.82 CBS
The Scarlet and the Black tf 2.2.83 CBS
An American Portrait ep Andy Lipkis 2.12.85 CBS
An American Portrait ep Emma Lazarus 3.25.85 CBS

PEEPLES, NIA*
Tales of the Gold Monkey ep The Sultan of Swat 1.5.83 ABC
T. J. Hooker ep Gang War 5.12.84 ABC
Fame sr 10.84 NN
Fame sr ret 10.85 NN

PELUCE, MEENO*
Night Cries tf 1.29.78 ABC
The Ghost of Flight 401 tf 2.18.78 NBC
The Incredible Hulk ep Married 9.22.78 CBS
The Pirate tf 11.21, 11.22.78 CBS
Lou Grant ep Denial 1.1.79 CBS
The Bad News Bears sr 3.24.79 CBS
Tenspeed and Brown Shoe ep The Millionaire's Life 3.16.80 ABC
Scout's Honor tf 9.30.80 NBC
The Love Boat ep Captive Audience 12.20.80 ABC

Best of the West sr 9.10.81 ABC
World War III tf 1.31, 2.1.82 NBC
Million Dollar Infield tf 2.2.82 CBS
Voyagers sr 10.3.82 NBC
Manimal ep Scrimshaw 12.3.83 NBC
The A-Team ep Pros and Cons 1.28.83 NBC
Scarecrow and Mrs. King ep The A.C.M. Kid 10.31.83 CBS
Silver Spoons ep Spare the Rod 1.21.84 NBC
Remington Steele ep A Pocketful of Steele 11.20.84 NBC
Punky Brewster ep Henry Falls in Love 2.3.85 NBC
Detective in the House sr 3.15.85 CBS

PENNINGTON, MARLA*
Charlie's Angels ep Bullseye 12.1.76 ABC
Magnum, P.I. ep Billy Joe Bob 10.8.81 CBS
Happy Days ep A Touch of Classical 2.2.82 ABC
Happy Days ep Hi Yo Fonzie ... Away 2.9.82 ABC
Private Benjamin ep Hero's Award 12.13.82 CBS
Herndon and Me pt 8.26.83 ABC
Small Wonder sr 9.85 NN

PENNY, JOE*
Delta County, U.S.A. tf 5.20.77 ABC
Death Moon tf 5.31.78 CBS
Mother, Juggs and Speed pt 8.17.78 ABC
The Girls in the Office tf 2.2.79 ABC
Samurai tf/pt 4.30.79 ABC
Lou Grant ep Influence 9.17.79 CBS
Paris ep 1.15.80 CBS
The Gossip Columnist tf/pt 3.21.80 OPT
Flamingo Road ep The Hostages 1.6.81 NBC
Vegas ep The Golden Gate Cop Killer 1.7.81 ABC
The Gangster Chronicles sr 2.12.81 NBC
Archie Bunker's Place ep 4.4.83 CBS
Tucker's Witch ep Dye Job 3.3.83 CBS
Savage in the Orient tf/pt 6.21.83 CBS
Lottery ep Denver: Following Through ("Matson Family" segment) 9.23.83 ABC
Matt Houston ep The Centerfold Murders 9.30.83 ABC
T. J. Hooker ep The Cheerleader Murders 10.22.83 ABC
Riptide sr 1.3.84 NBC
Riptide sr ret 10.2.84 NBC
Riptide sr ret 10.1.85 NBC

PENNY, SYDNEY*
The Night Rider tf/pt 5.11.79 ABC
The Big Stuffed Dog sp 2 8.80 NBC
It's Magic, Charlie Brown sp vo 4.28.81 CBS
Through the Magic Pyramid tf/pt 12.6, 12.13.81 NBC
The Patricia Neal Story tf 12.8.81 CBS
The Capture of Grizzly Adams tf 2.21.82 NBC

T. J. Hooker ep Mumbler 1.29.83 ABC
The Thorn Birds ms 3.27-3.30.83 ABC
St. Elsewhere ep Under Pressure 11.30.83 NBC
Silver Spoons ep Changes 3.3.84 NBC
Getting Physical tf 3.20.84 CBS
The Last Leaf sp 4.84 NN
Half Nelson ep Beverly Hills Princess 5.10.85 NBC
Hearts Island pt 8.31.85 NBC

PEPPARD, GEORGE
SUPP.:
The A-Team sr 1.23.83 NBC
The A-Team sr ret 9.20.83 NBC
The A-Team sr ret 9.18.84 NBC
The A-Team sr ret 9.26.85 NBC

PERLMAN, RHEA*
Stalk the Wild Child tf 11.3.76 NBC
I Want to Keep My Baby tf 11.19.76 CBS
Mary Jane Harper Cried Last Night tf 10.5.77 CBS
Having Babies II tf/pt 10.28.77 ABC
Intimate Strangers tf 11.11.77 ABC
Like Normal People tf 4.13.79 ABC
Taxi ep Louie's Fling 11.5.81 ABC
Dropout Father tf 9.27.82 CBS
Taxi ep Zena's Honeymoon 12.9.82 NBC
Taxi ep Celebration of Taxi 3.23.83 NBC
Cheers sr 9.20.82 NBC
Cheers sr ret 9.29.83 NBC
Cheers sr ret 9.27.84 NBC
The Ratings Game tf 12.15.84 TMC
St. Elsewhere ep Cheers 3.27.85 NBC
Cheers sr ret 9.26.85 NBC

PERREAU, GIGI
A&C, B.V.:
The Donna Reed Show ep Mary's Campaign 3.59 ABC
The Rifleman ep Heller 2.23.60 ABC
Gomer Pyle, USMC ep Arrivederci, Gomer 1.21.66 CBS
The Brady Bunch ep The Undergraduate 1.23.70 ABC

PERRINE, VALERIE
SUPP.:
Marian Rose White tf 1.19.82 CBS
Malibu tf/pt 1.23, 1.24.83 ABC
When Your Lover Leaves tf 10.31.83 NBC
Faerie Tale Theater ep The Three Little Pigs 2.12.85 SHO
George Burns Comedy Week ep The Couch 10.16.85 CBS

PERRY, ROGER*
You're Only Young Twice pt 8.1.60 CBS

Harrigan and Son sr 10.14.60 ABC
Arrest and Trial sr 9.15.63 ABC
Star Trek ep Tomorrow Is Yesterday 1.26.67 NBC
Crisis pt 9.2.68 CBS
The Outsider ep Take the Key and Lock Him Up 2.12.69 NBC
Lancer ep The Measure of a Man 4.8.69 CBS
The Bold Ones: The Doctors ep Giants Never Kneel 10.25.70 NBC
The D.A.: Conspiracy to Kill tf/pt 1.11.71 NBC
The Feminist and the Fuzz tf 1.26.71 ABC
Love, American Style ep 10.1.71 ABC
Alias Smith and Jones ep Something to Get Hung About 10.21.71 ABC
Revenge tf 11.6.71 ABC
The D.A. ep The People vs. Howard 12.3.71 NBC
Gidget Gets Married tf/pt 1.4.72 ABC
The FBI ep Arrangement with Terror 2.6.72 ABC
Ironside ep Hey Buddy, Can You Spare a Life? 11.16.72 NBC
Love, American Style ep 11.24.72 ABC
Beg, Borrow or Steal tf 3.20.73 ABC
Ironside ep Downhill all the Way 11.8.73 NBC
Room 222 ep 11.9.73 ABC
Tenafly ep The Widow That Wasn't 12.5.73 NBC
What Are Best Friends For? tf 12.18.73 ABC
Chase ep John Doe Bucks 1.16.74 NBC
Barnaby Jones ep Woman in the Shadows 3.10.74 CBS
Mannix ep The Ragged Edge 3.31.74 CBS
Emergency! 9.14.74 NBC
Movin' On ep Ammo 2.6.75 NBC
Emergency! ep 3.15.75 NBC
Conspiracy of Terror tf 12.29.75 NBC
The Bionic Woman ep A Thing of the Past 2.18.76 ABC
Most Wanted tf/pt 3.21.76 ABC
Hawaii Five-O ep Ready--Aim 1.20.77 CBS
Barnaby Jones ep Testament of Power 1.20.77 CBS
The Six Million Dollar Man ep Privacy of the Mind 2.27.77 ABC
The Man with the Power tf 5.24.77 NBC
Barnaby Jones ep Child of Danger 12.29.77 CBS
The Bionic Woman ep All for One 1.7.78 NBC
Operation Runaway ep Too Young to Love 5.18.78 NBC
The New Adventures of Wonder Woman ep The Richest Man in the World 2.19.79 CBS
Hanging By a Thread tf 5.8, 5.9.79 NBC
Quincy, M.E. ep The Money Plague 11.15.79 NBC
CHiPs ep 2.9.80 NBC
B.J. and the Bear ep Down and Dirty 2.3.81 NBC
The Facts of Life ep 12.2.81 NBC
The Facts of Life ep Growing Pains 3.10.82 NBC
The Facts of Life ep Read No Evil 5.5.82 NBC
Falcon Crest ep 10.15.82 CBS
The Facts of Life ep The Oldest Living Graduate 11.3.82 NBC

The Facts of Life ep Under Pressure 1.19.83 NBC
The Fall Guy ep Dirty Laundry 11.9.83 ABC
The Fall Guy ep Bite of the Wasp 1.18.84 ABC
Falcon Crest ep 1.6.84 CBS
Love Thy Neighbor tf 5.23.84 ABC
Falcon Crest ep Going Once, Going Twice 12.7.84 CBS
Falcon Crest ep Storm Warnings 11.22.85 CBS
Falcon Crest ep 11.29.85 CBS

PERSKY, LISA JANE*
KISS Meets the Phantom of the Park tf 10.28.78 NBC
The Choice tf 2.10.81 CBS
The ABC Afterschool Special ep A Matter of Time 2.11.81 ABC
Quincy, M.E. ep Sugar and Spice and Everything Nice 4.1.81 NBC
Trapper John, M.D. ep Ladies in Waiting 1.31.82 CBS
The Incredible Hulk ep A Minor Problem 5.12.82 CBS
Desperate Intruder tf 7.31.83 NN
Back Together pt 1.25.84 CBS
E/R ep 11.14.84 CBS
The Golden Girls ep Guess Who's Coming to the Wedding? 9.21.85 NBC
Amazing Stories ep The Main Attraction 10.6.85 NBC

PERSOFF, NEHEMIAH
A&C, Supp. 2:
Producers Showcase ep Mayerling 2.4.57 NBC
Playhouse 90 ep Death of Manolete 9.12.57 CBS
Alfred Hitchcock Presents ep Heart of Gold 10.27.57 CBS
Naked City ep The Scorpion Sting 6.2.59 ABC
Five Fingers ep Moment of Truth 10.17.59 ABC
Ford Startime ep The Young Juggler 3.29.60 NBC
Moment of Fear ep The Accomplice 8.26.60 NBC
Naked City ep Down the Long Night 11.2.60 ABC
Witness ep Lt. Charles Becker 11.24.60 CBS
The Dick Powell Show ep Death in a Village 1.2.61 NBC
Naked City ep Make Believe Man 5.17.61 ABC
Route 66 ep Incident on a Bridge 6.16.61 CBS
Naked City ep A Corpse Ran Down Mulberry Street 10.11.61 ABC
Route 66 ep First Class Movlick 10.20.61 CBS
Bus Stop ep The Glass Jungle 11.5.61 ABC
The New Breed ep How Proud the Guilt 2.27.62 ABC
Naked City ep And If Any Are Frozen, Warm Them 5.9.62 ABC
Sam Benedict ep Image of a Toad 2.23.63 NBC
Rawhide ep Incident of the White Eyes 5.3.63 CBS
Naked City ep One, Two, Three, Rita Rakahowski 5.15.63 ABC
Rawhide ep Incident of the Wanderer 2.27.64 CBS
The Bob Hope Chrysler Theater ep Echo of Evil 6.5.64 NBC
Burke's Law ep Who Killed Cassandra Cass? 9.30.64 ABC
Mr. Novak ep Enter a Strange Animal 1.19.65 NBC

The Nurses ep Act of Violence (Part 1) 2.23.65 CBS
For the People Act of Violence (Part 2) 2.28.65 CBS
Burke's Law ep Who Killed the Grand Piano? 4.28.65 ABC
Ben Casey ep Run for Your Lives, Dr. Galanos Practices Here! 10.4.65 ABC
Gilligan's Island ep The Little Dictator Fall 1965 CBS
Gunsmoke ep Ten Little Indians 10.9.65 CBS
The Bob Hope Chrysler Theater ep The Game 9.15.65 NBC
Amos Burke, Secret Agent ep Steam Heat 9.29.65 ABC
Gunsmoke ep The Pretender 11.20.65 CBS
Voyage to the Bottom of the Sea ep Deadly Creature Below 1.9.66 ABC
The Man from UNCLE ep The Master's Touch Affair 10.16.77 NBC
Gunsmoke ep Blood Money 1.22.68 CBS
Hawaii Five-O ep Deathwatch 12.25.68 CBS
The Bill Cosby Show ep The Killer Instinct 11.9.69 NBC
The Flying Nun ep A Convent Full of Miracles 11.69 ABC
The High Chaparral ep Fiesta 11.20.70 NBC
McCloud ep 1.23.77 NBC
Hawaii Five-O ep Hit Gun for Sale 2.25.75 CBS
Hawaii Five-O ep Dealer's Choice: Blackmail 2.3.77 CBS
SUPP.:
Sadat tf 10.31, 11.7.83 OPT
Scarecrow and Mrs. King ep Dead Ringer 2.6.84 CBS
Magnum, P.I. ep Torah, Torah, Torah 3.28.85 CBS
Hotel ep Passports 4.10.85 ABC

PESCOW, DONNA
SUPP.:
The Day the Bubble Burst tf 2.7.82 NBC
Cassie and Company ep Lover Come Back 8.13.82 NBC
The Love Boat ep Baby Talk 1.11.82 ABC
Fantasy Island ep The Songwriter 1.22.83 ABC
Trapper John, M.D. ep 1.23.83 CBS
Police Woman Centerfold tf 10.17.83 NBC
The Love Boat ep For Love or Money 10.22.83 ABC
Hotel ep Relative Loses 11.2.83 ABC
Fantasy Island ep Skin Deep 1.28.84 ABC
Finder of Lost Loves ep Echoes 10.27.84 ABC
Obsessed with a Married Man tf 2.11.85 ABC
The New Love, American Style ep Love and the Video Baby 12.27.85 ABC

PETERS, BERNADETTE
SUPP.:
Faerie Tale Theater ep Sleeping Beauty 7.7.83 SHO
An American Portrait ep Trevor Ferrell 12.17.84 CBS

PETERS, BROCK
SUPP.:
Agatha Christie's "A Caribbean Mystery" tf 10.22.83 CBS

Faerie Tale Theater ep Puss 'n' Boots 9.9.85 SHO
Magnum, P.I. ep Old Acquaintances 10.3.85 CBS

PETERSON, CASSANDRA (a.k.a. Elvira)*
Fantasy Island ep The Sheik 9.16.78 ABC
Elvira's Movie Macabre sr hos 1982 NN
Open All Night ep Sitting Ducks 2.5.82 ABC
CHiPs ep Rock Devil Rock 10.31.82 NBC
Alice ep 4.11.83 CBS
Last of the Great Survivors tf 1.3.84 CBS
The Fall Guy ep October the 31st 10.31.84 ABC
The Fall Guy ep October the 32nd 12.7.85 ABC

PETTET, JOANNA
A&C, Supp. 1:
Harry O ep Forty Reasons to Kill 12.5.74, 12.12.74 ABC
Harry O ep Group Terror 11.13.75 ABC
SUPP.:
Fantay Island ep Image of Celeste 3.20.82 ABC
The Love Boat ep Rhymes, Riddles and Romance 3.27.82 ABC
Knots Landing sr 2.17.83 CBS
Fantasy Island ep Death Games 3.12.83 ABC
Hotel ep Reflections 1.4.84 ABC
The Fall Guy ep Always Say Always 2.2.84 ABC
The Yellow Rose ep Running Free 2.25.84 NBC
Knight Rider ep Mouth of the Snake 4.8.84 NBC
Finder of Lost Loves ep Undying Love 11.10.84 ABC
Hotel ep Lost and Found 2.13.85 ABC

PEYSER, PENNY
SUPP.:
The Blue and the Gray ms 11.14-11.17.82 CBS
Knight Rider ep The Final Verdict 12.3.82 NBC
The Powers of Matthew Star ep 36 Hours 2.18.63 NBC
Emergency Room tf 7.17.83 NN
The A-Team ep Labor Pains 11.8.83 NBC
The Fall Guy ep Dirty Laundry 11.9.83 ABC
Masquerade ep Caribbean Holiday 1.12.84 ABC
Off Sides tf 7.6.84 NBC
Crazy Like a Fox sr 12.30.84 CBS
Crazy Like a Fox sr ret 9.29.85 CBS

PFLUG, JO ANN
A&C, Supp. 1:
The Beverly Hillbillies ep Granny Lives It Up 11.23.66 CBS
The Big Valley ep Down Shadow Street 1.23.67 ABC
Alias Smith and Jones ep Only Three to a Bed 1.13.73 ABC
SUPP.:
Fantasy Island ep The Spoilers 5.8.82 ABC
One Day at a Time ep 2.13.83 CBS
The Love Boat ep The Buck Stops Here 1.14.84 ABC

Knight Rider ep Diamonds Aren't a Girl's Best Friend 1.15.84 NBC
The Four Seasons ep 3.18.84 CBS
Matt Houston ep Cash and Carry 3.23.84 ABC
The Four Seasons ep 4.29.84 CBS
Rituals sr 9.84 NN

PHILLIPS, MACKENZIE
SUPP.:
The Love Boat ep Gopher's Roommate 1.23.82 ABC
One Day at a Time ep Orville and Family Strike Back 3.2.82 CBS
One Day at a Time ret to sr 9.26.82 CBS
One Day at a Time sr ret 10.2.83 CBS
Murder, She Wrote ep Murder in the Afternoon 10.13.85 CBS

PHILLIPS, MICHELLE*
Owen Marshall, Counselor at Law ep The Prowler 12.12.73 ABC
The Death Squad tf 1.8.74 ABC
The California Kid tf 9.25.74 ABC
Aspen ms 11.5-11.7.77 NBC
The Users tf 10.1.78 ABC
The French Atlantic Affair ms 11.15-11.18.79 ABC
Fantasy Island ep The Mermaid 12.1.79 ABC
Vegas ep Ladies in Blue 3.19.80 ABC
Moonlight tf/pt 9.14.82 CBS
Fantasy Island ep Legend 10.30.82 ABC
Matt Houston ep Shark Bait 11.21.82 ABC
The Fall Guy ep The Chameleon 4.6.83 ABC
Mickey Spillane's Mike Hammer: Murder Me, Murder You tf/pt 4.9.83 CBS
The Mississippi ep 10.18.83 CBS
Hotel ep Secrets 10.26.83 ABC
Fantasy Island ep Three's a Crowd 11.19.83 ABC
The Love Boat ep No More Alimony 1.7.84 ABC
Automan ep Murder Take One 3.19.84 ABC
Fantasy Island ep The Mermaid and the Matchmaker 3.24.84 ABC
The Love Boat ep Doc's Slump 9.22.84 ABC
Secrets of a Married Man tf 9.24.84 NBC
Finder of Lost Loves ep Yesterday's Child 9.29.84 ABC
Murder, She Wrote ep Death Casts a Spell 12.30.84 CBS
T. J. Hooker ep Love Story 2.16.85 ABC
Scene of the Crime ep Murder on the Half Shell 4.28.85 NBC
Covenant tf/pt 8.5.85 NBC

PICKENS, SLIM
A&C, B.V.:
The Westerner ep Line Camp 12.9.60 NBC
Alfred Hitchcock Presents ep Final Arrangements 6.20.61 CBS
Tall Man ep The Black Robe 5.5.62 NBC

The Fugitive ep Nowhere to Run 1.15.68 CBS
A&C, Supp. 2:
Switch ep Butterfly Mourning 2.6.77 CBS
Baretta ep Big Bad Charlie 3.30.77 ABC
SUPP.:
Filthy Rich sr 8.16.82 CBS
Sawyer and Finn pt 4.22.83 NBC

PICKETT, CINDY*
The Ivory Ape tf 4.18.80 ABC
Mickey Spillane's Margin for Murder tf/pt 10.15.81 CBS
The Cherokee Trail pt 11.28.81 CBS
Family in Blue pt 6.10.82 CBS
Cry for the Strangers tf 12.11.82 CBS
Cocaine and Blue Eyes tf/pt 1.2.83 NBC
Bring 'Em Back Alive ep 1.15.83 CBS
Riptide ep Somebody's Killing the Great Geeks of America 1.17.84 NBC
Simon and Simon ep 3.8.84 CBS
Magnum, P.I. ep Dream a Little Dream 3.29.84 CBS
Call to Glory sr 8.13.84 ABC

PIOLI, JUDY*
Laverne and Shirley ep Whatever Happened to the Class of '56? 2.16.82 ABC
Mork and Mindy ep Cheerleaders in Chains 4.22.82 ABC
Star of the Family sr 9.30.82 ABC
Happy Days ep Who Gives a Hootenanny 11.16.82 ABC
It Takes Two ep Lying Down on the Job 2.3.83 ABC
Shaping Up ep Ex Pede Herculem 3.20.84 ABC
Shaping Up ep Defusing the Muse 4.3.84 ABC
Simon and Simon ep Almost Fool Proof 1.3.85 CBS

PISCOPO, JOE*
George Burns Comedy Week ep Death Benefits 10.2.85 CBS

PLACE, MARY KAY
SUPP.:
The ABC Afterschool Special ep Mom's on Strike 11.14.84 ABC
For Love or Money tf 11.20.84 CBS

PLATO, DANA
SUPP.:
Diff'rent Strokes sr ret 10.2.82 NBC
High School, U.S.A. tf/pt 10.16.83 NBC
The Love Boat ep Baby Sister 12.1.84 ABC
Diff'rent Strokes ep Happy Birthday, Drummond 1.26.85 NBC
Diff'rent Strokes ret to sr 9.27.85 ABC
Growing Pains ep Mike's Madonna Story 11.5.85 ABC

PLEASENCE, DONALD

SUPP.:

Computercide tf/pt 8.1.82 NBC
Witness for the Prosecution tf 12.4.82 CBS
Master of the Game ms 2.19-2.21.84 CBS
The Barchester Chronicles sr 10.28.84 PBS
The Corsican Brothers tf 2.5.85 CBS
Arch of Triumph tf 5.29.85 CBS

PLESHETTE, SUZANNE

SUPP.:

Help Wanted: Male tf 1.16.82 CBS
Fantasies tf 1.18.82 ABC
Dixie: Changing Habits tf 2.16.83 CBS
One Cooks, the Other Doesn't tf 9.27.83 CBS
Suzanne Pleshette Is Maggie Briggs sr 3.4.84 CBS
For Love or Money tf 11.20.84 CBS
Kojak: The Belarus File tf/pt 2.10.85 CBS

PLUMB, EVE

SUPP.:

The Love Boat ep Command Performance 10.30.82 ABC
One Day at a Time ep 11.7.82 CBS
The Facts of Life ep Best Sister 2.16, 2.23.83 NBC
Masquerade ep Spying Down to Mexico 4.27.85 ABC

POLLAN, TRACY*

For Lovers Only tf 10.15.82 ABC
Sessions tf 9.26.83 ABC
Trackdown: Finding the Goodbar Killer tf 10.15.83 CBS
A Good Sport tf 2.8.84 CBS
The Baron and the Kid tf 11.21.84 CBS
Family Ties ep The Real Thing 9.26, 10.3.85 NBC

POLLARD, MICHAEL J.

A&C, B.V.:

Five Fingers ep The Unknown Town 10.24.59 NBC
The Many Loves of Dobie Gillis ep Maynard's Farewell to the Troops 11.3.59 CBS
The Many Loves of Dobie Gillis ep The Sweet Singer of Central High 11.10.59 CBS
Gunsmoke ep Journey for Three 6.4.64 CBS
Cimarron Strip ep The Battle of Bloody Stones 10.12.67 CBS

A&C, Supp. 1:

Get Christie Love ep The Longest Fall 12.11.74 ABC

PORTER, NYREE DAWN

A&C, B.V.:

The Man from Interpol ep Soul Peddlers 2.13.60 NBC

POST, MARKIE*
Barnaby Jones ep The Bigamist 2.22.79 CBS
The Incredible Hulk ep The Confession 5.4.79 CBS
The Lazarus Syndrome ep A Brutal Assault 9.11.79 ABC
Buck Rogers in the 25th Century ep The Plot to Kill a City 10.11, 10.18.79 NBC
Hart to Hart ep Cop Out 11.6.79 ABC
House Calls ep 1.21.80 CBS
Semi-Tough sr 5.29.80 ABC
The Gangster Chronicles sr 2.12.81 NBC
The Greatest American Hero ep The 200 Mile-an-Hour Fastball 10.28.81 ABC
Simon and Simon ep Details at 11 11.24.81 CBS
McClain's Law ep Requiem for a Narc 12.27.81 NBC
Code Red ep Wildfire 1.10.82 ABC
The Love Boat ep A Dress to Remember 5.8.82 ABC
Massarati and the Brain tf/pt 8.26.82 ABC
Not Just Another Affair tf 10.2.82 CBS
The Fall Guy sr 10.27.82 ABC
Fantasy Island ep No Friends Like Old Friends 2.26.83 ABC
Six Pack pt 7.24.83 NBC
The Fall Guy sr ret 9.21.83 ABC
The A-Team ep The Only Church in Town 10.11.83 NBC
The Love Boat ep Dee Dee Dilemma 12.3.83 ABC
Cheers ep Just Three Friends 12.15.83 NBC
Fantasy Island ep Dark Secret 3.3.84 ABC
Hotel ep Prisms 3.14.84 ABC
Glitter ep Glitter (pt) 9.13.84 ABC
The Love Boat Fall Preview Party sp 9.15.84 ABC
The Fall Guy sr ret 9.19.84 ABC
Scene of the Crime pt (untitled 1st segment) 9.30.84 NBC
Night Court ep Daddy for the Defense 10.4.84 NBC
The A-Team ep Hot Styles 12.11.84 NBC
Night Court sr (with ep Hello, Goodbye) 9.26.85 NBC

POSTON, TOM
SUPP.:
King's Crossing ep Home Front 2.27.82 ABC
Newhart sr 10.25.82 CBS
Newhart sr ret 10.17.83 CBS
The Love Boat ep The Prize Winner 12.3.83 ABC
Newhart sr ret 10.15.84 CBS
Newhart sr ret 9.30.85 CBS
Hotel ep Pathways 10.30.85 ABC

POTTS, ANNIE*
Hollywood High pt 7.21.77 NBC
Family ep 10.19.78 ABC
Flatbed Annie and Sweetiepie: Lady Truckers tf/pt 2.10.79 CBS
Goodtime Girls sr 1.22.80 ABC

In Security pt 7.7.82 CBS
Something So Right tf 11.30.82 CBS
Remington Steele ep Steele Crazy After All These Years 2.18.83 NBC
Magnum, P.I. ep 3.10.83 CBS
Cowboy tf 4.30.83 CBS
Why Me? tf 3.12.84 ABC
It Came Upon the Midnight Clear tf 12.15.84 NN
The Twilight Zone ep Word Play 10.4.85 CBS
Lime Street ep Diamonds Aren't Forever 10.12.85 ABC

POWELL, JANE
SUPP.:
The Love Boat ep Saving Grace 5.1.82 ABC

POWERS, MALA
A&C, B.V.:
Wanted: Dead Or Alive ep Till Death Do Us Part 11.8.58 CBS
Bewitched ep No Zip in My Zap Fall 1967 ABC
Here Come the Brides ep The Fetching of Jenny 12.5.69 ABC
A&C, Supp. 2:
Switch ep Camera Angels 1.30.77 CBS

POWERS, STEFANIE
A&C, Supp. 1:
Harry O ep Second Sight 11.7.74 ABC
The Rockford Files ep The Real Easy Red Dog 10.31.75 NBC
SUPP.:
Hart to Hart sr ret 9.28.82 ABC
Hart to Hart sr ret 9.27.83 ABC
Why Me? tf 3.12.84 ABC
Hollywood Wives ms 2.17-2.19.85 ABC
Deceptions tf 5.26, 5.27.85 NBC

PRANGE, LAURIE
A&C, Supp. 2:
Medical Center ep Death Grip 11.4.70 CBS
Marcus Welby, M.D. ep The Windfall 3.27.71 ABC
Baretta ep And Down Will Come Baby 11.19.75 ABC
Hawaii Five-O ep Elegy in a Rain Forest 1.27.77 CBS
Switch ep The Four Horsemen 2.13.77 CBS
SUPP.:
McClain's Law ep Sign of the Beast 1.29.82 NBC
American Playhouse ep Pilgrim, Farewell 3.23.82 PBS
Cagney and Lacey ep 11.22.82 CBS
T. J. Hooker ep The Return 10.1.83 ABC
The Mississippi ep 10.11.83 CBS
Cagney and Lacey ep 4.23.84 CBS
The Fourth Wise Man sp 3.30.85 ABC
Hardcastle and McCormick ep Duet for Two Wind Instruments 12.16.85 ABC

PRATT, DEBORAH*
Love Is Not Enough tf 6.12.78 NBC
Grambling's White Tiger tf 10.4.81 NBC
Benson ep Who's Arnold? 10.7.83 ABC
Gimme a Break ep The Way to a Man's Heart 10.13.83 NBC
Airwolf sr 1.22.84 CBS
Magnum, P.I. ep 2.2.84 CBS
Magnum, P.I. ep Echoes of the Mind 9.27.84 CBS
Magnum, P.I. ep Tran Quoc Jones 11.29.84 CBS

PRENTISS, PAULA
SUPP.:
Packin' It In tf 2.7.83 CBS
M.A.D.D.: Mothers Against Drunk Drivers tf 3.14.83 NBC

PRESLEY, PRISCILLA (a.k.a. Priscilla Beaulieu Presley)*
The Fall Guy ep Manhunter 1.19.83 ABC
Love Is Forever tf 4.3.83 NBC
Dallas sr 11.11.83 CBS
Dallas sr ret 9.28.84 CBS
Dallas sr ret 9.27.85 CBS

PRESSMAN, LAWRENCE
A&C, Supp. 2:
Cannon ep Killer on the Hill 1.29.75 CBS
Switch ep Maggie's Hero 12.14.76 CBS
SUPP.:
Hart to Hart ep Harts and Fraud 5.18.82 ABC
Rehearsal for Murder tf 5.26.82 CBS
Tucker's Witch ep The Corpse Who Knew Too Much 10.20.82 CBS
The Love Boat ep Father, Dear Father 12.4.82 ABC
Cry for the Strangers tf 12.11.82 CBS
The Winds of War ms 2.6-2.13.83 ABC
Dynasty ep The Vigil 2.29.84 ABC
Dynasty ep The Voice 3.21.84 ABC
Red Light Sting tf 4.5.84 CBS
Call to Glory ep Go/No Go 9.24.84 ABC
The Three Wishes of Billy Grier tf 11.1.84 ABC
Victims for Victims: The Theresa Saldana Story tf 11.12.84 NBC
For Love or Money tf 11.20.84 CBS
Murder, She Wrote ep My Johnnie Lies Over the Ocean 2.10.85 CBS

PRESTON, MIKE*
Agatha Christie's "A Caribbean Mystery" tf 10.22.83 CBS
Mickey Spillane's Mike Hammer ep Sex Trap 3.24.84 CBS
Hot Pursuit sr 9.22.84 NBC
Cover Up ep Jack of Spades 3.30.85 CBS
Blade in Hong Kong tf/pt 5.15.85 CBS

Scarecrow and Mrs. King ep Reach for the Sky 11.11.85 CBS
Airwolf ep Jennie 11.23.85 CBS

PRESTON, ROBERT
SUPP.:
Rehearsal for Murder tf 5.26.82 CBS
September Gun tf 10.8.83 CBS
Finnegan Begin Again tf 2.24.85 HBO

PRICE, VINCENT
A&C, B.V.:
F Troop ep V Is for Vampire 1.2.67 ABC
Get Smart ep Is This Trip Necessary? 12.69 NBC
The Brady Bunch ep The Tiki Caves 10.6.72 ABC
SUPP.:
Trapper John, M.D. ep 11.7.82 CBS
Faerie Tale Theater ep Snow White and the Seven Dwarfs 7.16.84 SHO
The Compleat Gilbert and Sullivan ep Ruddigore 4.3.85 PBS

PRINCE, WILLIAM
SUPP.:
Moonlight tf/pt 9.14.82 CBS
Joe Dancer: Murder One, Dance 0 tf/pt 6.5.83 NBC
Found Money tf 11.19.83 NBC
George Washington ms 4.8-4.11.84 CBS
Simon and Simon ep Manna from Heaven 10.25.84 CBS
The Fall Guy ep Seavers: Dead or Alive 12.14.85 ABC

PRINCIPAL, VICTORIA
A&C, Supp. 2:
The Rockford Files ep Sticks and Stones May Break Your Bones But Waterbury Will Bury You 1.14.77 NBC
Hawaii Five-O ep The Year of the Horse 4.5.79 CBS
SUPP.:
Dallas sr ret 10.1.82 CBS
Not Just Another Affair tf 10.2.82 CBS
Dallas sr ret 9.30.83 CBS
Dallas sr ret 9.28.84 CBS
Dallas sr ret 9.27.85 CBS

PRINE, ANDREW
A&C, B.V.:
Twelve O'Clock High ep Follow the Leader 9.25.64 ABC
A&C, Supp. 1:
Kung Fu ep The Gunman 1.3.74 ABC
The Night Stalker ep The Devil's Platform 11.15.74 ABC
Cannon ep Missing at F1-307 2.5.75 CBS
Hawaii Five-O ep Target? The Lady 10.3.75 CBS
SUPP.:
Darkroom ep Lost in the Translation 1.8.82 ABC

Hart to Hart ep Deep in the Hart of Dixieland 3.9.82 ABC
The Fall Guy ep One Hundred Miles a Gallon 3.9.83 ABC
V ms 5.1, 5.2.83 NBC
Trapper John, M.D. ep 1.15.84 CBS
Matt Houston ep On the Run 3.30.84 ABC
V: The Final Battle ms 5.6-5.8.84 NBC
Matt Houston ep Wanted Man 9.21.84 ABC
Cover Up ep The Million Dollar Face 10.6.84 CBS
Murder, She Wrote ep Lovers and Other Killers 11.18.84 CBS
On Our Way pt 6.29.85 CBS

PROWSE, JULIET
SUPP.:
The Devlin Connection ep Claudine 12.11.82 NBC
Fantasy Island ep Forbidden Love 10.8.83 ABC
The Love Boat ep Dream Boat 5.5.84 ABC
Glitter ep Glitter (pt) 9.13.84 ABC

PRYOR, RICHARD*
The Wild Wild West ep Night of the Eccentrics 9.16.66 CBS
The Wild Wild West ep The Night of the Golden Cobra 9.23.66 CBS
The Young Lawyers tf/pt 10.28.69 ABC
Carter's Army tf 1.27.70 ABC
The Partridge Family ep Save Our Firehouse 1971 ABC
The Mod Squad ep The Connection 9.14.72 ABC
Pryor's Place sr 9.15.84 CBS

PURCELL, LEE
A&C, Supp. 2:
The Young Rebels ep Alias Ben Toad 11.1.70 ABC
Lucas Tanner ep A Matter of Love 9.11.74 NBC
The Rockford Files ep The Dexter Crisis 11.15.74 NBC
Hawaii Five-O ep Turkey Shoot at Makapu 1.29.76 CBS
Hawaii Five-O ep Practical Jokes Can Kill You 5.5.77 CBS
SUPP.:
The Phoenix ep Presence of Evil 4.9.82 ABC
My Wicked, Wicked Ways.... The Legend of Errol Flynn tf 11.21.84 CBS
Magnum, P.I. ep Old Acquaintance 10.3.85 CBS
Hollywood Beat ep Fast Hustle 11.23.85 ABC

PURL, LINDA
A&C, Supp. 2:
Happy Days ep Wish Upon a Star 11.12.74 ABC
SUPP.:
Happy Days sr 9.28.82 ABC
Money on the Side tf 9.29.82 ABC
I Do, I Don't pt 9.2.83 ABC
The Last Days of Pompeii ms 5.6-5.8.84 ABC
Murder, She Wrote ep Murder at the Oasis 4.7.85 CBS

The Love Boat ep A Gentleman of Discrimination 5.4.85 ABC
Midas Valley tf/pt 6.27.85 ABC
Alfred Hitchcock Presents ep Revenge 9.29.85 NBC

PYLE, DENVER*
The Roy Rogers Show ep The Flying Bullets 6.15.52 CBS
Public Defender ep The Hobo Story 6.17.54 CBS
Public Defender ep Condemned 5.19.55 CBS
The Life and Legend of Wyatt Earp ep Mr. Earp Becomes Marshal 9.6.55 ABC
The Life and Legend of Wyatt Earp ep Mr. Earp Meets a Lady 9.13.55 ABC
The Life and Legend of Wyatt Earp ep Bill Thompson Gives In 9.20.55 ABC
Fury ep Joey's Father 12.3.55 CBS
The Life and Legend of Wyatt Earp ep Ben Thompson Returns 12.27.55 ABC
The Lone Ranger ep The Cross of Santo Domingo 10.11.56 ABC
The Adventures of Jim Bowie ep A Horse for Old Hickory 1.4.57 ABC
The Life and Legend of Wyatt Earp ep Witness for the Defense 1.22.57 ABC
The Adventures of Jim Bowie ep Master of Arms 1.25.57 ABC
Gunsmoke ep Liar from Blackhawk 6.22.57 CBS
The Restless Gun ep Rink 10.14.57 NBC
The Court of Last Resort ep The Wesley Ferguson Case 10.25.57 ABC
The Californians ep Magic Box 11.26.57 NBC
Broken Arrow ep Bad Boy 1.2.58 ABC
Perry Mason ep The Case of the Deadly Double 3.1.58 CBS
The Life and Legend of Wyatt Earp ep Dig a Grave for Ben Thompson 5.20.58 ABC
Jefferson Drum ep Prison Hill 12.4.58 NBC
The Life and Legend of Wyatt Earp ep A Good Man 1.6.59 ABC
Gunsmoke ep Mike Blocker 2.28.59 CBS
Bat Masterson ep Marked Deck 3.11.59 NBC
The Restless Gun ep The Pawn 4.6.59 NBC
Rescue 8 ep International Incident 5.13.59 NN
The Texan ep No Place to Stop 6.1.59 CBS
The Deputy ep Shadow of the Noose 10.3.59 NBC
Tales of Wells Fargo ep Double Reverse 10.19.59 NBC
The Texan ep 10.26.59 CBS
Two Faces West ep Hand of Vengeance 1960 NN
The Texan ep 3.28.60 CBS
Hotel de Paree ep Sundance and the Long Trek 4.22.60 CBS
Overland Trail ep The Baron Comes Back 5.15.60 NBC
Perry Mason ep The Case of the Ominous Outcast 5.21.60 CBS
The Man from Blackhawk ep The Man Who Wanted Everything 6.3.60 ABC
The Tall Man ep Garrett and the Kid 9.10.60 NBC

Gunsmoke ep The Wake 11.5.60 CBS
The Life and Legend of Wyatt Earp ep The Perfect Crime 12.6.60 ABC
Stagecoach West ep Three Wise Men 12.20.60 ABC
Maverick ep Family Pride 1.8.61 ABC
Bat Masterson ep End of the Line 1.26.61 ABC
The Deputy ep The Example 3.25.61 NBC
Checkmate ep Jungle Castle 4.1.61 CBS
The Rifleman ep The Clarence Debs Story 4.4.61 ABC
Bronco ep Guns of the Lawless 5.8.61 ABC
Cheyenne ep Winchester Quarantine 9.25.61 ABC
National Velvet ep The Tramp 10.23.61 NBC
The Rifleman ep The Decision 11.6.61 ABC
The Detectives ep Beyond a Reasonable Doubt 11.17.61 ABC
Thriller ep The Hollow Watcher 2.12.62 NBC
Ben Casey ep Among Others, a Girl Named Abilene 4.2.62 ABC
Empire ep The Day the Empire Stood Still 9.25.62 ABC
Cheyenne ep Sweet Sam 10.8.62 ABC
Bonanza ep A Hot Day for a Hanging 10.14.62 NBC
Gunsmoke ep Us Haggers 12.8.62 CBS
Laramie ep Vengeance 1.8.63 NBC
Gunsmoke ep The Odyssey of Jubal Tanner 5.18.63 CBS
Bonanza ep The Boss 5.19.63 NBC
Bonanza ep Little Man--Ten Feet Tall 5.26.63 NBC
The Dick Van Dyke Show ep Uncle George 10.63 CBS
Channing ep Dragon in the Den 10.23.63 ABC
Rawhide ep Incident of the Rawhiders 11.14.63 CBS
Dr. Kildare ep A Willing Suspension of Disbelief 1.9.64 NBC
The Twilight Zone ep Black Leather Jackets 1.31.64 CBS
Temple Houston ep The Case for William Gotch 2.6.64 NBC
Gunsmoke ep No Hands 2.8.64 CBS
Bonanza ep Bullet for a Bride 2.16.64 NBC
The Lieutenant ep The War Called Peace 4.11.64 NBC
Gunsmoke ep The Violators 10.17.64 CBS
Mr. Novak ep Johnny Ride the Pony--1,2,3 12.15.64 NBC
Gunsmoke ep Deputy Festus 1.6.65 CBS
Slattery's People ep What Did You Do Today, Mr. Slattery? 1.15.65 CBS
Tammy sr 9.17.65 ABC
Gunsmoke ep By Line 4.9.66 CBS
Gunsmoke ep The Gold Takers 9.24.66 CBS
Gunsmoke ep Mad Dog 1.4.67 CBS
The High Chaparral ep A Hanging Offense 11.12.67 NBC
Hondo ep Hondo and the Hanging Town 12.8.67 ABC
Cimarron Strip ep 12.14.67 CBS
Gunsmoke ep Baker's Dozen 12.25.67 CBS
The Guns of Will Sonnett ep The Warriors 3.1.68 ABC
The Doris Day Show sr 9.24.68 CBS
Bonanza ep The Passing of a King 10.13.68 NBC
The Doris Day Show sr ret 9.69 CBS
Here Come the Brides ep Bolt of Kilmaren 3.13.70 ABC

The Waltons ep 2.14.72 CBS
Gunsmoke ep Shadler 1.15.73 CBS
Hitched tf/pt 3.31.73 NBC
Kung Fu ep The Ancient Warrior 5.3.73 ABC
The Streets of San Francisco ep Winterkill 12.13.73 ABC
Cannon ep Duel in the Desert 1.16.74 CBS
The New Perry Mason ep The Case of the Violent Valley 1.20.74 CBS
The World of Disney ep Hog Wild 1.20, 1.27.74 NBC
Dirty Sally ep 2.8.74 CBS
Kung Fu ep Cross Ties 2.21.74 ABC
Sidekicks tf 3.21.74 CBS
Murder or Mercy? tf 4.19.74 ABC
The Manhunter ep The Baby-Faced Killers 9.25.74 CBS
Karen ep 1.30.75 NBC
Death Among Friends tf 5.20.75 NBC
The Family Holvak ep Remembrance of a Guest 9.28.75 NBC
Petrocelli ep Blood Money 2.11.76 NBC
The Life and Times of Grizzly Adams sr 2.9.77 NBC
The Life and Times of Grizzly Adams sr ret 9.28.77 NBC
Once Upon a Starry Night tf 12.19.78 NBC
The Dukes of Hazzard sr 1.26.79 CBS
How the West Was Won ep The Enemy 2.5.79 ABC
The Dukes of Hazzard sr ret 9.21.79 CBS
The Dukes of Hazzard sr ret 10.25.80 CBS
Enos ep Uncle Jesse's Visit 11.19.80 CBS
The Dukes of Hazzard sr ret 10.6.81 CBS
The Dukes of Hazzard sr ret 9.24.82 CBS
The Dukes sr vo 2.5.83 CBS
The Dukes of Hazzard sr ret 9.23.83 CBS
The Dukes of Hazzard sr ret 9.21.84 CBS

- Q -

QUALEN, JOHN

A&C, B.V.:

Maverick ep Lonesome Reunion 9.28.58 ABC
The Andy Griffith Show ep The Jinx 1.29.62 CBS

- R -

RAE, CHARLOTTE

SUPP.:

The Love Boat ep Getting to Know You 3.6.82 ABC
The Facts of Life Goes to Paris tf 9.25.82 NBC

The Facts of Life sr ret 10.6.82 NBC
The Facts of Life sr ret 9.21.83 NBC
The Love Boat ep Youth Takes a Holiday 10.15.83 ABC
The Facts of Life sr ret 9.26.84 NBC
Wonderworks ep Words By Heart 2.11.85 PBS
The Facts of Life sr ret 9.14.85 NBC
The Love Boat ep Your Money or Your Wife 10.5.85 ABC

RAFFIN, DEBORAH
SUPP.:
For Lovers Only tf 10.15.82 ABC
Running Out tf 1.26.83 CBS
Agatha Christie's "Sparkling Cyanide" tf 11.5.83 CBS
Lace II tf 5.5, 5.6.85 ABC

RAINS, CRISTINA
SUPP.:
Simon and Simon ep The List 2.17.83 CBS
T. J. Hooker ep Raw Deal 2.19.83 ABC
The Love Boat ep Set Up for Romance 11.19.83 ABC
Hotel ep Designs 12.28.83 ABC
Fantasy Island ep Goin' on Home 1.7.84 ABC
Matt Houston ep Death Match 2.24.84 ABC
The Return of Marcus Welby, M.D. tf/pt 5.16.84 ABC
Finder of Lost Loves ep Losing Touch 10.13.84 ABC
The Fall Guy ep Semi-Catastrophe 1.2.85 ABC
Murder, She Wrote ep Paint Me a Murder 2.17.85 CBS
The Love Boat ep The Perfect Arrangement 2.23.85 ABC
Generation tf/pt 5.24.85 ABC
Riptide ep 36 Hours Till Dawn 10.22.85 NBC
Streets of Justice tf 11.10.85 NBC
Alfred Hitchcock Presents ep You Gotta Have Luck 12.8.85 NBC

RALPH, SHERYL LEE*
Code Name: Foxfire pt ep Slay It Again, Uncle Sam 1.27.85 NBC
Code Name: Foxfire sr 2.8.85 NBC

RAMBO, DACK
SUPP.:
The Love Boat ep Two for Julie 3.14.82 ABC
All My Children sr 1983 ABC
Murder, She Wrote ep 10.7.84 CBS
Dallas sr 9.27.85 CBS

RANDALL, TONY
SUPP.:
Love, Sidney sr ret 9.15.82 NBC
Off Sides tf 7.6.84 NBC
Hitler's SS: Portrait in Evil tf 2.17.85 NBC

RATZENBERGER, JOHN*
Goliath Awaits tf 10.16, 10.17.81 OPT
Code Red ep All That Glitters 11.29.81 ABC
Wizards and Warriors ep To the Rescue 5.7.83 CBS
Cheers sr 9.30.82 NBC
Cheers sr ret 9.29.83 NBC
Cheers sr ret 9.27.84 NBC
Magnum, P.I. ep 10.18.84 CBS
St. Elsewhere ep Cheers 3.27.85 NBC
Cheers sr ret 9.26.85 NBC
The Love Boat ep A Day in Port 9.28.85 ABC

RAY, ALDO
A&C, B.V.:
Voyage to the Bottom of the Sea ep The Midst of Silence 10.5.64 ABC
Daniel Boone ep The Trek 10.21.65 NBC

RAYE, MARTHA
SUPP.:
Alice ep Sharples vs. Sharples 2.7.82 CBS
Alice ep My Mother, the Landlord 5.16.82 CBS
Alice ep 11.10.82, 1.9.83, 4.17.83, 1.29.84, 3.11.84 CBS
Pippin sp 4.83 SHO
Murder, She Wrote ep Armed Response 3.31.85 CBS

RAYMOND, PAULA
A&C, B.V.:
The Rough Riders ep The Double Dealers 3.19.59 ABC
The Life and Legend of Wyatt Earp ep The Pay Master 12.1.59 ABC
Bourbon Street Beat ep The House of Ledezan 2.22.60 ABC
Temple Houston ep 4.2.64 NBC

REDFORD, ROBERT
A&C, B.V.:
Whispering Smith ep The Grudge 5.15.61 NBC
The New Breed ep Lady Killer 12.12.61 ABC

REDGRAVE, LYNN
A&C, Supp. 2:
Kojak ep A Hair-Trigger Away 11.7.76 CBS
SUPP.:
Rehearsal for Murder tf 5.26.82 CBS
Teachers Only sr 4.14.82 NBC
The CBS Afternoon Playhouse ep The Shooting 6.1.82 CBS
The Love Boat ep The Anniversary Gift 10.16.82 ABC
Fantasy Island ep Face of Fire 11.20.82 ABC
Teachers Only sr ret 2.12.83 NBC
Hotel ep Relative Loses 11.2.83 ABC
Fantasy Island ep The High Cost of Loving 1.21.84 ABC

Murder, She Wrote ep It's a Dog's Life 11.4.84 CBS
An American Portrait ep James Hoban 12.18.84 CBS
The Fainthearted Feminist sr 1.27.85 A&E
The Bad Seed tf 2.7.85 ABC

REDGRAVE, VANESSA
SUPP.:
My Body, My Child tf 4.12.82 ABC
Faerie Tale Theater ep Snow White and the Seven Dwarfs 7.16.84 SHO
American Playhouse ep Three Sovereigns for Sarah 5.27, 6.3, 6.10.85 PBS

REED, DONNA
SUPP.:
Deadly Lessons tf 3.7.83 ABC
The Love Boat ep Polly's Poker Palace 2.4.84 ABC
Dallas sr 11.9.84 CBS

REED, ROBERT
A&C, B.V.:
The Danny Thomas Show ep Terry Comes Home 10.5.59 CBS
A&C, Supp. 1:
Chase ep Remote Control 2.27.74 ABC
Harry O ep Accounts Balanced 12.26.74 ABC
Hawaii Five-O ep The Moroville Convent 10.18.79 CBS
Hawaii Five-O ep Good Help Is Hard to Find 11.8.79 CBS
SUPP.:
The ABC Afterschool Special ep Between Two Loves 10.27.82 ABC
Fantasy Island ep Room and Bard 1.29.83 ABC
Hotel ep Secrets 10.26.83 ABC
The Mississippi ep 2.7.84 CBS
The Love Boat ep Seems Like Old Times 10.27.84 ABC
Hotel ep Transitions 11.14.84 ABC
Matt Houston ep Stolen 12.21.84 ABC
Cover Up ep A Subtle Seduction 12.29.84 CBS
Finder of Lost Loves ep From the Hearts 2.9.85 ABC
Murder, She Wrote ep Footnote to Murder 3.10.85 CBS
Half Nelson ep The Deadly Vase 3.29.85 NBC
International Airport tf/pt 5.25.85 ABC
The Love Boat ep Joint Custody 10.5.85 ABC
Glitter ep Suddenly Innocent 12.27.85 ABC

REED, SHANNA*
Gavilan ep Best Friend Money Can Buy 12.21.82 NBC
Legs tf 5.2.83 ABC
The Dukes of Hazzard ep 9.23.83 CBS
For Love and Honor ep Learning Experience 10.28.83 NBC
Newhart ep 2.19.83 CBS
Casablanca ep Jenny 4.24.83 NBC

For Love and Honor ep Mixed Signals 12.20.83 NBC
The Master ep Out-of-Time Step 1.27.84 NBC
T. J. Hooker ep Hooker's Run 2.4.84 ABC
Fantasy Island ep The Obsolete Man 3.24.84 ABC
Knight Rider ep Let It Be Me 5.13.84 NBC
Simon and Simon ep Manna from Heaven 10.25.84 CBS
Hotel ep Anniversary 2.20.85 ABC
Braker pt 4.28.85 ABC
Midas Valley tf/pt 6.27.85 ABC

REED, TRACY*
Journey to the Unknown ep The Indian Spirit Guide 10.10.68 ABC
Love, American Style sr 9.22.69 (through 9.14.73) ABC
Me and Benjy pt 7.27.70 NBC
Barefoot in the Park sr 9.24.70 ABC
Incident in San Francisco tf 2.28.71 ABC
The Great American Beauty Contest tf 2.13.73 ABC
Aloha Means Goodbye tf 10.11.74 CBS
Kojak ep I Want to Report a Dream 3.9.75 CBS
McCloud ep Three Guns for New York 11.23.75 NBC
That's My Mama ep 11.12.75 ABC
McCloud ep Bonnie and McCloud 10.24.76 NBC
Future Cop ep Fighting O'Haven 2.5.77 ABC
Future Cop ep 4.22.77 ABC
Tabitha ep 12.31.77 ABC
Top Secret tf/pt 6.4.78 NBC
Women in White sr 2.8.79 NBC
Doctors' Private Lives ep High Rollers 4.5.79 ABC
Turnover Smith tf/pt 6.8.80 ABC
Terror Among Us tf 1.12.81 CBS
The Fall Guy ep The Fall Guy (pt) 10.28.81 ABC
Death of a Centerfold: The Dorothy Stratton Story tf 11.1.81 NBC
The Quest ep Last One There Is a Rotten Heir 10.29.82 ABC
Cocaine and Blue Eyes tf/pt 1.2.83 NBC
Benson ep Boys Night Out 2.4.83 ABC
The Love Boat ep Daughter's Dilemma 2.16.83 ABC
The Love Boat ep Uncle Daddy 5.7.83 ABC
The New Odd Couple ep Night Stalker 5.26.83 ABC
Benson ep Embarrassing Moments 1.20.84 ABC
The A-Team ep Pure-Dee Poison 1.31.84 NBC
Sins of the Past tf 4.2.84 ABC
T. J. Hooker ep The Surrogate 1.12.85 ABC
Cover Up ep Murder Off Shore 1.12.85 CBS
Riptide ep Does Not Compute 10.29.85 NBC

REESE, DELLA*
The Voyage of the Yes tf 1.16.73 CBS
Twice in a Lifetime tf 3.16.74 NBC
McCloud ep This Must Be the Alamo 3.24.74 NBC

Police Woman ep Requiem for Bored Housewives 11.29.74 NBC
Petrocelli ep Once Upon a Victim 1.29.75 NBC
The Return of Joe Forrester tf 5.6.75 NBC
The Rookies ep 10.7.75 ABC
McCloud ep The Day New York Turned Blue 2.22.76 NBC
Medical Center ep Major Annie, M.D. 3.1.76 CBS
Flo's Place pt 8.9.76 NBC
Nightmare in Badham County tf 11.5.76 ABC
Roots: The Next Generations ms 2.18-2.25.79 ABC
The Love Boat ep The Pest 2.27.82 ABC
It Takes Two ep Promises in the Dark 11.4.82 ABC
It Takes Two ep An Affair to Remember 12.16.82 ABC
It Takes Two ep The Choice 1.20.83 ABC
It Takes Two ep Looks Bad, Feels Good 1.27.83 ABC
Crazy Like a Fox ep Fox Hunt 3.3.85 CBS
The A-Team ep Lease with an Option to Die 10.22.85 NBC
Crazy Like a Fox ep Is There a Fox in the House? 12.22.85 CBS

REEVE, CHRISTOPHER*
Faerie Tale Theater ep Sleeping Beauty 7.7.83 SHO
An American Portrait ep Robert H. Goddard 3.27.85 CBS
Anna Karenina tf 3.26.85 CBS
Dinosaur! sp hos 11.5.85 CBS

REGALBUTO, JOE*
The Associates sr 9.23.79 ABC
Lou Grant ep Pack 12.27.80 CBS
Bosom Buddies ep There's No Business 10.15.81 ABC
Divorce Wars tf 3.1.82 ABC
Barney Miller ep The Car 3.4.82 ABC
Mork and Mindy ep Gotta Run 5.6, 5.13, 5.20.82 ABC
Best of the West ep Sam's Life Is Threatened 6.14.82 ABC
Ace Crawford, Private Eye sr 3.15.83 CBS
The Other Woman tf 3.22.83 CBS
Baby Makes Five ep Eddie's Night Out 4.8.83 ABC
Baby Makes Five ep Jennie's Old Flame 4.29.83 ABC
Oh Madeline ep Ah Wilderness 1.3.84 ABC
Invitation to Hell tf 5.24.84 ABC
The Love Boat Fall Preview Party sp 9.15.84 ABC
Street Hawk sr 1.4.85 ABC
Detective in the House ep Down and Out 3.29.85 CBS
Love Lives On tf 4.1.85 ABC
Scene of the Crime ep Memory Game 4.14.85 NBC
Knots Landing ep The Longest Day 9.26.85 CBS
Knots Landing ep Here In My Arms 10.3.85 CBS
Hardcastle and McCormick ep The Yankee Clipper 10.7.85 ABC
Knots Landing ep While the Cat's Away 10.10.85 CBS
Knots Landing ep The Christening 10.17.85 CBS
Magnum, P.I. ep 10.31.85 CBS

REID, TIM*
Little Lulu pt 11.4.78 ABC
WKRP in Cincinnati sr 9.18.78 CBS
WKRP in Cincinnati sr ret 9.19.79 CBS
WKRP in Cincinnati sr ret 11.1.80 CBS
WKRP in Cincinnati sr ret 10.7.81 CBS
Teachers Only sr 2.12.83 NBC
Simon and Simon sr 11.10.83 CBS
Simon and Simon sr ret 9.27.84 CBS
Simon and Simon sr ret 10.3.85 CBS
Benson ep Thy Brother's Keeper 11.5.85 ABC

REILLY, JOHN*
The Mary Tyler Moore Show ep Lou Dates Mary 3.19.77 CBS
The Bionic Woman ep Long Live the King 3.25.78 NBC
Secrets of Three Hungry Wives tf 10.9.78 NBC
The Incredible Journey of Dr. Meg Laurel tf 1.2.79 CBS
A Man Called Sloane ep Demon's Triangle 10.20.79 NBC
The Secret War of Jackie's Girls tf/pt 11.29.80 NBC
Nero Wolfe ep The Murder in Question 4.17.81 NBC
Charlie and the Great Balloon Race tf 7.12.81 NBC
Quincy, M.E. ep Slow Boat to Madness 11.11.81 NBC
The Patricia Neal Story tf 12.8.81 CBS
The Powers of Matthew Star ep Experiment 11.26.82 NBC
Here's Boomer ep Flatfoots 7.3.82 NBC
Silver Spoons ep Falling in Love Again 12.11.82 NBC
Hart to Hart ep A Christmas Hart 12.21.82 ABC
Uncommon Valor tf 1.22.83 CBS
Tales of the Gold Monkey ep Boragora or Bust 3.25.83 ABC
Remington Steele ep Steele in the News 3.4.83 NBC
Silver Spoons ep Won't You Go Home, Bob Danish 3.5.83 NBC
Ryan's Four ep Couples 4.27.83 ABC
Missing Pieces tf 5.14.83 CBS
After George pt 6.6.83 CBS
Wishman pt 6.23.83 ABC
The Hamptons sr 7.27.83 ABC
Newhart ep It Happened One Afternoon 10.17, 10.24.83 CBS
Three's Company ep The Odd Couple 12.6.83 ABC
Simon and Simon ep 3.1.84 CBS
Benson ep Adventure in Hong Kong 9.21, 9.28.84 ABC
Dynasty ep The Rescue 10.24.84 ABC
Paper Dolls ep Episode Five 10.30.84 ABC
Cover Up ep Harper-Gate 10.13.84 CBS
Cagney and Lacey ep 10.15.84 CBS
Dynasty ep The Verdict 11.7.84 ABC
Who's the Boss? ep Dinner for Two 11.20.84 ABC

REINER, ROB
A&C, Supp. 1:
The Alfred Hitchcock Hour ep The Magic Shop 1.10.64 NBC
Gomer Pyle, USMC ep Gomer, the Recruiter Fall 1966 CBS

The Andy Griffith Show ep Goober's Contest 4.10.67 CBS
Gomer Pyle, USMC ep Lost, the Colonel's Daughter Spring 1967 CBS
Gomer Pyle, USMC ep Flower Power 3.28.69 CBS
The Beverly Hillbillies ep Back to the Hills 4.69 CBS
The Rockford Files ep The No-Cut Contrast 1.16.76 NBC
SUPP.:
Million Dollar Infield tf 2.2.82 CBS

REINHOLD, JUDGE*
A Piano for Mrs. Cimino tf 2.3.82 CBS
A Matter of Sex tf 1.16.84 NBC
Never Again pt 11.30.84 ABC

REMICK, LEE
SUPP.:
The Letter tf 5.3.82 ABC
The Gift of Love: A Christmas Story 12.20.83 CBS
A Good Sport tf 2.8.84 CBS
Rearview Mirror tf 4.26.84 NBC
An American Portrait ep Jacqueline Cochran 10.26.84 CBS
I Do! I Do! sp 1.8.85 A&E
Faerie Tale Theater ep The Snow Queen 3.11.85 SHO
Tough Love tf 10.13.85 ABC

RESCHER, DEE DEE*
Breaking Up Is Hard to Do tf 9.5, 9.7.79 ABC
Moviola: The Scarlett O'Hara War tf 5.4.80 NBC
Irene pt 8.19.81 NBC
Games Mother Never Taught You tf 11.27.82 CBS
Remington Steele ep Red Hot Steele 9.27.83 NBC
Empire ep 1.4.84 CBS
Hawaiian Heat ep Hawaiian Heat (pt) 9.14.84 ABC
Hotel ep Transitions 11.14.84 ABC
A Bunny's Tale tf 2.25.85 ABC
The Heart of a Champion: The Ray Mancini Story tf 5.1.85 CBS

RETTIG, TOMMY
A&C, B.V.:
Sugarfoot ep The Ghost 10.28.58 ABC

REUBENS, PAUL (a.k.a. Pee Wee Herman)*
The Pee Wee Herman Show sp 9.11.81 HBO
Mork and Mindy ep Long Before We Met 11.19.81 ABC
Open All Night ep Robin's Return 12.5.81 ABC
Faerie Tale Theater ep Pinocchio 5.14.84 SHO
Saturday Night Live ep hos 11.23.85 NBC

REY, ALEJANDRO
A&C, B.V.:
Voyage to the Bottom of the Sea ep The Midst of Silence

10.5.64 ABC
The Monroes ep Pawnee Warrior 12.28.66 ABC
The High Chaparral ep No Anger Greater Than Mine 9.18.70 NBC
SUPP.:
Cassie and Company ep Golden Silence 1.29.82 NBC
The Fall Guy ep The Adventures of Ozzie and Harold 2.3.82 ABC
The Love Boat ep The Duel 3.14.82 ABC
Herbie, the Love Bug ep 3.31.82 CBS
Bring 'Em Back Alive ep 10.5.82 CBS
The Devlin Connection ep Arsenic and Old Caviar 12.4.82 NBC
Knight Rider ep Forget Me Not 12.17.82 NBC
Grace Kelly tf 2.21.83 ABC
We Got It Made ep The Wedding (a.k.a. Mickey Gets Married) 11.3, 11.10.83 NBC
Rita Hayworth: The Love Goddess tf 11.2.83 CBS
Fantasy Island ep Don Juan's Last Affair 4.14.84 ABC
Masquerade ep Spanish Gambit 4.20.84 ABC
E/R ep 11.14.84 CBS
Cover Up ep Healthy, Wealthy and Dead 2.23.85 CBS

REYNOLDS, BURT
A&C, B.V.:
Perry Mason ep The Case of the Counterfeit Crank 4.28.62 CBS
Twelve O'Clock High ep Show Me a Hero, I'll Show You a Bum 10.25.65 ABC
The FBI ep Act of Violence 1.21.68 ABC
SUPP.:
Mickey Spillane's Mike Hammer ep A Death in the Family 11.24.84 CBS

REYNOLDS, DEBBIE
SUPP.:
Alice ep 10.6.82 CBS
The Love Boat ep First Impressions 1.8.83 ABC
Jennifer Slept Here ep Boo 11.1.83 NBC

RHOADES, BARBARA
A&C, Supp. 1:
Columbo ep Lady in Waiting 12.15.71 NBC
Toma ep "50" 1.18.74 ABC
Harry O ep Book of Charges 1.15.76 ABC
Switch ep Switch Hitter 12.7.76 CBS
SUPP.:
Magnum, P.I. ep The Elmo Ziller Story 3.25.82 CBS
Murder, She Wrote ep Birds of a Feather 10.14.84 CBS
Cagney and Lacey ep 1.14.85 CBS
Dallas ep 3.15.85 CBS
Scene of the Crime ep Memory Game 4.14.85 NBC
Crazy Like a Fox ep Eye in the Sky 10.6.85 CBS

Picking Up the Pieces tf 10.22.85 CBS
Trapper John, M.D. ep Friends and Lovers 10.27.85 CBS
Simon and Simon ep Have You Hugged Your Private Detective Today? 11.7.85 CBS

RHODES, DONNELLY*
Man with a Camera ep 2.1.60 ABC
The Twilight Zone ep The Little People 3.30.62 CBS
The Alfred Hitchcock Hour ep Ten Minutes from Now 5.1.64 NBC
The Alfred Hitchcock Hour ep The Trap 2.22.65 NBC
Dr. Kildare ep The Time Buyers 4.8.65 NBC
Run for Your Life ep The Night of the Terror 1.31.66 NBC
Laredo ep The Would-Be Gentleman of Laredo 4.14.66 NBC
The Road West ep Pariah 12.5.66 NBC
Run for Your Life ep Tears from a Glass Eye 12.12.66 NBC
The Girl from UNCLE ep The Fountain of Youth Affair 2.7.67 NBC
The Bob Hope Chrysler Theater ep Dead Wrong 4.5.67 NBC
Dundee and the Culhane ep 9.13.67 CBS
Mannix ep The Cost of a Vacation 10.21.67 CBS
Tarzan ep Hotel Hurricane 11.10.67 NBC
The Wild Wild West ep The Night of the Legion of Death 11.24.67 CBS
The Legend of Custer ep Dangerous Prey 12.6.67 ABC
Ironside ep Girl in the Night 12.21.67 NBC
Cimarron Strip ep 2.28.68 CBS
The Smugglers tf 12.24.68 NBC
The Wild Wild West ep The Night of the Cossacks 3.21.69 CBS
Here Come the Brides ep A Wild Colonial Boy 10.24.69 ABC
Mission: Impossible ep 11.18.72 CBS
Marcus Welby, M.D. ep The Working Heart 2.13.73 ABC
The New Adventures of Perry Mason ep The Case of the Wistful Widower 10.7.83 CBS
The Starlost ep 12.8.73 NN
Police Story ep The Ripper 2.12.74 NBC
Switch ep Fleece of Snow 10.5.76 CBS
Goldenrod tf 6.1.77 CBS
Soap sr 9.14.78 ABC
The New Adventures of Wonder Woman ep A Date with Doomsday 3.10.79 CBS
Soap sr ret 9.13.79 ABC
Soap sr ret 10.29.80 ABC
Making a Living ep Mann Is Mann 12.12.81 ABC
The Facts of Life ep Jo's Cousins 4.14.82 NBC
Cheers ep Sam's Women 10.7.82 NBC
Hill Street Blues ep A Hair of the Dog 11.25.82 NBC
Taxi ep Travels with My Dad 11.25.82 NBC
Hill Street Blues ep The Phantom of the Hill 12.2.82 NBC
It Takes Two ep Mr. Molly Quinn 1.6.83 ABC
Magnum, P.I. ep Of Sound Mind 1.6.83 CBS

Hill Street Blues ep Untitled 2.10.83 NBC
Amanda's ep You Were Meant for Me 2.17.83 ABC
Gimme a Break ep The Centerfold, Part 2 1.27.83 NBC
Alice ep 1.1.84 CBS
Flight #90: Disaster on the Potomac tf 4.1.84 NBC
Double Trouble sr 4.4.84 NBC
Double Trouble ep Where's Poppa? 3.30.85 NBC
The Hitchhiker ep Hired Help 3.30.85 HBO

RHUE, MADLYN
A&C, Supp. 1:
The Court of Last Resort ep The Steven Lowell Case 3.14.58 NBC
Black Saddle ep Client: Reynolds 5.23.59 NBC
Cheyenne ep The Prisoner of Moon Mesa 11.16.59 ABC
Tightrope ep The Money Fight 11.17.59 ABC
Gunsmoke ep Tag, You're It 12.19.59 CBS
The Troubleshooters ep Incident at Rain Mountain 2.26.60 NBC
Sugarfoot ep A Noose for Nero 10.24.60 ABC
The Westerner ep The Painting 12.30.60 NBC
The Fugitive ep Somebody to Remember 3.24.64 ABC
Hawaii Five-O ep Here Today ... Gone Tonight 1.23.73 CBS
Switch ep The Cold War Con 12.9.75 CBS
SUPP.:
Diff'rent Strokes ep The Model 11.12.81 NBC
Fantasies tf 1.18.82 ABC
Fame ep Street Kid 2.25.82 NBC
Fantasy Island ep Legend 10.30.82 ABC
Games Mother Never Taught You tf 11.27.82 NBC
Days of Our Lives sr 1983 NBC
CHiPs ep Country Action 1.23.83 NBC
Fame ep Blizzard 10.10.84 NN

RICH, ADAM
SUPP.:
The CBS Children's Mystery Theater ep The Zertigo Diamond Caper 9.28.82 CBS
Fantasy Island ep Natchez Bound 11.6.82 ABC
CHiPs ep Fallout 12.19.82 NBC

RICHARDS, KIM
A&C, Supp. 2:
The New Mickey Mouse Club ep The Mystery of Rustlers Cove 1977 NN
SUPP.:
Alice ep 1.17.82 CBS
CHiPs ep Tight Fit 10.17.82 NBC
The Love Boat ep Hyde and Seek 10.30.82 ABC
Magnum, P.I. ep Mixed Doubles 12.2.82 CBS
The Dukes of Hazzard ep 10.28.83 CBS
Lottery ep Boston: False Illusion ("Danziger Story" segment)

12.2.83 ABC
The Mississippi ep 1.24.84 CBS

RICHARDSON, PATRICIA*
Love, Sidney ep A Piece of the Rock 11.11.81 NBC
Double Trouble sr 4.4.84 NBC
The ABC Weekend Special ep The Adventures of Con Sawyer and Hucklemary Finn 9.7, 9.14.85 ABC

RICHMAN, PETER MARK
A&C, Supp. 1:
The FBI ep The Death Wind 12.25.66 ABC
Voyage to the Bottom of the Sea ep Secret of the Deep 2.11.68 ABC
Land of the Giants ep Panic 1.25.70 ABC
The Young Lawyers ep Legal Maneuver 1.20.71 ABC
Get Christie Love ep Market for Murder 9.11.74 ABC
Switch ep Big Deal in Paradise 2.24.76 CBS
SUPP.:
Fantasy Island ep Shadow Games 1.23.82 ABC
Dynasty ep Episode 25 2.3.82 ABC
Dynasty ep Episode 26 2.10.82 ABC
Dynasty ep Episode 31 3.24.82 ABC
Dynasty ep The Fragment 4.7.82 ABC
Hart to Hart ep The Harts at High Noon 11.9.82 ABC
Dynasty ep Battle Lines 2.23.83 ABC
Dynasty ep The Cabin 4.20.83 ABC
Fantasy Island ep The Sisters 5.14.83 ABC
Dempsey tf 9.28.83 CBS
Dynasty ep The Note 10.19.83 ABC
Dynasty ep The Hearing 11.2.83 ABC
Dynasty ep Tender Comrades 11.9.83 ABC
Dynasty ep Tracy 11.6.83 ABC
Dynasty ep The Wedding 12.28.83 ABC
Dynasty ep The Ring 1.4.84 ABC
Dynasty ep The Voice 3.21.84 ABC
Dynasty ep New Lady in Town 5.2.84 ABC
Santa Barbara sr 7.30.84 NBC
Dynasty ep The Mortgage 10.10.84 ABC
City Killer tf 10.28.84 NBC
The Fall Guy ep Baja 1,000 11.28.84 ABC
The Love Boat ep The Runaway 2.9.85 ABC
Hotel ep Anniversary 2.20.85 ABC
Finder of Lost Loves ep Connections 4.13.85 ABC
Knight Rider ep Many Happy Returns 11.15.85 NBC
Crazy Like a Fox ep Is There a Fox in the House? 12.22.85 CBS

RICHTER, DEBI*
The Waltons ep The Ferris Wheel 1.6.77 CBS
Aspen ms 11.5-11.7.77 NBC

Wheels ms 5.7-5.15.78 NBC
Charlie's Angels ep Teen Angels 2.28.79 ABC
The Rebels ms 5.14, 5.21.79 OPT
Portrait of a Stripper tf 10.2.79 CBS
Barnaby Jones ep Indoctrination Into Evil 11.1.79 CBS
Twirl tf 10.25.81 NBC
Hill Street Blues ep Some Like It Hot Wired 3.18.82 NBC
Hill Street Blues ep Midway to What? 12.1.83 NBC
Hill Street Blues ep Honk If You're a Goose 12.8.83 NBC
Hill Street Blues ep Ratman and Bobbin 1.19.84 NBC
Hill Street Blues ep The Count of Monty Tasco 3.8.84 NBC
Hill Street Blues ep Untitled 3.15.84 NBC
Hill Street Blues ep Lucky Ducks 5.10.84 NBC
Hill Street Blues ep Eva's Brawn 5.17.84 NBC
Hardcastle and McCormick ep You Would Cry Too, If It Happened to You 10.7.84 ABC
Mickey Spillane's Mike Hammer ep Kill Devil 10.13.84 CBS
T. J. Hooker ep Hardcore Connection 11.3.84 ABC
Hill Street Blues ep Blues in the Night 9.26.85 NBC
Alfred Hitchcock Presents ep Night Fever 10.6.85 NBC

RICKLES, DON

A&C, B.V.:

Hennessy ep Professional Soldier Spring 1962 CBS
The Addams Family ep Halloween with the Addams Family 10.30.64 ABC
The Dick Van Dyke Show ep "4½" 11.4.64 CBS
Gomer Pyle, USMC ep My Buddy--War Hero 3.12.65 CBS
The Andy Griffith Show ep The Luck of Newton Monroe 4.12.65 CBS
F Troop ep The Return of Bald Eagle 10.12.65 ABC

RIGBY, CATHY

SUPP.:

Challenge of a Lifetime tf 2.14.85 ABC

RIGG, DIANA

SUPP.:

Witness for the Prosecution tf 12.4.82 CBS
Bleak House sr 12.1.85 PBS
Laurence Olivier's King Lear sp 12.18.85 PBS

RINGWALD, MOLLY*

The Facts of Life sr 8.24.79 NBC
The Facts of Life sr ret 3.12.80 NBC
The Facts of Life sr ret 11.19.80 NBC
The Facts of Life sr ret 10.28.81 NBC
Packin' It In tf 2.7.83 CBS
Surviving tf 2.10.85 ABC

RITTER, JOHN
A&C, Supp. 2:
Kojak ep Deliver Us Some Evil 2.13.74 CBS
Hawaii Five-O ep Dealer's Choice ... Blackmail 2.3.77 CBS
SUPP.:
Pray TV tf 2.1.82 ABC
Three's Company sr ret 9.28.82 ABC
In Love with an Older Woman tf 11.24.82 CBS
Three's Company sr ret 9.27.83 ABC
Sunset Limousine tf 10.12.83 CBS
The Love Boat ep The Emperor's Fortune 11.5.83 ABC
Love Thy Neighbor tf 5.23.84 ABC
Secret World of the Very Young sp hos 9.12.84 CBS
Three's a Crowd sr 9.25.84 ABC
Pryor's Place ep 11.24.84 CBS
Letting Go tf 5.11.85 ABC

ROBARDS, JASON
SUPP.:
Hughie sp 9.81 SHO
The Day After tf 11.20.83 ABC
You Can't Take It With You sp 5.84 SHO
Sakharov tf 6.20.84 HBO
The Atlanta Child Murders tf 2.10, 2.12.85 CBS
The Long Hot Summer tf 10.6, 10.7.85 NBC

ROBERTS, DORIS*
The Mary Tyler Moore Show ep Phyllis Whips Inflation 1.25.75 CBS
All in the Family ep Edith's Night Out 3.8.76 CBS
The Streets of San Francisco ep The Thrill Killers 9.30.76 ABC
Rhoda ep Meet the Levys Fall 1976 CBS
Soap sr Fall 1977 ABC
Mary Hartman, Mary Hartman sr 1977 NN
The Story Teller tf 12.5.77 NBC
It Happened One Christmas tf 12.11.77 ABC
Ruby and Oswald tf 2.8.78 CBS
Angie sr 2.8.79 ABC
Jennifer: A Woman's Story tf 3.5.79 NBC
Angie sr ret 9.11.79 ABC
Fantasy Island ep 9.14.79 ABC
The Diary of Anne Frank tf 11.17.80 NBC
The Love Boat ep Sergeant Bull 10.25.80 ABC
Fantasy Island ep 4.11.81 ABC
In Trouble pt 8.24.81 ABC
Alice ep Alice's Big Four-Oh! 11.8.81 CBS
St. Elsewhere ep Cora and Arnie 11.23.82 NBC
Another Woman's Child tf 1.19.83 CBS
The Love Boat ep Our Son, the Lawyer 1.29.83 ABC
Cagney and Lacey ep 2.14.83 CBS

The New Odd Couple ep The Perils of Pauline 5.13.83 ABC
The New Odd Couple ep The Night Stalker 5.26.83 ABC
Remington Steele sr 9.20.83 NBC
Me and Mrs. C pt 3.18.84 NBC
Remington Steele sr ret 9.25.84 NBC
The Love Boat ep Call Me a Doctor 10.6.84 ABC
Faerie Tale Theater ep The Three Little Pigs 2.12.85 SHO
California Girls tf 3.24.85 ABC
Remington Steele sr ret 9.24.85 NBC
A Letter to Three Wives tf 12.16.85 NBC

ROBERTS, PERNELL
A&C, Supp. 2:
Cheyenne ep Misfire 12.10.57 ABC
Sugarfoot ep Man Wanted 2.18.58 ABC
Zane Grey Theater ep Utopia, Wyoming 6.6.58 CBS
Trackdown ep The Reward 1.3.58 CBS
Shirley Temple's Storybook ep Hiawatha 10.5.58 NBC
Zane Grey Theater ep Pressure Point 12.4.58 CBS
Northwest Passage ep The Assassin 11.16.58 NBC
Alcoa Presents ep The Vision 3.24.59 ABC
Bronco ep The Belles of Silver Flat 3.24.59 ABC
Lawman ep The Posse 3.28.59 ABC
Bonanza sr ret 9.10.60 NBC
Bonanza sr ret 9.24.61 NBC
Bonanza sr ret 9.23.62 NBC
Naked City ep The S.S. American Dream 5.8.63 ABC
Bonanza sr ret 9.22.63 NBC
Route 66 ep Child of the Night 1.3.64 CBS
Bonanza sr ret 9.20.64 NBC
The Girl from UNCLE ep The Little John Doe Affair 12.13.66 NBC
Gunsmoke ep Strangers in Town 11.20.67 CBS
The Big Valley ep Run of the Cat 10.21.68 ABC
Alias Smith and Jones ep Exit from Wickenburg 1.28.71 ABC
Hawaii Five-O ep The Grand Stand Play 3.3.71, 3.10.71 CBS
Alias Smith and Jones ep 21 Days to Tenstrike 1.6.72 ABC
Bronk ep Deception 12.7.75 CBS
Switch ep Camera Angels 1.30.77 CBS
SUPP.:
Trapper John, M.D. sr ret 9.26.82 CBS
Trapper John, M.D. sr ret 10.2.83 CBS
Trapper John, M.D. sr ret 9.30.84 CBS
Trapper John, M.D. sr ret 10.6.85 CBS

ROBERTS, TANYA
SUPP.:
The Love Boat ep Past Perfect Love 1.30.82 ABC
Fantasy Island ep The Ghost's Story 5.8.82 ABC
Mickey Spillane's Mike Hammer: Murder Me, Murder You tf/pt 4.9.83 CBS

ROBERTS, TONY
SUPP.:
A Question of Honor tf 4.28.82 CBS
Trapper John, M.D. ep 1.30.83 CBS
Packin' It In tf 2.7.83 CBS
The Four Seasons sr 1.29.84 CBS
Finder of Lost Loves ep Tricks 2.23.85 ABC
Trapper John, M.D. ep 3.3.85 CBS
The Lucie Arnaz Show sr 4.2.85 CBS

ROBERTSON, CLIFF
SUPP.:
Two of a Kind tf 10.9.82 CBS
Falcon Crest sr 9.30.83 CBS
The Key to Rebecca tf 4.29, 5.6.85 OPT

ROBERTSON, DALE
SUPP.:
Dallas ep 10.22.82 CBS
Big John pt 12.3.83 NBC
Airwolf ep Eagles 11.9.85 CBS

ROBINSON, EDWARD G.
A&C, B.V.:
The Silent Force ep The Courier 12.7.70 ABC

ROCCO, ALEX
A&C, Supp. 1:
Get Smart ep How to Succeed in the Spy Business Without Really Trying 3.67 NBC
Cannon ep Hear No Evil 11.29.72 CBS
Circle of Fear ep Spare Parts 2.3.73 NBC
Get Christie Love ep Death on Delivery 10.9.74 ABC
Police Story ep The Test of Brotherhood 11.14.75 NBC
A&C, Supp. 2:
Police Story ep Nightmare on a Sunday Morning 1.18.77 NBC
The Rockford Files ep The Birds, the Bees and T. T. Flowers! 1.21.77, 1.28.77 NBC
SUPP.:
Simon and Simon ep Ashes to Ashes and None Too Soon 1.19.82 CBS
The First Time tf 11.8.82 ABC
The Love Boat ep Salvaged Romance 1.29.83 ABC
Small and Frye ep 6.15.83 CBS
The Facts of Life ep Second Time Around 12.14.83 NBC
T. J. Hooker ep Hooker's Run 2.4.84 ABC
Matt Houston ep Cash and Carry 3.23.84 ABC
Hardcastle and McCormick ep Ties My Father Sold Me 9.30.84 ABC
Simon and Simon ep 10.11.84 CBS
The Love Boat ep Seems Like Old Times 10.27.84 ABC

Hot Pursuit ep Identity Crisis 12.28.84 NBC
The A-Team ep The Champ! 1.22.85 NBC
Murder, She Wrote ep Tough Guys Don't Die 2.24.85 CBS
The Facts of Life ep Sisters 3.20.85 NBC
Braker pt 4.28.85 ABC
Badge of the Assassin tf 11.2.85 CBS
The Golden Girls ep That Was No Lady.... 11.16.85 NBC
The Golden Girls ep 12.21.85 NBC

ROCHE, EUGENE
A&C, Supp. 2:
East Side/West Side ep The Name of the Game 3.23.64 CBS
Kojak ep Acts of Desperate Men 1.2.75 CBS
Hawaii Five-O ep A Woman's Work Is With a Gun 1.21.75 CBS
Harry O ep Victim 3.4.76 ABC
Medical Center ep If Dreams Were Horses 3.15.76 CBS
SUPP.:
Mr. Merlin ep Change of Menu 2.22.82 CBS
Taxi ep The Road Not Taken 4.29.82 ABC
Chicago Story ep Dutton's Law 5.7.82 NBC
Farrell for the People tf/pt 10.18.82 NBC
Cocaine and Blue Eyes tf/pt 1.2.83 NBC
Quincy, M.E. ep Guilty Till Proved Innocent 1.12.83 NBC
Baby Makes Five ep The Matchmakers 4.22.83 ABC
Johnny Blue pt 9.4.83 CBS
Magnum, P.I. ep Luther Gillis File #521 10.6.83 CBS
Gimme a Break ep The Chief's Gay Evening 11.13.83 NBC
Masquerade ep Girls for Sale 12.29.83 ABC
Airwolf ep Airwolf (pt) 1.29.84 CBS
Magnum, P.I. ep The Return of Luther Gillis 2.16.84 CBS
Off Sides tf 7.6.84 NBC
Airwolf ep Firestorm 9.29.84 CBS
Webster sr (with ep Moving On) 11.2.84 ABC
Magnum, P.I. ep 12.6.84 CBS
Night Court ep Daddy for the Defense 10.4.84 NBC
Hardcastle and McCormick ep Something's Going On on This Train 10.14.85 ABC
Night Court ep Dad's First Date 10.17.85 NBC

RODD, MARCIA*
The New Dick Van Dyke Show ep 12.11.71 CBS
All in the Family ep Cousin Maude 2.22.72 CBS
Medical Center ep The Torn Man 10.11.72 CBS
Barnaby Jones ep Fatal Witness 11.14.75 CBS
The Dumplings sr 1.28.76 NBC
How to Break Up a Happy Divorce tf 10.6.76 NBC
Phyllis ep 2.13.77 CBS
Maude ep 10.17.77 CBS
Lou Grant ep The Samaritan 2.12.79 CBS
13 Queens Blvd. sr 3.20.79 ABC
The ABC Afterschool Special ep A Movie Star's Daughter

10.10.79 ABC
Quincy, M.E. ep Sweet Land of Liberty 10.25.79 NBC
Trapper John, M.D. ep 2.10.80 CBS
Flamingo Road ep Bad Girl 3.3.81 NBC
Flamingo Road ep Secrets 3.10.81 NBC
Flamingo Road ep They Drive By Night 3.17.81 NBC
Flamingo Road ep Hell Hath No Fury 3.24.81 NBC
Flamingo Road ep Bad Chemistry 4.2.81 NBC
Maggie ep 10.24.81 ABC
Bret Maverick ep The Yellow Rose 12.22.81 NBC
Lou Grant ep 1.25.82 CBS
Cassie and Company ep A Ring Ain't Always a Circle 8.20.82 NBC
Trapper John, M.D. ep 10.3, 10.10.83 CBS
Laverne and Shirley ep The Playboy Show 11.9.82 ABC
Trapper John, M.D. ep Life, Death & Vinnie Duncan 1.2.83 CBS
Hart to Hart ep Pasts Imperfect 2.20.83 ABC
Trapper John, M.D. ep 10.23.83, 11.20.83 CBS
The Four Seasons sr 1.29.84 CBS
Gimme a Break ep Carl's Delicate Moment 11.24.84 NBC
Trapper John, M.D. ep Buckaroo Bob Rides Again 1.20.85 CBS
Trapper John, M.D. ep So Little, Gone 2.17.85 CBS
Trapper John, M.D. ep Bad Breaks 2.24.85 CBS
Trapper John, M.D. ep The Second Best Man 12.15.85 CBS
Between the Darkness and the Dawn tf 12.23.85 NBC

RODRIGUES, PERCY
SUPP.:
Dynasty ep Episode 25 2.3.82 ABC
Benson ep The Party's Over 4.30.82 ABC
T. J. Hooker ep Lady in Blue 5.7.83 ABC
Cutter to Houston ep Cutter to Houston (pt) 10.1.83 CBS
Benson ep Full Court Press 10.21.83 ABC
This Girl for Hire tf/pt 11.1.83 CBS
Benson ep The Inheritance 9.28.84 ABC
Cutter to Houston ep The Life You Save 12.31.84 CBS
The Atlanta Child Murders tf 2.10.85 CBS
Benson ep Benson the Hero 10.4.85 ABC

ROGERS, GINGER
SUPP.:
Glitter ep Queen of the Soaps 9.27.84 ABC

ROGERS, KENNY*
The Dream Makers tf 1.7.75 NBC
Kenny Rogers as the Gambler tf 4.8.80 CBS
Coward of the Country tf 10.7.81 CBS
Grandpa, Will You Run with Me? sp 4.3.83 NBC
Kenny Rogers as the Gambler: The Adventure Continues tf

11.28, 11.29.83 CBS
An American Portrait ep Joseph Gidden 11.13.84 CBS
Wild Horses tf 11.12.85 CBS

ROGERS, MIMI*
Hill Street Blues ep Rites of Spring 8.11, 8.18, 8.25.81 NBC
Quincy, M.E. ep Slow Boat to Madness 11.11, 11.18.81 NBC
Magnum, P.I. ep Italian Ice 2.4.82 CBS
Hart to Hart ep Hartstruck 4.12.83 ABC
The Rousters sr 10.1.83 NBC
The Rousters sr ret 6.9.84 NBC
Paper Dolls sr 9.23.84 ABC
Embassy tf/pt 4.21.85 NBC

ROGERS, WAYNE
A&C, Supp. 2:
Law of the Plainsman ep Full Circle 10.8.59 CBS
Gunsmoke ep False Witness 12.12.59 CBS
Law of the Plainsman ep Calculated Risk 12.31.59 NBC
Wanted: Dead Or Alive ep Angela 1.9.60 CBS
Law of the Plainsman ep Dangerous Barriers 3.10.60 NBC
Gunsmoke ep Cody's Code 1.20.62 CBS
The Dick Powell Show ep The Clocks 3.27.62 NBC
Alfred Hitchcock Presents ep The Big Kick 6.19.62 CBS
Have Gun--Will Travel ep The Debutantes 1.19.63 CBS
Great Adventure ep The Hunley 9.27.63 CBS
Gunsmoke ep Taps for Old Jeb 10.16.65 CBS
Twelve O'Clock High ep A Distant Cry 10.7.66 ABC
Men at Law ep View from the Top 3.24.71 CBS
The Starlost ep Circuit of Death 11.30.73 NN
Medical Center ep If Dreams Were Horses 3.15.76 CBS
SUPP.:
Chiefs ms 11.13-11.16.83 CBS
He's Fired, She's Hired tf 12.18.84 CBS
The Lady form Yesterday tf 5.14.85 CBS
I Dream of Jeannie: 15 Years Later tf/pt 10.20.85 NBC

ROLLE, ESTHER
SUPP.:
Flamingo Road ep The Bad and the Beautiful 4.13.82 NBC
Flamingo Road ep The Harder They Fall 4.27.82 NBC
The New Odd Couple ep Tales of April 10.29.82 ABC
The Love Boat ep He Ain't Heavy 2.26.83 ABC
Finder of Lost Loves ep Goodbye, Sara 11.3.84 ABC
Mickey Spillane's Mike Hammer ep Deadly Reunion 1.12.85 CBS
The Love Boat ep Daughter's Dilemma 2.16.85 ABC
MacGruder and Loud ep Act of War 4.23.85 ABC

ROMERO, CESAR
A&C, B.V.:
G.E. True ep Five Tickets to Hell 5.26.63 CBS

Burke's Law ep Who Killed Billy Joe? 11.8.63 ABC
Alias Smith and Jones ep The McCreedy Bust--Going, Going Gone 1.13.72 ABC
Alias Smith and Jones ep The McCreedy Feud 9.30.72 ABC
SUPP.:
The Rainbow Girl pt 6.4.82 NBC
Matt Houston ep Who Killed Ramona? 10.31.82 ABC
Fantasy Island ep The Tallowed Image 1.29.83 ABC
Hart to Hart ep Chamber of Lost Harts 2.1.83 ABC
Fantasy Island ep The Big Show 11.12.83 ABC
The Love Boat ep Authoress! Authoress! 1.7.84 ABC
Magnum, P.I. ep Little Games 1.3.85 CBS
The Love Boat ep Love on the Line 1.26.85 ABC
Murder, She Wrote ep Paint Me a Murder 2.17.85 CBS
Half Nelson ep The Deadly Vase 3.29.85 NBC
Riptide ep Arrivederci Baby 5.17.85 NBC
Falcon Crest sr (with ep Blood Brothers) 10.18.85 CBS

ROONEY, MICKEY
SUPP.:
One of the Boys sr 1.23.82 NBC
O'Malley pt 1.8.83 NBC
Bill on His Own tf 11.9.83 CBS
It Came Upon the Midnight Clear tf 12.15.84 NN

ROSE, JAMIE*
Twirl tf 10.25.81 NBC
Falcon Crest sr 12.4.81 CBS
Falcon Crest sr ret 10.1.82 CBS
In Love with an Older Woman tf 11.24.82 CBS
Falcon Crest sr ret 9.30.83 CBS
Fantasy Island ep Forbidden Love 10.8.83 CBS
Flight #90: Disaster on the Potomac 4.1.84 NBC
Jessie ep Flesh Wounds 10.9.84 ABC
Matt Houston ep Caged 10.26.84 ABC
Never Again pt 11.30.84 ABC
Simon and Simon ep Simon Without Simon 1.24, 1.31.85 CBS
Lady Blue pt 4.15.85 ABC
Lady Blue sr 9.26.85 ABC
Amazing Stories ep Vanessa in the Garden 12.29.85 NBC

ROSS, KATHARINE
A&C, B.V.:
Gunsmoke ep Crooked Mile 10.3.64 CBS
SUPP.:
Marian Rose White tf 1.19.82 CBS
The Shadow Riders tf 9.28.82 CBS
Wait Until Dark sp 12.29.82 HBO
Travis McGee tf 5.18.83 ABC
Secrets of a Mother and Daughter tf 10.4.83 CBS
Dynasty ep 11.13.85 ABC
Dynasty II: The Colbys sr 11.20.85 ABC

ROSS, MARION

A&C, Supp. 2:

The George Burns and Gracie Allen Show ep Gracie Runs for City Council Spring 1959 CBS

The George Sanders Mystery Theater ep You Don't Live Here 7.13.57 NBC

Perry Mason ep The Case of the Romantic Rogue 2.14.59 CBS

M Squad ep High School Bride 5.29.59 NBC

The Donna Reed Show ep Flowers for the Teacher Fall 1959 ABC

Philip Marlowe ep You Kill Me 3.29.60 ABC

Father Knows Best ep Jim's Big Surprise Spring 1960 CBS

Markham ep The Snowman 9.1.60 CBS

The Loretta Young Theater ep No Margin for Error 11.13.60 NBC

The Barbara Stanwyck Theater ep We Are the Women Who Wait 12.5.60 NBC

Dante ep Dante in the Dark 3.20.61 NBC

Thriller ep The Prisoner in the Mirror 5.23.61 NBC

Mrs. G Goes to College sr 10.4.61 CBS

Route 66 ep 1800 Days to Justice 1.26.62 CBS

The Detectives ep Finders Keepers 4.13.62 ABC

Rawhide ep Gold Fever 5.4.62 CBS

Mystery Theater ep Night Panic 7.18.62 NBC

Channing ep Exercise in a Shark Tank 9.25.63 ABC

Great Adventure ep The Outlaw and the Nun 12.6.63 CBS

Dr. Kildare ep Charlie Wade Makes Lots of Shade 12.12.63 NBC

The Eleventh Hour ep Is Mrs. Martin Coming Back? 12.25.63 NBC

Great Adventure ep The Henry Bergh Story 3.20.64 CBS

The Fugitive ep Trial By Fire 10.5.65 ABC

Hawaii Five-O ep Blind Tiger 12.31.69 CBS

Hawaii Five-O ep Air Cargo--Dial for Murder 10.26.71 CBS

The Streets of San Francisco ep The Thriller Killers 9.30.76, 10.7.76 ABC

SUPP.:

Happy Days sr ret 10.6.81 ABC

Joanie Loves Chachi ep Chicago 3.23.82 ABC

The Love Boat ep Command Performance 10.30.82 ABC

Happy Days sr ret 9.28.82 ABC

The ABC Afterschool Special ep Have You Ever Been Ashamed of Your Parents? 3.16.83 ABC

Happy Days sr ret 9.27.83 ABC

Fantasy Island ep Final Adieu 4.14.84 ABC

Sins of the Father tf 1.13.85 NBC

Hotel ep Rallying Cry 10.2.85 ABC

The Love Boat ep Picture from the Past 10.12.85 ABC

Glitter ep The Bag Lady of Rodeo Drive 12.27.85 ABC

ROTH, LILLIAN

A&C, B.V.:

Matinee Theater ep Woman Across the Hall 10.23.56 NBC

ROUNDTREE, RICHARD
SUPP.:
Magnum, P.I. ep Birds of a Feather 3.17.83 CBS
The Baron and the Kid tf 11.21.84 CBS
A.D. ms 3.31-4.4.85 NBC

ROWE, MISTY*
Blood Sport tf 12.5.73 ABC
The Story of Pretty Boy Floyd tf 5.7.74 ABC
SST--Death Flight tf 2.25.77 ABC
Kojak ep I Could Kill My Wife's Lawyer 12.24.77 CBS
Flying High ep Brides and Grooms 12.15.78 CBS
Young Maverick ep 1.16.80 CBS
Fantasy Island ep Unholy Wedlock 1.12.80 ABC
The Love Boat ep Rent a Romeo 1.26.80 ABC
Fantasy Island ep High Off the Hog 1.10.81 ABC
Fantasy Island ep Volcano 11.21.81 ABC
Darkroom ep A Quiet Funeral 12.18.81 ABC
Fantasy Island ep Tattoo the Matchmaker 2.20.82 ABC
Matt Houston ep Recipe for Murder 11.7.82 ABC
The Love Boat ep Just Plain Folk Medicine 4.30.83 ABC
Silver Spoons ep The Trouble with Grandfather 11.4.84 NBC
Airwolf ep Out of the Sky (a.k.a. Rock 'n' Roll Heaven) 3.2.85 CBS

ROWLANDS, GENA
SUPP.:
Thursday's Child tf 2.1.83 CBS
Faerie Tale Theater ep Rapunzel 2.5.83 SHO
An Early Frost tf 11.11.85 NBC

RUBINSTEIN, JOHN
A&C, Supp. 1:
Room 222 ep Flu 10.15.69 ABC
Cannon ep A Deadly Quiet Town 2.15.72 CBS
SUPP.:
Trapper John, M.D. ep Hear Today, Gone Tomorrow 1.23.83 CBS
Emerald Point, N.A.S. ep 10.31.83 CBS
Fantasy Island ep Dick Turpin's Last Ride 4.7.84 ABC
Crazy Like a Fox sr 12.30.84 CBS
Crazy Like a Fox sr ret 9.29.85 CBS

RUBINSTEIN, ZELDA*
Jennifer Slept Here ep One of Our Jars Is Missing 11.25.83 NBC
Matt Houston ep Target: The Most Beautiful Girls in the World 12.23.83 ABC
The Whiz Kids ep Amen to Amen-Re 1.28.84 CBS
CBS Storybreak ep The Roquefort Gang vo 11.9.85 CBS

RUNYON, JENNIFER*
Six Pack pt 7.24.83 NBC
The Fall Guy ep Hollywood Shorties 11.30.83 ABC
The Master ep Hostages 2.17.84 NBC
Charles in Charge sr 10.3.84 CBS

RUSH, BARBARA
A&C, B.V.:
The Fugitive ep Landscaping with Running Figures 11.16.65, 11.23.65 ABC
A&C, Supp. 2:
The Eddie Capra Mysteries ep Dying Declaration 12.15.78 NBC
SUPP.:
Fantasy Island ep Curse of the Moreaus 10.16.82 ABC
Matt Houston ep Who's Party Is This Anyway? 1.23.83 ABC
Fantasy Island ep The Sweet Life 1.14.84 ABC
Masquerade ep Sleeper 4.13.84 ABC
At Your Service pt 8.1.84 NBC
Magnum, P.I. ep Blind Justice 11.8.84 CBS
Finder of Lost Loves ep A Gift 12.8.84 ABC
Hotel ep Anniversary 2.20.85 ABC
Scene of the Crime ep Education in Murder 4.14.85 NBC
Glitter ep The Rivals 12.26.85 ABC

RUSSELL, JOHN
A&C, B.V.:
Maverick ep Lonesome Reunion 9.28.58 ABC
Alias Smith and Jones ep Which Way to the O.K. Corral? 2.10.72 ABC
Alias Smith and Jones ep The Day the Amnesty Came Through 11.25.72 ABC
Alias Smith and Jones ep Witness to a Lynching 12.16.72 ABC
SUPP.:
Simon and Simon ep Rough Rider Rides Again 11.18.82 CBS
The Yellow Rose ep Divide and Conquer 1.7.84 NBC
The Yellow Rose ep Sacred Ground 3.10.84 NBC

RUSSELL, KURT
A&C, Supp. 2:
Gunsmoke ep Blue Heaven 9.26.64 CBS
Gilligan's Island ep 2.6.65 CBS
Then Came Bronson ep The Spitball Kid 12.17.69 NBC
The High Chaparral ep The Guns of Johnny Rondo 2.6.70 NBC
The Storefront Lawyers ep 11.8.70 CBS
Room 222 ep Paul Revere Rides Again 3.31.71 ABC

RUTTAN, SUSAN*
Best of the West ep The New Jail 9.24.81 ABC
Thursday's Child tf 2.1.83 CBS
Packin' It In tf 2.7.83 CBS
The Fighter tf 2.19.83 CBS

After George pt 6.6.83 CBS
Second Sight: A Love Story tf 3.13.84 CBS
Buffalo Bill ep Have Yourself a Very Degrading Christmas 3.21.84 NBC
Benson ep The Scandal 9.21.84 ABC
Benson ep Adventure in Hong Kong 9.28.84 ABC
Remington Steele ep Lofty Steele 10.2.84 NBC
Newhart ep 12.31.84 CBS
The Jeffersons ep 4.2.85 CBS
Murder: By Reason of Insanity tf 10.1.85 CBS

RYAN, MITCHELL
A&C, Supp. 2:
Naked City ep The Well-Dressed Termites 2.8.61 ABC
N.Y.P.D. ep The Boy Witness 11.28.67 ABC
The High Chaparral ep Jelks 1.23.70 NBC
The Rockford Files ep Two Into 5.56 Won't Go 11.21.75 NBC
SUPP.:
King's Crossing ep Long Ago Tomorrow 2.13.82 ABC
Uncommon Valor tf 1.22.83 CBS
High Performance sr 3.2.83 ABC
Kenny Rogers as the Gambler: The Adventure Continues tf 11.28, 11.29.83 CBS
Hart to Hart ep Highland Fling 11.29.83 ABC
Robert Kennedy and His Times ms 1.27-1.30.84 CBS
Hardcastle and McCormick ep The Homecoming 3.4, 3.11.84 ABC
Dallas ep 9.28.84 CBS
Hot Pursuit ep Home Is the Heart 10.20, 10.27.84 NBC
Fatal Vision tf 11.18, 11.19.84 NBC
Murder, She Wrote ep Capitol Offense 1.6.85 CBS
Riptide ep Boz Busters 2.5.85 NBC
Hostage Flight tf 11.17.85 NBC
North and South ms ep 11.3.85 ABC
Hell Town ep 11.25.85 NBC

- S -

SABELLA, ERNIE*
Cagney and Lacey ep 12.27.82 CBS
The New Odd Couple ep My Strife in Court 1.28.83 ABC
Knots Landing ep 2.17.83 CBS
Newhart ep View from the Bench 2.21.83 CBS
13 Thirteenth Avenue pt 8.15.83 CBS
Newhart ep The Stratford Wives 11.7.83 CBS
Newhart ep 12.12, 12.19.83 CBS
Alice ep 1.8.84 CBS
Oh Madeline ep Monday Night Madeline 1.10.84 ABC

Mickey Spillane's Mike Hammer ep Vicki's Song 2.18.84 CBS
Cagney and Lacey ep 3.26.84 CBS
Domestic Life ep 5.23.84 CBS
100 Center Street pt 8.31.84 ABC
It's Your Move sr (with ep Dating Game) 10.17.84 NBC
Punky Brewster ep Parents Night 10.28.84 NBC
Hill Street Blues ep Queen for a Day 4.11.85 NBC
Hardcastle and McCormick ep Strange Hold 11.18.85 ABC
Cheers ep 11.21.85 NBC
Copacabana tf 12.3.85 CBS

SAGAL, JEAN*
Double Trouble sr 4.4.84 NBC
Double Trouble sr ret 12.1.84 NBC
Simon and Simon ep Facets 12.26.85 CBS

SAGAL, KATEY*
Mary sr 12.11.85 CBS

SAGAL, LIZ*
Double Trouble sr 4.4.84 NBC
Double Trouble sr ret 12.1.84 NBC

SAINT, EVA MARIE
SUPP.:
Malibu tf/pt 1.23, 1.24.83 ABC
The Love Boat ep Poor Rich Man 2.5.83 ABC
Jane Doe tf 3.12.83 CBS
Fatal Vision tf 11.18, 11.19.84 NBC
An American Portrait ep Chester Carlson 1.30.85 CBS

St. JACQUES, RAYMOND
A&C, Supp. 2:
Little House on the Prairie ep The Fighter 11.21.77 NBC
SUPP.:
Strike Force ep Turnabout 2.26.82 ABC
Fantasy Island ep Curse of the Moreaus 10.16.82 ABC
Gavilan ep Sarah and the Buzz 10.26.82 NBC
Voyagers ep Buffalo Bill and Annie Play the Palace 1.9.83 NBC
The Love Boat ep The Senior Sinners 1.22.83 ABC
The Powers of Matthew Star ep Dead Man's Hand 2.11.83 NBC
Matt Houston ep Get Houston 2.20.83 ABC
Falcon Crest ep The Motive 9.30.83 CBS
Falcon Crest ep Forgiveness 10.14.83 CBS
Falcon Crest ep 10.21.83, 11.4.83 CBS
Trapper John, M.D. ep 11.6.83 CBS
The Fall Guy ep Best of the Wasp 1.18.84 ABC
Airwolf ep They Are Us 3.31.84 CBS
Murder, She Wrote ep Murder, She Wrote (pt) 9.30.84 CBS
Cagney and Lacey ep 12.10.84 CBS
The Fall Guy ep Spring Back 2.20.85 ABC

Hardcastle and McCormick ep Undercover McCormick 3.11.85 ABC
Murder, She Wrote ep Will No One Weep for Me? 9.29.85 CBS
The Love Boat ep Hidden Treasure 10.12.85 ABC

SAINT JAMES, SUSAN
SUPP.:
The Kid from Nowhere tf 1.4.82 NBC
I Take These Men tf 1.5.83 CBS
After George pt 6.6.83 CBS
Kate and Allie sr 3.19.84 CBS
Kate and Allie sr ret 10.8.84 CBS
Kate and Allie sr ret 9.30.85 CBS

St. JOHN, JILL
A&C, B.V.:
The Life of Riley ep Teenage Troubles 1958 NBC
The Bob Hope Chrysler Theater ep Russian Roulette 11.17.65 NBC
SUPP.:
The Love Boat ep Live It Up 2.20.82 ABC
Two Guys from Muck pt 3.29.82 NBC
Magnum, P.I. ep Three Minus Two 4.1.82 CBS
Fantasy Island ep Forget-Me-Not 4.10.82 ABC
Rooster tf/pt 8.19.82 ABC

SALDANA, THERESA*
240-Robert ep The Applicant 11.26.79 ABC
Sophia Loren: Her Own Story tf 10.26.80 NBC
The Gangster Chronicles sr 2.12.81 NBC
Nurse ep The Gift 4.9.81 CBS
Seven Brides for Seven Brothers ep 1.5.83 CBS
T. J. Hooker ep Too Late for Love 1.15.83 ABC
Victims for Victims: The Theresa Saldana Story tf 11.12.84 NBC
The Twilight Zone ep Dead Woman's Shoes 11.22.85 CBS
Cagney and Lacey ep Bold Ghosts 12.9.85 CBS
The New Love, American Style ep Gotta Dance 12.24.85 ABC

SALMI, ALBERT
A&C, B.V.:
The Eleventh Hour ep Angie, You Made My Heart Stop 11.14.62 NBC
Stoney Burke ep The Wanderer 12.3.62 ABC
Destry ep The Nicest Girl in Gomorrah 3.13.64 ABC
The Monroes ep Wild Dog of the Tetons 10.5.66 ABC
Cimarron Strip ep The Last Wolf 12.14.67 CBS
A&C, Supp. 1:
Toma ep A Funeral for Max Berlin 2.22.74 ABC
SUPP.:
The Fall Guy ep Guess Who's Coming to Town 3.17.82 ABC

Dallas ep 11.19, 11.26.82 CBS
St. Elsewhere ep Legionnaires I 12.7.82 NBC
Simon and Simon ep The Club Murder Vacation 1.27.83 CBS
Bring 'Em Back Alive ep The Shadow Woman of Chung Tui 1.29.83 CBS
Simon and Simon ep The Secret of the Chrome Eagle 3.3.83 ABC
Ace Crawford, Private Eye ep 3.29.83 CBS
Small and Frye ep 6.15.83 CBS
The A-Team ep Diamonds 'n' Dust 9.20.83 NBC
Knight Rider ep Custom KITT 11.13.83 NBC
Hart to Hart ep Highland Fling 11.29.83 ABC
Scarecrow and Mrs. King ep 12.19.83 CBS
The Best Kept Secrets tf 3.26.84 ABC
Knots Landing ep Tomorrow Never Knows 11.22.84 CBS
Trapper John, M.D. ep 12.30.84 CBS
Murder, She Wrote ep Murder Takes the Bus 3.17.85 CBS

SAMMS, EMMA*
More Wild Wild West tf/pt 10.7, 10.8.80 CBS
Goliath Awaits tf 10.16, 10.17.81 OPT
Hotel ep Tomorrows 1.11.84 ABC
Ellis Island ms 11.12-11.14.84 CBS
Hotel ep Crossroads 1.30.85 ABC
Dynasty ep Kidnapped 4.10.85 ABC
Dynasty ep 11.20.85 ABC
Dynasty II: The Colbys sr 11.20.85 ABC

SAND, PAUL*
The Mary Tyler Moore Show ep 1040 or Fight 11.28.70 CBS
Story Theater sr 9.71 NN
Friends and Lovers pt 5.16.74 CBS
Paul Sand in Friends and Lovers sr 9.14.74 CBS
The New Adventures of Wonder Woman ep Disco Devil 10.20.78 CBS
Flying High ep The Vanishing Point 11.3.78 CBS
Fantasy Island ep 11.4.78 ABC
The Legend of Sleepy Hollow tf 10.31.80 NBC
Taxi ep Fledgling 11.26.81 ABC
Alice ep 3.7.83 CBS
The Love Boat ep For Love or Money 10.22.83 ABC
St. Elsewhere sr (with ep Under Pressure) 11.30.83 NBC
Domestic Life ep 1.25.84 CBS
Cagney and Lacey ep 1.14.85 CBS
Murder, She Wrote ep Footnote to Murder 3.10.85 CBS
Trapper John, M.D. ep 5.5.85 CBS
I Had Three Wives ep 8.21.85 CBS
Who's the Boss? ep Tony the Matchmaker 10.29.85 ABC

SANDERS, BEVERLY
SUPP.:
The Fall Guy ep The Adventures of Ozzie and Harold 2.3.82 ABC

It Takes Two ep Promises in the Dark 11.4.82 ABC
The Other Woman tf 3.22.83 CBS
E/R ep 9.16.84 CBS
Cover Up ep Who's Trying to Kill Miss Globe? 3.9.85 CBS

SANDERS, RICHARD*
McCloud ep London Bridges 3.6.77 NBC
Alexander: The Other Side of Dawn tf 5.16.77 NBC
Good Against Evil tf 5.22.77 ABC
Rafferty ep The Wild Child 10.31.77 CBS
Ruby and Oswald tf 2.8.78 CBS
Keefer tf 3.16.78 ABC
WKRP in Cincinnati sr 9.18.78 CBS
Bud and Lou tf 11.15.78 NBC
WKRP in Cincinnati sr ret 9.17.79 CBS
Diary of a Hitchhiker tf 9.21.79 ABC
Trouble in High Timber Country tf/pt 6.27.80 ABC
WKRP in Cincinnati sr ret 11.1.80 CBS
WKRP in Cincinnati sr ret 10.7.81 CBS
The ABC Weekend Special ep The Joke's On Mr. Little 2.6.82 ABC
Gloria ep 11.28.82 CBS
It Takes Two ep Anniversary 1.13.83 ABC
Gimme a Break ep The Custody Suit 2.10.83 NBC
The Invisible Woman tf/pt 2.13.83 NBC
Alice ep 10.23.83 CBS
The Love Boat ep 12.11.83 ABC
Found Money tf 12.19.83 NBC
Goodnight Beantown ep 12.25.83 CBS
Simon and Simon ep 2.9.84 CBS
Newhart ep 3.19.84 CBS
Spencer sr 12.1.84 NBC
Murder, She Wrote ep We're Off to Kill the Wizard 12.9.84 CBS
Under One Roof ep Crazy Girl 4.20.85 NBC
Under One Roof ep Wayne's Nose Job 5.11.85 NBC
Who's the Boss? ep It Happened One Summer 9.24, 10.1.85 ABC

SANDY, GARY
A&C, Supp. 2:
Harry O ep Anatomy of a Frame 9.11.75 ABC
Medical Center ep The Happy State of Depression 3.8.76 CBS
SUPP.:
Murder, She Wrote ep Capitol Offense 1.6.85 CBS
Hearts Island pt 8.31.85 NBC

SANFORD, ISABEL
SUPP.:
The Jeffersons sr ret 9.82 CBS
The Love Boat ep Women's Best Friend 3.26.83 ABC
The Jeffersons sr ret 10.2.83 CBS
The Jeffersons sr ret 10.4.84 CBS

SANTONI, RENI

A&C, Supp. 2:

Hawaii Five-O ep A Death in the Family 5.4.78 CBS

The Rockford Files ep A Different Drummer 4.13.79 NBC

SANTOS, JOE*

Room 222 ep 10.20.72 ABC

Nightside pt 4.15.73 ABC

Toma ep The Oberon Contract 10.4.73 ABC

The Blue Knight ms 11.13-11.16.73 NBC

Police Story ep Countdown 1.15, 1.22.74 NBC

Barnaby Jones ep Rendezvous with Terror 2.24.74 CBS

The Streets of San Francisco ep Rampage 2.28.74 ABC

The Rockford Files tf/pt 3.27.74 NBC

The Girl on the Late, Late Show tf 4.1.74 NBC

The Rockford Files sr 9.13.74 (through 7.25.80) NBC

Police Story ep Robbery: 48 Hours 9.27.74 NBC

Kung Fu ep 1.11.75 ABC

Baretta ep The Secret of Terry Lake 4.16.75 ABC

Police Story ep Spanish Class 1.2.76 NBC

Joe Forrester ep A Game of Love 2.16.76 NBC

A Matter of Wife ... And Death tf 4.10.76 NBC

Police Story ep Two Frogs on a Mongoose 10.12.76 NBC

Police Story ep Monster Manor 11.30.76 NBC

Police Story ep Trial Board 1.4.77 NBC

Lou Grant ep Barrio 11.1.77 CBS

David Cassidy--Man Undercover ep Running the Hill 11.2.78 NBC

Police Story ep River of Promises 1.14.78 NBC

The Black Sheep Squadron ep The Show Must Go On--Sometimes 3.22.78 NBC

Eischied ep Spanish Eight 12.7.79 NBC

Power tf 1.14, 1.15.80 NBC

Paris ep 1.15.80 CBS

Me and Maxx sr 3.22.80 NBC

The Hustler of Muscle Beach tf/pt 5.16.80 ABC

The Greatest American Hero ep Space Ranger 1.27.83 ABC

Masquerade ep Five Days 1.19.84 ABC

a.k.a. Pablo sr 3.6.84 ABC

Hill Street Blues ep Lucky Ducks 5.10.84 NBC

Hill Street Blues ep Eva's Brawn 5.17.84 NBC

Cover Up ep Cover Up (pt) 9.22.84 CBS

The A-Team ep Trouble on Wheels 10.30.84 NBC

Hardcastle and McCormick ep Do Not Go Gentle.... 11.4.84 ABC

Hardcastle and McCormick ep Hardcastle, Hardcastle, Hardcastle and McCormick 2.4.85 ABC

T. J. Hooker ep The Bribe 2.9.85 ABC

Hardcastle and McCormick ep Games People Play 11.11.85 ABC

Hardcastle and McCormick ep Strange Hold 11.18.85 ABC

Hardcastle and McCormick ep Duet for Two Wind Instruments 12.16.85 ABC

Hardcastle and McCormick ep If You Could See What I See 1.6.86 ABC

SARRAZIN, MICHAEL
SUPP.:
Murder, She Wrote ep Joshua Peabody Died Here 10.6.85 CBS

SAVALAS, TELLY
A&C, B.V.:
Kraft Suspense Theater ep The Watchman 5.14.64 NBC
SUPP.:
American Playhouse ep My Palikari 5.4.82 PBS
The Cartier Affair tf 11.4.84 ABC
The Love Boat ep Too Many Isaacs 2.2.85 ABC
Kojak: The Belarus File tf/pt 2.16.85 CBS
George Burns Comedy Week ep The Assignment 10.30.85 CBS

SAXON, JOHN
SUPP.:
Dynasty ep Episode 21 1.6.82 ABC
Dynasty ep Episode 22 1.13.82 ABC
Rooster tf/pt 8.19.82 ABC
The A-Team ep The Children of Jamestown 1.30.83 NBC
Savage in the Orient pt 6.21.83 CBS
Prisoners of the Lost Universe tf/pt 8.15.83 SHO
Scarecrow and Mrs. King ep Scarecrow and Mrs. King (pt) 10.3.83 CBS
Scarecrow and Mrs. King ep The Kidnapping of Amanda 11.28.83 CBS
Magnum, P.I. ep 1.5.84 CBS
Dynasty ep The Voice 3.28.84 ABC
Masquerade ep The French Connection 3.30.84 ABC
Fantasy Island ep Surrogate Mother 5.19.84 ABC
Finder of Lost Loves ep White Lies 10.20.84 ABC
Murder, She Wrote ep Hooray for Homicide 10.28.84 CBS
Dynasty ep Domestic Intrigue 11.28.84 ABC
The A-Team ep Prey 2.12.85 NBC
Brothers-in-Law pt 4.28.85 ABC
Glitter ep The Matriarch 12.19.85 ABC

SCANNELL, SUSAN*
Ryan's Hope sr Summer-Fall 1985 ABC
The A-Team ep Uncle Buckle-Up 12.17.85 NBC

SCHAAL, WENDY*
It's a Living sr 10.30.80 ABC
Fantasy Island sr (with ep The Devil and Mr. Roarke) 10.17.81 ABC
Making a Living sr 10.24.81 ABC
Strike Force ep Chinatown 4.9.82 ABC
Love, Sidney ep Sidney's Cousin 10.30.82 NBC

The Love Boat ep Love Will Find a Way 11.20.82 ABC
Happy Days ep Since I Don't Have You 11.28.82 ABC
AfterMASH ep 9.26.83, 10.3.83, 12.12.83, 12.19.83, 2.13.84 CBS
The Love Boat ep Love on Strike 12.17.83 ABC
Fatal Vision tf 11.18, 11.19.84 NBC
Cover Up ep Midnight Highway 12.8.84 CBS
Knight Rider ep The 19th Hole 3.10.85 NBC
Finder of Lost Loves ep Connections 4.13.85 ABC
The A-Team ep Lease with an Option to Die 10.22.85 NBC
The Insiders ep 12.4.85 ABC

SCHALLERT, WILLIAM

A&C, Supp. 2:

The George Burns and Gracie Allen Show ep Gracie, the Artist Early 1955 CBS
The George Burns and Gracie Allen Show ep Gracie Wants the House Painted Spring 1955 CBS
The George Burns and Gracie Allen Show ep Cyrano de Bergerac Early 1956 CBS
You Are There ep Halley's Comet 4.29.56 CBS
Combat Sergeant ep Destruction at Dawn 8.3.56 ABC
The Adventures of Jim Bowie ep The Captain's Chimp 3.8.57 ABC
The Adventures of Jim Bowie ep The Pearl and the Crown 4.5.57 ABC
The Adventures of Jim Bowie ep The Bounty Hunter 5.17.57 ABC
Have Gun--Will Travel ep The Long Night 11.16.57 CBS
The Adventures of Jim Bowie ep Close Shave 1.10.58 ABC
Jefferson Drum ep Matter of Murder 7.11.58 NBC
Father Knows Best ep Betty, the Pioneer Woman 11.17.58 CBS
Steve Canyon ep Operation Crash Landing 12.6.58 NBC
Wanted: Dead Or Alive ep Call Your Shot 2.7.59 CBS
Wanted: Dead Or Alive ep Littlest Client 4.25.59 CBS
The Donna Reed Show ep All Mother's Worry Fall 1959 ABC
Richard Diamond ep Act of Grace 10.12.59 CBS
Johnny Ringo ep The Accused 10.15.59 CBS
Black Saddle ep Blood Money 12.18.59 ABC
Bat Masterson ep Deadly Diamonds 2.11.60 NBC
Wagon Train ep The Amos Gibbon Story 4.20.60 NBC
Black Saddle ep End of the Line 5.6.60 ABC
The Rifleman ep 10.25.60 ABC
Hennessy ep Admiral and Son Spring 1961 CBS
The Andy Griffith Show ep Quiet Sam 5.1.61 CBS
The Dick Van Dyke Show ep A Word a Day 2.7.62 CBS
Gunsmoke ep Daddy Went Away 5.11.63 CBS
Here Come the Brides ep Man of the Family 10.16.68 ABC
Get Smart ep With Love and Twitches 11.9.68 NBC
Here Come the Brides ep A Far Cry from Yesterday 9.26.69 ABC

The Girl with Something Extra ep No Benefit of Doubt 11.73 NBC
Switch ep The Argonaut Special 10.12.76 CBS
SUPP.:
Lou Grant ep Blacklist 4.5.82 CBS
Magnum, P.I. ep Basket Case 2.3.83 CBS
Grace Kelly tf 2.21.83 ABC
Through Naked Eyes tf 12.11.83 ABC
Matt Houston ep Waltz of Death 1.13.84 ABC
Amazons tf 1.29.84 ABC
Gidget's Summer Reunion tf/pt 6.85 NN
The Duck Factory ep Call Me Responsible 7.11.85 NBC

SCHEEDEN, ANNE*
Get Christie Love ep Market for Murder 9.11.74 ABC
Marcus Welby, M.D. ep Last Flight to Babylon 9.24.74 ABC
Aloha Means Goodbye tf 10.11.74 CBS
Ironside ep Speak No Evil 12.12.74 NBC
Lucas Tanner ep Merry Gentlemen 12.25.74 NBC
You Lie So Deep, My Love tf 2.25.75 ABC
Switch tf/pt 3.21.75 CBS
McCloud ep Park Avenue Pirates 9.21.75 NBC
Marcus Welby, M.D. ep Calculated Risk 11.11.75 ABC
Marcus Welby, M.D. ep Killer of Dreams 11.18.75 ABC
Marcus Welby, M.D. ep Go Ahead and Cry 12.16.75 ABC
Marcus Welby, M.D. ep The Highest Mountain 2.17.76 ABC
Marcus Welby, M.D. ep Vanity Case 4.27, 5.4, 5.11.76 ABC
Emergency! ep 10.30.76 NBC
Flight to Holocaust tf 3.27.77 NBC
Kingston: Confidential ep Seed of Corruption 4.6.77 NBC
Family ep 5.3.77 ABC
Exo-Man tf/pt 6.18.77 NBC
Switch ep Dangerous Curves 1.2.78 CBS
Baretta ep Why Me? 1.11.78 ABC
Project UFO ep Sighting 4001 2.19.78 NBC
Champions: A Love Story tf 1.13.79 CBS
Never Say Never pt 7.11.79 CBS
Semi Tough ep 6.5.80 ABC
Simon and Simon ep The $100,000 Deductible 11.4.82 CBS
Cheers ep Norman's Conquest 2.23.84 NBC
E/R ep 9.18.84 CBS
Paper Dolls sr 9.23.84 ABC
Braker pt 4.28.85 ABC

SCHNEIDER, JOHN*
The Dukes of Hazzard sr 1.26.79 CBS
The Dukes of Hazzard sr ret 10.25.80 CBS
The Dukes of Hazzard sr ret 10.6.81 CBS
Dream House tf 11.28.81 CBS
The Dukes of Hazzard ret to sr 2.25.83 CBS
The Dukes of Hazzard sr ret 9.23.83 CBS

The Dukes of Hazzard sr ret 9.21.84 CBS
Gus Brown and Midnight Brewster tf/pt 6.2.85 NBC

SCHRODER, RICKY*
Silver Spoons sr 9.25.82 NBC
Faerie Tale Theater ep Hansel and Gretel 11.20.82 SHO
Silver Spoons sr ret 10.15.83 NBC
Silver Spoons sr ret 9.23.84 NBC
A Reason to Live tf 1.7.85 NBC
Silver Spoons sr ret 9.15.85 NBC

SCHUCK, JOHN
SUPP.:
Earthbound sp 1.31, 2.7.82 NBC
Simon and Simon ep The Uncivil Servant 1.26.82 CBS
The New Odd Couple sr 10.29.82 ABC
St. Elsewhere ep Untitled 11.28.84 NBC
Murder, She Wrote ep We're Off to Kill the Wizard 12.9.84 CBS
St. Elsewhere ep The Children's Hour 12.12.84 CBS
E/R ep 12.12.84 CBS

SCHULTZ, DWIGHT*
CHiPs ep The Hawk and the Hunter 4.5.81 NBC
The A-Team sr 1.23.83 NBC
The A-Team sr ret 9.20.83 NBC
The A-Team sr ret 9.18.84 NBC
The A-Team sr ret 9.24.85 NBC

SCOGGINS, TRACY*
Twirl tf 10.25.81 NBC
McClain's Law ep A Matter of Honor 1.15.82 NBC
The Dukes of Hazzard ep New Deputy in Town 2.19.82 CBS
The Devlin Connection ep The Lady on the Billboard 10.9.82 NBC
Tucker's Witch ep Abra Cadaver 11.10.82 CBS
The Fall Guy ep Hell on Wheels 12.8.82 ABC
The A-Team ep The Rabbit Who Ate Las Vegas 3.1.83 NBC
Remington Steele ep Steele in the News 3.4.83 NBC
The Renegades sr 3.4.83 ABC
The New Odd Couple ep The Only Way to Fly 5.20.83 ABC
Dallas ep 10.21.83 CBS
Manimal ep High Stakes 11.4.83 NBC
Hardcastle and McCormick ep Killer B's 11.6.83 ABC
The A-Team ep There's Always a Catch 11.15.83 NBC
The Big Easy pt 12.3.83 NBC
Mickey Spillane's Mike Hammer ep 24 Karat Dead 1.28.84 CBS
T. J. Hooker ep Exercise in Murder 1.28.84 ABC
Blue Thunder ep Skydiver 2.24.84 ABC
Hawaiian Heat sr 9.14.84 ABC
Crazy Like a Fox ep Fox in Wonderland 3.17.85 CBS
Dynasty ep 11.13.85 ABC
Dynasty II: The Colbys sr 11.20.85 ABC

SCOLARI, PETER*
The Goodtime Girls sr 1.22.80 ABC
The Further Adventures of Wally Brown pt 8.21.80 NBC
Bosom Buddies sr 11.27.80 ABC
Bosom Buddies sr ret 10.8.81 ABC
Remington Steele ep Steele Waters Run Deep 10.22.82 NBC
Happy Days ep May the Best Man Win 2.22.83 ABC
Baby Makes Five sr 4.1.83 ABC
Newhart sr 1.30.84 CBS
Newhart sr ret 10.15.84 CBS
Finder of Lost Loves ep A Gift 12.8.84 ABC
Newhart sr ret 9.30.85 CBS

SCOTT, BRENDA
A&C, Supp. 1:
The Donna Reed Show ep Just a Little Wedding 1.13.63 ABC
Gunsmoke ep Anybody Can Kill a Marshal 3.8.63 CBS
Wagon Train ep The Molly Kincaid Story 9.16.63 ABC
Here Come the Brides ep A Wild Colonial Boy 10.24.69 ABC
Alias Smith and Jones ep Witness to a Lynching 12.16.72 ABC
Get Christie Love ep A Deadly Sport 1.8.75 ABC
SUPP.:
Simon and Simon ep 3.31.83 CBS

SCOTT, DEBRALEE
A&C, Supp. 1:
Isis ep 9.20.75 CBS

SCOTT, GEORGE C.
SUPP.:
Oliver Twist tf 3.23.82 CBS
China Rose tf 10.18.83 CBS
A Christmas Carol tf 12.17.84 CBS
Mussolini: The Untold Story ms 11.24-11.26.85 NBC

SCOTT, JEAN BRUCE*
Magnum, P.I. sr 9.30.82 CBS
Knight Rider ep A Nice, Indecent Little Town 2.18.83 NBC
St. Elsewhere ep All About Eve 12.14.83 NBC
St. Elsewhere ep A Pig Too Far 1.11.84 NBC
St. Elsewhere ep In Sickness and in Health 2.8.84 NBC
St. Elsewhere ep Attack 2.22.84 NBC
Airwolf sr 9.22.84 CBS
Kids Don't Tell tf 3.5.85 CBS
Airwolf sr ret 9.28.85 CBS

SCOTT, JUDSON*
Strike Force ep Fallen Angel 2.12.82 ABC
The Phoenix sr 3.26.82 ABC
The Powers of Matthew Star ep Jackal 9.17.82 NBC
Voyagers ep World's Apart 11.7.82 NBC

The Greatest American Hero ep It's Only Rock 'n' Roll 2.10.83 ABC
The Dukes of Hazzard ep 2.18.83 CBS
T. J. Hooker ep Exercise in Murder 1.28.84 ABC
The Dukes of Hazzard ep 12.14.84 CBS
V: The Series ep The Hero 1.11.85 NBC
V: The Series ep The Champion 2.1.85 NBC
V: The Series ep The Wildcats 2.15.85 NBC
V: The Series ep War of Illusions 3.8.85 NBC
V: The Series ep The Secret Underground 3.15.85 NBC
The A-Team ep Incident at Crystal Lake 5.14.85 NBC

SCOTT, MARTHA
A&C, B.V.:
Slattery's People ep Color Him Red 11.26.56 CBS
SUPP.:
Summer Girl tf 4.12.83 CBS
Adam tf 10.10.83 NBC
Hotel ep Obsessions 10.31.84 ABC

SCRUGGS, LINDA*
The Whiz Kids ep Programmed for Murder 10.5.83 CBS
The Whiz Kids ep Computer Thief 10.19.83 CBS
The Whiz Kids ep Candidate for Murder 11.2.83 CBS
The Whiz Kids ep Red Star Rising 12.21.83 CBS
The Whiz Kids ep The Network 1.7.84 CBS

SEGAL, GEORGE
A&C, B.V.:
Arrest and Trial ep He Ran for His Life 4.5.64 ABC
SUPP.:
Death Game sp 7.23.82 HBO
Not My Kid tf 1.15.85 CBS

SEGALL, PAMELA*
The Facts of Life ep Halloween 10.26.83 NBC
The Facts of Life ep Small But Dangerous 11.16.83 NBC
The Facts of Life ep Store Games 11.3.83 NBC
The Facts of Life ep Big Fish/Little Fish 2.8.84 NBC
The Fantastic World of D.C. Collins tf 2.10.84 NBC
E/R ep 12.19.84 CBS
The Jeffersons ep 12.23.84 CBS

SELLECCA, CONNIE
SUPP.:
The Greatest American Hero sr ret 10.29.82 ABC
Hotel sr 9.21.83 ABC
The Love Boat Fall Preview Party sp 9.14.84 ABC
Hotel sr ret 9.26.84 ABC
Finder of Lost Loves ep Goodbye, Sara 11.3.84 ABC
International Airport tf/pt 5.25.85 ABC
Hotel sr ret 9.25.85 ABC

SELLECK, TOM

A&C, Supp. 2:

The Streets of San Francisco ep Spooks for Sale 12.11.75 ABC

Doctors' Hospital ep And Hear a Sudden Cry 1.6.76 NBC

The Rockford Files ep White on White and Nearly Perfect 10.20.78 NBC

The Rockford Files ep Heartaches of a Fool 9.22.78 NBC

SUPP.:

Divorce Wars tf 3.1.82 ABC

The Shadow Riders tf 9.28.82 CBS

Magnum, P.I. sr ret 10.7.82 CBS

Simon and Simon ep 10.7.82 CBS

Taxi ep Celebration of Taxi 3.23.83 NBC

Magnum, P.I. sr ret 9.29.83 CBS

Magnum, P.I. sr ret 9.27.84 CBS

Magnum, P.I. sr ret 9.26.85 CBS

SEYMOUR, JANE

SUPP.:

The Scarlet Pimpernel tf 11.9.82 CBS

Phantom of the Opera tf 1.29.83 CBS

The Haunting Passion tf 10.24.83 NBC

Dark Mirror tf 3.5.84 ABC

The Sun Also Rises tf 12.9, 12.10.84 NBC

An American Portrait ep John Alexander 1.31.85 CBS

Obsessed with a Married Man tf 2.11.85 ABC

Jamaica Inn tf 6.3.85 NN

SHATNER, WILLIAM

A&C, B.V.:

Kraft Mystery Theater ep The Man Who Didn't Fly 7.16.58 NBC

The Reporter ep 10.30.64 CBS

SUPP.:

Mork and Mindy ep Mork, Mindy & Mearth Meet Milt 2.18.82 ABC

T. J. Hooker sr 3.13.82 ABC

T. J. Hooker sr ret 9.25.82 ABC

The Magic Planet sp hos/nar 3.17.83 ABC

T. J. Hooker sr ret 10.1.83 ABC

The Love Boat Fall Preview Party sp 9.15.84 ABC

T. J. Hooker sr ret 10.6.84 ABC

Heroes and Sidekicks--Indiana Jones and the Temple of Doom sp hos/nar 11.27.84 CBS

T. J. Hooker sr ret 9.25.85 CBS

North Beach and Rawhide tf 11.12, 11.13.85 CBS

SHAVER, HELEN

SUPP.:

Between Two Brothers tf 3.9.82 CBS

Hill Street Blues ep Officer of the Year 10.28.82 NBC

Hill Street Blues ep A Hair of the Dog 11.25.83 NBC

Hill Street Blues ep The Phantom of the Hill 12.2.82 NBC
T. J. Hooker ep Shadow of Truth 3.17.84 ABC

SHEEN, MARTIN
A&C, B.V.:
Arrest and Trial ep We May Be Better Strangers 12.1.63 ABC
SUPP.:
In the Custody of Strangers tf 5.26.82 ABC
Kennedy ms 11.20-11.22.83 NBC
Choices of the Heart tf 12.5.83 NBC
Consenting Adult tf 2.4.85 ABC
The Atlanta Child Murders tf 2.10, 2.12.85 CBS
The Fourth Wiseman sp 4.30.85 ABC
An American Portrait ep Roger Nash Baldwin 4.8.85 CBS
Out of the Darkness tf 10.12.85 CBS
Alfred Hitchcock Presents ep Method Actor 11.10.85 NBC

SHELLEY, BARBARA
A&C, B.V.:
Twelve O'Clock High ep Falling Star 1.3.66 ABC

SHEPHERD, CYBILL*
A Guide for the Married Man tf 10.13.78 ABC
Fantasy Island ep No Friends Like Old Friends 2.26.83 ABC
The Yellow Rose sr 10.2.83 NBC
Moonlighting pt 3.3.85 ABC
Moonlighting sr 3.5.85 ABC
Seduced tf 3.12.85 CBS
Moonlighting sr ret 9.24.85 ABC
The Long Hot Summer tf 10.6, 10.7.85 NBC

SHERMAN, BOBBY
A&C, B.V.:
Honey West ep The Princess and the Pauper 10.29.65 ABC
SUPP.:
The Love Boat ep New York A.C. 2.20.82 ABC
Murder, She Wrote ep Murder to a Jazz Beat 2.3.85 CBS

SHERMAN, JENNY*
Waikiki tf/pt 4.21.80 ABC
Lobo ep The Fastest Woman Around 3.10.81 NBC
The Seal pt 11.27.81 NBC
Quincy, M.E. ep For Love of Joshua 2.3.82 NBC
Dallas ep Anniversary 2.12.82 CBS
The Fall Guy ep The Silent Partner 4.28.82 ABC
Matt Houston ep The Showgirl Murders 3.20.83 ABC
Three's Company ep Hair Today, Gone Tomorrow 4.5.83 ABC
Scarecrow and Mrs. King ep Dead Ringer 2.6.84 CBS
Matt Houston ep Cash and Carry 3.23.84 ABC
Matt Houston ep Blood Money 11.30.84 ABC
T. J. Hooker ep The Cheerleader Murders 10.22.83 ABC
Hollywood Beat ep Fast Hustle 11.23.85 ABC

SHERWOOD, MADELEINE
A&C, B.V.:
Alfred Hitchcock Presents ep Make My Death Bed 6.27.61 NBC

SHIELDS, BROOKE
SUPP.:
Wet Gold tf 10.28.84 ABC

SHIGETA, JAMES
SUPP.:
Tomorrow's Child tf 3.22.82 ABC
Strike Force ep Chinatown 4.9.82 ABC
The Renegades tf/pt 8.11.82 ABC
Masquerade ep Girls for Sale 12.29.83 ABC

SHIRRIFF, CATHEE*
The Cabot Connection pt 5.10.77 CBS
The New Adventures of Wonder Woman ep Gault's Brain 12.29.78 CBS
Friendships, Secrets and Lies tf 12.3.79 NBC
She's Dressed to Kill tf 12.10.79 NBC
Magnum, P.I. ep Skin Deep 1.15.81 CBS
Lewis and Clark ep Opposites Attract 11.5.81 NBC
Today's FBI ep Kidnap 4.4.82 ABC
One Shoe Makes It Murder tf 11.6.82 CBS
Taxi ep Alex Gets Burned By an Old Flame 3.30.83 NBC
Shaping Up sr 3.12.84 ABC
Riptide ep Boz Busters 2.5.85 NBC
Murder in Space tf 7.28.85 SHO

SHOOP, PAMELA SUSAN
A&C, Supp. 2:
The Interns ep Mondays Can Be Fatal 11.27.70 CBS
SUPP.:
Knight Rider ep Knight Rider (pt) 9.26.82 NBC
The Fall Guy ep Bail and Bond 10.27.82 ABC
T. J. Hooker ep A Cry for Help 11.27.82 ABC
Fame ep Relationships 1.6.83 NBC
Tales of the Gold Monkey ep Force of Habit 2.2.83 ABC
Masquerade ep Oil 1.26.84 ABC
The Whiz Kids ep The Sufi Project 3.17.84 CBS
I Had Three Wives ep 8.28.85 CBS
Scarecrow and Mrs. King ep Fast Food for Thought 12.16.85 CBS

SIDNEY, SYLVIA
SUPP.:
Sense of Humor pt 2.16.82 PBS
Having It All tf 10.13.82 ABC
Magnum, P.I. ep Birman of Budapest 2.10.83 CBS
Ryan's Four ep Never Say Never 4.6.83 ABC

Domestic Life ep 1.11.84 CBS
The Whiz Kids ep The Lollipop Gang Strikes Back 2.25.84 CBS
Trapper John, M.D. ep 5.6.84 CBS
Finnegan Begin Again tf 2.4.85 HBO
An Early Frost tf 11.11.85 NBC

SIERRA, GREGORY
SUPP.:
Lou Grant ep Immigrants 2.15.82 CBS
Gloria ep 2.20.82 CBS
McClain's Law ep The Last Hero 3.20.82 NBC
Cassie and Company ep Anything for a Friend 6.22.82 NBC
Quincy, M.E. ep Baby Rattlesnakes 9.29.82 NBC
Farrell for the People tf/pt 10.18.82 NBC
Uncommon Valor tf 1.22.83 CBS
Simon and Simon ep The Club Murder Vacation 1.27.83 ABC
Hill Street Blues ep Untitled 2.10.83 NBC
Hill Street Blues ep The Belles of St. Mary's 2.17.83 NBC
Hill Street Blues ep Life in the Minors 2.24.83 NBC
Hill Street Blues ep Eugene's Comedy Empire Strikes Back 3.3.83 NBC
High Performance ep Ice on the Road 3.9.83 ABC
Zorro and Son sr 4.6.83 CBS
Kenny Rogers as the Gambler: The Adventure Continues tf 11.28, 11.29.83 CBS
Hart to Hart ep Max's Waltz 1.17.84 ABC
Masquerade ep Oil 1.26.84 ABC
Blue Thunder ep The Long Flight 3.16.84 ABC
Miami Vice ep Miami Vice (pt) 9.16.84 NBC
Miami Vice ep Heart of Darkness 9.28.84 NBC
Miami Vice ep Cool Runnin' 10.5.84 NBC
Miami Vice ep Hit List 10.12.84 NBC
Murder, She Wrote ep Broadway Malady 1.13.85 CBS
Cover Up ep The Assassin 1.26.85 CBS
Cagney and Lacey ep 3.18.85 CBS
Stingray tf/pt 7.14.85 NBC
MacGyver ep The Gauntlet 10.20.85 ABC
Simon and Simon ep The Enchilada Express 10.24.85 CBS

SIKES, CYNTHIA*
The Rockford Files ep A Portrait of Elizabeth 1.13.76 NBC
Jigsaw John ep Promise to Kill 2.2.76 NBC
Columbo ep Now You See Him 2.29.76 NBC
Captains and the Kings ms 9.30-10.11.76 NBC
Big Shamus, Little Shamus sr 9.29.79 CBS
Archie Bunker's Place ep Bosom Partners 10.21.79 CBS
Archie Bunker's Place ep 1.13.80 CBS
Hart to Hart ep Tis the Season to Be Murdered 12.16.80 ABC
Flamingo Road ep The Intruder 11.24.81 NBC
Falcon Crest ep Kindred Spirits 1.1.82 CBS
Flamingo Road ep Strange Bedfellows 1.12.82 NBC

Flamingo Road ep The Explosion 2.9.82 NBC
The Fall Guy ep Soldiers of Misfortune 2.10.82 ABC
Flamingo Road ep Chance of a Lifetime 2.16.82 NBC
Flamingo Road ep Double Exposure 2.23.82 NBC
Flamingo Road ep The Dedication 3.2.82 NBC
Flamingo Road ep Sins of the Father 3.16.82 NBC
Flamingo Road ep The Bad and the Beautiful 4.13.82 NBC
Bring 'Em Back Alive ep 9.24.82 CBS
St. Elsewhere sr 10.26.82 NBC
St. Elsewhere sr ret 10.26.83 NBC
Poor Richard pt 1.21.84 CBS
His Mistress tf 10.21.84 NBC
Hotel ep Imperfect Union 10.9.85 ABC
Magnum, P.I. ep The Kona Winds 10.10.85 CBS

SILVA, HENRY
A&C, B.V.:
Route 66 ep Two in the House 4.26.62 CBS
The High Chaparral ep The Terrorist 12.17.67 NBC
The Sixth Sense ep Shadow in the Wall 4.15.72 ABC

SILVERA, FRANK
A&C, B.V.:
Wanted Dead Or Alive ep Sheriff of Red Rock 11.29.58 CBS
The Man From Blackhawk ep The Gypsy Story 11.6.59 ABC
Johnny Ringo ep Shoot the Moon 6.2.60 CBS
Kraft Suspense Theater ep A Truce to Terror 1.9.64 NBC
Daniel Boone ep Daughter of the Devil 4.15.65 NBC

SILVERS, CATHY*
Happy Days sr 11.11.80 ABC
Happy Days sr ret 10.6.81 ABC
Happy Days sr ret 9.28.82 ABC
High School, U.S.A. tf/pt 10.16.83 NBC
T.L.C. pt 8.8.84 NBC
The Love Boat ep No Dad of Mine 3.30.85 ABC
Sam pt 6.11.85 ABC
Punky Brewster ep Baby Buddies, Inc. 10.6.85 NBC
First and Ten ep Sins of the Quarterback 11.5.85 HBO
Foley Square sr 12.11.85 CBS

SIMMONS, JEAN
A&C, Supp. 2:
Hawaii Five-O ep The Cop on the Cover 9.29.77 CBS
SUPP.:
The Thorn Birds ms 3.22.83 CBS
Hotel ep Deceptions 11.30.83 ABC
Hotel ep Hearts and Minds 5.8.85 ABC
Midas Valley tf/pt 6.27.85 ABC
North and South ms 11.3-11.10.85 ABC

SIMPSON, O. J.
A&C, Supp. 2:
Medical Center ep The Last Ten Yards 9.24.69 CBS
SUPP.:
Cocaine and Blue Eyes tf/pt 1.2.83 NBC

SLATER, HELEN*
The ABC Afterschool Special ep Amy and the Angel 9.22.82 ABC
Supergirl--The Making of the Movie sp 12.29.85 ABC

SLAVIN, MILLIE*
The Bob Newhart Show ep 1.19.74 CBS
The Stranger Who Looks Like Me tf 3.6.74 ABC
6 RMS RIV VU sp 3.17.74 CBS
Sons and Daughters ep The Rejection 10.16.74 CBS
Black Bart pt 4.4.75 CBS
The Rookies ep 12.9.75 ABC
Raid on Entebe tf 1.9.77 NBC
Rafferty sr 9.5.77 CBS
Eight Is Enough ep 9.20.77 ABC
Family ep 2.7.78 ABC
Visions ep Blessings 10.30.78 PBS
Struck by Lightning sr 9.19.79 CBS
Landon, Landon & Landon pt 6.14.80 CBS
Lou Grant ep Nightside 9.22.80 CBS
Revenge of the Stepford Wives tf 10.12.80 NBC
Lou Grant ep Search 2.9.81 CBS
The People vs. Jean Harris tf 5.7, 5.8.81 NBC
Quick and Quiet pt 8.18.81 CBS
Hart to Hart ep Harts Under Glass 11.24.81 ABC
Benson ep Kraus Falls in Love 1.15.82 ABC
The Rules of Marriage tf 5.10, 5.11.82 CBS
Farrell for the People tf/pt 10.18.82 NBC
Summer Girl tf 4.12.83 CBS
Riptide ep The Twisted Cross 3.12.85 NBC

SLOANE, EVERETT
A&C, B.V.:
Wanted: Dead Or Alive ep The Give Away Gun 10.11.58 CBS
Zorro ep Treasure for the King 4.16.59 ABC
Wanted: Dead Or Alive ep Reckless 11.7.59 CBS
Arrest and Trial ep We May Be Better Strangers 12.1.63 ABC
Jonny Quest ep (vo) Shadow of the Condor 11.20.64 ABC
Wagon Train ep The Andrew Elliott Story 2.10.64 ABC
Jonny Quest ep (vo) Tieru the Terrible 12.25.64 ABC

SLOYAN, JAMES*
Honor Thy Father tf 3.1.73 CBS
The Streets of San Francisco ep A String of Puppets 2.7.74 ABC

The Family Kovack tf 4.5.74 CBS
Cannon ep Kelly's Song 9.11.74 CBS
Panic on the 5:22 tf 11.20.74 ABC
Manhunter ep The Wrong Man 2.5.75 CBS
The Million Dollar Rip-off tf 9.22.76 NBC
Delvecchio ep Board of Rights 10.17.76 CBS
The Disappearance of Aimee tf 11.17.76 NBC
Centennial sr 10.1.78 NBC
Kaz ep Trouble on the South Side 2.21.79 CBS
The New Adventures of Wonder Woman ep The Girl with the Gift for Disaster 3.17.79 CBS
Blind Ambition ms 5.20-5.23.79 CBS
Buck Rogers in the 25th Century ep The Plot to Kill a City 10.11, 10.18.79 NBC
Act of Violence tf 11.10.79 CBS
Tenspeed and Brown Shoe ep The Millionaire's Life 3.16.80 ABC
Trouble in High Timber Country tf/pt 6.27.80 ABC
Lou Grant ep Depression 4.13.81 CBS
The Violation of Sarah McDavid tf 5.19.81 CBS
Callie and Son tf 10.13.81 CBS
A Long Way Home tf 12.10.81 ABC
Falcon Crest ep Lord of the Manor 1.22.82 CBS
Oh Madeline sr 9.27.83 ABC
Ryan's Hope sr 1984 ABC
Hawaiian Heat ep The Island 10.12.84 ABC
The Love Boat ep Honey Beats the Odds 10.13.84 ABC
Knots Landing ep A Little Help 11.1.84 CBS
Partners in Crime ep Duke 10.20.84 NBC
Code Name: Foxfire ep Pick a Hero, Any Hero 3.8.85 NBC
Cagney and Lacey ep 3.11.85 CBS
Moonlighting ep The Next Murder You Hear 3.19.85 ABC
Amos tf 9.29.85 CBS
The Misfits of Science ep Guess What's Coming to Dinner 10.25.85 NBC

SMART, JEAN*
Piaf sp 9.6.82 TEC
Teachers Only sr 2.12.83 NBC
Goodnight Beantown ep 4.17.83 CBS
Reggie sr 8.2.83 ABC
The Facts of Life ep Next Door 12.21.83 NBC
Alice ep 4.1.84 CBS
Maximum Security sr 3.9.85 HBO
Remington Steele ep Steele in the Chips 3.19.85 NBC
Royal Match pt 8.2.85 CBS
Lime Street ep Diamonds Aren't Forever 10.12.85 ABC

SMITH, ALEXIS
SUPP.:
The Love Boat ep Papa Doc 11.13.82 ABC
Dallas sr 3.16.84 CBS

The Love Boat ep The Parents 5.5.84 ABC
A Death in California tf 5.12, 5.13.85 ABC
The Love Boat ep The Villa 11.2.85 ABC

SMITH, ALLISON*
Evita Peron tf 2.23, 2.24.81 NBC
The CBS Library ep Orphans, Waifs and Wards 11.26.81 CBS
Silver Spoons ep The Toy Wonder 1.22.83 NBC
Kate and Allie sr 3.19.84 CBS
Kate and Allie sr ret 10.8.84 CBS
Kate and Allie sr ret 9.30.85 CBS

SMITH, BUBBA*
Superdome tf 1.9.78 ABC
Vegas ep A Deadly Victim 12.3.80 ABC
Fighting Back tf 12.7.80 ABC
Joe Dancer: The Big Black Pill tf/pt 1.29.81 NBC
Open All Night sr 11.28.81 ABC
Taxi ep Tony's Comeback 3.4.82 ABC
Hart to Hart ep Bahama Bound Harts 2.22.83 ABC
Blue Thunder sr 4.6.84 ABC
Mickey Spillane's Mike Hammer ep Bone Crunch 11.3.84 CBS
Half Nelson sr 3.29.85 NBC

SMITH, JACLYN
A&C, Supp. 2:
Get Christie Love ep High Fashion Heist 3.12.75 ABC
Switch tf/pt 3.21.75 CBS
Switch ep The Old Diamond Game 9.16.75 CBS
Switch ep The Late Show Murders 9.23.75 CBS
Switch ep Death Heist 10.21.75 CBS
SUPP.:
Rage of Angels tf 2.20, 2.21.83 NBC
George Washington ms 4.8-4.11.84 CBS
The Night They Saved Christmas tf 12.13.84 ABC
Florence Nightingale tf 4.7.85 NBC

SMITH, LANE*
Kojak ep Queen of the Gypsies 1.19.75 CBS
The Rockford Files ep Claire 1.31.75 NBC
A Death in Canaan tf 3.1.78 CBS
Crash tf 10.29.78 ABC
American Short Story ep The Displaced Person 12.10.78 PBS
The Rockford Files ep The Battle Ax and the Exploded Cigar 1.12.79 NBC
The Solitary Man tf 10.9.79 CBS
Disaster on the Coastliner tf 10.28.79 ABC
City in Fear tf 3.3.80 ABC
Gideon's Trumpet tf 4.30.80 CBS
A Rumor of War tf 9.24, 9.25.80 CBS
The Georgia Peaches tf/pt 11.8.80 CBS

Mark, I Love You tf 12.10.80 CBS
Dark Night of the Scarecrow tf 10.24.81 CBS
Prime Suspect tf 1.20.82 CBS
Thou Shalt Not Kill tf/pt 4.12.82 NBC
Lou Grant ep Unthinkable 5.3.82 CBS
Chicago Story ep 6.4.82 NBC
Quincy, M.E. ep Science for Sale 11.24.82 NBC
Special Bulletin tf 3.20.83 NBC
Chiefs ms 11.13-11.16.83 CBS
Something About Amelia tf 1.9.84 ABC
Beverly Hills Cowgirl Blues tf/pt 10.5.85 CBS
Bridge Across Time tf 11.22.85 NBC

SMITH, MARTHA*
Quincy, M.E. ep Go Fight City Hall to Death 10.3.76 NBC
Ebony, Ivory & Jade tf/pt 8.3.79 CBS
The Dukes of Hazzard ep To Catch a Duke 2.6.80 CBS
Alex and the Doberman Gang pt 4.11.80 NBC
Fantasy Island ep Hard Knocks 5.9.81 ABC
Dallas ep 11.12.82 CBS
Love, Sidney ep Alison 5.16.83 NBC
Scarecrow and Mrs. King sr 10.3.83 CBS
Scarecrow and Mrs. King sr ret 10.1.84 CBS
Scarecrow and Mrs. King sr ret 9.23.85 CBS

SMITH, SAMANTHA*
Charles in Charge ep The Slumber Party 11.14.84 CBS
Lime Street sr 9.28.85 ABC

SMITH, SAVANNAH*
Vegas ep The Lido Girls 2.6.80 ABC
The Oklahoma City Dolls tf 1.23.81 ABC
Bret Maverick ep A Night at the Red Ox 2.23.82 NBC
The Devlin Connection ep The Corpse in the Corniche 10.23.82 NBC
T. J. Hooker ep The Two Faces of Betsy Morgan 10.20.84 ABC
Sweet Revenge tf 10.31.84 CBS
St. Elsewhere ep 12.4.85 NBC

SMITH, SHAWNEE*
Silver Spoons ep Growing Pains 9.30.84 NBC
Not My Child tf 1.15.85 CBS
Crime of Innocence tf 10.27.85 NBC

SMITH, SHELLEY
<u>SUPP.</u>:
Fantasy Island ep A Very Strange Affair 1.2.82 ABC
Hart to Hart ep Pounding Harts 1.18.83 ABC
Tales of the Gold Monkey ep High Stakes Lady 1.26.83 ABC
Simon and Simon ep The Club Murder Vacation 1.27.83 ABC
Simon and Simon ep The Secret of the Chrome Eagle 3.3.83 CBS

For Love and Honor sr 9.23.83 NBC
The Fantastic World of D. C. Collins tf 2.10.84 NBC
Fantasy Island ep Lady of the House 2.25.84 ABC
Cover Up ep The Million Dollar Face 10.6.84 CBS
Hotel ep Vantage Point 12.5.84 ABC

SMITH, WILLIAM* (a.k.a. Bill Smith)
The Asphalt Jungle sr 4.2.61 ABC
Zero One sr 1962 NN
Stoney Burke ep Point of Entry 3.4.63 ABC
Wagon Train ep The Bob Stewart Story 9.20.64 ABC
Tom, Dick & Mary ep 10.5.64 NBC
Wagon Train ep The Richard Bloodgood Story 11.29.64 ABC
The Virginian ep Timberland 3.10.65 NBC
The Virginian ep We've Lost a Train 4.21.65 NBC
Laredo sr 9.16.65 NBC
Laredo sr ret 9.66 NBC
The Legend of Custer ep Death Hunt 11.22.67 ABC
Daniel Boone ep A Matter of Blood 12.28.67 NBC
Batman ep Minerva, Money & Millionaires 3.4.68 ABC
The Virginian ep Silver Image 9.25.68 NBC
Daniel Boone ep Big, Black & Out There 11.14.68 NBC
The Felony Squad ep Blind Terror 1.24.69 ABC
Ironside ep Poole's Paradise 10.2.69 NBC
The Over-the-Hill Gang tf 10.7.69 ABC
The Mod Squad ep Never Give the Sucker an Even Break 12.23.69 ABC
Crowhaven Farm tf 11.24.70 ABC
The Most Deadly Game ep Model for Murder 12.19.70 ABC
The Mod Squad ep We Spy 3.16.71 ABC
Dan August ep The Meal Ticket 3.18.71 ABC
Longstreet ep The Shape of Nightmares 10.28.71 ABC
Mission: Impossible ep Encounter 10.30.71 CBS
The Mod Squad ep The Loser 11.30.71 ABC
Alias Smith and Jones ep 10.28.72 ABC
Mission: Impossible ep Movie 11.4.72 CBS
Columbo ep The Greenhouse Jungle 11.4.72 NBC
Gunsmoke ep The Gang 12.1.72 CBS
Search ep The 24 Karat Hit 1.24.73 NBC
The Fuzz Brothers pt 3.5.73 ABC
Kung Fu ep The Chalice 10.11.73 ABC
Ironside ep Downhill All the Way 11.8.73 NBC
The Streets of San Francisco ep Commitment 1.3.74 ABC
The Six Million Dollar Man ep Survival of the Fittest 1.25.74 ABC
The Rockford Files tf/pt 3.27.74 NBC
The Sex Symbol tf 9.17.74 ABC
Planet of the Apes ep The Gladiators 9.20.74 CBS
The Night Stalker ep Matchemonedo 12.13.74 ABC
Death Among Friends tf 5.20.75 NBC
S.W.A.T. ep Time Bomb 10.4.75 ABC

Barnaby Jones ep Hostage 1.15.76 CBS
Rich Man, Poor Man ms 2.1-3.15.76 ABC
The Blue Knight ep Mariachi 2.11.76 CBS
City of Angels ep A Lovely Way to Die 3.2.76 NBC
Bert D'Angelo/Superstar ep A Concerned Citizen 4.3.76 ABC
The Manhunter tf 4.3.76 NBC
Rich Man, Poor Man--Book II sr 9.21.76 ABC
Police Woman ep Brain Wash 11.16.76 NBC
Logan's Run ep Half Life 10.31.77 CBS
Fantasy Island ep 3.18.78 ABC
The Eddie Capra Mysteries ep Murder Plays a Dead Hand 11.17.78 NBC
Vegas ep Demand and Supply 2.14.79 ABC
The Rebels tf 5.14, 5.21.79 OPT
Hawaii Five-O sr (with ep A Lion in the Streets) 10.4.79 CBS
Wild Times tf 1.24, 1.31.80 NN
Buck Rogers in the 25th Century ep Buck's Duel to the Death 3.20.80 NBC
Hagen ep Jeopardy 4.10.80 CBS
Fantasy Island ep The Lady and the Monster 10.31.81 ABC
The Dukes of Hazzard ep The Ten Million Dollar Sheriff 10.20.81 CBS
The Fall Guy ep License to Kill 1.13, 1.20.82 ABC
Tales of the Apple Dumpling Gang pt 1.16.82 CBS
Code Red ep Trial By Fire 2.28.82 ABC
Matt Houston ep Who Killed Ramona? 10.3.82 ABC
The A-Team ep Pros and Cons 2.8.83 NBC
CHiPs ep 3.20.83 NBC
Knight Rider ep Short Notice 5.6.83 NBC
Benson ep Katie's Cookies 11.18.83 ABC
The Jerk, Too tf/pt 1.6.84 NBC
Masquerade ep 1.12.84 ABC
Wildside sr 3.21.85 ABC
Simon and Simon ep Quint Is Art 12.5.85 CBS
Hunter ep Think Blue 12.14.85 NBC

SMITHERS, JAN*
Love Story ep Beginner's Luck 11.28.73 NBC
Starsky and Hutch ep Running 2.25.76 ABC
WKRP in Cincinnati sr 9.18.78 CBS
WKRP in Cincinnati sr ret 9.17.79 CBS
The Love Tapes tf 5.9.80 ABC
WKRP in Cincinnati sr ret 11.1.80 CBS
WKRP in Cincinnati sr ret 10.7.81 CBS
The Love Boat ep Papa Doc 11.13.82 ABC
The Fall Guy ep Spaced Out 2.16.83 ABC
The Love Boat ep Long Time No See 11.12.83 ABC
Legmen ep Legmen (pt) 1.20.84 NBC
Hotel ep Encores 3.7.84 ABC
Finder of Lost Loves ep Old Friends 11.17.84 ABC
The Love Boat ep Don't Get Mad, Get Even 11.17.84 ABC

Mickey Spillane's Mike Hammer ep Firestorm 1.5.85 CBS
Cover Up ep The Assassin 1.26.85 CBS
Murder, She Wrote ep Sudden Death 3.3.85 CBS
The Comedy Factory ep The Columnist 6.28.85 ABC

SMOTHERS, DICK
SUPP.:
Terror at Alcatraz tf/pt 7.4.82 NBC
Benson ep Solid Gold 2.1.85 ABC

SMOTHERS, TOM
SUPP.:
Terror at Alcatraz tf/pt 7.4.82 NBC
Benson ep Solid Gold 2.1.85 ABC

SNODGRASS, CARRIE
SUPP.:
Quincy, M.E. ep The Face of Fear 3.24.82 NBC
The ABC Afterschool Special ep Andrea's Story: A Hitchhiking Tragedy 12.7.83 ABC
Nadia tf 6.11.84 NN
Highway to Heaven ep To Touch the Moon 9.26.84 NBC
A Reason to Live tf 1.7.85 NBC

SOMERS, SUZANNE
A&C, Supp. 2:
Ben Casey ep If There Were Dreams to Sell 10.9.63 ABC
The Rockford Files ep The Big Ripoff 10.25.74 NBC
SUPP.:
Hollywood Wives ms 2.17-2.19.85 ABC
Goodbye, Charlie pt 6.4.85 ABC

SOMMARS, JULIE
A&C, Supp. 2:
The Loretta Young Theater ep The Trouble with Laury's Men 3.13.60 NBC
Gunsmoke ep The Warden 5.9.64 CBS
Great Adventure ep Teeth of the Lion 1.17.64 CBS
Slattery's People ep How Do You Fall in Love with a Town? 1.22.65 CBS
Flipper ep Bud Minds Bud 3.20.65 NBC
Gunsmoke ep Dry Road to Nowhere 4.3.65 CBS
Mr. Novak ep The Firebird 4.13.65 NBC
Gunsmoke ep The Pretender 11.20.65 CBS
Gunsmoke ep The Jailor 10.1.66 CBS
The Bob Hope Chrysler Theater ep Storm Crossing 12.7.66 NBC
The FBI ep The Conspirators 2.5.67 ABC
He and She ep The Background Man Fall 1967 CBS
The Falony Squad ep The Love Victim 2.5.68 ABC
Switch ep The James Caan Con 9.9.75 CBS

The Family Holvak ep Remembrance of a Guest 9.28.75 NBC
SUPP.:
Magnum, P.I. ep Texas Lightning 2.18.82 CBS
Cave-In tf 6.19.83 NBC
Emergency Room tf 7.17.73 NN
Rituals sr 9.84 NN
Partners in Crime ep Partners in Crime (pt) 10.13.84 NBC

SOMMER, ELKE
SUPP.:
Inside the Third Reich tf 5.9, 5.10.82 ABC
The Love Boat ep Lady in the Window 9.29.84 ABC
Jenny's War tf 10.28, 11.4.85 NN

SOREL, LOUISE
A&C, Supp. 2:
The Doctors and the Nurses ep A39846 4.20.65 CBS
The Big Valley ep Hide the Children 12.19.66 ABC
Occasional Wife ep 1.24.67 NBC
The Flying Nun ep A Bell for San Tanco 9.28.67 ABC
The Eddie Capra Mysteries ep Murder Plays a Dead Hand 12.22.78 NBC
SUPP.:
Simon and Simon ep Ashes to Ashes and None Too Soon 1.19.82 CBS
Magnum, P.I. ep One More Summer 2.11.82 CBS
Hart to Hart ep Blue and Broken Harted 2.23.82 ABC
Trapper John, M.D. ep A Piece of the Action 4.11.82 CBS
Knots Landing ep Encounters 10.14.82 CBS
Dallas ep 10.29.82 CBS
Knots Landing ep 10.29.82 CBS
Rona Jaffe's "Mazes and Monsters" tf 12.28.82 CBS
Diff'rent Strokes ep Parents Have Rights Too 1.15.83 NBC
Sunset Limousine tf 10.12.83 CBS
Oh Madeline ep Chances Are 11.29.83 ABC
Simon and Simon ep Corpus Delecti 3.22.84 CBS
Matt Houston ep Eye Witness 10.12.84 ABC
Santa Barbara sr 1985 NBC

SOTHERN, ANN
A&C, B.V.:
Alias Smith and Jones ep Everything Else You Can Steal 12.17.71 ABC
SUPP.:
A Letter to Three Wives tf 12.16.85 NBC

SOUL, DAVID
SUPP.:
World War III tf 1.31, 2.1.83 NBC
Casablanca sr 4.10.83 NBC
The Yellow Rose sr 10.2.83 NBC

Through Naked Eyes tf 12.11.83 ABC
The Key to Rebecca tf 4.29, 5.6.85 NN

SPANG, LAURETTE
A&C, Supp. 2:
Alias Smith and Jones ep Only Three to a Bed 1.13.73 ABC
SUPP.:
The Dukes of Hazzard ep The Fugitive 11.3.81 CBS
Three's Company ep Downhill Chaser 12.22.81 ABC
The Day the Bubble Burst tf 2.7.82 NBC
Magnum, P.I. ep 1.19.84 CBS

SPELMAN, SHARON*
The Rockford Files ep Profit and Loss 12.20, 12.27.77 NBC
Barnaby Jones ep Image of Evil 2.18.75 CBS
Barnaby Jones ep Voice in the Night 12.2.76 CBS
Calling Dr. Storm, M.D. pt 8.25.77 NBC
The Girl in the Empty Grave tf 9.20.77 NBC
Deadly Game tf 12.3.77 NBC
Peeping Times pt 1.25.78 NBC
Barnaby Jones ep The Enslaved 1.18.79 CBS
The Rockford Files ep The Deuce 1.25.79 NBC
Angie sr 2.8.79 ABC
Angie sr ret 9.11.79 ABC
The Big Stuffed Dog sp 2.8.80 NBC
The ABC Afterschool Special ep Schoolboy Father 10.15.80 ABC
Terror Among Us tf 1.12.81 CBS
Twirl tf 10.25.81 NBC
Lou Grant ep Execution 11.9.81 CBS
Quincy, M.E. ep The Shadow of Death 2.24.82 NBC
Barney Miller ep Old Love 4.2.82 ABC
Scarecrow and Mrs. King ep There Goes the Neighborhood 10.10.83 CBS
Trauma Center ep Out of Control 12.8.83 ABC
Gimme a Break ep Flashback 1.26.84 NBC
Second Edition pt 7.17.74 CBS
Crazy Like a Fox ep Suitable for Framing 3.31.85 CBS
Suburban Beat pt 8.17.85 NBC

SPIELBERG, DAVID
SUPP.:
Maid in America tf 9.22.82 CBS
Tucker's Witch ep The Curse of the Tolric Death Mask 10.27.82 CBS
Quincy, M.E. ep Dying for a Drink 11.3.82 NBC
Family Ties ep Give Uncle Arthur a Kiss 11.10.82 NBC
Games Mother Never Taught You tf 11.27.82 CBS
Police Woman Centerfold tf 10.17.83 NBC
Blue Thunder ep Revenge in the Sky 1.27.84 ABC
Automan ep Death By Design 4.2.84 ABC
The CBS Weekend Special ep Hear Me Cry 10.16.84 CBS

Magnum, P.I. ep 12.13.84 CBS
Hardcastle and McCormick ep Too Rich and Too Thin 1.14.85 ABC
Airwolf ep And a Child Shall Lead 10.12.85 CBS
The Love Boat ep Couples 10.19.85 ABC
Highway to Heaven ep The Smile in the Third Row 11.20.85 NBC

STACK, ROBERT
SUPP.:
Hotel ep The Wedding 2.22.84 ABC
George Washington ms 4.8-4.11.84 CBS
Hotel ep New Beginnings 1.23.85 ABC
An American Portrait ep Jean Nguyen 1.24.85 CBS
Hollywood Wives ms 2.17-2.19.85 ABC
Brothers ep Donald's Dad 5.16.85 SHO
Midas Valley tf/pt 6.27.85 ABC
It's a Great Life sr 10.85 NN

STACY, JAMES
SUPP.:
St. Elsewhere ep 12.4.85 NBC

STANLEY, KIM
A&C, B.V.:
You Are There ep The Death of Cleopatra 10.18.53 CBS

STANWYCK, BARBARA
SUPP.:
Dynasty ep The Californians 10.9.85 ABC
Dynasty ep The Man 10.16.85 ABC
Dynasty II: The Colbys sr 11.20.85 ABC

STAPLETON, JEAN
A&C, B.V.:
The Robert Herridge Theater ep The End of the Beginning Summer 1960 CBS
Dennis the Menace ep Mr. Wilson's Housekeeper Spring 1962 CBS
SUPP.:
Eleanor, the First Lady of the World tf 5.12.82 CBS
Something's Afoot sp 12.82 SHO
Faerie Tale Theater ep Jack and the Beanstalk 9.8.83 SHO
A Matter of Sex tf 1.16.84 NBC
Scarecrow and Mrs. King ep The Legend of Das Gesterschloss (The Ghost Castle) 10.22.84 CBS
Scarecrow and Mrs. King ep The Three Wishes of Emily 12.31.84 CBS
Faerie Tale Theater ep Cinderella 8.14.85 SHO
Grown Ups sp 11.25.85 SHO

STAPLETON, MAUREEN
SUPP.:
The Electric Grandmother sp 1.17.82 NN
Little Gloria ... Happy at Last tf 10.24, 10.25.82 NBC
Family Secrets tf 5.13.84 NBC
Private Sessions tf/pt 3.18.85 NBC

STEEL, AMY*
The Powers of Matthew Star sr 9.17.82 NBC
Seven Brides for Seven Brothers ep 9.22.82 CBS
Women of San Quentin tf 10.23.83 NBC
First Steps tf 3.19.85 CBS
Scene of the Crime ep Dead Wrong 4.28.85 NBC
Stir Crazy ep The Sulky Race 10.23.85 CBS

STEENBURGEN, MARY*
Faerie Tale Theater ep Little Red Riding Hood 11.10.83 SHO
Tender Is the Night sr 10.27.85 SHO

STEIGER, ROD
SUPP.:
Cook and Perry: The Race to the North Pole 2.13.83 CBS
An American Portrait ep Jacob Riis 11.20.84 CBS
Hollywood Wives ms 2.17-2.19.85 ABC

STEPHENS, JAMES
SUPP.:
The Mysterious Two tf/pt 5.31.82 NBC
The Paper Chase: The Second Year sr 5.22.84 SHO
Murder, She Wrote ep We're Off to Kill the Wizard 12.9.84 CBS
The Paper Chase: The Third Year sr 5.11.85 SHO

STEPHENS, LARAINE
A&C, Supp. 1:
Dobie Gillis ep The Ugliest American 10.17.62 CBS
Hawaii Five-O ep Death Is a Company Policy 2.13.73 CBS
SUPP.:
McClain's Law ep To Save the Queen 1.8.82 NBC
Fantasy Island ep The Case Against Mr. Roarke 2.6.82 ABC
Fantasy Island ep Beautiful Skeptic 11.27.82 ABC
Seven Brides for Seven Brothers ep 12.8.82 CBS
T. J. Hooker ep Thieves Highway 12.4.82 ABC
Fantasy Island ep Room and Bard 11.29.83 ABC

STERLING, JAN
SUPP.:
Riptide ep Fuzzy Vision 3.19.85 NBC

STERLING, ROBERT
SUPP.:
Simon and Simon ep The Last Time I Saw Michael 12.9.82

CBS
Hotel ep Tomorrows 1.11.84 ABC

STEVENS, ANDREW
SUPP.:
Two of a Kind tf 10.9.82 CBS
Journey's End sp 1.83 SHO
Emerald Point, N.A.S. sr 9.26.83 CBS
Hotel ep Obsessions 10.31.84 ABC
Murder, She Wrote ep Lovers and Other Killers 11.18.84 CBS
Hollywood Wives ms 2.17-2.19.85 ABC
The Love Boat ep A Gentleman of Discrimination 5.4.85 ABC

STEVENS, CONNIE
SUPP.:
The Love Boat ep A Wife for Wilfred 2.13.82 ABC
The Love Boat ep The Same Wave Length 10.23.82 ABC
Hotel ep Choices 10.5.83 ABC
Detective in the House ep Whatever Happened to.... 3.15.85 CBS
The Love Boat ep Your Money or Your Wife 10.5.85 ABC
Murder, She Wrote ep Murder Digs Deep 12.29.85 CBS

STEVENS, CRAIG
SUPP.:
Quincy, M.E. ep When Luck Runs Out 1.20.82 NBC
Happy Days ep Hello, Pfisters 1.4.83 ABC
Fantasy Island ep Second Time Around 11.19.83 ABC
Hotel ep The Offer 12.7.83 ABC
Hotel ep Crossroads 1.30.85 ABC
The Love Boat ep The Villa 11.2.85 ABC

STEVENS, STELLA
SUPP.:
The Love Boat ep Off-Course Romance 2.19.83 ABC
Fantasy Island ep Eternal Flame 3.5.83 ABC
Newhart ep It Happened One Afternoon 10.17, 10.24.83 CBS
The Love Boat ep One Last Time 10.22.83 ABC
Women of San Quentin tf 10.23.83 NBC
Fantasy Island ep Saturday's Child 12.10.83 ABC
Amazons tf 1.29.84 ABC
No Man's Land tf 5.27.84 NBC
Hotel ep Flesh and Blood 10.10.84 ABC
Highway to Heaven ep Help Wanted: Angel 11.21.84 NBC
Night Court ep Last Madam in New York (a.k.a. Harry and the Madam) 11.22.84 NBC
Murder, She Wrote ep Murder at 50 Mile 4.21.85 CBS

STEVENSON, McLEAN
SUPP.
Condo sr 2.10.83 ABC

Hotel ep Reflections 1.4.84 ABC
The Love Boat ep The Buck Stops Here 1.14.84 ABC

STEVENSON, VALERIE*
Dreams sr 10.3.84 CBS
The A-Team ep There Goes the Neighborhood 12.3.85 NBC

STEWART, JAMES
SUPP.:
Air Force One sp nar 12.4.84 PBS

STEWART, MEL
SUPP.:
Mr. Merlin ep Alex Goes Popless 1.25.82 CBS
The Kid with the 200 I.Q. tf 2.6.83 NBC
The Invisible Woman tf/pt 2.13.83 NBC
The Love Boat ep Women's Best Friend 3.26.83 ABC
Scarecrow and Mrs. King sr 10.3.83 CBS
The Outlaws tf/pt 7.9.84 ABC
Scarecrow and Mrs. King sr ret 10.1.84 CBS
Scarecrow and Mrs. King sr ret 9.23.85 CBS

STIERS, DAVID OGDEN
SUPP.:
The Day the Bubble Burst tf 2.7.82 NBC
M*A*S*H sr ret 10.25.82 CBS
Anatomy of an Illness tf 5.15.84 CBS
The Return of the Man from UNCLE: The 15 Years Later Affair tf/pt 5.16.84 CBS
The Bad Seed tf 2.7.85 ABC
North and South ms 11.3-11.10.85 ABC

STOCKWELL, DEAN
A&C, B.V.:
Restless Gun ep Mercy Day 10.6.58 NBC
SUPP.:
The A-Team ep A Small and Deadly War 2.15.83 NBC
Miami Vice ep 11.22.85 NBC

STOCKWELL, GUY
SUPP.:
Tales of the Gold Monkey ep Shanghaied 9.29.82 ABC
Voyagers ep Agents of Satan 1.31.82 NBC
T. J. Hooker ep Thieves Highway 12.4.82 ABC
Simon and Simon ep The Club Murder Vacation 1.27.83 CBS
Knight Rider ep Knight Moves 3.11.83 NBC
Knight Rider ep Return to Cadiz 10.30.83 NBC
The Whiz Kids ep Sabotage 11.9.83 CBS
The Fall Guy ep The Finish 12.7.83 ABC
Simon and Simon ep Deep Cover 12.6.84 CBS
Scene of the Crime ep Memory Game 4.14.85 NBC

Hell Town ep I Will Abide 10.23.85 NBC
Hell Town ep The Porno Racket 12.11.85 NBC

STONE, CHRISTOPHER
A&C, Supp. 2:
Here Come the Brides ep A Hard Card to Play 10.23.68 ABC
Here Come the Brides ep Loggerheads 3.26.69 ABC
Here Come the Brides ep The Soldier 10.10.69 ABC
The Mod Squad ep A Place to Run--a Heart to Hide 12.2.69 ABC
SUPP.:
Harper Valley ep Flora's Dinner Party 3.6.82 NBC
Fantasy Island ep Image of Celeste 3.20.82 ABC
Father Murphy ep Stopover in a One-Horse Town 10.26.82 NBC
The Blue and the Gray ms 11.14-11.17.82 CBS
Manimal ep Illusion 10.14.83 NBC
The Whiz Kids ep Red Star Rising 12.21.83 CBS
Simon and Simon ep 2.2.84 CBS
Airwolf ep They Are Us 3.31.84 CBS
Riptide ep Catch of the Day 10.23.84 NBC
Dallas ep 11.9, 11.16, 11.23.84 CBS
Simon and Simon ep Marlowe, Come Home 2.28.85 CBS
Code Name: Foxfire ep Robin's Egg Blues 3.15.85 NBC
The A-Team ep Incident at Crystal Lake 5.14.85 NBC
T. J. Hooker ep Death Is a Four Letter Word 11.6.85 ABC
Murder, She Wrote ep Sticks and Stones 12.15.85 CBS

STORCH, LARRY*
Car 54, Where Are You? ep Remember St. Petersburg 10.28.62 NBC
Car 54, Where Are You? ep That's Show Business 11.4.62 NBC
Car 54, Where Are You? ep Pretzel Mary 12.2.62 NBC
The Alfred Hitchcock Hour ep An Out for Oscar 4.5.63 NBC
The Greatest Show on Earth ep Clancy 2.25.64 ABC
The Kraft Suspense Theater ep The Jack Is High 11.19.64 NBC
The Baileys of Balboa ep 12.10.64 CBS
Gilligan's Island ep 1.23.65 CBS
F-Troop sr 9.14.65 ABC
F-Troop sr ret 9.8.66 ABC
I Dream of Jeannie ep Monkey Into Man 9.12.67 NBC
The Mothers-in-Law ep 11.12.68 NBC
Garrison's Gorillas ep The Magnificent Forger 12.19.67 ABC
Get Smart ep 1.13.68 NBC
Mannix ep Another Final Exit 2.10.68 CBS
He and She ep 2.21.68 CBS
The Name of the Game ep Nightmare 10.18.68 NBC
That Girl ep 12.12.68 ABC
Gomer Pyle, U.S.M.C. ep 12.15, 12.22.68 CBS
The Queen and I sr 1.16.69 CBS
Love, American Style ep Love and the Joker 10.6.69 ABC
The Flying Nun ep 10.29.69 ABC

The Name of the Game ep Give Till It Hurts 10.31.69 NBC
The Doris Day Show ep 1.5.70, 3.23.70, 11.9.70 CBS
Hunters Are for Killing tf 3.12.70 CBS
Love, American Style ep 2.5.71, 9.24.71 ABC
The Groovie Goolies sr vo 9.21.71 CBS
The Brady Kids sr vo 9.9.72 ABC
Alias Smith and Jones ep The Long Chase 9.16.72 ABC
The Woman Hunter tf 9.19.72 CBS
Emergency ep 10.21.72, 12.22.73 NBC
The Couple Takes a Wife tf 12.5.72 ABC
All in the Family ep 1.20.73 CBS
Tenafly ep Joyride to Nowhere 10.10.73 NBC
Mannix ep Portrait in Blues 9.22.74 CBS
The Night Stalker ep Vampire 10.4.74 ABC
Columbo ep Negative Reaction 10.6.74 CBS
Police Story ep Love, Mabel 11.26.74 NBC
McCloud ep Return to the Alamo 3.30.75 NBC
The Ghost Busters sr 9.6.75 CBS
Switch ep The Case of the Purloined Case 3.2.76 CBS
Rosetti and Ryan ep 11.10.77 NBC
The Life and Times of Grizzly Adams ep 11.23.77 NBC
The Hardy Boys Mysteries ep The Mystery of the Silent Scream 11.27.77 ABC
The Incredible Rocky Mountain Race tf 12.17.77 NBC
The Love Boat ep Tony's Family 11.12.78 ABC
Fantasy Island ep 3.3.79, 5.17.80 ABC
CHiPs ep CHiPs Goes Roller Disco 9.22.79 NBC
The Misadventures of Sheriff Lobo ep 11.27.79 NBC
Better Late Than Never tf 10.17.79 NBC
Jack Frost sp vo 12.13.79 NBC
CHiPs ep Go-Cart Terror 9.21.80 NBC
Phyl and Mikhy ep 6.30.80 CBS
Aloha Paradise ep 3.11.81 ABC
Fantasy Island ep House of Dolls 1.9.82 ABC
The Adventures of Huckleberry Finn tf 7.9.81 NBC
Harper Valley ep The Show Must Go On 1.23.82 NBC
Trapper John, M.D. ep Maybe Baby 3.7.82 CBS
Two Guys from Muck pt 3.29.82 NBC
Small and Frye ep 6.1.83 CBS
The Fall Guy ep Losers Weepers 9.19.84 ABC
Knight Rider ep Knight Sting 11.8.85 NBC

STOSSEL, LUDWIG

A&C, B.V.:

Man with a Camera ep Six Faces of Satan 12.19.58 ABC
Man with a Camera ep Lady on the Loose 1.23.59 ABC
Man with a Camera ep The Big Squeeze 1.30.59 ABC

STRAIGHT, BEATRICE

SUPP.:

Robert Kennedy and His Times ms 1.27-1.30.84 CBS
Chiller tf 5.22.85 CBS

STRANGIS, JUDY*
The Twilight Zone ep The Bard 5.23.63 CBS
Room 222 sr 9.17.71 ABC
Congratulations, It's a Boy tf 9.21.71 ABC
Women in Chains tf 1.25.72 ABC
The Mod Squad ep The Tangled Web 2.22.72 ABC
Medical Center ep 9.13.72, 10.4.72 CBS
Love, American Style ep 10.20.72 ABC
All My Darling Daughters tf 11.22.72 ABC
Love, American Style ep 3.2.73 ABC
Barnaby Jones ep 4.1.73 CBS
My Darling Daughter's Anniversary tf 11.7.73 ABC
Barnaby Jones ep Mary Had More Than a Little 1.2.76 CBS
Electra Woman and Dyna Girl sr 9.11.76 ABC
Eight is Enough ep 12.14.77 ABC
Loose Change ms 2.26-2.28.78 NBC
Lobo ep Airsick 2.3.81 NBC
CHiPs ep Moonlight 10.18.81 NBC
Not Just Another Affair tf 10.2.82 CBS
The A-Team ep In Plane Sight 1.3.84 NBC
The ABC Weekend Special ep Bad Cat vo 4.14.84 ABC
Matt Houston ep High Fashion Murders 11.16.84 ABC

STRASBERG, SUSAN
SUPP.:
The Love Boat ep An 'A' for Gopher 4.10.82 ABC
Mickey Spillane's Mike Hammer ep Cold Target 12.1.84 CBS
Tales from the Darkside ep Effect and Cause 12.7.85 NN

STRASSMAN, MARCIA
A&C, Supp. 2:
Ironside ep The Man Who Believed 11.23.67 NBC
Love Story ep Mirabelle's Summer 11.7.73 NBC
SUPP.:
Magnum, P.I. ep Heal Thyself 12.16.82 CBS
At Ease ep Love Sick 4.8.83 ABC
Shadow Chasers ep Shadow Chasers (pt) 11.14.85 ABC

STRAUSS, PETER*
The Man Without a Country tf 4.24.73 ABC
The Mary Tyler Moore Show ep Angels in the Snow 9.22.73 CBS
The Streets of San Francisco ep For the Love of God 9.27.73 ABC
Hawaii Five-O ep Death with Father 1.22.74 CBS
Cannon ep The Cure That Kills 2.20.74 CBS
Cannon ep A Killing in the Family 11.6.74 CBS
Attack on Terror: The FBI vs. the Ku Klux Klan tf 2.20, 2.21.75 CBS
Medical Center ep Survivors 3.3.75 CBS
Rich Man, Poor Man ms 2.1-3.15.76 ABC

Young Joe: The Forgotten Kennedy 9.18.77 ABC
The Jericho Mile tf 3.18.79 ABC
Angel on My Shoulder tf 5.11.80 ABC
A Whale for the Killing tf 2.1.81 ABC
Masada ms 4.5-4.8.81 ABC
Heart of Steel tf 12.4.83 ABC
An American Portrait ep Guy Bradley 10.29.84 CBS
Tender Is the Night sr 10.27.85 SHO
Kane and Abel ms 11.17-11.19.85 CBS

STRICKLAND, GAIL
A&C, Supp. 2:
Kojak ep Both Sides of the Law 2.22.76 CBS
SUPP.:
Trapper John, M.D. ep Doctors and Other Strangers 3.28.82 CBS
Alice ep Give My Regards to Broadway 4.4.82 CBS
My Body, My Child tf 4.12.82 NBC
Cagney and Lacey ep Suffer the Children 4.25.82 CBS
Eleanor, the First Lady of the World tf 5.12.82 CBS
Hill Street Blues ep Invasion of the Third World Mutant Body Snatchers 5.13.82 NBC
The ABC Afterschool Special ep Amy and the Angel 9.22.82 ABC
Life of the Party: The Story of Beatrice 9.29.82 CBS
Starflight: The Plane That Couldn't Land tf 2.27.83 ABC
Hardcastle and McCormick ep Flying Down to Rio 12.4.83 ABC
Night Court ep All You Need Is Love 1.4.84 NBC
Family Ties ep Ladies' Man 2.2.84 NBC
Hill Street Blues ep The Other Side of Oneness 2.9.84 NBC
Emerald Point, N.A.S. ep 2.13.84 CBS
Cagney and Lacey ep 11.12.84 CBS
Dallas ep 1.11.85, 2.22.85, 4.12.85 CBS
On Our Way pt 6.29.85 CBS
The Insiders sr 9.25.85 ABC

STROUD, DON*
Ironside ep An Inside Job 10.19.67 NBC
Split Second to Death tf 9.26.68 NBC
The Outsider ep A Time to Run 10.30.68 NBC
Something for a Lonely Man tf 11.26.68 NBC
The FBI ep The Savage Wilderness 10.18.70 ABC
Hawaii Five-O ep The Late John Louisana 11.11.70 CBS
The D.A.: Conspiracy to Kill tf 1.11.71 NBC
The Deadly Dream tf 9.25.71 ABC
O'Hara: United States Treasury ep Operation: Smoke Screen 3.10.72 CBS
The Daughters of Joshua Cabe tf/pt 9.13.72 ABC
Rolling Man tf 10.4.72 ABC
Jigsaw ep The Bradley Affair 11.2.72 ABC
Ironside ep Nightmare Trip 11.9.72 NBC

Adam-12 ep The Surprise 11.15.72 NBC
Hec Ramsey ep The Mystery of the Yellow Rose 1.28.73 NBC
Owen Marshall, Counselor at Law ep They've Got to Blame Somebody 2.14.73 ABC
Ironside ep The Best Laid Plans 3.15.73 NBC
Banacek ep No Stone Unturned 10.3.73 NBC
The FBI ep Break 10.7.73 ABC
Cannon ep Come Watch Me Die 10.24.73 CBS
The Streets of San Francisco ep Blockade 1.24.74 ABC
Barnaby Jones ep Programmed for Killing 1.27.74 CBS
The Elevator tf 2.9.74 ABC
Manhunter ep The Ma Gentry Gang 9.11.74 CBS
Police Woman ep Warning: All Wives 9.27.74 NBC
Petrocelli ep A Fallen Idol 1.22.75 NBC
The Return of Joe Forrester tf 5.6.75 NBC
S.W.A.T. ep Deadly Tide 9.13.75 ABC
Police Woman ep Blaze of Glory (a.k.a. Hostage) 11.11.75 NBC
Harry O ep Group Terror 11.13.75 ABC
Police Woman ep Task Force: Cop Killer 3.2, 3.9.76 NBC
High Risk tf/pt 5.15.76 ABC
Hawaii Five-O ep Target--A Cop 12.23.76 CBS
Katie: Portrait of a Centerfold tf 10.28.78 NBC
Kate Loves a Mystery sr 10.18.79 NBC
Fantasy Island ep Dr. Jekyll and Miss Hyde 2.2.80 ABC
The Dukes of Hazzard ep Carnival of Thrills 9.16.80 CBS
Fantasy Island ep 11.15.80 ABC
Hart to Hart ep Homemade Murder 3.3.81 ABC
Vegas ep The Golden Gate Cop Killer 1.7.81 ABC
The Incredible Hulk ep Danny 5.15.81 CBS
The Fall Guy ep Colt's Angels 12.2.81 ABC
Knight Rider ep Good Day at White Rock 10.8.82 NBC
Simon and Simon ep Rough Rider Rides Again 11.18.82 CBS
The Powers of Matthew Star ep Mother 11.26.82 NBC
Fantasy Island ep Beautiful Skeptic 11.27.82 ABC
The Fall Guy ep Win One for the Gipper 1.5.83 ABC
Mickey Spillane's Mike Hammer: Murder Me, Murder You tf/pt 4.9.83 CBS
I Want to Live tf 5.9.83 ABC
The A-Team ep A Nice Place to Visit 5.10.83 NBC
The Rousters ep Finders Keepers 10.22.83 NBC
Mickey Spillane's Mike Hammer: More Than Murder tf/pt 1.26.84 CBS
Mickey Spillane's Mike Hammer sr 1.29.84 CBS
Mickey Spillane's Mike Hammer sr ret 9.29.84 CBS
Murder, She Wrote ep Murder Takes the Bus 3.17.85 CBS
Gidget's Summer Reunion tf/pt 6.85 NN
Hunter ep The Biggest Man in Town 10.5.85 NBC
Hell Town ep I Will Abide 10.23.85 NBC

STRUTHERS, SALLY

SUPP.:

Archie Bunker's Place ep Gloria Comes Home 2.28.82 CBS

Gloria sr 10.3.82 CBS
The Secret World of the Very Young sp 9.12.84 CBS
The Charmkins pt vo 4.85 NN
The Teller and the Tale pt hos 10.85 NN
Alice in Wonderland tf 12.9, 12.10.85 CBS

STUART, RANDY
A&C, B.V.:
The Life and Legend of Wyatt Earp ep Tombstone 9.15.59 ABC
The Life and Legend of Wyatt Earp ep Wyatt's Decision 9.22.59 ABC
The Life and Legend of Wyatt Earp ep Lineup for Battle 9.29.59 ABC
The Life and Legend of Wyatt Earp ep The Nugget and the Epitaph 10.6.59 ABC
The Life and Legend of Wyatt Earp ep The Matchmaker 12.15.59 ABC
The Life and Legend of Wyatt Earp ep John Clum, Fighting Editor 4.12.60 ABC
The Life and Legend of Wyatt Earp ep The Judge 4.19.60 ABC
The Life and Legend of Wyatt Earp ep My Enemy, John Beehan 5.31.60 ABC

SULLIVAN, BARRY
A&C, B.V.:
Arrest and Trial ep A Shield Is for Hiding Behind 10.6.63 ABC
A&C, Supp. 1:
The Streets of San Francisco ep The Thrill Killers 9.30.76, 10.7.76 ABC
A&C, Supp. 2:
Little House on the Prairie ep Author, Author 11.26.79 NBC

SULLIVAN, JENNY*
Adam-12 ep Jimmy Eisley's Dealing Smack 1.11.69 NBC
Cannon ep Call Unicorn 1.28.71 CBS
All in the Family ep 2.23.71 CBS
Cannon ep 9.28.71 CBS
Barnaby Jones ep Divorce--Murder's Style 10.28.73 CBS
The Waltons ep 2.8.73 CBS
Mission: Impossible ep 2.16.73 CBS
Ironside ep All About Andrea 2.22.73 NBC
Hawaii Five-O ep Murder Is a Taxing Affair 10.16.73 CBS
Firehouse ep The Hottest Place in Town 1.31.74 ABC
Movin' On ep Fraud 1.30.75 NBC
Katherine tf 10.5.75 ABC
Cannon ep The Melted Man 11.12.75 CBS
Starsky and Hutch ep Coffin for Starsky 3.3.76 ABC
Starsky and Hutch ep Bounty Hunter 4.21.76 ABC
Captains and the Kings ms 9.30-11.11.76 NBC
Project UFO ep Sighting 4017: The Devilish Lights Incident 9.28.78 NBC

Lucan ep Creature from Beyond the Door 11.27.78 ABC
Little House on the Prairie ep Someone Please Love Me 3.5.79 NBC
Friendly Fire tf 4.22.79 ABC
Lou Grant ep 11.24.79 CBS
The Seal pt 11.27.81 NBC
Falcon Crest ep Kindred Spirits 1.1.82 CBS
Falcon Crest ep 1.8.82 CBS
V ms 5.1, 5.2.83 NBC
The Fall Guy ep Just a Small Circle of Friends 5.4.83 ABC
V: The Final Battle ms 5.6-5.8.84 NBC
Highway to Heaven ep Dust Child 11.28.84 NBC
SUPP.:
Fantasy Island ep The Perfect Husband 11.21.81 ABC
Falcon Crest sr 12.4.81 CBS
Falcon Crest sr ret 10.1.82 CBS
Cave-In tf 6.19.83 NBC
Falcon Crest sr ret 9.30.83 CBS
Falcon Crest sr ret 9.28.84 CBS
Falcon Crest sr ret 10.4.85 CBS

SUPIRAN, JERRY*
Archie Bunker's Place ep 1.23.82 CBS
Love, Sidney ep Sail Away 2.3.82 NBC
Happy Days ep A Little Case of Revenge 11.9.82 ABC
Lottery ep Phoenix: Blood Brothers 10.7.83 ABC
Newhart ep Animal Attractions 10.31.83 CBS
Trapper John, M.D. ep 2.12.84 CBS
Obsessive Love tf 10.2.84 CBS
Small Wonder sr 9.85 NN
George Burns Comedy Week ep Christmas Carol II: The Sequel 12.11.85 CBS

SUSMAN, TODD
A&C, Supp. 1:
Room 222 ep I Hate You, Silas Marner 3.10.71 ABC
Room 222 ep You Can't Take a Boy Out of the Country But.... 3.17.71 ABC
SUPP.:
Lou Grant ep Jazz 1.4.82 CBS
Barney Miller ep Altercation 4.9.82 ABC
Here's Boomer ep Flatfoots 7.3.82 NBC
Star of the Family sr 9.30.82 ABC
Remington Steele ep Steele Crazy After All These Years 2.18.83 NBC
Amanda's ep I Ain't Got No Body 3.3.83 ABC
Goodnight Beantown ep 10.16, 10.23.83 CBS
Newhart ep 11.19.84 CBS
Alice ep 11.20.83, 4.29.84, 5.6.84 CBS
Goodnight Beantown ep 12.11.83 CBS
Webster ep Burn-Out 10.26.84 ABC

I Married a Centerfold tf 11.11.84 NBC
Cagney and Lacey ep 1.28.85 CBS
Newhart ep 4.8.85 CBS
Fame ep Leroy and the Kid 10.20.85 NN
St. Elsewhere ep Slice o' Life 11.6.85 NBC
Newhart ep Lock, Stock and Noodlehead 11.11.85 CBS

SUTORIUS, JAMES*
The Andros Targets sr 1.31.77 CBS
Kojak ep A Death in Canaan tf 3.1.78 CBS
Siege tf 4.26.78 CBS
A Question of Love tf 11.26.78 NBC
Operating Room pt 10.4.79 NBC
Hellinger's Law tf/pt 3.10.81 CBS
Skokie tf 11.17.81 CBS
Shannon ep Curtain Calls 4.7.82 CBS
Gloria ep 2.27.83 CBS
St. Elsewhere ep Craig in Love 4.12.83 NBC
Ryan's Four ep Couples 4.27.83 ABC
T. J. Hooker ep The Return 10.1.83 ABC
Simon and Simon ep 11.10.83 CBS
Prototype tf 12.7.83 CBS
Family Ties ep To Snatch a Keith 12.21.83 NBC
The Mississippi ep 1.17.84 CBS
My Mother's Secret Life tf 2.5.84 ABC
The Rousters ep Snake Eyes 6.30.84 NBC
Call to Glory ep Blackbird 8.27.84 ABC
Jessie ep In the Line of Duty 11.13.84 ABC
Dynasty ep Swept Away 12.12.84 ABC
Space ms 4.14-4.18.85 CBS
No Complaints pt 7.24.85 NBC
Murder, She Wrote ep School for Scandal 10.20.85 CBS

SVENSON, BO*
The Name of the Game ep Love-in at Ground Zero 1.31.69 NBC
Lost Treasure pt 6.28.71 CBS
The Bravos tf 1.9.72 ABC
Banyon ep Meal Ticket 10.13.72 NBC
The Mod Squad ep A Gift for Jenny 10.5.72 ABC
Frankenstein tf 1.16, 1.17.73 ABC
You'll Never See Me Again tf 2.28.73 ABC
Hitched tf/pt 3.31.73 NBC
Kung Fu ep The Spirit Helper 11.8.73 ABC
The Snoop Sisters ep Fear Is a Free Throw 1.29.74 NBC
Target Risk tf 1.6.75 NBC
Snowbeast tf 4.28.77 NBC
Gold of the Amazon Women tf 3.6.79 NBC
Walking Tall sr 1.17.81 NBC
Magnum, P.I. ep 9.30.82 CBS
I Do, I Don't pt 9.2.83 ABC
Jealousy tf 1.23.84 ABC

Hunter ep A Long Way from L.A. 10.12.84 NBC
Crazy Like a Fox ep Motor Homicide 2.3.85 CBS
The Fall Guy ep Seavers: Dead or Alive 12.14.85 ABC

SWEET, DOLPH
A&C, Supp. 2:
The Defenders ep The Eye of Fear 2.23.62 CBS
The Nurses ep The Helping Hand 11.7.63 CBS
Stone ep The Man in the Full Toledo 2.4.80 ABC
SUPP.:
Trapper John, M.D. ep Victims 1.10.82 CBS
Gimme a Break sr ret 10.2.82 NBC
Gimme a Break sr ret 9.29.83 NBC
Gimme a Break ret to sr (with ep Samantha's First Love) 10.27.84 NBC

SWENSON, INGA
SUPP.:
Benson sr ret 10.22.82 ABC
Benson sr ret 9.16.83 ABC
The Love Boat Fall Preview Party sp 9.15.84 ABC
Benson sr ret 9.21.84 ABC
Benson sr ret 10.4.85 ABC
North and South ms 11.3-11.10.85 ABC

SWIT, LORETTA
SUPP.:
The Kid from Nowhere tf 1.4.82 NBC
M*A*S*H sr ret 10.25.82 CBS
Games Mother Never Taught You tf 11.27.82 CBS
First Affair tf 10.25.83 CBS
The Best Christmas Pageant Ever sp 12.5.83 ABC
The Love Boat ep The Present 11.24.84 ABC
The Execution tf 1.14.85 NBC
Sam pt 6.11.85 ABC
Wonderworks ep Miracle at Mareaux 12.8.85 PBS

SWOFFORD, KEN
A&C, Supp. 1:
The Big Valley ep A Day of Terror 12.12.66 ABC
Cimarron Strip ep Nobody 12.7.67 CBS
Gunsmoke ep Wonder 12.18.67 CBS
Gunsmoke ep Lobo 12.16.68 CBS
Here Come the Brides ep The Wealthiest Man in Seattle 10.3.69 ABC
Here Come the Brides ep Land Grant 11.21.69 ABC
The Girl with Something Extra ep It's So Peaceful in the Country 11.73 NBC
The Rockford Files ep The Aaron Innwood School of Success 9.12.75 NBC
Switch ep The Late Show Murders 9.23.75 CBS

Switch ep Stung from Behind 9.30.75 CBS
Switch ep Through the Past Deadly 12.16.75 CBS
Switch ep The Walking Bomb 1.6.76 CBS
Switch ep One of Our Zeppelins Is Missing 2.10.76 CBS
The Rockford Files ep The Family Hour 10.8.76 NBC
A&C, Supp. 2:
Police Story ep Spitfire 1.11.77 NBC
The Rockford Files ep The Queen of Peru 12.16.77 NBC
The Rockford Files ep The Hawaiian Headache 11.23.79 NBC
SUPP.:
The Fall Guy ep License to Kill 1.13, 1.20.82 ABC
Trapper John, M.D. ep John's Other Life 5.2.82 CBS
Voyagers ep Cleo and the Babe 10.17.82 NBC
Simon and Simon ep Sometimes Dreams Come True 12.2.82 CBS
M.A.D.D.: Mothers Against Drunk Drivers tf 3.14.83 NBC
I Want to Live tf 5.9.83 ABC
The Rousters ep A Picture's Worth a Thousand Dollars 10.29.83 NBC
Kenny Rogers as the Gambler: The Adventure Continues 11.28, 11.29.83 CBS
Fame sr 10.84 NN
Hardcastle and McCormick ep The Game You Learn from Your Father 3.18.85 ABC
The A-Team ep Incident at Crystal Lake 5.14.85 NBC
Murder, She Wrote ep Joshua Peabody Died Here 10.6.85 CBS
Fame sr ret 10.13.85 NN
Bridge Across Time tf 11.22.85 NBC
Riptide ep Home for Christmas 12.17.85 NBC

SWOPE, TRACY BROOKS
SUPP.:
Voyagers ep The Voyagers of the Titanic 2.27.83 NBC
Mickey Spillane's Mike Hammer ep Satin, Cyanide and Arsenic 4.14.84 CBS
The A-Team ep Timber 10.16.84 NBC
Hardcastle and McCormick ep Too Rich and Too Thin 1.14.85 ABC

- T -

TABORI, KRISTOFFER
SUPP.:
Chicago Story sr 3.6.82 NBC
T. J. Hooker ep Terror at the Academy 11.6.82 ABC
Trapper John, M.D. ep Life, Death and Vinnie Duncan 1.2.83 CBS
Trapper John, M.D. ep 2.12.84 CBS
The Facts of Life ep Taking a Chance on Love 11.7.84 NBC

The Fall Guy ep Baja 1,000 11.28.84 ABC
Murder, She Wrote ep We're Off to Kill the Wizard 12.9.84 CBS
Murder, She Wrote ep Sing a Song of Murder 10.27.85 CBS
The Twilight Zone ep Her Pilgrim Soul 12.13.85 CBS

TACKER, FRANCINE
SUPP.:
Oh Madeline sr 9.27.83 ABC
Empire sr 1.18.84 CBS
Ryan's Hope sr 9.85 ABC

TAGGART, RITA*
James Dean tf 2.19.76 NBC
David Cassidy--Man Undercover ep Night Work 7.5.79 NBC
Seizure: The Story of Kathy Morris 1.19.80 CBS
Rape and Marriage: The Rideout Case tf 10.30.80 CBS
Inmates: A Love Story tf 2.13.81 ABC
Knots Landing ep Moment of Truth 2.26.81 CBS
Every Stray Dog and Kid pt 9.21.81 NBC
Born to Be Sold tf 11.2.81 NBC
The Other Victim tf 11.4.81 CBS
Mae West tf 5.2.82 ABC
Filthy Rich ep 10.13.82 CBS
Cagney and Lacey ep 11.22.82 CBS
St. Elsewhere ep Legionnaires I 12.7.82 NBC
Wait Till Your Mother Gets Home! tf 1.17.83 NBC
Night Court ep Santa Goes Downtown 1.11.84 NBC
Night Court ep Once in Love with Harry 2.22.84 NBC
Steambath pt 8.16.84 SHO
Night Court ep Harry on Trial 11.15.84 NBC
Cagney and Lacey ep Thank God It's Monday 12.3.84 CBS
Eye to Eye ep The Suicide 3.28.85 ABC
Hunter ep Case X 9.21.85 NBC
Hill Street Blues ep Blues in the Night 9.26.85 NBC
Kate and Allie ep Make Mine Mink 10.7.85 CBS

TALBOT, NITA
A&C, B.V.:
Lawless Years ep Triple Cross 9.1.61 NBC
Ensign O'Toole ep Operation Stowaway Spring 1963 NBC
Daniel Boone ep The Search 3.3.66 NBC
Gomer Pyle, USMC ep A Marriage of Convenience 11.15.68 CBS
SUPP.:
CHiPs ep Trained for Trouble 4.4.82 NBC
The Other Woman tf 3.22.83 CBS
Matt Houston ep Blood Ties 3.2.84 ABC
Trapper John, M.D. ep 3.18.84 CBS
Scarecrow and Mrs. King ep Murder Between Friends 5.6.85 CBS

TALMAN, WILLIAM

A&C, B.V.:

Telephone Time ep The Sgt. Boyd Story 12.23.56 CBS
Trackdown ep Like Father 11.1.57 CBS
Tombstone Territory ep The Return of the Outlaw 3.12.58 ABC
Perry Mason sr ret 9.20.58 CBS
Perry Mason sr ret 9.17.60 CBS
Gunsmoke ep Don't Sleep 10.12.63 CBS
Perry Mason sr ret 9.24.64 CBS

TANDY, JESSICA

SUPP.:

The Gin Game sp 4.81 SHO

TAYBACK, VIC

A&C, Supp. 2:

F Troop ep Corporal Agarn's Farewell 10.5.65 ABC
Daniel Boone ep 11.3.66 NBC
Gunsmoke ep Ladies from St. Louis 3.25.67 CBS
Cimarron Strip ep The Hunted 10.5.67 CBS
Here Come the Brides ep Here Come the Brides 9.25.68 ABC
The Bill Cosby Show ep The Fatal Phone Call 9.14.69 NBC
Here Come the Brides ep Debt of Honor 1.23.70 ABC
The Partridge Family ep Danny and the Mob 11.6.70 ABC
Police Story ep The Ten-Year Honeymoon 10.23.73 NBC
Hawaii Five-O ep Bones of Contention 1.7.75 CBS
Khan! sr 2.7.75 CBS
Switch ep The Body at the Bottom 11.4.75 CBS
Cannon ep Wedding March 11.19.75 CBS
Medical Center ep A Touch of Sight [illegible].10.70 CBS
Hawaii Five-O ep Angel in Blue 3.9.78 CBS
The Eddie Capra Mysteries ep How Do I Kill Thee? 11.3.78 NBC

SUPP.:

T. J. Hooker ep Hooker's War 4.3.82 ABC
The Mysterious Two tf/pt 5.31.82 NBC
Alice sr ret 10.6.82 CBS
Matt Houston ep Deadly Fashion 10.17.82 ABC
Fantasy Island ep Roller Derby Dolls 12.4.82 ABC
Alice sr ret 10.2.83 ABC
Fantasy Island ep The Big Switch 10.15.83 ABC
Hotel ep Relative Loses 11.2.83 ABC
The Love Boat ep Love Below Decks 12.10.83 ABC
The Jesse Owens Story tf 7.9, 7.16.84 NN
Finder of Lost Loves ep Finder of Lost Loves (pt) 9.22.84 ABC
Alice sr ret 10.14.84 CBS
The Love Boat ep Unmade for Each Other 1.5.85 ABC
The Love Boat ep Your Money or Your Wife 10.5.85 ABC

TAYLOR, ELIZABETH
SUPP.:
Between Friends tf 9.15.83 HBO
Hotel ep Intimate Strangers 9.26.84 ABC
Malice in Wonderland tf 5.12.85 CBS
North and South ms 11.3-11.10.85 ABC

TAYLOR, HOLLAND*
Bosom Buddies sr 11.27.80 ABC
The ABC Afterschool Special ep My Mother Was Never a Kid 3.18.81 ABC
The Royal Romance of Charles and Diana tf 9.20.82 CBS
I Was a Mail Order Bride tf 12.14.82 CBS
The Love Boat ep A Booming Romance 11.22.83 ABC
Kate and Allie ep Diner 10.22.84 CBS
Me and Mom sr 4.5.85 ABC
Perry Mason Returns tf 12.1.85 NBC

TAYLOR, KENT
A&C, B.V.:
My Little Margie ep The Hawaii Story 1954 NBC
Restless Gun ep Imposter for a Day 2.17.58 NBC
Zorro ep The Cross of Andes 5.15.58 ABC

TAYLOR, ROD
SUPP.:
Charles and Diana: A Royal Love Story tf 9.17.82 ABC
Masquerade sr 12.22.83 ABC
Half Nelson ep 3.29.85 NBC

TAYLOR-YOUNG, LEIGH*
The Love Boat ep Legal Eagle 12.2.78 ABC
Marathon tf 1.30.80 CBS
Hart to Hart ep Deep in the Hart of Dixieland 3.9.82 ABC
The Devlin Connection ep 10.2.82 NBC
The Hamptons sr 7.27.83 ABC
Hotel ep Secrets 10.26.83 ABC
Hotel ep Identities 3.20.85 ABC

TEWES, LAUREN
SUPP.:
The Love Boat sr ret 10.2.82 ABC
The Love Boat sr ret 10.1.83 ABC
Fantasy Island ep Lady of the House 2.25.84 ABC
Hotel ep Flesh and Blood 10.10.84 ABC
Mickey Spillane's Mike Hammer ep Firestorm 1.5.85 CBS
T. J. Hooker ep Lag Time 3.23.85 ABC
Anything for Love pt 8.7.85 NBC
Murder, She Wrote ep A Lady in the Lake 11.10.85 CBS
The Love Boat ep Trouble in Paradise 11.30.85 ABC

THICKE, ALAN*
The Love Boat ep No More Alimony 1.7.84 ABC
The Calendar Girl Murders tf 4.8.84 ABC
Masquerade ep Sleeper 4.13.84 ABC
Scene of the Crime ep A Vote for Murder 5.26.85 NBC
Growing Pains sr 9.24.85 ABC

THINNES, ROY
A&C, B.V.:
The Reporter ep The Lost Lady Blues 12.11.64 CBS
SUPP.:
Falcon Crest sr 10.22.82 CBS
Hotel ep Memories 2.29.84 ABC
The Love Boat ep Frat Brothers Forever 12.8.84 ABC
Murder, She Wrote ep Dead Heat 11.24.85 CBS

THOMAS, BETTY*
Outside Chance tf 12.2.78 CBS
Hill Street Blues sr 1.15.81 NBC
Nashville Grab tf 10.18.81 NBC
Hill Street Blues sr ret 10.29.81 NBC
Hill Street Blues sr ret 9.30.82 NBC
Hill Street Blues sr ret 10.13.83 NBC
When Your Lover Leaves tf 10.31.83 NBC
Hill Street Blues sr ret 9.27.84 NBC
The ABC Afterschool Special ep No Greater Gift 9.11.85 ABC
Hill Street Blues sr ret 9.26.85 NBC

THOMAS, DANNY
A&C, B.V.:
The Dick Van Dyke Show ep It May Look Like a Walnut 2.6.63 CBS
SUPP.:
Benson ep Quest for Retire 11.12.82 ABC
An American Portrait ep Selman Abraham Waksman 11.7.84 CBS
Benson ep Let's Play Doctor 5.4.85 ABC

THOMAS, HEATHER*
Coed Fever pt 2.4.79 CBS
B.J. and the Bear ep The Girls on the Hollywood High 7.5.80 NBC
The Fall Guy sr 10.28.81 ABC
The Fall Guy sr ret 10.27.82 ABC
The Fall Guy sr ret 9.21.83 ABC
Trauma Center ep Notes About Courage 9.29.83 ABC
The Love Boat ep When Worlds Collide 11.5.83 ABC
The Love Boat Fall Preview Party sp 9.15.84 ABC
The Fall Guy sr ret 9.19.84 ABC
T. J. Hooker ep Hardcore Connection 11.3.84 ABC
Cover Up ep Murder in Malibu 12.1.84 CBS
The Fall Guy sr ret 9.26.85 ABC

THOMAS, MARLO

A&C, B.V.:

The Danny Thomas Show ep Everything Happens to Me (pilot to "The Joey Bishop Show") 3.27.61 CBS

SUPP.:

Love, Sex ... And Marriage sp 5.11.83 ABC
The Lost Honor of Kathryn Beck tf 1.24.84 CBS
Consenting Adult tf 2.4.85 ABC
An American Portrait sp 1.3.85 CBS

THOMAS, RICHARD

SUPP.:

Barefoot in the Park sp 3.21.82 HBO
The Fifth of July sp 10.14.82 SHO
Johnny Belinda tf 10.19.82 CBS
Living Proof: The Hank Williams Jr. Story tf 3.7.82 NBC
Hobson's Choice tf 12.21.83 CBS
The Master of Ballantrae tf 1.31.84 CBS
An American Portrait ep Joe Delaney 12.7.84 CBS
Final Jeopardy tf 12.8.85 NBC

THOMAS, ROSEMARIE*

Cover Up sr 9.22.84 CBS
Hunter ep Hot Grounder (a.k.a. The Real Tough Murder Case) 10.5.84 NBC
Hotel ep Obsessions 10.31.84 ABC
Hardcastle and McCormick ep The Birthday Present 2.25.85 ABC
Who's the Boss? ep Thanksgiving in Brooklyn 11.25.85 ABC
Trapper John, M.D. ep Promises, Promises 12.9.85 CBS

THOMERSON, TIM*

Starsky and Hutch ep The Avenger 10.31.78 ABC
Fantasy Island ep The Class of '69 ABC
Nero Wolfe ep Death on the Doorstep 1.23.81 NBC
In Trouble pt 8.24.81 ABC
The Two of Us sr 9.15.81 CBS
Private Benjamin ep Me, Me 4.19.82 CBS
His Mistress tf 10.21.84 NBC
Hunter ep Pen Pals 11.16.84 NBC
Hardcastle and McCormick ep The Game You Learn from Your Father 3.18.85 ABC
Murder, She Wrote ep Sudden Death 3.3.85 CBS

THOMPSON, HILARY

A&C, Supp. 2:

Room 222 ep I Hate You, Silas Marner 3.10.71 ABC

SUPP.:

Automan ep Murder Take One 3.19.84 ABC

THOMSON, GORDON*

Ryan's Hope sr Summer 1983 ABC

Dynasty sr 9.28.83 ABC
Fantasy Island ep The Wedding Picture 11.26.83 ABC
Dynasty sr ret 9.26.84 ABC
Dynasty sr ret 9.25.85 ABC
The Love Boat ep A Day in Port 9.28.85 ABC
Glitter ep 12.18.85 ABC

THORSON, LINDA
SUPP.:
The Two of Us ep The Advice to the Lovelorn Business 10.26.81 CBS
The Lost Honor of Kathryn Beck tf 1.24.84 CBS
Lime Street ep Diamonds Aren't Forever 10.12.85 ABC
St. Elsewhere ep Lost and Found in Space 11.13.85 NBC

TICOTIN, RACHEL*
For Love and Honor sr 9.23.83 NBC
Love, Mary tf 10.8.85 CBS

TILTON, CHARLENE
SUPP.:
The Love Boat ep The Courier 2.9.85 ABC
The Fall of the House of Usher tf 7.25.82 NBC
Dallas sr ret 10.1.82 CBS
Dallas sr ret 9.30.83 CBS
Hotel ep Relative Loses 11.2.83 ABC
Dallas sr ret 9.28.84 CBS
Dallas sr ret 9.27.85 CBS

TOBIN, MICHELE
SUPP.:
Code Red ep From One Little Spark 1.3.82 ABC
T. J. Hooker ep Vengeance Is Mine 2.5.83 ABC
The Powers of Matthew Star ep Swords and Quests 4.8.83 NBC
The Love Boat ep The Fountain of Youth 5.7.83 ABC

TODD, HALLIE*
Who Will Love My Children? tf 2.14.83 ABC
The ABC Afterschool Special ep Have You Ever Been Ashamed of Your Parents? 3.16.83 ABC
The Best of Times pt 8.29.83 CBS
Brothers sr 7.13.84 SHO
Brothers sr ret 4.25.85 SHO
Highway to Heaven ep Cindy 10.23.85 NBC

TOLBERT, BERLINDA*
The Streets of San Francisco ep For Good or Evil 11.14.74 ABC
The Jeffersons sr 1.17.75 (through 7.23.85) CBS
Fantasy Island ep Basin Street 5.2.81 ABC
The Love Boat ep Radioactive Isaac 11.28.81 ABC
Today's FBI ep Serpent in the Garden 2.14.82 ABC

Fantasy Island ep Cotton Club 2.26.83 ABC
Fantasy Island ep Games People Play 1.14.84 ABC
Airwolf ep They Are Us 3.31.84 CBS
Hotel ep Resolutions 10.24.84 ABC
The Love Boat ep BOS 1.5.85 ABC
International Airport tf/pt 5.25.85 ABC

TOMPKINS, ANGEL*
The Wild Wild West ep The Night of the Death Maker 2.23.68 CBS
Bonanza ep The Night Virginia City Died 9.13.70 NBC
The Name of the Game ep A Sister from Napoli 1.8.71 NBC
O'Hara: United States Treasury ep Operation: Big Stone 9.17.71 CBS
Probe pt 2.12.72 NBC
Search sr 9.13.72 NBC
The Starlost ep 11.15.73 NN
Police Woman ep Anatomy of Two Rapes 10.11.74 NBC
You Lie So Deep, My Love tf 2.25.75 ABC
Kojak ep Case Without a File 12.17.77 CBS
Charlie's Angels ep Angels on Horseback 12.21.77 ABC
Three's Company ep 10.5.78 ABC
The Eddie Capra Mysteries ep And the Sea Shall Give Up Her Dead 10.20.78 NBC
The Buffalo Soldiers pt 5.26.79 NBC
CHiPs ep 11.24.79 NBC
Eischied ep The Buddy System 1.27.80 NBC
Knight Rider ep Nobody Does It Better 4.29.83 NBC
Knight Rider ep Custom KITT 11.13.83 NBC
The Rousters ep Cold Streak 7.17.84 NBC
Simon and Simon ep Enter the Jaguar 1.17.85 CBS
Hardcastle and McCormick ep The Birthday Present 2.25.85 ABC
Simon and Simon ep Down Home Country Blues 11.2.85 CBS

TOOMEY, REGIS
A&C, B.V.:
Trackdown ep Matter of Justice 10.17.58 CBS
Wanted: Dead Or Alive ep Ricochet 11.22.58 CBS
Trackdown ep Guilt 12.19.58 CBS

TORN, RIP
A&C, B.V.:
Great Adventure ep The Pathfinder 3.6.64 CBS

TRAVANTI, DANIEL J.
A&C, Supp. 2:
East Side/West Side ep The Name of the Game 3.23.64 CBS
The Nurses ep Park Runs Into Vreeland 6.11.64 CBS
The Patty Duke Show ep Block That Statue 11.25.64 ABC
The Defenders ep The Siege 12.3.64 CBS

The Doctors and the Nurses ep The Witness 4.27.65 CBS
Gidget ep Now There's a Face 12.65 ABC
Perry Mason ep The Case of the Midnight Howler 1.16.66 CBS
Love on a Rooftop ep 10.25.66 ABC
The FBI ep Death of a Fixer 10.20.68 ABC
Here Come the Brides ep A Jew Named Sullivan 11.20.68 ABC
The FBI ep The Diamond Millstone 1.18.70 ABC
Medical Center ep The Savage Image 12.30.70 CBS
Men at Law ep The Climate of Doubt 2.3.71 CBS
The Interns ep The Choice 3.26.71 CBS
The Bob Newhart Show ep The Battle of the Groups 1.19.74 CBS
Kojak ep The Frame 2.1.76 CBS
SUPP.:
Hill Street Blues sr ret 9.30.82 NBC
Adam tf 10.10.83 NBC
Hill Street Blues sr ret 10.13.83 NBC
A Case of Libel sp 10.83 SHO
Hill Street Blues sr ret 9.27.84 NBC
Hill Street Blues sr ret 9.26.85 NBC

TRAVOLTA, ELLEN
A&C, Supp. 2:
All in the Family ep The Unemployment Story 10.13.76 CBS
SUPP.:
Quincy ep For Love of Joshua 2.3.82 NBC
Joanie Loves Chachi sr 3.23.82 ABC
Joanie Loves Chachi sr ret 10.28.82 ABC
Allison Sidney Harrison pt 8.19.83 NBC

TREAS, TERRI*
Seven Brides for Seven Brothers sr 10.6.82 CBS
The Master ep High Rollers 3.2.84 NBC
Knight Rider ep The Rotten Apples 11.11.84 NBC
Crazy Like a Fox ep Till Death Do Us Part 1.20.85 CBS
Simon and Simon ep Down Home Country Blues 11.21.85 CBS

TREVOR, CLAIRE
SUPP.:
The Love Boat ep The Misunderstanding 12.10.83 ABC

TUCKER, FORREST
SUPP.:
The Love Boat ep A Dress to Remember 5.8.82 ABC
Filthy Rich sr 10.13.82 CBS
The Love Boat ep Love Finds Florence Nightingale 1.8.83 ABC
Blood Feud tf 4.25, 5.2.83 OPT
Murder, She Wrote ep It's a Dog's Life 11.4.84 CBS

TUCKER, TANYA
SUPP.:
Fantasy Island ep Sing Melancholy Baby 3.10.84 ABC

Masquerade ep Sleeper 4.13.84 ABC
The Love Boat ep Hits and Missus 4.30.84 ABC

TURKEL, ANN*
Matt Helm tf/pt 5.7.75 ABC
Death Ray 2000 tf/pt 3.5.81 NBC
Fantasy Island ep The Whistle 1.30.82 ABC
Strike Force ep The John Killer 3.5.82 ABC
Massarati and the Brain tf/pt 8.26.82 ABC
The Fall Guy ep The Ives Have It 11.3.82 ABC
Fantasy Island ep Candy Kisses 1.15.83 ABC
The Love Boat ep Loser and Still Champ 3.5.83 ABC
Knight Rider ep Soul Survivor 11.27.83 NBC
Masquerade ep Caribbean Holiday 1.12.84 ABC
Mickey Spillane's Mike Hammer ep Cat Fight 10.20.84 CBS
Knight Rider ep Knight in Retreat 3.29.85 NBC
Street Hawk ep Female of the Species 5.9.85 ABC

TURMAN, GLYNN*
Carter's Army tf 1.27.70 ABC
Men at Law ep Marathon 2.10.71 CBS
In Search of America tf 3.23.71 ABC
The Rookies ep Blood Brother 10.29.73 ABC
The Blue Knight tf 5.9.75 CBS
Minstrel Man tf 3.22.77 CBS
The ABC Afterschool Special ep The Rag Tag Champs 3.22.78 ABC
Centennial sr 10.1.78 NBC
Visions ep Charlie Smith and the Fritter Tree 10.9.78 PBS
Katie: Portrait of a Centerfold tf 10.23.78 NBC
The Paper Chase ep Moot Court 11.21.78 CBS
Attica tf 3.2.80 ABC
The White Shadow ep A Few Good Men 4.1.80 CBS
Palmerstown, U.S.A. ep The Old Sister 4.3.80 CBS
Thornwell tf 1.28.81 CBS
The Greatest American Hero ep The Devil and the Deep Blue Sea 2.24.82 ABC
Cass Malloy pt 7.21.82 CBS
Fame ep Class Act 10.21.82 NBC
Lottery ep Detroit: The Price of Freedom ("The Prisoner" segment) 9.30.83 ABC
Poor Richard pt 1.21.84 CBS
Fantasy Island ep Bojangles and the Dancer 5.12.84 ABC
T. J. Hooker ep Anatomy of a Killing 10.6.84 ABC
Hot Pursuit ep Goodbye, I Love You 12.21.84 NBC
Murder, She Wrote ep Murder to a Jazz Beat 2.3.85 CBS
American Playhouse ep Charlotte Forten's Mission 2.25.85 PBS
Detective in the House ep Whatever Happened to...? 3.15.85 CBS
The Twilight Zone ep Paladin of the Lost Hour 11.8.85 CBS

TURNER, JANINE*
The Master ep The Good, the Bad and the Priceless 3.23.84 NBC
Mickey Spillane's Mike Hammer ep Bone Crunch 11.3.84 CBS
Knight Rider ep KITTnapp 9.27.85 NBC

TURNER, LANA
SUPP.:
Falcon Crest ep Family Reunion 2.19.82 CBS
Falcon Crest ep 11.12.82, 12.17.82, 12.31.82, 1.7.83, 3.11.83 CBS
The Love Boat ep Call Me Grandma 5.4.85 ABC

TWEED, SHANNON*
Fantasy Island ep Castaways 11.26.83 ABC
The Dukes of Hazzard ep Welcome, Whelan Jennings 9.28.84 CBS
Three's a Crowd ep King for a Day 3.5.85 ABC

TWOMEY, ANNE*
Shannon ep Curtain Calls 4.21.82 CBS
The Staff of "Life" pt 5.17.85 ABC
No Complaints! pt 7.24.85 NBC
The Twilight Zone ep Her Pilgrim Soul 12.13.85 CBS
Behind Enemy Lines tf/pt 12.29.85 NBC

TYRRELL, SUSAN
SUPP.:
Jealousy tf 1.23.84 ABC
MacGruder and Loud ep MacGruder and Loud (pt) 1.20.85 ABC

TYSON, CICELY
SUPP.:
Benny's Place tf 5.31.82 ABC
An American Portrait ep Rosa Parks 3.26.85 CBS
Playing with Fire tf 4.14.85 NBC

- U -

UGGAMS, LESLIE
SUPP.:
Magnum, P.I. ep 2.9.84 CBS

URICH, ROBERT
SUPP.:
Take Your Best Shot tf 10.12.82 CBS
Gavilan sr 10.26.82 NBC

Princess Daisy tf 11.6, 11.7.83 NBC
Invitation to Hell tf 5.24.84 ABC
His Mistress tf 10.21.84 NBC
Scandal Sheet tf 1.21.85 ABC
Spenser: For Hire sr 9.20.85 ABC

URSETH, BONNIE*
WKRP in Cincinnati ep Straight from the Heart 11.4.81 CBS
WKRP in Cincinnati ep Who's on First 11.11.81 CBS
Cassie and Company ep Gorky's Army 2.19.82 NBC
Gimme a Break ep Hot Muffins 3.11.82 NBC
Gimme a Break ep Take My Baby, Please 10.30.82 NBC
Mama's Family ep Family Feud 2.19.83 NBC
Voyagers ep Destiny's Choice 3.13.83 NBC
We Got It Made sr 9.8.83 NBC
Punky Brewster ep Take Me Out to the Ballgame 10.24.84 NBC
Hardcastle and McCormick ep One of the Girls from Accounting 11.25.84 ABC
Punky Brewster ep The Gift 11.24.85 NBC

USTINOV, PETER
SUPP.:
Agatha Christie's "Thirteen at Dinner" tf 10.19.85 CBS

- V -

VACCARO, BRENDA
SUPP.:
The Love Boat ep Shop Ahoy 2.4.84 ABC
St. Elsewhere ep The Women 3.28.84 NBC
The Love Boat Fall Preview Party sp 9.15.84 ABC
Paper Dolls sr 9.23.84 ABC
Deceptions tf 5.26, 5.27.85 NBC

VALENTINE, KAREN
SUPP.:
Muggable Mary: Street Cop tf 2.25.82 CBS
Goodbye Doesn't Mean Forever pt 5.28.82 NBC
Money on the Side tf 9.29.82 ABC
Skeezer tf/pt 12.27.82 NBC
Illusions tf 1.18.83 CBS
Jane Doe tf 3.12.83 CBS
Adams House pt 7.14.83 CBS
A Girl's Life pt 8.4.83 NBC
Children in the Crossfire tf 12.3.84 NBC
He's Fired, She's Hired tf 12.18.84 CBS
Our Time sr hos 7.27.85 NBC

VAN ARK, JOAN
A&C, Supp. 2:
The Mod Squad ep Twinkle, Twinkle Little Starlet 12.17.68 ABC
Gunsmoke ep Stryker 9.29.69 CBS
The FBI ep The Condemned 9.20.70 ABC
The Silent Force ep A Deadly Game of Love 10.5.70 ABC
Hawaii Five-O ep 12.16.70 CBS
Cannon ep Country Blues 10.5.71 CBS
Medical Center ep Adults Only 9.9.74 CBS
Manhunter ep The Deadly Brothers 10.30.74 CBS
The Six Million Dollar Man ep The Seven Million Dollar Man 11.1.74 ABC
Medical Center ep Too Late for Tomorrow 11.3.75 CBS
SUPP.:
Knots Landing sr ret 10.4.82 CBS
Knots Landing sr ret 9.29.83 CBS
Glitter ep Glitter (pt) 9.13.84 ABC
Knots Landing sr ret 10.4.84 CBS
The Love Boat ep Seems Like Old Times 10.27.84 ABC
Knots Landing sr ret 9.26.85 CBS

VAN CLEEF, LEE
A&C, B.V.:
Lawman ep The Deputy 10.5.58 ABC
Lawman ep Conclave 6.14.59 ABC
Wanted: Dead Or Alive ep The Empty Cell 10.17.59 CBS
Black Saddle ep The Cabin 4.1.60 ABC
The Rifleman ep The Prodigal 4.26.60 ABC
Colt .45 ep The Trespasser 6.21.60 ABC
Branded ep The Richest Man in Boot Hill 10.31.65 NBC
Branded ep Call to Glory 2.27.66, 3.6.66, 3.13.66 NBC
SUPP.:
The Master sr 1.20.84 NBC

VAN DUSEN, GRANVILLE
SUPP.:
This Is Kate Bennett tf/pt 5.28.82 ABC
The Astronauts pt 8.11.82 CBS
Bare Essence ms 10.4, 10.5.82 CBS
Three's Company ep Breaking Up Is Hard to Do 1.4.83 ABC
It Takes Two ep The Choice 1.20.83 ABC
Hotel ep Transitions 11.14.84 ABC
A Death in California tf 5.12, 5.13.85 ABC
The Staff of "Life" pt 5.17.85 ABC
Magnum, P.I. ep The Hotel Dick 10.17.85 CBS

VAN DYKE, DICK
SUPP.:
The Country Girl sp 5.82 SHO
Drop Out Father tf 9.27.82 CBS

The CBS Library ep The Wrong Way Kid 3.15.83 CBS
Found Money tf 12.19.83 NBC
An American Portrait ep Squanto 11.22.84 CBS
American Playhouse ep Breakfast with Les and Bess 8.28.85 PBS

VAN DYKE, JERRY
A&C, Supp. 2:
The Dick Van Dyke Show ep I Am My Brother's Keeper 3.21.62 CBS
The Dick Van Dyke Show ep The Sleeping Brother 3.28.62 CBS
Perry Mason ep The Case of the Woeful Widower 3.26.64 CBS
The Dick Van Dyke Show ep Stacey Petrie 1.20.65, 1.27.65 CBS
The Andy Griffith Show ep Banjo Playing Deputy 5.3.65 CBS
Gomer Pyle, USMC ep Gomer and the Night Club Comic 1968 CBS
Good Morning World ep Partner My Feet Partner 1968 CBS
SUPP.:
The Love Boat ep The Groupies 11.6.82 ABC
Newhart ep You're Homebody Till Somebody Loves You 3.27.83 CBS

VAN PATTEN, DICK*
I Remember Mama sr 6.1.49 CBS
I Remember Mama sr ret 8.4.50 CBS
I Remember Mama sr ret 9.7.51 CBS
I Remember Mama sr ret 9.5.52 CBS
I Remember Mama sr ret 9.4.53 CBS
I Remember Mama sr ret 9.13.54 CBS
I Remember Mama sr ret 10.7.55 CBS
I Remember Mama sr ret 12.16.56 CBS
Rawhide ep Incident of the Power and the Plow 2.13.59 CBS
Arnie ep 9.21.70 CBS
Love, American Style ep 2.5.71 ABC
The Partners sr 9.18.71 NBC
Medical Center ep 2.23.72 CBS
Sanford and Son ep 3.3.72 NBC
The Streets of San Francisco ep 45 Minutes from Home 10.7.72 ABC
Hec Ramsey: The Century Turns tf/pt 10.8.72 NBC
The Crooked Hearts tf 11.8.72 ABC
Banyon ep Time to Kill 11.10.72 NBC
Love, American Style ep 11.17.72 ABC
Emergency ep 11.23.72 NBC
McMillan and Wife ep No Hearts, No Flowers 1.4.73 NBC
Cannon ep Murder for Murder 2.7.73 CBS
Banacek ep Rocket to Oblivion 2.12.73 NBC
The Paul Lynde Show ep 2.21.73 ABC
The Rookies ep Tribute to a Veteran 2.26.73 ABC
The New Dick Van Dyke Show sr 9.10.73 CBS
Adam's Rib ep 10.12.73 ABC

Chopper One ep 2.21.74 ABC
The Girl with Something Extra ep 3.15.74 NBC
Ernie, Madge and Artie pt 8.15.74 ABC
Sierra ep 9.12.74 NBC
The Night Stalker ep U.F.O. 9.27.74 ABC
Barnaby Jones ep Odd Man Loses 10.8.74 CBS
Adam-12 ep Alcohol 12.10.74 NBC
The Rookies ep S.W.A.T. 2.17.75 ABC
The Six Million Dollar Man ep E.S.P. Spy 3.2.75 ABC
Grandpa Max pt 3.28.75 CBS
When Things Were Rotten sr 9.10.75 ABC
Medical Center ep Street Girl 10.20.75 CBS
Ellery Queen ep The Adventure of the Eccentric Engineer 1.18.76 NBC
Emergency ep 2.7.76 NBC
Barnaby Jones ep Deadly Reunion 2.12.76 CBS
The Streets of San Francisco ep Clown of Death 2.26.76 ABC
Ace pt 7.26.76 NBC
Charo and the Sergeant pt 8.24.76 ABC
The Love Boat I tf/pt 9.17.76 ABC
Phyllis ep 9.20.76 CBS
The Streets of San Francisco ep The Thrill Killers 9.30, 10.7.76 ABC
The New, Original Wonder Woman ep Beauties on Parade 10.13.76 ABC
The ABC Afterschool Special ep Blind Sunday 10.27.76 ABC
The Six Million Dollar Man ep The Bionic Boy 11.7.76 ABC
Maude ep 11.10.76 CBS
What's Happening!! ep 11.20.76 ABC
The Tony Randall Show ep 12.23.76 ABC
Happy Days ep 2.8, 2.15.77 ABC
Eight Is Enough sr 3.15.77 ABC
Eight Is Enough sr ret 8.10.77 ABC
The Love Boat ep The Congressman Was Indiscreet 1.28.78 ABC
With This Ring tf 5.5.78 ABC
Eight Is Enough sr ret 9.6.78 ABC
This One's for Dad sp 2.23.79 NN
Eight Is Enough sr ret 9.5.79 ABC
Diary of a Teenage Hitchhiker tf 9.21.79 ABC
CHiPs ep CHiPs Goes Roller Disco 9.22.79 NBC
Eight Is Enough sr ret 10.29.80 ABC
The Love Boat ep 11.15.80 ABC
State Fair, U.S.A. sp 9.5.81 NN
Walt Disney ... One Man's Dream sp 12.12.81 CBS
The Love Boat ep His Girls Friday 2.13.82 ABC
Snowbird sp 4.18.82 NN
Fit for a King pt 6.11.82 ABC
The Love Boat ep When the Magic Disappears 4.2.83 ABC
Too Close for Comfort ep Don't Rock the Boat 4.28.83 ABC
Hotel ep Choices 10.19.83 ABC
The Love Boat ep How Do I Love Thee? 1.7.84 ABC

Masquerade ep Sleeper 4.13.84 ABC
Finder of Lost Loves ep Undying Love 11.10.84 ABC
Wonderworks ep The Hoboken Chicken Emergency 11.19.84 PBS
Mickey Spillane's Mike Hammer ep Cold Target 12.1.84 CBS
Crazy Like a Fox ep Murder Is a Two Stroke Penalty 10.27.85 CBS
The Midnight Hour tf 11.1.85 ABC

VAN VALKENBURGH, DEBORAH

SUPP.:

Too Close for Comfort sr ret 10.14.82 ABC
Too Close for Comfort sr ret 10.83 NN
Too Close for Comfort sr ret 10.84 NN
Hotel ep Resolutions 10.24.84 ABC
A Bunny's Tale tf 2.25.85 ABC
Going for the Gold: The Bill Johnson Story tf 5.8.85 CBS
Too Close for Comfort sr ret 10.85 NN
Glitter ep Rock 'n' Roll Heaven 12.12.85 ABC

VAUGHN, ROBERT

A&C, B.V.:

The Rifleman ep The Apprentice Sheriff 12.9.58 ABC
Tales of Wells Fargo ep Treasure Coach 10.14.61 NBC
The Dick Van Dyke Show ep It's a Shame She Married Me 4.17.63 CBS

SUPP.:

Fantasies tf 1.18.82 ABC
The Day the Bubble Burst tf 2.7.82 NBC
A Question of Honor tf 4.28.82 CBS
Inside the Third Reich tf 5.9, 5.10.82 ABC
The Blue and the Gray ms 11.14-11.17.82 CBS
Intimate Agony tf 3.21.83 ABC
Will There Ever Be a Morning? tf 2.22.83 CBS
The Return of the Man from UNCLE: The 15 Years Later Affair tf/pt 4.5.83 CBS
Emerald Point, N.A.S. sr 12.5.83 CBS
Evergreen ms 2.24-2.26.85 NBC
Private Sessions tf/pt 3.18.85 NBC
International Airport tf 5.25.85 ABC
Murder, She Wrote ep Murder Digs Deep 12.29.85 CBS

VERDUGO, ELENA

A&C, B.V.:

Love That Bob ep Bob and the Ravishing Realtor Fall 1958 NBC
Love That Bob ep Bob Helps Harry Von Zell 6.2.59 NBC
Law of the Plainsman ep The Innocent 12.10.59 NBC

VEREEN, BEN*

Louis Armstrong--Chicago Style tf 1.25.76 ABC
Roots ms 1.23-1.30.77 ABC
Ten Speed and Brown Shoe sr 1.27.80 ABC

The Love Boat ep Pal-I-Mony-O-Mine 4.10.82 ABC
Pippin sp 4.83 SHO
Webster ep That's Entertainment 11.18.83 ABC
Webster ep Uncle Philip 2.24.84 ABC
The Love Boat ep Dreamboat 5.5.84 ABC
The Jesse Owens Story tf 7.9, 7.16.84 NN
Secret World of the Very Young sp 9.12.84 CBS
Webster ep Re: Webster Long 9.21, 9.28.84 ABC
Ellis Island ms 11.12-11.14.84 CBS
Webster ep God Bless the Child 11.23.84 ABC
Webster ep It's a Dog's Life 1.4.85 ABC
Webster ep What Is Art? 2.22.85 ABC
A.D. ms 3.31-4.4.85 NBC
The Charmkins pt vo 4.85 NN
An American Portrait ep Fannie Lou Hamer 4.16.85 CBS
Webster ep Great Expectations 11.8, 11.15.85 ABC
Lost in London tf 11.20.85 CBS

VIGODA, ABE
A&C, Supp. 2:
Dark Shadows two episodes Early 1969 ABC
Toma ep The Street 5.3.74 ABC
The Rockford Files ep The Kirkoff Case 9.13.74 NBC
Hawaii Five-O ep The Two-Faced Corpse 10.29.74 CBS
The Rockford Files ep Rosenthal and Gilda Stern Are Dead 9.29.79 NBC
SUPP.:
Mickey Spillane's Mike Hammer ep A Bullet for Benny 12.8.84 CBS

VILLECHAIZE, HERVE*
Fantasy Island tf/pt 1.14.77 ABC
Return to Fantasy Island tf/pt 1.20.78 ABC
Fantasy Island sr 1.28.78 ABC
Fantasy Island sr ret 9.16.78 ABC
Fantasy Island sr ret 9.7.79 ABC
Fantasy Island sr ret 10.25.80 ABC
Fantasy Island sr ret 10.10.81 ABC
Faerie Tale Theater ep Rumplestiltskin 10.16.82 SHO
Diff'rent Strokes ep Arnold the Entrepreneur 11.17.84 NBC

VINCENT, JAN-MICHAEL
A&C, Supp. 1:
Toma ep Blockhouse Breakdown 11.8.73 ABC
SUPP.:
The Winds of War ms 2.6-2.13.83 ABC
Airwolf sr 1.28.84 CBS
Airwolf sr ret 9.22.84 CBS
Airwolf sr ret 9.28.85 CBS

- W -

WAGGONER, LYLE

SUPP.:

The Love Boat ep A Dress to Remember 5.8.82 ABC
Fantasy Island ep No Friends Like Old Friends 2.26.83 ABC
Gun Shy ep 3.29.83 CBS
Happy Days ep Like Mother, Like Daughter 1.24.84 ABC
Murder, She Wrote ep Hooray for Homicide 10.28.84 CBS

WAGNER, LINDSAY

A&C, Supp. 1:

The Rockford Files ep Aura Lee, Farewell 1.3.75 NBC

SUPP.:

Memories Never Die tf 12.15.82 CBS
The Fall Guy ep Devil's Island 9.21.83 ABC
I Want to Live tf 5.9.83 ABC
Princess Daisy tf 11.6, 11.7.83 NBC
Two Kinds of Love tf 11.8.83 CBS
The Love Boat Fall Preview Party sp 9.15.84 ABC
Jessie sr 9.18.84 ABC
Passions tf 10.1.84 CBS
The Other Love tf 9.24.85 CBS
This Child Is Mine tf 11.4.85 NBC

WAGNER, ROBERT

SUPP.:

Hart to Hart sr ret 9.28.82 ABC
Hart to Hart sr ret 9.27.83 ABC
To Catch a King tf 2.12.84 HBO
Lime Street sr 9.28.85 ABC

WAITE, RALPH*

The Borgia Stick tf 2.25.67 NBC
N.Y.P.D. ep Murder for Infinity 11.7.67 ABC
N.Y.P.D. ep 'L' Is for Love and Larceny 12.24.68 ABC
Nichols ep The Dirty Half Dozen Run Amuck 10.28.71 NBC
The Waltons sr 9.14.72 CBS
The Waltons sr ret 9.13.73 CBS
The Waltons sr ret 9.12.74 CBS
The Waltons sr ret 9.11.75 CBS
The Waltons sr ret 9.30.76 CBS
The Secret Life of John Chapman tf 12.27.76 CBS
Roots ms ep 1.23, 1.24.77 ABC
Red Alert tf 5.18.77 CBS
The Waltons sr ret 9.15.77 CBS
The Waltons sr ret 9.21.78 CBS
The Waltons sr ret 9.20.79 CBS
Ohms tf 1.2.80 CBS
Angel City tf 11.12.80 CBS

The Waltons sr ret 11.20.80 CBS
The Gentleman Bandit tf 5.6.81 CBS
The Mississippi sr 3.25.83 CBS
The Mississippi sr ret 9.27.83 CBS
Growing Pains sp 12.10.84 NN
Crime of Innocence tf 10.27.85 NBC

WALDEN, ROBERT
SUPP.:
Memorial Day tf 11.27.83 CBS
Brothers sr 4.25.85 SHO
Murder, She Wrote ep Murder in the Afternoon 10.13.85 CBS

WALDEN, SUSAN*
Three's Company ep Hearing Is Believing 11.8.83 ABC
The Dukes of Hazzard ep 3.24.84 CBS
Half Nelson ep The Deadly Vase 3.29.85 NBC

WALKER, JIMMIE
SUPP.:
Today's FBI ep Bank Job 3.7.82 ABC
Fantasy Island ep Beautiful Skeptic 11.27.82 ABC
At Ease sr 3.4.83 ABC
Cagney and Lacey ep 3.14.83 CBS
The Jerk, Too tf/pt 1.6.84 NBC
The Fall Guy ep Losers Weepers 9.19.84 ABC
The Love Boat ep Ashes to Ashes 3.30.85 ABC

WALKER, NANCY
SUPP.:
Trapper John, M.D. ep "42" 1.3.82 CBS
The Love Boat ep A Honeymoon for Horace 10.23.82 ABC
Fame ep Sunshine Again 1.20.83 NBC
The ABC Weekend Special ep Jeeter Mason and the Magic Headset 10.5.85 ABC
The ABC Weekend Special ep Columbus Circle 11.23.85 ABC

WALLACE, DEE*
The Waltons ep 2.23.73 CBS
Police Woman ep Do You Still Beat Your Wife? 10.25.77 NBC
Barnaby Jones ep Terror on a Quiet Afternoon 2.9.78 CBS
Police Story ep A Chance to Live 5.28.78 NBC
Lou Grant ep Hooker 10.16.78 CBS
Trapper John, M.D. ep 10.7.79 CBS
Hart to Hart ep Jonathan Hart Jr. 10.6.79 ABC
Kate Loves a Mystery ep Love on Instant Replay 10.18.79 NBC
Young Love, First Love tf 11.20.79 CBS
Skag ep The Working Girl 1.31, 2.7.80 NBC
Dribble pt 8.21.80 NBC
The Secret War of Jackie's Girls tf/pt 11.29.80 NBC
A Whale for the Killing tf 2.1.81 ABC

The ABC Afterschool Special ep Run, Don't Walk 3.14.81 ABC
The Five of Me tf 5.12.81 CBS
The CBS Afternoon Playhouse ep Help Wanted 10.12.82 CBS
Child Bride of Short Creek tf 12.7.81 NBC
Skeezer tf/pt 12.27.82 NBC
I Take These Men tf 1.5.83 CBS
Wait Till Your Mother Gets Home! tf 1.17.83 NBC
Harpy tf 10.26.83 CBS
The Sky's the Limit tf 2.7.84 CBS
100 Center Street pt 8.31.84 ABC
Hotel ep Intimate Strangers 9.26.84 ABC
Suburban Beat pt 8.17.85 NBC
Simon and Simon ep Love and/or Marriage 10.3.85 CBS
The Twilight Zone ep The Wish Bank 10.18.85 CBS
Hostage Flight tf 11.17.85 NBC

WALLACH, ELI

SUPP.:

The Wall tf 2.16.82 CBS
The Executioner's Song tf 11.28, 11.29.82 NBC
Anatomy of an Illness tf 5.15.84 CBS
An American Portrait ep Tommy Howell 4.14.85 CBS
Embassy tf/pt 4.21.85 NBC
Christopher Columbus tf 5.19, 5.20.85 CBS
Our Family Honor sr 9.17.85 ABC
Murder: By Reason of Insanity tf 10.1.85 CBS

WALSH, LORY*

Sticking Together tf/pt 4.14.78 ABC
The MacKenzies of Paradise Cove sr 3.27.79 ABC
Charlie's Angels ep Angels on Skates 11.21.79 ABC
Barnaby Jones ep The Killin' Cousin 4.3.80 CBS
The Asphalt Cowboy pt 12.7.80 NBC
Simon and Simon ep 2.23.84 CBS
Legmen ep The Poseidon Indenture 2.24.84 NBC
Airwolf ep Santini's Millions 2.2.85 CBS

WALSTON, RAY

A&C, B.V.:

You Are There ep D-Day 3.6.55 CBS

SUPP.:

The Kid with the Broken Halo tf/pt 4.5.82 NBC
Fame ep A Big Finish 4.15.82 NBC
The Fall of the House of Usher tf 7.25.82 NBC
Hart to Hart ep Hart's Desire 11.16.82 ABC
Simon and Simon ep Murder Between the Lines 1.6.83 CBS
Fantasy Island ep The Devil Stick 3.19.83 ABC
This Girl for Hire tf/pt 11.1.83 CBS
The Jerk, Too tf/pt 1.6.84 NBC
Oh Madeline ep My Mother the Carnal 1.31.84 ABC
Newhart ep 10.15.84 CBS

Night Court ep Harry on Trial 11.15.84 NBC
For Love or Money tf 11.20.84 CBS
The Love Boat ep Santa, Santa, Santa 12.15.84 ABC
Trapper John, M.D. ep 1.20.85 CBS
Otherworld ep Rules of Attraction 1.26.85 CBS
Matt Houston ep New Orleans Nightmare 2.8.85 ABC
Amos tf 9.29.85 CBS
Silver Spoons sr (with ep Trouble with Uncle Harry) 11.3.85 NBC
The Misfits of Science ep Steer Crazy (a.k.a. Old Folk) 11.29.85 NBC

WALTER, JESSICA
<u>A&C, Supp. 1</u>:
Hawaii Five-O ep The Two-Faced Corpse 10.29.74 CBS
<u>SUPP.</u>:
Knots Landing ep Reunion 2.18.82 CBS
Trapper John, M.D. ep Cause for Concern 4.18.82 CBS
Trapper John, M.D. ep Don't Rain on My Charade 9.26.82 CBS
Joanie Loves Chachi ep Everybody Loves Aunt Vanessa 11.4.82 ABC
Matt Houston ep Joey's Here 12.5.82 ABC
Thursday's Child tf 2.1.83 CBS
Bare Essence sr 2.8.83 NBC
Trapper John, M.D. ep 10.23.83 CBS
The Return of Marcus Welby, M.D. tf/pt 5.16.84 ABC
T.L.C. pt 8.8.84 NBC
Trapper John, M.D. ep My Son, the Doctor 10.14.84 CBS
Three's a Crowd ep The Maternal Triangle 10.16.84 ABC
Three's a Crowd ep Jack's Problem 10.30.84 ABC
Three's a Crowd ep A Foreign Affair 12.18.84 ABC
Trapper John, M.D. ep 11.25.84 CBS
Three's a Crowd ep Father Knows Nothing 1.8.85 ABC
The Execution tf 1.14.85 NBC
Day to Day Affairs sp 2.4.85 HBO
Three's a Crowd ep Deeds of Trust 2.19.85 ABC
Three's a Crowd ep The New Mr. Bradford 2.26.85 ABC
Three's a Crowd ep King for a Day 3.5.85 ABC
Murder, She Wrote ep Murder in the Afternoon 10.13.85 CBS

WALTER, TRACEY*
Charlie's Angels ep An Angel's Trail 2.27.80 ABC
Best of the West sr (with ep The Prisoner) 9.17.81 ABC
The Fall Guy ep The Silent Partner 4.28.82 ABC
Hill Street Blues ep Shooter 5.6.82 NBC
Seven Brides for Seven Brothers ep 10.13.82 CBS
Filthy Rich ep 11.10.82 CBS
Oh Madeline ep The Write Stuff 12.6.83 ABC
Cagney and Lacey ep 3.28.83 CBS
Hill Street Blues ep Here's Adventure, Here's Romance 10.13.83 NBC

Hunter ep Pen Pals 11.9.84 NBC
Amazing Stories ep Mummy, Daddy 10.27.85 NBC
The Insiders ep 11.20.85 ABC

WALTERS, LAURIE*
The People tf 1.22.72 ABC
Returning Home tf 4.29.75 ABC
Medical Story ep Test Case 9.25.75 NBC
Cannon ep The Hero 11.26.75 CBS
Eight Is Enough sr 3.15.77 (through 8.29.81) ABC
The Love Boat ep The Kissing Bandit 10.21.78 ABC
Fantasy Island ep Tattoo the Matchmaker 2.20.82 ABC
Lottery ep Kansas City: Protected Winner ("The Library" segment) 10.28.83 ABC
Cheers ep Bar Bet 3.14.85 NBC
Hollywood Beat ep Girls, Girls, Girls 11.30.85 ABC
The New Love, American Style ep Love and the Night Watchman 12.30.85 ABC

WARD, RACHEL*
Christmas Lillies of the Field tf 12.16.79 NBC
The Thorn Birds ms 3.27, 3.28, 3.29, 3.30.83 ABC
Fortress tf 11.24.85 HBO

WARDEN, JACK*
Mr. Peepers sr 9.13.53 NBC
Mr. Peepers sr ret 12.18.54 NBC
The Philco Television Playhouse ep Shadow of the Champ 3.20.55 CBS
Bonanza ep The Paiute War 10.3.59 NBC
The Twilight Zone ep The Lonely 11.13.59 CBS
The Twilight Zone ep The Mighty Casey 6.17.60 CBS
Stagecoach West ep A Fork in the Road 11.1.60 ABC
The Outlaws ep Starfall 11.24, 12.1.60 NBC
Route 66 ep The Clover Throne 1.27.61 CBS
The Asphalt Jungle sr 4.2.61 NBC
Bus Stop ep Accessory by Consent 11.19.61 ABC
Naked City ep The Face of the Enemy 1.3.62 ABC
Route 66 ep A Feat of Strength 5.18.62 CBS
Target: The Corruptors ep The Organizer 5.18, 5.25.62 ABC
Naked City ep The King of Venus Will Take Care of You 5.30.62 ABC
The Virginian ep Throw a Long Rope 10.3.62 NBC
Going My Way ep Not Good Enough for My Sister 11.14.62 ABC
Ben Casey ep Hear America Singing 12.10.62 ABC
Naked City ep Spectre of the Rose Street Gang 12.19.62 ABC
Route 66 ep Two Strangers and an Old Enemy 9.27.63 CBS
The Breaking Point ep No Squares in My Family Circle 2.10.64 ABC
Great Adventure ep Escape 4.17.64 CBS
Kraft Suspense Theater ep The Watchman 5.14.64 NBC

Bewitched ep 10.8.64 ABC
The Bob Hope Chrysler Theater ep On the Outskirts of Town 11.6.64 NBC
Slattery's People ep Is Laura the Name of the Game? 11.9.64 CBS
Dr. Kildare ep No Mother to Guide Them 2.4.65 NBC
The Virginian ep Shadows of the Past 2.24.65 NBC
The Wackiest Ship in the Army sr 9.16.65 NBC
The Fugitive ep Concrete Evidence 1.24.67 ABC
N.Y.P.D. sr 9.5.67 ABC
N.Y.P.D. sr ret 10.1.68 ABC
The Face of Fear tf 10.8.71 CBS
Brian's Song tf 11.30.71 ABC
What's a Nice Girl Like You...? tf 12.18.71 ABC
Man on a String tf 2.18.72 CBS
Lieutenant Schuster's Wife tf 10.11.72 ABC
Wheeler and Murdock pt 5.9.73 ABC
Remember When tf 3.23.74 NBC
The Godchild tf 11.26.74 ABC
Journey from Darkness tf 2.25.75 NBC
They Only Come Out at Night tf 4.29.75 NBC
Jigsaw John sr 2.2.76 NBC
Raid on Entebbe tf 1.9.77 NBC
The Bad News Bears sr 3.24.79 CBS
The Bad News Bears sr ret 9.15.79 CBS
Topper tf/pt 11.9.79 ABC
A Private Battle tf 10.7.80 CBS
Hobson's Choice tf 12.21.83 CBS
Robert Kennedy and His Times ms 1.27-1.30.84 CBS
Helen Keller: The Miracle Continues tf 4.23.84 OPT
A.D. ms 3.31-4.4.85 NBC
Crazy Like a Fox sr 12.30.84 CBS
Crazy Like a Fox sr ret 9.29.85 CBS
Alice in Wonderland tf 12.9, 12.10.85 CBS

WARREN, JENNIFER
SUPP.:
Paper Dolls tf/pt 5.24.82 ABC
Confessions of a Married Man tf 1.31.83 ABC
Cagney and Lacey ep 3.7.83 CBS
Amazons tf 1.29.84 ABC
Celebrity ms 2.12-2.14.84 NBC
The Love Boat Fall Preview Party sp 9.15.84 ABC
Paper Dolls sr 9.23.84 ABC
Double Dare ep Double Negative 4.10.85 CBS

WARREN, LESLEY ANN
A&C, Supp. 2:
For the People ep Dangerous to the Public Peace and Safety 3.21.65 CBS
Gunsmoke ep Harvest 3.22.66 CBS

Columbo ep A Deadly State of Mind 4.27.75 NBC
SUPP.:
Portrait of a Showgirl tf 5.4.82 CBS
Evergreen ms 2.24-2.26.85 NBC
An American Portrait ep George Perkins Marsh 3.18.85 CBS

WASHBURN, BEVERLY
A&C, B.V.:
The Schlitz Playhouse of Stars ep The Closed Door 11.27.53 CBS
Fury ep Joey Sees Through It 1.21.56 NBC
The Texan ep No Tears for the Dead 12.8.58 CBS
Leave it to Beaver ep Blind Date Committee 10.3.59 ABC
Thriller ep Parasite Mansion 4.25.61 NBC
Target: The Corruptors ep Nobody Gets Hurt 6.1.62 ABC
Hawaiian Eye ep Passport 4.2.63 ABC
Gidget ep Take a Lesson 3.10.66 ABC
The Streets of San Francisco ep Most Feared in the Jungle 12.20.73 ABC
Manhunter ep The Ma Gentry Gang 9.11.74 CBS
SUPP.:
Scarecrow and Mrs. King ep Remembrance of Things Past 1.9.84 CBS

WATKINS, CARLENE*
The Two-Five tf/pt 4.14.78 ABC
Little Women tf/pt 10.2, 10.3.78 NBC
Quincy, M.E. ep A Night to Raise the Dead 12.7.78 NBC
The Dukes of Hazzard ep High Octave 2.23.79 CBS
Cliffhangers: Stop Susan Williams sr 2.27.79 NBC
B.J. and the Bear ep Snow White and the Seven Lady Truckers 9.29, 10.6.79 NBC
B.J. and the Bear ep 3.1.80 NBC
Fantasy Island ep 5.17.80 ABC
Condominium tf 11.20, 11.24.80 OPT
Nero Wolfe ep The Golden Spider 1.16.81 NBC
Best of the West sr 9.10.81 ABC
The Love Boat ep The Floating Bridge Game 12.12.81 ABC
Taxi ep The Schloogel 9.30.82 NBC
Remington Steele ep In the Steele of the Night 12.3.82 NBC
It Takes Two ep An Affair to Remember 12.16.82 ABC
Magnum, P.I. ep Legacy from a Friend 3.10.83 CBS
It's Not Easy sr 9.29.83 ABC
Hotel ep Mistaken Identities 2.1.84 ABC
Mary sr 12.11.85 CBS

WATSON, MILLS
A&C, Supp. 2:
Mission: Impossible ep 3.3.68 CBS
Here Come the Brides ep The Log Jam 1.8.69 ABC
Here Come the Brides ep The Wealthiest Man in Seattle 10.3.69

ABC
Here Come the Brides ep Absalom 3.20.70 ABC
San Francisco International Airport ep We Once Came Home to Paradise 11.4.70 NBC
The Interns ep The Oath 11.6.70 CBS
Alias Smith and Jones ep The McCreedy Bust 1.21.71 ABC
Alias Smith and Jones ep The Root of It All 4.1.71 ABC
Police Story ep War Games 1.4.76 NBC
McCoy ep In Again, Out Again 1.4.76 NBC
Barnaby Jones ep The Eyes of Terror 3.11.76 CBS
The Six Million Dollar Man ep Danny's Inferno 1.23.77 ABC
The Six Million Dollar Man ep Deadly Countdown 9.25.77, 10.3.77 ABC
SUPP.:
Voyagers ep An Arrow Pointing East 12.12.82 NBC
Simon and Simon ep 10.6.83 CBS
The A-Team ep When You Comin' Home, Range Rider? 10.25.83 NBC
The Fall Guy ep Old Heroes Never Die 5.2.84 ABC
The A-Team ep Trouble on Wheels 10.30.84 NBC
Cover Up ep Murder in Malibu 12.1.84 CBS
Benson ep On the Road 1.11.85 ABC
The Fall Guy ep Spring Break 2.20.85 ABC
Murder, She Wrote ep Murder Takes the Bus 3.17.85 CBS
Half Nelson ep Half Nelson (pt) 3.29.85 NBC
Airwolf ep Eruption 4.6.85 CBS
T. J. Hooker ep Return of a Cop 10.2.85 CBS
Hunter ep The Big Fall 11.23.85 NBC

WATSON, VERNEE*
Welcome Back, Kotter sr 9.9.75 ABC
The Boy in the Plastic Bubble tf 11.12.76 ABC
Vegas ep Yours Truly, Jack the Ripper 1.24.79 ABC
Love's Savage Fury tf 5.20.79 ABC
The Love Boat ep Till Death Do Us Part 11.17.79 ABC
Vegas ep The Hunter Hunted 3.5.80 ABC
Fantasy Island ep The Children of Mentu 5.17.80 ABC
Dribble pt 8.21.80 NBC
The Violation of Sarah McDonald tf 5.19.81 CBS
Fantasy Island ep Mr. Nobody 11.7.81 ABC
Chicago Story ep Half a Chance 6.11.82 NBC
London and Davis in New York pt 9.9.84 CBS
The Love Boat ep Only the Good Die Young 10.13.84 ABC
Punky Brewster ep A Visit to the Doctor 10.21.84 NBC
Benson ep Taking It to the Max 11.30.84 ABC
Benson ep Reunion 12.7.84 ABC
Hill Street Blues ep Passage to Libya 2.14.85 NBC
Foley Square sr 12.11.85 CBS

WAYNE, DAVID
A&C, B.V.:
Wagon Train ep The Sharack Bennington Story 6.22.60 NBC

Batman ep The 13th Hat ... Batman Stands Pat 2.66 ABC
SUPP.:
Matt Houston ep Heritage 9.9.83 ABC
Matt Houston ep Houston Is Dead 1.20.84 ABC
Matt Houston ep Blood Ties 3.2.84 ABC
St. Elsewhere ep Whistle Wylie Works 1.2.85 NBC
Murder, She Wrote ep Murder Takes a Bow 3.17.85 CBS
Crazy Like a Fox ep The Man Who Cried Fox 4.7.85 CBS
Newhart ep Pirate Pete 9.30.85 CBS
The Love Boat ep No More Mr. Nice Guy 11.30.85 ABC

WAYNE, PATRICK
A&C, Supp. 2:
Voyage to the Bottom of the Sea 1.2.66 ABC
SUPP.:
Fantasy Island ep Nancy and the Thunderbirds 5.1.82 ABC
Fantasy Island ep Let Them Eat Cake 2.12.83 ABC
The Love Boat ep Loser and Still Champ 3.5.83 ABC
Lottery ep Kansas City: Protected Winner ("The Library" segment) 10.28.83 ABC
Matt Houston ep Cash and Carry 3.23.84 ABC
The Love Boat ep By Hook or Crook 11.17.84 ABC
The New Love, American Style ep Love and the Sauna 12.30.85 ABC

WEATHERLY, SHAWN*
The Dukes of Hazzard ep 2.4.83 CBS
Happy Days ep Where the Guys Are 10.18.83 ABC
T. J. Hooker ep A Matter of Passion 11.26.83 ABC
T. J. Hooker ep Carnal Express 12.31.83 ABC
Shaping Up sr 3.12.84 ABC
T. J. Hooker ep Shadow of Truth 3.17.84 ABC
Hunter ep The Shooter 1.4.85 NBC
Ocean Quest sr 8.18.85 NBC
Amazing Stories ep Remote Control Man 12.8.85 NBC

WEAVER, DENNIS
SUPP.:
Don't Go to Sleep tf 12.10.82 ABC
Cocaine: One Man's Seduction tf 2.27.83 NBC
Emerald Point, N.A.S. sr 9.26.83 CBS
Magnum, P.I. ep Let Me Hear the Music 2.21.85 CBS
Looking for the Gold: The Bill Johnson Story tf 5.8.85 CBS

WEAVER, FRITZ
SUPP.:
Maid in America tf 9.22.82 CBS
The Love Boat ep A Match Made in Heaven 10.20.84 ABC
Hawaiian Heat ep Ancient Fires 11.9.84 ABC
Hot Pursuit ep Portrait of a Lady Killer 11.17.84 NBC
Tales from the Darkside ep Inside the Closet 11.17.84 NN

The Hearst and Davies Affair tf 1.14.85 ABC
Murder, She Wrote ep Tough Guys Don't Die 2.14.85 CBS
A Death in California tf 5.12, 5.13.85 ABC
The Twilight Zone ep The Star 12.20.85 CBS

WEBBER, ROBERT
A&C, Supp. 1:
Robert Montgomery Presents the Lucky Strike Theater ep Machinal 1.18.54 NBC
The Rifleman ep The Retired Gun 1.20.59 ABC
Play of the Week ep A Palm Tree in a Rose Garden 4.4.60 NN
The Dick Powell Show ep Three Soldiers 1.25.61 NBC
Straightaway ep Panic Wagon 12.7.61 ABC
Alfred Hitchcock ep Burglar Proof 2.27.62 NBC
Thriller ep Portrait Without a Face 11.1.62 NBC
Stoney Burke ep Spin a Golden Web 11.26.62 ABC
The Dick Powell Show ep The Court-Martial of Captain Wycliffe 12.11.62 NBC
Route 66 ep Give the Old Cat a Tender Mouse 12.21.62 CBS
The Defenders ep Ordeal 2.2.63 CBS
Naked City ep Golden Lads and Girls 5.22.63 ABC
The Greatest Show on Earth ep Silent Love, Secret Love 9.24.63 ABC
Arrest and Trial ep The Witnesses 11.3.63 CBS
The Bob Hope Chrysler Theater ep The Candidate 12.6.63 NBC
The Defenders ep The Seal of Confession 11.30.63 CBS
Ben Casey ep It Is Getting Dark and We Are Lost 12.18.63 ABC
The Fugitive ep The Garden House 1.14.64 ABC
Kraft Suspense Theater ep Leviathan 5 1.30.64 NBC
Espionage ep The Liberators 3.11.64 NBC
Mr. Broadway ep Don't Mention My Name in Shaboygab 11.7.64 CBS
The Outer Limits ep Keeper of the Purple Twilight 12.5.64 ABC
The Rogues ep Wherefore Art Thou, Harold? 3.21.65 NBC
Kraft Suspense Theater ep Kill No More 4.29.65 NBC
The Men from Shiloh ep The Mysterious Mr. Tate 10.14.70 NBC

WEITZ, BRUCE*
The White Shadow ep 1.27.79 CBS
Paris ep Once More for Free 12.11.79 CBS
Hill Street Blues sr 1.15.81 NBC
Every Stray Dog and Kid pt 9.21.81 NBC
Hill Street Blues sr ret 10.29.81 NBC
Death of a Centerfold: The Dorothy Stratton Story tf 11.1.81 NBC
Hill Street Blues sr ret 9.30.82 NBC
Hill Street Blues sr ret 10.13.83 NBC
Hill Street Blues sr ret 9.27.84 NBC
A Reason to Live tf 1.7.85 NBC
Hill Street Blues sr ret 9.26.85 NBC

WELCH, RAQUEL
SUPP.:
The Legend of Walks Far Woman tf 5.30.82 NBC

WELD, TUESDAY
A&C, B.V.:
Dobie Gillis ep Birth of a Salesman 3.6.62 CBS
SUPP.:
The Rainmaker sp 10.22.82 HBO
John Steinbeck's "The Winter of Our Discontent" tf 12.6.83 CBS
Scorned and Swindled tf 10.9.84 CBS

WELLES, ORSON
SUPP.:
Magnum, P.I. ep J. Digger Doyle vo 4.16.81 CBS
Magnum, P.I. ep Double Jeopardy vo 2.25.82 CBS
Scene of the Crime pt hos 9.30.84 NBC
Scene of the Crime sr hos 4.14.85 NBC
Moonlighting ep Dream Sequences Always Ring Twice 10.15.85 ABC

WELLS, AARIKA*
Love's Savage Fury tf 5.20.79 ABC
The Death of Ocean View Park tf 10.19.79 ABC
The Six O'Clock Follies sr 4.24.80 NBC
Mickey Spillane's Margin for Murder tf/pt 10.15.81 CBS
Fantasies tf 1.18.82 ABC
Two of a Kind tf 10.9.82 CBS
Archie Bunker's Place ep 10.24.82 CBS
Tucker's Witch ep Abra Cadaver 11.10.82 CBS
The Jeffersons ep 11.6.83 CBS
Hart to Hart ep Meanwhile, Back at the Ranch 5.22.84 ABC
Knight Rider ep Dead of Knight 12.2.84 NBC
Knots Landing ep 5.23.85 CBS
The Hugga Bunch sp 7.85 NN
Knots Landing ep The Longest Day 9.26.85 CBS
Knots Landing ep Here in My Arms 10.3.85 CBS
Crazy Like a Fox ep Fox in 3/4 Time 11.3.85 CBS

WELLS, CLAUDIA*
Rise and Shine pt 8.25.81 CBS
Strike Force ep Magic Man 12.11.81 ABC
Herbie, the Love Bug sr 3.17.82 CBS
Lovers and Other Strangers pt 7.22.83 ABC
Anatomy of an Illness tf 5.15.84 CBS
Off the Rack pt 12.7.84 ABC
Trapper John, M.D. ep 1.6.85 CBS
Simon and Simon ep Slither 2.7.85 CBS
Off the Rack sr 3.15.85 ABC

WELLS, TRACY*
Mr. Belvedere sr 3.15.85 ABC
Mr. Belvedere sr ret 9.27.85 ABC

WENDELL, HOWARD
A&C, Supp. 2:
The George Burns and Gracie Allen Show ep Gracie Enrolls George in College Spring 1954 CBS
The George Burns and Gracie Allen Show ep George's Insurance Exam Spring 1954 CBS
The George Burns and Gracie Allen Show ep Harry's Alumni Banquet December 1954 CBS
The George Burns and Gracie Allen Show ep Gracie Gets an Extension Visa for Jeanette DuVal Spring 1955 CBS
The George Burns and Gracie Allen Show ep Harry's Cocktail Party Fall 1955 CBS
The Life and Legend of Wyatt Earp ep The Suffragette 3.27.56 ABC
The Life and Legend of Wyatt Earp ep They Hired Some Guns 2.26.57 ABC
The George Burns and Gracie Allen Show ep With or Without Glasses Fall 1957 CBS
The Life and Legend of Wyatt Earp ep Remittance Man 11.4.58 ABC
Leave It to Beaver ep Wally's Haircomb 1959 ABC
Bachelor Father ep Bentley Goes to Europe Spring 1961 NBC
The Dick Van Dyke Show ep One Angry Man 3.7.62 CBS
The Alfred Hitchcock Hour ep Diagnosis: Danger 3.1.63 NBC
The Dick Van Dyke Show ep I'm No Henry Walden 3.27.63 CBS
The Alfred Hitchcock Hour ep A Matter of Murder 4.3.64 NBC
The Dick Van Dyke Show ep October Eve 4.8.64 CBS
Gunsmoke ep Old Man 10.17.64 CBS
The Dick Van Dyke Show ep Stacey Petrie 1.20.65 CBS
The Dick Van Dyke Show ep 100 Terrible Hours 5.5.65 CBS
The Munsters ep Herman, the Master Spy Fall 1965 CBS
The Dick Van Dyke Show ep The Great Petrie Fortune 10.27.65 CBS
The Dick Van Dyke Show ep I Do Not Choose to Run 1.19.66 CBS
The Big Valley ep The Man from Nowhere 11.14.66 ABC
Get Smart ep The Whole Tooth and.... Spring 1967 NBC

WENDT, GEORGE*
Making the Grade sr 4.5.82 CBS
Alice ep 4.18.82 CBS
Cheers sr 9.30.82 NBC
M*A*S*H ep 11.1.82 CBS
Cheers sr ret 9.29.83 NBC
The Ratings Game tf 12.15.84 TMC
Cheers sr ret 9.27.84 NBC

St. Elsewhere ep Cheers 3.27.85 NBC
Cheers sr ret 9.26.85 NBC

WEST, ADAM
A&C, B.V.:
Colt .45 ep Don't Tell Joe 6.14.59 ABC
Colt .45 ep The Devil's Godson 10.18.59 ABC
Gunsmoke ep Ash 2.16.63 CBS
Alias Smith and Jones ep The Man That Corrupted Hadleyburg 1.27.72 ABC
SUPP.:
Laverne and Shirley ep The Gymnast 12.14.82 ABC
I Take These Men tf 1.5.83 CBS
The Love Boat ep A Booming Romance 1.22.83 ABC
Hart to Hart ep Love Game 11.8.83 ABC
Fantasy Island ep Lost and Found 4.7.84 ABC

WHELAN, JILL
SUPP.:
The Love Boat sr ret 10.2.82 ABC
Matt Houston ep Who Killed Ramona? 10.31.82 ABC
Fantasy Island ep Candy Kisses 1.15.83 ABC
The Love Boat sr ret 10.1.83 ABC
Trapper John, M.D. ep 10.30.83 ABC
The Love Boat sr ret 9.22.84 ABC
The Love Boat sr ret 9.25.85 ABC

WHELCHEL, LISA
SUPP.:
The Facts of Life Goes to Paris tf 9.25.82 NBC
The Facts of Life sr ret 10.6.82 NBC
The Wild Women of Chastity Gulch tf/pt 10.31.82 ABC
The Love Boat ep Poor Rich Man 2.5.83 ABC
The Facts of Life sr ret 9.21.83 NBC
The Facts of Life sr ret 9.26.84 NBC
Back to Next Saturday sp 9.12.85 NBC
The Facts of Life sr ret 9.14.85 NBC
The Love Boat ep The Racer's Edge 11.2.85 ABC

WHITE, BETTY
SUPP.:
Love, Sidney ep Charlotte's Web 1.13.82 NBC
Best of the West ep Mail Order Bride 1.28.82 ABC
Eunice sp 3.15.82 CBS
The Love Boat ep My Friend, the Executrix 12.11.82 ABC
Fame ep Sunny Again 1.20.83 NBC
Mama's Family sr 1.22.83 NBC
Mama's Family sr ret 9.29.83 NBC
The Love Boat ep Authoress! Authoress! 1.7.84 ABC
St. Elsewhere ep Red, White, Black and Blue 2.13.85 NBC
Who's the Boss? ep Eye on Angela 2.19.85 ABC

The Golden Girls sr 9.14.85 NBC
St. Elsewhere ep Close Encounters 12.20.85 NBC
The Love Boat ep Soap Star 11.23.85 ABC

WHITMAN, STUART
A&C, B.V.:
Trackdown ep The Town 12.13.57 CBS
The Bob Hope Chrysler Theater ep The Highest of All 12.1.65 NBC
A&C, Supp. 1:
Harry O ep Mysterious Case of Lester and Dr. Fong 3.18.76 ABC
SUPP.:
Matt Houston ep Stop the Presses 10.3.82 ABC
Fantasy Island ep Curse of the Moreaus 10.16.82 ABC
Simon and Simon ep Rough Rider Rides Again 11.18.82 CBS
The A-Team ep West Coast Turnaround 4.15.83 NBC
The Master ep Juggernaut 3.16.84 NBC
Fantasy Island ep Deuces Are Wild 5.12.84 ABC
Knight Rider ep Big Iron 5.27.84 NBC
Murder, She Wrote ep Hit, Run and Homicide 11.25.84 CBS
Matt Houston ep Deadly Games 12.7.84 ABC
Cover Up ep Midnight Highway 12.8.84 CBS
Hotel ep Hearts and Minds 5.8.85 ABC
Beverly Hills Cowgirl Blues tf/pt 10.5.85 CBS
Hunter ep The Biggest Man in Town 10.5.85 NBC
The A-Team ep Blood, Sweat and Cheers 11.19.85 NBC

WHITMORE, JAMES
A&C, B.V.:
Zane Grey Theater ep The Fearful Courage 10.12.56 CBS
Twelve O'Clock High ep The Hero 5.7.65 ABC
The Monroes ep The Hunter 10.26.66 ABC
The Big Valley ep Target 10.31.66 ABC
SUPP.:
Celebrity ms 2.12-2.14.84 NBC
The Twilight Zone ep Night Crawlers 10.18.85 CBS
George Burns Comedy Week ep Christmas Carol II: The Sequel 12.11.85 CBS
Riptide ep Home for Christmas 12.17.85 NBC

WIDMARK, RICHARD
SUPP.:
An American Portrait ep Richard M. Hunt 3.6.85 CBS

WILCOX, LARRY
A&C, Supp. 2:
Hawaii Five-O ep The Young Assassins 9.10.74 CBS
SUPP.:
Deadly Lessons tf 3.7.83 ABC
Hotel ep Memories 2.29.84 ABC

Fantasy Island ep Dark Secret 3.3.84 ABC
Hardcastle and McCormick ep Outlaw Companion 9.23.84 ABC
Hotel ep Ideals 12.12.84 ABC
The Dirty Dozen: The Next Mission tf/pt 2.4.85 NBC

WILCOX, SHANNON*
Thou Shalt Not Commit Adultery tf/pt 11.1.78 NBC
The Mysterious Two tf/pt 5.31.82 NBC
Remington Steele ep Etched in Steele 11.19.82 NBC
Ryan's Four ep Heartaches 4.20.83 ABC
When Your Lover Leaves tf 10.31.83 NBC
Crazy Like a Fox ep Premium for Murder 1.13.85 CBS
Magnum, P.I. ep A Pretty Good Dancing Chicken 4.4.85 CBS

WILDE, CORNELL
SUPP.:
The Love Boat ep Don't Leave Home Without It 10.15.83 ABC
Masquerade ep Sleeper 4.13.84 ABC

WILHOITE, KATHLEEN*
Family Ties ep Ready or Not 2.9.84 NBC
Not My Kid tf 1.15.85 CBS
The Jeffersons ep 4.23.85 CBS
Just Married pt 5.10.85 ABC
Goodbye Charlie pt 6.4.85 ABC

WILKES, DONNA
SUPP.:
Father Murphy ep The First Miracle 4.4, 4.11.82 NBC
T. J. Hooker ep King of the Hill 10.2.82 ABC
Teachers Only ep Praise the Lord and Pasta Ammunition 3.5.83 NBC
Partners in Crime ep Fantasyland 11.24.84 NBC
Hell Town ep The Porno Racket 12.11.85 NBC

WILLIAMS, ANSON
SUPP.:
Happy Days sr ret 9.28.82 ABC
Fantasy Island ep The Song Writer 1.22.83 ABC
Happy Days sr ret 9.27.83 ABC
I Married a Centerfold tf 11.11.84 NBC

WILLIAMS, BILLY DEE*
The Defenders ep Survival 3.14.64 CBS
The Doctors and the Nurses ep The Witnesses 4.27.65 CBS
Coronet Blue ep Six Months to Mars 8.14.67 CBS
The FBI ep Eye of the Storm 1.5.69 ABC
The FBI ep The Sanctuary 11.16.69 ABC
The New People ep Prisoner of Romano 12.29.69 ABC
Carter's Army tf 1.27.70 ABC
The FBI ep The Architect 10.11.70 ABC

The Most Deadly Game ep War Games 11.28.70 ABC
Dan August ep The Manufactured Man 3.11.71 ABC
The Mod Squad ep The Medicine Men 10.19.71 ABC
Mission: Impossible ep 10.23.71 CBS
Brian's Song tf 11.30.71 ABC
Shooting Stars tf/pt 7.28.83 ABC
Dynasty sr 9.26.84 ABC
An American Portrait ep Charles Drew 4.5.85 CBS
Double Dare sr 4.10.85 CBS

WILLIAMS, CARA
SUPP.:
In Security pt 7.7.82 CBS

WILLIAMS, CINDY
A&C, Supp. 1:
Room 222 ep The Exchange Teacher 12.17.69 ABC
Room 222 ep I Love You Charlie, I Love You Abbie 2.25.70 ABC
Room 222 ep Laura Fay, You're OK! 3.31.71 ABC
Hawaii Five O ep Secret Witness 1.15.74 CBS
SUPP.:
Joanna pt 4.30.85 ABC
When Dreams Come True tf 5.28.85 ABC

WILLIAMS III, CLARENCE
SUPP.:
T. J. Hooker ep Sweet Sixteen 2.12.83 ABC
T. J. Hooker ep Deadlock 5.5.84 ABC
Wonderworks ep The House of Dies Drear 11.12.84 PBS
The ABC Afterschool Special ep The Hero Who Couldn't Read 1.9.85 ABC
T. J. Hooker ep Homecoming 3.9.85 ABC
The Cosby Show ep Cliff's Birthday 5.9.85 NBC
Miami Vice ep Tale of the Goat 11.15.85 NBC

WILLIAMS, HAL
A&C, Supp. 2:
The Waltons ep John-Boy Comes Home 3.16.78 CBS
SUPP.:
T. J. Hooker ep T. J. Hooker (pt) 3.13.82 ABC
Private Benjamin sr ret 9.28.82 CBS
The ABC Weekend Special ep All the Money in the World 3.19.83 ABC
The ABC Afterschool Special ep The Celebrity and the Arcade Kid 11.9.83 ABC
The Dukes of Hazzard ep 3.24.84 CBS
Webster ep Webster Long, Part 3 9.28.84 ABC
The Jeffersons ep 11.18.84 CBS
227 sr 9.14.85 NBC

WILLIAMS, JO-BETH*
Fun and Games tf 5.26.80 ABC
Joe Dancer: The Big Black Pill tf/pt 1.29.81 NBC
Adam tf 10.10.83 NBC
The Day After tf 11.20.83 ABC
An American Portrait ep John Walsh 10.26.84 CBS
Kids Don't Tell tf 3.5.85 CBS

WILLIAMS, PAUL
SUPP.:
The Love Boat ep Rhymes, Riddles and Romance 3.27.82 ABC
Fantasy Island ep The Perfect Gentleman 10.30.82 ABC
The Fall Guy ep How Do I Kill Thee? Let Me Count the Ways 12.15.82 ABC
The Night They Saved Christmas tf 12.13.84 ABC
Silver Spoons ep Hotshot 3.3.85 NBC

WILLIAMS, ROBIN
SUPP.:
Faerie Tale Theater ep The Tale of the Frog Prince 9.11.82 SHO
Mork and Mindy sr vo 9.25.82 ABC
E.T. and Friends--Magical Movie Visitors sp hos/nar 12.14.82 CBS
Pryor's Place ep 10.27.84 CBS

WILLIAMS, VANESSA*
The Love Boat ep Hit or Miss America 2.25.84 ABC
Partners in Crime ep Celebrity 9.29.84 NBC

WILLIS, BRUCE*
Miami Vice ep No Exit (a.k.a. The Three-Eyed Turtle) 11.9.84 NBC
Moonlighting pt 3.3.85 ABC
Moonlighting sr 3.5.85 ABC
Moonlighting sr ret 9.24.85 ABC
The Twilight Zone ep Shatterday 9.27.85 CBS

WILLS, CHILL
A&C, B.V.:
Trackdown ep The Samaritan 2.18.59 CBS
Burke's Law ep 3.6.64 ABC

WILSON, DEMOND*
Sanford and Son sr 1.14.72 (through 9.2.77) NBC
Baby, I'm Back pt 10.22.77 CBS
Baby, I'm Back sr 1.30.78 CBS
The Love Boat ep 11.17.79 ABC
The Love Boat ep 2.28.81 ABC
Today's FBI ep Terror 11.22.81 ABC
The New Odd Couple sr 10.29.82 ABC

WILSON, FLIP
SUPP.:
Charlie and Company sr 9.18.85 CBS

WILSON, JEANNIE*
Vegas tf/pt 4.25.78 ABC
The Dukes of Hazzard ep Mary Kaye's Baby 2.9.79 CBS
The Dukes of Hazzard ep The Treasure of Hazzard County 1.25.80 CBS
Marriage Is Alive and Well tf/pt 1.25.80 NBC
Fantasy Island ep The Wedding Picture 11.26.83 ABC
The Love Boat ep Looking for Mr. Wilson 12.17.83 ABC
The A-Team ep It's a Desert Out There 2.7.84 NBC
The Love Boat ep Why Johnny Can't Read 10.6.84 ABC
Street Hawk sr 1.11.85 ABC
Stir Crazy sr 9.25.85 CBS

WINDOM, WILLIAM
A&C, B.V.:
Guestward Ho ep Spirit of Christmas 12.22.60 ABC
The Donna Reed Show ep All Is Forgiven 11.61 ABC
The Donna Reed Show ep Wide Open Spaces 3.62 ABC
SUPP.:
Fantasy Island ep Daddy's Little Girl 1.30.82 ABC
Desperate Lives tf 3.3.82 CBS
The Rules of Marriage tf 5.10, 5.11.82 CBS
Hart to Hart ep With This Hart, I Thee Wed 10.12.82 ABC
Trapper John, M.D. ep 10.31.82 CBS
Matt Houston ep The Good Doctor 12.12.82 ABC
The Love Boat ep Here Comes the Bride ... Maybe 1.15.83 ABC
The Greatest American Hero ep Live at Eleven 1.20.83 ABC
The A-Team ep The A-Team (pt) 1.23.83 NBC
Mama's Family ep Mama's Boyfriend 3.19.83 NBC
The Tom Swift and Linda Craig Mystery Hour pt 7.3.83 ABC
The Facts of Life ep Store Games 11.30.83 NBC
Lottery ep Boston: False Illusion ("Danziger Story" segment) 12.2.83 ABC
St. Elsewhere ep In Sickness and Health 2.8.84 NBC
Simon and Simon ep 2.23.84 CBS
Why Me? tf 3.12.84 ABC
Off Sides tf 7.6.84 NBC
Hunter ep Hot Grounder (a.k.a. The Real Tough Murder Case) 10.5.84 NBC
Surviving tf 2.10.85 ABC
Hotel ep Anniversary 2.20.85 ABC
Hardcastle and McCormick ep Surprise at Seagull Beach 3.4.85 ABC
Murder, She Wrote ep Murder at 50 Mile 4.21.85 CBS
Dirty Work pt 6.6.85 CBS
Murder, She Wrote ep Joshua Peabody Died Here 10.6.85 CBS
Airwolf ep Eagles 11.9.85 CBS

Murder, She Wrote ep A Lady in the Lake 11.10.85 CBS
Knight Rider ep Knight Racer 11.29.85 NBC
Murder, She Wrote ep Sticks and Stones 12.15.85 CBS
Glitter ep The Bag Lady of Rodeo Drive 12.27.85 ABC
Murder, She Wrote ep Murder Digs Deep 12.29.85 CBS

WINDSOR, MARIE
A&C, B.V.:
Markham ep The Duelists 7.18.59 CBS
Destry ep The Nicest Girl in Gomorrah 3.13.64 ABC
Gunsmoke ep Trafton 10.25.71 CBS
SUPP.:
Simon and Simon ep Murder Between the Lines 1.6.83 CBS
Scarecrow and Mrs. King ep Remembrance of Things Past 1.19.84 CBS
Simon and Simon ep Manna from Heaven 10.25.84 CBS
J.O.E. and the Colonel tf/pt 9.11.85 ABC

WINKLER, HENRY
SUPP.:
Laverne and Shirley with the Fonz sr vo 9.25.82 ABC
Happy Days sr ret 9.28.82 ABC
Joanie Loves Chachi ep Fonzie's Visit 9.30.82 ABC
Happy Days sr ret 9.27.83 ABC

WINKLER, K. C.*
Lobo ep The Cowboy Connection 3.31.81 NBC
CHiPs ep In the Best of Families 2.21.82 NBC
Simon and Simon ep The Last Time I Saw Michael 12.9.82 CBS
The Fall Guy ep Strange Bedfellows 2.23.83 ABC
Cutter to Houston ep From the Smallest Crystal, from the Smallest Stone 10.15.83 ABC
The Love Boat ep Ace in the Hole 1.28.84 ABC
Riptide ep Diamonds Are for Never 2.21.84 NBC
Riptide ep There Goes the Neighborhood 2.28.84 NBC
Three's Company ep Friends and Lovers 9.18.84 ABC
Growing Pains ep The Weekend Fantasy 11.12.85 ABC

WINNINGHAM, MARE
SUPP.:
Missing Children: A Mother's Story tf 12.1.82 CBS
The Thorn Birds ms 3.27, 3.28, 3.29, 3.30.83 ABC
Helen Keller: The Miracle Continues tf 4.23.84 OPT
The ABC Afterschool Special ep One Too Many 10.23.84 ABC
Love Is Never Silent tf 12.9.85 NBC

WINTER, EDWARD*
Big Daddy pt 6.19.73 CBS
Adam's Rib sr 9.14.73 ABC
The New Adventures of Perry Mason ep The Case of the Furious Father 11.11.73 CBS

M*A*S*H ep 12.8.73 CBS
The Magician ep The Stainless Steel Lady 1.28.74 NBC
M*A*S*H ep 3.2.74 CBS
The Disappearance of Flight 412 tf 10.1.74 NBC
Marcus Welby, M.D. ep The Outrage 10.8.74 ABC
The Bob Newhart Show ep 10.19.74 CBS
Karen sr 1.30.75 ABC
Eleanor and Franklin tf 1.11, 1.12.76 ABC
The Invasion of Johnson County tf 7.31.76 NBC
Bell, Book and Candle pt 9.8.76 NBC
Never Con a Killer tf/pt 5.13.77 ABC
The Girl in the Empty Grave tf 9.20.77 NBC
Maude ep 11.14.77 CBS
Charlie's Angels ep Angel Baby 11.16.77 ABC
Barnaby Jones ep Shadow of Fear 11.24.77 CBS
Lou Grant ep House Warming 11.29.77 CBS
Alice ep That Old Black Magic 12.4.77 CBS
The Gathering tf 12.4.77 ABC
Woman on the Run pt 12.17.77 CBS
Police Woman ep Sixth Sense 2.8.78 NBC
Project UFO sr 3.26.78 NBC
Project UFO sr ret 9.21.78 NBC
The Love Boat ep Rocky 9.23.78 ABC
Salvage 1 ep Golden Orbit 3.12, 3.19.79 ABC
Little House on the Prairie ep The Odyssey 3.19.79 NBC
Rendezvous Hotel tf/pt 7.11.79 CBS
The Second Time Around pt 7.24.79 ABC
Lou Grant ep Influence 9.17.79 CBS
Mother and Daughter: The Loving War tf 1.25.80 ABC
Trapper John, M.D. ep If You Can't Stand the Heat 2.17.80 CBS
Moviola: The Scarlett O'Hara War tf 5.19.80 NBC
Joe Dancer: The Big Black Pill tf/pt 1.29.81 NBC
Lou Grant ep Business 3.23.81 CBS
Fly Away Home tf/pt 9.18.81 ABC
Dallas ep Little Boy Lost 10.30.81 CBS
Dallas ep Sweet Smell of Revenge 11.6.81 CBS
The Greatest American Hero ep Classical Gas 12.2.81 ABC
Trapper John, M.D. ep Angel of Mercy 1.17.82 CBS
Fantasy Island ep The Whistle 1.30.82 ABC
The Adventures of Pollyana pt 4.10.82 CBS
The First Time tf 11.8.82 ABC
Magnum, P.I. ep Heal Thyself 12.16.82 CBS
Wait Until Dark sp 12.29.82 HBO
Hart to Hart ep Pounding Harts 1.18.83 ABC
The A-Team ep Holiday in the Hills 3.15.83 NBC
Simon and Simon ep 3.31.83 CBS
Dynasty ep The Cabin 4.20.83 ABC
Dynasty ep The Arrest 9.28.83 ABC
The Rousters ep Two-and-a-Half Days of the Condor 11.5.83 NBC
Hardcastle and McCormick ep Killer B's 11.6.83 ABC

Empire sr 1.4.84 CBS
The Lost Honor of Kathryn Beck tf 1.24.84 CBS
Fantasy Island ep Mrs. Brandell's Favorites 2.24.84 ABC
Riptide ep #1 with a Bullet 3.20.84 NBC
Call to Glory ep Blackbird 8.27.84 ABC
Finder of Lost Loves ep Undying Love 11.10.84 ABC
Falcon Crest ep The Triumbirate 12.14.84 CBS
Falcon Crest ep Winner Take All 12.21.84 CBS
Falcon Crest ep Suitable for Framing 12.28.84 CBS
Cagney and Lacey ep 1.28.85 CBS
The A-Team ep Road Games 2.5.85 NBC
Cagney and Lacey ep 3.11.85 CBS
Detective in the House ep 4.5.85 CBS
Scene of the Crime ep A Vote for Murder 5.26.85 NBC

WINTERS, SHELLEY
SUPP.:
The Love Boat ep Venetian Love Song 10.2.82 ABC
Hotel ep Trials 5.2.84 ABC
Hawaiian Heat ep Andy's Mom 11.23.84 ABC
Alice in Wonderland tf 12.9, 12.10.85 CBS

WITT, KATHRYN*
Flying High tf/pt 8.28.78 CBS
Flying High sr 9.29.78 CBS
Rendezvous Hotel tf/pt 7.11.79 CBS
Massarati and the Brain tf/pt 8.26.82 ABC
Riptide ep Diamonds in the Rough 2.21.84 NBC
Matt Houston ep The Honeymoon Murders 1.25.85 ABC
Midas Valley tf/pt 6.27.85 ABC

WOLF, KELLY*
The CBS Schoolbreak Special ep The Alfred E. Graebner Memorial High School Book of Rules and Regulations 6.12.84 CBS
The ABC Afterschool Special ep Don't Touch 11.6.85 ABC

WOLTER, SHERILYN*
B.J. and the Bear sr 1.13.81 NBC
General Hospital sr 1983 ABC
The A-Team ep The Children of Jamestown 1.30.83 NBC
The Devlin Connection ep Of Nuns and Other Black Birds 11.13.82 NBC

WOOD, LANA
A&C, Supp. 2:
Police Story ep Ice Time 5.10.77 NBC
SUPP.:
Capitol sr 6.83 CBS
The Fall Guy ep Always Say Always 2.22.84 ABC
Mickey Spillane's Mike Hammer ep Deadly Reunion 1.12.85 CBS

WOODARD, ALFRE*
What Really Happened to the Class of '65 ep The Girl Nobody Knew 12.29.77 NBC
Freedom Road tf 10.29, 10.30.79 NBC
Enos ep 4.22.81 CBS
The Sophisticated Gents ms 9.29-10.1.81 NBC
The Ambush Murders tf 1.5.82 CBS
Tucker's Witch sr 10.6.82 CBS
Hill Street Blues ep Doris in Wonderland 11.10.83 NBC
Hill Street Blues ep Praise Dilaudid 11.17.83 NBC
Hill Street Blues ep Goodbye, Mr. Scripps 11.24.83 NBC
Sweet Revenge tf 10.31.84 CBS
Sara sr 1.23.85 NBC
Wonderworks ep Words By Heart 2.11.85 PBS
Faerie Tale Theater ep Puss 'n' Boots 9.9.85 SHO
St. Elsewhere sr (with ep Remembrance of Things Past) 9.18.85 NBC

WOODWARD, JOANNE
SUPP.:
An American Portrait ep Jane Adams 4.15.85 CBS
Passions tf 10.1.84 CBS
Do You Remember Love? tf 5.21.85 CBS

WOPAT, TOM*
The Dukes of Hazzard sr 1.26.79 CBS
The Dukes of Hazzard sr ret 10.25.80 CBS
Fantasy Island ep 11.1.80 ABC
The Dukes of Hazzard sr ret 10.6.81 CBS
The Dukes of Hazzard ret to sr 2.25.83 CBS
The Dukes of Hazzard sr ret 9.23.83 CBS
The Dukes of Hazzard sr ret 9.21.84 CBS
Burning Rage tf 9.21.84 CBS

WORLEY, JO ANNE
A&C, Supp. 1:
Dobie Gillis ep Baby Talk 10.18.60 CBS
Dobie Gillis ep Goodbye Mr. Promfitt--Hello Mr. Chips 6.13.62 CBS
Get Christie Love ep Murder on High C 2.5.75 ABC
Hawaii Five-O ep Blood Money Is Hard to Wash 3.3.77 CBS
SUPP.:
The Love Boat ep Putting on the Dog 3.26.83 ABC
Murder, She Wrote ep My Johnnie Lies Over the Ocean 2.10.85 CBS

WRAY, FAY
A&C, B.V.:
Caribe ep Assault on the Calavera 5.12.75 ABC

WRIGHT, MAX*
Playing for Time tf 9.30.80 CBS

For Ladies Only tf 11.9.81 NBC
Hart to Hart ep Hart of Diamonds 2.2.82 ABC
The Wall tf 2.16.82 CBS
WKRP in Cincinnati ep 2.24.82 CBS
Code Red ep No Escape 3.21.82 ABC
Taxi ep The Road Not Taken 5.6.82 ABC
Buffalo Bill sr 6.2.83 NBC
I Gave at the Office pt 8.15.84 NBC
E/R ep 11.21.84 CBS
Code Name: Foxfire ep Slay It Again, Uncle Sam (pt) 1.27.85 NBC
Code Name: Foxfire sr 2.8.85 NBC
Benson ep Mid-Life Cowboy 2.15.85 ABC
The Misfits of Science sr 10.4.85 NBC

WRIGHT, TERESA

SUPP.:
Mornings at Seven sp 9.82 SHO
The Love Boat ep The Christmas Presence 12.18.82 ABC
Bill on His Own tf 11.9.83 CBS

WYATT, JANE

SUPP.:
Happy Days ep Empty Nest 10.19.82 ABC
Missing Children: A Mother's Story tf 12.1.82 CBS
The Love Boat ep Here Comes the Bride ... Maybe 1.15.83 ABC
Fantasy Island ep Midnight Waltz 2.12.83 ABC
St. Elsewhere ep A Wing and a Prayer 11.23.83 NBC
The Love Boat ep Love on the Line 1.26.85 ABC
St. Elsewhere ep Cheers 3.27.85 NBC
St. Elsewhere ep Santa Claus Is Dead 12.18.85 NBC

WYMAN, JANE

SUPP.:
Falcon Crest sr ret 10.1.82 CBS
Falcon Crest sr ret 9.30.83 CBS
Falcon Crest sr ret 9.28.84 CBS
Falcon Crest sr ret 10.4.85 CBS

WYNN, ED

A&C, B.V.:
Burke's Law ep 3.6.64 ABC

WYNN, KEENAN

SUPP.:
A Piano for Mrs. Cimino tf 2.3.82 CBS
The Capture of Grizzly Adams tf 2.21.82 NBC
The Greatest American Hero ep The Good Samaritan 3.31.82 ABC
The Love Boat ep The Christmas Presence 12.18.82 ABC

St. Elsewhere ep Family History 2.8.83 NBC
The Return of the Man from UNCLE: The 15 Years Later Affair tf/pt 4.5.83 CBS
Taxi ep Tony's Baby 4.20.83 NBC
Quincy, M.E. ep Whatever Happened to Morris Perlmutter? 5.4.83 NBC
Manimal ep Scrimshaw 12.3.83 NBC
The Mississippi ep 12.13.83 CBS
Call to Glory sr 8.13.84 ABC
Code of Vengeance tf/pt 6.30.85 NBC
Tales form the Darkside ep I'll Give You a Million 10.6.85 NN
Highway to Heaven ep Popcorn, Peanuts and Crackerjacks 11.13.85 NBC

WYNTER, DANA
SUPP.:
Magnum, P.I. ep Double Jeopardy 2.25.82 CBS
The Royal Romance of Charles and Diana tf 9.20.82 CBS
Magnum, P.I. ep Foiled Again 11.11.82 CBS

WYSS, AMANDA*
This House Possessed tf 2.6.81 ABC
Buck Rogers in the 25th Century ep The Crystals 3.5.81 NBC
The ABC Afterschool Special ep She Drinks a Little 9.23.81 ABC
The Other Victim tf 11.4.81 CBS
Jessica Novak ep The Boy Most Likely 11.12.81 CBS
Teachers Only ep Quote Unquote 5.5.82 NBC
Cass Malloy pt 7.21.82 CBS
Star of the Family ep The Critic 10.7.82 ABC
Star of the Family ep Making Time 10.14.82 ABC
The Powers of Matthew Star ep Matthew Star: D.O.A. 1.21.83 NBC
The Tom Swift and Linda Craig Mystery Hour pt 7.3.83 ABC
A Killer in the Family tf 10.30.83 ABC
My Mother's Secret Life tf 2.5.84 ABC
Otherworld ep Rules of Attraction 1.26.85 CBS
Cheers ep Woody Goes Belly Up 10.3.85 NBC
St. Elsewhere ep Lost and Found in Space 11.13.85 NBC
St. Elsewhere ep 12.11.85 NBC
Glitter ep The Runaway 12.26.85 ABC

- Y -

YATES, CASSIE
A&C, Supp. 2:
Marcus Welby, M.D. ep The One Face in the Wind 12.9.75 ABC

SUPP.:
The Gift of Life tf 3.16.82 CBS
Trapper John, M.D. ep Getting to Know You 12.12.82 CBS
Listen to Your Heart tf 1.4.83 CBS
Simon and Simon ep Pirate's Key 1.20.83 CBS
Family Tree sr 1.22.83 NBC
Agatha Christie's "A Caribbean Mystery" tf 10.22.83 CBS
Simon and Simon ep 12.8.83 CBS
Knots Landing ep 12.15.83 CBS
Hotel ep Memories 2.29.84 ABC
Fantasy Island ep The Imposter 3.17.84 ABC
Love Thy Neighbor tf 5.23.84 ABC
Simon and Simon ep A Little Wine with Murder 10.4.84 CBS
Murder, She Wrote ep Deadly Lady 10.7.84 CBS
Magnum, P.I. ep 12.13.84 CBS
Finder of Lost Loves ep Forgotten Melodies 12.22.84 ABC
Detective in the House sr 3.15.85 CBS
Hell Town ep The One Called Daisy 11.13.85 CBS
Perry Mason Returns tf 12.1.85 NBC

YORK, DICK
A&C, B.V.:
The Outlaws ep Night Riders 11.2.61 NBC

YORK, FRANCINE*
Any Second Now tf 2.11.69 NBC
Adam-12 ep Log 88: Reason to Run 4.1.71 NBC
Adam-12 ep Sub-Station 2.16.72 NBC
Hec Ramsey ep The Mystery of the Yellow Rose 1.28.73 NBC
I Love a Mystery tf/pt 2.27.73 NBC
Kojak ep Slay Ride 10.13.74 CBS
The Streets of San Francisco ep Bird of Prey 11.21.74 ABC
Petrocelli ep The Sleep of Ransom 1.15.75 NBC
The Adventures of the Queen tf 2.14.75 CBS
Columbo ep The Forgotten Lady 9.14.75 NBC
The Barbary Coast ep An Iron-Clad Plan 10.31.75 ABC
Time Travelers tf 3.19.76 ABC
The Quest ep Prairie Woman 11.10.76 NBC
Flood tf 11.24.76 NBC
Masquerade ep The French Connection 3.30.84 ABC
The Love Boat ep There'll Be Some Changes Made 2.2.85 ABC
Riptide ep Harmony and Grits 5.14.85 NBC

YORK, MICHAEL
SUPP.:
The Phantom of the Opera tf 1.29.83 CBS
The Master of Ballantrae tf 1.31.84 CBS
An American Portrait ep Samuel Howe 2.15.85 CBS
Space ms 4.14-4.18.85 CBS

YORK, SUSANNAH
SUPP.:
The Love Boat ep There'll Be Some Changes Made 2.2.85 ABC

YOTHERS, TINA*
The Cherokee Trail pt 11.28.81 CBS
Father Murphy ep The Dream Day 3.2.82 NBC
Family Ties sr 9.22.82 NBC
Your Place or Mine tf 3.2.83 CBS
Family Ties sr ret 9.28.83 NBC
Domestic Life ep 1.4.84 CBS
Domestic Life ep 4.15.85 CBS
Family Ties sr ret 9.27.84 NBC
A Christmas Carol tf 12.17.84 CBS
Family Ties Vacation tf 9.23.85 NBC
Family Ties sr ret 9.26.85 NBC

YOUNG, ALAN
SUPP.:
The Love Boat ep A Booming Romance 1.22.83 ABC
Sitcom pt 10.2.83 HBO

YOUNGFELLOW, BARRIE
SUPP.:
It Takes Two ep The Choice 1.20.83 ABC
Trapper John, M.D. ep 11.27.83 CBS
It Came Upon the Midnight Clear tf 1.15.84 NN
The ABC Weekend Special ep The Adventures of a Two-Minute Werewolf 2.23, 3.2.85 ABC
The Lady from Yesterday tf 5.14.85 CBS
It's a Living sr ret 9.29.85 NN

- Z -

ZABRISKIE, GRACE*
The Concrete Cowboys tf/pt 10.17.79 CBS
Freedom Road tf 10.29, 10.30.79 NBC
The CBS Afternoon Playhouse ep Lost in Death Valley 4.19.80 CBS
Blinded by the Light tf 12.16.80 CBS
East of Eden ms 2.8-2.11.81 ABC
Hart to Hart ep A Couple of Harts 10.13.81 ABC
The Executioner's Song tf 11.28, 11.29.82 NBC
M.A.D.D.: Mothers Against Drunk Drivers tf 3.14.83 NBC
My Mother's Secret Life tf 2.5.84 ABC
The Burning Bed tf 10.8.84 NBC
The ABC Afterschool Special ep One Too Many 3.6.85 ABC
Beverly Hills Cowgirl Blues tf/pt 10.5.85 CBS

North Beach and Rawhide tf 11.12, 11.13.85 CBS
Shadow Chasers ep Shadow Chasers (pt) 11.14.85 ABC

ZADORA, PIA*
Pajama Tops sp 3.18.83 SHO

ZERBE, ANTHONY
A&C, B.V.:
The Wild Wild West ep The Night of the Legion of Death 11.24.67 CBS
SUPP.:
Rascals and Robbers--The Secret Adventures of Tom Sawyer and Huck Finn tf 2.27.82 CBS
A Question of Honor tf 4.28.82 CBS
Nurse ep Fevers 5.7.82 CBS
Little House: A New Beginning ep The Wild Boy 11.1, 11.8.82 NBC
The Man from UNCLE: The 15 Years Later Affair tf/pt 4.5.83 CBS
George Washington ms 4.8-4.11.84 CBS
A.D. ms 3.31-4.4.85 NBC
Highway to Heaven ep The Devil and Jonathan 10.30.85 NBC
Our Family Honor ep 11.29.85 ABC

ZIMBALIST, EFREM JR.
SUPP.:
Beyond Witch Mountain pt 2.20.82 CBS
Family in Blue pt 6.10.82 CBS
Charley's Aunt sp 2.6.83 TEC
Baby Sister tf 3.6.83 ABC
Remington Steele ep Sting of Steele 4.5.83 NBC
Shooting Stars tf/pt 7.28.83 ABC
Fantasy Island ep The Butler's Affair 11.12.83 ABC
The Love Boat ep Polly's Poker Palace 2.4.84 ABC
Hardcastle and McCormick ep The Georgia Street Motors 2.5.84 ABC
Partners in Crime ep Murder in the Museum 10.6.84 NBC
Hotel ep Flesh and Blood 10.10.84 ABC
Remington Steele ep Blue-Blooded Steele 10.30.84 NBC
Cover Up ep Writer's Block 11.24.84 CBS
Remington Steele ep Steele Searching 10.1.85 NBC

ZIMBALIST, STEPHANIE
SUPP.:
Tomorrow's Child tf 3.22.82 ABC
Remington Steele sr 10.1.82 NBC
Remington Steele sr ret 9.20.83 NBC
Remington Steele sr ret 9.25.84 NBC
Remington Steele sr ret 9.24.85 NBC
Love on the Run tf 10.21.85 NBC
A Letter to Three Wives tf 12.16.85 NBC

ZMED, ADRIAN*
Flatbush sr 2.26.79 CBS
The Goodtime Girls sr 1.22.80 ABC
Riker ep Gun Run 3.28.81 CBS
T. J. Hooker sr 3.13.82 ABC
T. J. Hooker sr ret 9.25.82 ABC
T. J. Hooker sr ret 10.1.83 ABC
Glitter ep Glitter (pt) 9.13.84 ABC
The Love Boat Fall Preview Party sp 9.15.84 ABC
T. J. Hooker sr ret 10.6.84 ABC
Victims for Victims: The Theresa Saldana Story tf 11.12.84 NBC

ABOUT THE AUTHORS

JAMES ROBERT PARISH, Los Angeles-based vice president of marketing for a national direct marketing firm, was born in Cambridge, Massachusetts. He attended the University of Pennsylvania and graduated Phi Beta Kappa with a degree in English. A graduate of the University of Pennsylvania Law School, he is a member of the New York Bar. As president of Entertainment Copyright Research Co., Inc. he headed a major research facility for the film and television industries. Later he was a film reviewer-interviewer for *Motion Picture Daily* and *Variety*. He is the author of over sixty volumes, including: *The Fox Girls*, *Good Dames*, *The Slapstick Queens*, *The RKO Gals*, *The Tough Guys*, *The Jeanette MacDonald Story*, *The Elvis Presley Scrapbook*, and *The Hollywood Beauties*. Among those he has co-written are *The MGM Stock Company*, *The Debonairs*, *Liza!*, *Hollywood Character Actors*, *The Hollywood Reliables*, *The Funsters*, *The Best of MGM*, *The Great Western Pictures*, *The Great Spy Pictures*, *The Great Sci Fi Pictures*, *Hollywood on Hollywood*, and *Film Director Guide: The U.S.*

VINCENT TERRACE, a native New Yorker, is a graduate of the New York Institute of Technology and holds a Bachelor's Degree in Fine Arts. He is the author of *The Complete Encyclopedia of Television Programs, 1947-1979*, *Radio's Golden Years, 1930-1960*, *Television: 1970-1980*, and the three-volume *Television: Series, Pilots and Specials, 1937-1984*. Mr. Terrace has also worked with Mr. Parish on a number of other books and together they co-authored *Actors' Television Credits, Supplement II, 1977-1981*.